From Sacrament to Contract,

Second Edition

ALSO BY JOHN WITTE JR.

Christianity and Democracy in Global Context (ed.)

Christianity and Human Rights: An Introduction (ed. with F. S. Alexander)

Christianity and Law: An Introduction (ed. with F. S. Alexander)

Covenant Marriage in Comparative Perspective (ed. with E. Ellison)

The Equal-Regard Family and Its Friendly Critics (ed. with M. C. Green and A. Wheeler)

Family Transformed: Religion, Values, and Family Life in Interdisciplinary Perspective (ed. with S. M. Tipton)

God's Joust, God's Justice: Law and Religion in the Western Tradition

Human Rights in Judaism: Cultural, Religious, and Political Perspectives (ed. with M. J. Broyde)

Law and Protestantism: The Legal Teachings of the Lutheran Reformation

Modern Christian Teachings on Law, Politics, and Human Nature, 3 vols. (ed. with F. S. Alexander)

No Establishment of Religion: America's Original Contribution to Religious Liberty (ed. with T. J. Gunn)

Proselytism and Orthodoxy in Russia: The New War for Souls (ed. with M. Bourdeaux)

The Reformation of Rights: Law, Religion, and Human Rights in Early Modern Calvinism

Religion and Human Rights: An Introduction (ed. with M. C. Green)

Religion and the American Constitutional Experiment, 3rd ed. (with J. A. Nichols)

Religious Human Rights in Global Perspective, 2 vols. (ed. with J. D. van der Vyver)

Sex, Marriage, and Family in John Calvin's Geneva, 2 vols. (with R. M. Kingdon)

Sharing the Book: Religious Perspectives on the Rights and Wrongs of Proselytism (ed. with R. C. Martin)

The Sins of the Fathers: The Law and Theology of Illegitimacy Reconsidered

To Have and to Hold: Marrying and Its Documentation in Western Christendom, 400–1600 (ed. with P. L. Reynolds)

The Weightier Matters of the Law: Essays on Law and Religion (ed. with F. S. Alexander)

From Sacrament to Contract

Marriage, Religion, and Law in the Western Tradition

Second Edition

JOHN WITTE JR.

WJK WESTMINSTER JOHN KNOX PRESS
LOUISVILLE • KENTUCKY

First edition published in 1997 by Westminster John Knox Press

Second edition
Published by Westminster John Knox Press
Louisville, Kentucky

12 13 14 15 16 17 18 19 20 21—10 9 8 7 6 5 4 3 2 1

Except as otherwise identified, quotations from Scripture and from the Apocryphal/Deuterocanonical books are from the New Revised Standard Version of the Bible, copyright © 1989 by the Division of Christian Education of the National Council of the Churches of Christ in the U.S.A., and are used by permission.

Book design by Sharon Adams
Cover design by Dilu Nicholas
Cover Art: Ms 251, f.16r: The marriage of Adam and Eve from
'Des Proprietes De Choses', c.1415 (gold leaf, gold ink & tempera
on parchment) (detail of 276966) by Boucicaut Master (fl.1390–1430)
(and workshop) / Fitzwilliam Museum, University of Cambridge,
UK / The Bridgeman Art Library International

Library of Congress Cataloging-in-Publication Data

Witte, John, 1959–
    From sacrament to contract : marriage, religion, and law in the Western tradition / John Witte, Jr. — 2nd ed.
      p.   cm.
    Includes bibliographical references (p.   ) and indexes.
    ISBN 978-0-664-23432-4 (alk. paper)
    1. Marriage law—Religious aspects.   2. Marriage—Religious aspects—Christianity.
3. Marriage (Canon law)   I. Title.
    K675.W57 2011
    234'.16509—dc23

                                                      2011039952

∞ The paper used in this publication meets the minimum requirements
of the American National Standard for Information Sciences—
Permanence of Paper for Printed Library Materials, ANSI Z39.48-1992.

Most Westminster John Knox Press books are available at special
quantity discounts when purchased in bulk by corporations,
organizations, and special-interest groups. For more information,
please e-mail SpecialSales@wjkbooks.com.

For my parents,
John and Gertie Witte

Contents

Preface to the Second Edition

"The apt and cheerful conversation of man with woman is the chief and noblest purpose of marriage," wrote the seventeenth-century English poet and philosopher John Milton. "Where loving [conversation] cannot be, there can be left of wedlock nothing but the empty husk of an outside matrimony,"[1] dry, shriveled, and dispensable. Aptness can strain cheerfulness: candid conversations between spouses can be very painful to endure. Cheerfulness can strain aptness: blissful domestic ignorance can be very tempting to pursue. But aptness and cheerfulness properly belong together in a marriage, Milton tells us. Where they fail, the marriage fails.

An apt and cheerful conversation *about* marriage must be part of our dialogue today. For marriage is one of the great mediators of individuality and community, revelation and reason, tradition and modernity. Marriage is at once a harbor of the self and a harbinger of the community, a symbol of divine love and a structure of reasoned consent, an enduring ancient mystery and a constantly modern invention.

To be "apt," our conversation cannot wax nostalgic about a prior golden age of marriage and the family, nor wax myopic about modern ideals of liberty, privacy, and autonomy. We cannot be blind to the patriarchy, paternalism, and plain prudishness of the past. Nor can we be blind to the massive social, psychological, and spiritual costs of the modern sexual revolution. To be apt, participants in the conversation on marriage must seek to understand both traditional morals and contemporary mores of marriage on their own terms and in their own context—without deprecating or privileging either form or norm. Traditionalists must heed the maxim of church historian Jaroslav Pelikan

---

1. John Milton, *The Doctrine and Discipline of Divorce*, 2nd ed. (London, 1644), in *The Complete Prose Works of John Milton* (New Haven: Yale University Press, 1959), 2:235–56 (spelling modernized); see further discussion of Milton in chap. 7 herein.

that "tradition is the living faith of the dead; traditionalism is the dead faith of the living."[2] Wooden antiquarianism, a dogmatic indifference to the changing needs of marriages and families, is not apt. Modernists must heed the instruction of legal historian Harold Berman that "we must walk into the future with an eye on the past."[3] Chronological snobbery, a calculated disregard for the wisdom of the past, also is not apt.

To be "cheerful," our conversation must proceed with the faith that the crisis of modern marriage and family life can be overcome. Traditional norms and forms of marriage and the family are in trouble today. Statistics tell the bald American story, which has parallels in other Western cultures. Since 1975, roughly one-quarter of all pregnancies were aborted. One-third of all children were born to single mothers. One-half of all marriages ended in divorce. Two-thirds of all African American children were raised without a father present. Children from broken homes proved two to three times more likely to have behavioral and learning problems than children from two-parent homes. Single mothers faced four times the rates of bankruptcy and eviction. More than two-thirds of juveniles and young adults convicted of major felonies came from single- or no-parent homes. So much is well known. Though these numbers have improved over the past decade, they bring little cheer.

What is less well known, and what brings more cheer, is that the Western tradition has faced family crises on this scale before. And apocalyptic jeremiads about the end of civil society have been uttered many times before. What brings cheer is that the Western tradition of marriage has always found the resources to heal and reinvent itself, to strike new balances between orthodoxy and innovation, order and liberty, with regard to our enduring and evolving sexual, marital, and familial norms and habits. The prospect of healing and reinvention is no less likely today— so long as academics, activists, advocates, and political, religious, and civic leaders ponder these problems in good faith and direct their resources to good works.

This volume makes a small contribution to this apt and cheerful conversation on marriage. The main argument of this volume is that modern Western marriage law was founded on ancient classical and biblical ideas and forged by a series of Christian and Enlightenment traditions. Each of these traditions contributed a variety of familiar legal ideas and institutions about marriage—some overlapping, some conflicting. It is in the overlapping and creatively juxtaposed legal contributions of the various classical, Christian, and Enlightenment traditions that one sees some of the ingredients of a third way to conceive and govern marriage in a modern Western culture that is increasingly post-Christian and constitutionally committed to the establishment of no religion.

I wrote the first edition of this volume as a brash youngster, audacious enough to try to cover 2,000 years of history in 250 pages of text. Happily, my

2. Jaroslav Pelikan, *The Vindication of Tradition* (New Haven: Yale University Press, 1984), 65.
3. Harold J. Berman, *Law and Revolution: The Formation of the Western Legal Tradition* (Cambridge, MA: Harvard University Press, 1983), vii.

great mentors at the time, Harold Berman and Don Browning, spared me from making too many mistakes in drawing the big picture, and I learned a great deal about the rest of the story from the many expert scholars gathered in the annual conferences of the Religion, Culture, and Family Project at the University of Chicago, which commissioned this study. It was gratifying to see the generous reception and reviews of the book by students and scholars of theology, ethics, history, law, and family studies, and its translation into several foreign languages.

In the ensuing two decades, I have continued to work on the history, law, and theology of sex, marriage, and family life and to learn from leading scholars in the field. Particularly edifying has been the privilege of directing two large research projects of the Center for the Study of Law and Religion at Emory University, with the generous support of The Pew Charitable Trusts, Inc.—one on "Sex, Marriage, and Family & the Religions of the Book" (2000–2007), codirected with Don Browning, the second on "The Child in Law, Religion, and Society" (2003–2010), codirected with Martin Marty. Also deeply edifying has been the privilege of directing four successive projects since 2000 on "Christian Jurisprudence," with the support of Pew, the Lilly Endowment, Inc., and the Alonzo L. McDonald Family Agape Foundation. Some 100 scholars, 200 lecturers, and 2,000 conferees have been part of these projects over the past decade, and they have collectively yielded some 150 new volumes of scholarship.

This new edition takes account of some of this new scholarship produced in our projects and in many other academies around the world. I have updated, revised, and streamlined the argument of the book throughout, trimmed and updated the notes, and corrected several mistakes in the first edition. I have sprinkled new material throughout the volume and have added new chapters on classical, biblical, and patristic sources of Western marriage, which did not receive enough attention in the first edition. I have also expanded the last chapter and concluding reflections section a bit to address more fully some of the debates about sex, marriage, and family life that now challenge and divide church, state, and society alike.

Some of these revisions are distilled from more extensive recent writings on the history of marriage and family life that I have had the privilege to prepare over the past two decades. Readers interested in the classical and biblical themes covered in chapter 1 can read more in a book that Don Browning and I just sent to press, tentatively titled *From Private Order to Public Covenant: What Can Christianity Offer to Modern Marriage Law?* I do more with these ancient sources, and with the medieval legal sources covered in chapter 4, in a recent monograph *The Sins of the Fathers: The Law and Theology of Illegitimacy Reconsidered* (2009) and in an anthology coedited with Philip Reynolds, *To Have and to Hold: Marrying and Its Documentation in Western Christendom, 400–1600* (2007). Those interested in the Lutheran themes of chapter 5 might wish to consult further my *Law and Protestantism: The Legal Teachings of the Lutheran Reformation* (2002) as well as my *God's Joust, God's Justice: Law and Religion in the Western Tradition* (2006). Those interested in the Calvinist themes of chapter 6 can read more analysis and hundreds of freshly translated sources in a two-volume work prepared with Robert M. Kingdon, *Sex, Marriage, and Family in John Calvin's Geneva* (2005, 2012). Those interested in marriage, family, and childhood themes viewed in broader social science and comparative cultural perspective might find helpful three other volumes, coedited with my colleagues: *Sex, Marriage, and Family in the World Religions* (2006, with Don Browning and M. Christian Green); *Covenant Marriage in Comparative Perspective* (2005, with Eliza Ellison); and *Family Transformed: Religion, Values, and Family Life in Interdisciplinary Perspective* (2005, with Steven M. Tipton).

Preparation of this new edition was made possible by generous grants from the Lilly Endowment, Inc., and the Alonzo L. McDonald Family Agape Foundation. Profound thanks are due to Craig Dykstra and his colleagues in the Religion Division at Lilly for their support of this project as well as my related projects on law, religion, and the Protestant tradition. Profound thanks as well go to Alonzo McDonald, Suzie McDonald, Peter McDonald, and Bob Pool of the McDonald Foundation for their uncommonly generous support of my writing and lectures.

I enjoyed working with Stephanie Egnotovich of Westminster John Knox Press on the first edition of this volume, and I am grateful for her invitation to prepare this second edition. I have missed her sage editorial advice in the months since her untimely death, but I have enjoyed working with Marianne Blickenstaff, Daniel Braden, and their colleagues as we brought this new edition to press.

Finally, I wish to express my gratitude to the excellent professional staff of our Center for the Study of Law and Religion at Emory University—April Bogle, Linda King, Anita Mann, and Amy Wheeler—and my research assistants—Thomas Buck, Andy Mayo, Jamie Schickler, and Matthew Tuininga—for their help with this new edition.

John Witte Jr.

Preface to the First Edition

I would like to express my gratitude to a number of persons and institutions who have supported the preparation of this text. It has been a privilege to be a part of The Religion, Culture, and Family Project at the University of Chicago Divinity School, which commissioned this text. I am especially grateful to Don S. Browning for his brilliant leadership of the Family Project as a whole and his sage mentorship of this text in particular. I have learned much from my interactions with him and with the dozens of scholars associated with this Project over the past four years, particularly those gathered in the annual fall seminars convened by the Project. I want to thank Carol Browning, Anne Carr, Bertram Cohler, Ian S. Evison, and John Wall for their leadership of this Project, and the Lilly Endowment, Inc., for its most generous financial support.

I was grateful to receive a Max Rheinstein Fellowship and Research Prize from the Alexander von Humboldt-Stiftung in Bonn, which allowed me to conduct research at several libraries in Brussels, Cologne, Dresden, Frankfurt am Main, Heidelberg, Tübingen, Leiden, and The Hague during the past two years. I was also grateful for the opportunity to serve as a visiting scholar at the Protestant Interdisciplinary Research Institute in Heidelberg in February and March 1995 and as the Jerald Brauer Seminar Scholar at the University of Chicago in April 1995, which provided splendid opportunities for research, writing, and lectures on various parts of this book.

Several friends and colleagues were kind enough to lend liberally of their advice and criticism. I would like especially to thank Harold J. Berman, R. H. Helmholz, Martin E. Marty, Max L. Stackhouse, and Steven E. Ozment, who each read large portions of the manuscript and made numerous edifying suggestions. Their comments have greatly improved my understanding of the subject, and I hope the quality of the book begins to approximate the quality of their advice. Several other friends have helped me with specific criticisms and suggestions, for which I am grateful. These include Frank Alexander, Tom Arthur, Wolfgang Bock, Michael Broyde, Rebecca Chopp, Nathaniel Gozansky, Peter Hay, Timothy Jackson, Harriet King, Charles Reid, and Wolfgang Vögele.

Several joint degree candidates in the Law and Religion Program at Emory University have provided able and ample research assistance. I would like especially to thank Julia Belian, Scott Blevins, Heidi Hansan, M. Christian Green, and Joel Nichols for their invaluable help. I am also grateful for the stalwart support of my dean, Howard O. Hunter, and for the research support of the Emory Law Library staff, particularly Holliday Osborne and Will Haines.

It was a special pleasure to write a book about the virtues of marriage and family life, while enjoying the same in such abundance. My dear wife, Eliza, and our daughters, Alison and Hope, have given me constant love and support. Eliza has improved many of my ideas with her critical insights and many of my passages with her keen editorial eye. Most important, she has improved all my life with her love, and for that I am most grateful of all.

This book is dedicated to my parents, John and Gertie Witte, who have provided me with a pristine model of marriage and parentage.

John Witte Jr.

The Wedding of King Philip II of Macedonia and Olympias, the parents of Alexander the Great. From the *History of Alexander the Great*. France, 15th. CE. Dutui 456, f.8r. Photo: Bulloz. Musee du Petit Palais, Paris, France. Réunion des Musées Nationaux / Art Resource, NY. Used by permission of Art Resource, New York.

A Proposal by Otto Erdmann (1834–1905). Private Collection / Photo © Christie's Images / The Bridgeman Art Library. Nationality / copyright status: German / out of copyright. Used by permission of the Bridgeman Art Library, London.

Introduction

Oliver Wendell Holmes Jr. once said that all the great questions of theology and philosophy must ultimately come to the law for their resolution. Holmes's claim, while overstated, has merit for this book. While theologians and philosophers have debated questions of the origin, nature, and purpose of marriage, jurists and judges have had to resolve them—in general statutes as well as in concrete cases. Such legal formulations have invariably reflected, and sometimes reified, prevailing theological ideas and ideals respecting marriage.

This book explores this interplay among law, theology, and marriage in the Western tradition. Its principal topical foci are Christian theological norms and Western legal principles of marriage and family life. Its principal geographical focus is Western Europe and its extension overseas to America. Its principal goal is to uncover some of the main theological beliefs that have helped to form Western marriage law in the past, and so to discover how such beliefs might help to inform Western marriage law in the future.

This book is, by design, more of a theological analysis than a sociological analysis of Western marriage law. It dwells principally on official lore and dips only intermittently into social practice. It draws more on marital statutes and summae than on testamentary documents and confessional practices. You will read more about the Marriage Acts of Lutheran Germany than about the acts of marriage by German gentlemen, more about papal pronouncements on lay sexual practices than about plaintiff petitions on clerical sexual abuse. For my principal interest is to come to terms with the cardinal religious sources and dimensions of the Western marriage law on the books.

To select this genre of writing is not to deprecate the great value of local and social histories of marriage and family life. Nor is it to ignore the dangers of writing a naked history of magisterial ideas. I do ground my analysis of marriage law and theology in concrete cases and other social data. I also fully acknowledge that not only theology but also economics, politics, psychology, and numerous other factors have helped to shape Western ideas and institutions of marriage and family life. My principal goal, however, is to pull out of this thick fabric of family experience in the West the slender interwoven threads of Christian theology and marriage law and to examine some of their colors and patterns.

MODELS OF MARRIAGE

The Western Christian Church has, from its apostolic beginnings, offered four perspectives on marriage. A *spiritual perspective* regards marriage as a sacramental or covenantal association, subject to the creed, cult, and canons of the church community. A *social perspective* treats marriage as a social estate, subject to the expectations and exactions of the local community and to special state laws of contract, property, and inheritance. A *contractual perspective* describes marriage as a voluntary association, dependent upon the consent of the parties, and subject to the wills and preferences of the couple, their children, and their household. Hovering in the background is a *naturalist perspective*, which treats marriage as a created institution, subject to the natural laws of reason, conscience, and the Bible. According to Voltaire's quip, "Among Christians, the family is either a little church, a little state, or a little club" blessed by nature and nature's God.

In an important sense, these four perspectives are complementary, for they each emphasize one aspect of marriage—its religious sanction, communal legitimation, voluntary formation, and natural origin, respectively. These perspectives, however, have also come to stand in considerable tension, for they are linked to competing claims of ultimate authority over the form and function of marriage—claims by the church, by the state, by family members, and by God and nature. Some of the deepest fault lines in the historical formation and in the current transformations of Western marriage ultimately break out from this central tension of perspective. Which perspective of marriage dominates a culture, or at least prevails in an instance of dispute—the religious, the social, the contractual, or the natural? Which authority wields preeminent, or at least peremptory, power over marriage and family questions—the church, the state, the marital couple, or God and nature operating through one or more of these parties?

Historically, Catholics, Lutherans, Calvinists, Anglicans, and Enlightenment thinkers constructed systematic models of marriage to address these cardinal questions. Each group recognized multiple perspectives on marriage but gave priority to one perspective in order to achieve an integrated understanding. Their efforts have yielded five models of marriage for the modern West. These I have labeled (1) the Catholic sacramental model, (2) the Lutheran social model, (3) the Calvinist covenantal model, (4) the Anglican commonwealth model, and (5) the Enlightenment contractarian model.

These models of marriage are offered not as Weberian ideal types but as Niebuhrian conceptual constructs—ways of "stopping the endless Western dialogue" on marriage "at certain points," in H. Richard Niebuhr's apt phrase, to test its theological meaning and to take its legal measure.[1] A full exposition of the details of any of these models could easily fill a long shelf of books. The sources are rich enough and the differences of perspective wide enough, even among close coreligionists, that one could easily subdivide these models into a battery of subtypes and hybrid types. Moreover, a full exposition of these models in action—portraying the day-to-day intimacies of the bedroom and courtroom, the patterns of paternity and inheritance, the indicia of wife and child abuse, the connivings of clerics and magistrates, the forms and forums of domestic stability and sexual discipline, the beauties and mysteries of marital and parental love, and much more—could easily fill several more long bookshelves. Selection, distillation, and truncation are necessary evils.

As our "Niebuhrian stopping points," I have chosen the mid-twelfth to mid-thirteenth centuries, the sixteenth and early seventeenth centuries, and the mid-nineteenth century and thereafter. These are watershed periods in the Western tradition of marriage—eras when powerful new theological models of marriage were forged that helped to transform the prevailing law of marriage. I have sought to sketch out just enough of the theology of each model to demonstrate its unique contribution to the Western legal tradition of marriage. And, in laying these models alongside each other, I have sought to give just enough of an account of the Western tradition of marriage to demonstrate its cardinal ideas and institutions.

All five of these models started with several basic assumptions about marriage inherited from classical Greco-Roman sources that were retrieved and reconstructed each time a new model emerged. Already in the centuries before Christ, classical Greek philosophers treated marriage as a natural and necessary institution designed to foster the mutual love, support, and friendship of husband and wife, and to produce legitimate children who would carry on the family name and property. Foundational to the Western Christian tradition were Aristotle's insights that monogamous marriage is a natural institution for most men and woman, that it is at once "useful," "pleasant," and "moral" for their lives, that it provides efficient pooling and division of specialized labor

1. H. Richard Niebuhr, *Christ and Culture* (New York: Harper & Row, 1951), 39–40.

and resources within the household, and that it serves for the fulfillment, happiness, and lasting friendship of husbands and wives, parents and children. Also essential were Aristotle's insights that the marital household was the foundation of the polis, the first school of justice and education, the private font of public virtue. These views were echoed and elaborated by later Roman Stoic philosophers who described marriage as a "sacred and enduring union" that entailed a complete sharing of the persons, properties, and pursuits of husband and wife in service of marital affection and friendship, mutual caring and protection, and mutual procreation and education of children. These philosophical ideas of marriage entered pre-Christian Roman law, which defined "lawful marriage" as "the union of a man and a woman, a partnership for life involving divine as well as human law" and restricted marriage to men and women who were of the age, fitness, and capacity to marry each other.

The Bible provided the Western tradition with a set of religious teachings about marriage that complemented the philosophical teachings of the Greeks and Romans but also went beyond them. The creation narratives in Genesis 1 and 2 treated marriage as a creation and commandment of God, a one-flesh union between a man and woman whom God called to be "fruitful and multiply." The later Hebrew prophets described marriage as an enduring covenant of love, modeled on the covenant between God and his chosen people of Israel. The New Testament confirmed the natural origins and orientation of marriage as the one-flesh union of male and female. But it also insisted on the essential mutuality of marriage, the need for both husbands and wives to sacrifice themselves and their bodies for the other and to respect and meet the other's physical, sexual, material, and moral needs. This Christian ethic confirmed the procreative goods and goals of marriage so celebrated in the Jewish and Greco-Roman traditions. But it now treated children as new cocreations of God and humanity, as new models of faith in the church community. This ethic confirmed the traditional injunctions against adultery and other illicit sexual unions that corrupted the blood, commingled the property, and compromised the legacy of the family. But it also now called husbands and wives to flee all fornication and to purify their hearts and minds in loving service of each other, their children, and the Christian community.

The *Catholic sacramental model* began with the insights offered by fifth-century Latin Father, Augustine of Hippo, who described marriage as a natural God-given institution that served the goods of children, fidelity, and sacramental stability. But the model assumed definitive theological and legal form in the High Middle Ages from the twelfth to fifteenth centuries. Catholic writers in this period came to treat marriage and the family in a threefold manner—at once as a natural, contractual, and sacramental unit. First, marriage was a natural association, created by God to enable man and woman to "be fruitful and multiply" and to raise children in the service and love of God. Since the fall into sin, marriage had also become a remedy for lust, a channel to direct one's natural passion to the service of the community and the church. Second, marriage was a contractual unit, formed by the mutual consent of the parties. This contract prescribed for couples a lifelong relation of love, service, and devotion to each other and proscribed unwarranted breach or relaxation of their duties to each other and their children. Third, marriage between Christians was an indissoluble sacrament. The temporal union of body, soul, and mind within the marital estate symbolized the eternal union between Christ and the church and brought sanctifying grace to the couple, the church, and the community. This sacramental perspective helped to integrate the natural and the contractual dimensions of marriage and to render marriage a central concern of the church.

Though a sacrament and a sound way of Christian living, marriage, however, was not considered to be particularly spiritually edifying. Marriage was more of a remedy for sin than a recipe for righteousness. Marital life was considered less commendable than celibate life, propagation less virtuous than contemplation. Clerics, monastics, and other church officials were thus to forgo marriage as a condition for church service. Those who could not forgo marriage were not worthy of the church's holy orders and offices. Celibacy was something of a litmus test of spiritual discipline and social superiority.

From the twelfth century forward, the Catholic Church built upon this conceptual foundation a comprehensive canon law of marriage that was enforced by church courts throughout much of Western Christendom. By the fifteenth century, the church's canon law was the predominant law governing marriage in much of the West; state-administered civil law or common-law norms were generally supplemental and subordinate. Consistent with the natural perspective on marriage, the canon law punished contraception and abortion as violations of the created marital functions of propagation and childrearing. It proscribed unnatural acts such as incest, bestiality, and buggery, and unjust acts such as polygamy, polygyny, and abuses of wives and children. Consistent with the contractual perspective, the canon law ensured voluntary unions by dissolving marriages formed through mistake, duress, fraud, or coercion, and by granting husband and wife alike equal rights to enforce conjugal debts that had been voluntarily assumed. Consistent with the sacramental perspective, the church protected the sanctity and sanctifying purpose of marriage by declaring valid marital bonds to be indissoluble and by dissolving invalid unions between Christians and non-Christians or between parties related by various legal, spiritual, blood, or familial ties. This canon law of marriage was formalized and systematized by the Council of Trent in 1563 and greatly influenced Western marriage law for centuries thereafter. Only in 1917 and again in 1983 did the Catholic Church issue new codes of canon law but leave in place many of the traditional provisions on sex, marriage, and family life forged in the High Middle Ages.

The Lutheran, Calvinist, and Anglican traditions gave birth to three *Protestant models* of marriage. Like Catholics, Protestants retained the naturalist perspective of marriage as an association created for the procreation of children and mutual protection of both parties from sexual sin. They also retained the contractual perspective of marriage as a voluntary association formed by the mutual consent of the couple. Unlike Catholics, however, Protestants rejected the subordination of marriage to celibacy and the celebration of marriage as a sacrament. According to common Protestant lore, the person was too tempted by sinful passion to forgo God's remedy of marriage. The celibate life had no superior virtue and was no prerequisite for clerical service. It too easily led to fornication and concubinage and too often impeded the access to and activities of the clerical office. Moreover, marriage was not a sacrament on the order of baptism. It was instead an independent social institution ordained by God and equal in dignity and social responsibility with the church, state, and other estates of society. Participation in marriage required no prerequisite faith or purity and conferred no sanctifying grace, as did true sacraments.

From this common critique, the Lutheran, Calvinist, and Anglican traditions constructed their own models of marriage. Each Protestant tradition provided a different theological formula for integrating the inherited contractual, natural, and religious perspectives on marriage. Lutherans emphasized the social dimensions of marriage; Calvinists, the covenantal dimensions; and Anglicans, the commonwealth dimensions. Each Protestant tradition also assigned principal legal responsibility for marriage quite differently. Lutherans consigned legal authority mostly to the state; Calvinists, to both state and church; and Anglicans, mostly to the church. These differences in emphasis and authority among early Protestants were based, in part, on differences among their theological models of marriage.

From 1517 onward, the *Lutheran tradition* developed a *social model* of marriage, grounded in the Lutheran doctrine of the heavenly and earthly kingdoms. Marriage, Luther and his colleagues taught, was a social estate of the earthly kingdom of creation, not a sacred estate of the heavenly kingdom of redemption. Though divinely ordained, marriage was directed primarily to human goods, ends, and needs. Marriage revealed to persons their sexual sinfulness and their need for God's marital gift. It deterred prostitution, promiscuity, and other public sexual sins. It taught love, restraint, and other public virtues. All fit men and women were free to enter such unions, clerical and lay alike. Indeed, all persons were encouraged to marry when they came of age unless they had the rare gift of continence.

As part of the earthly kingdom, marriage was governed primarily by the state and its civil law, not the church and its canon law. State officials were God's vice-regents in the earthly kingdom, called to apply justly and equitably the divine and natural laws of sex, marriage, and family life. Church officials were still required to counsel magistrates about God's law and to cooperate with them in publicizing and disciplining marriage. Pastors were still required to minister to families in their congregations. All church members, as part of the priesthood of believers, were required to counsel those who contemplated marriage and to admonish those who sought annulment or divorce. But the church no longer had formal legal authority over marriage.

This social model of marriage was reflected in the transformation of marriage law in sixteenth-century Germany and Scandinavia. Civil marriage courts replaced church courts. Civil marriage statutes replaced canon-law rules. Lutheran jurists published treatises and opinions on marriage law, affirming and drawing out the legal implications of the new evangelical marriage theology. The new state marriage law of Lutheran lands, like the new evangelical marriage doctrine, remained indebted to the Catholic canon law tradition. Traditional canon law rules, like prohibitions against unnatural relations and against infringement of marital functions, remained in effect. The new state law retained most of the impediments that protected free consent, implemented biblical prohibitions against marriage of relatives, and governed the couple's physical relations. Such laws were as consistent with the Catholic sacramental model as with the Lutheran social model of marriage.

But changes in marriage doctrine also yielded changes in marriage law. Because the Lutheran reformers rejected the subordination of marriage to celibacy, they rejected laws that forbade clerical and monastic marriage, denied remarriage to those who had married a cleric or monastic, and permitted vows of chastity to annul promises of marriage. Because they rejected the sacramental nature of marriage, the Reformers allowed for interreligious marriage, for divorce on grounds of adultery, desertion, and other serious fault, and remarriage at least for the innocent party. Because persons by their lustful nature were in need of God's remedy of marriage, the reformers removed numerous impediments to marriage not countenanced by Scripture and encouraged the single and the widowed to get married. Because of their emphasis on the godly responsibility of the prince, the pedagogical role of the church and the family, and the priestly calling of all believers, the Reformers insisted that both the formation of marriage and the dissolution of marriage through annulment or divorce be public. The validity of marriage promises depended upon parental consent, witnesses, church consecration and registration, and priestly instruction. Parties who wanted to annul their union or divorce their spouse had to announce their intentions in the church and community and to petition a civil judge to dissolve the bond after open hearings. Secret marriages and private dissolutions were considered dangerous and easily abused. These changes in the laws of marital formation and dissolution introduced in Lutheran Germany—featuring parental consent, two witnesses, civil registration, church consecration, limited impediments, divorce for cause, and remarriage for those men or women who were divorced or widowed—were widely advocated in all Protestant communities after the sixteenth century.

The *Calvinist tradition*, established in mid-sixteenth-century Geneva and eventually spread throughout Europe and North America, set out a *covenantal model* of marriage. This model confirmed many of the Lutheran theological and legal reforms but cast them in a new ensemble. Marriage, Calvin and his followers taught, was not a sacramental institution of the church, but a covenantal association of the entire community. A variety of parties participated in the formation of this covenant. The marital parties themselves confirmed their engagement promises and marital vows before each other and God—rendering all marriages triparty agreements, with God as third-party witness, participant, and judge. The couple's parents, as God's lieutenants for children, gave their consent to the union. Two witnesses, as God's priests to their peers, served as witnesses to the marriage. The minister, holding God's spiritual power of the Word, blessed the couple and admonished them in their spiritual duties. The magistrate, holding God's temporal power of the sword, registered the couple and protected them in their person and property. Each of these parties was considered essential to the legitimacy of the marriage, for they each represented a different dimension of God's involvement in the covenant. To omit any such party was, in effect, to omit God from the marriage covenant.

The covenant of marriage was grounded in the order of creation and governed by the law of God, Calvinists believed. At creation, God ordained the structure of marriage to be a lifelong union between a fit man and a fit woman of the age of consent. God assigned to this marriage the interlocking purposes of mutual love and support of husband and wife, mutual procreation and nurture of children, and mutual protection of both parties from sexual sin. Thereafter, God set forth in reason, conscience, and the Bible a whole series of commandments and counsels for proper adherence to this ideal-created structure and purpose of marriage.

God's moral law for the covenant of marriage set out two tracks of marital norms: civil norms, which are common to all persons; and spiritual norms, which are distinctly Christian. This moral law, in turn, gave rise to two tracks of marital morality: a simple morality of duty demanded of all persons regardless of their faith; and a higher morality of aspiration demanded of believers in order to reflect their faith. It was the church's responsibility to teach aspirational spiritual norms for marriage and family life. It was the state's responsibility to enforce mandatory civil norms. This division of responsibility was reflected in Geneva in the procedural divisions between the church consistory and the city council. In marriage cases, the consistory was the court of first instance; it would call parties to their higher spiritual duties, backing their recommendations with (threats of) spiritual discipline. If such spiritual counsel failed, the parties were referred to the city council to compel them, using civil and criminal sanctions, to honor at least their basic civil duties for marriage.

This Calvinist covenantal model mediated both sacramental and contractual understandings of marriage inherited from the Catholic tradition. On the one hand, this covenantal model confirmed the sacred and sanctifying qualities of marriage without ascribing to its sacramental functions. Marriage was regarded as a holy and loving fellowship, a compelling image of the bond between Yahweh and Israel, between Christ and the church. But marriage was no sacrament, for it confirmed no divine promise. On the other hand, this covenantal model confirmed the contractual and consensual qualities of marriage without subjecting it to the personal preferences of the parties alone. Marriage depended for its validity and utility on the voluntary consent of the parties. But marriage was more than a mere contract, for God was a third party to every marriage covenant, and God set its basic terms in the order and law of creation. Freedom of contract in marriage was thus effectively limited to carefully choosing which party to marry—with no real choice about the form, forum, or function of marriage once a fit spouse was chosen.

Calvinists also modified the Lutheran social model of marriage. By superimposing the doctrine of covenant on the two-kingdom framework, Calvinists in effect added a spiritual dimension to marriage life in the earthly kingdom, a marital obligation to spiritual life in the heavenly kingdom, and complementary marital roles for both church and state in the governance of both kingdoms. On the strength of this, Calvinist communities added a variety of refinements to the Protestant marriage law inherited from Lutheran lands. The laws of marital formation, maintenance, and dissolution were tightened to ensure that only fit parties entered this covenant, that only right conduct attended the household, and that only innocent spouses could dissolve the covenant. Consistory, magistracy, and community alike were made responsible for the proper functioning of the marital covenant and the proper enforcement of God's moral laws for marriage.

The *Anglican tradition*, which took shape gradually in the sixteenth and seventeenth centuries, brought forth a *commonwealth model* of marriage. This model embraced the sacramental, social, and covenantal models but went beyond them. For Anglicans, marriage was at once a gracious symbol of the divine, a social unit of the earthly kingdom, and a solemn covenant with one's spouse. But the essential cause, condition, and calling of the family was that it served and symbolized the common good of the couple, the children, the church, and the state all at once. Marriage was appointed by God as "a little commonwealth" to foster the mutual love, service, and security of husband and wife, parent and child. It was likewise appointed by God as a "seedbed and seminary" of the broader commonwealth to teach church, state, and society the essential Christian and political norms and habits.

In the sixteenth century, this commonwealth model served to rationalize the traditional hierarchies of husband over wife, parent over child, church over household, state over church. After three decades of experimentation, Anglican England in the mid-sixteenth century had formally rejected most Protestant reforms of marriage. It returned to much of the medieval canon law of marriage administered by the church, but now under the supreme headship of the English Crown. Calling the marital household "a little commonwealth" signaled its subordinate place within the new hierarchy of social institutions that comprised "the great commonwealth" of England. It also called the household to an internal hierarchy of offices that matched the royal and episcopal offices of the greater commonwealth, all under the "supreme headship" of the monarchy. The commonwealth model was thus used to integrate a whole network of parallel domestic and political duties rooted in the Bible and the English tradition. Moralists expounded at great length the reciprocal duties of husband and wife, parent and child, and master and servant that would produce a well-ordered little commonwealth. And, in keeping with the tradition of stability in the great commonwealth, they prohibited the dissolution of any little commonwealth by divorce.

As the political concept of the English commonwealth was revolutionized and democratized in the seventeenth century, however, so was the English commonwealth model of marriage. The traditional hierarchies of husband over wife, parent over child, and church over family were challenged with a revolutionary new principle of equality. The biblical duties of husband and wife and of parent and child were recast as the natural rights of each household member against the other. The traditional idea of a created natural order of marriage, society, and state met with a new idea of marriage, society, and state formed voluntarily by contracts by individuals moving from the state of nature. Just as the English commonwealth could be rent asunder by force of arms when it abused the people's natural rights, so the family commonwealth could be put asunder by suits at law when it abused the couple's marital rights. Just as the king could be beheaded for abuses in the commonwealth, so the paterfamilias could be removed from the head of the little commonwealth for abuses in the household. This revolutionary construction of the commonwealth model provided the rationale for the incremental liberalization of English marriage law in the course of the next two centuries. It also provided a stepping-stone for the development of the contractarian model of marriage during the Enlightenment era.

After the sixteenth century, these four models of marriage—each with multiple variants—lay at the heart of Western marriage law. The Catholic sacramental model flourished in Italy, Spain, Portugal, and France and in their colonies in Latin America, the Caribbean, Louisiana, Quebec, and other outposts. The Lutheran social model dominated portions of Germany, Austria, Switzerland, and Scandinavia, together with their colonies. The Calvinist covenantal model came to strong expression in Calvinist Geneva and in dispersed Huguenot, Pietist, Presbyterian, and Puritan communities in Western Europe and North America. The Anglican commonwealth model prevailed in much of Great Britain and its many colonies across the Atlantic.

The *Enlightenment contractarian model* of marriage was adumbrated in the eighteenth century, elaborated theoretically in the nineteenth century, and implemented legally in the twentieth century. In various quarters of the Continent, England, and America, exponents of the Enlightenment gave increasing emphasis to the contractual perspective of marriage. The essence of marriage, Enlightenment thinkers argued, was not its sacramental symbolism, nor its covenantal associations, nor its social service to the community and commonwealth. The essence of marriage was the voluntary bargain struck between two parties who wanted to come together into an intimate association. The terms of their marital bargain were not preset by God or nature, church or state, tradition or community. The terms of the marital bargain were set by the parties themselves, in accordance with general rules of contract formation and general norms of a civil society. Such rules and norms demanded respect for the life, liberty, and property interests of other parties, and compliance with general standards of health, safety, and welfare in the community. But the terms of marriage were to be left to the parties themselves. Couples should now be able to make their own marital beds and then to lie in them or leave them as they saw fit.

On the strength of these contractarian convictions, Enlightenment thinkers eventually advocated the abolition of much that was considered sound and sacred in the Western legal tradition of marriage. In the eighteenth and early nineteenth centuries, most Enlightenment writers still maintained traditional ideas of sex, marriage, and family life, which they defended with arguments from nature, utility, and common sense. But in the later nineteenth and twentieth centuries, Enlightenment-based writers began to call for the abolition of the requirements of parental consent, church consecration, and formal witnesses for marriage. They questioned the exalted status of heterosexual monogamy. They called for the absolute equality of husband and wife to receive, hold, and alienate property, to enter into contracts and commerce, to participate on equal terms in the workplace. They castigated the state for leaving annulment practice to the church and urged that the laws of annulment and divorce be both merged and expanded under exclusive state jurisdiction. They urged that paternal abuse of children be severely punished and that the state intervene where necessary to ensure the proper physical and moral nurture and education of children.

This contractarian gospel for the reformation of Western marriage law was too radical to transform much of the law of the nineteenth century, though it did induce greater protections for wives and children in their persons and properties and easier suits for divorce. But this contractarian gospel anticipated much of the agenda for the transformation of marriage law in the twentieth century, particularly in America. In the early part of the twentieth century, sweeping new laws were passed to govern marriage formalities, divorce, alimony, marital property, wife abuse, child custody, adoption, child support, child abuse, juvenile delinquency, education of minors, among other subjects. Such sweeping legal changes had several consequences. Marriages became easier to contract and easier to dissolve. Wives received greater independence in their relationships outside the family. Children received greater protection from the abuses and neglect of their parents and greater access to benefit rights. And the state began to replace the church as the principal external authority governing marriage and family life. The Catholic sacramental concept of the family governed principally by the church and the Protestant concepts of the family governed by the church and broader Christian community both began to give way to a new concept of the private family in which the wills of the marital parties became primary. Neither the church nor the local community nor the paterfamilias could override the reasonable expressions of will of the marital parties themselves.

In the last third of the twentieth century and continuing into the twenty-first, the early Enlightenment call for the privatization of marriage and the family has come to greater expression in new cultural and constitutional norms and habits of privacy, equality, and sexual autonomy. Prenuptial contracts, determining in advance the respective rights and duties of the parties during and after marriage, have gained prominence. No-fault divorce statutes are in place in virtually every state. Legal requirements of parental consent and witnesses to marriage have become largely dead letters. The functional distinction between the rights of the married and the unmarried has been narrowed by a growing constitutional law of sexual autonomy and privacy. Same-sex, nonmarital, and other intimate associations have gained increasing acceptance at large, and at law.

Although *consensual* intimate relationships between adults have become increasingly impervious to state scrutiny, *nonconsensual* conduct has become increasingly subject to state sanction. Many state courts have opened their dockets to civil and criminal cases of physical abuse, rape, embezzlement, conversion, and fraud by one spouse or lover against the other. The ancient "marital exemption" in the law of rape, which often protected abusive husbands from criminal prosecution, is falling into desuetude. Fading, too, is the ancient spousal exemption in evidence law that discouraged spouses from testifying against each other. The arm of the state no longer knocks at the bedroom door with the same ease that it did in the past. But today, if a distressed party opens the bedroom door and calls for help, the state will reach deeply into the intimacies of bed and board and punish severely those who have abused their autonomy.

FROM SACRAMENT TO CONTRACT

This is the grand movement of Western marriage law in the course of the past millennium. It is a movement "from sacrament to contract"—from a sacramental model that prioritizes canonical norms and ecclesiastical structures to a contractarian model that prioritizes private choice and contractual strictures. It is a movement fueled, in part, by the reciprocating shifts in the dominant theological models and legal structures of marriage.

This is a movement not so much of incremental secularization as of intermittent resacralization of Western marriage. The medieval Catholic model was every bit as secular—that is worldly, corporeal, and material—in its theology and law of marriage as the Enlightenment contractarian model. The modern contractarian construction of marital equality was every bit as religious in inspiration as earlier Christian constructions of marital hierarchy—dependent on faith-like beliefs in liberty, equality, autonomy, and more. Each model struck its own balances between church and state, clergy and laity, rights and duties, order and liberty, dogma and adiaphora in matters of sex, marriage, and family life. These balances were struck on the basis of deep religious convictions—whether Catholic, Protestant, Enlightenment libertarian, or some combination of the same. To laicize, temporalize, or politicize marriage is not the same thing as to secularize marriage.

Historians will recognize that my book title, *From Sacrament to Contract*, is a play on the words of Sir Henry Sumner Maine's thesis that legal history altogether moves "from status to contract." In a series of nineteenth-century classics,

Maine argued that all law must be viewed as part and product of the spirit of a people and their times—of a *Volksgeist und Zeitgeist*, as his German counterparts put it. As the spirit of a people changes, so inevitably does their law. Moreover, Maine had argued that, in earlier eras, a person's religious and familial status was a critical source of legal identity, rights, and duties and that, by contrast, in his own day individually negotiated contracts were a more important source for the same.[2] These two general insights of Maine find a place in this book. The shifts in prevailing Western marriage law were, in part, products of shifts in the prevailing spirit and theology of a people, although they did not always follow the neat *post hoc ergo propter hoc* development that Maine sometimes suggested. Moreover, a person's marital status was historically defined much more fully by one's standing in the sacramental, covenantal, or commonwealth communities than is the case today.

Maine, however, pressed his logic to all manner of fanciful conclusions that play no part in this book. For example, his descriptions of grand movements from religious primitivism to cultural custom to legal codes and from fiction to equity to legislation, in my view depend on far too schematic and selective a treatment of the historical data. His preferences for legislation over natural law, individuals over communities, equality over hierarchy, rights over duties led him to a Whiggish historicism that seemed to render Enlightenment liberalism the aspirational apex of every law and civilization. His repeated insistence that "the basic unit of an ancient society was the Family, and of a modern society the Individual" does justice neither to the place of the individual in ancient societies nor to the place of the family in modern societies.[3] It is going too far to call Maine "a reactionary, a laissez-faire extremist in the [Herbert] Spencerian tradition, an ethnocentric imperialist, and a scholar whose British-based prejudices tainted his investigations of law and kinship with strong infusions of ideology."[4] But Maine must certainly be used with great caution.

Historians will also recognize that the beginning and end of this story of Western marriage law, represented by the terms "sacrament" and "contract" in my book title, are well known. A long tradition of distinguished medievalists—represented in America today by James A. Brundage, Charles Donahue, R. H. Helmholz, John T. Noonan, and Philip Reynolds—has brought the medieval sacramental theology and canon law of marriage to vivid light and life.

2. See Henry Sumner Maine, *Ancient Law* (London: J. Murray, 1861); idem, *Village Communities in the East and the West* (London: J. Murray, 1871); idem, *Lectures on the Early History of Institutions* (London; J. Murray, 1875); idem, *Dissertations on Early Law and Customs* (New York: Henry Holt, 1883). See studies in Paul Vinogradoff, *The Teaching of Sir Henry Maine* (Oxford: Oxford University Press, 1904); R. C. J. Cocks, *Sir Henry Sumner Maine: A Study in Victorian Jurisprudence* (Cambridge: Cambridge University Press, 1988).

3. Maine, *Ancient Law*, 121.

4. Kenneth Bock, "The Moral Philosophy of Sir Henry Sumner Maine," *Journal of History of Ideas* 37 (1976):147, 149. Also see Henry Orenstein, "The Ethnological Theories of Henry Sumner Maine," *American Anthropologist* 70 (1968): 264; Mark Francis, "Henry Sumner Maine: Victorian Evolution and Political Theory," *History of European Ideas* 19 (1994): 753.

Their research has made clear that much of what we today call the "traditional family" and the "classic law" of the family was forged by canon lawyers and scholastic theologians from 1100–1350. The great medieval tradition of marriage—amply amended over the centuries, particularly by the Second Vatican Council in the early 1960s and various modern papal declarations—lives on within the canon law of the Catholic Church today and in muted form within the civil law of many nations where Catholicism was strong. Given the rich literature on the subject, I have provided only a relatively brief summary in chapter 4 of the sacramental model that emerged in the Middle Ages, culminating in the Council of Trent, directing readers to the many authoritative studies at hand. I have also spent more time in chapters 1–3 documenting the classical, biblical, and patristic sources on which medieval writers drew heavily to create their unique synthesis.

Likewise, a long tradition of distinguished historians—represented in America today by David Blankenhorn, Margaret Brinig, Don Browning, Jean Bethke Elshtain, Mary Ann Glendon, and others—has described the rise of the modern contractarian model in Anglo-American law. Their research has made clear what Professor Glendon saw already in 1977: "Beginning in the 1960s, there has been an unparalleled upheaval in the family law systems of Western industrial societies [that] equals and surpasses in magnitude that which occurred when family matters passed from ecclesiastical to secular authorities in the age that began with the Protestant Reformation."[5] The past two generations of scholarship have produced innumerable books and articles describing, decrying, and defending these massive changes in the modern family. Again, to avoid redundancy, I have given only a brief summary in chapter 8 of the rise of the contractarian model of marriage, directing the reader to the more substantial treatments readily at hand.

What is far less known to all but specialists are the chronological and conceptual movements between "sacrament" and "contract"—the "to" in my book title *From Sacrament to Contract*. I have thus devoted a good deal of this book to mining the theologies and laws of marriage in the Lutheran, Calvinist, and Anglican traditions and in the classical, biblical, and patristic sources on which they drew, parsing many dusty old collections of canons, commentaries, and cases in the process. The stories of Luther burning the canon-law books in 1520 and later condemning "jurists as bad Christians" has, for many, obscured the reality that the Lutheran Reformation profoundly transformed Western public and private law, including the law of sex, marriage, and family life. I have thus devoted chapter 5 to giving the reader something of a tour of the rich German Reformation sources on marriage, pointing the reader to comparable materials on Reformation Scandinavia. The early Calvinist sources of covenant theology and laws of marriage have been almost entirely lost on modern historians outside

5. Mary Ann Glendon, *State, Law, and Family: Family Law in Transition in the United States and Western Europe* (Boston and Dordrecht: Martinus Nijhoff Publishers, 1977), 1.

of narrow Protestant circles, and I have thus devoted chapter 6 to a close case study of Calvin's marital theology and the marriage law of sixteenth-century Geneva that he helped to create and implement. The remarkable evolution of early modern Anglican commonwealth understandings of marriage—from Thomas Becon in the mid-sixteenth century to John Locke in the later seventeenth—is now known only in fragments to specialists, and I have thus devoted chapter 7 to a long discussion of this topic.

To bring to light all these historical models of marriage is not to wax nostalgic about a golden age of Western marriage, but to point to a rich resource for the lore and law of modern marriage that is too little known and too little used today. Too much of contemporary society seems to have lost sight of the rich and diverse Western theological heritage of marriage and of the uncanny ability of the Western legal tradition to strike new balances between order and liberty, orthodoxy and innovation, with respect to our enduring and evolving sexual and familial norms and habits. Too many contemporary churches seem to have lost sight of the ability of their theological ancestors to translate their enduring and evolving perspectives on marriage and family life into legal forms, both canonical and civil. There is a great deal more in those dusty old tomes and canons than idle antiquaria or dispensable memorabilia. These ancient sources ultimately hold the theological genetic code that has defined the contemporary family for what it is—and what it can be.

Chapter 1

Classical Foundations of Western Marriage

The Western tradition inherited from ancient Greece and Rome the idea that marriage is a union of a single man and single woman who unite for the purposes of mutual love and friendship and mutual procreation and nurture of children. Classical philosophers and jurists alike regarded monogamous marriage as both a private good for members of the household and a public good for the broader community or polis. This idea was reflected in early Greek laws already in the sixth century BCE and became a staple of Greek philosophy from the fifth century onward.[1] In the opening centuries of the new millennium, various Roman Stoics and Roman jurists repeated these Greek ideas of the goods of monogamous marriage, grounding them more fully in a theory of natural law. And in the first four centuries CE, before the Christianization of Rome, the Roman emperors put in place a sophisticated law of sex, marriage, and family life.

---

1. See the laws of Solon described in Susan Lape, "Solon and the Institution of the 'Democratic' Family Form," *Classical Journal* 98 (2002/3): 117–39 and other early Greek legislation in Cynthia B. Patterson, *The Family in Greek History* (Cambridge, MA: Harvard University Press, 1998), 22–27; W. Scheidel, "A Peculiar Institution? Greco-Roman Monogamy in Global Context," *The History of the Family* 14 (2009): 280–91.

These classical sources were a critical foundation for Western marriage. Some of these classical teachings found a place in the writings and canons developed by the church fathers in the first five centuries CE, particularly in the writings of Augustine of Hippo, as we will see in chapter 3. More were preserved in the Eastern Empire that eventually came to be known as the Byzantine Empire and the world of Orthodox Christianity. But after the sixth century CE, many of these classical Greek philosophical and Roman law texts were lost to the West for half a millennium. They were preserved principally by Arabic and Muslim scholars from the seventh to eleventh centuries, before they were rediscovered and reintroduced into the first Western universities in the later eleventh and twelfth centuries. Thereafter, these classic texts became staple parts of high medieval canon law and theological discourses on marriage. These ancient texts were reworked anew in the later fifteenth and sixteenth centuries by humanists and legal scholars, who used them to spur the reformation movements of the sixteenth and seventeenth centuries, which shaped both Continental civil and Anglo-American common law.

In this chapter, I sample some of the main teachings on marriage in Plato and Aristotle, the Roman Stoics, and the Roman law.

PLATO AND ARISTOTLE

Plato (ca. 428–ca. 347 BCE) said it was obvious that a "just republic . . . must arrange [for] marriages, sacr[ed] so far as may be. And the most sacred marriages would be those that were most beneficial."[2] When advising young men on how to choose a wife, Plato wrote further: "A man should 'court the tie' that is for the city's good, not that which most takes his own fancy."[3] Once married, the man should restrict "procreative intercourse to its natural function, . . . and the result will be untold good. It is dictated, to begin with, by nature's own voice, leads to the suppression of the mad frenzy of sex, as well as marriage breaches of all kinds, and all manner of excess in meats and drinks, and wins men to affection of their wedded wives. There are also numerous other blessings which will follow."[4] Plato further underscored the natural human need for dyadic love as a way for humans to complete themselves. "This then is the source of our desire to love each other. Love is born into every human being; it calls back the halves

2. Plato, *Republic* 5.458E, in *The Collected Dialogues of Plato, Including the Letters,* ed. and trans. Edith Hamilton and Huntingdon Cairns (New York: Pantheon Books, 1961), 575, 698. My colleague Philip Reynolds has pointed out that Greek term *hieros,* which appears back-to-back in this quotation, is better translated as "sacred" both times rather than as "sacrament" the first time and "sacred" the second as the translator has done. I am grateful for his correction of this translation, which I have used in prior publications.

3. Plato, *Laws* 6. 773B, in *The Collected Dialogues,* 1350.

4. Plato, *Laws* 8. 839A-B, in *The Collected Dialogues,* 1404.

of our original nature together; it tries to make one out of two and heal the wound of human nature. . . . Why should this be so? It's because . . . we used to be complete wholes in our human nature, and now 'Love' is the name for our pursuit of wholeness, for our desire to be complete."[5]

Plato's student Aristotle (384–321 BCE) viewed marriage as the foundation of the polis and the prototype of friendship. He envisioned humans as political or communal animals who form states and other associations "for the purpose of attaining some good."[6] "Every state is composed of households," Aristotle wrote famously in his *Politics*.[7] Every household, in turn, is composed of "a union or pairing of those who cannot exist without one another. A male and female must unite for the reproduction of the species—not from deliberate intention, but from the natural impulse. . . to leave behind them something of the same nature as themselves."[8] Aristotle extended this view in his *Ethics*, now emphasizing the natural inclinations and goods of dyadic marriage beyond its political and social expediency:

> The love between husband and wife is evidently a natural feeling, for nature has made man even more of a pairing than a political animal in so far as the family is an older and more fundamental thing than the state, and the instinct to form communities is less widespread among animals than the habit of procreation. Among the generality of animals male and female come together for this sole purpose [of procreation]. But human beings cohabit not only to get children but to provide whatever is necessary to a fully lived life. From the outset the partners perform distinct duties, the man having one set, the woman another. So by pooling their individual contributions [into a common stock] they help each other out. Accordingly there is general agreement that conjugal affection combines the useful with the pleasant. But it may also embody a moral ideal, when husband and wife are virtuous persons. For man and woman have each their own special excellence, and this may be a source of pleasure to both. Children too, it is agreed, are a bond between the parents—which explains why childless unions are more likely to be dissolved. The children do not belong to one parent more than the other, and it is the joint ownership of something valuable that keeps people from separating.[9]

To ensure that marital couples would remain bonded together for the sake of their children, Aristotle (echoing Plato's *Laws*) prescribed a whole series of rules

5. Plato, *Symposium*, trans. Alexander Nehmans and Paul Woodruff (Indianapolis: Hackett Publishers, 1989), 25–31.

6. Aristotle, *Politica* 1.1.1, in *The Politics of Aristotle*, ed. and trans. Ernest Barker (New York: Oxford University Press, 1962).

7. Ibid., 1.3.1.

8. Ibid., 1.2.2.

9. Aristotle, *The Nicomachean Ethics* 8.12, in *The Ethics of Aristotle*, trans. and ed. J. A. K. Thomson (repr., New York: Penguin Books, 1965). The interpolation "into a common stock" is an alternative translation that appears in several other translations of this passage.

about the ideal ages, qualities, and duties of husband and wife to each other and to their children.[10]

Aristotle rejected Plato's passing suggestion in *The Republic* that children be raised by state nurses, without maintaining any ties to their parents. Plato had speculated that this arrangement of anonymous parentage would help overcome tribalism and nepotism, the chief cause of civic strife and partisanship. But by the time he wrote his *Laws*, Plato had abandoned this suggestion and again commended monogamous marriage and joint parentage of children.[11] Aristotle rejected Plato's earlier suggestion, too, arguing that parents will better identify with and invest in their children and kin if they are certain that the children are theirs, that they carry their "blood" and bodily "substance":

> Whereas in a state having women and children in common, love will be watery, and the father will certainly not say "my son," or the son "my father." As a little sweet wine mingled with a great deal of water is imperceptible in the mixture, so, in this sort of community, the idea of relationship which is based upon these names will be lost; there is no reason why the so-called father should care about the son, or the son about the father, or brother about one another. Of the two qualities which chiefly inspire regard and affection—that a thing is your own and that it is your only one—neither can exist in such a state as this.[12]

Plato's purported utopian society contemplated in *The Republic*, which failed to privilege these natural family ties, would actually work out to be anything but utopian, Aristotle argued. Such a society would "water down" parental recognition and investment to the detriment of children. Moreover, it would unleash greater violence within society because parties would lack the natural restraint that most persons have about harming their known blood kin. "Evils such as assaults, unlawful loves, homicides, will happen more," Aristotle wrote, "for they will no longer call the members of the class they have left brothers, and children, and fathers, and mothers, and will not, therefore, be afraid of committing any crimes" against them.[13]

THE ROMAN STOICS

In the centuries after Plato and Aristotle, the Roman Stoics repeated and glossed these classical Greek views about marriage, even while many of them celebrated celibacy as the higher ideal for philosophers seeking quiet contemplation. For

10. Ibid., 8.10–12; also see Plato, *Laws* 6. 773-774. See further Sarah Pomeroy, *Families in Classical and Hellenistic Greece: Representations and Realities* (Oxford: Clarendon Press, 1997), and the discussions of comparable sentiments of Xenophon in Sarah Pomeroy, *Xenophon, "Oeconomicus": A Social and Political Commentary* (Oxford: Clarendon Press, 1994).

11. Plato, *Republic* 459D–461E.

12. Aristotle, *Politics* 2.4.

13. Ibid.

example, Musonius Rufus (b. ca. 30 CE), an influential Stoic moralist, described monogamous marriage in robust companionate terms that prefigured the familiar language of the Western marriage liturgy:

> The husband and wife. . . should come together for the purpose of making a life in common and of procreating children, and furthermore of regarding all things in common between them, and nothing peculiar or private to one or the other, not even their own bodies. The birth of a human being which results from such a union is to be sure something marvelous, but it is not yet enough for the relation of husband and wife, inasmuch as quite apart from marriage it could result from any other sexual union, just as in the case of animals. But in marriage there must be above all perfect companionship and mutual love of husband and wife, both in health and in sickness and under all conditions, since it was with desire for this as well as for having children that both entered upon marriage.[14]

Musonius further insisted that sexual intercourse was "justified only when it occurs in marriage and is indulged in for the purpose of begetting children." He was almost unique among first-century writers in condemning the sexual double standards of the ancient Greco-Roman world of his day that treated a wife's extramarital sex with anyone as adultery but allowed a husband to consort freely with prostitutes or slaves. Both husband and wife had to remain faithful to each other in body and soul, he insisted. Musonius was also distinctive in condemning the Roman toleration of leaving unwanted infants exposed to die. He praised those lawgivers who "considered the increase of the homes of the citizens [through procreation] the most fortunate thing for the cities and the decrease of them [through infanticide] the most shameful thing." Indeed, he wrote, "whoever destroys human marriage destroys the home, the city, and the whole human race."[15]

Musonius's student, Hierocles (early second century CE), argued more strongly than his teacher that it was incumbent upon all men, even philosophers seeking quiet contemplation, to marry and to maintain a household. For "the married couple is the basis of the household, and the household is essential for civilization," he wrote, echoing Aristotle.[16] While procreation remained the ultimate ideal of marriage, in Hierocles' view, the consistent companionship and mutual care of husband and wife was no less important, even in the absence of children:

> The beauty of a household consists in the yoking together of a husband and wife who are united to each other by fate, are consecrated to the gods who preside over weddings, births, and houses, agree with each other and have all things in common, including their bodies, or rather their souls, and who exercise appropriate rule over their household and servants, take care in

14. Musonius Rufus, *Musonius Rufus: The Roman Socrates*, trans. and ed. Cora E. Lutz (New Haven, CT: Yale University Press, 1947), 89.

15. Ibid., 87, 93, 97. See further Roy B. Ward, "Musonius and Paul on Marriage," *New Testament Studies* 36 (1990): 281–89.

16. Judith Evans Grubbs, *Law and Family in Late Antiquity: The Emperor Constantine's Marriage Legislation* (Oxford: Clarendon Press, 1995), 59.

rearing their children, and pay an attention to the necessities of life which is neither intense nor slack, but moderate and fitting.[17]

The prolific Roman historian and moralist Plutarch (46–120 CE) extolled the pleasures of marital love, intimacy, and friendship. The ideal marriage, he wrote, is "a union for life between a man and a woman for the delights of love and the getting of children." "In the case of lawful wives, physical union is the beginning of friendship, a sharing, as it were, in great mysteries. The pleasure [of sexual intercourse] is short; but the respect and kindness and mutual affection and loyalty that daily spring from it . . . [renders] such a [marital] union a 'friendship.'" And again: "No greater pleasures derived from others, nor more continuous services are conferred on others than those found in marriage, nor can the beauty of another friendship be so highly esteemed or so enviable as when a man and wife keep house in perfect harmony."[18]

The ideal marital household, Plutarch continued in his *Advice to the Bride and Groom*, is a sharing of the person, property, and pursuits of its members under the gentle leadership of the paterfamilias:

> When two notes are struck together, the melody belongs to the lower note. Similarly, every action performed in a good household is done by the agreement of the partners, but displays the leadership and decision of the husband. . . .
>
> Plato says that the happy and blessed city is one in which the words "mine" and "not mine" are least to be heard, because the citizens treat everything of importance, so far as possible, as their common property. Even more firmly should these words be banished from a marriage. Doctors tell us that an injury on the left side refers the sensation to the right. Similarly, it is good for a wife to share her husband's feelings, and a husband his wife's, so that, just as ropes gain strength from the twisting of the strands, so their communion may be the better preserved by their joint effort, through mutual exchanges of goodwill. Nature joins you together in your bodies, so that she may take a part of each, and mixing them together give you a child that belongs to you both, such that neither of you can say what is his or her own, and what the other's. Community of resources also is particularly appropriate for the married; they should pour everything into one fund, mix it all together, and not think of one part as belonging to one and another to the other, but of the whole as their own, and none of it anyone else's.[19]

Plutarch also wrote at length about the natural affinity and affection of parents to their children. Among "the first mothers and fathers . . . there was no law ordering them to have families, no expectation of advantages or return to be

17. Ibid., 59–60, quoting Hierocles.

18. Plutarch, *Life of Solon* 20.4, in *Plutarch's Lives*, trans. Bernadotte Perrin (London: William Heinemann, 1928); Plutarch, *The Dialogue of Love* §§769–770, in *Plutarch's Moralia*, trans. L. Pearson (London: W. Heinemann, 1960). See further *Plutarch's "Advice to the Bride and Groom," and "A Consolation to His Wife,"* ed. Sarah B. Pomeroy (New York: Oxford University Press, 1999).

19. *Plutarch's "Advice,"* 6–10.

got out of them." "But the love of one's offspring implanted by nature moves and influences" parents even then both to have nurture and care for their children, much like it moves many other animals. "There is no power or advantage to be got from children, but that the love of them, alike in mankind as among the animals, proceeds entirely from nature." Nature also teaches that mothers should nurse and nurture their own infant children, and that both mother and father should cooperate in the upbringing, discipline, and education of their children.[20] Although Plutarch, like most of the ancient philosophers, advocated what he called "lawful marriage," he did not believe that law creates marriage or parenthood. Marital relationships spring from the natural inclinations of attraction and attachment between a man and a woman, which the law of the state then recognizes, sanctions, channels, and thereby promotes.

Not only law but also liturgy served to sanction these natural inclinations and appetites for marriage. For example, an early Greek handbook, attributed to Menander Rhetor of Laodicea (third century CE), included some telling instructions on what should be included in the wedding hymn, sung by an official when the couple is formally joined. The liturgy described by Menander underscores the philosophical beliefs in the transcendent sources and ends of marriage:

> After the proemia there should follow a sort of thematic passage on the god of marriage, including the general consideration of the proposition that marriage is a good thing. You should begin far back, telling how Marriage was created by Nature immediately after the dispersal of Chaos, and perhaps also how Love too was created then. . . . You should go on to say that the ordering of the universe . . . took place because of Marriage. . . . [Marriage] also made ready to create man, and contrived to make him virtually immortal, furnishing successive generations to accompany the passage of time. . . . Marriage gives us immortality. . . . It is due to Marriage that the sea is sailed, the land is farmed, philosophy and knowledge of heavenly things exist, as well as laws and civil governments—in brief, all human things.[21]

Later Menander advised the rhetor to pray that the couple be able to fulfill the good of procreation:

> Add a prayer, asking the gods to grant them goodwill and harmony, happiness [?] in their union, a mingling of souls as of bodies, so that the children may be like both parents. . . . And you may add: "so that you can provide children for the city, who will flourish in letters, in generosity, in charitable benefactions."[22]

20. *The Complete Works of Plutarch*, 6 vols. (New York: Kelmscott Society, 1909), 5:1–27.

21. *Menander Rhetor*, trans. and ed. D. A. Russell and N. G. Wilson (Oxford: Oxford University Press, 1981), 136–39.

22. Ibid., 150–52, with analysis in Grubbs, *Law and Family*, 63–64. On other marriage rites in the ancient Greco-Roman world, see Karen K. Hersch, *The Roman Wedding: Ritual and Meaning in Antiquity* (Cambridge, MA: Harvard University Press, 2010).

CLASSICAL ROMAN LAW

Some of these philosophical views about marriage were also reflected in classical Roman law. Marriage was a prominent public concern for Rome from the beginning, and monogamous marriage was considered "an honorable and desirable condition . . . that ensured the continuation of the human race and provided a sort of communal immortality" for Rome itself and for the extended families (*familiae*) that made it up.[23] A number of Roman jurists had "a sentimental ideal" of marriage "focused on a standard of companionate (but not necessarily equal) marriage and a delight in children as individuals and as symbols of home comforts" and perpetuators of the family's name, property, and household.[24]

Unlike the philosophers who focused on the functions and ethics of marriage, the jurists focused on the form of marriage and the formalities that attended its proper formation, maintenance, and dissolution. The first Roman emperor, Caesar Augustus (27 BCE—14 CE), put in place several strong new laws on marriage and family life that systematized, reformed, and expanded the half millennium of laws inherited from the Roman Republic, going back to the Twelve Tables (ca. 450 BCE). Caesar's laws, in turn, catalyzed sundry commentaries and imperial edicts over the next five centuries, which were later compiled in Emperor Justinian's *Corpus iuris civilis* (ca. 529–534). This massive legal text, while lost to the West after the fall of Rome in the fifth century, was rediscovered in the late eleventh century and became an important foundation of the canon-law, civil-law, and common-law traditions alike.

Well before the Christianization of the Roman Empire in the fourth century, classical Roman law defined a "lawful marriage" as "the union of a man and a woman, a partnership for life involving divine as well as human law."[25] This mid-third-century formulation, by the Stoic jurist Herennius Modestinus, was of a piece with the Stoic teachings of his teacher, Ulpian, who called marriage an "inseparable communion" and "a sacred and enduring union," to be "voluntarily contracted" for the sake of "marital affection" and the "propagation of offspring."[26] Modestinus and Ulpian were typical of some of the classical Roman jurists who regarded marriage as a mandate of the natural law. Justinian's *Institutes* later distilled the prevailing view: "Natural law is the law instilled by nature in all creatures. It is not merely for mankind but for all creatures of the

23. Grubbs, *Law and Family*, 64.

24. Suzanne Dixon, "The Sentimental Ideal of the Roman Family," in *Marriage, Divorce, and Children in Ancient Rome*, ed. Beryl Rawson (Oxford: Oxford University Press, 1991), 99–113; see also idem, *The Roman Family* (Baltimore: Johns Hopkins University Press, 1992).

25. *The Digest of Justinian*, ed. Theodor Mommsen and Paul Krueger, trans. Alan Watson, 4 vols. (Philadelphia: University of Pennsylvania Press, 1985), 23.2.1 (hereafter cited as *Dig.*).

26. Ibid.; 24.1.32; 25.1; 35.1; *Justinian's Institutes*, ed. Paul Kruger, trans. Peter Birks and Grant McLeod (Ithaca, NY: Cornell University Press, 1987), 1.9–10 (hereafter, *Inst.*).

sky, earth, and sea. From it comes [the union] between male and female, which we call marriage, and also the bearing and bringing up of children."[27]

To form a "lawful marriage," classical Roman law required that the man and woman be of the age of puberty and have the fitness and capacity (*conubium*) to enter into marriage with each other. This latter requirement of *conubium* precluded marriage between parties of different ranks or classes, notably between Roman citizens and noncitizens and between noncitizen freemen and slaves (slaves were forbidden marriage altogether, even with each other, until the third century CE). The requirement of *conubium* also precluded marriage between parties related by blood, marriage, or adoption—the impediments of consanguinity and affinity, as they came to be called, whose violation constituted the crime of incest.

At least among aristocratic citizens, marriage was a two-step process, involving both a formal engagement and a later celebratory wedding and public feast. Between the engagement and wedding day, the couple's families or guardians would often negotiate and exchange marital property—the woman's family contributing a dowry to the budding marital household, the man's family in turn contributing betrothal gifts to his fiancée and her family. It was customary, at least in parts of the empire, to prepare a dotal, or marital, contract that set out these property contributions and their disposition in case the engagement or marriage was broken. These marital contracts included specific language that the marriage was entered into "for the private and public good" and "in order to bring forth children." But throughout the imperial period, Roman law maintained the traditional belief that "reciprocal affection constitutes marriage, without it being necessary to enter into a dotal contract" or to hold a public ceremony.[28]

One of the main purposes of marriage in classical Rome was to bear legitimate children who would serve as heirs to the family property, name, lineage, and household religion. Continuity of the family across the generations was of paramount importance in ancient Rome—a local expression of Rome's broader ideal of "communal immortality." The children born to or adopted by a married couple were legitimate; those born outside of marriage (through

---

27. *Inst.* 1.1.2 (rendering *conjunctio* as "the union" rather than "the intercourse," as the translators put it). See also Gaius, *Gaius' Institutiones*, ed. Paul Krüger and William Studemund (Berlin: Weidmann, 1877), 1.1.1: "What natural reason establishes among all men and is observed by all people alike, is called the Law of Nations, as being the law which all nations employ." See also 1.7.55–87, describing the various civil laws of marriage and family life in Rome and their consonance with this law of nations.

28. *The Code of Justinian* 5.4–9, in Paul Krüger, ed., *Corpus iuris civilis* (Berlin: Weidmann, 1928–29) (hereafter, *CJ*). See further Judith Evans Grubbs, "Marrying and Its Documentation in Later Roman Law," in *To Have and to Hold: Marrying and Its Documentation in Western Christendom, 400–1600*, ed. Philip L. Reynolds and John Witte Jr. (Cambridge: Cambridge University Press, 2007), 43–94; Bruce W. Frier and Thomas A. J. McGinn, *A Casebook on Roman Family Law* (Oxford: Oxford University Press, 2004).

fornication, adultery, incest, concubinage, or other illicit unions) were illegitimate. Legitimate children came automatically within the authority of their father (*patria potestas*), who had near absolute power over their person, property, and activities until his death or their emancipation. He also had responsibilities for them: caring for and supporting them, facilitating their later marriages and their entry into a proper profession, and making presumptive provision for them in his last will and testament—though he could disinherit any of his children by name. Legitimate children also automatically came to be members of the formal legal family or extended household, called the *familia*, which was headed by a paterfamilias. These legitimate children were related to the siblings, aunts, uncles, nieces, nephews, and other relatives by blood or adoption within this extended Roman *familia*. All these relatives had mutual rights and responsibilities to each other and could have claims to various parts of the others' estates, especially if one of their kin died without a valid last will and testament.

Much to the dismay of the early church fathers, Roman law recognized the institution of concubinage. Concubinage was a quasi-marital relation that was generally reserved for men of ample means who sought a long-standing monogamous relationship with a woman for sex and companionship. This could be a young man not yet ready for the responsibilities of a wife and children, or a widower or divorced man who already had enough children. It could also be a man who had fallen in love with a woman whom he could not marry because of the social disparities between them.[29] Such was the case with Augustine of Hippo, who took a lowborn woman as a concubine before he converted to Christianity. He could not marry her because of her inferior social status, and he painfully dismissed her after he turned to the faith and turned against concubinage as a violation of the Christian view of marriage.[30]

Most concubines in the Roman Empire were freeborn or freedwomen but of lower status and sometimes of doubtful origin. But concubines kept by men of *dignitas*, such as senators, governors, and even occasional emperors, could be rich women who were citizens. While single men rather freely fornicated with single women of lower classes, including their slaves, Roman law, already before the Christian era, discouraged this promiscuity by a male patron who had a concubine. And this same pre-Christian law—confirmed famously by the first Christian emperor, Constantine, early in the fourth century—prohibited a patron from keeping a concubine once he had become married to another woman. A man could marry his concubine if she was of proper status and not a relative, but he could not have a concubine and a wife at the same time.[31] Men could give gifts to their concubines during their lifetimes, but most could not leave them

29. Paul Meyer, *Der römischen Konkubinat nach den Rechtsquellen und den Inschriften* (Leipzig: G. B. Teubner, 1895).

30. Augustine, *Confessions* 4.2; 6.12–15; Philip L. Reynolds, *Marriage in the Western Church: The Christianization of Marriage during the Patristic and Early Medieval Periods* (Leiden: E. J. Brill, 1994), 101–20.

31. *CJ* 5.26.1 (quoting Constantine in 326); see Grubbs, *Law and Family*, 294–304.

property in their last wills and testaments. Nor could they support any children born to their concubines; they remained illegitimate and the responsibility of their mothers and her *familia*. Concubines were expected to remain faithful to their patrons and could be punished severely for fornicating with others. They could also be dismissed by their male patron or his paterfamilias without cause and left without support from them or legal recourse against them thereafter.

Although the Roman law continued to recognize concubinage, it banned bigamy and polygyny—marriage of one man to two or more women at the same time. In the republic and early centuries of the empire, "Roman law assumed monogamy; so strong and basic was this assumption that classical Roman law simply ignored the possibility of bigamy" as a valid form of marriage and initially imposed no special penalties on it.[32] Extramarital sex by a married woman was punished as adultery, by a married man as fornication.[33] No-fault unilateral divorce could be pursued without formal notice, procedure, or documentation, except in cases of adultery where civil and criminal sanctions could be imposed on the adulteress. Thus, if a man held out another woman as his new wife, it was assumed either that she was a prostitute or concubine or that he had divorced the first wife and married the second. In the latter case, the public and private rights and duties of marriage attached to the second union and no longer to the first. Having two wives at the same time was impossible by the law of the Roman Republic and the early empire.

Beginning in 258 CE, the Roman emperors became more explicit in prohibiting and punishing polygyny per se, eventually putting it alongside adultery and incest as "abominable," "wicked," "unnatural," and "execrable" sexual offenses that were against the law of God and the state.[34] A series of new third- and fourth-century laws provided that parties who knowingly entered into an engagement or marriage agreement while already engaged or married to another would be charged with "fornication" (*stuprum*) and would incur *infamia*—a legal black mark that precluded them from holding public office or other positions of trust or authority, from appearing or testifying in court to press a number of private claims, and from exercising a number of private and public rights, even if they were citizens.[35] A father or guardian could also be brought up on charges of *infamia* if he knowingly ordered those under his authority to enter into a bigamous union.[36] No engagement or marriage could proceed without a legitimate breaking of the prior engagement or a successful divorce from the prior marriage. Until that time a second woman or her family could not keep or claim property from her purported fiancé, and the man in turn could reclaim

32. James A. Brundage, *Law, Sex, and Christian Society in Medieval Europe* (Chicago: University of Chicago Press, 1987), 37–38.

33. Jane Gardner, *Women in Roman Law and Society* (London: Croom Helm, 1986), 91–93.

34. *CJ* 6.57.5.1. See further 5.27.2; and Paul Krüger, ed., *Codex Theodosianus* 4.4.6 (Berlin: Weidmann, 1923–26).

35. *Dig.* 3.2.1; 3.2.13.1–4; *CJ* 9.9.18; 5.3.5; Grubbs, *Law and Family*, 167–69.

36. *Dig.* 3.2.1 (Julian); 3.2.13.1–4 (Ulpian).

any property from his purported second fiancée or wife and her family.[37] Both parties could be punished for their *infamia* in attempting or practicing bigamy, though an innocent single woman who had been coerced or tricked into joining a polygynous relationship would be spared.[38]

After the Christianization of the empire in the fourth century, the Christian emperors repeated and extended these provisions against polygamy. They also repeated and extended traditional prohibitions of sexual dalliances that could border on or encourage polygamy. First, men were again forbidden from having both a wife and a concubine at the same time.[39] Second, convicted adulterers, both men and women, were forbidden from ever marrying their former paramours, even after separation or divorce from, or death of, the innocent spouse.[40] Third, a new widow was forbidden to remarry until after a suitable one-year period of mourning on pain of losing her legacy from her late husband and having any child born of another man during this mourning period declared illegitimate.[41]

Later Roman laws took special aim at Jewish polygyny.[42] While monogamy was the norm among the vast majority of Jews, polygyny "existed in a small number of noble families side by side with monogamy among the people at large. Josephus, for instance, tells his Roman readers of the long-standing Jewish custom to marry many wives, while various rules in the Mishnah, especially concerning levirate [marriage—the requirement of a brother to marry his late brother's widow], point to the existence of polygynous families at that period. . . . The vast majority of Jews concurred with the trend towards monogamy, yet no general prohibition against polygyny was laid down" as Jewish law during the Roman period. Indeed Jewish law did not formally renounce polygyny altogether until the twelfth century CE.[43]

The Roman emperors sought to ban the Jewish practice of polygyny. In 393, Emperor Theodosius and others announced: "None of the Jews shall . . . enter into several marriages at the same time."[44] In 535, Emperor Justinian repeated this prohibition, calling polygyny "contrary to nature" and "abominable," again declaring

37. *CJ* 9.9.18; 5.3.5.

38. Ibid.; Susan Treggiari, *Roman Marriage: Iusti Coniuges from the Time of Cicero to the Time of Ulpian* (Oxford: Clarendon Press, 1991), 279.

39. *CJ* 5.26.1.

40. See earlier formulation by Modestinus, in *Dig.* 23.2.24.

41. *CJ* 5.9.1–3. See Judith Evans Grubbs, "Promoting Pietas in Roman Law," in *A Companion to Families in the Greek and Roman Worlds*, ed. Beryl Rawson, Blackwell Companions to the Ancient World (Chichester: John Wiley & Sons, 2011).

42. Adiel Schremer, "How Much Polygyny in Roman Palestine?" *Proceedings of the American Academy for Jewish Research* 63 (1997–2001): 181–223.

43. Ze'ev W. Falk, *Jewish Matrimonial Law in the Middle Ages* (Oxford: Oxford University Press, 1966), 2–6 (internal citations omitted). See further Michael L. Satlow, *Jewish Marriage in Antiquity* (Princeton, NJ: Princeton University Press, 2001), 189–92; Louis M. Epstein, *Marriage Laws in the Bible and the Talmud* (Cambridge, MA: Harvard University Press, 1942), 12–33; and sample contracts in Mordechai Akiva Friedman, *Jewish Marriage in Palestine: A Cairo Geniza Study*, 2 vols. (Tel Aviv and New York: Jewish Theological Seminary of America, 1981).

44. *CJ* 1.9.7.

all children born of the second wife to be illegitimate and ordering the seizure of one-quarter of the property of practicing polygynists.[45] By the ninth century, Byzantine Emperor Theophilus declared the practice of polygyny to be a capital crime, which it remained in much of the West until the nineteenth century.[46]

Before the fourth-century establishment of Christianity, Roman law granted husband or wife alike the right to unilateral no-fault divorce. One partner would send the other a written repudiation, witnessed by seven others. Absent fault, the wife would recover her dowry and the man his marital gifts. If the wife was at fault, particularly for adultery, the husband would retain a portion of the dowry and retain custody of the children. If the husband was at fault, he was required to repay the dowry, sometimes on accelerated terms, and could in extreme cases lose custody of their children. Both parties were free to remarry thereafter.

The first Christian emperor, Constantine, put severe restrictions on these traditional rights to unilateral divorce, especially for women. Unilateral divorce thereafter was allowed only on proof of adultery, poisoning, pimping, or conviction for a grave crime. A man who brought false charges against his wife or procured an illegal divorce was denied the right to remarry; a wife who acted similarly against her husband would lose her dowry and could be exiled. Later Christian emperors expanded the fault grounds for unilateral divorce somewhat, though they still made it procedurally more difficult for wives to divorce. These later emperors, with the exception of Justinian, also retained the traditional view that divorce by mutual consent was permissible, with both parties holding rights to regain their properties brought into the marriage and to remarry someone else thereafter.

SUMMARY AND CONCLUSIONS

Such were some of the sentiments and regulations concerning marriage among selected pre-Christian writers and legal sources. These classical sources illustrate that the West has long recognized that marriage has natural goods and benefits for the couple, their children, and the broader community. Particularly perceptive were Aristotle's insights that marriage is a natural institution that is fundamental and foundational to any republic; that marriage is at once "useful," "pleasant," and "moral" in its own right; that it provides efficient pooling and division of specialized labor and resources within the household; and that it

45. *The Novels [New Laws] of Justinian,* in *The Civil Law,* ed. S. P. Scott, 17 vols. (Cincinnati: The Central Trust Company, 1932), Novel 12; and Novel 89.5.12 [hereafter Nov.]. Two years later, however, Justinian granted a narrow exception for the Jews living in the region of Tyre to continue to practice polygyny, contrary to the general law: Nov. 139. But this exemption ended with his death.

46. *Institutionum graeca paraphrasis Theophilo antecessori vulgo tributa ad fidem librorum manu,* ed. Cantadori Ferrini (Berlin: S. Calvary, 1884), 1.10.6. See Percy Ellwood Corbett, *The Roman Law of Marriage* (1930; repr., Oxford: Clarendon Press, 1969), 143.

serves both for the fulfillment and happiness of spouses, and for the procreation and nurture of children. Also influential was the Stoic idea that marriage is a "sacred and enduring union" that entails a sharing of the persons, properties, and pursuits of husband and wife in service of marital affection and friendship, mutual caring and protection, and mutual procreation and education of children. Roman law distilled these ideas about marriage and defined its basic legal form and valid formation. Marriage was formed by the mutual consent of a fit man and a fit woman and their families; it also involved a complex exchange of property and prerogatives. Children born to or adopted by the married couple were legitimate and heritable; they came under the authority of the paterfamilias, who had obligations for their nurture, care, and education. A breakdown or betrayal of the marriage could lead to unilateral or mutual divorce, with rights to remarry thereafter, at least for the innocent party.

These classical sources illustrate that the Christian tradition, from the beginning, had at its disposal a natural logic and language about the goods and goals of enduring monogamous marriage. To be sure, these classical reflections were only very small fragments within a vast Greco-Roman literature, which also tolerated sexual norms and habits among the elite that the Christian tradition condemned: prostitution, concubinage, sodomy, pedophilia, mixed bathing, group sex, casual consortium with slaves, infanticide, and more.[47] But in these classical sources, the Christian tradition found ready touchstones for a theory of the natural goods and goals of marriage that would prove helpful to their broader theological formulations about marriage. Natural arguments about marriage could not provide the Christian tradition with a complete theology of marriage. But a theology of marriage could not be complete or cogent without some natural foundation and corroboration.

These classical sources further illustrate that the Christian tradition, from the beginning, had a sophisticated system of Roman law at hand to govern sex, marriage, and family life. To be sure, Christian writers from the beginning urged reforms of some features of this Roman legal system, reforms that slowly soaked into Roman law after the fourth-century Christianization of the empire. But a good deal of the Roman law of marriage, much of it forged already before the time of Christ, would find a place in the emerging Christian canon. And in the second millennium, Catholic canon law, Continental civil law, and Anglo-American common law would take as axiomatic many of its legal postulates about marriage.

47. Brundage, *Law, Sex, and Christian Society*, 38–40, 156–72.

Chapter 2

Biblical Foundations
of Western Marriage

The Western tradition of marriage was shaped not only by Greek philosophy and Roman law, but even more by Jewish theology and Mosaic law and its reinterpretation by Jesus and the apostle Paul. The Old Testament, or Hebrew Bible, reported that God created the first marriage between Adam and Eve, calling them to become "two in one flesh" and "to be fruitful and multiply." God wrote the laws for marriage first on the hearts of all men and women (Rom. 2:14-15), then in greater detail in the law given to Moses on Mount Sinai. And God exemplified the ideals of marriage by analogizing it to the special covenant of faith between God and his chosen people, Israel. In the New Testament, both Jesus and Paul echoed the creation story of marriage, lifting up the union of male and female in "one flesh" as the normative ideal for Christian marriages. They elaborated the Mosaic law of marriage, now calling the faithful to live both by its letter and by its spirit. And they introduced a new ideal of marriage by analogizing it to the mysterious and sacrificial union between Christ and the church. The New Testament provided detailed instruction on sexual ethics, calling husbands and wives to love and honor each other, to be faithful and respect their spouse's bodily and spiritual needs, and to abstain from all sexual immorality within and beyond marriage. All these biblical teachings would become anchor texts for the emerging Christian theology, law, and ethics of sex, marriage, and family life and be subject to endless interpretations and elaborations.

MARRIAGE AS CREATION MANDATE

The two creation stories in Genesis 1 and 2 were a critical source for Christian teachings on marriage. Biblical scholars now believe that these two chapters, written several hundred years apart, first appeared together in the Second Temple period in the sixth century BCE. This was the time when a remnant of the Jews returned to Israel from Babylonian exile, rebuilt the temple in Jerusalem, and reissued the Torah (the Jewish law), now with these Genesis texts prominently placed at the head of the Torah.[1] These creation narratives were both a celebration of the divine origins of marriage and, for later interpreters, the starting point for a natural law governing men and women, husbands and wives.[2]

The older, Yahwistic account of the creation of man and woman, written in the tenth or ninth century BCE, appears in Genesis 2:18–24. The first verses of Genesis 2 recount how God created the heavens and the earth and placed the first man in a paradise, called the garden of Eden. But this paradise was not complete without the creation of the first woman. The narrator in Genesis writes:

> Then the LORD God said, "It is not good that the man should be alone; I will make him a helper as his partner." So out of the ground the LORD God formed every animal of the field and every bird of the air, and brought them to the man to see what he would call them; and whatever the man called every living creature, that was its name. The man gave names to all cattle, and to the birds of the air, and to every animal of the field; but for the man there was not found a helper as his partner. So the LORD God caused a deep sleep to fall upon the man, and he slept; then he took one of his ribs and closed up its place with flesh. And the rib that the LORD God had taken from the man he made into a woman and brought her to the man. Then the man said,
>
> > "This at last is bone of my bones
> >   and flesh of my flesh;
> > this one shall be called Woman,
> >   for out of Man this one was taken."
>
> Therefore a man leaves his father and his mother and clings to his wife, and they become one flesh.[3]

1. See John J. Collins, "Marriage, Divorce, and Family in Second Temple Judaism," in Leo G. Perdue et al., *Families in Ancient Israel* (Louisville, KY: Westminster John Knox Press, 1997), 104, 127–28.
2. See David Novak, *Natural Law in Judaism* (Cambridge: Cambridge University Press, 1998).
3. Gen. 2:18–24.

One-flesh union meant more than just the sexual coupling between a man and a woman, though that would become an important dimension of their relationship if done licitly. The Hebrew word for "flesh" (*basar*) is better translated as "human substance" or "real human life."[4] To be joined in one flesh signifies "the personal community of man and woman in the broadest sense—bodily and spiritual community, mutual help and understanding, joy and contentment in each other."[5] Especially when read in the context of Adam's searching for a proper mate, the passage underscores that it was only in the woman, and not in any other creature, that the man found someone like him, someone with whom he could ultimately discover and discern his humanity. Before the creation of Eve, there was no creature to which Adam could compare or join himself. God was above humanity; the beasts of paradise were below it. With the creation of Eve, Adam had a mirror in which to see himself, a creature with whom to compare and complete himself. To be fully human thereafter, Adam and Eve needed each other.[6] That is what was signified in the phrase "one-flesh union" between a man and a woman. That is what Adam was celebrating when he said of Eve, "This at last is bone of my bones and flesh of my flesh." And that is the fundamental human good that the institution of marriage serves to confirm, channel, and celebrate. The ancient rabbis, and a few of the early church fathers with them, taught that it is "only after marriage and the union of man and woman into one person that the image of God may be discerned in them. An unmarried man, in their eyes, is not a whole man."[7] The writer of Ecclesiastes (ca. 400 BCE) also underscored this: "Two are better than one, because they have a good reward for their toil. For if they fall, one will lift up the other. . . . Again, if two lie together, they keep warm; but how can one keep warm alone?"[8]

The description of the woman, Eve, as man's "helper" (*ezer*) did not change the natural quality and equality of the primordial relationship of men and women. In the Bible, to be a "helper" is not necessarily to be in an inferior role—as many later Christian teachings on "male headship" within the home, church, and society would assume.[9] The Hebrew word for "helper" (*ezer*) is the same word that the Hebrew Bible uses fifteen more times to describe God's helping role in human life. Psalm 70:5, for example, describes God this way: "You are my help [*ezer*] and my deliverer." Again, read in context, the emphasis of Genesis 2 is on the woman's unique "suitability" (*kenegdo*) to be the man's helper or partner—unlike any other creature in paradise whom Adam had already

---

4. Michael G. Lawler, *Secular Marriage, Christian Sacrament* (New York: Twenty-Third Publications, 1985), 6–8.

5. Claus Westermann, *Genesis 1–11: A Commentary*, trans. J. J. Scullion, SJ (Minneapolis: Augsburg Publishing House, 1984), 232.

6. John E. Coons and Patrick M. Brennan, *By Nature Equal: The Anatomy of a Western Insight* (Princeton, NJ: Princeton University Press, 1999), 55–62.

7. Lawler, *Secular Marriage, Christian Sacrament*, 7–8.

8. Eccl. 4:9–11.

9. See David Blankenhorn, Don Browning, and Mary Stewart van Leeuwen, eds., *Does Christianity Teach Male Headship?* (Grand Rapids: Wm. B. Eerdmans Publishing Co., 2004).

classified and named. The Hebrew phrase *ezer kenegdo* is usually translated as someone suitable, a "help meet" (KJV) or even a "helpmate" (Darby). But properly it means that the woman is a helper who is like the man, who corresponds to him, who is suitable for and needed by him. The book of Sirach in the Apocrypha underscored this insight: "He who acquires a wife gets his best possession, a helper fit for him and a pillar of support. Where there is no fence, the property will be plundered, and where there is no wife, a man will become a fugitive and a wanderer."[10] Moreover, it is symbolically significant that this Genesis story describes the woman as being created from man's rib, from his midsection. A later Quaker adage, echoing the Talmud, would underscore the equality of men and women implicit in this image: "God did not take Eve out of Adam's head, that she might lord it over him, nor from his heel, that he might trample on her, but out of his rib, nearest his heart, that he might cherish her."[11]

A later Priestly account of creation, written in the sixth century BCE and recorded in Genesis 1, emphasizes anew the equality of the man and the woman as image bearers of God and co-stewards with God of new life thereafter:

> Then God said, "Let us make humankind in our image, according to our likeness; and let them have dominion over the fish of the sea, and over the birds of the air, and over the cattle, and over all the wild animals of the earth, and over every creeping thing that creeps upon the earth."

> So God created humankind in his image,
>   in the image of God he created them,
>   male and female he created them.

> God blessed them, and God said to them, "Be fruitful and multiply, and fill the earth and subdue it.". . . God saw everything that he had made, and indeed, it was very good.[12]

Genesis 5:1–2 repeated this account more cryptically: "When God created humankind, he made them in the likeness of God. Male and female he created them, and he blessed them and named them 'humankind' [*adam*] when they were created." And Genesis 9:1, 7 repeated the admonition for humankind to "be fruitful and multiply, abound on the earth and multiply in it."

Part of the point of creating men and women as image bearers of God, Genesis 1 makes clear, is that they, together, were designed to be God's instruments in producing children and cultivating the earth. God's command to "be fruitful and multiply, and fill the earth and subdue it" was a mandate not only for

10. Sir. 36:29–30. See further Sir. 25:1; 26:1–3, 14; 36:26; Prov. 18:22; 30:18–19; Song 2:16; 6:3; and analysis in David R. Blumenthal, "The Images of Women in the Hebrew Bible," in *Marriage, Sex, and Family in Judaism*, ed. Michael J. Broyde and Michael Ausubel (Lanham, MD: Rowman & Littlefield, 2005), 15–60.

11. Quoted and discussed in Peter Coleman, *Christian Attitudes toward Marriage from Ancient Times to the Third Millennium* (London: SCM Press, 2004), 28.

12. Gen. 1:26–31.

the first man and the first woman, the Christian tradition would later teach. It is also a mandate for all humanity to this day. The union of male and female is not only for their personal completion and fulfillment. It is also designed to allow humanity to continue God's act of creation through their procreation of children—"dressing and keeping" their children as a special procreative responsibility within the general mandate of "dressing and keeping" all of God's creation as stewards and trustees.

These Genesis narratives, of course, are not about marriage per se, except for the oblique reference to a man's "clinging" to his "wife," rather than to just any woman, and "multiplying" with her to form a new family. But the Jewish and Christian traditions saw these creation narratives as a source and sanction of the institution of marriage, whose rules, procedures, and aspirations are laid out more fully in the rest of the Bible. Both traditions saw God's ceremonial presentation of Eve to Adam as a celebration of the first wedding feast. The book of Tobit, from the fourth or third century BCE, celebrates this in the wedding prayer that Tobias offers to his new wife, Sarah:

> Blessed are you, O God of our ancestors.
>   And blessed is your name in all generations forever.
> Let the heavens and the whole creation bless you forever.
> You made Adam, and for him you made his wife Eve
>   as a helper and support.
> From the two of them the human race has sprung.
> You said, "It is not good that the man should be alone;
>   let us make a helper for him like himself."
> I am now taking this kinswoman of mine,
>   not because of lust,
>   but with sincerity.
> Grant that she and I may find mercy
>   and that we may grow old together.[13]

This passage eventually would find a prominent place in Christian wedding liturgies, especially among Eastern Orthodox Christians as well as the Amish and other Anabaptists.[14]

MARRIAGE AS LEGAL RELATION

Much more specific direction on sex, marriage, and family life came through the Mosaic law, or Torah. Particularly the biblical books of Leviticus and Deuteronomy include a large number of rules, procedures, cases, and moral admonitions on point, some of which were echoed and elaborated in the writings of the prophets and sages gathered in the later books of the Hebrew Bible.

13. Tob. 8:5–7.
14. Kenneth W. Stevenson, *Nuptial Blessing: A Study of Christian Marriage Rites* (London: SPCK, 1982).

Included in these many biblical passages are detailed teachings on marital formation, maintenance, and dissolution; on proper sexual behavior by men and women before, within, and after marriage; on the prohibition and punishment of sexual crimes like adultery, fornication, incest, rape, sodomy, interreligious marriage, and more; on the special roles and duties of boy and girl, man and woman, fiancé and fiancée, husband and wife, parent and child, master and servant, brother and sister-in-law, householder and patriarch; on the proper habits of sexual, bodily, and ritual cleanliness for men and women in different seasons; on the special marital and sexual restrictions and responsibilities imposed on priests and Levites; on dowries, marital property, child support, and family inheritance, including primogeniture (the testamentary privileging of the eldest male); on the special care owing to widows, orphans, strangers, slaves, and conquered persons within the household and community; on the complex social, economic, and ritual relationships within and among the marital household, the patriarchal family, the clan or tribe, and the evolving religious and political communities and their leaders. These many Mosaic laws and their prophetic echoes and elaborations provided the Western tradition with a perennial treasure trove of domestic norms and practices to mine in crafting their law, theology, and ethics.

Later Western jurists and theologians, however, understood that the Mosaic law was given by God to the elect people of ancient Israel, not to all humanity. Already the earliest church fathers argued that the Mosaic law had many distinct ceremonial provisions concerning diet, dress, ritual life, and the like that were specific to the time and place of this ancient tribal people. These ceremonial laws, they argued, were fulfilled with the coming of Christ. But the early church fathers also understood that this Mosaic law was, in part, a reflection and elaboration of the natural or moral law that God has "written on [the] hearts" and consciences of all persons.[15] As such, the Mosaic law was a valuable prototype for a Christian law, theology, and ethics of sex, marriage, and family life. Particularly important was the Decalogue, or Ten Commandments, which many Christian writers saw as a source and summary of both the moral law of the ancient Israelites and the natural law of all peoples. Four of the Ten Commandments deal with issues of sex, marriage, and family life. They reiterate the basic structure and obligation of the marital household and the demand for love and fidelity to God and neighbor, parent and spouse, child and servant.

> Remember the sabbath day, and keep it holy. Six days you shall labor and do all your work. But the seventh day is a sabbath to the LORD your God; you shall not do any work—you, your son or your daughter, your male or female slave, your livestock, or alien resident in your town. . . .
>
> Honor your father and your mother, so that your days may be long in the land which the LORD your God is giving you. . . .
>
> You shall not commit adultery. . . .

15. Rom. 2:14–15.

> You shall not covet your neighbor's house; you shall not covet your neighbor's wife, or male or female slave, or ox, or donkey, or anything that belongs to your neighbor.[16]

Also important for the Western Christian tradition was the realization that a number of Mosaic laws of sex, marriage, and family life were comparable to the pre-Christian Roman law. Like the Roman law, the Mosaic law largely presumed marriage to be a monogamous union of a man and a woman,[17] designed for the procreation of children, and it likewise punished adultery and other sexual offenses that betrayed marriage and its fundamental purposes. Like Roman law, Jewish law prohibited incestuous unions of relatives and mixed marriages between parties from different classes and cultures (with Judaism adding interreligious marriage among the prohibited unions). Like Roman law, Jewish law envisioned a two-step marital process of an engagement and a wedding, featuring the exchange of marital gifts, dowry, and other property transactions negotiated by the families or guardians of the newly engaged man and woman. Like Roman law, Jewish law allowed for unilateral divorce at least for the man, and the right to remarriage for both parties thereafter, with the requirement that the father continue to care for and support the children of his first marriage during his lifetime and in devising his testamentary estate. Like Roman law, Jewish law obligated members of the extended Jewish family to care for their kin (though Judaism was unique in requiring "levirate marriage," marrying the widowed wife of one's brother). And like Roman law, Jewish law tended to privilege men in the laws of sexuality, courtship, marriage, divorce, and inheritance and in the adulation of the paterfamilias and the firstborn son (though Jewish law was more tolerant of polygyny than Roman law). A number of Christian writers would later see these and other parallels between Jewish law and Roman law as evidence that these two legal traditions were drawing on a common natural law of sex, marriage, and family life, a natural law whose basic norms were part of the foundation of Christian marriage.

---

16. Exod. 20:8–9, 12, 14, 17.

17. There is enough slippage in some of the Mosaic law texts to allow for polygynous interpretations. As the authoritative *Anchor Bible Dictionary* reports: "Exodus 20:17 and Deut. 5:21 list several things one ought not to covet, and all the objects the individual is warned against coveting are in the singular. If it is possible for a man to have more than one manservant, maidservant, ox, or ass, he could have more than one wife. Or again Lev. 18:8, 11, 14, 15, 16, 20 all refer to uncovering the nakedness of somebody's wife, always again in the singular as well. In fact, Lev. 18:9 warns against uncovering the nakedness of one's sister, who is further identified as "the daughter of your father or the daughter of your mother," indicating that a man could have multiple wives, providing sons and daughters from different mothers. . . . [And] there is one law in the Deuteronomic code (Deut. 21:15–17) which does allow for one man to be married simultaneously to two wives." David Noel Freedman et al., eds., *Anchor Bible Dictionary* (New York: Doubleday, 1992), 4:565. Also, Deut. 21:15–17 sets inheritance rules for children in cases where "a man has two wives" (though some scholars read this as "one wife" and one "ex-wife"). And Deut. 17:17 instructs a king: "He shall not multiply wives for himself" (RSV). Some Jewish rabbis used these texts to justify the practice of polygyny, a pattern that persisted in Jewish communities until the twelfth century CE.

MARRIAGE AS COVENANT

All the commandments of the Mosaic law, including those on sex, marriage, and family life, were considered to be part and product of Israel's covenant obligations to God. The Hebrew Bible relates that God entered into a special new covenant relationship with his chosen people of Israel, building on earlier covenant promises to Noah and Abraham.[18] In this new covenant, God promised the people of Israel divine favor and blessing in return for their obedience to the Mosaic law. But God also threatened divine condemnation and punishment if the people disobeyed the law and went after other gods.

The biblical term "covenant" (Heb. *berith*; Gk. *diathēkē*; Lat. *foedus*) is more than simply a contract or agreement. In a covenant, both sides yield a portion of their natural freedom to the other: they agree to limit and direct their actions thereafter in accordance with the terms of their covenant. Both sides agree on the dire consequences to them and their descendents of noncompliance with the terms of their covenant. In the ancient world, peace treaties and alliances between tribes and peoples were sometimes formed by covenants of this sort. Their formation often featured elaborate ceremonies and sacrifices, communal oath swearings, and the erection or dedication of a physical marker signifying the covenant and sometimes recording its terms. As Daniel Elazar puts it: "A covenant is a morally informed agreement or pact based upon voluntary consent, established by mutual oaths or promises, involving or witnessed by some transcendent authority, between peoples or parties having independent status, equal in connection with the purposes of the pact, that provides for joint action or obligation to achieve defined ends (limited or comprehensive) under conditions of mutual respect, which protect the individual integrities of all the parties to it."[19]

This was the special covenant relationship that God had entered into with his chosen people of Israel. Moses' charge to the people of Israel in Deuteronomy, as part of an elaborate public recitation and ceremony, was one of several statements of this mutual covenant between God and Israel:

> This very day, the LORD your God is commanding you to observe these statutes and ordinances; so observe them diligently with all your heart and with all your soul. Today you have obtained the LORD's agreement: to be your God; and for you to walk in his ways, to keep his statutes, his commandments, and his ordinances, and to obey him. Today the LORD has obtained your agreement: to be his treasured people, as he promised you, and to keep his commandments; for him to set you high above all nations that he has made, in praise and in fame and in honor; and for you to be a people holy to the LORD your God, as he promised.[20]

18. Gen. 9:8–19; 15:1–6, 18; 17:2; 22:16–18.

19. See Daniel J. Elazar, *Covenant and Polity in Biblical Israel: Biblical Foundations and Jewish Expressions* (London: Transaction Publishers, 1998), 163; Delbert R. Hillers, *Covenant: The History of a Biblical Idea* (Baltimore: Johns Hopkins University Press, 1969), 25–39.

20. Deut. 26:16–19; see further 29:13; Exod. 6:7; Lev. 26:12.

Though the Mosaic law itself did not draw this analogy, the later Hebrew Prophets Hosea, Jeremiah, Ezekiel, Isaiah, and Malachi all analogized this covenant relationship between God and Israel to the marital relationship between a husband and wife. Just as God chose to give up his divine freedom to bind himself to his chosen people of Israel, the prophets argued, so a man chooses to give up his natural freedom to bind himself to his wife, to become "one flesh" with her. Just as Israel chose Yahweh out of all the other gods of the ancient pantheon to be its God and to make sacrifices only to this God, so a woman chooses her husband from all the other men in the universe to be her only husband, and to sacrifice and dedicate herself to him alone. Just as God and Israel swore to bind themselves together by a special covenant, with each side promising to be faithful and obedient to the other, so a husband and wife enter into a special marital covenant, with each side promising to be faithful and obedient to the other in accordance with the terms of their agreement and with the laws of the Torah. Just as breach of the divine covenant between God and his chosen people will hurt the parties and have devastating consequences upon later generations, so also will breach or betrayal of a marital covenant between husband and wife hurt the innocent spouse and have devastating consequences for each of them and for the children of that union.[21]

The prophet Hosea, who wrote in the mid-eighth century BCE, was the first to use this covenant-marriage metaphor.[22] Hosea preached against Israel's worship in the cult of Baal. Baal was a Canaanite fertility god, whom his worshipers regarded as the LORD of the earth. Baal's sexual intercourse with the goddess Anat was regarded as the source of all things on earth. This creative act of divine intercourse was celebrated by temple prostitutes, both male and female. They were joined by the faithful worshipers of Baal in ritual acts of sexual intercourse in the temple, sometimes evidently in massive orgies of collective worship. The Mosaic law had already sought to stamp out this cult of Baal.[23] The later prophets repeatedly denounced the Jews for succumbing to its temptations. Jewish women who served as temple prostitutes of Baal were treated as harlots and were to be shunned.

One such temple harlot was a woman named Gomer. Yet God told the prophet Hosea to take her as his wife. After Hosea and Gomer had married and produced children, however, Gomer eventually committed adultery by returning to "play the harlot" in the temple of Baal.[24] Yet Hosea, acting under divine instruction, forgave her and called her back into marital covenant with him

21. Hos. 2:2–23; Isa. 1:21–22; 54:5–8; 57:3–10; 61:10–11; 62:4–5; Jer. 2:2–3; 3:1–25; 13:27; 23:10; 31:32; Ezek.16:1–63; 23:1–49; Mal. 1–2. See further Gordon P. Hugenberger, *Marriage as a Covenant: A Study of Biblical Law and Ethics Governing Marriage Developed from the Perspective of Malachi* (Leiden: E. J. Brill, 1994); Michael G. Lawler, "Marriage as Covenant in the Catholic Tradition," in *Covenant Marriage in Comparative Perspective*, ed. John Witte Jr. and Eliza Ellison (Grand Rapids: Wm. B. Eerdmans Publishing Co., 2005), 70–92.

22. Lawler, *Secular Marriage, Christian Sacrament*, 8–9.

23. Deut. 23:17.

24. Hos. 2:5.

and to faithful care of their three children. Hosea used this personal experience of marriage, adultery, and reconciliation with Gomer as the foundation and exemplification of his prophecy about Israel's relationship with God. Before the giving of the Mosaic law, Israel was involved with false gods, yet God had called her to be his chosen ones. God entered into a special covenant relationship with them, calling them to abide by the Mosaic law. Israel, however, played the harlot by going after false gods, committing idolatry. Yet God maintained his steadfast covenant faithfulness and love for Israel. "Yahweh's love for unfaithful Israel," Michael Lawler writes, "is a love that is the opposite of hatred (9:15), a helping love (11:1), a healing love (14:5 [4E]), a love that wins back an unfaithful wife (3:4–5), a covenantal love that is 'loyalty, service, and obedience.'"[25] Hosea used the loaded Hebrew term *khesed* for this special kind of covenantal love. It means "love, goodness, and inward feeling of tenderness and mercy," as several other passages in the Hebrew Bible illustrate.[26] He also used the Hebrew term *emunah*, which means "faithfulness, devotion, unflinching and enduring support."[27]

The prophet Jeremiah, writing at the turn of the sixth century BCE, also used this marital covenant metaphor to condemn the idolatry of the Jews in consorting with false gods and foreign peoples.[28] But now Israel had compounded its sins of idolatry with the sins of false sacrifice and child murder. Rather than offering to God the burnt sacrifices of animals prescribed in the Torah, the Israelites of Jeremiah's day were sacrificing their first children to Baal as a thanksgiving offering.[29] Through Jeremiah's prophecy, God now rejected his chosen people of Israel and presented them with a bill of divorce, as a husband is permitted to do under the Mosaic law.[30] But when a remnant of the people proved faithful, God ultimately retreated from this threat of divorce and pledged his eternal love and covenant faithfulness to Israel and to her children who remain faithful: "I have loved you with an everlasting love; therefore I have continued my faithfulness to you."[31]

The prophet Ezekiel gave the covenant marriage metaphor more elaborate expression still, now imputing graphic emotions to God, the metaphorical lover, then husband, and then victim of his wife's adultery. Ezekiel wrote in the early sixth century BCE at the time when Jerusalem had fallen to Nebuchadnezzar and the Israelites were in exile in Babylon. He described the metaphorical marriage of God and Israel in graphic terms. He depicted God wistfully recounting the birth of Israel, her puberty, their happy courtship, betrothal, wedding, and happy cohabitation, only to be devastated by Israel's infidelity and her need for severe punishment:

25. Lawler, *Secular Marriage, Christian Sacrament,* 8–9, citing Edward Schillebeeckx, *Marriage: Human Reality and Saving Mystery* (New York: Sheed & Ward, 1965), 37–44.

26. Ibid., 63, citing Isa. 63:7; Joel 2:13; Mic. 7:18; Pss. 5:7; 36:5; 48:9; Jer. 3:12.

27. Schillebeeckx, *Marriage,* 63, citing Deut. 7:9; Isa. 49:7; Jer. 42:5; Hos.11:12.

28. Jer. 2:18.

29. Jer. 2:34; 7:32; 19:5; 32:35.

30. Jer. 3.7–8; cf. Deut. 24:1–4.

31. Jer. 31:3; cf. Ezek. 16:62–63; Isa. 54:7–8.

I passed by you again, and looked on you; you were at the age for love. I spread the edge of my cloak over you, and covered your nakedness: I pledged myself to you and entered into a covenant with you, says the LORD God, and you became mine. Then I bathed you with water and washed off the blood from you, and anointed you with oil. I clothed you with embroidered cloth and with sandals of fine leather; I bound you in fine linen and covered you with rich fabric. I adorned you with ornaments: I put bracelets on your arms, a chain on your neck, a ring on your nose, earrings in your ears, and a beautiful crown upon your head. You were adorned with gold and silver, while your clothing was of fine linen, rich fabric, and embroidered cloth. You had choice flour and honey and oil for food. You grew exceedingly beautiful, fit to be a queen. Your fame spread among the nations on account of your beauty, for it was perfect because of my splendor that I bestowed on you, says the LORD God.

But you trusted in your beauty, and played the whore because of your fame, and lavished your whorings on any passer-by.[32]

And on and on this narrative went with the same raw emotion imputed to God. Ezekiel devoted many chapters to documenting Israel's betrayal of the law of God and her union with false gods and foreign peoples. His running metaphor eventually shifted to a divorce court, where God, the aggrieved husband, presents evidence against his wife, Israel, whose "uncleanness" has led to her necessary repudiation and exile. But eventually God forgave his wayward bride and promised her "a new covenant of peace," whose terms he lays out in great detail in later chapters of Ezekiel. He promised that, despite her unfaithfulness and exile, Israel "will soon come home," and "the LORD is there," waiting as a faithful and forgiving husband.[33] Exactly the same metaphorical pattern of courtship, marriage, betrayal, divorce proceedings, and eventual reconciliation between God and Israel can be found in the writings of the prophet Isaiah.

All four of these prophets—Hosea, Jeremiah, Ezekiel, and Isaiah—used this marriage metaphor for anthropomorphic reasons. By casting in graphic human and emotional terms that everyone could understand what it must feel like to God to be betrayed by his beloved chosen people, the prophets hoped to shake the wayward people from sin and bring them back to covenant faithfulness.

Malachi, the last of the prophets to use this marital covenant image[34] in his mid-fifth century BCE text, repeats this story of marital formation, betrayal, and reconciliation, but then he drew direct lessons from this image for human marriages as well. In the opening verses of his prophecy, Malachi started out the same way as the earlier prophets had done, depicting God's angry lamentation about Israel's infidelity. This time it was their many ritual impurities and fraudulent sacrifices that ran contrary to the "covenant of life and peace." God

32. Ezek. 16:8–15.

33. Ezek. 36:8; 37:26; 48:35.

34. The Book of Daniel, which is usually dated to the second century BCE, uses the language of "covenant" in books 9:4, 27; 11:22, 28, 30, 32, but does not use the image of a marital covenant as earlier prophets had done.

lashes out angrily at this latest act of infidelity by his bride: "I will rebuke your offspring, and spread dung on your faces, the dung of your offerings, and I will put you out of my presence."[35]

But then Malachi flipped this covenant marital metaphor on its head, using it to offer moral instructions about human marriages. He now called each human marriage a special covenant relationship in its own right, indeed an echo and expression of God's loving covenant with Israel. He now called humans to be faithful to their covenant marriage with each other, just as God had been faithful in his covenant relationship with his chosen people. And he now called breach of one's own marital covenant with a spouse a breach of the broader covenant with God, which God will punish—in this case by refusing their sacrifices, even if these sacrifices follow the ritual laws. Malachi 2:13-16 is the key passage:

> You cover the LORD's altar with tears, with weeping and groaning because he no longer regards the offering or accepts it with favor at your hand. You ask, "Why does he not?" Because the LORD was a witness [to the covenant] between you and the wife of your youth, to whom you have been faithless, though she is your companion and your wife by covenant. Did not one God make her? Both flesh and spirit are his. And what does the one God desire? Godly offspring. So look to yourselves, and do not let anyone be faithless to the wife of his youth. For I hate divorce, says the LORD, the God of Israel, and covering one's garment with violence, says the LORD of hosts. So take heed to yourselves and do not be faithless.[36]

The King James or Authorized Version of this same passage highlights other aspects in its translation:

> And this have ye done again, covering the altar of the LORD with tears, with weeping, and with crying out, insomuch that he regardeth not the offering any more, or receiveth it with good will at your hand. Yet ye say, Wherefore? Because the LORD hath been witness between thee and the wife of thy youth, against whom thou hast dealt treacherously: yet is she thy companion, and the wife of thy covenant. And did not he make one? Yet had he the residue of the spirit. And wherefore one? That he might seek a godly seed. Therefore take heed to your spirit, and let none deal treacherously against the wife of his youth. For the LORD, the God of Israel, saith that he hateth putting away: for one covereth violence with his garment, saith the LORD of hosts: therefore take heed to your spirit, that ye deal not treacherously.

There is a lot packed into this passage, and it has long been an exegetical battleground among interpreters.[37] But parsed closely, this passage, read together with the earlier prophetic teachings on the marital metaphor of covenant, holds

---

35. Mal. 2:3.

36. Mal. 2:13–16.

37. Hugenberger, *Marriage as a Covenant.* For a range of other metaphors and interpretations at work in these texts, see Sharon Moughtin-Mumby, *Sexual and Marital Metaphors in Hosea, Jeremiah, Isaiah, and Ezekiel* (Oxford: Oxford University Press, 2008).

major lessons for human marriage, integrating and elevating some of the other biblical teachings on marriage.

First, the covenant metaphor confirms the created form of marriage as a monogamous union between one man and one woman. Even God, who had the perfect right to pick as many brides as he wished, chose only one bride, his beloved Israel, with whom to produce godly descendents. Malachi 2, just quoted, ties this norm directly to the primordial creation stories of Genesis 1–2. At creation, God could have created two or more wives for Adam, but he chose just one wife. God could have created three or four types of humans to be the image of God, but he created two types: "Male and female he created them."[38] In the law, God could have commanded his people to worship two or more gods, but he commanded them to worship one God. Marriage, as an order of creation and a symbol of God's special relationship with his elect, involves two parties and two parties only.

Second, the covenant metaphor confirms that God participates in each marriage. The passage in Malachi again underscores this, echoing the Genesis story of creation. Just as God gave the first man Adam and the first woman Eve "the spirit of life" and brought them together, so God gives each man and each woman a spirit of love and witnesses and solemnizes their union. God is not only the creator of the institution of marriage, Malachi makes clear. God is also the "witness" to each marriage, whose presence and testimony legitimates the formation of each new marital covenant that follows prescribed forms and norms. God is also the guarantor of the marriage, on whom the couple can call to ensure that the terms of the marital agreement are fulfilled. And God is the exemplar of a faithful covenant marriage as he shows in his metaphorical covenant marriage with the bride of Israel. To enter into a marriage, the prophets teach, is to enter into a new relationship not only with one's spouse but also with God.

Third, the covenant metaphor confirms the created procreative function of marriage. Even God, who had the power to create as many faithful followers as he wished for as many generations as he wanted, chose instead to produce "godly seed" through his chosen bride Israel, operating under the normative terms of the covenant. This, too, echoes the creation story, where God delegates the power of creating the next generation of humans to Adam and Eve, calling them to be "fruitful and multiply" and fill the earth. Covenant marriage underscores this created procreative purpose of marriage. But Malachi emphasizes further that faithful married couples are called to produce not just any children but "godly offspring," the next generation of God's covenant faithful, who love God and live by the laws of God's covenant.

Fourth, the covenant metaphor confirms the divine laws governing marriage formation, as set out in both the Mosaic law and in the natural law revealed before Moses. Even God, who had the perfect right to take whatever bride by whatever means he wanted, obeys his own laws for proper courtship and

38. Gen. 1:27.

marriage. He chooses his spouse carefully and takes his time in courting and getting to know her. He seeks her consent and that of her father, Abraham. He provides her with engagement and wedding gifts. He rehearses for her the terms of the marital covenant before their wedding day so that they both understand what they are getting into. And the couple then celebrates their covenant union in an elaborate public ceremony and public exchange of vows before the whole community, with an authorized official, Moses, presiding. The metaphorical story of God's covenant marriage with Israel, as told by the prophets, cleverly underscores the very Mosaic laws of marriage that the covenanted people of Israel were required to follow in forming their own marriages.

Fifth, the covenant metaphor elevates these Mosaic laws of marriage, both by adding new provisions and by exemplifying how to live by the spirit of the law. God goes beyond the letter of the Mosaic law of marital formation in forming his relationship with Israel, thereby setting a moral example for his people. For example, Mosaic law, following the customs of ancient times, took very little account of the woman's consent, allowing a man to sell his daughter to the highest dowry bidder and providing that even a rapist could marry his victim so long as her father accepted the bride-price for her.[39] God, by contrast, takes time to get to know Israel and to seek her consent to the marital covenant, while also seeking the consent of her metaphorical father, the ancient patriarch, Abraham. Mosaic law, again following ancient customs, treated marital gifts effectively as a bride-price paid directly by the man to his fiancée's father, not unlike transactions used to sell slaves or cattle.[40] God, by contrast, bestows his gifts directly upon his chosen fiancée and bride, making them a sign and token of his love for her. Mosaic law made little provision for the public celebration of a marriage or public recitation of reciprocal marital vows.[41] God, by contrast, connects the formation of marriage to the elaborate public ceremonies that attended the formation of other covenants; a covenant marriage is a public celebration in which the whole community must be involved.[42] Mosaic law gave the man the exclusive right to divorce a woman who was "unclean."[43] God, by contrast, chooses to forgive his "unclean" spouse and to continue in loving covenant union with her, notwithstanding her idolatrous adultery. God does get sad, hurt, and angry, and he even files for divorce. But he ultimately waives his divorce rights under

---

39. Exod. 22:16–17; Deut. 22:28–29.

40. See the scattered passages within and beyond the Torah in Joseph Blenkinsopp, "The Family in Old Testament Israel," in Leo G. Perdue et al., *Families in Ancient Israel* (Louisville, KY: Westminster John Knox Press, 1996), 48, 60-63. See further T. M. Lemos, *Marriage Gifts and Social Change in Ancient Palestine, 1200 BCE to 200 CE* (Cambridge: Cambridge University Press, 2010).

41. See the detailed evidence and arguments for and against marital ceremonies and oaths in ancient Israel as discussed in Hugenberger, *Marriage as a Covenant*, 168–215.

42. See Daniel J. Elazar, *Covenant and Commonwealth: From Christian Separation through the Protestant Reformation* (New Brunswick, NJ: Transaction Publishers, 1996), and his earlier writings cited and distilled therein.

43. Deut. 24:1–4 KJV.

the covenant and reconciles with his wife despite her "uncleanness" and betrayal. Mosaic law required a man who was divorced and remarried to support the children of his first wife as much as those of his second.[44] God, by contrast, chooses to remain married to his first wife, if for no other reason than to be there to support their "children and children's children" more effectively. The covenant of marriage confirms and conforms to the natural and Mosaic laws for marriage, but it also integrates and elevates them, calling the faithful to live by the letter and spirit of these laws.

Sixth, the covenant metaphor makes clear that each individual marital covenant between husband and wife is part and product of a much larger covenantal relationship between God and humanity. Both the husband and the wife must be faithful to this covenant, Malachi makes clear. This is a new egalitarian ethic. The earlier prophets, echoing the Genesis account of humanity's fall into sin through the failings of Eve, had always focused on Israel, the wayward wife, the adulteress who had gone after other gods and produced illegitimate children, who could not be supported and who would die out.[45] That image of the fallen woman comes through as late as Proverbs 2:16, a book produced a century before the book of Malachi: "You will be saved from the loose woman, from the adulteress with her smooth words, who forsakes the partner of her youth and forgets her sacred covenant."

Malachi turns the tables and focuses on the husband, too, calling him to be faithful to his wife, just as God is faithful to Israel. For a husband to wander after another woman—whether a lover, prostitute, or concubine—is now not just an act of adultery, but also an act of blasphemy, an insult to the divine example of covenant marriage that God, the metaphorical husband, offers to each human husband living under God's covenant. Husbands are now to follow God's example of offering "covenant love" (*khesed*) to their wives, remaining faithful to them even in the face of "violence," trouble, or betrayal. Husbands are also to follow God's example in living both by the letter and the spirit of the traditional law of divorce. There is still a place for divorce in cases of deep rupture of the relationship. "God hates divorce," Malachi says, but God does not prohibit it. Instead, God calls husbands not to divorce lightly on grounds of mere "uncleanness" (as Deuteronomy 24 puts it), nor to divorce harshly, "covering one's garment with violence" (as Malachi 2 puts it). To breach one's marital covenant lightly or violently, Malachi teaches, is tantamount to breaching one's covenant with God. For those who do so, God "no longer regards or accepts" their offerings or worship—a sure sign of divine condemnation. In Malachi's formulation, marital fidelity has now become a part of one's religious duty, a part of living in covenant community, a part of one's expression of true love (*khesed*) of God, neighbor, and self.

44. Deut. 21:15–17.
45. Hos. 2:4–5; Sir. 23:24–26; Wis. 3:16–17; 4:16; with discussion in John Witte Jr., *The Sins of the Fathers: The Law and Theology of Illegitimacy Reconsidered* (Cambridge: Cambridge University Press, 2009), 11–16.

NEW TESTAMENT TEACHINGS

These same Hebrew Bible lessons about the creation, commandments, and covenant of marriage recur in the New Testament.[46] The New Testament opened by illustrating the equitable application of the Mosaic law. Joseph had the right to have Mary, his fiancée, stoned for committing presumptive premarital adultery that led to her pregnancy. Instead, he endeavored to break the engagement quietly, without dishonoring her—before God intervened and encouraged him to marry Mary and join her in raising Jesus.[47] When he began his ministry, Jesus participated in the wedding at Cana and performed his first miracle there, thus incarnating and dramatizing God's own participation in the formation of a human marriage.[48] Jesus repeated and condoned the created structure of marriage as a one-flesh union between a man and a woman, designed for their mutual affection and support and mutual procreation of children. He used this image to rebuke the Pharisees of his day who allowed for easy unilateral divorce by a husband: "The one who made them at the beginning 'made them male and female,' and said, 'For this reason a man shall leave his father and mother and be joined to his wife, and the two shall become one flesh.'"[49]

Jesus further used the image of a wedding feast repeatedly to illustrate the coming of the kingdom of God and the union of God and his elect.[50] "The kingdom of heaven may be compared to a king who gave a wedding banquet for his son," he proclaimed. Only those who are invited may come to the feast. Only those who are ready for the feast when the bridegroom comes will gain entrance.[51] The kingdom of God may also be viewed as an extended spiritual family. "My mother and my brothers are those who hear the word of God and do it."[52] "Let the little children come to me, and do not stop them; for it is to such as these that the kingdom of God belongs."[53] For Jesus, children are models of piety, fidelity, and purity, and he reserved a special place in hell for those who harm or mislead children.[54] And even when children stray, the most "prodigal son" and daughter who come back to their father in childlike faith to seek forgiveness remain part of the Christian family.[55] To be both a child of God and a brother or sister in Christ were the defining features of the new Christian community.

---

46. Matt. 22:1–14; 25:1–13; 2 Cor. 11:2; see also Mark 2:19–20; John 3:29; Rev. 19:6–8; 21:9–10.

47. Deut. 22:13–21; 24:1–4; Matt. 1:18–19; see also Hos. 2:19–20; 3:1–3.

48. John 2:1–12.

49. Matt. 19:4–6.

50. Matt. 22:1–14; 25:1–13.

51. Ibid.

52. Luke 8:21.

53. Luke 18:16–17.

54. See sundry verses and interpretations in Marcia Bunge, ed., *The Child in the Bible* (Grand Rapids: Wm. B. Eerdmans Publishing Co., 2009); and Patrick M. Brennan, ed., *The Vocation of the Child* (Grand Rapids: Wm B. Eerdmans Publishing Co., 2008).

55. Luke 15:11–32.

Jesus' followers were not, however, to elevate the temporal demands of their own families above the spiritual demands of the kingdom of God. Jesus drove this lesson home in several jarring texts: "Do not think that I have come to bring peace on earth; I have not come to bring peace, but a sword. For I have come to set a man against his father, and a daughter against her mother, and daughter-in-law against her mother-in law; and one's foes will be members of one's own household. Whoever loves his father and mother more than me is not worthy of me; and whoever loves son or daughter more than me is not worthy of me; and whoever does not take up the cross and follow me is not worthy of me."[56] Jesus commanded his twelve disciples to leave their families and vocations behind them and follow him. He commanded a man mourning the death of his father: "Follow me, and let the dead bury their own dead."[57] "Truly, I tell you," he said to his disciples, "there is no one who has left house or wife or brothers or parents or children, for the sake of the kingdom of God, who will not get back very much more in this age, and in the age to come eternal life."[58] His followers need to recognize, Jesus put it bluntly, that "those who belong to this age marry and are given in marriage; but those who are considered worthy of a place in that age [to come] and in the resurrection from the dead neither marry nor are given in marriage."[59] These and other passages would become important sources for the later Christian traditions of celibacy and asceticism, particularly in the early centuries, when Christians were anticipating the imminent return of Christ.

Jesus's followers were also not to subordinate the moral laws of marriage and sexuality taught by Moses to sinful calculus, but instead to live by the spirit of the law. "You have heard that it was said, 'You shall not commit adultery,'" Jesus said. "But I say to you that everyone who looks at a woman with lust has already committed adultery with her in his heart. . . . It was also said, 'Whoever divorces his wife, let him give her a certificate of divorce.' But I say to you that anyone who divorces his wife, except on the ground of unchastity, causes her to commit adultery; and whoever marries a divorced woman commits adultery."[60] "What . . . God has joined together, let not man or woman put asunder."[61]

Living by the spirit of the law, Jesus made clear, also means applying it equitably. The Pharisees wanted to stone an adulteress who had been caught in the act. Instead, Jesus challenged her accusers: "Let anyone among you who is without sin be the first to throw a stone at her." Thereafter, however, he ordered the accused woman to sin no more.[62] The Pharisees prohibited the Jews of their day from interacting with Samaritans. Jesus not only interacted with them, but also offered "living water" to an infamous Samaritan woman who had already been

56. Matt. 10:34–39.
57. Matt. 8:21–22.
58. Luke 18:29–30.
59. Luke 20:34–35; Matt. 22:29–30.
60. Matt. 5:27–32.
61. Matt. 19:6 RSV.
62. John 8:7, 11.

married five times and was now cohabiting with yet another man. It was her faith that was critical, not her works.[63]

In the generation after Jesus' death, the apostle Paul and his school elaborated these Gospel teachings for the new Christian churches, writing various letters that are preserved in the New Testament. Paul glossed Jesus' words on divorce, with an admonition that Christians must remain in marriages even with unbelievers, in the hope that they might convert their wayward spouses to the faith. But "if the unbelieving partner separates, let it be so," Paul wrote; "in such a case the brother or sister is not bound. It is to peace that God has called you."[64] Later Christians understood this passage to mean that "spiritual desertion" was a second ground for divorce or separation in addition to the ground of adultery or "unchastity," which Christ had recognized. But Paul's more general admonition was that each spouse should remain faithful to the other. As he put it in his famous letter to the Romans: "Thus a married woman is bound by the law to her husband as long as he lives; but if her husband dies, she is discharged from the law concerning the husband. Accordingly, she will be called an adulteress if she lives with another man while her husband is alive. But if her husband dies, she is free from that law, and if she marries another man, she is not an adulteress."[65]

Paul glossed Christ's prohibitions on adultery and lust with a number of specific prohibitions against sexual sins outside of marriage that violate the norm of the one-flesh union between husband and wife. These sins included incest, sodomy, prostitution, polygamy, seduction, immoderate dress and grooming, and other forms of sexual "immorality" and "perversion."[66] "Flee fornication!" was his most famous admonition to the new Christians of his day.[67]

> Do you not know that your bodies are members of Christ? Should I therefore take the members of Christ and make them members of a prostitute? Never! Do you not know that whoever is united to a prostitute becomes one body with her? For it is said, "The two shall be one flesh." But anyone united to the Lord becomes one spirit with him. Shun fornication [RSV, immorality]! Every sin that a person commits is outside the body; but the fornicator [RSV, immoral] sins against the body itself. Or do you not know that your body is a temple of the Holy Spirit within you, which you have from God, and that you are not your own? For you were bought with a price; therefore glorify God in your body.[68]

This emphasis upon bodily purity and exclusive, sacrificial bodily union with one's spouse was even more prominent in Paul's two most famous statements

63. John 4:7–26.
64. See 1 Cor. 7:15.
65. Rom. 7:2–3.
66. Rom. 1:24–27; 1 Cor. 5:1; 6:9, 15–20; Eph. 5:3–4; Col. 3:5–6; 1 Tim. 2:9–10; 3:2; 1 Thess. 4:3–8. See also Heb. 13:4: "Let marriage be held in honor among all, and let the marriage bed be undefiled; for God will judge the immoral and the adulterous" (RSV).
67. In 1 Cor. 6:18 KJV.
68. From 1 Cor. 6:15–20.

on marriage in 1 Corinthians 7 and Ephesians 5. In 1 Corinthians 7, Paul followed Jesus in teaching and illustrating in his own life that marriage is not for everyone: "It is well for a man not to touch a woman. . . . I wish that all were [celibate] as I myself am." He repeated this counsel of celibacy to widow(er)s and divorcees.[69] But Paul condoned marriage for those tempted by sexual sin, saying it was "better to marry than to burn."[70] And within marriage, he instructed the husband and wife alike to have equal regard for the rights and needs of the other, including the other's sexual and bodily needs:

> Because of cases of sexual immorality, each man should have his own wife and each woman her own husband. The husband should give to the wife her conjugal rights, and likewise the wife to her husband. For the wife does not have authority over her own body, but the husband does; likewise the husband does not have authority over his own body, but the wife does. Do not deprive one another except perhaps by agreement for a set time, to devote yourselves to prayer, and then come together again, lest Satan may not tempt you because of your lack of self-control. This I say by way of concession, not of command.[71]

This important passage echoed the Hebrew Bible in commending sex to marital couples, but also went beyond it in pressing this ethic in egalitarian terms. The Mosaic law, for example, gave new husbands an exemption from military service to "be free at home one year, to be happy with the wife whom he has married."[72] "Rejoice in the wife of your youth," the ancient Proverb said. "May her breasts satisfy you at all times; may you be intoxicated always by her love"[73]—a sensual admonition underscored by whole chapters of sensuality gathered in the Song of Songs. But all these passages in the Hebrew Bible were focused on the husband, and some other passages are downright misogynist in their steamy depictions of women and preoccupation with the female form. Malachi had already turned the tables on husbands and pressed for a more egalitarian understanding of the marital covenant. Paul widened this egalitarian trajectory in 1 Corinthians 7. He underscored the mutual rights of both the wife and the husband to sexual bonding, the mutual sacrifice expected for the body of the other, and the mutual need for husband and wife to agree together to abstain from sex, and then only for a set time, lest the unused marital bed tempt either of them to test the neighbor's bed.

This egalitarian language of mutuality and equality was even more pronounced in Ephesians 5:21–33, a passage written either by Paul or by one of his disciples in the later first century CE. The full passage bears quotation:

69. See 1 Cor. 7:1, 7, 25–35, 39–40; 1 Tim. 3:2, 12; Titus 1:6; 1 Tim. 5:9–16. See a detailed study in Will Deming, *Paul on Marriage and Celibacy: The Hellenistic Background of 1 Corinthians 7*, 2nd ed. (Grand Rapids: Wm. B. Eerdmans Publishing Co., 2004).

70. See 1 Cor. 7:9 KJV.

71. See 1 Cor. 7:2–7.

72. Deut. 24:5.

73. Prov. 5:18–19.

Be subject to one another out of reverence for Christ.

Wives, be subject to your husbands as you are to the Lord. For the husband is the head of the wife just as Christ is the head of the church, the body of which he is the Savior. Just as the church is subject to Christ, so also wives ought to be, in everything, to their husbands.

Husbands, love your wives, just as Christ loved the church and gave himself up for her, in order to make her holy by cleansing her with the washing of water by the word, so as to present the church to himself in splendor, without a spot or wrinkle or anything of the kind—yes, so that she may be holy and without blemish. In the same way, husbands should love their wives as they do their own bodies. He who loves his wife loves himself. For no one ever hates his own body, but he nourishes and tenderly cares for it, just as Christ does for the church, because we are members of his body. "For this reason a man will leave his father and mother and be joined to his wife, and the two will become one flesh." This is a great mystery, and I am applying it to Christ and the church. Each of you, however, should love his wife as himself, and a wife should respect her husband.[74]

This passage echoes many of the same teachings of the marital covenant. Marriage, the author of Ephesians 5 emphasized, is a divinely sanctioned union in which God participates and which God exemplifies in his loving sacrificial union with his chosen people in the church. Marriage is a monogamous one-flesh union between a man and a woman, grounded in the creation order and created in part, as Ephesians 6 went on to say, for the procreation and nurture of children. Marriage is a union based on mutual consent and respect for the other but even more on a "tender" and "sacrificial love" for one's spouse as if that spouse were one's own body, a love modeled on Christ's sacrificial love for the church, in which Christ is embodied on earth. Marriage is fundamentally a communal relationship, being part of a broader body of Christ on earth, and an echo and reflection of God's mysterious union with his church. These are all familiar themes of the marital covenant that had been described more than a half millennium earlier by the Hebrew prophets. This famous passage in Ephesians would become an anchor text for all Christian groups in succeeding centuries.

The last verse, Ephesians 5:32, has long been used by Catholics and Orthodox Christians as the biblical source for the idea that marriage is a sacrament on the order of baptism and the Eucharist. In his famous fifth-century translation of the Bible from the Greek Septuagint into the Latin Vulgate, the church father Jerome for the first time translated the Greek word for "mystery" (*mystērion*) into the Latin word for "sacrament" (*sacramentum*). This rendered Ephesians 5:32 as: "This is a great sacrament [*mystērion→sacramentum*], and I am applying it to Christ and the church." Church fathers like John Chrysostom and Augustine in the fifth century experimented with the idea of marriage as a sacrament, though neither regarded marriage as a sacrament like baptism or the Eucharist.[75] In the

---

74. Eph. 5:21–33.

75. See pp. 65–75, on Augustine; and see Don S. Browning and John Witte Jr., *From Private Contract to Public Covenant: What Can Christianity Offer to Modern Marriage Law?* (Cambridge: Cambridge University Press, forthcoming), chaps. 3, 13.

twelfth century, however, the leading French theologian, Peter Lombard, in gathering the wisdom of the preceding centuries into his *Books of Sentences*, famously spoke of marriage as one of the seven sacraments of the church, and various medieval theologians and local church councils echoed and elaborated this view.[76] This position also shaped the medieval canon law of the church, which treated sacramental marriage as an indissoluble union that could be formed only between baptized Christians in good standing who were governed by the church. In 1563, the Council of Trent made these sacramental teachings part of Catholic dogma, and they remain at the heart of Catholic theology and canon law to this day. The sacramental nature of marriage would become a major point of controversy during the Protestant Reformation, whose theologians tended to treat marriage as covenant or social estate rather than as a sacrament.

SUMMARY AND CONCLUSIONS

The Bible, particularly the New Testament, provided the Christian tradition with a set of core religious teachings that confirmed the core philosophical teachings of the Greeks and Romans but also went beyond them. Early Christians noted the substantial overlaps between the teachings on marriage and family life in the Mosaic law and the classical Roman law: their comparable understandings of engagement and marriage, husband and wife, sex and procreation, parent and child, household and community, property and legacy, death and inheritance, divorce and remarriage. Early Christians saw these substantial overlaps in part as confirmations of a common natural law at work in both these ancient legal systems, a natural law written by God onto the hearts and minds of all persons, regardless of their faith. These legal provisions gave further concreteness to the natural core of marriage so celebrated by the ancient Greek and Roman philosophers.

Already the Hebrew Bible, however, went beyond these common natural teachings with its unique images of marriage as a creation of God and as a covenant modeled on the love between God and Israel. Particularly the covenant metaphor used by the Hebrew prophets underscored the natural origin, monogamous form, mutual ethic, procreative function, and spiritual mandates of marriage. These Hebrew Bible teachings provided the starting point for an emerging New Testament ethic that saw marriage as a reflection and expression of the mysterious and sacrificial love between Christ and his church. This New Testament ethic confirmed the natural origins and orientation of marriage. But it rooted marriage in a more primordial order that God had created and that Christ had redeemed. This ethic confirmed the essential unity of the one-flesh union of male and female in marriage. But it also insisted on the essential mutuality of marriage, the need for both husbands and wives to sacrifice themselves and their bodies for the other, to respect and meet the other's physical, sexual,

76. See Philip L. Reynolds, *Marriage and the Schoolmen* (forthcoming).

material, and moral needs. This ethic confirmed the procreative goods and goals of marriage so celebrated in Hebrew and Greco-Roman traditions. But it now treated children not only as the next generation in the family's lineage, but also as the new cocreations of God and humanity, the new "godly offspring," who were at the heart of the emerging family and kingdom of God. This ethic confirmed the traditional injunctions against impurity, adultery, and other illicit unions that corrupted the blood, commingled the property, and compromised the legacy of the family. But it also now called husbands and wives to flee all sexual immorality and to purify their bodies, hearts, and minds in loving service of each other, their children, and the community. This ethic allowed a couple to separate and divorce in the event of fundamental betrayal of the essence of marriage. But it also called both parties, especially husbands who may claim a unilateral right to divorce, to reconcile with each other if at all possible in emulation of God's abiding covenant love for Israel and Christ's eternal love for his church.

Chapter 3

Patristic Foundations
of Western Marriage

These provocative biblical passages set out the first principles of Christian marriage and were influential in the early church long before the various biblical texts were compiled into the final biblical canon. Beginning in the second century, the bishops and councils of the early church used these passages to develop a host of canon-law rules and aids to spiritual discipline to guide the sex, marriage, and family lives of the Christian faithful. These early canons would become important prototypes for the laws of church and state in succeeding centuries. Even more important for the Western tradition was the ample stock of commentaries and sermons on these biblical passages offered by the church fathers of the first five centuries.[1] The early church fathers were largely content to show the ample overlaps between Greco-Roman and Christian teachings on marriage and those teachings' continuity with the natural law. But these early fathers also used the Bible to criticize prevailing Roman practices of concubinage, homosexuality,

1. See a good sampling of patristic texts in David G. Hunter, ed., *Marriage in the Early Church* (Minneapolis: Fortress Press, 1992); and detailed analysis in Philip L. Reynolds, *Marriage in the Western Church: The Christianization of Marriage during the Patristic and Early Modern Periods* (Leiden: E. J. Brill, 1994).

infanticide, child abuse, arranged marriages, raucous weddings, and the deprecation of wives, slaves, and noncitizens.

The later church fathers repeated and embellished these themes at greater length—and eventually helped to effectuate modest reforms of the prevailing Roman law, albeit only partially and gradually. But these later fathers, especially Augustine of Hippo in the early fifth century, developed new and deeper reflections on the natural, social, legal, and spiritual dimensions of marriage, and the goods of children, fidelity, and sacrament that marriage afforded to the couple, the church, and the broader community. These fuller Augustinian teachings served in part as the theological foundation on which medieval Catholics and early modern Protestants would later build their sacramental, covenantal, and social models of marriage, and their accompanying laws of church and state.

This chapter analyzes and illustrates these patristic teachings on marriage. It must be emphasized, however, that a good number of church fathers treated marriage as an inferior option for Christians. As Ambrose of Milan put it in the fifth century: "The virtue of chastity is threefold: one kind that of married life, a second that of widowhood, and a third that of virginity"—in escalating order of virtue.[2] This "trajectory of celibacy"[3] in the early church built on Christ's statements that "marriage has no place" in the eternal kingdom, and the apostle Paul's encouragement for Christians "to be celibate as I am."[4] It found further support in the virginity of Mary, the mother of Jesus, whose chaste example inspired later traditions of "sexless marriage."[5] And it built on various Greco-Roman schools that regarded sex, marriage, and family life as a distraction from a life of virtuous philosophical contemplation. These early patristic ideals of celibacy and chastity found their strongest expression in the development of monasteries and occasional practices of hermitage as well as in the growing demand for clerical celibacy.

THE EARLY CHURCH FATHERS

A good example of early Christian thinking on marriage can be seen in the work of the distinguished church father Clement of Alexandria (ca. 150–ca.

---

2. Ambrose, *Concerning Widows* 4.23, in *A Select Library of Nicene and Post-Nicene Fathers of the Christian Church: Second Series*, ed. Philip Schaff and Henry Wace (repr., Grand Rapids: Wm. B. Eerdmans Publishing Co., 1952), 10:395 (hereafter, *NPNF*[2]). See also Gregory of Nyssa, *On Virginity*, in *NPNF*[2] 5:342–371; Jerome, Letters, in *NPNF*[2] 6:22–42, 66–79, 102–11, 141–48, 260–72, and idem, *Against Jovianus*, in *NPNF*[2] 6:346–86.

3. This language is from Stanley Harakas, "Covenant Marriage: Reflections from an Eastern Orthodox Perspective," in *Covenant Marriage in Comparative Perspective*, ed. John Witte Jr. and Eliza Ellison (Grand Rapids: Wm. B. Eerdmans Publishing Co., 2005), 92–123, here 98, drawing on John Meyendorff, "Christian Marriage in Byzantium: The Canonical and Liturgical Tradition," *Dumbarton Oaks Papers* 44(1990): 99 (Washington, DC: Dumbarton Oaks Research Library and Collection, 1990).

4. See detailed study in Will Deming, *Paul on Marriage and Celibacy: The Hellenistic Background of 1 Corinthians 7*, 2nd ed. (Grand Rapids: Wm. B. Eerdmans Publishing Co., 2004).

5. Dyan Elliott, *Spiritual Marriage: Sexual Abstinence in Medieval Wedlock* (Princeton, NJ: Princeton University Press, 1993).

215). Clement, was particularly well schooled in Platonism, and he worked hard to show that Christianity was a form of philosophy that was consonant with this ancient Greek philosophy but superior on discrete points. He developed his views on sex, marriage, and family life against the antimarital teachings of various gnostics and Encratites in Alexandria and against the anti-Christian teachings of various Jewish and Greek philosophers of his day. Clement held up marriage as both a natural and spiritual good, which all rational adults should embrace, regardless of their divergent philosophies. Indeed, he insisted, marriage is commended and governed by a common natural law, embraced by Christians, Jews, and Greeks alike.

To reject marriage is both to deny human nature and "to blaspheme" "the holy Creator" of marriage, Clement argued. "Nature has adapted us for marriage, as is evident from the structure of our bodies, which are male and female." And "nature urges us to have children." We are born with a physical capacity to unite with the opposite sex. We are born with a natural desire to have sex and to produce a child in our own "likeness," who "attains to our same nature," and who eventually becomes "a proper successor in our place." Procreation is not only personally fulfilling, however, allowing us to produce heirs to carry on the family name, property, and lineage. Procreation is also socially fulfilling, allowing us to produce the next generation of citizens to carry on our civilization and way of life. The Greek philosophers understood these combined personal and social goods of marriage, Clement wrote, and they thus commended marriage and procreation as a good form of living. Indeed, "the renowned Plato orders the man who has not married to pay a wife's maintenance into the public treasury, and to give to the magistrates a suitable sum of money as expenses. For if they shall not beget children," there will be "a scarcity of men, and states will dissolve." "The possession of children is consequently a good thing; and if it be so, so also is marriage."[6]

Christianity confirms but elevates these natural goods of marriage, Clement insisted. Christianity teaches that procreation is not only a form of self-generation, but more importantly a form of "divine generation." "The human being becomes the image of God, by cooperating in the creation of another human being." A new father or mother "shares in the divine work of creation." Christian believers can never interrupt this divine creativity by aborting their offspring or exposing them upon birth, as Roman law allowed. A child is a special gift of God to his creation, an act of divine creativity with and within us, which must be cherished. Christianity further teaches that procreation serves to produce not only the next generation of citizens within the state, but more importantly the next generation of saints within the church. When they bring up children in the Lord, parents become "ambassadors of Christ," engaged in the work of the Great Commission: making new disciples and teaching them to observe all that Christ has taught us.[7]

6. Clement of Alexandria, *Stromata, or Miscellanies* 2.23; 3.6, in *The Ante-Nicene Fathers: The Writings of the Fathers Down to A.D. 325*, ed. Alexander Roberts and James Donaldson, 10 vols. (1885; repr., Peabody, MA: Hendrickson Publishers, 1995), 2:377–79, 389–91 (hereafter, *ANF*).

7. Ibid., 2.23; Clement, *The Instructor* 2.10.83, 90, in *ANF* 2:259–63.

Nature not only commends marriage and procreation, Clement continued. It also commands that we maintain basic sexual morals, which Christians hold in common with other traditions. Jews, Greeks, Romans, and Christians alike make clear that the motivation for "marriage is the desire for procreation, but it is not the random, illicit, or irrational scattering of seed."[8] Procreation is more than an accident of sexual intercourse; marriage is more than an incidence of sexual coupling. Our sexual and marital lives are much more naturally structured than this, and they must be much more morally disciplined, Clement insisted. For they are governed by a common natural law, whose contents can be seen in parallel classical and biblical sources:

> Those who indulge in excess violate the laws of nature and harm themselves in illegitimate unions. Above all, it is never right to have intercourse with young boys as if they were girls. . . . The Logos has proclaimed this loudly and clearly through Moses: "*Do not lie with a male as with a female, for it is an abomination.*" . . . That is why the philosopher [Plato], following Moses' lead, said: "Do not sow seeds on rocks and stones because it will never take root and achieve the fruitfulness of its nature." . . . Our LORD wanted humanity to *multiply*, but he did not say that people should engage in licentious behavior, nor did he intend for them to give them[selves]over to pleasure as if they were born for rutting. Rather, let the Pedagogue put us to shame with the words of Ezekiel: "*Put away your fornications.*" Even irrational animals have a proper time for sowing seed. . . . Our entire life will be spent observing the law of nature, if we control our desires from the start.[9]

Moreover, within the estate of marriage itself, Clement continued, this common law of nature teaches a basic morality of faithfulness to one's spouse. This is particularly important for husbands whose sexual roving sometimes makes them "more licentious than the irrational creatures."[10]

> When the noble Plato [in his *Laws*] recommended that "you shall abstain from every female field that is not your own," he derived this from his reading of the biblical injunction: "*You must not lie with your neighbor's wife or defile yourself with her.*" "There should be no sowing of sterile, bastard seed with concubines," [Plato says]. Do not sow "where you do not wish your seed to grow." "Do not touch anyone except your wedded wife." Only with a wife are you permitted to enjoy physical pleasure for the purpose of producing descendents, for all this the Logos allows. We who have a share in the divine work of creation must not scatter seed randomly, nor should we act disrespectfully or sow what cannot grow. . . . To have intercourse without intending to have children is to violate nature, which we must take as our teacher. We should observe the wise precepts that her pedagogy has established.[11]

8. Ibid., 2.10.95.

9. Ibid., 2.10.83, 90–95; quoting Plato, *Laws* 8.838E, 839A, 841; Gen. 1:28; Lev. 18:20, 22; Ezek. 43:9; using the translation in Hunter, *Marriage in the Early Church*, 41–42.

10. Clement, *Stromata* 2.23.137.

11. Clement, *The Instructor* 2.10.90–91; using the translation in Hunter, *Marriage in the Early Church*, 41–42.

Christianity again confirms this natural law of sex and marriage, Clement continued, but also elevates it. The natural law "is not at variance with the Gospel but agrees with it," since God is "the author of both." But the gospel goes beyond the natural law, forbidding some acts that are naturally permissible and commanding other acts that are not naturally necessary but are spiritually expedient. In particular, the gospel condones marriage as "a sacred image" of Christ and his church, "that must be kept pure from those things which defile it." Like the divine mystery which it symbolizes, a Christian marriage must be kept chaste and pure. Christians must marry fellow believers and not become "unequally yoked" to nonbelievers. They must marry those who are single or widowed, not those who are married or divorced, for that is adultery, as Christ made clear in his disputation on divorce in Matthew 19. Once married, husbands must be attentive to their wives throughout their lives and avoid all impurity, including having sex while their wives are menstruating. They must care for their wives when they become sick or weak, and they must love their wives even as they age and become barren or when they sometimes lose their mental or physical capacities. Wives, in turn, should dress modestly, work and pray assiduously at home, and tend to their husbands and children. "A wife's care and constancy" are more endearing and enduring than "all other relations and friends" that a man can have. Finally, Christian couples should not divorce, even though that is permitted by the laws of the Jews, Greeks, and Romans. "Scripture counsels marriage, and allows no release from the union," save in the case of adultery. Adultery should lead to execution of the adulterer, releasing the innocent spouse to remarry (although Clement, like other church fathers, counseled against remarriage, especially for widows). Properly, Clement concluded, "marriage provides help . . . and self-restraint for the whole of life."[12]

Writing a century after Clement, the Latin apologist Lactantius (ca. 260–ca. 340), offered a similar blend of rational and religious teachings on marriage. Lactantius was a tutor to the son of the first Christian emperor, Constantine, and he evidently influenced some of Constantine's ample new legislation on marriage.[13] He was also an accomplished philosopher, and he developed what he called the first Latin summa of Christian theology, the *Divine Institutes*, which he dedicated to Emperor Constantine. Lactantius was known in his day as "the Christian Cicero," and he worked hard to show the compatibility between Stoic and Christian ideas on many matters, including their ideas of sex, marriage, and family life.

The common point of departure for Stoics and Christians was the natural law, which Lactantius defined with Cicero as a rule of "true, right reason, agreeing with nature, diffused among all, unchanging, everlasting, which calls to duty by commanding, deters from wrong by forbidding." The source of this natural law is "the one common Master and Ruler of all, even God, the framer, arbitrator,

---

12. Ibid., 2.10.90–97; Clement, *Stromata* 2.23.137.

13. See Judith Evans Grubbs, *Law and Family in Late Antiquity: The Emperor Constantine's Marriage Legislation* (Oxford: Clarendon Press, 1995), 88–94.

and proposer of this law."[14] Using their "right reason," Lactantius argued, Stoics and Christians alike have understood and applied this law of nature, and they have developed overlapping teachings on what is commanded for marriage and what is "contrary both to nature and to the institution which God has created."[15]

Like the Stoics, Christians condone marriage between a fit man and a fit woman of the age of consent, and they form unions with the consent of their parents and the participation of their families. Like the Stoics, Christians do not permit incest, adultery, prostitution, concubinage, homosexuality, sodomy, pederasty, or other such "lustful furies" and "libidinous excesses," which are "nefarious," "abominable," "execrable," even "insane." And like the Stoics, Christians do not kill their wives in order to seize their dowries or engage in random coupling and procreation outside of marriage.[16]

In particular, Christians like Stoics reject the idea of open sex and anonymous parentage set out in Plato's *Republic* (although, evidently unknown to Lactantius, Plato had rejected this idea in his later *Laws,* the text that Clement had celebrated in expounding his natural law of marriage). In the *Republic,* as Lactantius reported it, Plato said that "the state will be in harmony and bound together with the bonds of mutual love if all should be the husbands, and fathers, and wives, and children of all." This scheme, in Lactantius' judgment, encouraged "many men to flock together like dogs to the same woman." It ensured that men "superior in strength shall succeed in obtaining her" or that other men superior in cunning will set up a brothel or barter system for sex. To Lactantius, such open sex with "no fixed marriage" could only lead to rampant "adulteries, lusts [and] promiscuous pleasures." It could only breed animosity and violence among men and women who rival for prized mates. The lack of stability and commitment provided by marriage would not be good for adults or children. "What man would love a woman, or what woman a man, unless they always lived together, unless a devoted mind and fidelity mutually preserved has made *caritas* inseparable." What incentive, moreover, would either party have to care for their children or vice versa. "Only if a man truly knows that his children are really his, will he be able to love them," Lactantius argued, echoing Aristotelian themes.[17] And only if a child knows who his father and mother are will that child be able to love, honor, and obey them, and tend to them when they grow old and decrepit. "Nature herself cries out against" this Platonic system, Lactantius concluded. Even the birds know better. "For almost all birds make marriages, and equals join together, and they make their own nests like nuptial beds with harmonious mind; and they love their own offspring, since they are certainly their own; and if you should substitute someone's children, they drive them off."[18]

---

14. Lactantius, *Divine Institutes* 6.8, in *ANF* 7, quoting in part from Cicero, *De republica* 3.22.16.
15. Lactantius, *Divine Institutes* 6.23.
16. Ibid., 3.21.5–8; 6.18–19.
17. Ibid., 3.21–3.22.
18. Ibid., 3.21, 22; 6.23; using the translation in Grubbs, *Law and Family,* 89.

While nature and the natural law have taught Stoics and Christians a great deal in common about marriage and family life, Lactantius continued, "it is divine instruction only which bestows wisdom." Indeed, without the wisdom of God revealed in Scripture, a person can be "overpowered by nature" and natural philosophy and bewildered by its immense variety. The "precepts of God, because of their simplicity and truth," help us sort through the teachings of nature and philosophy, and thereby exert "the best influence on the minds of men."[19]

One such simple biblical truth, said Lactantius, is that we must not kill. That should lead Christians to denounce the exposure of unwanted infants, which Stoic philosophers and Roman jurists allowed, particularly if the child was born deformed or illegitimate or if the parents were impoverished or incapable of caring for it. Lactantius called infanticide a crime of "the greatest impiety," an act "wicked and unjust" in every respect. "It is better to abstain from marriage than with wicked hands to mar the work of God by strangling or exposing children" born through marriage or through extramarital sex. It is better to support a child born out of wedlock, rather than compound the sin of sexual immorality with the sin of homicide. The slaying of innocent children, while perhaps natural, is demonstrably unchristian, Lactantius insisted, especially given the premium that Christ attached to such children as models of piety.[20]

Another simple biblical truth is that we must not commit adultery. That should lead Christians to denounce the prevailing double standard of sexual morality that punishes an adulteress severely but often winks at the husband who consorts with slaves and prostitutes. God's command against adultery applies equally to husband and wife, said Lactantius, and it should be equally enforced "in public law" and "within private walls." A Christian man "who has a wife should not wish to have, in addition, either a slave or a free woman, but should keep faith with his marriage. Indeed, it is not as the reasoning of public law has it, that only the woman who has another man is an adulteress, but the husband, even if he has many women, has been absolved from the crime of adultery. But divine law so joins the two in marriage, that is, in one body," each with an equal duty of fidelity to the other, each with an equal right of care from the other. That is what Christ meant when he called all persons to abide by the Golden Rule. That is what the apostle Paul meant when he called Christian spouses to love and sacrifice for each other as Christ loved and sacrificed for his church. "Let the behavior of the two spouses begin to influence one another, let them bear the yoke with equal commitment. Let us imagine ourselves in the other's place. For this is virtually the summit of justice; not to do to another what you yourself do not wish to suffer from another."[21]

A final simple biblical truth is that marital sex is a good thing and should never be shunned or disparaged. Paul had already taught this, Lactantius noted,

19. Lactantius, *Divine Institutes* 3.26.
20. Ibid., 6.20.
21. Ibid., 6.23.23–30, using the translation in Grubbs, *Law and Family*, 90–91.

in calling husbands and wives to give up their bodies for the other and to honor the other's conjugal rights to sex.[22] The author of Hebrews had underscored this point by saying that, while the "marital bed [should] be kept undefiled,"[23] it should be well used. More than Clement, and indeed more than any other church father before him, Lactantius thus extolled sexual expression and pleasure within marriage as a sublime and essential expression of Christian love. He rejected the old Jewish laws of sexual purity in the name of Christian freedom, allowing sexual intercourse and intimacy with one's spouse even during menstruation and pregnancy. And he urged older or sterile couples to maintain healthy sex lives, even after the window of fertility had closed. This not only protected the couple from sexual sin but also fostered in them mutual love and harmony.[24]

Clement and Lactantius were typical of the early church fathers who wrote on marriage and family life. In the first four centuries of the Christian era, the fathers did not write systematically on this topic. They instead confirmed various natural and philosophical teachings and practices on sex and marriage, particularly selected Platonic, Aristotelian, and Stoic views. But they reformed and supplemented these views in light of gospel imperatives. Part of this effort, especially before the fourth-century establishment of Christianity by Roman law, was an exercise in apologetics—showing how Christianity was compatible with much of the prevailing Greco-Roman family and not necessarily a cultural threat. But part of this was an exercise in prophecy—showing how Christianity offered a more demanding and rewarding ethic of liberty, equality, and morality within the home, often for the betterment of wives and children.

EARLY CHURCH LAWS AND LITURGIES

The early church fathers not only defended Christian ideas of marriage, based on the teachings of the Bible. They also developed the rudiments of a church law of marriage for governance of the Christian community. Like their early theological writings, which confirmed prevailing natural philosophies but went beyond them on certain points, these early church laws presupposed the Roman law of marriage but added new provisions based on biblical imperatives. Early church laws that have survived—from the *Didache* (ca. 90–120) to the Canons of Elvira (ca. 300–309)—prohibited the sins of sodomy, adultery, and fornication, and commend chastity, modesty of dress, and separation of the sexes during bathing and education.[25] In the third century, local synods and councils

22. See 1 Cor. 7:3–5.
23. Heb. 13:4.
24. Lactantius, *Divine Institutes* 6.23; see other texts in Hunter, *Marriage in the Early Church*, 72–76.
25. *The Teaching of the Twelve Apostles, Didache, or The Oldest Church Manual*, ed. and trans. Philip Schaff, 3rd, rev. ed. (New York: Funk & Wagnalls, 1889), 161, 168, 172; *Didascalia Apostolorum*, trans. R. Hugh Connolly (Oxford: Clarendon Press, 1929), chaps. 2–4, 14; Hamilton Hess, *Sexuality and Power: The Emergence of Canon Law at the Synod of Elvira* (Philadelphia: University of Pennsylvania Press, 1972), with canons trans. Kenneth Pennington, http://faculty.cua.edu/pennington/Canon%20Law/ElviraCanons.htm.

began to order bishops, priests, monks, and other leaders of the church to be chaste, heterosexual, and monogamous. By the fourth century, some councils ordered high clerics to be celibate and to avoid prostitution, concubinage, and other sexual activities on pain of losing their clerical offices. Lay Christians in turn were repeatedly enjoined to live in peaceful, monogamous, and heterosexual unions and threatened with spiritual discipline escalating to excommunication for betraying Christian sexual and marital ideals. They were prohibited from sexual immorality, with Paul's long lists of sexual sins repeated and sometimes supplemented with strong and more specific rules against incest, bestiality, polygamy, abortion, infanticide, child prostitution, pedophilia, pederasty, and abuse of wives, children, servants, and slaves. Lay Christians were further forbidden from marrying Jews, heretics, or heathens and from marrying parties with whom they had fornicated (save in certain cases of pregnancy). And the church laws discouraged and sometimes prohibited remarriage after death or divorce, particularly for women beyond childbearing years.[26]

The fullest surviving example of this early church law came from the Council of Elvira in Spain, which issued a collection of disciplinary canons around 300–309 CE. This canonical collection emerged just before the issuance of the Edict of Milan (313), the promulgation of the new Christian Emperor Constantine that for the first time granted toleration to Christians as a "licit religion." Given that timing, the Elvira canons provide a good sense of what canon laws the church had developed for itself, even while as an "illicit religion" it faced periodic persecution by the Roman authorities.

More than a third of the 81 canons from Elvira that have survived dealt with issues of sex, marriage, and family life, most of them threatening severe spiritual discipline for their violation. A number of the Elvira canons dealt with questions of proper marital formation and dissolution:

8. Women who without acceptable cause leave their husbands and join another man may not receive communion even when death approaches.
9. A baptized woman who leaves an adulterous husband who has been baptized, for another man, may not marry him. If she does, she may not receive communion until her former husband dies, unless she is seriously ill.
10. If an unbaptized woman marries another man after being deserted by her husband who was a catechumen, she may still be baptized. This is also true for female catechumens. If a Christian woman marries a man in the knowledge that he deserted his former wife without cause, she may receive communion only at the time of her death.

26. See illustrative provisions in *The Seven Ecumenical Councils*, in *NPNF*[2] 14:11, 46–51, 70, 73, 79, 81–82, 92, 95, 98, 129, 149, 156, 157, 279, 280, 452, 460–62, 569–70, 604–13. See discussion in David Balch and Carolyn Osiek, *Families in the New Testament World: Households and House Churches* (Louisville, KY: Westminster John Knox Press, 1997); David Balch and Carolyn Osiek, eds., *Early Christian Families in Context: An Interdisciplinary Dialogue* (Grand Rapids: Wm. B. Eerdmans Publishing Co., 2005).

11. If a female catechumen marries a man in the knowledge that he deserted his former wife without cause, she may not be baptized for five years unless she becomes seriously ill.

61. A man who, after his wife's death, marries her baptized sister may not commune for five years unless illness requires that reconciliation be offered sooner.

The Council of Elvira also prohibited interreligious marriage:

15. Christian girls are not to marry pagans, no matter how few eligible men there are, for such marriages lead to adultery of the soul.

16. Heretics shall not be joined in marriage with Catholic girls unless they accept the Catholic faith. Catholic girls may not marry Jews or heretics, because they cannot find a unity when the faithful and the unfaithful are joined. Parents who allow this to happen shall not commune for five years.

17. If parents allow their daughter to marry a pagan priest, they shall not receive communion even at the time of death.

A number of canons dealt with issues of sexual immorality, particularly the burning issues of fornication and adultery, on which the council came down hard:

7. If a Christian completes penance for a sexual offense and then again commits fornication, he or she may not receive communion even when death approaches.

31. Young men who have been baptized and then are involved in sexual immorality may be admitted to communion when they marry if they have fulfilled the required penance.

44. A former prostitute who has married and who seeks admission to the Christian faith shall be received without delay.

47. If a baptized married man commits adultery repeatedly, he is to be asked as he nears death whether or not he will reform should here cover. If he so promises, he may receive communion. If he recovers and commits adultery again, he may not commune again, even as death approaches.

64. A woman who remains in adultery to the time of her death may not commune. If she breaks the relationship, she must complete ten years' penance before communing.

65. If a cleric knows of his wife's adultery and continues to live with her, he shall not receive communion even before death in order not to let it appear that one who is to exemplify a good life has condoned sin.

69. A married person who commits adultery once may be reconciled after five years' penance unless illness necessitates an earlier reconciliation.

70. A husband who knows of his wife's adultery and who remains with her may not commune even prior to death. If he lived with his wife

for a period of time after her adultery and then left her, he may not commune for ten years.

72. If a widow has intercourse and then marries the man, she may only commune after five years' penance. If she marries another man instead, she is excluded from communion even at the time of death. If the man she marries is a Christian, she may not receive communion until completing ten years' penance, unless illness makes earlier communion advisable.

78. If a Christian confesses adultery with a Jewish or pagan woman, he is denied communion for some time. If his sin is exposed by someone else, he must complete five years' penance before receiving the Sunday communion.

Several other canons also dealt directly with children, providing a modicum of spiritual and physical protection from delinquent or abusive parents, including adulteresses who might be tempted to abort or smother their illegitimate children:

12. Parents and other Christians who give up their children to sexual abuse are selling others' bodies, and if they do so or sell their own bodies, they shall not receive communion even at death.

22. If people fall from the Catholic Church into heresy and then return, let them not be denied penance, since they have acknowledged their sin. Let them be given communion after ten years' penance. If children have been led into heresy, it is not their own fault, and they should be received back immediately.

54. Parents who fail to keep the betrothal agreement and who break their child's engagement are to be kept from communion for three years. If the bride or groom has committed a serious crime, the parents are justified in such an action. If both the bride and groom are involved in the sin, the first rule applies and the parents may not interfere.

63. If a woman conceives in adultery and then has an abortion, she may not commune again, even as death approaches, because she has sinned twice.

68. A catechumen who conceives in adultery and then suffocates the child may be baptized only when death approaches.

66. A man who marries his stepdaughter is guilty of incest and may not commune even before death.

71. Those who sexually abuse boys may not commune even when death approaches.[27]

In addition to these internal canon laws, some early Christians evidently also developed their own distinct wedding rituals, although the earliest full

---

27. Hess, *Sexuality and Power*, with canons trans. Pennington. Historians dispute whether these canons were issued by a single council or produced by several councils and later compiled.

Christian marriage liturgies that have survived are from the eighth century.[28] Already in the second century, some Christians who intended to marry were required to seek the permission of a bishop, presbyter, deacon, or widow. Others were required to profess and celebrate their marriages publicly "before the church."[29] Tertullian, writing in the early third century, hinted at the operation of an even fuller public wedding ritual that confirmed the mutual love and companionship of Christian marriage and was to be celebrated with parents and priests alike:

> What words can describe the happiness of that marriage which the church unites, the offering strengthens, the blessing seals, the angels proclaim, and the Father declares valid? For even on earth children do not rightly and lawfully wed without their fathers' consent. What a bond this is: two believers who share one hope, one desire, one discipline, the same service! The two are brother and sister, fellow servants. There is no distinction of spirit or flesh, but truly they are *two in one flesh* (Gen. 2:24; Mark 10:8). Where there is one flesh, there is also one spirit. . . . Side by side in the church of God and at the banquet of God, side by side in difficulties, in times of persecution, and in times of consolation. Neither hides anything from the other, neither shuns the other, neither is a burden to the other. They freely visit the sick and sustain the needy. They give alms without anxiety, attend the sacrifice without scruple, perform their daily duties unobstructed. They do not have to hide the sign of the cross, or be afraid of greeting their fellow Christians, or give blessings in silence. They sing psalms and hymns to one another and strive to outdo each other in chanting to their Lord. He gives them his peace.[30]

By the fourth century, patristic authority David Hunter reports, Christians in Rome "regularly celebrated rituals in which the bishop placed a veil over the head of the bride and offered a nuptial blessing."[31] And a growing number of church fathers in this same period urged their fellow believers to avoid the excessive drunkenness, dancing, sumptuousness, and pagan rituals featured in some Roman weddings.[32] The Greek father John Chrysostom offered a typical critique when urging his congregants: "Throw out the lewd songs, the corrupt melodies, the disorderly dances, the uproar, . . . the hymns to Aphrodite, songs

---

28. Mark Searle and Kenneth W. Stevenson, *Documents of the Marriage Liturgy* (Collegeville, MN: Liturgical Press, 1992).

29. Tertullian, *De pudicitia* 4.4, in *Tertullian: Treatises on Penance*, trans. William P. Le Saint (Westminster, MD: Newman Press, 1959), 62. See sources in Edward Schillebeeckx, *Marriage: Human Reality and Saving Mystery* (New York: Sheed & Ward, 1965), 347–49.

30. Tertullian, *To His Wife* 1.1.8, in Hunter, *Marriage in the Early Church*, 38–39.

31. David G. Hunter, "Marrying and the *Tabulae Nuptiales* in Roman North Africa from Tertullian to Augustine," in *To Have and to Hold: Marrying and Its Documentation in Western Christendom, 400–1600*, ed. Philip L. Reynolds and John Witte Jr. (Cambridge: Cambridge University Press, 2007), 95–113. See also Schillebeeckx, *Marriage*, 260–72, 344–56; John Meyendorff, *Marriage: An Orthodox Perspective* (Crestwood, NY: St. Vladimir's Press, 1975), 23–32.

32. On these, see Karen K. Hersch, *The Roman Wedding: Ritual and Meaning in Antiquity* (Cambridge, MA: Harvard University Press, 2010).

full of adultery, corruption of marriages, illicit loves, unlawful unions, and many other impious and shameful themes. . . . When you invoke demons by your songs, when you fulfill their desires by your shameful speeches, when you bring mimes and effeminate actors and the whole theater into your house, and when you fill your house with harlots and arrange for the whole chorus of demons to make merry there, what good can you expect?"[33]

AUGUSTINE AND THE GOODS OF MARRIAGE

In the later fourth century and thereafter, these early patristic rites, rules, and reflections were woven into more elaborate models of Christian marriage, which slowly reshaped the law and culture of the newly Christianized Roman Empire. The most expansive and enduring formulations came from the pen of Augustine (354–430), the bishop of Hippo (in North Africa), who set the tone for the marital teachings of Western Catholicism and parts of Protestantism as well.

Augustine came to Christianity only after immersing himself in various Manichean, Stoic, Skeptic, Platonic, and other philosophies. And he came to a Christian understanding of marriage and family life only after leading what he later described as a rather profligate youthful life, which included keeping a concubine and fathering an illegitimate son with her.[34] After his conversion to Christianity in 386, however, he resolved to lead a pious and celibate life and to distinguish Christian teachings from what he now considered the heretical and pagan teachings of his youth, including several such teachings on sex, marriage, and family life. He became a parish priest in 391 and bishop of Hippo in North Africa in 395. Over the next three decades, he penned a staggering number of works on Christian theology, philosophy, and ethics, many of which would become foundational texts for Western Christianity. He peppered these writings with keen insights into the origin, nature, and function of marriage. His fullest expositions came in his tracts *On the Good of Marriage* (ca. 401),[35] *On Marriage and Concupiscence* (ca. 419),[36] and *On Adulterous Marriages* (419).[37]

Augustine sought to define a middle way between the robustly pro-marital teachings of a Roman monk named Jovinian and the stridently antimarital teachings of

---

33. John Chrysostom, *Sermon on Marriage*, in idem, *On Marriage and Family Life*, trans. Catherine P. Roth and David Anderson (Crestwood, NY: St. Vladimir's Seminary Press, 1986), 82–83.

34. Augustine, *Confessions* 4.2; 6.12–15; Reynolds, *Marriage in the Western Church*, 101–20. Despite his later self-castigation, Augustine had been faithful to his concubine and supported his illegitimate son until he was emancipated as an adult.

35. Augustine, *On the Good of Marriage*, in *Early Church Fathers: Nicene and Post-Nicene Fathers: First Series*, ed. and trans. Philip Schaff (repr., Peabody, MA: Hendrickson Publishers, 1994), 3:397–413 (hereafter, *NPNF*[1]); and in *St. Augustine: Treatises on Marriage and Other Subjects*, ed. Roy J. Deferrari, trans. Charles T. Wilcox (Washington, DC: Catholic University of America Press, 1969), 9–54 (hereafter, *GM*).

36. Augustine, *On Marriage and Concupiscence*, in *NPNF*[1] 5:258–309 (hereafter, *MC*).

37. Augustine, *On Adulterous Marriages*, in *Treatises on Marriage*, 61–134 (hereafter, *AM*).

Jovinian's many opponents. Jovinian had stirred up great controversy in Rome in the 380s when he described marriage and nonmarriage as equal in merit and virtue when faithfully pursued by baptized Christians. And he had criticized sharply other church fathers who had converted Paul's instructions in 1 Corinthians 7 into a strong preference for virginity, celibacy, and chastity over marriage—sometimes to the point of outright opposition to sexual intercourse, even to marriage itself. Jovinian's views sparked instant denunciation from various church councils and from such distinguished church fathers as Jerome and Ambrose. Their diatribes against Jovinian sometimes treated marriage and marital sex as inferior and irrational, if not outright sinful and scandalous for pious Christians. Their antimarital sentiments rested atop an already-ample stack of antimarital writings penned by Manicheans, Encratites, Pelagians, and various earlier church fathers and Greco-Roman writers in the first centuries of the Common Era.[38]

Augustine steered a middle course between these two extremes. Like Clement, Lactantius, and others, Augustine regarded marriage as a God-given "natural society" created for the procreation of children and the protection of parties from sexual sin and governed by what he called "a secret law of nature." Also like other church fathers, Augustine called marriage the most "intimate and sincere" form of "human fellowship," "an order of charity," "a faithful friendship," "a friendly and true union," "a fellowship of faith," a "bond of love" that fosters "domestic peace" and "household bliss" if properly nurtured and maintained. He, too, insisted that couples continue to "remain permanently joined" in body, mind, and property, abstain from sexual intercourse only by mutual consent "for the sake of the Lord," avoid unnecessary separation from bed and board for fear of temptation, and reject the easy divorce available under Mosaic and Roman laws. Like Aristotle, the Stoics, and the Roman jurists, in turn, Augustine called marriage "the first natural bond of human society," "the first step in the organization of men," the "first school" of justice, virtue, and order—a veritable "seedbed of the republic." When marriage is properly formed by "a publicly attested contract," one that is "read in the presence of all attesting witnesses," Augustine declared, it provides a disciplined and "orderly lifestyle" that anticipates and "ministers to the ordered agreement concerning command and agreement among citizens."[39]

Marriage is a good institution, Augustine continued, even if celibacy might be better for those who have the gift of continence. Marriage is not just a lesser form of sin than fornication. That would be like calling health a lesser evil than sickness. Rather, "marriage and continence are two goods, whereof the second is better," just as "health and immortality are two goods, whereof the second is better." God created marriage, before the fall into sin, and enjoined men and

38. David G. Hunter, *Marriage, Celibacy, and Heresy in Ancient Christianity: The Jovinianist Controversy* (Oxford: Oxford University Press, 2007).

39. Augustine, *The City of God against the Pagans*, ed. and trans. R. W. Dyson (Cambridge and New York: Cambridge University Press, 1998), 14.10, 22; 15.16; 19.14 (hereafter, *CG*); *GM*, 1–6, 9, 20; *MC*, I.5–9; *Sermon 1: On the Agreement of the Evangelists Matthew and Luke in the Generations of the Lord* 20–29, in *NPNF*[1] 6:252–56; *AM* 1.19.

women to join together "in one flesh" and to "be fruitful and multiply." Those original goods and goals of marriage continued after the fall into sin. "When a woman is lawfully united to her husband, in accordance with the true constitution of marriage, and they remain faithful to what is due, and the flesh is kept free from the sin of adultery and children are lawfully conceived, it is actually the very same marriage which God instituted at the beginning." As a creation and gift of God, marriage is and remains a "great and natural good."[40]

Marriage actually offers three interrelated goods (*bona*), Augustine wrote in an effort to distill and integrate earlier classical and patristic teachings. These goods are the procreation and nurture of children (*proles*), the faithfulness of spouses toward each other (*fides*), and the sacramental stability of the marital household within the city of God (*sacramentum*). The first two goods of children and fidelity are taught by the natural law and known to all persons. The third good of sacrament, known principally through Scripture, is a distinct (though not necessarily exclusive) quality of a Christian marriage.[41] These three goods of marriage are mutually reinforcing, Augustine insisted, and together help create an integrated understanding of marriage.

The first good of marriage is children (*proles*). The procreation of children is a perennial and natural duty of humankind, Augustine maintained, echoing Plato and Clement. Marriage is the proper institution for discharging that duty. Each generation must produce children for the human race to survive, and for the city of God to grow. In the ancient world of the Old Testament, when the earth was nearly empty, this duty of procreation bound everyone. Mosaic law thus made no provision for celibacy or for the virginal life, nor indeed did it insist on monogamous marriage alone. But in this new dispensation after Christ, with the earth filled with people, procreation has been confined exclusively to marital couples, and marriage itself has become optional. Marriage remains a good vocation to pursue, even though it is better for those who are widowed or naturally continent to pursue higher spiritual goods without domestic distractions.[42]

Before the fall into sin, Augustine continued, humans could procreate innocently, perhaps even "sexlessly," he mused in his early writings before abandoning this view as "unnatural." But since the fall into sin, human sexuality, like all of human nature, has been corrupted. Lust pervades every human act, and the libido has become unruly, "animalistic," and indiscriminate in the objects of its desire. God provided marriage to school fallen desire, to pardon sexual sinfulness, and to direct the natural but corrupted passions of a man and a woman to the good of procreation. Indeed, once they become parents, "the lust of their flesh is repressed, . . . being tempered by parental affection. When they become a father and mother, husband and wife unite more closely." Their lust for others

---

40. *GM*, 8–12; *MC*, I. 23–24; 2.13, 54; *AM* 1.25.
41. *GM*, 32; *MC*, 1.11, 19.
42. *GM*, 3, 9; *CG*, 22.1;14.23; *MC*, 1.5, 14; *AM*, 2.12. On the nonmarital life, see works by Augustine, *Of Continence*; *Of Holy Virginity*; *Of the Good of Widowhood*; *Of the Work of Monks*; all in *NPNF*[1] 3:379–93, 417–54, 503–24.

is blunted by the "glowing pleasure" of rearing their own children together. Children are thus a marital good in two complementary ways. They are the good fruit born of what could otherwise be the sexual sins of their parents. And their very presence in the household tempers the lust of their parents. Marriage channels the procreation of children. Children foster the preservation of marriage.[43]

In this sense, children are a "natural good of marriage," a "palpable blessing of nature," Augustine wrote, that complement the two other goods of fidelity and sacrament. This first good of marriage is evident even among animals, who are governed by the natural law. Sundry animals and birds "preserve a certain kind of federation of pairs, and a social combination of skill" in building their nests, protecting their infants, rearing their offspring, and driving away rival adults. Similarly, among human beings governed by the natural law, "males and females are united together as associates for procreation, and consequently they do not defraud each other" but develop "a natural abhorrence for a fraudulent companion."[44]

The marital household is the proper place to bear and raise children, Augustine continued, whether one's own children or other needy children who are adopted as one's own. Both parents—with the help of their extended families, friends, nurses, and servants—are to feed, clothe, discipline, and educate their children, preparing them for their independent lives as adults. Christian parents, Augustine emphasized, need to pay special attention to the spiritual welfare of their children, "imbuing them" in the sacramental life of the church. For all children are "conceived and born in sin," and even newborn infants carry the contagion of the original sin of Adam and Eve.[45] The sacraments, beginning with infant baptism, provide remedies for sin and relief from its threats of divine condemnation. "For no other reason are infants carried by pious hands [of their parents] to Jesus, that is to Christ, Savior and Physician, than that they be healed of the plague of their sin by the medication of his sacraments."[46]

Second, marriage offers not only the good of children, but also the good of fidelity between husband and wife. While children help foster fidelity in marriage, fidelity is also a good of marriage in its own right, and a sufficient natural good if the couple is not blessed with children:

> [Marriage] does not seem to me to be a good solely because of the procreation of children, but also because of the natural companionship between the two sexes. Otherwise, we could not speak of marriage in the

43. *GM*, 3, 9 (my trans.); *CG*, 22.1; 14.23; *MC*, 1.5;2.14.
44. *MC*, 1.5.
45. Ibid., 1.21–22, 27, 37–39; 2.15, 20, 49; *GM*, 22.
46. Augustine, *De peccatorum meritis* 3.4.8, using the translation and analysis of William Harmless, SJ, "Christ the Pediatrician: Augustine on the Diagnosis and Treatment of the Injured Vocation of the Child," in *The Vocation of the Child*, ed. Patrick M. Brennan (Grand Rapids: Wm. B. Eerdmans Publishing Co., 2008), 127–53, here 140. On Augustine's views of adoption as a charitable form of procreation, see John Witte Jr., *The Sins of the Fathers: The Law and Theology of Illegitimacy Reconsidered* (Cambridge and New York: Cambridge University Press, 2009), 39–45.

case of old people, especially if they had either lost their children or had begotten none at all. But, in a good marriage, although one of many years, even if the ardor of youths has cooled between man and woman, the order of charity still flourishes between husband and wife. . . . There is observed that promise of respect and of services due to each other by either sex, even though both members weaken in health and become almost corpse-like, the chastity of souls rightly joined together continues the purer, the more it has been proved, and the more secure, the more it has been calmed.[47]

In expounding this second good of fidelity, Augustine focused especially on the need for sexual fidelity between husband and wife. Glossing Paul's discussions of the "conjugal debt" in 1 Corinthians 7 and the calling to mutuality in Ephesians 5, he emphasized that marriage gives husband and wife an equal power over the other's body, an equal right to demand that the other spouse avoid adultery, and an equal claim to the "service, in a certain measure, of sustaining each other's weakness, for the avoidance of illicit intercourse." Marriage is "a contract of sexual fidelity," said Augustine, and couples could and should maintain active sexual lives for "the larger good of continence," even if procreation is not or is no longer possible. To be sure, it is best for couples to avoid sex altogether if they can no longer procreate. But it is better to remain sexually active than to court the temptations of lust and adultery. Sex within marriage is, at most, a venial sin; adultery in betrayal of marriage is a mortal sin. Marriage is furthermore a "hard knot" that should not be "unloosed," even if the couple proves barren or if one spouse strays into adultery or loses sexual or physical capacity. The marital good of "fidelity" calls for acceptance of barrenness, forgiveness of fault, and reconciliation to the inevitable fragility and erosion of age.[48]

Third, among Christians, marriage offers not only the goods of procreation and fidelity, but also the good of a "sacrament." For Christians, marriage is not only a natural union of couples into "one flesh" for the good of "being fruitful and multiplying," as Genesis 1 and 2 provided. Nor is it only a "contract of sexual fidelity," which should not be "rent asunder," except in the case of adultery, as Matthew 19 taught. For Christians, marriage is also a reflection and expression of the enduring sacrificial love that Christ has for his church, described in Ephesians 5. "Accordingly," Augustine wrote, "the apostle commands, 'Husbands, love your wives even as Christ also loved the Church.' Of this bond, the essence of the sacrament (*res sacramenti*) is undoubtedly that the man and the woman who are joined together in marriage should remain inseparable as long as they live."[49]

Going beyond the marital metaphors of Christ and Paul, Augustine treated the mysterious union of Christ the bridegroom with his bride the church as the very paradigm of marriage, the marriage par excellence, which every human marriage should seek to imitate. He treated each marriage between Christian believers as a

47. *GM* 3, trans. Deferrari.
48. Ibid., 6–11; *MC* 1.15–18; *AM* 1.2;2.12–17.
49. *MC* 1.11–12, my trans.

miniature version of this great divine marriage, a visible expression of this invisible mystery, this *sacramentum*. "It was said in Paradise before sin: 'A man shall leave his father and mother and be joined to his wife and they will be two in one flesh,' which the Apostle says is a 'great sacrament in Christ and in the Church.' Therefore what is great in Christ and in the Church is very small in individual husbands and wives, but is nevertheless a sacrament of an inseparable union."[50]

The sacramental good of marriage confirms the marital goods that natural law provides, but also curbs the sexual sins that natural law permits. The natural law permits any fit and able adults to join together for the good of procreation. The sacrament of marriage, however, as a symbol of Christ's union with his faithful church, commands that only baptized, faithful Christians join together in marriage within the city of God, an injunction against interreligious marriage already anticipated in the covenant laws of ancient Israel. Similarly, the natural law of paradise taught that the "two shall become one flesh." Yet many ancient patriarchs, operating under the natural law, practiced polygyny for the sake of producing many children and heirs. So do many higher animals still today who gather in large herds of one male with several females and their offspring. The sacrament of marriage, as a symbol of Christ's union with his one true church, calls Christians to return to the primeval natural law of monogamy and to spurn polygyny, concubinage, and sexual unions with anyone but one's spouse. Finally, the natural law teaches parents to remain faithful to each other for the sake of their children, who need them, but allows for separation when there are no children. The ancient patriarchs, operating under both the natural law and the Mosaic law, thus practiced divorce and remarriage, particularly when their wives proved barren. So do many animals today who drive out those mates who cannot produce offspring. The sacrament of marriage, in imitation of God's eternal faithfulness to his elect, calls Christians to remain faithful to their spouses to the end, regardless of their procreative capacity. "For this is what is preserved 'in Christ and in the Church': that they [i.e., Christ and the Church] should live together for eternity with no divorce. The observance of this sacrament is so great . . . in the Church of Christ and in each and every married believer, for they are without doubt Christ's members, that even when women marry or men take wives 'for the sake of procreating children,' a man is not allowed to put away a barren wife in order to take another, fruitful one."[51]

The sacramental good of marriage confirms the good of fidelity in the marriage contract, but also goes beyond it. Earlier church fathers had occasionally used the term *sacramentum* to describe the "solemn vow," "binding pledge," and "spiritual commitment" demanded of a Christian marriage.[52] Lactantius further

---

50. Ibid., 1.23, trans. Reynolds, *Marriage in the Western Church*, 292. See also Augustine, *On the Gospel of St. John*, Tract 44, 9.2, in *NPNF*[1], 7:245.

51. *GM*, 17, 21; *AM*, 1.21; *Sermon 1: On the Agreement of the Evangelists* 23–26; *MC*, 1.10–11; Augustine, *De Genesi ad litteram* 9.7, in Patrologia latina 34:397 (hereafter, PL).

52. Theodore Mackin, SJ, *Marriage in the Catholic Church: The Marital Sacrament* (New York: Paulist Press, 1989), 83–189, discussing the concept of the marital *sacramentum* in Tertullian, Lactantius, Ambrosiaster, Jerome, and Ambrose.

urged marital couples to keep "the sacraments of a chaste and inviolate bed."[53] Augustine sometimes used the term *sacramentum* in this way, too. But this largely repeated his formulation of the second good of fidelity (*fides*), which marks all marriages. The deeper quality of a Christian sacramental marriage, Augustine argued, lies in its also being a "covenant" (*foedus*), a "bond" (*vinculum*), or a "bond of covenant" (*vinculum foederis*). Once contracted between Christians, he declared, "marriage bears a kind of sacred bond," like the eternal bond between Christ and his church. Even if the Christian couple does not produce children, even if they separate and divorce, even if one of them purports to marry another, "there remains between the partners as long as they live some conjugal thing [*quiddam coniugale*] that neither separation nor remarriage can remove." "So enduring, in fact, are the rights of marriage between those [Christians] who have contracted them, that they remain husband and wife" even if they divorce and marry others. The sacrament of marriage ends only when one spouse dies.[54]

In this sense, but only in this sense, Augustine argued, marriage is like the sacrament of baptism. A person who is baptized by the church remains a child of God, even if that person is excommunicated from the church and is never reconciled to God. The promise of the sacrament of baptism remains with that person until death, because "God never dies," and his covenant seal given in baptism is indelible. So too, said Augustine, two Christians who marry remain spouses of the other, even if they divorce on grounds of adultery and never reconcile. But at this point, the symmetry between marriage and baptism breaks down. Augustine did not say, as later Catholic medieval theologians would say, that a Christian marriage remains indissoluble because God's mysterious union with his church is permanent even if its members fall into sin. Nor did he say, as later Protestant theologians would say, that Christian marriage is presumptively permanent just as Yahweh's covenantal bond with Israel was enduring, despite Israel's proclivity for "playing the harlot." For Augustine, it is not the divine participation in marriage that makes a Christian marriage permanent—God's holding the married couple together despite their divorce, just as God holds the baptized sinner fast despite one's excommunication. Nor is it the divine quality of marriage as a representation of the union of Christ and his church that makes it permanent, as Thomas Aquinas would argue. Instead, marriage among Christians is indissoluble because "it affects what it signifies."[55]

Augustine said that Christian marriage is permanent, but he did not clearly say why. He just repeatedly said that among Christians the "bond of the marital contract persists in itself"; the "conjugal thing" (the *quiddam coniugale*), the "essential quality" (the *res*) of being married, remains with each spouse regardless of what they say or do or with whom else they join. Marriage is an ineradicable status, a permanent mark of a married Christian man or woman. And that is what

53. Lactantius, *Epitome* 61, in *Corpus scriptorum ecclesiasticorum latinorum* 19:748 (hereafter, CSEL), quoted by Reynolds, *Marriage in the Western Church*, 282.

54. *MC*, 1.11; *GM*, 6, 7, 15, 17, 32; *AM* 1.12; 2.9–11.

55. See pp. 82–87, under "Marriage as Natural."

makes the good of fidelity at work in Christian marriage so unique. Christians not only should remain faithful to their marriage, as the natural law teaches. They cannot help but remain married, for that is the mysterious nature, the *mystērion* or *sacramentum*, of a Christian marriage. Their marriage is a permanent status, an ontological condition that ends only with the death of one spouse.[56]

The issue that remained for Augustine was how to deal with the right to divorce for adultery or desertion, which Jesus and Paul had allowed. Even if the "sacrament" of marriage remains indissoluble until the death of one spouse, does the "bond of covenant" remain indissoluble too, precluding divorce and/or remarriage? For Augustine, was there ultimately still a difference between calling marriage a sacrament that cannot be dissolved and a covenant that can be dissolved when its essence is betrayed? Moreover, if Christians should not exercise their rights to divorce because they cannot, didn't Augustine simply conflate "is" and "ought"? Augustine did not fully and finally resolve these questions, which would divide Catholics and Protestants alike in succeeding centuries.[57] But he charted something of a middle way that later Catholic moralists and jurists would develop into the canonical Catholic understanding of divorce and remarriage, which still prevails today.[58]

In his earlier writings, Augustine followed traditional patristic readings of the "exception" clause in Matthew 19:9 and allowed for divorce on grounds of adultery. He also hinted that 1 Corinthians 7:15 can be read to condone divorce on the ground of spiritual desertion. Although the adulterous or departing spouse cannot remarry without committing adultery, the innocent spouse can eventually remarry with impunity. This was traditional Christian teaching in his day. But it stood in tension with Augustine's insistence that a Christian marriage remains indissoluble until the death of one spouse. In his later writings, particularly in his substantial tract *On Adulterous Marriages* (419), Augustine argued that a Christian operating under divine law was still permitted to divorce an adulterous or spiritually deserting spouse. But such a divorcing person could

56. *AM* 2.3–5, 10; *MC*, 1.11. *GM* 32 compares the permanence of marriage and ordination.

57. A few later first-millennium writers also used the term covenant (*foedus*) of marriage, sometimes equating it with sacrament or viewing it as the essence or product (*res*) of the sacrament, as does Augustine. See, e.g., Arnobius, *Adversus gentes* 4.20, in PL 5:1040; Leo the Great, *Epistola* 167, Inq. 4, in PL 54:1204–5; Nicolas I, *Responsa ad Consulta Bulgarorum* 3, in PL 119:979–80, with discussion in Mackin, *The Marital Sacrament*, 169–70; Michael G. Lawler, "Marriage as Covenant in the Catholic Tradition," in *Covenant Marriage*, 75–76. Lawler disputes the argument of Paul F. Palmer, "Christian Marriage: Contract or Covenant," *Theological Studies* 33 (1972): 617–65, that marriage was frequently viewed as a covenant among first-millennium theologians. My electronic search of the Patrologia latina for references to covenant marriage also produced considerably fewer instances than Palmer's essay implies; most of those are references to the metaphorical marital covenant discussed by the Hebrew prophets discussed pp. 38–45. "Sacrament" was the preferred language of the later fathers, and even more so of medieval and early modern Catholic writers. Discussion of the "covenant" of marriage would emerge prominently in Catholic circles only in the documents of the Second Vatican Council and would become the language of choice of Protestants, particularly among Calvinists discussed in chapter 6.

58. On this development, see the detailed study of Theodore Mackin, SJ, *Marriage in the Catholic Church: Divorce and Remarriage* (New York: Paulist Press, 1984).

not remarry another until the spouse had died. For despite their divorce at law, the couple remained married in fact, and to marry another would be to commit adultery and polygamy in violation of the indissoluble marital bond that still remained. Augustine thereby preserved the indissolubility of marriage, even if the actual relationship between husband and wife was now broken. He preserved the right to divorce, but now in the form of what came to be called separation from bed and board. And he preserved the right to remarriage, but now only if and when one's spouse had died.[59]

Augustine, moreover, treated these limited rights of divorce and remarriage as concessions to human frailty that pious Christians should strive to forgo. It was best for a Christian not to divorce on any grounds and not to remarry at any time. Such rights "are lawful, but not necessarily expedient," Augustine wrote, adducing Paul's counsel of Christian prudence.[60] While the teaching of Christ allows for divorce in the case of adultery, it is better for an innocent spouse to forgive and reconcile with the other, just as God forgives mortal sinners. While the counsels of Paul permit a pious believer to "let a faithless spouse depart,"[61] it is better to remain joined in marriage, so that the unbelieving spouse is "sanctified by the faith" of the other, and their children are brought up in the Lord.[62] In his treatise, *Adulterous Marriages*, Augustine presented this "good/better" balance as a dialectic between justice and charity, rule and mercy, law and Gospel, command and counsel, precept and prudence, the law of the state and the law of Christ. And while his strong preference was for no divorce and no remarriage in the church, he also recognized that "it is difficult to draw with some universal dividing line the distinction between what is unlawful, and therefore inexpedient, and what is lawful, although inexpedient."[63]

Augustine thus used the concept of the marital sacrament in a number of ways: as a sign and expression of the eternal union of Christ and his church, as a covenant or bond that binds the parties for life, as an ineradicable quality or ontological status akin to the seal of baptism, as an "essential reality" that transcends the existential relationship of husband and wife, as a miniature visible expression of the mysterious invisible marriage of Christ and the church. "The sense of the word *sacramentum* in his treatment of marriage," distinguished patristic authority Philip Reynolds concludes, "was neither clear nor fixed."[64] Moreover, although he compared marriage to the sacraments of baptism and ordination for purposes of showing some of their analogous qualities, Augustine preferred to call marriage not a sacrament per se, but "a kind of [*quoddam*] sacrament," or "what might be called a sacrament." Sometimes he also referred to

59. *AM* 1.6–12; 2.4–5, 13.
60. See 1 Cor. 10:23.
61. See 1 Cor. 7:15.
62. *AM* 1.13–15.
63. *AM* 2.8, 10, 17, 19, 22.
64. Reynolds, *Marriage in the Western Church*, 309. See also Mackin, *The Marital Sacrament*, 226–27.

the "sacrament-like" qualities, benefits, and virtues of marriage.[65] Nowhere in his writings, so far as I have found, did he list marriage as one of the seven sacraments like baptism or the Eucharist, as the Council of Trent would do canonically for the time in 1563. Nor did he impute to marriage the supernatural and salvatory meaning associated with later medieval sacramental theology. There is far more ambiguity and plasticity in Augustine's views of the sacramental qualities of marriage. This had the ironic effect of allowing Catholics, Protestants, and Orthodox Christians alike to weave some of his profound insights about sex, marriage, and family life into their theology and jurisprudence. Augustine's work was a perennial touchstone for Christian marriage.[66]

Procreation, fidelity, and sacrament: These are the three goods of marriage, in Augustine's view. They are why the institution of marriage is good. They are why participation in marriage is good. They are the goods and goals that a person can hope and expect to realize upon marrying. They are three integrated, interacting, and reinforcing goods. They are all important individually, and they are all important to each other. This integrated interdependence of the goods of marriage is seen in the variations he gave in listing them. Augustine usually listed the goods of marriage by giving first place to the good of procreation and childrearing in the Christian context. At least twice, he underscored this priority by writing that "the procreation of children is itself the primary, natural, legitimate purpose of marriage."[67] But he did not regard the others as secondary. He sometimes changed the order of marital goods to "fidelity, procreation, and sacrament";[68] such passages inspired later canonists and theologians to develop theories of "marital affection" as the primary marital good.[69] Even when he listed procreation as the first marital good, Augustine made clear that spousal fidelity and sacramental stability are essential for marriage and sufficient when married couples are childless or their children have left the household.[70] In doing so, he followed the classical Greek and Roman authors in highlighting some of the benefits of marriage to the couple themselves.

Augustine's integrated understanding of the three goods of children, fidelity, and sacrament also highlighted three dimensions of marriage: the natural, the contractual, and the spiritual. For him, marriage is a natural institution, rooted in the created order and designed for the procreation of children. Marriage is a contractual institution, designed with a formal set of rights and duties that the couple needs to discharge faithfully. And marriage is a spiritual institution, modeled on the enduring mysterious covenant between Yahweh and Israel, Christ

65. *GM* 7, 17; *MC* 1.11–12.

66. See several articles by Philip L. Reynolds in *The Oxford Guide to the Historical Reception of Augustine*, ed. W. Otten and K. Pollman (Oxford: Oxford University Press, forthcoming).

67. *AM* 2.12.

68. Augustine, *De Genesi ad litteram* 9.7.

69. Jean Leclercq, *Monks on Marriage: A Twelfth Century View* (New York: Seabury Press, 1982), 11–38, 71–81; John T. Noonan Jr., "Marital Affection among the Canonists," *Studia Gratiana* 14 (1967): 480–99.

70. *GM* 12–13.

and his church. It was left to the medieval theologians and canonists, notably Thomas Aquinas, to bring these various goods and dimensions of marriage together into a more elaborate integration centered on marriage as a sacrament. And their work provided the enduring teaching on Christian marriage in the Catholic tradition, as we shall see in the next chapter.

SUMMARY AND CONCLUSIONS

The church fathers at work before the time of Augustine, were important fulcrums in the Western tradition of Christian marriage. These church fathers were the first Christians to strike balances between the cultural and the confessional, the rational and the religious, the natural and the spiritual dimensions of marriage. And they developed their views on Christian marriage as religious and cultural minorities, sometimes as victims of bitter persecution. That forced them to decide what features of Greco-Roman marriage were worth adopting and what reforms of Christian marriage were worth dying for. What emerged among Christians of the first four centuries was the Greco-Roman marriage with a strong "Christian spin or twist," in the apt phrase of marriage authority Don S. Browning.[71] Early Christian writers accepted the Greco-Roman ideal of marriage as a heterosexual, monogamous union designed for the procreation of children and the cultivation of virtuous citizens. And they selectively adduced Greek and Roman writers who extolled marital love, healthy procreation, family allegiance, and household stability. But, using Scripture and moral casuistry, they also criticized the prevailing Roman legal culture of the family. They strove for greater equality between husband and wife, for better treatment for women and children, and for greater restraint in sexual expression. They inveighed against the sexual double standard of Roman marriages, against the unchecked power of the paterfamilias, against infanticide and child enslavement, against sexual immorality, and against extravagant weddings, easy divorces, and routine remarriages.

Later church fathers wove these early patristic productions into more elaborate orchestrations. For the Western tradition, Augustine's formulations would become axiomatic. Augustine, too, contrasted philosophical and biblical approaches to marriage; on the strength of biblical teachings, he recommended discrete reforms of prevailing Greco-Roman customs and laws. But his main focus concerned what marriage was for and why it remained a good creation of God despite human sinfulness. He portrayed marriage as offering three main goods: the procreation of children, the preservation of faith, and the permanence of a sacrament. Children, faith, and sacrament were what made marriage good, and they were the goods that marriage offered to its members and to the

71. Don S. Browning, "Family Law and Christian Jurisprudence," in *Christianity and Law: An Introduction*, ed. John Witte Jr. and Frank S. Alexander (Cambridge: Cambridge University Press, 2008), 163–83, here 163–64.

communities they occupied. All three of these goods of marriage, Augustine believed, were designed to complement and complete the others. Each could be understood through philosophical and theological arguments. What ultimately made any marriage a Christian marriage, however, was the good of the sacrament. And this good could be sufficient to preserve a Christian marriage, even if the other two goods were lacking.

In the second millennium of the Common Era, both Catholics and Protestants built on these patristic teachings in constructing their own more elaborate Christian marriage theories. Catholics and Protestants deepened each of these aspects of marriage and combined them in various ways to achieve a fuller integrative theory. Catholics used the metaphor of sacrament to achieve their integration; Protestants used the metaphor of covenant. Catholics and Protestants also differentiated the associations and professions that bore principal responsibility for each aspect of marriage. In medieval times, Catholics gave more emphasis to the role of the church; in early modern times, Protestants gave more emphasis to the role of the state in governing and guiding marriage. Such is the story of the next four chapters.

Chapter 4

Marriage as Sacrament in the Medieval Catholic Tradition

The patristic theology and Roman law of marriage came to their fullest expression in the fifth and sixth centuries, just at the time when the Western church and state were the least able to implement them effectively. Already in the later fourth century, the Western Empire gradually eroded in its power and reach, and the city of Rome itself ultimately fell in 476 with the death of the final emperor. While Roman law lived on in the Eastern Empire, with its capital in Constantinople, in the West it became increasingly a legal relic and found only fragmentary application in the many Germanic legal systems that emerged. At the same time, the Western church fell under increasing control of Germanic kings and local feudal lords, leading to both clerical indiscipline and ample variation in the church's teachings and practices across the West. Moreover, the sophisticated theology of Augustine and other later fathers, the early canon laws of the church, and the deep philosophical writings of the Greeks and Romans were all increasingly lost on and to the church.

This is not to say that the Christian West became a wasteland after 500. The royal courts of the Frankish ruler Charlemagne and of the Anglo-Saxon ruler Alfred produced important new legal and theological literature, including some discussions of marriage. The monastic communities of the day preserved and collected a number of canon laws and theological treatises from the earlier centuries and also developed an important new penitential literature, with elaborate norms on sexual and marital ethics. Various popes, bishops, and church councils continued to issue canons and decrees on various aspects of sex, marriage, and family life, which had at least regional influence. Some Germanic groups also made striking legal, scientific, literary, military, artistic, and architectural contributions. But at least in the field of marriage law and theology, much of this was a rather pale shadow of what went on before.[1]

After 1100, the West developed a much more sophisticated and systematic sacramental theology and canon law of marriage. Beginning with Pope Gregory VII (r. 1073–85), the church's leaders threw off their royal, feudal, and civil rulers and established the church as an autonomous legal and political corporation within Western Christendom, centered in the Roman papacy. This dramatic reform of church-state relations was part and product of an enormous transformation of Western society. The West was renewed through the rediscovery and study of ancient texts of Roman law, Greek philosophy, and patristic theology that had been preserved in the intervening centuries by Arabic and Muslim scholars and traders. The first Western universities were established in Bologna, Rome, and Paris, with their core faculties of theology, law, and medicine. A number of towns were transformed into city-states. Trade and commerce boomed. A new dialogue was opened with the sophisticated cultures of Judaism and Islam. Great advances were made in the natural sciences, in mechanics, in literature, in music, art, and architecture. This "revolutionary era" of the twelfth and thirteenth centuries, the great legal historian Harold Berman tells us, was the "first modern age" of the West.[2]

It was in this era that the church developed a full sacramental model of marriage. From the twelfth century forward, the church's theology of marriage was categorized, systematized, and refined, notably in Hugh of St. Victor's *On the Sacraments of the Christian Faith* (ca. 1143),[3] Peter Lombard's *Books of Sentences* (ca. 1155–58),[4] and Thomas Aquinas's commentaries on Lombard's

1. In the vast literature, see James A. Brundage, *Law, Sex, and Christian Society in the Middle Ages* (Chicago: University of Chicago Press, 1987), 124–75; Philip L. Reynolds, *Marriage in the Western Church* (Leiden: E. J. Brill, 1994), 386–412; Angeliki E. Laiou, ed., *Consent and Coercion to Sex and Marriage in Ancient and Medieval Societies* (Washington, DC: Dumbarton Oaks Research Library and Collection, 1993).

2. Harold J. Berman, *Law and Revolution: The Formation of the Western Legal Tradition* (Cambridge, MA: Harvard University Press, 1983).

3. Hugh of St. Victor, *On the Sacraments of the Christian Faith*, pt. 2, trans. R. Deferrari (Cambridge, MA: Harvard University Press, 1951).

4. *Sententiae in IV libris distinctae*, bk. 4, dist. 26–42, in Patrologia latina (hereafter, PL), vol. 192; republished, 3rd ed., 2 vols. in 3, Spicilegium Bonaventurianum 4–5 (Rome: Collegii S. Bonaventura ad Claras Aquas, 1971–81) (hereafter, Lombard, *Sent.*). On its pervasive medieval influence, see Philipp W. Rosemann, *The Story of a Great Medieval Book: Peter Lombard's Sentences* (Peterborough, ON: Broadview Press, 2007).

Sentences,[5] together with his massive *Summa contra gentiles* (ca. 1258–64)[6] and *Summa theologica* (ca. 1265–73). These early theological masterworks, among others, became anchor texts that inspired many generations of commentaries and glosses thereafter. Also from the twelfth century forward, the church's canon law of marriage was systematized, first in Gratian's *Decretum* (ca. 1140)[7] and Gregory IX's *Decretales* (1234),[8] then in a welter of other papal and conciliar laws that were later compiled into the *Corpus iuris canonici* (ca. 1586).[9] These canon-law texts became the basis for a sophisticated marital jurisprudence developed by the canon lawyers as well as a sophisticated marital litigation in church courts spread throughout the West.[10] These new theological and legal teachings on marriage were communicated not only through formal theological and legal tracts. They also found their way into sermons, catechisms, confessional books, household manuals, and illustrated handbooks of domestic etiquette and decorum that allowed these teachings to penetrate deeply into the lives of the laity.

The hundreds of medieval Catholic theologians, philosophers, and jurists between 1100 and 1500 who wrote on marriage drew on a number of common sources from the first millennium.[11] They often integrated these texts by using the famous dialectical method—first collating and juxtaposing sundry conflicting texts from earlier centuries and then harmonizing them into systematic principles and precepts that became the premises for later commentary and legislation.

5. Thomas Aquinas, *Scriptum super Libros Sententiarum Petri Lombardiensis*, in *Opera omnia sancti Thomae Aquinatis Doctoris Angelici*, 13 vols. (Rome: C. de Propagandae Fidei, 1882), vol. 7, pt. 2 (hereafter, Aquinas, *Comm. Sent.*); partly translated in Thomas Aquinas, *On Love and Charity: Readings from the Commentary on the Sentences of Peter Lombard*, trans. Peter A. Kwasniewski, Thomas Bolin, and Joseph Bolin (Washington, DC: Catholic University Press of America, 2009). Thomas Aquinas's commentary on Lombard's discussion of marriage is reprinted almost verbatim in the Supplement to idem, *Summa theologica*, trans. Fathers of the English Dominican Province, first complete American ed., 3 vols. (New York: Benziger Bros., 1947–48), vol. 3, qq. 41–68 (hereafter, Aquinas, *ST* Supp.).

6. Thomas Aquinas, *Summa contra Gentiles*, trans. Vernon J. Bourke, 4 vols. (Notre Dame, IN: University of Notre Dame Press, 1975) (hereafter, Aquinas, *SCG*).

7. Gratian, *Decretum*, causae 27–36, reprinted in *Corpus iuris canonici*, ed. Emil Friedberg (Leipzig: Bernard Tauchnitz, 1879), pt.1 (hereafter, *Decretum*). Anders Winroth has convincingly argued that there were two texts of the *Decretum*, a much simpler and systematic earlier text that was then heavily amended, sometimes at the cost of coherence. It is the latter amended text that has survived; amid the ten cases on marriage, it has buried a short treatise on penance that has no clear bearing on any of the surrounding material. See Anders Winroth, *The Making of Gratian's "Decretum"* (Cambridge: Cambridge University Press, 2000).

8. *Decretales Gregorii*, bk. 5, tit. 1–19, in Friedberg, *Corpus iuris canonici*, pt. 2 (hereafter, *Decretales*).

9. On the development of the *Corpus iuris canonici* (first so named in 1671), see Knut Wolfgang Nörr, "Die Entwicklung des *Corpus iuris canonici*," in *Handbuch der Quellen und Lteratur der neueren europäischen Privatrechtsgeschichte*, ed. Helmut Coing, 4 vols. (Munich: Beck, 1977), 1:835–46.

10. See Charles Donahue, *Law, Marriage and Society in the Later Middle Ages* (Cambridge: Cambridge University Press, 2007); Richard H. Helmholz, *Marriage Litigation in Medieval England* (Cambridge: Cambridge University Press, 1974).

11. A good sampling of the best medieval literature on marriage is collected in *Tractatus universi iuris, duce, & auspice Gregorio XIII*, 25 vols. (Venice: Società dell'Aquila che si rinnova, 1584–86).

The Bible was their most common point of departure and reference. Genesis 1 and 2 were axiomatic: marriage was created as a one-flesh union between a man and a woman and was designed for them to "be fruitful and multiply." So was Matthew 19: a lawful marriage could not be "rent asunder," "except in the case of adultery." So was 1 Corinthians 7, which stipulated the "conjugal rights" that husband and wife could enjoy in order to avoid "burning" with lust. So were the Mosaic family laws and the Pauline household codes and the scattered biblical examples of natural law in action among the pre-Mosaic patriarchs and the apostolic churches. The crowning text for medieval marriage was Ephesians 5, with its call for the mutual sacrificial love of husband and wife, modeled on the mysterious union of Christ and his church. Particularly among medieval theologians, Ephesians 5 became the basis for a rich sacramental theology that rendered marriage one of the church's canonical sacraments, on the order of baptism and the Eucharist.[12] This sacramental theology of marriage was firmly entrenched by the thirteenth century, though not canonically confirmed until the Council of Trent in 1563.

A second common point of departure and reference for medieval writings on marriage was the Roman law, especially as compiled in the sixth-century *Corpus iuris civilis* of Emperor Justinian. Through trade and interaction between Christians and Muslims, the *Corpus iuris civilis* resurfaced in the West in the later eleventh century. This vast legal resource proved invaluable to medieval scholars of marriage. Often quoted was the Roman law's definition of marriage, taken from the mid-third century Stoic jurist Modestinus: "Marriage is the union of a man and a woman, a partnership for the whole of life, involving divine as well as human law"; this text still appears verbatim in the canonical statements on marriage of the Catholic Church today.[13] Also regularly used were various Roman law rules of marital consent and capacity, marital property and contracts, marital impediments and dissolution, illegitimacy and legitimation, inheritance and succession, and more. Medieval Catholics supplemented and reformed these inherited rules and procedures, and they rejected the Roman laws of divorce, remarriage, concubinage, and various forms of sexual permissiveness. But a good deal of the Roman law, in both its pre- and post-Christian forms, remained at the foundation of the medieval church's canon law.

---

12. See Theodore Mackin, SJ, *Marriage in the Catholic Church: The Marital Sacrament* (New York: Paulist Press, 1989), 274–378.

13. *The Digest of Justinian*, ed. Theodor Mommsen and Paul Krueger, trans. Alan Watson, 4 vols. (Philadelphia: University of Pennsylvania Press, 1985), 23.2.1; *Justinian's Institutes*, ed. Paul Krüger, trans. Peter Birks and Grant McLeod (Ithaca, NY: Cornell University Press, 1987), 1.9.1; *Decretum*, c. 27, q. 2, 1; *Decretales* 2.23.11. See *Code of Canon Law* (Washington, DC: Canon Law Society of America, 1983), Canon 1055.1; *Catechism of the Catholic Church*, 2nd ed. (Washington, DC: Libraria Editrice Vaticana, 2000), n. 1601. See other modern formulations quoted and discussed in David E. Fellhauer, "The *consortium omnis vitae* as a Juridical Element of Marriage," *Studia Canonica* 13 (1979): 117; John McAreavey, *The Canon Law of Marriage and the Family* (Dublin: Four Courts Press, 1997), 18–29.

A third common point of departure and reference was Augustine's writings on marriage, particularly his theory of the three goods of marriage, which became axiomatic. Augustine's works as a whole were not available; medieval writers knew him primarily through various sentences and fragments of his writings compiled in the early twelfth century. Yet even as abridged, Augustine was the most frequently cited church father on marriage in the writings of medieval theologians and canonists. Peter Lombard, for example, devoted a long "distinction" of his *Books of Sentences* to Augustine's three marital goods of "faith, procreation, and sacrament" (note Lombard's ordering of the goods), making this trope a commonplace for centuries of Catholic commentators thereafter. Among them was Thomas Aquinas, whose most sustained writing on marriage came in his 4,000-page commentary on Lombard's *Sentences*.[14] Similarly, Gratian's *Decretum* cited Augustine 82 times in his discussion of marriage alone. Raymond of Penyafort (ca. 1180–1275), the principal author of the *Decretales* (1234), also took Augustine as axiomatic: "The goods of marriage are principally three," Raymond wrote, quoting Augustine: "fidelity, offspring, and sacrament."[15] Among Christians, "the first two goods sometimes accompany marriage, sometimes not, but the third adheres inseparably as long as the marriage lasts."[16]

A final common point of departure and reference for medieval writers was Aristotle. His rich natural philosophy and ethical reflections on human reproductive strategies, on marriage and family life, and on the place of the household in broader society—these all provided a good deal of the rational reflection and natural law foundation of medieval marriage theory. Other classical writers on marriage—such as Plato, Plutarch, and others—came in for repeated citation, too. But Aristotle was the preeminent philosophical sage for many later medieval writers on marriage, particularly for Thomas Aquinas, who drew Aristotelian philosophy, Christian theology, and canon law into an exquisite synthesis.

MARRIAGE AS NATURAL, CONTRACTUAL, AND SACRAMENTAL

Although their views were wide-ranging, many medieval theologians and jurists came to treat marriage as a three-dimensional institution, subject to three types of law: (1) as a created, natural association, subject to the laws of nature; (2) as

---

14. Lombard, *Sent.*, bk. 4, dist. 31.1–9.

15. Raymond of Penyafort (Peñafort), *Summa on Marriage*, trans. Pierre J. Payer (Toronto: Pontifical Institute of Medieval Studies, 2005), bk. 2, tit. 12, quoting Augustine, *The Literal Meaning of Genesis* 9.7.12. Lombard and Aquinas also sequenced Augustine's goods as fidelity, children, and sacrament. See Lombard, *Sent.*, bk. 4, dist. 31.1; Aquinas, *Comm. Sent.*, dist. 31.1.

16. Raymond of Penyafort, *Summa on Marriage*, bk. 2, tit. 12–13. His canonical discussion of marriage, which also cites Augustine regularly, is in *Decretales*, bk. 4, tit. 1–21. See also S. Raimundus de Pennaforte (Raymond of Peñafort), *Summa de iure canonico*, ed. Xaverio Ochoa and Aloisio Díez (Rome: Commentarium pro religiosis, 1975), pt. 2, tit. 5 and 22.

a consensual contract, subject to the laws of contract; and (3) as a sacrament of faith, subject to the laws of the church.

Marriage as Natural

First, medieval writers argued, marriage was a natural association, formed by the one-flesh union of a man and a woman. Marriage served, in Augustine's famous phrase, both as "a duty for the sound and a remedy for the sick." Already in paradise, God had commanded man and woman to "be fruitful and multiply." He had created them as social beings, naturally inclined to one another and endowed with the physical capacity to join together and beget children. God had commanded them to help and nurture each other and to inculcate within their children the highest virtue and love of the Divine. These qualities and duties continued after the fall into sin, medieval writers insisted. But after the fall, marriage also came to serve as a remedy for the individual sinner to allay lustful passion, to heal incontinence, and to substitute a bodily union with a spouse for the lost spiritual union with the Father in paradise. Rather than allow sinful people to burn with lust, God provided the institution of marriage, wherein couples could direct their natural drives and desires toward the service of each other, their children, the church, and the broader society.

Many medieval writers, however, subordinated the duty of propagation to that of celibate contemplation, and the natural drive for sexual union to the spiritual drive for beatitude. For, as Peter Lombard put it:

> The first institution [of marriage in Paradise] was commanded, the second permitted . . . to the human race for the purpose of preventing fornication. But this permission, because it does not select better things, is a remedy, not a reward; if anyone rejects it, he will deserve judgment of death. An act which is allowed by permission, however, is voluntary, not necessary. Now permission is received in various ways, as concession, as remission, as toleration. And there is toleration in the New Testament, for lesser good deeds and lesser evils; among the lesser good deeds is marriage, which does not deserve a palm, but is a remedy.[17]

After the fall into sin, marriage remained a good and dutiful institution, but only for those tempted by sexual sin. For those not so tempted, marriage was an inferior option. It was better and more virtuous to pursue the spiritual life of celibacy and contemplation than to seek the temporal life of marriage and family. Marriage served primarily for the protection of the human community, not for the perfection of the individual. Participation in it merely kept a person free from sin and vice, rather than contributing directly to his virtue. The celibate, contemplative life, by contrast, increased a person's virtue and aided the pursuit of beatitude. It was particularly important for clerics, monastics, and other

---

17. Lombard, *Sent.*, bk. 4, sent. 26.3.

servants of the church to forgo sex, marriage, and family life as a condition for ecclesiastical service. Those who could not do so were not worthy of the church's holy orders and offices.[18]

The laity who did choose to marry found their first and most basic guidance in the natural law. For medieval writers, natural law was not only, as Emperor Justinian had put it, "the law that nature has taught all animals," giving them "natural inclinations" to protect, preserve, and perpetuate themselves through natural procreative means.[19] Natural law was also what Gratian called the "natural instincts" or "intuitions" that are unique to humans, and the "common customs" and "conventions" that have emerged among humans over time.[20] These distinctly human qualities of natural law are known through reason and conscience and often confirmed, illustrated, and sometimes corrected by the Bible.

Natural law, in this fuller human sense, defined the natural drive and determination that fit persons marry when they reach the age of puberty, that they conceive children and nurture and educate them until adulthood, and that they remain bonded to their kin, who by nature are inclined to serve and support each other, especially in times of need, frailty, and old age. The natural law prescribed heterosexual, lifelong unions between a couple, featuring mutual support and faithfulness. It proscribed incest, bestiality, buggery, sodomy, pederasty, masturbation, contraception, abortion, and other unnatural and nonprocreative sexual activities and relations.[21]

Writing in the mid-thirteenth century, Thomas Aquinas gave a particularly insightful account of the natural foundations of human marriage as a monogamous, exclusive, and indissoluble union. Thomas built his account in part on the extensive observations of his teacher, Albert the Great, on the reproductive strategies of various animals.[22] He also built on Aristotle's teaching that humans are "marital animals" as much as they are "political animals," and that most men and women have a natural attraction to each other and have a natural inclination to produce "copies of themselves."[23] But in building on Albert's observations of nature, Thomas added several new insights into the unique strategies of human reproduction through enduring pair-bonding.

18. See sources and discussion in Christopher N. L. Brooke, "The Cult of Celibacy in the Eleventh and Twelfth Centuries," in *The Medieval Idea of Marriage* (Oxford and New York: Oxford University Press, 1991), 61–92; Helen Parish, *Clerical Celibacy in the West, c. 1100–1700* (Burlington, VT: Ashgate, 2010), 87–142.

19. *Inst.* 1.1.2; *Dig.* 1.1.3. See the Ordinary Gloss on *Decretum*, Dist. 1.6–7, in *Gratian: The Treatise on Laws with the Ordinary Gloss*, trans. James Gordley and Augustine Thompson, OP (Washington, DC: Catholic University of America Press, 1993), 6–7.

20. Gratian, *Decretum*, Dist. 1, c. 7.

21. See sample texts in Rudolf Weigand, *Die Naturrechtslehre die Legisten und Dekretisten von Irenaeus bis Johannes Teutonicus* (Berlin: Hueber, 1967), 283–98.

22. See Albertus Magnus, *Quaestiones super animalibus*, trans. as *Questions concerning Aristotle's "On Animals,"* trans. Irven M. Resnick and Kenneth F. Kitchell Jr. (Washington, DC: Catholic University of America Press, 2008), esp. bks. 5, 9, 10, 15, and 67.

23. See pp. 19–20.

Thomas first observed that humans are unique among other animals in producing utterly fragile and helpless infants, who depend on their parents' support for a very long time:

> There are animals whose offspring are able to seek food immediately after birth, or are sufficiently fed by their mother; and in these there is no tie between male and female; whereas in those whose offspring needs the support of both parents, although for a short time, there is a certain tie, as may be seen in certain birds. In man, however, since the child needs the parents' care for a long time, there is a very great tie between male and female, to which ties even the generic nature inclines.[24]

"Among some animals where the female is able to take care of the upbringing of offspring, male and female do not remain together for any time after the act of generation." This is the case with cats, dogs, cattle, and other herding animals, where newborns quickly become independent after a brief nursing period. "But in the case of animals of which the female is not able to provide for upbringing of children, the male and female do stay together after the act of generation as long as is necessary for the upbringing and instruction of the offspring." In these latter cases, this inclination to stay and help with the feeding, protection, and teaching of the offspring is "naturally implanted in the male," said Thomas. Birds are a particularly good example of this: they pair for the entire mating season and cooperate in building their nests, in brooding their eggs, and in feeding, protecting, and teaching their fledglings until they finally take flight.[25]

Human beings push this natural pattern of pair-bonding and reproduction much further, Thomas continued, not only because their children remain dependent for so much longer but also because these children place heavy and shifting demands on their parents as they slowly mature. This requires the effort of both parents. "The female in the human species is not at all able to take care of the upbringing of offspring by herself, since the needs of human life demand many things which cannot be provided by one person alone. Therefore it is appropriate to human nature to remain together with a woman after the generative act, and not leave her immediately to have such relations with another woman, as is the practice of fornicators." For this reason, human males and females are naturally inclined to remain together for the sake of their dependent human infant.[26]

A man will remain with the mother and care for the child, however, only if he is certain that he is the father, Thomas continued. A woman will know that a child is hers because she carries it to term for nine months and then nurses the child thereafter. A man will know that a child is his only if he is sure that his wife has been sexually faithful to him alone. Only with an exclusive monogamous relationship can a man be sure that if his wife becomes pregnant, he is the father.

24. Aquinas, *ST* Supp. q. 41, art. 1.
25. Aquinas, *SCG* III-II.122.6; 124.3.
26. Ibid., 122.6; 124.3.

And only then will a man be likely to join his wife in care for their child. "Man naturally desires to know his offspring," Thomas declared, "and this knowledge would be completely destroyed if there were several males for one female. Therefore that one female is for one male is a consequence of a natural instinct."[27]

Thomas recognized that paternal certainty alone was often not enough to bind a man to his wife and child. Echoing his teacher Albert, Thomas believed that human males, like other male animals, craved sex with many females much more than they craved permanent attachment to their consorts and children. But rational men were further induced to care for their children because of their natural instinct for self-preservation. A father is naturally inclined to remain with the mother and care for their children indefinitely, Aquinas argued, because his child is literally an extension of himself, a part and product of his own body. Once a human male recognizes that the infant is his, that it shares his very "substance"—indeed is a part and product of his own being—he will care for the infant as he is inclined to care for his own body. And once he begins this parental process, his attachment to that child will deepen, and he will remain with the child and its mother. He will enjoy the interaction with and growth of his child, and he will enjoy the sexual intimacy and domestic support of his wife as the family remains together. Both faithful and indissoluble marriage, Aquinas concluded, provides the context for this parental lifelong investment in children. Faithful marriage provides paternal certainty, ensuring a man that he is investing in his own children, not those with whom he has no biological tie. Indissoluble marriage provides parental investment, ensuring children of their parents' support for their many years of maturation, which these children will later reciprocate when their parents grow old and fragile and enter into their second childhood.[28]

To these two arguments from the nature of human reproduction and attachment, Thomas added a third argument from natural justice. He pressed this natural justice argument to show that monogamy was superior to polyandry, polygyny, and other forms of extramarital procreation that were rampant among some other animals. Thomas rejected polyandry (one female with multiple males), a practice that Plato had briefly contemplated in his *Republic*, because it was naturally unjust to children. If a woman had sex with several husbands, he argued, it removed the likelihood that the children born to that woman will clearly belong to any one husband. This will undermine paternal certainty and consequent paternal investment in their children's care. The children will suffer from neglect, and the wife will be overburdened in trying to care for them and tend to her multiple husbands at once.[29]

Thomas rejected polygyny (one male with multiple females) because it was unjust to wives. Polygyny did not necessarily erode paternal certainty, Thomas

27. Ibid., 124.1; see also Aquinas, *ST* Supp. q. 41, art. 1.
28. Aquinas, *SCG* III-II, 122–123.
29. Aquinas, *ST* Supp, qq. 41, 65–66; idem, *SCG* III-II, 123.3; 124.3–8.

recognized. So long as his multiple wives remained faithful to him alone, a man could be assured of being the father of children born in his household. But polygyny betrayed the requirement of mutuality and equality that should exist between husband and wife. It also undercut the undivided and undiluted love and friendship between husband and wife that become a proper marriage. In polygymous households, wives are reduced to servants if not slaves of the household, and set in perennial competition with each other for resources and access to their shared husband. This is not marriage, but servitude, Thomas concluded. True marital "friendship consists in an equality" that must remain undivided. "So, if it is not lawful for the wife to have several husbands, since this is contrary to the certainty as to offspring, it would be not lawful, on the other hand, for a man to have several wives, for the friendship of husband and wife would not be free, but somewhat servile. And this argument is corroborated by experience, for among husbands having plural wives, the wives have a status like that of servants." Natural law and natural justice teach otherwise.[30]

Thomas used a similar argument from natural justice to denounce extramarital sex and unilateral divorce. Extramarital sex through fornication, prostitution, adultery, or concubinage is inherently unjust to the children often born of such unions, Aquinas insisted. Such children are "bastards" who must bear "the sins of their fathers and mothers" for a lifetime. Absent successful legitimation, these children bear the permanent stigma of their extramarital birth, noted on certificates of baptism, confirmation, marriage, and death as well as on tax rolls, court records, and property registrations. In Thomas's day and for many centuries before and after, these children born out of wedlock lived in a sort of legal limbo, with some claims to charity and support, but with severely truncated rights to inherit or devise property, to hold high clerical, political or military offices, to sue or testify in court, and more. These formal legal disabilities were often compounded by the chronic poverty, neglect, and abuse that these children faced, assuming that they escaped the not-so-uncommon historical practice of being secretly smothered or exposed upon birth, or sent out to be nursed by and eventually to work for others with modest odds of survival.[31] For Thomas, the natural injustice to children was one strong argument for restricting procreation to monogamous marriages.

Unilateral divorce, in turn, was naturally unjust to wives who were left vulnerable to their husband's right to divorce them when they became barren or lost their youthful beauty. In the patriarchal society of his day, Aquinas recognized, divorce was a male prerogative that would almost always work to the disadvantage of the wife. She would often be left in middle age, without support either from her husband, who would go on to other women, or from her father, who would likely be dead at that point. This made divorce "naturally wrong," said

---

30. Aquinas, *ST* III, qq. 41, 65–66; idem, *SCG* III-II, 123.3; 124.3–8.

31. See sources and discussion in John Witte Jr., *The Sins of the Fathers: The Law and Theology of Illegitimacy Reconsidered* (Cambridge: Cambridge University Press, 2009), chap. 3. See further Nicholas Orme, *Medieval Children* (New Haven, CT: Yale University Press, 2001).

Thomas: "So if a man took a woman in the time of her youth, when beauty and fecundity were hers, and then sent her away after she had reached an advanced age, he would damage that woman, contrary to natural equity."[32]

This combination of natural arguments for monogamous, exclusive, and presumptively permanent marriage, and against polygamy, adultery, and other extramarital unions, would become axiomatic in the Western tradition. The core of the natural argument was focused on the natural needs and tendencies of men, women, and human infants and the premium placed on stable marriage as the proper site for sexual exchange, mutual adult dependency, procreation and nurture of long-dependent children. The core of the natural-justice argument was focused on the injustice and harm done to women and children by polygyny, unilateral divorce, desertion, concubinage, promiscuity, and illegitimacy.

To these natural arguments, we will see in a moment, Thomas added his theological arguments about marriage as a sacrament. This strengthened his case for the exclusive and indissoluble marriages of Christians. But even stripped of its theological overlay and left to stand alone, his naturalist arguments for enduring monogamous marriages and against polygamy and other extramarital unions were powerful. Many later Western jurists and philosophers would build on these early arguments in defending monogamy and denouncing polygamy. And today, a number of anthropologists and evolutionary scientists have shown that reproduction through enduring pair-bonding is the most expedient means for humans to reproduce, given the realities of long and demanding infant dependency. Indeed, human reproduction by enduring pair-bonding is now described by primatologist Bernard Chapais and others as the "deep structure" of survival that the human species has evolved.[33] In his own prescientific way, Thomas already saw this 750 years ago.

Marriage as Contractual

Many medieval writers treated marriage not only as a natural association, but also a contract, subject to general rules of contract formation. In its essence, marriage depended on the mutual consent of the parties to be legitimate and binding. "What makes a marriage is not the consent to cohabitation nor the carnal copula," wrote Peter Lombard; "it is the consent to conjugal society that does." The form and function of this conjugal society, and the requirements for valid entrance into it, were preset by the laws of nature, as amended and emended by the laws of the church. But the choice of whether to enter this

32. Aquinas, *ST* Supp. q. 67; idem, *SCG* III-II, 123.

33. Bernard Chapais, *Primeval Kinship: How Pair-Bonding Gave Birth to Human Society* (Cambridge, MA: Harvard University Press, 2008), 10. See also Peter B. Gray and Kermyt G. Anderson, *Fatherhood: Evolution and Human Paternal Behavior* (Cambridge, MA: Harvard University Press, 2010); Melvin A. Konner, *The Evolution of Childhood: Relations, Emotions, Mind* (Cambridge, MA: Harvard University Press, 2010).

conjugal society lay first and foremost with the man and the woman.[34] "Marriage, therefore," said Peter Lombard, "is the marital union between persons legitimate according to the [natural] law, who persevere in a single sharing of life."[35] In the fourteenth century, John Duns Scotus glossed Lombard's definition with a reference to the conjugal debt: "Marriage is an indissoluble bond between a man and his wife arising from the mutual exchange of authority over one another's bodies for the procreation and proper nurture of children. The contract of marriage is the mutual exchange by a man and wife of their bodies for perpetual use in the procreation and nurture of children."[36] Hugh of St. Victor stressed the requirement of conjugal fidelity: "What else is marriage but the legitimate association between a man and woman, an association in which each partner obligates [*debet*] himself to the other by virtue of mutual consent? This obligation can be considered in two ways, that one reserve oneself for the spouse, and that one not refuse oneself to the spouse. That is, he reserves himself in that after giving consent he does not go now to another union. He does not refuse himself in that he does not separate himself from that mutual association of one with the other."[37]

Thomas Aquinas elaborated on this tie between the marital contract and the marital good of "fidelity." Marital fidelity is not a spiritual faith, but a faith of justice, Thomas argued. It means keeping faith, being faithful, holding faithfully to one's promises made in the contract of marriage. Marital faith requires, as Augustine had said, forgoing sexual contact with others and honoring the conjugal debt to one's spouse. But marital faith also involves, as Aristotle and the Stoics had said, the commitment to be indissolubly united with one's spouse in body and mind, to be the "greatest of friends," to be willing to share fully and equally in the person, property, lineage, and reputation of one's spouse—indeed, in the "whole life" of one's spouse. To be faithful is to be and to bear with each other in youth and in old age, in sickness and in health, in prosperity and adversity. It is to be "solicitous" for one's marital household and common possessions and to develop "solid affection" for one's relatives and families.[38]

As a contract, marriage was subject to the general principles of contract that prevailed in medieval canon and civil law. One such principle was freedom of contract, and this applied to marriage contracts just the same.[39] The validity of the marriage contract in its essence depended on the free and voluntary con-

34. Lombard, *Sent.*, bk. 4, dist. 27.2; 28.4.

35. Ibid., bk. 4, dist. 27.2.

36. Quoted by Theodore Mackin, *Marriage in the Catholic Church: What Is Marriage?* (New York: Paulist Press, 1982), 186.

37. Hugh of St. Victor, *De beatae Mariae Virginis virginitate*, in PL 176:859, quoted and discussed in Mackin, *What Is Marriage?* 155.

38. Aquinas, *Comm. Sent.*, bk. 4, dist. 26.2; 27.1; 31.1; 33.1; 41.1; idem, *ST* Supp., qq. 41, 49.5–6, 64; idem, *SCG* III-II, 123.3, 4, 8; 124.4–5; 125.6; 126.1–6. See further John Finnis, *Aquinas: Moral, Political, and Legal Theory* (Oxford: Oxford University Press, 1998), 143–48.

39. See X.4.1.29; C. 31, q. 2, c. 1; and Hostiensis, *Summa aurea*, quoted by Richard H. Helmholz, *The Spirit of the Classical Canon Law* (Athens, GA: University of Georgia Press, 1996), 237.

sent of both the man and the woman. Marriage contracts entered into by force, fear, or fraud, or through undue influence or inducement by parents, masters, or lords—such contracts were thus not binding, at least in theory, though the medieval practice of arranged marriages, especially for children of aristocratic and political families, sometimes strained this theory to the breaking point. A second general principle of medieval contract law was that consensual agreements, entered into with or without formalities, were legally binding. Absent proof of mistake or frustration, or of some condition that would render the marital contract unjust, either party could petition a court to enforce its terms. This general principle also applied to marriage contracts. Both husband and wife had an equal right to sue in court for enforcement even of a "naked promise" (*nudum pactum*) of marriage, for discharge of an essential and licit condition to marriage, and for vindication of their conjugal rights to sexual intercourse. Rights to spousal support and maintenance set in automatically after the couple was married, even if their marriage was not consummated. Conjugal rights to future sexual performance set in only after their first act of consensual sexual intercourse within marriage.[40]

A prominent issue in medieval canon law concerned conditional contracts to engagement and marriage.[41] What was the status of a contract when a party promised something like the following? I shall marry you "if my parents agree"; "after you have secured a job"; "provided you quit your military service"; "so long as the wedding takes place within six months"; "if we can live in my hometown"; "provided you pay me certain property"; "after my father dies"; "if God preserves me"; "so long as we have no children"; "if you can touch the sky"; "whenever a woman becomes pope"; "if you can drink the sea empty"; "provided you kill my rival"—or any number of other such conditions. Did those promises automatically lapse if the condition was not met, or would the parties have to litigate? What if the conditions in question were impossible, silly, or downright illegal?

The canonists gathered a complex jurisprudence around these questions.[42] They eventually distinguished three types of conditional marriage contracts. "Honest possible" conditions ("if my parents consent"; "so long as you move to my hometown by September 1"; "provided you buy me a horse and carriage

---

40. James A. Brundage, "Implied Consent to Intercourse," in *Consent and Coercion to Sex and Marriage in Ancient and Medieval Societies,* ed. Angeliki E. Laiou (Washington, DC: Dumbarton Oaks Research Library and Collection, 1993), 245–56; Charles J. Reid Jr., *Power over the Body, Equality in the Family: Rights and Domestic Relations in Medieval Canon Law* (Grand Rapids: Wm. B. Eerdmans Publishing Co., 2004), 25–68; Rudolf Weigand, *Die bedingte Eheschliessung im kanonischen Recht,* 2 vols. (Munich: Max Hueber, 1963); John T. Noonan, *Canons and Canonists in Context* (Goldbach: Keip, 1997), 173–98.

41. See Weigand, *Die bedingte Eheschliessung,* vol. 1; Bartholomew T. Timlin, *Conditional Matrimonial Consent: An Historical Synopsis and Commentary* (Washington, DC: Catholic University of America Press, 1934).

42. Good early modern summaries are provided in Sanchez, bk. 5, disp. 1–19; Henry Swinburne, *A Treatise of Spousals, or Matrimonial Contracts* (London: S. Roycroft, 1686), 109.

before the wedding") were valid, and engagement or marriage promises would be voided on their breach. "Dishonest possible" conditions that vitiated an essential dimension of marriage ("so long as we have no children"; "provided I may maintain a concubine"; "so long as you remain unbaptized") were invalid and automatically voided the promises. All other conditions were generally disregarded, and the marital contracts would be enforced as if the condition had not been made. These included "dishonest possible" conditions that did not go to the essence of the marriage ("so long as you kill my rival") as well as conditions that were considered impossible to fulfill ("if you empty the sea"; "when a woman becomes pope").[43]

Marital contracts were often accompanied by contracts concerning marital property, though these two contracts were independent.[44] The prospective husband gave to his fiancée (and sometimes to her father or family as well) a betrothal gift, sometimes a very elaborate and expensive gift. He often followed this with a gift to his new wife on the day of their wedding or the morning after (sometimes called the "morning gift"). These were residues of older traditions that required a man to pay a bride-price to a father for his daughter's hand. But they were also symbolic ways by which a man could express his love and commitment to his chosen woman. A whole cluster of medieval love poetry and courtship etiquette books eventually gathered around this crucial step in marital formation. Through her family, the wife in turn brought into the marital household her dowry. This was at minimum her basic living articles, often a great deal more, including sometimes an advance on any inheritance she had coming from her father or guardian. The husband was obligated to preserve a substantial part of this dowry, known as "the marriage portion," that would be returned to the wife's family if she predeceased him or if their marriage was annulled. The husband was also required to preserve a substantial portion of his own property, known as a dower, to support his wife and their children if he predeceased her. The parties could negotiate about the exact terms of these presumptive marital property arrangements. They could also negotiate about inheritance of the marital estate, confirming or tailoring the default rules requiring that marital property be left to the surviving spouse and children, with priority for the eldest son under the laws of primogeniture, which had persisted since biblical times. These marital property contracts, which drew on a complex blend of canon laws, civil laws, feudal laws, and local customary laws, were not absolute conditions for the validity of the marriage contract. For parties of modest means, marital property agreements could be easily bypassed or the default rules of canon and civil law simply accepted. But for parties with

---

43. Helmholz, *Marriage Litigation*, 50.
44. This is the key insight of Richard H. Helmholz, "Marriage Contracts in Medieval England," in *To Have and to Hold: Marrying and Its Documentation in Western Christendom, 400–1600*, ed. Philip L. Reynolds and John Witte Jr. (Cambridge: Cambridge University Press, 2007), 260–86, and is evident in several other regions of Europe described in other chapters in this work.

greater means, these economic dimensions of marriage were serious business. The negotiation about them, which often involved the extended families and matchmakers or lawyers on both sides, could delay and derail a prospective marriage. And breach of a contract to deliver property in consideration of a marriage could lead to annulment at least of the engagement contract, and occasionally of a newly formed marital contract too.[45]

Marriage as Sacramental

Marriage was not only a natural and contractual union, medieval writers argued. When contracted between two baptized Christians in conformity with the laws of nature and contract, marriage was also raised to the dignity of a sacrament. Unlike other sacraments, such as baptism or the Eucharist, the sacrament of marriage required no formalities and no clerical or lay instruction, witnesses, or participation. The two parties, if properly baptized in the faith, were themselves "ministers of the sacrament." Their consciences instructed them in the taking of the sacrament, and their own testimony was considered sufficient evidence to validate their sacramental marriage in cases of dispute.[46] This was an "astonishingly individualistic" view of how the marital sacrament could be formed, but it remained the consensus view until the reforms of the sixteenth century.[47]

Medieval church councils, particularly the Fourth Lateran Council of 1215, did strongly encourage the couple to seek their parents' consent, draw upon the counsel of witnesses, publicize their engagement through banns, and seek premarital counseling from a priest. The church also offered a variety of wedding liturgies to be presided over by ordained priests and to take place at home, in the church, or at the door of the church (*in facie ecclesiae*). In medieval England and France, where church weddings were more common, the wedding liturgies featured a final pronouncement of the banns, an invitation for anyone to state objections to the marriage or "forever hold your peace," a confirmation of the mutual consent of the couple, an exchange of marital vows with words in the present tense to live together "in sickness and in health, for richer or poorer," the blessing and exchange of rings, and sometimes the celebration of the Eucharist. Some late medieval wedding liturgies also included ritual exchanges of property—the husband providing his bride with silver coins and the wife providing a token of her dowry, both gifts to be blessed by the priest. Some liturgies also

45. For examples, see ibid., passim; Mia Korpiola, *Between Betrothal and Bedding: Marriage Formation in Sweden, 1200–1600* (Leiden: E. J. Brill, 2009); Katherine L. Jansen, Joanna Drell, and Frances Andrews, eds., *Medieval Italy: Texts in Translation* (Philadelphia: University of Pennsylvania Press, 2009), 421–58; and discussion in Shannon McSheffrey, *Marriage, Sex, and Civic Culture in Late Medieval London* (Philadelphia: University of Pennsylvania Press, 2006), 21–35, 88–97.

46. Aquinas, *ST* II-II, q. 100, art. 2; *Decretales* 4.1.14.

47. The phrase is from Michael M. Sheehan, *Marriage, Family, and Law in Medieval Europe: Collected Studies*, ed. James K. Farge (Toronto: University of Toronto Press, 1996), 76.

included a postwedding blessing of the bridal chamber and a prayer imploring God to bless the couple with children.[48]

It was not until 1563, however, that the Council of Trent required a priest to witness the union, to join the spouses using whatever form of words was customary in the region, and to offer the couple a "sacerdotal benediction." None of this was required in the High Middle Ages.[49] "In the celebration of this sacrament," Peter Lombard wrote, "there are certain things which belong to the substance of the sacrament, including the words of present consent, which of themselves suffice to form a marriage. There are other things which belong only to the dignity and solemnity of the sacrament, such as the delivery of the bride by her parents, the priestly blessing, and the like." But none of these latter activities affects the validity and legality of the marriage.[50]

Like the other sacraments, medieval writers argued, marriage was an instrument of sanctification, a channel of grace that caused God's gracious gifts and blessings to be poured upon humanity. Marriage sanctified the Christian couple by allowing them to comply with God's law for marriage and by providing them with an ideal model of marriage in Christ the bridegroom, who took the church as his bride and accorded it his highest love, devotion, and sacrifice, even to the point of death. It sanctified their children by welcoming them as legitimate members of church, state, and society and by providing them with a chrysalis of nurture, support, and education that sustained them until they reached adulthood. And marriage sanctified the Christian community by enlarging the church and by educating the next generation of children as people of God and parishioners of the church.

In medieval theory, the sacrament of marriage transformed the relationship of a married couple, much like baptism transformed the character of the baptized. In baptism, the seemingly simple ritual act of sprinkling water on the forehead spiritually transformed the baptized party—cancelling the original sin of Adam, promising the baptized party divine aid and protection in life, and welcoming the baptized believer into the sanctuary of the church, into the spiritual care of the parents and godparents, and into the communion of saints. Similarly, in marriage the simple ritual act of a Christian man and woman coming

---

48. See good samples in Mark Searle and Kenneth W. Stevenson, *Documents of the Marriage Liturgy* (Collegeville, MN: Liturgical Press, 1992). For an English case study of public weddings, often featuring church consecration, see McSheffrey, *Marriage, Sex, and Civic Culture,* esp. 20–48. On the alternative Italian tradition of notarization of marriages, rather than church wedding, see David D'Avray, "Marriage Ceremonies and the Church in Italy after 1215," in *Marriage in Italy, 1300–1650,* ed. T. Dean and K. J. P. Lowe (Cambridge: Cambridge University Press, 1998), 105–15.

49. Several regional councils of the church also listed marriage as a sacrament, beginning with the Council of Verona (1184). *Enchiridion Symbolorum Definitionum et Declarationum de rebus Fidei et Morum,* ed. H. Denzinger and A. Schoenmetzer, 3rd ed. (Fribourg: Herder, 1965), 1327. See Michael G. Lawler, *Marriage and the Catholic Church: Disputed Questions* (Collegeville, MN: Liturgical Press, 2002), 1–24.

50. Lombard, *Sent.,* bk., 4, dist. 28.2. See other views in G. H. Joyce, SJ, *Christian Marriage: An Historical and Doctrinal Study,* 2nd ed. (London: Sheed & Ward, 1948), 191–92.

together consensually in a sacramental marriage spiritually transformed their relationship—removing the sin of sexual intercourse, inviting them into the new creative act of procreation, promising them divine help in fulfilling their marital and parental duties, and welcoming them into the hierarchy of institutions that comprised the church. Just as the mother church communicated to the new couple the forms of nurture, education, and worship they needed to thrive as Christian believers, so the married couple now communicated to each other and to their children the nurture, education, and worship they needed to thrive as members of a Christian household.[51]

Twelfth- and thirteenth-century writers endlessly debated what step in the marital formation process rendered it sacramental. Several writers, building on Gratian's *Decretum*, insisted that sacramental grace was conferred only on consummation of the marriage through sexual intercourse, the final act of marriage. After all, the most startling feature of the sacrament was that it transformed sexual intercourse from an otherwise sinful act of lust into a spiritual act of great symbolic value. Moreover, it was well understood that a simple promise to marry in the future followed by intercourse rendered the couple married.[52] But the purely carnal act of intercourse, which was prone to great sinfulness even within marriage, seemed to be a most unlikely channel of grace. Moreover, some couples, such as Mary and Joseph, were truly married even though they purportedly did not have sexual intercourse. Such "spiritual marriages" seemed to be more worthy of sacramental designation, rather than being unworthy.[53]

Other writers, notably John Duns Scotus, insisted that it was the blessing of the priest during the church wedding that rendered marriage sacramental. This view was appealing because it matched the role of the priest in other sacraments—the priest's sprinkling of water in baptism, his declaration of absolution from sin in penance, or his offering of bread and wine in the Eucharist.[54] But this view stood in tension with the social and legal reality that many marriages were contracted and consummated without priestly consecration. To declare such marriages "nonsacramental" was tantamount to removing them from the spiritual jurisdiction and sacramental care of the church. It also jeopardized the legality of a great number of "marriages" that had been contracted and celebrated outside of the church, and it threatened illegitimacy to the many children born of such unions.

---

51. See texts in Mackin, *What Is Marriage?* 20–33, 332–33. On the critical symbolism of sacramental marriage, see David D'Avray, *Medieval Marriage: Symbolism and Society* (Oxford: Oxford University Press, 2005).

52. Gratian, *Decretum*, causa 27, q. 2; Vincentius Hispanus, *Lectura*, ad X.1.21.5, quoted by Brundage, *Law, Sex, and Christian Society*, 433n; Albert the Great, *Commentary on the Sentences*, bk. 4, dist. 26.11 and dist. 31.37; discussed in John T. Noonan Jr., *Contraception: A History of Its Treatment by the Catholic Theologians and Canonists* (Cambridge, MA: Belknap Press, 1965), 286–88.

53. See generally Dyan Elliott, *Spiritual Marriage: Sexual Abstinence in Medieval Wedlock* (Princeton, NJ.: Princeton University Press, 1993).

54. John Duns Scotus, *Quaestiones in IV libros Sententiarum*, bk. 4, dist. 26.14, in his *Opera omnia*, repr. ed. (Farnbourgh: Gregg, 1969), 19:168.

By the later thirteenth century, it became widely accepted that it was the simple exchange of present promises between the parties that rendered the marriage a sacrament. This view became canonical. Neither consecration of the marriage through a church wedding nor consummation of the marriage through sexual intercourse was critical in the sacramental process. Even a secretly contracted, unconsummated marriage between a man and a woman capable of entering conjugal society in accordance with natural law could be an instrument of sacramental grace. It was the mutual exchange of wills, the genuine union of mind to be married, that triggered the conferral of sacramental grace. The fruits of that sacramental grace pervaded the institution from that time forward.[55]

Once this channel of sacramental grace was properly opened, it could no longer be closed, medieval writers argued. A marriage between baptized Christians in compliance with natural, contractual, and spiritual laws was an indissoluble union, a permanently open channel of grace. God would not close this channel of grace, given his faithfulness to his church. Neither spouse could close this channel, no matter how faithless to the other they became. Because Christ's gracious love for his church is indissoluble, medieval writers argued, a Christian husband's love for his wife must remain indissoluble as well. Because the church is a permanent embodiment of Christ on earth, a Christian wife must remain permanently joined to the body of her husband, part of one being and one flesh with him. For as a sacrament, a Christian marriage not only reflected and symbolized Christ's marriage with his church, it actually participated in this eternal mystery of the incarnation, taking on its essential qualities. The mysterious and enduring union of Christ and his church was thus duplicated in each Christian marriage. Its unique quality of indissolubility remained part of this sacramental association, regardless of what the husband and wife did or said.[56] Thomas Aquinas captured this in a critical passage on the indissolubility of marriage:

> Since the sacraments effect what they figure, it is to be believed that grace is conferred through this sacrament on the spouses, whereby they might belong to the union of Christ and the Church. And this is very necessary to them so that as they concern themselves with carnal and earthly matters, they do not become detached from Christ and the Church. Now since the union of husband and wife designates the union of Christ and the Church, the figure must correspond with that which it signifies. Now the union of Christ and the church is a union of one to another, and it is to last in perpetuity. For there is only one Church, . . . and Christ will never be separated from His Church. As he himself says in the last chapter of Matthew, "Behold I am with you even unto the end of the world. . . ." It

55. Aquinas, *ST* II–II, q. 100, art. 2; *Decretales* 4.1.14. See discussion in Charles Donahue Jr., "The Policy of Alexander the Third's Consent Theory of Marriage," *Proceedings of the Fourth International Congress of Medieval Canon Law*, ed. Stephan Kuttner (Vatican City: Biblioteca Apostolica Vaticana, 1976), 251–81.

56. See texts in Edward Schillebeeckx, OP, *Marriage: Human Reality and Saving Mystery*, trans. N. D. Smith (New York: Sheed & Ward, 1965), 319–27; and discussion of the emerging medieval understanding in D'Avray, *Medieval Marriage*, 74–130.

follows necessarily then that a marriage, in so far as it is a sacrament of the Church, must be one holding to another indivisibly.[57]

Thomas bolstered this sacramental argument for the indissolubility of marriage with the arguments from nature that we have already sampled: "According to nature's intent, marriage is oriented to the nurture of offspring. Thus it is according to the law of nature that parents save for their children and that children be heirs for their parents. Therefore, since offspring are the good of both husband and wife together, the latter's union must remain permanently, according to the dictate of the law of nature."[58] He also added a contractual argument that the couple had consensually agreed to remain together "in sickness and in health, for better and for worse" and that preserving the marital bond was more advantageous to the couple, their children, and the broader community.[59] But it was the argument from the sacramental quality of marriage that gave his arguments for indissolubility their final cogency and canonical force.

The sacramental understanding of marriage both elevated and integrated the natural and the contractual dimensions of marriage. In the first place, the sacramental quality of Christian marriage helped to elevate the natural acts of marriage to spiritual significance. At minimum, it helped to remove the stigma of sin in sexual intercourse and to elevate the procreation and nurture of children into an act useful for the church. More fully conceived, the sacramental quality effectively placed the natural institution of marriage into the hierarchy of church orders as something of an institution and instrument of grace, although one clearly subordinate to the celibate clerical and monastic orders. It rendered each Christian household something of a "domestic church," the first school of virtue and faith, with the parents serving as the first teachers, catechists, and moral exemplars for their children.

Moreover, the sacramental quality of Christian marriage helped to elevate the marriage contract into more than just a bargained-for exchange between two parties. At minimum, it rendered marriage an "adhesion contract." The terms of the marital bargain, as a heterosexual monogamous union between a fit man and a fit woman with freedom and capacity to join together, were already preset by the laws of nature and the laws of contract. And the conditions for marriage—as an enduring union of their persons, properties, and labors and an enduring communion of marital love, fidelity, and sacrifice—were already prefigured in the sacrament between Christ and the church. More fully conceived, the exchange of consent between the couple also signified an exchange of consent of the couple with God and the church. Viewed from this perspective, marriage was an indissoluble promise because it went beyond the contract and consent of the couple with one another. In essence, the parties consented to bind themselves to

57. Aquinas, *SCG* IV.78.
58. Quoted by Theodore Mackin, SJ, *Marriage in the Catholic Church: Divorce and Remarriage* (New York: Paulist Press, 1984), 342.
59. Ibid.

each other, to God, and to the church and thus to accept God's grace and the church's spiritual guidance and legal governance of their marriage.

This understanding of the marriage sacrament, which became entrenched in the West by the thirteenth century, echoed but went beyond the fifth-century formulations of Augustine of Hippo. Augustine had called marriage a sacrament in order to demonstrate its symbolic stability. Thirteenth-century writers called marriage a sacrament to demonstrate its spiritual efficacy. Augustine had said that marriage as a symbol of Christ's bond to the church *should* not be dissolved. Thirteenth-century writers said that marriage as a permanent channel of sacramental grace *could* not be dissolved.[60] Augustine had simply scattered throughout his writings reflections on the natural, contractual, and spiritual dimensions of the marriage without fully integrating them. Thirteenth-century writers wove these three dimensions of marriage into an integrated framework, with sacrament as the linchpin.

A few critics of the day—and more of them during the sixteenth-century Protestant Reformation, as we will see in the next chapters—considered this new theology of marriage to be a self-serving attempt to bring marriage within the domain and power of the church.[61] Given the revolutionary climate of the day and the great battles between popes and emperors and between bishops and lords over power and jurisdiction, there may be something to this. But whatever the inspiration of twelfth- and thirteenth-century writers might have been, their theological construction of a sacramental model of marriage was a work of genius. It integrated nearly a millennium of inherited theological reflections on marriage and anticipated many of the hardest questions that would confront the church in subsequent centuries. The thirteenth-century sacramental model of marriage lies at the heart of Catholic theology still today—amply amended and emended over the centuries, but unchanged in its fundamental form.[62]

THE MEDIEVAL CANON LAW OF MARRIAGE

One reason why the Catholic sacramental model of marriage has had such an enduring influence in the West was that it was not only a theological but also a legal model. The theological formulations of monks and professors were translated into the canon laws of popes and church councils. New canon laws of marriage were in turn given new theological and philosophical elaboration. Since

60. Joseph Martos, *Doors to the Sacred: A Historical Introduction to Sacraments in the Catholic Church* (Garden City, NY: Image Books, 1982), 430–32.

61. See, e.g., the attack of the Cathars in the thirteenth century as discussed in Brundage, *Law, Sex, and Christian Society*, 431–32; and of Marsilius of Padua, *Defensor pacis*, disc. 2, chaps. 10, 25, 26, in Alan Gewirth, *Marsilius of Padua: The Defender of the Peace*, vol. 2, *The Defensor Pacis*, translated, with an introduction (New York: Columbia University Press, 1956).

62. See, e.g., Mackin, *What Is Marriage?* 225–327; Karl Rahner, "Marriage as Sacrament," in *Theological Investigations*, trans. D. Bourke (New York: Herder & Herder, 1973), 10:199–221.

the late eleventh century, there was a constant cross-fertilization between the theology and law of marriage in the Catholic Church.

Marital Jurisdiction

It was the church's new legal and political prominence in the West that rendered this alliance of theology and law so powerful. In the Western world of 1200–1500, the church was not merely a voluntary association of like-minded believers gathered for worship. Its canon law was not simply an internal code of spiritual discipline to guide the faithful. The church was the one universal sovereign of the West that governed all of Christendom. The canon law was the one universal law of the West that was common to jurisdictions and peoples throughout Europe. The great nation-states of Western Europe were not yet fully born. The Holy Roman Empire was not yet fully real. In that interim, the Catholic Church with its canon law often held preeminent authority.

The church claimed a vast jurisdiction—a power to proclaim and enforce law, literally "to speak the law" (*jus dicere*) for Western Christendom.[63] The church claimed personal jurisdiction over clerics, pilgrims, students, heretics, Jews, and Muslims. It claimed subject-matter jurisdiction over doctrine, liturgy, ecclesiastical property, patronage, education, charity, inheritance, oral promises, oaths, moral crimes, and marriage. The church predicated these jurisdictional claims partly on Christ's famous delegation of the keys to Peter (Matt. 16:18–19)—a key of knowledge to discern God's word and will, and a key of power to implement and enforce that word and will by law. The church also predicated these new claims on its traditional authority over the form and function of the Christian sacraments. By the fifteenth century, the church had gathered whole systems of canon law around the seven sacraments of baptism, Eucharist, penance, orders, extreme unction, confirmation, and marriage.[64]

These jurisdictional claims rendered the church both legislator and judge of Christendom. Popes and bishops, councils and synods issued a steady stream of new canon laws. Periodically the pope or a strong bishop would deploy itinerant ecclesiastical judges, called *inquisitores*, with original jurisdiction over discrete questions that would normally lie within the competence of the church courts. The pope also sent out his legates, who could exercise a variety of judicial and administrative powers in the name of the pope. Church courts adjudicated cases (*causae*) in accordance with the substantive and procedural rules of the canon law. Most cases were generally heard first in the court of the archdeaconry, generally called the consistory court, presided over by the archdeacon or a provisory judge. Major disputes involving annulment or sexual felonies committed

---

63. On the medieval concept of jurisdiction, see generally Berman, *Law and Revolution*, 221–24; Udo Wolter, "Amt und Officium in mittelalterlichen Quellen von 13. bis 15. Jahrhunderts," *Zeitschrift der Savigny-Stiftung für Rechtsgeschichte: Kanonistische Abteilung* 74 (1988): 246.

64. See sources and discussion in John Witte Jr., *Law and Protestantism: The Legal Teachings of the Lutheran Reformation* (Cambridge: Cambridge University Press, 2002), chap.1.

by or against clergy were generally heard by the consistory court of the bishop, presided over by the bishop himself or by his principal official. These courts operated with sophisticated rules of procedure, evidence, and equity; they had a battery of sharp spiritual weapons on hand to enforce their judgments and to put down their secular rivals. Cases could be appealed up the hierarchy of church courts, ultimately to the papal rota. Cases raising novel questions could be referred to distinguished canonists or law faculties called assessors, whose learned opinions (*consilia*) on the questions were often taken by the church court as edifying if not binding.[65]

The church's canon law of marriage was the supreme law of marriage in much of the West from 1200 to 1500. Temporal laws of marriage—whether issued by imperial, royal, customary, urban, feudal, or manorial authorities—were considered supplemental and subordinate. In the event of conflict, civil courts and councils were to relinquish their jurisdiction over marriage to church courts and councils. The church could not always make good on its claim to exclusive jurisdiction and peremptory power over marriage. In polities governed by strong kings or dukes and weak bishops, civil authorities often enjoyed concurrent jurisdiction over marriage—doubly so when the papacy and church leadership came to be wracked with scandal in the fourteenth and fifteenth centuries. But as a sacrament, marriage was at the heart of the church's jurisdiction, and the canon law of marriage was pervasive and powerful.

Engagements and Marriages

The medieval canon law included complex and comprehensive rules to govern the formation and dissolution of a marriage. The canonists distinguished two types of contracts: contracts of engagement and contracts of marriage—betrothals (*sponsalia de futuro*) and espousals (*sponsalia de praesenti*), as these two contracts were historically called. An engagement contract or betrothal was a promise to be married in the future: "I, John, *promise to take you*, Mary, to be my wife." A marriage contract or espousal was a promise to marry here and now: "I, John, *now take you*, Mary, to be my lawfully wedded wife."

Neither the engagement nor the marital contract required much formality to be valid and enforceable at medieval canon law. Parties were required simply to exchange these or similar formulaic words—or where parties were mute, deaf, or incapable of de facto exchange, some symbolic equivalent thereof. Parties could add much more to either contract. They could attach conditions. They could seek their parents' consent. They could draw on witnesses. They could have a wedding in church or at home, and a public celebration thereafter. They could seek the counsel and blessing of a priest. But none of this was required at medieval canon

---

65. See, e.g., John T. Noonan Jr., *The Power to Dissolve: Lawyers and Marriage in the Courts of the Roman Curia* (Cambridge, MA: Harvard University Press, 1972); Rudolf Weigand, "Zur mittelalterlichen kirchlichen Ehegerichtsbarkeit: Rechtsvergleichende Untersuchung," *Zeitschrift der Savigny-Stiftung für Rechtsgeschichte: Kanonistische Abteilung* 67 (1981): 218–47.

law. As both the theologians and canonists of the day had made clear, a private voluntary exchange of promises between a fit man and fit woman of the age of consent was a valid and enforceable marriage at medieval canon law—and this was doubly true if the parties had consummated their vows and the woman was now pregnant. Clandestine or secret marriages, contracted without the involvement of any third parties, were perennially frowned upon and could be occasionally prohibited by unusually firm and severe church courts.[66] But they were generally considered to be valid marriages, with the marital promises implied and imputed to the parties. Concubinage was a more problematic category for canonists. While immoral and illegal, it was such a widespread practice that most canonists before the fifteenth century tended to view a man's long-standing cohabitation with a concubine, featuring "marital affection," as a form of clandestine marriage that could be later ratified through a formal marriage ceremony. Here, too, marital contracts were imputed to the couple, and marital rights and duties attached.[67]

Impediments to Engagement

Not all parties were free and fit to make such engagement and marital promises, however, and not all such promises had to be enforced or could be enforced. The parties needed to have the freedom, fitness, and capacity to marry each other—*ius conubium*, "the right to marry," as the classical Roman lawyers had put it. Certain relationships or experiences could disqualify the parties from engagement and marriage, altogether or at least with each other. Certain actions or conditions discovered after the exchange of promises could, and sometimes had to, lead to the dissolution of these promises.

These disqualifying and disabling factors were called impediments. Impediments provided the two parties, and sometimes third parties as well, with grounds to seek annulment of the engagement or marriage contract. An annulment was an order by a church court or a qualified religious official that declared the engagement or marital contract to be null and void and the relationship between the parties dissolved. A declaration of annulment meant that the engagement or marriage never formally existed at law; it was never a legally binding union, however contrary to fact that might appear. In cases involving serious impediments, even fully consummated long-standing marriages that had yielded children could be annulled.

The late medieval canon law recognized a variety of impediments to the engagement contract. Although canonists differed widely in emphasis and in nomenclature, most cited fourteen impediments to engagement: (1) infancy, where one or both parties were below the age of consent at the time they exchanged promises; (2) precontract or polygamy, where either party was already betrothed

---

66. See Joyce, *Christian Marriage*, 103–46.

67. See Brundage, *Law, Sex, and Christian Society*, 206–7, 225–26, 297–300, 341–33, 369–70, 441–47.

or married to another; (3) incest, which prevented a party from marrying a relative by blood or marriage; (4) disease or deformity, the contracting or discovery of a physical or mental disease or deformity that would endanger the other or preclude intercourse; (5) physical desertion by either party for more than two years (in some formulations, three years); (6) failure of a condition that went to the essence of the marriage; (7) expiration of the agreed-upon period of engagement; (8) cruelty or dissent, where either party exhibited excessive hatred, cruelty, or abuse of the other; (9) bodily fornication, either party's voluntary sexual contact with a third party; (10) special affinity, where after engagement either party had sexual intercourse with a relative of the other—a special and more serious case of bodily fornication; (11) spiritual fornication, one party's abandonment of the faith, particularly one's conviction for heresy, apostasy, or infidelity; (12) entry of the man into the clergy; (13) entry of either party into a religious order; and (14) mutual consent of the parties to dissolve their engagement.

During the period of engagement, the man and the woman, separately or together, had standing in a church court to press a case for annulment at any time. Third parties had standing as well, particularly parents, guardians, or relatives of the parties. A final invitation for any person to allege an impediment came during the formal wedding service (if there was one), where the priest invited the congregation: "If any man or woman knows of any . . . impediment standing in the way of this marriage, let them say so now, before we proceed any further."[68] Other late medieval marriage rituals concluded with the still-familiar words, "or let him forever hold his peace."

Not all these cases of annulment of engagements required litigation. The expiration of a set engagement time or the breach of an essential condition automatically dissolved the engagement. Similarly, where one party entered the clergy or a religious order involving religious vows and orders, the engagement was automatically dissolved. The final case of dissolution by mutual consent generally required church involvement only when the engagement had been made public.

A public or private future promise to marry, followed by sexual intercourse, was viewed as a consummated marriage at canon law. The parties were now in a valid marriage, even though the act of premarital sex was punishable as fornication. Intercourse after engagement raised the presumption that the parties had implicitly consented to be married and to consummate their marriage. A woman could defeat this presumption of marriage by pleading that her fiancé had raped her, which would lead to annulment.

Impediments to Marriage and Annulment

The canon law also recognized several impediments to the marital contract. These were of two main types: prohibitive impediments and absolute (or diriment)

---

68. "Ritual from the Abbey of Barbeau," in Searle and Stevenson, *Documents of the Marriage Liturgy*, 156–62, at 158.

impediments. *Prohibitive* impediments were less serious. They rendered the marriage contract voidable, but their violation did not necessarily render the marriage void unless the innocent party insisted on pressing for an annulment. Seven prohibitive impediments were commonly recognized: (1) rape, the man's rape or violent abduction of a relative of his fiancée; (2) uxoricide, the husband's (suspected) killing of his prior wife; (3) priesticide, either party's (suspected) killing of an ordained priest or monastic; (4) solemn penance, where either party had been assigned public penance for a mortal sin; (6) former monasticism, which precluded marriage to a former nun or monk who had renounced their vows; and (7) age, either too wide a disparity in age between the parties or a discovery that one or both of the parties was too young to give one's consent to the union.

Discovery of any of these conditions after the couple had already been married gave the innocent spouse standing in a church court to press a case for annulment. An annulment suit based on one of these impediments was relatively easy to win if it was brought shortly after the marriage by a spouse who knew nothing of this impediment beforehand. It was harder, though not impossible, to win if a party had entered the marriage with full knowledge of this impediment and then had a change of heart, or learned of the impediment after the marriage but delayed long in suing for annulment on that basis. This case became doubly difficult to press if the woman was now pregnant or had given birth, since their child would be rendered illegitimate by the annulment order.

Absolute (or diriment) impediments were more serious. They prohibited the contracting of marriage altogether and, upon discovery, rendered the marriage void, regardless of what the parties wished. Two clusters of absolute impediments were commonly maintained. One set of impediments preserved the freedom of consent by both parties. Proof of extreme duress, fear, compulsion, or fraud to get married—by a parent, the engaged partner, or a third party—impinged on consent and invalidated the marriage contract. Similarly, a mistake about the identity of the other party (think of Jacob's discovery of Leah rather than Rachel under the bridal veil) or a mistake about the presumed virginity of the new wife—this was also a ground for annulment.

A second and larger set of absolute impediments defined which parties were free to give their consent to marriage. Clerics and monastics could not marry or have sex with anyone. Christians could not have sex or contract marriage with infidels, Jews, or pagans. Persons related by blood (consanguinity), by adoption, or by marriage (affinity) up to the fourth degree[69] could not marry each other. These impediments of consanguinity and affinity, as they were called, included rules of Mosaic law but also many other rules of natural law not included in the

69. This was per the rules of the Fourth Lateran Council (1215), canon 50. Earlier canon laws had prohibited marriages up to six or seven degrees, a formidable barrier to marriage in a small town or isolated community. "First degree" means parent, daughter, sibling, et al.; "second degree" means first cousin, niece, aunt, et al.

Torah. The rules of affinity applied also to the close relatives of parties who were related by engagement or even by sexual contact of any sort: this was the impediment of public honesty or public propriety, as it came to be called. (Notably, this impediment included the prohibition of a brother from marrying the widow or fiancée of his deceased brother—the impediment against levirate marriage, which was at the heart of Henry VIII's dispute with the papacy over his marriage to Catherine of Aragon, as we will see in chap. 7 below.) Godparents could not marry their godchildren. Adulterers could not later marry their former paramours. Eunuchs and castrati could not marry anyone because they lacked the physical capacity for sex. Nor could the insane, possessed, bewitched, or severely retarded marry because they lacked the mental capacity to consent. And those already engaged or married to one spouse could not betroth or marry another because of the impediment of precontract or polygamy.

Discovery of any of these absolute impediments could lead to a suit for annulment in a church court. The court's annulment not only broke the marriage but also could sometimes saddle the parties with serious criminal charges of sacrilege, incest, or polygamy. A church court judge, or a higher religious official, had power to dispense some of these absolute impediments in individual cases and allow the marriage to continue. But the spouses themselves had no corresponding right to forgive the impediment and continue the marriage without the church's approval. All children born of such improper marriages were presumptively illegitimate.

This thick canon-law tangle of impediments to marriage—particularly the attenuated impediments of consanguinity, affinity, and public honesty that defined the expansive canon-law crime of incestuous and other prohibited unions—sometimes left pious innocent couples and their children in a quandary. The couple had married out of love, had celebrated their wedding with the blessing of the church, and lived their lives together with their children as a Christian family. Now suddenly, because of an arcane and attenuated impediment understood only by lawyers or judges, the husband and wife were forced to separate and to face charges of sin and crime, and their children were declared illegitimate.[70] After an exhaustive review of the records of several medieval church courts, Charles Donahue has shown that such involuntary dissolutions happened much less frequently than critics of the medieval canon law have supposed.[71] Yet such involuntary annulments did happen on occasion. To overcome this undue harshness, medieval canon lawyers introduced the concept of the "putative marriage." This was defined as an invalid marriage contracted in good faith, celebrated in a church wedding, and with at least one party ignorant of the impediment. Children born of a putative marriage were declared

70. For examples of the attenuated laws of incest in action, see Donahue, *Law, Marriage, and Society*, 562–98.

71. See analysis and citations to authors who have concluded similarly in ibid., 563–64, 596–97.

legitimate, even if their parents were ultimately forced to annul their marriage and to remain separated from each other thereafter.[72]

Today the canon-law doctrine of annulment is sometimes described as the virtual equivalent of the common-law doctrine of fault-based divorce. Any enterprising canon lawyer, it is said, can sift through the multiple impediments to marriage recognized at canon law and find one that applies sufficiently to allow an unhappy couple to dissolve their union. Historians have often assumed that the same was true in the canon law of the twelfth through the fifteenth centuries. They have been encouraged in this belief by sixteenth-century Protestant Reformers, who constantly pummeled the canonists with this charge, as we will see in succeeding chapters. "The conclusion has seemed logically to follow," writes leading medieval legal historian, R. H. Helmholz, "that energetic genealogical research coupled with legal ingenuity would almost always have produced sufficient grounds for the annulment of a marriage." But, says Helmholz on the strength of a career of close archival research, "the evidence of actual court practice . . . does not support this seemingly compelling conclusion. Court records from the Middle Ages produce many fewer cases in which such divorces occurred than expected." There are spectacular examples of ingeniously crafted arguments for annulment—not least that of Henry VIII in his attempts to escape his marriage to Catherine of Aragon, which we'll see in chapter 7. But one cannot write "history by anecdote," Helmholz warns, and the surviving records of more typical cases suggest that annulments were not so easily procured.[73]

Marital Breakdown and Divorce

The relationship of the parties once properly married was more closely regulated by the confessional norms of the internal forum than by the canon laws of the external forum.[74] The confessional books of the fourteenth and fifteenth centuries—along with various informal household manuals and books on domestic economy and etiquette—went on at great length in describing the appropriate household duties of husbands and wives, parents and children, masters and servants. Long sections of these confessional books were devoted to proper sexual etiquette within marriage: the proper "time, place, and manner" of sexual contact between husband and wife; the appropriate rules of dress, language, and decorum; the Christian response to impotence, sexual disease, and pregnancy;

---

72. The precise origin of this rule in the twelfth century is disputed, but it was fully operative by the end of the twelfth century. See summary in Gilbert J. McDevitt, *Legitimacy and Legitimation: An Historical Synopsis and Commentary* (Washington, DC: Catholic University of America Press, 1941), 23–29.

73. Helmholz, *Spirit of Classical Canon Law*, 241.

74. Winfried Trusen, "Forum internum und gelehrten Rechts im Spätmittelalter: Summae confessorum und Traktate als Wegbereiter der Rezeption," *Zeitschrift der Savigny-Stiftung für Rechtsgeschichte: Kanonistische Abteilung* 57 (1971): 83.

and more. These same confessional books also glossed and illustrated at length the biblical lists of sexual sins—particularly Paul's injunctions against lust, fornication, concubinage, prostitution, sodomy, and "sexual perversion."[75] Many of the more mundane aspects of daily marital living were thus left to the private control of the sacrament of penance. At least once annually, parties were to confess their sins secretly, including their sexual and marital sins. Once absolved, they were expected to do appropriate penitential works of purgation.

The canon law and the church courts became more actively and openly involved when the conduct of the marital parties rose to the level of a canon-law crime. Neglect of a child's physical needs, spiritual nurture, or education might lead to intervention by a church court, particularly if pastoral reproof proved ineffective. Illegal transfers of marital property through contract or testament, which breached obligations of minimal care for one's spouse or children, could likewise trigger judicial intervention. Most important, violence against a wife or child, marital rape or incest, malicious desertion of one's spouse and family, and the commission of adultery, sodomy, or other grave sexual sins had dramatic legal effect. These actions, if proved, constituted serious felonies, which could be severely sanctioned—by both the church and any number of civil authorities. Moreover, proof of adultery, desertion, and cruelty could also support an action for divorce by the innocent spouse.

Divorce in the modern sense was not permitted at canon law. The sacramental bond, once consummated, remained indissoluble at least till the physical death of one of the parties. Divorce at canon law meant separation from bed and board (*a mensa et thoro*) alone. Both husband and wife were given standing to sue for this type of divorce in church courts. During pendency of the divorce case, a church court could order a husband to pay his wife temporary alimony to sustain her, particularly if she had already moved out of the marital home out of fear or under pressure from her husband. If a church court found adequate grounds for divorce, it would order the estranged parties to live separately and sometimes make further orders respecting custody and support of the children.

A separated spouse, although freed from the physical bond of marriage, was not freed from the spiritual bond. "Separation can be of two kinds, corporeal and spiritual," reads a thirteenth-century canon-law text, echoing Peter Lombard. "Spouses can be separated corporeally because of adultery, or by mutual consent in order to enter religious life, whether for a time or permanently. But they cannot be separated sacramentally as long as both live, provided they are married legitimately. For the marital bond remains between them even though, on separating, they should seek to marry other partners."[76] A subsequent marriage

---

75. The most influential confessional books on marriage included *Summa Raymundi de Penaforti de poenitentia et matrimonio* (c. 1280), *Summa pisana casuum conscientiae* (c. 1338), and *Summa angelica de casibus conscientiae* (1486). See Josef Georg Ziegler, *Die Ehelehre der Pönitentialsummen von 1200–1350* (Regensburg: Friedrich Pustet, 1956); Thomas N. Tentler, *Sin and Confession on the Eve of the Reformation* (Princeton, NJ: Princeton University Press, 1977).

76. Lombard, *Sent.*, bk. 4, dist. 33.4.

contracted before the death of one's estranged spouse was an act of bigamy—a mortal sin at canon law, and a serious if not capital crime at civil law. Even remarriage of widows and widowers was frowned upon; many medieval canonists regarded it as a form of serial polygamy or "digamy."

THE TRIDENTINE SYNTHESIS

The Roman Catholic tradition provided its own systematic distillation of these medieval teachings on marriage in the work of the Council of Trent (1545–63). This great council brought unity and reform to the Catholic Church on the scale of the great ecumenical councils of the past. And it set the basic theological and legal tone of the Catholic contribution to the Western tradition of marriage, which lasted until the canon-law revisions of 1917 and 1983 and the theological and structural transformations of the Second Vatican Council (1962–65).

As Pope Paul III's 1542 Bull of Convocation made clear, the Council of Trent was prompted by "the many distresses [of] pastoral solicitude and vigilance" within the church and the many new "schisms, dissensions, and heresies" by which the "Christian commonwealth" was "well-nigh rent and torn asunder."[77] From the mid-fourteenth century forward, strong kings and princes in France, England, Spain, and Germany had challenged the church's expansive property holdings, lucrative jurisdiction, and swollen bureaucracy. Humanists had challenged the authenticity of some of the Catholic Church's canons and called for a renaissance of classical Greek and Roman texts and teachings, freed from medieval glosses and interpretations. Pietists had challenged the church's monopoly on education, its harsh censorship laws, and its prohibitions on vernacular translations of the Bible. Various propagandists, armed with the new power of the printing press, had exposed all manner of moral and material excesses of the clergy and papacy, whether real or imagined. These criticisms and others proved to be storm signals of the Protestant Reformation, which broke out with Martin Luther's posting of the 95 Theses in 1517 and his public burning of the canon-law books in 1520.

Included in this swelling tide of dissent were attacks on the Catholic Church's law and theology of marriage, which had been developed over the past millennium. Several Catholic dissenters, later joined by the Protestant Reformers, challenged the idea of marriage as a sacrament and the church's claims to marital jurisdiction based upon sacramental theology. Others attacked the church's toleration of secret marriages contracted without parental consent, peer witness, civil registration, or church consecration. Some attacked the church's capacious law of impediments and its sometimes capricious system of annulments and dispensations. Some attacked the church's exultation of celibacy over marriage,

77. Henry Joseph Schroeder, OP, *Canons and Decrees of the Council of Trent* (St. Louis: B. Herder Book Co., 1941), 1, 10.

chastity over sexuality, and a sexual ethic that severely limited the opportunities and motivations for licit sex even within marriage. Some attacked the abolition of divorce even on biblical grounds of adultery and malicious desertion, and the severe restrictions on remarriage of widows and widowers, plus the divorced, for whom it was foreclosed altogether. And some attacked the patriarchal excesses of the traditional rules of household governance, marital property, and family inheritance.

The Council of Trent—the most important Catholic Church council between the Fourth Lateran Council of 1215 and the Second Vatican Council of 1962–65—responded forcefully to these attacks in a series of decrees designed "for the extirpation of heresies, for the peace and unity of the Church, [and] for the reform of the clergy and Christian people."[78] In 1563, the Council of Trent issued a lengthy decree, called *Tametsi*, to restore and reform the church's theology and law of marriage. Confirming the occasional statements about the marital sacrament issued by local medieval synods going back to 1184, this 1563 decree for the first time declared canonically that marriage is one of the seven canonical sacraments of the Catholic Church universal. Indeed, said the Council of Trent, marriage was the first sacrament that had already been created by God the Father in paradise and was then sanctified and symbolized by God the Son's union with the church. Weaving together the familiar texts of Genesis 1–2 and Ephesians 5, the Council declared:

> The perpetual and indissoluble bond of matrimony was expressed by the first parent of the human race, when, under the influence of the divine Spirit, he said: "This now is bone of my bones and flesh of my flesh. Wherefore a man shall leave his father and mother and shall cleave to his wife, and they shall be two in one flesh." But that by this bond two only are united and joined together, Christ the Lord taught more plainly when referring to those last words, as having been spoken by God, he said: Therefore now they are not two, but one flesh, and immediately ratified the firmness of the bond. . . .
>
> But the grace which was to perfect the natural love, and confirm that indissoluble union, and sanctify the persons married, Christ Himself, the instituter and perfecter of the venerable sacraments, merited for us by His passion, which Paul the Apostle intimates when he says: "Husbands, love your wives, as Christ also loved the Church, and delivered himself up for it"; adding immediately: "This is a great sacrament, but I speak in Christ and in the Church."
>
> Since therefore matrimony in the evangelical law surpasses in grace through Christ the ancient marriages, our holy Fathers, the councils, and the tradition of the universal Church, have with good reason always taught that it is to be numbered among the sacraments of the New Law.[79]

On the strength of this decree, the council issued a dozen canons that confirmed conventional medieval teaching and practice and condemned with "anathema" critics and customs to the contrary. Polygamy was forbidden. Mandatory

78. Ibid., 11.
79. Ibid., 180.

clerical celibacy was confirmed. The spiritual superiority of celibacy and virginity to marriage was underscored. Medieval canon law impediments to betrothal and marriage, and traditional prohibitions against marriage in certain seasons were confirmed. The church's power to grant dispensations from impediments was confirmed. Divorce meant only separation from bed and board, with no right of remarriage. Ecclesiastical judges were to enjoy exclusive marital jurisdiction.[80]

In the same decree *Tametsi*, the Council of Trent also instituted several reforms to put down abuses that "experience teaches" have crept into the church. In an effort to curb the "evil" of clandestine marriages, the church sought to apply a "more efficacious remedy," based on earlier conciliar and patristic teachings. Minor children—who were above the age of consent, but below the age of majority—were to procure the consent of their parents to marry. Local parish priests were to announce the banns of marriage of a prospective couple on three successive festival days, forgoing such announcements only if "there should be a probable suspicion that a marriage might be maliciously hindered." Betrothed parties were to postpone cohabitation until after their wedding. Three days before consummation of their marriage, they were to make full and "careful" confession in the sacrament of penance and to "approach most devoutly the most holy sacrament of the Eucharist." Weddings were to be contracted in the church before a priest and "in the presence of two or three witnesses"—save during the seasons of Lent and Advent, when marriage was forbidden. Failure to comply with these requirements was a great sin, which "shall at the discretion of the ordinary [priest] be severely punished." And if the marriage contract was not consecrated by a priest, it was deemed automatically "invalid and null," and the parties subject to spiritual and temporal sanctions. If the marriage was contracted properly, the priest was to record the names of the couple and their witnesses in the local parish register.[81]

To remedy some of the abuses of marital impediments and of dispensations from the same, the council also instituted a number of changes. Baptized parties were to have only one godfather or godmother, with whom marriage was prohibited and whose name was to be recorded in the local parish register. The impediment of public honesty (which could preclude marriage to and of a nonvirgin) was removed. The impediment of affinity (which precluded marriage to the relatives of a person with whom one had intercourse) was limited to relatives only in the second degree. Dispensations from impediments could be granted retroactively (allowing consummated marriages to stand) only if the parties had innocently violated these impediments. Persons who consummated their marriages in knowing violation of an impediment were subject to severe punishment and foreclosed from any dispensation.[82]

80. Canons 1–12, in ibid., 181–82. See also "Decree concerning Reform" (November 11, 1563), chap. 20, in ibid., 211, on matrimonial jurisdiction.

81. Chaps.1, 10, in ibid., 183–85, 189–90.

82. Chaps. 2–5, in ibid., 185–87.

To protect against the "singularly execrable" abuses of the freedom of marital contract, the council commanded "all, of whatever rank, dignity and profession they may be, under penalty of anathema to be incurred *ipso facto*, that they do not in any manner whatever, directly or indirectly, compel their subjects or any others whomsoever in any way that will hinder them from contracting marriage freely."[83] This provision was designed especially to end the practice of coerced and arranged marriages instituted by feudal or manorial lords, overbearing parents, or aristocratic or dynastic guardians eager to solemnize treaties and alliances with rivals through arranged or coerced marriages of their children or wards.

To deter the problems of abduction, rape, and kidnapping of young maidens, the council imposed the ultimate sanction, declaring that any such party and his accomplices "shall be *ipso jure* excommunicated and forever infamous and disqualified for all dignities of any kind; and if they be clerics, they shall forfeit all rank." The woman who was abducted had no obligation to marry her abductor, although a despoiled virgin often had few choices besides marriage or entering a monastery. If she chose to marry her abductor, she could request an ecclesiastical judge to order him to pay her an endowment.[84]

To curb the common custom of concubinage, the council also invoked the ultimate sanction of excommunication. Clergy were empowered to admonish concubinaries of their sin and demand them to separate. Those who persisted in their concubinage after three warnings "shall be punished with excommunication, from which they shall not be absolved till they have in fact obeyed the admonition given them." Those who return to concubinage are to be punished "with a severity in keeping with the character of the crime."[85]

The marital reforms of the Council of Trent went beyond stark legal pronouncements that would guide the clergy and educated laity. The council also authorized the preparation of a comprehensive new catechism aimed at children and uninstructed adults, "who are in need of milk rather than solid food."[86] The Tridentine Catechism, issued in 1566, included instructions on the "efficacy and use" of the seven sacraments, translated "into the language of the people and explained to the people by all parish priests."[87]

This catechism provided a convenient distillation and integration of the contractual, natural, and sacramental dimensions of marriage.[88] Citing the "general opinion of the theologians," the catechism defined marriage as "the conjugal union of man and woman, contracted between two qualified persons, which obliges them to live together throughout life." A "perfect" marital contract

---

83. Chap. 9, in ibid., 189.

84. Chap. 6, in ibid., 187–88.

85. Chap. 8, in ibid., 188–89.

86. Quoted in the introduction to *Catechism of the Council of Trent for Parish Priests*, trans. John A. McHugh and Charles J. Callan (Rockford, IL: Tan Books & Publishers, 1982), xxiii. The following quotations are based on this authorized translation.

87. "Decree concerning Reform" (November 11, 1563), chap. 7, in Schroeder, *Canons and Decrees*, 197–98; cf. also ibid., 255.

88. All quotes are from the Tridentine *Catechism*, 338–55.

requires "internal consent, [an] external compact expressed by words, the obligation and tie which arise from the contract, and the marriage debt by which it
is consummated." Consent alone is not enough for marriage. There must be a
"mutual agreement," freely entered into and declared in words stated in the present tense one to the other—or where parties were deaf or mute, by some other
token of genuine consent. "The marriage promise is not a mere promise, but a
transfer of right, by which the man actually yields the dominion of his body to
the woman, the woman the dominion of her body to the man." Consummation
of the marriage is not necessary to render it true and valid, although it is expected.

A marriage once contracted, the Tridentine Catechism continued, must be
understood both "as a natural union, since it was not invented by man but instituted by nature," and "as a Sacrament, the efficacy of which transcends the order
of nature." As a natural union, created by God in paradise, marriage has three
reasons for its existence: (1) the "companionship of husband and wife," (2) "an
antidote to avoid sins of lust," and (3) "the desire of family, not so much, however, with a view to leave after us heirs to inherit our property and fortune, as to
bring up children in the true faith and service of God." This latter reason automatically renders contraception and abortion "a most heinous crime—nothing
less than wicked conspiracy to commit murder."

As a sacramental union, marriage "is far superior . . . and aims at an incompa-
rably higher end." "For as marriage, as a natural union, was instituted from the
beginning to propagate the human race; so was the sacramental dignity subsequently conferred upon it in order that a people might be begotten and brought
up for the service and worship of the true God and of Christ our Saviour." As
a symbol of Christ's eternal bond to the church, marriage introduces an indissoluble bond between husband and wife, a bond "of the greatest affection and
love." The sacrament of marriage was anticipated already at creation, but it was
not completed till the time of Christ. Christ perfected the institution and outlawed prior sinful practices of polygamy and divorce with his proclamation that
"the two shall become one flesh" (Matt. 19:5) and "what . . . God has joined
together, let no man put asunder" (19:6 RSV).

Marriage brings three blessings, the catechism stated, echoing Augustine: offspring, if it is the Lord's will; fidelity, which is "a special, holy, and pure love";
and "sacrament," now in the Augustinian sense of stability and permanence.
God confers those blessings where couples abide by his duties for marriage, as set
out in the natural law and elaborated in the Bible. "It is the duty of the husband
to treat his wife generously and honorably," to be "constantly occupied in some
honest pursuit with a view to provide necessaries for his family and to avoid idle-
ness, the root of almost every vice." Wives in turn must "never forget that next
to God they are to love their husbands, to esteem them above all others, yielding
to them in all things not inconsistent with Christian piety, a willing and ready
obedience." Anyone who wanted further instruction could turn to Thomas
Sanchez's massive 1,300-page *Disputation on the Sacred Sacrament of Marriage*
(1637), which described and defended in copious detail the new sacramental

theology and canon law of marriage for the newly reformed Catholic Church.[89] This was but one book in a vast new library of new scholarship on marriage that emerged among the neoscholastics in early modern Spain and Portugal.

In the centuries thereafter, this Tridentine synthesis of marriage theology and law became a rallying point for Catholic communities. Translated into multiple languages and widely disseminated, the Council of Trent's teachings on marriage provided a common and familiar guide not only for the inner marital lives of Catholic believers but also for the public marriage law of Catholic countries. The rich sacramental model of marriage that was crisply summarized in these documents came to be accepted throughout much of the early modern Catholic world—in Italy, Spain, and Portugal, and eventually in their colonies in Latin America, Mexico, Florida, Louisiana, New Mexico, California, and beyond. Even though the French objected strongly to Trent's legal formulations on political grounds, French authorities eventually stipulated even firmer rules of Catholic marriage formation and dissolution, which it propagated widely through its local catechetical and theological writings and transmitted to its colonies in Quebec and the Caribbean, and eventually in the Middle East and Africa as well.

This Catholic sacramental model of marriage, while not prominent in early America, came to direct application in parts of the colonial American south and southwest from the sixteenth century onward.[90] Before the United States acquired the territories of Louisiana (1803), the Floridas (1819), Texas (1836), New Mexico (1848), and California (1848), these colonies were under the formal authority of Spain and thus under the formal jurisdiction of the Catholic Church. Most of the areas east of the Mississippi River came within the ecclesiastical provinces of San Domingo or Havana; most of those west of that river came within the ecclesiastical province of Mexico. The Catholic clergy and missionaries taught the sacramental theology of marriage. The ecclesiastical hierarchy sought to enforce the canon laws of marriage, particularly the decree *Tametsi*, issued by the Council of Trent.[91]

To be sure, there was ample disparity between the law on the books and the law in action, particularly on the vast and sparsely populated American frontier. Religious and political authorities alike often had to recognize the validity of private marriages formed simply by mutual consent, particularly if the union had brought forth children. Yet the church hierarchy sought to enforce

89. Ibid.

90. Hans W. Baade, "The Form of Marriage in Spanish North America," *Cornell Law Review* 61 (1975): 1–89.

91. This was not true of American Catholic communities, outside of Spanish territory, that came within the ecclesiastical provinces of Baltimore, Philadelphia, New York, and Boston and, later, ecclesiastical provinces in the West. The original settlers in these non-Spanish communities were from Britain, Scotland, or other parts of northern Europe where the Decree *Tametsi* was not in effect. They thus continued to recognize the pre-Tridentine Catholic canon law that a secret marriage formed by mutual consent was valid, even without priestly consecration. This disparity continued among some American Catholics until the Tridentine legislation was written into the 1918 Code of Canon Law. See Baade, "Marriage in Spanish North America," 19–24, 36–38.

the marital-formation rules of *Tametsi*—mutual consent of the couple, parental consent on both sides, two witnesses to betrothals and espousals, and priestly consecration in the face of the church (or in the absence of a priest, which was not uncommon, a substitute "marital bond," pending later consecration). Privately or putatively married couples that had defied these rules sometimes faced sanctions. Intermarriage between Catholics and non-Catholics, in open defiance of the sacrament, led to involuntary annulment of the union and the illegitimating of children born of the same. Church authorities also grudgingly acceded to the reality of divorce and remarriage, particularly in distant regions to the north and west that lay beyond their practical reach. Yet their persistent teaching was that a marriage, once properly contracted, was an indissoluble union, to be maintained until the death of one of the parties.

SUMMARY AND CONCLUSIONS

The Catholic Church first systematized its sacramental theology and canon law of marriage in the twelfth and thirteenth centuries. For the first time in that era, the church came to treat marriage systematically as a natural, contractual, and sacramental unit. First, the church taught, marriage is a *natural association*, created by God to enable man and woman to "be fruitful and multiply" and to raise children in the service and love of God. Since the fall into sin, marriage has also become a remedy for lust, a channel to direct one's natural passion to the service of the community and the church. The laws of nature taught that a man and a woman enter into an exclusive and enduring relationship for the mutual support of each other and their children, who would remain dependent upon them for a very long time. The laws of natural justice also taught that humans avoid adultery, fornication, prostitution, concubinage, polygamy, and unilateral divorce because of the inherent injustice that all these acts pose for women and children. Later medieval writers began to speak of the natural rights of women and children vis-à-vis their husbands and parents—early prototypes to what we now call "women's rights" and "children's rights."[92]

Second, the church taught, marriage is a *contractual unit*, formed by the voluntary and mutual consent of each of the two parties. The marital contract prescribed for couples a lifelong relation of love, service, and devotion to each other, both in sickness and in health, and for better or for worse. It also called on parties to respect the conjugal rights to the body and sexual needs of the spouse and to be faithful and loyal to the other in all things, not least in their sexual lives. Especially among the well heeled, the marital contract was often accompanied by an independent marital property contract, which stipulated and protected the rights of the parties and their families to the gifts of betrothal and

---

92. See Timothy P. Jackson, *The Best Love of the Child: Being Loved and Being Taught to Love as the First Human Right* (Grand Rapids: Wm. B. Eerdmans Publishing Co., 2011).

marriage, to dowry and dower, and to various property distributions after the dissolution of the marriage by annulment or death. These early marital property contracts were important prototypes of what we now call prenuptial agreements.

Third, marriage, when properly contracted between baptized Christians, rises to the dignity of a *sacrament*. The temporal union of body, soul, and mind within the marital estate symbolizes the eternal union between Christ and his church. Participation in this sacrament confers sanctifying grace upon the couple and the community. Couples could perform this sacrament privately, provided they had the fitness, capacity, and freedom to marry. Their mutual consent to marry is what opens the channel of sacramental grace, which is poured out upon their couple, their children, their families, and the broader communities of which they are part. Only baptized believers, in good standing within the church, could enter into a sacramental marriage, and once they did, their marriages remained binding until the death of one of the parties. This sacramental theology placed marriage squarely within the social hierarchy of the church. The Catholic Church claimed jurisdiction over marriage formation, maintenance, and dissolution. It exercised this jurisdiction through both the penitential rules of the sacrament of penance and the canon-law rules of the church courts.

The medieval canon law built on these theological foundations and on their classical and patristic antecedents. And church courts and officials enforced them throughout Western Christendom prior to the sixteenth-century Reformation. At canon law, marriage was a heterosexual monogamous union for life. It was formed by the free and mutual consent of a man and woman who have the fitness and capacity to marry and are not too closely related by blood, family, spiritual, or other ties. The couple first exchanged an engagement promise to be married in the future, with or without conditions, then a formal promise of marriage, using verbs in the present tense. The church encouraged the couple to seek their parents' consent, to secure the testimony of witnesses, to publish banns of their pending nuptials, to negotiate marital property contracts, and to get married in a church wedding. But none of this was required. According to medieval canon law, a valid marriage was formed either by an engagement promise followed by consensual sex or by an actual promise to marry even if not sexually consummated. Children born of a valid marriage were legitimate, supportable, and heritable. Children born out of wedlock were bastards, with severely truncated rights and limited means of support and legitimation. Absolute divorce, with a subsequent right to remarry, was not permitted, even in cases of adultery, desertion, or cruelty. *Divortium* meant only separation from bed and board until the death of one's spouse. Full marital dissolution with a subsequent right to remarry was possible only on proof of a serious impediment to marriage, which could trigger an annulment, a declaration that the marriage was and always had been null and void. The laws on impediments and annulments were—and still are—tremendously complex in theory. But in medieval practice, annulment was not nearly so brisk a business in church courts as was once thought.

Chapter 5

Marriage as Social Estate
in the Lutheran Reformation

Questions of marriage occupied Protestant theologians and jurists from the beginning of the Reformation. The founding fathers of the sixteenth-century Continental and English Reformations—Martin Luther and Philipp Melanchthon, Martin Bucer and John Calvin, Thomas Cranmer and Thomas Becon—all prepared lengthy sermons and pamphlets on the subject. Scores of leading jurists and judges took up legal questions of marriage in their legal opinions and commentaries, often working under the direct inspiration of early Protestant theology and theologians.

The Protestants' early preoccupation with marriage was driven in part by their theology. Many of the core issues of the Protestant Reformation were implicated by the Roman Catholic theology and canon law of marriage that prevailed throughout much of the West on the eve of the Reformation. The Catholic Church's jurisdiction over marriage was, for the Reformers, a particularly flagrant example of the church's usurpation of the magistrate's authority. The Catholic sacramental concept of marriage, on which the church predicated its jurisdiction, raised deep questions of sacramental theology and scriptural interpretation. The canon-law impediments to marriage, its prohibitions against complete divorce, its close regulations of sexuality, parenting, and education all stood in considerable tension with the Reformers' interpretation of biblical teaching. That a child could enter marriage without church consecration betrayed the Reformers' views of the basic responsibilities of the family, church, and state to children. Issues of marriage doctrine and law thus implicated and epitomized some of the cardinal theological issues of the Protestant Reformation.

The Protestants' early preoccupation with the theology and law of marriage was also driven by their politics. A number of early leaders of the Reformation faced aggressive prosecution by the Catholic Church and its political allies for violating the canon law of marriage. Among the earliest Protestant leaders were ex-priests and ex-monastics, who had forsaken their orders and vows and often married shortly thereafter. One of the important symbolic acts of solidarity with the new Protestant cause thereafter was to marry, divorce, and remarry in open violation of canon-law rules. King Henry VIII of England's famous flouting of the traditional canon law of annulment and Philip of Hesse's knowing violation of the canon laws of bigamy were only the most sensational cases.[1] Such acts of deliberate disobedience were quite common in the early years of the Reformation, among the highborn and lower classes alike. As Catholic Church courts began to prosecute these canon-law offenses, Protestant theologians and jurists rose to the defense of their coreligionists—producing a welter of briefs, letters, sermons, and pamphlets denouncing traditional norms and pronouncing a new gospel of marriage.

Political leaders rapidly translated this new Protestant gospel into civil law. Just as the act of marriage came to signal a person's conversion to Protestantism, so a political community's marriage act came to symbolize its acceptance of Protestantism. Political leaders—long envious of the church's lucrative jurisdiction over marriage and inspired by the new Protestant teachings—were quick to establish new civil marriage statutes. In Lutheran, Calvinist, and Anglican polities alike, a new civil law of marriage was promulgated within a generation after official acceptance of Protestantism. Protestant theologians and jurists played prominent roles both in formulating this new law and in defending it against detractors.

The following two chapters take up the contributions of the Continental and English Reformations to the development of Western marriage law. This chapter analyzes the contribution of the Lutheran Reformation to the marriage law of sixteenth-century Germany, with passing attention to Swiss and Scandinavian developments.[2] The following chapters take up, in turn,

---

1. On Henry VIII, see chap. 7 below. On Philip of Hesse, see Paul Mikat, *Die Polygamiefrage in der frühen Neuzeit* (Opladen: Westdeutscher Verlag, 1988), 13-24; Hasting Eells, *The Attitude of Martin Bucer toward the Bigamy of Philip of Hesse* (New Haven, CT: Yale University Press, 1924), and discussion below, pp. 128–30.

2. On Scandinavian developments, see Mia Korpiola, *Between Betrothal and Bedding: Marriage Formation in Sweden, 1200–1600* (Leiden: Brill, 2009); idem, "Lutheran Marriage Norms in Action: The Example of Post-Sweden, 1520–1600," in *The Lutheran Reformation and the Law*, ed. Virpi Mäkinen (Leiden: Brill, 2006), 131–69; Agnes S. Arnórsdóttor, *Property and Virginity: The Christianization of Marriage in Medieval Iceland, 1200–1600* (Aarhus: Aarhus University Press,

the contribution of the Calvinist and Anglican Reformations to Western marriage law.[3]

Despite their differences in theological orientation and legal emphasis, these three Protestant Reformations of marriage had two broad features in common. First, they all replaced the traditional sacramental model of marriage with a new model that played up another dimension of marriage besides its spiritual qualities. Lutherans spoke of marriage as one of the three foundational social estates of the earthly kingdom, alongside the clergy and the magistracy. Calvinists called it a covenantal association of the civil and ecclesiastical order. Anglicans regarded it as a domestic commonwealth within the church and Commonwealth of England. The common effect of these reconceptualizations was to reduce the role of the church and to increase the role of the state and the community in marriage formation, governance, and dissolution. Lutherans consigned much of the legal responsibility for marriage to the state and local community. Calvinists vested the law of marriage equally in the church and state. Anglicans ultimately returned much of the jurisdiction over marriage to the church courts, but now guided by ample Parliamentary legislation and occasional intervention from the royal and common-law courts.

Second, despite the fiery anti-Catholic and anticanonical rhetoric of their early leaders—symbolized most poignantly in Martin Luther's 1520 public burning of the canon-law books and Henry VIII's 1533 revolutionary rejection of the pope's legal authority over marriage—each of these Protestant Reformations eventually accepted and appropriated a great deal of the medieval canon law of marriage. This could only be expected. Roman Catholic institutions had, after all, ruled effectively and efficiently in Europe for centuries. The canon law was a sophisticated system of law well known to the jurists and theologians who had joined the Reformation cause. Courses in canon law were regularly offered in both the law faculties and theology faculties of European universities, in both Catholic and Protestant lands. Indeed, canon law remained part of the common law (*jus commune*) of Protestant and Catholic Europe until the legal reforms and codification movements of the later eighteenth and nineteenth centuries.[4] To be sure, in Protestant polities more than in Catholic polities, theologically offensive ecclesiastical structures and legal provisions, such as those directly rooted in notions of papal supremacy or spurned sacraments, were discarded. And to be

---

2010); Anne Irene Riisøy, *Sexuality, Law, and Legal Practice and the Reformation in Norway* (Leiden: Brill, 2009); Anu Pylkkänen, "Feminism and the Challenge to Religious Truths on Marriage: The Case of Nordic Protestantism," in *Law and Religion in the 21st Century: Nordic Perspectives*, ed. Lisbet Christoffersen, Kjell A. Modéer, and Svend Andersen (Copenhagen: Djøf Publishing, 2009), 525–45.

3. I have not included Anabaptist contributions to the Western legal tradition of marriage, partly because they were by design not so politically influential and partly because the subject has been authoritatively analyzed in George Huntston Williams, *The Radical Reformation*, 3rd ed., Sixteenth Century Essays and Studies (Kirksville, MO: Sixteenth Century Journal Publishers, 1992), 756–98.

4. See Richard H. Helmholz, ed., *Canon Law in Protestant Lands* (Berlin: Duncker & Humblot, 1992).

sure, some of the practices of the medieval church courts, particularly the variant uses of spiritual sanctions and equitable dispensations, were reined in. What remained, however, was readily used in service of the new Protestant theology and state law of marriage.

THE CASE OF JOHANN APEL

A 1523 case involving Johann Apel of Nuremberg provides an illuminating window on the budding reformation of marriage law in early sixteenth-century Germany.[5] Johann Apel was a canonist and a canon. He was trained first in his native Nuremberg, then at a Latin school in Wittenberg. In 1514, he enrolled at the University of Wittenberg, where he had passing acquaintance with a new professor of theology, Martin Luther. In 1516, he transferred to the University of Leipzig for legal studies. Like many law students in his day, Apel studied for a joint degree in canon law and civil law; he was awarded the doctorate in both laws (*doctor utriusque juris*) in 1519.[6] After a brief apprenticeship, Apel took holy orders and swore an oath of celibacy. Conrad, Bishop of Würzburg and Duke of Francken, appointed him as a cathedral canon in Würzburg in 1523. He also licensed him as an advocate in all courts in his domain, both ecclesiastical and civil.

Shortly after his ecclesiastical appointment, Apel became enamored of a nun (whose name is not revealed in the records) at the local St. Marr cloister. The couple saw each other secretly for several weeks and carried on a brisk correspondence. The letters read into the court record hint that she became pregnant. Ultimately she forsook the cloister and her vows and secretly married Apel. After a few weeks of further secrecy, the couple cohabited openly as a married couple.

This was an outrage. Clerical concubinage was one thing. The local records show that at least three other priests in Conrad's diocese kept concubines and paid Conrad the standard concubinage tax for that privilege. Earlier that very same year (1523), another priest had fathered a child, paid the bishop the standard cradle tax, and oblated the infant in the very same St. Marr's cloister that the new Mrs. Apel had just forsaken. Clerical concubinage and clerical fatherhood were known and were tolerated by some obliging bishops of the day. But clerical marriage was an outrage, particularly when it involved both a priest and a nun—a prima facie case of double spiritual incest. Thus, upon hearing of these

5. The case is recounted in Theodore Muther, *Doctor Johann Apell: Ein Beitrag zur Geschichte der deutschen Jurisprudenz* (Köningsberg: Universitätsdruckerei, 1861), 14. Excerpts from the pleadings and court records are included in *Politische Reichs Händel: Das ist, Allerhand gemeine Acten, Regimentssachen, und weltlichen Discursen*, compiled from the library of Melchior Goldast of Haiminsfeld (Frankfurt am Main: Johann Bringern, 1614), 785–95. Unless otherwise noted, all quotes from the case record are from this source. The record also touches on a companion case involving Apel's fellow Würzburg canon and advocate, Friedrich Fischer, which I do not analyze.

6. See generally Karl Heinz Burmeister, *Das Studium der Rechte im Zeitalter des Humanismus im deutschen Rechtsbereich* (Wiesbaden: G. Pressler, 1974).

developments, Bishop Conrad privately annulled Apel's marriage and admonished him to confess his sin, return his putative wife to the cloister, and resume his duties. Apel refused, insisting that his marriage, though secretly contracted, was valid. Unconvinced, the bishop indicted Apel and temporarily suspended him from clerical office. Apel offered a spirited defense of his conduct in a frank letter to the bishop.

In response, Bishop Conrad had Apel indicted in the church court of audience, for breach of holy orders and the oath of celibacy, and for defiance of his episcopal dispensation and injunction. Apel adduced conscience and Scripture in his defense, much as Luther had done two years before at the Diet of Worms. "I have sought only to follow the dictates of conscience . . . and the Gospel," Apel insisted, not to defy episcopal authority and canon law. Scripture and conscience condone marriage for fit adults as "a dispensation against lust and fornication." Apel and his wife had availed themselves of this dispensation and entered and consummated their marriage "in chasteness and love." Contrary to Scripture, canon law commands celibacy for clerics and monastics, and thereby introduces all manner of impurity among them. "Who does not see the fornication and concubinage? Who does not see the defilement and the adultery?" My alleged sin and crime of breaking "this little man-made rule of celibacy," Apel insisted, "is very slight when compared to these sins of fornication and breaking the law of the Lord." "The Word of the Lord is what will judge between you and me," Apel declared to the bishop, and such Word commands my acquittal.

The bishop took the case under advisement. Apel took his cause to the new Lutheran community. He sought support for his claims among Lutheran theologians and jurists in Nuremberg, Wittenberg, and elsewhere, who had already spoken against celibacy and monasticism. He published his remarks at trial under the title *Defense of Johannes Apel*, adorned with a preface by Martin Luther.[7]

Two weeks after publication of the tract, Bishop Conrad had Apel arrested and put in the tower, pending further proceedings. Apel's family pleaded in vain with the bishop to release him. The local civil magistrate, Archduke Ferdinand, brother of the emperor, twice mandated that Apel be released, again to no avail. Jurists and councilmen wrote letters that denounced the bishop's actions "as unduly savage and contrary to canon and imperial law" and that defended Apel's conduct as consistent with "the equitable commands of divine, natural, and human laws" and the "dictates and liberties of conscience." Emperor Charles V himself weighed in with a brief letter, urging the bishop not to protract Apel's harsh imprisonment in violation of imperial law, but to try him and release him if found innocent. Apel himself wrote at least four supplications to

7. Johann Apel, *Defensio Johannis Apelli ad Episcopum Herbipolensem pro suo coniugio* (Wittenberg: Johann Rau-Grunenberg, 1523). See also Luther's correspondence in *D. Martini Luthers Werke: Kritische Gesamtausgabe*, 78 vols. (repr., Weimar: Hermann Böhlaus Nachfolger, 1964–2000), *Briefe*, 2:353, 354, 357 (hereafter Weimarer Ausgabe is cited as WA). On the long publication history of Apel's tract, see Muther, *Doctor Johann Apell*, 72.

the bishop, arguing ever more sharply that lawful marriage is a "biblical commandment," whereas unlawful incarceration is a "diabolical connivance." Apel was finally tried three months later and was found guilty of several violations of the canon law and of heretically participating in "Luther's damned teachings." He was defrocked and excommunicated. Thereafter, Apel made his way to Wittenberg; at the urging of Luther and others, he was appointed to the law faculty at the university there. Two years later, Apel served as one of the four witnesses to the marriage of ex-monk Martin Luther to ex-nun Katharina von Bora—another case of double spiritual incest according to prevailing canon law.

For all of his bitter experience, however, Apel did not urge the abolition of the canon law of marriage. He collaborated with another fellow reformer, Lazarus Spengler, to publish a collection of early canon-law texts for use at the University of Wittenberg faculty.[8] Despite Luther's heated protestations—which eventually prompted his famous remark that "jurists are bad Christians"[9]—Apel also insisted that the Wittenberg law faculty continue to offer lectures and the doctoral program in canon law. Apel himself offered lectures on the canon law from his first year of appointment, and in 1528 he developed a special course on the canon law of marriage, with his University of Wittenberg colleague Kaspar von Teutleben. His two famous books on legal science are peppered throughout with discussion of the canon law.[10]

Apel's case provides a miniature portrait of both the prevailing sacramental model and the budding social model of marriage in the sixteenth century. It illustrates the most pressing issues that divided proponents of these models—celibacy, concubinage, clerical marriage, secret marriage, easy annulments—issues that pressed with equal force in Calvin's Geneva, Zwingli's Zurich, and Henry VIII's England. The Apel case also illustrates the organic connections that remained between these two models. Even while Luther was burning the canon-law books, Apel, though badly burned by the canon law, insisted that this source remain at the core of the new Protestant theory and law of marriage. Even Luther would eventually come grudgingly to accept a good deal of the canon law, as did the many German theologians and jurists whom he inspired.

---

8. Lazarus Spengler, *Eyn kurtzer ausszug aus dem Bebstlichen rechten der Decret und Decretalen, in den artickeln, die ungeverlich Gottes Wort un[d] Euangelio gemess sein* (Nuremberg: Jobst Gutknecht, 1530). See other examples of the heavy use of canon law in Lutheran Germany in John Witte Jr., *Law and Protestantism: The Legal Teachings of the Lutheran Reformation* (Cambridge: Cambridge University Press, 2002), chaps. 2, 4.

9. See Luther, in the WA *Tischreden* [*Table Talk*], 2:219 (hereafter, WA TR) and discussion in Roderich von Stintzing, *Das Sprichwort "Juristen böse Christen" in seinen geschichtlichen Bedeutung* (Bonn: Marcus, 1875); Karl Köhler, *Luther und die Juristen: Zur Frage nach dem gegenseitigen Verhältniss des Rechtes und Sittlichheit* (Gotha: R. Besser, 1873).

10. Johann Apel, *Methodica dialectices ratio, ad jurisprudentiam accommodata* (Nuremburg: Fridericus Peypus, 1535); and idem, *Isagoge per dialogum in quatuor libros Institutionum D. Justiniani Imperatoris* (Bratislaviae: A. Vincleri, 1540). On the history and influence of these two publications, see Roderich von Stintzing, *Geschichte der deutschen Rechtswissenschaft: Erste Abteilung* (Munich: Oldenbourg, 1880), 287–96.

THE NEW LUTHERAN THEOLOGY OF MARRIAGE

The Attack on the Canon Law

In his early writings, Martin Luther attacked the traditional Catholic theology and canon law of marriage repeatedly. "The estate of marriage has fallen into awful disrepute," he declared in a sermon of 1522:

> There are many pagan books which treat of nothing but the depravity of woman kind and the unhappiness of the estate of marriage. . . . Every day one encounters parents who forget their former misery because, like the mouse, they have now had their fill. They deter their children from marriage and entice them into priesthood and nunnery, citing the trials and troubles of married life. Thus do they bring their own children home to the devil, as we daily observe; they provide them with ease for the body and hell for the soul. . . .
>   [Furthermore,] the shameful confusion wrought by the accursed papal law has occasioned so much distress, and the lax authority of both the spiritual and the temporal swords has given rise to so many dreadful abuses and false situations that I would much prefer neither to look into the matter nor to hear of it. But timidity is no help in an emergency.[11]

According to Luther, evidence for the decrepit estate of marriage and marriage law was all around.[12] Germany, he charged, had suffered through more than a century of sexual immorality brought on by the neglect and corruption of church and state officials alike. Prostitution was rampant. Clergy and laity regularly kept concubines, sired illegitimate children, and then abandoned them. The small fines imposed by the bishops on sexually active clerics and monks— the so-called "whore tax" (*Hurenzins*) and "cradle tax" (*Wigenzins*)—provided little deterrence to clerics and ample income to bishops.[13] The stern laws against adultery, fornication, sodomy, and other sexual crimes had become largely dead letters. Lewd pamphlets and books exalting sexual liberty and license were published with virtual impunity. Writings extolling celibacy and deprecating marriage and sex dissuaded many couples from marriage and persuaded many parents to send their children to monasteries and cloisters. The numbers of single men and women, of monasteries and cloisters, of monks and nuns have reached new heights, Luther charged. Within the marital household itself, mass confusion reigned over the laws of marital formation, maintenance, and dissolution, and over the laws of care of parents, children, and spouses.

---

11. Jaroslav Pelikan and Helmut T. Lehmann, eds., *Luther's Works*, American ed., 55 vols. (Philadelphia: Muhlenberg Press/Fortress Press; St. Louis: Concordia Publishing House, 1955–86), 45:36–37 (hereafter, *LW*).

12. *LW* 44:3, 153, 176, 184, 215; 45:141, 243ff, 385ff; 36:99ff; see further Steven Ozment, *When Fathers Ruled: Family Life in Reformation Europe* (Cambridge, MA: Harvard University Press, 1983), 3–24; idem, *Protestants: The Birth of a Revolution* (New York: Doubleday, 1992), 151–58; Scott Hendrix, "Masculinity and Patriarchy in Reformation Germany," *Journal of the History of Ideas* 56 (1995): 177–93.

13. *LW* 39:290–91.

Luther's lengthy indictment of prevailing German patterns of sex, marriage, and family life, while hyperbolic, had ample support. Already in the previous two centuries, a number of theologians and canonists had issued similar attacks on prevailing marital and family laws; they had already inspired a good number of reforms at canon law and increasingly at civil law as well.[14] The canon law of monastic and clerical celibacy was a sore subject that occupied several Lutheran Reformers in the 1520s, and it would become a major institution ripe for reform. The Bavarian noblewoman Argula von Grumbach, for example, regarded mandatory clerical celibacy laws as sources of great sin: "The pope has followed the advice of the devil; he has forbidden [his clergy] to have wives, but for the sake of money permitted them to have concubines."[15] The distinguished criminal law jurist Johann Freiherr von Schwarzenberg denounced a Bamberg monastery that kept his daughter from leaving the "hellish prison" of a cloister[16] and then wrote a long exposé on what he called "the diabolical teachings of those monkish snakes," which inspired "the perverted and profligate living" of some monks and nuns.[17] The evangelical (Lutheran) pamphleteer Hans Schwalb pressed even further: "If a married man sleeps with another woman, one of them must leave the city [i.e., be banished]. But our squires, the worthy clergy, forcefully seize the wives and daughters of pious townsmen and peasants, holding them against God, honor, and law. . . . Why are such pastors—and it is not an isolated case but many—not excommunicated?"[18] No one was harsher in his rebuke of clerical celibacy than Erasmus of Rotterdam, himself the illegitimate son of an enterprising priest. Celibate priests who casuistically defended their celibacy while living sexually active lives were for Erasmus no less than "barbarians, monkeys, asses, hypocrites, philistines, pharisees, scribes, publicans, Essenes, sycophants, pseudo-apostles, prophets, [and] demons."[19]

Luther and his followers went beyond these conventional critics, however, in attributing much of the decay of marriage not only to the negligence of

14. See Witte, *Law and Protestantism*, chap. 1.

15. Argula von Grumbach, *Ein christe[n]liche Schrifft einer erbaren Frawen vom Adel* (Bamberg: [Erlinger], 1523), iii–v, using the translation of Gerald Strauss, *Law, Resistance, and the State: The Opposition to Roman Law in Reformation Germany* (Princeton, NJ: Princeton University Press, 1986), 6. See also the lengthy tract against monasticism attributed to her: *Grund und Ursach auss göttlichem Rechten, warumb Prior und Convent in Sant. Annen Closter zu Augspurg ihren Standt verändert haben* (Augsburg, 1526). Luther urged a more gentle and gradual approach to dissolving the monasteries in *LW* 45:169–72, 341.

16. Johann von Schwarzenberg, *Ein schöner Sendbrieff des wolgebornen und Edeln herrn Johannsen, herrn zu Schwartzenberg, an Bischoff zu Bamberg ausgangen* (Nuremberg: Hans Hergot, 1524), giving Christian reasons why his daughter should leave the cloister.

17. Idem, *Diss Büchlyn Kuttenschlang genant die Teüffels lerer macht bekant* (Nuremberg: Friedrich Peypus, 1526).

18. Hans Schwalb, *Beklagung eines Laien, gennant Hans Schwalb über viel Missbräuche christlichen Lebens* (Nuremberg: Johann Stuchs, 1521), using the translation in Joel F. Harrington, *Reordering Marriage and Society in Reformation Germany* (Cambridge: Cambridge University Press, 1995), 37.

19. See Harrington, *Reordering Marriage*, 36–37, 61–63; and detailed discussion in Émile V.-Telle, *Érasme de Rotterdam et le septième sacrement* (Geneva: Droz, 1954), 81, 233.

authority and the laxness of society but also to the paradoxes in the traditional canon law and theology of marriage. According to Luther and other evangelical reformers, the canon law purported to govern in accordance with natural law and Scripture. Yet it was filled with provisions not prefigured in natural law or Scripture. The canon law discouraged and prevented mature persons from marrying by its celebration of celibacy, its proscription against breach of vows to celibacy and chastity, its permission to breach oaths of betrothal, and its numerous impediments, which led to marital annulment. Yet it encouraged marriages between the immature by declaring valid secret unions consummated without parental permission as well as oaths of betrothal followed by sexual intercourse. The canon law highlighted the sanctity and solemnity of marriage by deeming it a sacrament. Yet it permitted a couple to enter this holy union without clerical or parental witness, instruction, or participation. Celibate and impeded persons were thus driven by their sinful passion to incontinence and all manner of sexual deviance. Married couples, not taught the biblical norms for marriage, adopted numerous immoral practices. A true reformation of the law of marriage, therefore, required a new theological foundation. Accordingly, Luther and several other theologians worked assiduously in the early years of the Reformation to lay this new theological foundation—often working in direct collaboration with like-minded jurists.[20]

Maintaining Some Traditions

Following the medieval Catholic tradition, the Lutheran Reformers viewed marriage as at once a natural, contractual, and spiritual estate. Marriage was created and ordered by God as a monogamous union between a fit man and fit woman, presumptively for life. In its essence marriage depended on the voluntary consent of both parties. Marriage brought spiritual comfort and edification to its faithful participants.

Moreover, the Lutheran Reformers agreed with Augustine and the medieval theologians that marriage was both "a duty for the sound and a remedy for the sick." God had created Adam and Eve to be naturally inclined and attracted to each other.[21] He had commanded them to be "fruitful and multiply," to fill the earth with their kind, and to teach their children the meaning and measure of God's faith, law, and order. This commandment to join together in marriage became doubly imperative after the fall into sin, lest persons succumb to the evil temptations of lust and lasciviousness. Luther put this traditional lore strongly in his *Large Catechism* (1529):

20. For detailed lists of these theological and legal writings, and the secondary literature on them, see the first edition of this volume, John Witte, Jr., *From Sacrament to Contract: Marriage, Religion, and Law in the Western Tradition* (Louisville: Westminster John Knox Press, 1997), 227–31.

21. See *LW* 45:18: "For it is not a matter of free choice or decision, but a natural and necessary thing, that whatever is a man must have a woman and whatever is a woman must have a man."

How gloriously God honors and extols this estate, inasmuch as by his commandments, He both sanctions and guards it. . . . He also wishes us to honor it, and to maintain and conduct it as a divine and blessed estate; because, in the first place, He has instituted it before all others, and therefore created man and woman separately (as is evident), not for lewdness, but that they should live together, be fruitful, beget children, and nourish and train them to the honor of God. Therefore God has also most richly blessed this estate above all others, and in addition, has bestowed on it and wrapped up in it everything in the world, to the end that this estate might be well and richly provided for. Married life therefore is no jest or presumption; but it is an excellent thing and a matter of divine seriousness. For it is of the utmost importance to Him that persons be raised who may serve the world and promote the knowledge of God, godly living, and all virtues, to fight against wickedness and the devil.[22]

Luther's distinguished colleague in Wittenberg, Philipp Melanchthon, echoed these sentiments in 1531, adding that marriage was not only a natural duty and remedy but also a natural facility and right that no human ordinance should discourage or impede:

Genesis 1:28 teaches that persons were created to be fruitful, and that one sex in a proper way should desire another. For we are speaking not of concupiscence, which is sin, but of the appetite which would have existed in nature even if it had remained uncorrupted, which they call physical love. And this love of one sex for the other is truly a divine ordinance. . . .

Because this creation or divine ordinance is a natural right (*ius naturale*), jurists have accordingly said wisely and correctly that the union of male and female belongs to the [order of] natural laws (*iuris naturalis*). But since natural law is immutable, the right to contract marriage (*ius contrahendi conjugi*) must always remain. For where nature does not change, that ordinance with which God has endowed nature does not change, and cannot be removed. . . . Moreover a natural right is truly a divine right (*ius divinum*), because it is an ordinance divinely impressed upon nature. But inasmuch as this right cannot be changed without an extraordinary work of God, it is necessary that the right to contract marriage remains, because the natural desire of [one] sex for [the other] sex is an ordinance of God (*ordinatio Dei*) in nature, and for this reason is a right.[23]

These catechetical and confessional statements on marriage were widely known in the Lutheran world and echoed repeatedly in the more specialized writings of theologians and jurists.

Following tradition further, the Lutheran Reformers taught that marriage has three inherent goods. They too, echoing Augustine and Aquinas, put these marital goods in varying orders of priority, depending on what dimension of marriage they were emphasizing. The Reformers' preferred formula of these marital

22. *Triglot Concordia: The Symbolic Books of the Evangelical Lutheran Church; German-Latin-English* (St. Louis: Concordia Publishing House, 1921), 639 (hereafter, *TC*); see also *LW* 21:89; 45:17, 43.

23. *TC*, 366–67.

goods, however, was not the Augustinian trilogy of children, faith, and sacrament (*proles, fides, et sacramentum*). Instead, most of the Reformers preferred to speak of the three marital goods of (1) mutual love and support of husband and wife; (2) mutual procreation and nurture of children; and (3) mutual protection of both spouses from sexual sin.[24]

This trilogy of love, procreation, and protection was no invention of the Reformation. It had already appeared more than a millennium earlier, in late patristic and Roman law texts, ably distilled by Isidore of Seville in his *Etymologies* (ca. 633).[25] Some medieval moralists had adopted this trilogy to describe the reasons (*causae*) for a person to marry, as distinguished from the inherent goods (*bona*) of the institution of marriage itself. The Reformers rejected this medieval distinction. From God's point of view, they argued, marriage has built-in purposes or reasons that God wishes to see achieved among his human creatures. From humanity's point of view, these are the created goods that we need to realize. To make fine distinctions between the goods and purposes or the causes and effects of marriage was ultimately to engage in idle casuistry, most Reformers believed. The essential formula was love, procreation, and protection.

This Lutheran formula of the marital goods of love, procreation, and protection overlapped with Augustine's formula of faith, children, and sacramentality, but it also amended and emended it in critical ways.

Marital Love

Like Augustine, the Lutheran reformers emphasized the good of marital faithfulness (*fides*). Parties were to be faithful to their marital promises and loyal to their spouses. A marriage once properly contracted was presumptively binding on both parties for life. Infidelity to the marriage contract—whether sexual, physical, spiritual, or emotional—was a sin against this good of fidelity. The breakup of a marriage was also a sin against this good, even if sometimes justified as the lesser of two evils.

Unlike Augustine, however, the Lutheran Reformers often cast this good of *fides* in overt terms of marital love, intimacy, friendship, and companionship—adducing passages from Aristotle, the Roman Stoics, and Thomas Aquinas to drive home their point. Luther was among the strongest proponents for the good of marital love. "Over and above all [other loves] is marital love," he wrote. Marital love drives husband and wife to say to each other, "'It is you whom I want, not what is yours. I want neither your silver nor your gold. I want neither. I want only you. I want you in your entirety, or nor at all.' All other kinds of love seek something other than the loved one: this kind wants only to have the beloved's own self completely. If Adam had not fallen, the love of bride and

24. WA 34:52.

25. *The Etymologies of Isidore of Seville*, trans. Stephen A. Barney (Cambridge: Cambridge University Press, 2006), 9.7.27.

groom would have been the loveliest thing."[26] "There's more to [marriage] than
a union of the flesh," Luther wrote, although he considered sexual intimacy and
warmth to be essential to the flourishing of marriage. "There must [also] be
harmony with respect to patterns of life and ways of thinking."[27]

> The chief virtue of marriage [is] that spouses can rely upon each other
> and with confidence entrust everything they have on earth to each other,
> so that it is as safe with one's spouse as with oneself. . . . God's Word is
> actually inscribed on one's spouse. When a man looks at his wife as if she
> were the only woman on earth, and when a woman looks at her husband
> if he were the only man on earth; yes, if no king or queen, not even the
> sun itself sparkles any more brightly and lights up your eyes more than
> your own husband or wife, then right there you are face to face with God
> speaking. God promises to you your wife or husband, actually gives your
> spouse to you, saying: "The man shall be yours; the woman shall be yours.
> I am pleased beyond measure! Creatures earthly and heavenly are jumping
> for joy." For there is no jewellery more precious than God's Word; through
> it you come to regard your spouse as a gift of God and, as long as you do
> that, you will have no regrets.[28]

Luther did not press these warm sentiments to the point of denying the traditional leadership of the paterfamilias within the marital household. Luther
had no modern egalitarian theory of marriage. But Luther also did not betray
these warm sentiments to the point of becoming the grim prophet of patriarchy,
paternalism, and procreation über alles that some modern critics make him out
to be. For Luther, love was a necessary and sufficient good of marriage. He supported marriages between loving couples, even those between young men and
older women beyond childbearing years or between couples who knew full well
that they could have no children.[29] He repeatedly stressed that husband and wife
were spiritual, intellectual, and emotional "partners," each to have regard for the
needs and strengths of the other. He called his own wife, Katharina, respect-
fully "Mr. Kathy" and said more than once of her: "I am an inferior Lord, she
the superior; I am Aaron, she is my Moses."[30] He repeatedly told husbands and
wives alike to tend to each other's spiritual, emotional, and sexual needs and to
share in all aspects of childrearing and household maintenance—from changing
their children's diapers to helping their children establish their own new homes
when they had grown up.[31]

26. WA 2:167; see also 13:11; 17/2:350.

27. WA TR 5, No. 5524; LW 54:444.

28. WA 34:52.5–9, 12–21, using the translation of Scott Hendrix, "Luther on Marriage,"
Lutheran Quarterly 14 (2000): 335–50, at 338. See also LW 31:351.

29. See, e.g., WA TR 4, No. 5212; LW 2:301.

30. Quoted by Steven E. Ozment, Ancestors: The Loving Family in Old Europe (Cambridge,
MA: Harvard University Press, 2001), 36–37. See the interesting portrait of Katharina and other
Reformation women in Kirsi Irmeli Stjerna, Women and the Reformation (Malden, MA: Blackwell
Publishers, 2009).

31. LW 45:39.

Several other German Reformers wrote with equal flourish about the good of marital love and fidelity. The Zurich reformer, Heinrich Bullinger, for example, who was influential both in Germany and in England, wrote similarly that God planted in a married man and woman "the love, the heart, the inclination and natural affection that is right to have with the other. . . . Marital love ought to be (next unto God) above all loves," with couples rendering to each other "the most excellent and unstinting service, diligence and earnest labor, . . . one doing for another, one loving, depending, helping, and forbearing another, always rejoicing and suffering one with another."[32] The Strasbourg reformer, Martin Bucer, who was also influential in Lutheran, Calvinist, and Anglican circles alike, wrote effusively about marital love. Marital couples, he wrote, must be

> united not only in body but in mind also, with such an affection as none may be dearer and more ardent among all the relations of mankind, nor of more efficacy to the mutual offices of love, and of loyalty. They must communicate and consent in all things both divine and human, which have any moment to well and happy living. The wife must honor and obey her husband, as the Church honors and obeys Christ her head. The husband must love and cherish his wife, as Christ his Church. Thus they must be to each other, if they will be true man and wife in the sight of God, whom certainly churches must follow in their judgment. Now the proper and ultimate end of marriage is not copulation, or children, for then there was no true matrimony between Joseph and Mary the mother of Christ, nor between many holy persons more, but the full and proper and main end of marriage is the communicating of all duties, both divine and human, each to the other, with utmost benevolence and affection.[33]

Children

Like Augustine, the Lutheran Reformers emphasized the good of children, if such a blessing were naturally possible and divinely granted. But the Reformers amended Augustine's account with Thomas Aquinas's heavy gloss that the good of procreation must include the Christian nurture and education of children, a responsibility that fell on husband and wife alike as well as on the broader communities of church and state. And they repeated Thomas's argument that children were best born in faithful monogamous marriages that ensured paternal certainty and parental investment in the children. Thomas's argument about the natural goods of exclusive monogamous marriage and joint parental responsibilities for children was as axiomatic for early Protestants as it was for medieval Catholics.[34]

32. Heinrich Bullinger, *Der christlich E[h]estand* (Zurich: Froschouer, 1540); translated by Myles Coverdale as *The Christen State of Matrimonye* (London, 1541), fol. iii.b–iiii. For further on Bullinger, see pp. 234–38 below.

33. Martin Bucer, *De regno Christi* (1555), in *Melanchthon and Bucer*, ed. Wilhelm Pauck (Philadelphia: Westminster Press, 1969), bk. 2, chap. 38 (hereafter, Bucer, *RC*). For further on Bucer, see pp. 238–41 below and Herman J. Selderhuis, *Marriage and Divorce in the Thought of Martin Bucer*, trans. John Vriend and Lyle D. Biersma (Kirksville, MO: Thomas Jefferson University Press, 1999).

34. WA TR 5, No. 5513; *LW* 54:441–42.

Luther treated procreation as an act of cocreation and coredemption with God. He wished for all marital couples the joy of having children, not only for their own sakes but for the sake of God as well. Childrearing, he wrote, "is the noblest and most precious work, because to God there can be nothing dearer than the salvation of souls. . . . You can see how rich the estate of marriage is in good works. God has entrusted to its bosom souls begotten of its own body on whom it can lavish all manner of Christian works. Most certainly, father and mother are apostles, bishops, [and] priests to their children, for it is they who make them acquainted with the Gospel. See therefore how good and great is God's work and ordinance."[35] This last image—of parents serving as priests to their children—was a new and further application of the familiar Protestant doctrine of the priesthood of all believers. It added further concreteness to the Protestant effort to soften the hard medieval distinction between a superior clergy and a lower laity: all persons are priests to their peers, and all parents are priests to their children, called to care for them in body, mind, and soul alike.

The education of children fell not only to parents. The Lutheran Reformers also were pioneers in creating public schools for the religious and civic education of all children and producing a welter of catechisms, textbooks, and household manuals to assist in the same. For the Reformers, each child was called to a unique Christian vocation, and it was the responsibility of the parent, priest, and prince alike to ensure that each child was given the chance to discern his or her special gifts and prepare for the particular vocation that best suited those gifts. This teaching drove the creation of public schools in early modern Protestant lands. It added a crucial public dimension to the parents' private procreation and nurture of their children. Philipp Melanchthon, the so-called "teacher of Germany," called the public school a "civic seminary" designed to allow families, churches, and states alike to cooperate in imbuing both civic learning and spiritual piety in children.[36]

Protection from Sin

Unlike Augustine, the early Protestant Reformers emphasized protection from sexual sin as a marital good in itself, not just a function of *fides*. Since the fall into sin, they argued, lust has pervaded the conscience of every person. Marriage has become not only an option but also a necessity for sinful humanity. For without it, the person's distorted sexuality becomes a force capable of overthrowing the most devout conscience. A person is enticed by his or her own nature to prostitution, masturbation, voyeurism, and sundry other sinful acts. "You can't be without a wife and remain without sin," Luther blurted out at one of his famous

35. *LW* 45:46.
36. See Witte, *Law and Protestantism*, 257–92.

table talks.[37] Anyone who chooses to "live alone undertakes an impossible task, . . . counter to God's Word and the nature that God has given and preserves in him."[38] The calling of marriage, Luther wrote, should be declined only by those who have received God's gift of continence. "Such persons are rare, not one in a thousand [later he said, 'a hundred thousand'], for they are a special miracle of God." The apostle Paul has identified this group as the permanently impotent and the eunuchs; few others can claim such a unique gift.[39]

This understanding of the protective good of marriage undergirded the Reformers' bitter attack on the traditional canon-law rules of mandatory celibacy.[40] To require celibacy of clerics, monks, and nuns, the Reformers believed, was beyond the authority of the church and ultimately a source of great sin. Celibacy was for God to give, not for the church to require. It was for each individual, not for the church, to decide whether he or she had received this gift.[41] By demanding monastic vows of chastity and clerical vows of celibacy, the church was seen to be intruding on Christian freedom and violating Scripture, nature, and common sense.[42] By institutionalizing and encouraging celibacy, the church was seen to prey on the immature and the uncertain. By holding out food, shelter, security, and opportunity, the monasteries enticed poor and needy parents to condemn their children to celibate monasticism. Mandatory celibacy, Luther taught, was hardly a prerequisite to true service of God. Instead it led to "great whoredom and all manner of fleshly impurity and . . . hearts filled with thoughts of women day and night."[43] For the consciences of Christians and non-Christians alike are infused with lust, and a life of celibacy and monasticism only heightens the temptation.[44]

Furthermore, to impute superior spirituality and holier virtue to the celibate contemplative life was, for the Reformers, contradicted by the Bible. Scripture teaches that each person must perform his or her calling with the gifts that God provides. The gifts of continence and contemplation are but two among many, and they are by no means superior to the gifts of marriage and child-rearing. Each calling plays an equally important, holy, and virtuous role in the drama of redemption, and its fulfillment is a service to God.[45] Luther agreed with the apostle Paul that the celibate person "may better be able to preach and care for God's Word." But "it is God's Word and the preaching which makes

---

37. WA TR 1, No. 233; *LW* 54:31.

38. WA 18:276.

39. *LW* 45:18–22; 28:9–12, 27–31.

40. *LW* 44:243–400; 46:139; Philipp Melanchthon, *Loci communes* (1521), translated in Pauck, *Melanchthon and Bucer*, 59 [hereafter *LC* (1521)]; Johannes Bugenhagen, *Von dem ehelich en Stande der Bischoffe vnd Daiken* (Wittenberg: Josef Klug, 1525); idem, *Was man vom Closter leben halten sol* (Wittenberg: G. Rhaw, 1529); *TC*, 363, 419.

41. *TC*, 499, 501.

42. This is the heart of Luther's 1521 diatribe against monastic vows in *LW* 44:243; 46:139.

43. WA 12:98.

44. Ibid. See also Apel, *Defensio*, A11–A12.

45. *LC* (1521), 60–61; see also *TC*, 501.

celibacy—such as that of Christ and of Paul—better than the estate of marriage. In itself, however, the celibate life is far inferior."[46]

This understanding of the good of marriage as a protection against sexual sin also informed the Reformers' repeated counsel that widows, widowers, and divorcees could and sometimes should remarry, after a suitable period of grieving. Medieval writers, building on the apostle Paul and some of the church fathers, had discouraged all such remarriages, arguing that these were forms of "digamy" or "serial polygamy." The Reformers taught the opposite. A grieving and lonely widow, widower, or divorcee often benefits from a new spouse, especially if he or she still has children to care for. Even more important, this now-single party who has known the pleasures and warmth of sexual intimacy will be doubly tempted to sexual sin in its sudden absence. Paul's instruction that "it is better to marry than to burn" becomes doubly imperative for them. "I'm astonished that the lawyers, and especially the canonists, are so deeply offended by digamy," Luther wrote. "Lawyers interpret digamy in an astonishing way if somebody marries a widow, etc. Oh, how vast is the ignorance of God in man's heart that he can't distinguish between a commandment of God and a tradition of men. To have one, two, three, or four wives in succession is [in every case] a marriage and isn't contrary to God, but what's to prevent fornication and adultery, which are against God's command?"[47]

Luther, Bucer, and Melanchthon sometimes pressed this counsel to even more adventuresome, if not scandalous, ends of condoning private bigamy as a lesser sin than public adultery or concubinage.[48] Luther hinted at this in several entries in his letters and *Table Talk*.[49] A 1532 case in his *Table Talk* reads thus:

> A certain man took a wife, and after bearing several children, she contracted syphilis and was unable to fulfill her marital obligation. Thereupon her husband, troubled by the flesh, denied himself beyond his ability to sustain the burden of chastity. It is asked, Ought he be allowed a second wife? I reply that one or another of two things must happen: either he commits adultery or he takes another wife. It is my advice that he take a second wife; however, he should not abandon his first wife but should provide for her sufficiently to enable her to support her life. There are many cases of this kind, from which it ought to be clearly seen and recognized that this is the law and that is the gospel.[50]

This might be read as a case of serial marriages rather than as bigamy. It might be understood that the "second wife" was to be taken after divorce from the first wife, who was still to be cared for despite the divorce. As we shall see in a moment, divorce would presumably be warranted in this case on account of the wife's adultery, which had evidently been the cause of her syphilis.

46. *LW* 45:47.
47. WA TR 3, No. 3609B; *LW* 54:243–44. See Bucer, *RC*, bk. 2, chaps. 23, 24, 34, 41, 44.
48. WA 29:144, 303.
49. See, e.g., WA TR 1, No. 611; WA TR 2, No. 1461; *LW* 50:33.
50. WA TR 1, No. 414; *LW* 54:65–66.

Luther and his colleagues went further in their advice to Landgrave Philip of Hesse. Philip had been diplomatically married at the age of nineteen to Christina, the daughter of Duke George of Albertine Saxony. He claimed that "he had never any love or desire for her on account of her form, fragrance, and manner," though this did not prevent him from producing seven children with her. Throughout his married life, and especially when his wife grew frigid in later life, Philip admitted to robust intercourse with prostitutes and paramours of all sorts, and he was rewarded with a rash of syphilis. He was now deeply ashamed of his conduct, confessed it fully, and sought to do better. He insisted that he still needed a sexual outlet, or he would again be driven to resort to fraternizing with his maids and prostitutes. He had taken a single concubine and wanted to marry her, thinking that contracting such a second marriage would be better than breaking the first, let alone fornicating indiscriminately. Philip asked Martin Bucer for his advice and blessing on this bigamous arrangement. Bucer instead counseled divorce from his first wife, with remarriage to his concubine. Divorce was licit if for no other reason than Philip's own repeated and fully confessed adultery. But Philip apparently did not want to risk public confession of such conduct. He preferred to keep and support his first wife and to marry and support the second as well, in the tradition of David, Solomon, and the other patriarchs of Israel. A troubled Bucer took the case to Luther and Melanchthon for their counsel.[51] Luther reports what happened thereafter:

> Martin Bucer brought [us] a certified statement which set forth that the landgrave was unable to remain chaste on account of certain defects in his wife. Accordingly, he had lived so and so, which was not good, especially for an Evangelical, and indeed one of the most prominent Evangelical princes. He swore before God and on his conscience that he was unable to avoid such vice unless he was permitted to take another wife. The account of his life and purpose shocked us in view of the vicious scandal that would follow and we begged His Grace not to do it. We were then told he was unable to refrain and would carry out his intention in spite of us by appealing to the emperor or pope. To prevent this, we humbly requested him, if he insisted on doing it or (as he said) was unable to do otherwise before God and his conscience, at least to do it secretly because he was constrained by his need, for it could not be defended in public and under imperial law. We were promised that he would do so. Afterward we made an effort to help as much as we could to justify it before God with examples of [the relative virtues of bigamy over concubinage evident in the story of] Abraham, etc. All this took place and was negotiated under seal of confession, and we cannot be charged with having done this willingly, gladly, or with pleasure. It was exceedingly difficult for us to do, but because we could not prevent it, we thought that we ought at least to ease his conscience as much as possible.[52]

51. See Eells, *The Attitude of Martin Bucer toward Bigamy.*
52. "Letter to Elector John of Saxony (June 10, 1540)," in *D. Martin Luthers Werke: Briefwechsel,* 17 vols. (Weimar: Bohlau, 1930-83), 9:131-35 (hereafter, WA BR), using the translation in *Luther: Letters of Spiritual Counsel,* ed. Theodore G. Tappert (Philadelphia: Westminster Press, 1955), 288–91. See further WA BR 8:631; WA TR 4, No. 5038, 5046, 5096.

Philip apparently shared the Reformers' counsel with others and publicly celebrated his second wedding in open defiance of his own territorial laws as well as more general imperial laws against bigamy. This caused a great scandal in Germany. Both the emperor and the pope eventually weighed in to condemn Philip for his actions and to rebuke Luther and his colleagues for their counsel. In defense of Luther and his colleagues, this was supposed to have been quiet private pastoral counsel, reluctantly given to an obviously troubled soul, who could keep neither his continence nor his confidence. And allowing bigamy in cases of extreme necessity had long been recognized in the tradition as an equitable exception to the general prohibition against it. But it must also be said that this advice was of a piece with the Reformers' broader insistence that one of the fundamental goods and goals of marriage was to protect parties from sexual sin.

Marriage Is Not a Sacrament

While the Reformers endorsed, with ample amendment, Augustine's two goods of *fides* and *proles*, they had no place for the good of *sacramentum*—either in the medieval sense of a permanent channel of sanctifying grace or even in Augustine's own sense of symbolic stability. For the Reformers, marriage was neither a sacrament of the church on the order of baptism or the Eucharist, nor a permanent union dissolvable only upon the death of one of the parties.

For the Reformers, marriage was a social institution of the earthly kingdom, not a sacrament of the heavenly kingdom. Though divinely ordained to serve a holy purpose, marriage remained, in Luther's words, "a natural order," "an earthly institution," "a secular and outward thing."[53] "No one can deny that marriage is an external, worldly matter, like clothing and food, house and property, subject to temporal authority, as the many imperial laws enacted on the subject prove."[54] To be sure, Luther agreed, marriage can symbolize the union of Christ with his Church, as Paul wrote in Ephesians 5:32. The sacrifices that husband and wife make for each other and for their children can express the sacrificial love of Christ on the cross. A "blessed marriage and home" can be "a true church, a chosen cloister, yes, a paradise" on earth.[55] But these analogies and metaphors do not make marriage a sacrament on the order of baptism and the Eucharist. Sacraments are God's gifts and signs of grace, ensuring Christians of the promise of redemption, available only to those who have faith.[56] Marriage carries no such promise and demands no such faith. "Nowhere in Scripture," wrote Luther, "do we read that anyone would receive the grace of God by getting married; nor does the rite of matrimony contain any hint that the ceremony

---

53. *LW* 21:93.
54. *LW* 46:265. See further Hartwig Dieterich, *Das protestantische Eherecht in Deutschland bis zur Mitte des 17. Jahrhunderts* (Munich: Claudius, 1970), 80; Walter Köhler, *Zürcher Ehegericht und Genfer Konsistorium* (Leipzig: M. Heinsius Nachfolger, 1942), 2:427.
55. *LW* 44:85.
56. See *LW* 36:11; *TC*, 310.

is of divine institution."[57] Scripture teaches that only baptism and the Eucharist (and perhaps penance) confer this promise of grace. All other so-called sacraments are "mere human artifices" that the church has created to augment its legal powers and to fill its coffers with court fees and fines.[58]

The Catholic Church, Luther continued, has based its entire sacramental theology and canon law of marriage on a misunderstanding of Ephesians 5:32: "This is a great mystery [mystērion], and I am applying it to Christ and the church." The Greek term mystērion means "mystery," not "sacrament." Jerome had just misunderstood it a millennium earlier when he translated the Greek word mystērion as the Latin word sacramentum and included that in the standard Latin translation of the Bible, the Vulgate. The Catholic Church has gotten it wrong ever since. In this famous Ephesians passage, Luther argued, the apostle Paul is simply describing the loving and sacrificial union of a Christian husband and wife as a reflection, an echo, a foretaste of the perfect mysterious union of Christ and his church. But the analogy does not make marriage a sacrament that confers sanctifying grace. The Bible is filled with analogies and parables that are designed to provide striking images to drive home lessons: "Faith is like a mustard seed": it grows even if tiny. "The kingdom of heaven is like yeast": it leavens even if you can't see it. Or "the Son of Man will come like a thief in the night": so be ready at all times for his return. And the examples go on. The marriage analogy is similar: "Marital love is like the union of Christ and the church": So be faithful and sacrificial to your spouse. Paul is not divining a new sacrament here, Luther insisted, but driving home, with a familiar rhetorical move, a lesson about marital love that he has spent much of Ephesians 5 explicating.[59]

Moreover, Luther argued, it made no sense for the Catholic Church to call marriage a sacrament without giving the clergy a role in this sacrament or providing a liturgy of preparation and celebration. Neither the husband nor the wife are ordained as clergy, nor can they be if they seek marriage. Yet, regardless of what they know or intend, both perform a sacrament just by making a present promise to marry or making a future promise to marry and then having sex. And that purported sacramental act binds them for life. This just piles fiction upon self-serving fiction, Luther concluded. The Catholic Church forbids its clergy to marry because it is a natural association and beneath them in dignity. Yet it pretends that marriage is a sacrament even if the clergy do not participate in its formation or if the marriage does not take place in the church. "This is an insult to the sacraments," Luther charged. The church's "real goal is jurisdictional [and] not theological" in declaring marriage to be a canonical sacrament. There is no valid biblical or theological basis for this claim.[60]

Denying the sacramental quality of marriage had dramatic implications for how a marriage should be formed, maintained, and dissolved. First, the Lutheran

57. *LW* 36:92–93.
58. *LW* 36:97.
59. Ibid.
60. Ibid.

Reformers argued, there should be no formal religious tests for marriage. Parties would certainly do well to marry within the faith for the sake of themselves and their children. But this is not an absolute condition. Religious differences should not be viewed as an impediment to a valid marriage that can lead to annulment, but a challenge to be more faithful within marriage and to induce proper faith in each other.

> Marriage is an outward, bodily thing, like any other worldly undertaking. Just as I may eat, drink, sleep, walk, ride with, buy from, speak to, and deal with a heathen, Jew, Turk, or heretic, so I may also marry and continue in wedlock with him. Pay no attention to the precepts of those fools who forbid it. You will find plenty of Christians—and indeed the greater part of them—who are worse in their secret unbelief than any Jew, heathen, Turk, or heretic. A heathen is just as much a person—God's good creation—as St. Peter, St. Paul, and St. Lucy, not to speak of slack or spurious Christians.[61]

Second, because marriage is not a sacrament, divorce and remarriage are licit, and sometimes even necessary. To be sure, the Lutheran Reformers, like their Catholic counterparts, insisted that marriages should be stable and presumptively indissoluble. But this presumption could be overcome if one of the essential marital goods were chronically betrayed or frustrated. If there were a breach of marital love by one of the parties—by reason of adultery, desertion, or cruelty—the marriage was broken. The innocent spouse who could not forgive this breach could sue for divorce and remarry. If there were a failure of procreation—by reason of sterility, incapacity, or disease discovered shortly after the wedding—the marriage was also broken. Spouses who could not reconcile themselves to this condition could end the marriage, and at least the healthy spouse could marry another. And if there were a failure of protection from sin—by reason of frigidity, separation, desertion, cruelty, or crime—the marriage was again broken. If the parties could not be reconciled to regular cohabitation and consortium, they could divorce and seek another marriage.[62] In each instance, divorce was painful, sinful, and sad, and it was a step to be taken only after ample forethought and counsel. But it was a licit and sometimes essential step to take.

Martin Bucer put this case for divorce and remarriage more flatly than most. But his argument signals the striking changes born of the rejection of marriage as a sacrament. Marriage has "four necessary properties," he declared:

> 1. That the [couple] should live together. . . . 2. That they should love one another in the height of dearness. . . . 3. That the husband bear himself as the head and preserver of the wife, instructing her to all godliness and integrity of life; that the wife also be to her husband a help, according to her place, especially furthering him in the true worship of God, and next in all

61. *LW* 45:25.
62. WA BR 3:288–90; WA 15:558; Martin Brecht, *Martin Luther,* trans. James L. Schaaf, 3 vols. (Philadelphia and Minneapolis: Fortress Press, 1985–93), 2:93–94.

the occasions of civil life. 4. That they not defraud each other of conjugal benevolence.

Marriages that exhibit these four properties must be maintained and celebrated. But even "where only one [property] be wanting in both or either party, . . . it cannot then be said that the covenant of matrimony holds good between such." To perpetuate the formal structure of marriage after a necessary property is lost, Bucer argued, is not only unnecessary but often destructive.[63]

Third, because marriage is not a sacrament, it also does not belong primarily within the jurisdiction of the church, that is, within the lawmaking authority of the clergy, consistory, and congregation. Luther underscored this several times in his sermons and instructions to fellow pastors:

> First, we [pastors] have enough work to do in our proper office. Second, marriage is outside the church, is a civil matter, and therefore should belong to the government. Third, these cases [of marital dispute] have no limits, extend to the height, the breadth, and the depth, and produce many offences that bring disgrace to the gospel. . . . We prefer to leave this business to civil officials. The responsibility rests on them. Only in cases of conscience should pastors give counsel to godly people. Controversies and court cases [respecting marriage] we leave to the lawyers.[64]

This did not mean that marriage was beyond the pale of God's authority and law, nor that it should be beyond the influence and concern of the church. "It is sheer folly," Luther opined, to treat marriage as "nothing more than a purely human and secular state, with which God has nothing to do."[65] The civil magistrate holds his authority from God. His will is to reflect God's will. His law is to reflect God's law. His rule is to respect God's creation ordinances and institutions. His civil calling is no less spiritual than that of the church. Marriage is thus still completely subject to godly law, but this law is now to be administered by the state, not the church.[66]

Moreover, questions of the formation, maintenance, and dissolution of marriage remain important public concerns, in which church officials and members must still play a key role. First, Luther and other Reformers took seriously the duty of pastoral counseling in marriage disputes that raised matters of conscience. As pastors themselves, many of the Reformers issued scores of private letters to parishioners who came to them for counsel. Second, theologians and preachers were to communicate to magistrates and their subjects God's law and will for marriage and the family, and press for reforms when prevailing marital laws violated God's law. As a theologian, Luther published an ample series of pamphlets and sermons

---

63. Bucer, *RC*, bk. 2, chaps. 26, 38, 39.
64. WA TR 3, No. 4716; *LW* 54:363–64. See also WA TR 2, No. 3267; *LW* 54:194.
65. *LW* 21:95.
66. See Dieterich, *Das protestantische Eherecht*, 44, 81; Reinhard Seeberg, "Luthers Anschauung von dem Geschlechtsleben der Ehe und ihre geschichtliche Stellung," *Luther-Jahrbuch* 7 (1925): 77, 93.

on questions of marriage and marriage law, sometimes wincing about how often his interventions were still needed. Third, to aid church members in their instruction and care and to give notice to all members of society of a couple's marriage, the local parish church clerk was to develop a publicly available marriage registry, which all newly married couples would be required to sign. Fourth, the pastors and teachers of the local church were to instruct and discipline the marriages of its church members by pronouncing the public banns of betrothal, by blessing and instructing the couple at their public church wedding ceremony, and by punishing sexual turpitude or egregious violations of marriage law with public reprimands, bans, or, in serious cases, excommunication. Fifth, it was incumbent upon all members of the church to participate in the spiritual upbringing and counsel of all new children, as their collective baptismal vows required.[67]

Marriage as Social Estate

The linchpin of prevailing Catholic teaching was that marriage was a sacrament of the church. This understanding both integrated and elevated the natural and contractual dimensions of marriage and elevated marriage into an institution and instrument of grace. The linchpin of the Lutheran teaching was that marriage was the founding social estate of the earthly kingdom, the first order of creation, in which God revealed his law and authority, his love and charity. Luther and a number of his followers believed that God had ordained three main estates (*drei Stände*) for the governance of the earthly kingdom: household, church, and state; *Hausvater, Gottesvater,* and *Landesvater, paterfamilias, patertheologicus,* and *paterpoliticus.* Here were the three natural estates or offices through which God revealed himself and reflected divine authority in the world. These three offices and orders stood equal before God and before each other, but the marital household was the "oldest," "most primal," and "most essential" of the three estates. Marriage is the "mother of all earthly laws," Luther wrote, and the source from which the church, the state, and other earthly institutions flow. "God has most richly blessed this estate above all others, and in addition, has bestowed on it and wrapped up in it everything in the world, to the end that this estate might be well and richly provided for. Married life therefore is no jest or presumption; it is an excellent thing and a matter of divine seriousness."[68]

---

67. See Dieterich, *Das protestantische Eherecht*, 47, 86; Roland Kirstein, *Die Entwicklung der Sponsalienlehre und der Lehre vom Eheschluss in der deutschen protestantischen Eherechtslehre bis zu J.H. Böhmer* (Bonn: Röhrscheid, 1966), 39ff.; Walter Köhler, "Die Anfänge des protestantischen Eherechtes," *Zeitschrift der Savigny-Stiftung für Rechtsgeschichte: Kanonistische Abteilung* 30 (1941): 271, 278.

68. *TC*, 639–41; WA 30/1:152. See WA TR 3, No. 3528; *LW* 54:222–23: marriage is "a divine institution from which everything proceeds and without which the whole world would have remained empty, and all creatures would have been meaningless." See similar views in *TC*, 611; WA 49:297; WA 2:734; *LW* 44:81; Philipp Melanchthon, *Melanchthon on Christian Doctrine: Loci Communes, 1555,* trans. and ed. Clyde L. Manschreck (New York and Oxford: Oxford University Press, 1965), 323 (hereafter, *LC 1555*); *TC*, 363–83.

This Lutheran understanding rendered marriage both a private and a public institution, whose proper formation and maintenance were essential to the just and orderly instruction and operation of all other institutions. "The estate of marriage is the spring from which all authority originates and flows," wrote George Spalatin, a leading Saxon official and jurist.[69] Marriage "is not only placed on an equality with other estates, but it [also] precedes and surpasses them all, whether they be that of emperor, princes, bishops, or whoever you please. For both ecclesiastical and civil estates must humble themselves and all be found in this estate."[70] Philipp Melanchthon put it thus:

> The earthly life has orders [*Stände*] and works [*Werke*] which serve to keep the human race, and are ordained by God, within certain limits and means. Matrimony is first, for God does not want human nature simply to run its course as animals do. Therefore, God has ordained marriage, Genesis 2 and Matthew 19 and 1 Corinthians 7, as an eternal inseparable fellowship of one husband and one wife. . . . Matrimony is a very lovely, beautiful fellowship and church of God if two people in true faith and obedience toward God live together, together invoke God, and rear children in the knowledge of God and virtue.[71]

"All orders of human society," the Frankfurt jurist Justin Göbler concurred, "derive from the first estate, matrimony, which was instituted by God himself. On this origin and foundation, stand all other estates, communities, and associations of men. . . . From the administration of the household, which we call *oeconomia*, comes the administration of a government, a state being nothing more than the proliferation of households."[72]

The Lutheran Reformers believed that the social estate of the family was to teach Christian values, morals, and mores to all persons, particularly children. It was to exemplify for a sinful society a community of love and cooperation, meditation and discussion, song and prayer. It was to hold out for the church and the state an example of firm but benign parental discipline, rule, and authority. It was to take in and care for wayfarers, widows, and destitute persons, a responsibility previously assumed largely by monasteries and cloisters. The social estate of marriage was thus as indispensable an agent in God's redemptive plan as the church had been for the Catholics. It no longer stood within the orders of the church but alongside it. Moreover, the social estate of marriage was as indispensable an agent of social order and communal cohesion as the state should be. It was not simply a creation of the civil law, but a godly creation, designed to aid the state in

69. Georg Spalatin, *Vierzehen ursachen, die billich yederman bewegen sollen, den Ehestand lieb und hoch zuhaben und achten* (Erfurt: Andreas Rauscher, 1531), 2a, translated in Harrington, *Reordering Marriage*, 25.

70. *TC*, 639–41.

71. *LC 1555*, 323–24.

72. Justin Göbler, *Der Rechten Spiegel* (Frankfurt am Main: Egenolff, 1550), translated in Gerald Strauss, *Luther's House of Learning: Indoctrination of the Young in the German Reformation* (Baltimore: Johns Hopkins University Press, 1986), 118.

discharging its divine mandate. Thus marriage should be viewed not an inferior option but as a divine calling and a social status desirable for all people.[73]

The best example of such an idealized marital household was the local parsonage, the home of the married Lutheran minister. The Reformers had already argued that pastors, like everyone else, should be married—lest they be tempted by sexual sin, deprived of the joys of marital love, and precluded from the great act of divine and human creativity in having children. Such arguments, coupled with a theology of the priesthood of all believers and the equality of clergy and laity, proved strong enough for the early Reformers to institute and encourage clerical marriage, even in the face of a millennium of canon law to the contrary. Here was an even stronger argument for clerical marriage: the clergy were to be exemplars of marriage. The minister's household was to be a source and model for the right order and government of the local church, state, and broader community. As Adolf von Harnack put it a century ago: "The Evangelical parsonage, founded by Luther, became the model and blessing of the entire German nation, a nursery of piety and education, a place of social welfare and social equality. Without the German parsonage, the history of Germany since the sixteenth century is inconceivable."[74]

THE NEW CIVIL LAW OF MARRIAGE

The Reformers' new theology of marriage helped to transform prevailing German marriage law. The new marital theology was something of a self-executing program of action. It required civil authorities to divest the Catholic Church of its jurisdiction over marriage and assured them that this was a mandate of Scripture, not a sin against the church. It called for new civil marriage laws that were consonant with God's Word but required that the church (and thus the Reformers themselves) advise the civil authorities on what God's Word commands. Both the magistrates' seizure of jurisdiction over marriage and the Reformers' active development of new marriage laws were thus seen as divine tasks.

In the early years of the Reformation, the theology faculties and law faculties of the new Protestant German universities became major catalysts for the development of a new civil law of marriage. Lutheran theologians throughout Protestant Germany, several themselves trained in law, joined with university jurists to debate detailed questions of marriage raised by Scripture, Roman law, canon law, and local custom. At the University of Wittenberg, for example, Luther, Melanchthon, Bugenhagen, Jonas, and several other theologians gave courses and public lectures on marriage law, along with such renowned jurists as Melchior Kling, Konrad Lagus, Johannes Apel, Hieronymus Schürpf, and

---

73. WA 34:73; 50:651–52; *LW* 41:176–77; *TC*, 393.

74. Quoted by Carter Lindberg, "The Future of a Tradition: Luther and the Family," in *All Theology Is Christology: Essays in Honor of David P. Scaer*, ed. Dean O. Wenthe et al. (Fort Wayne, IN: Wayne State University Press, 2000), 133–51, here 141. See Harrington, *Reordering Marriage*, 83.

several others. By 1570, the Wittenberg theology and law professors together published more than eighty tracts on marriage-law questions, disseminating their ideas throughout Germany and beyond. Law professors and theology professors at other Lutheran universities became equally active throughout the sixteenth century in developing a learned civil law of marriage.[75]

This learned law did not remain confined to the academy or to books. Three channels allowed it to penetrate directly into the law of the courts and the councils of Lutheran cities and territories. First, civil courts regularly consulted both the law and theology faculties of local universities throughout the sixteenth century by use of what was called the "file-sending" (*Aktenversendung*) procedure. Courts sent the written records of marital cases raising difficult legal and moral issues to the law and theology faculties, who would discuss the case and submit separate or joint judgments. These judgments were frequently accepted by the courts and issued as formal judgments. This *Aktenversendung* procedure had major influence on substantive marriage law.[76]

Second, courts, councils, and litigating parties solicited opinions (*consilia*) from prominent individual jurists,[77] as well as from the early theological leaders.[78] Particularly the opinions of the new authorities on marriage law were eagerly sought after, for they were frequently dispositive of issues raised in court. For example, the Wittenberg jurist Hieronymus Schürpf—Luther's advocate at the Diet of Worms and the best man at Luther's wedding to Katharina—was famous throughout Germany and beyond for his learned *consilia* on difficult marriage questions.[79] When not teaching at the University of Wittenberg, he traveled extensively throughout Germany, Scandinavia, and Switzerland to dispense his

75. The most authoritative tracts beyond those already cited are Joachim von Beust, *Tractatus connubiorum praestantiss: Iuris consultorum* (vol. 1, Jena, 1606; vols. 2–3, Frankfurt, 1617–18, 1742), bound with tracts by Konrad Mauser and Johannes Schneidewin; Nicolaus Hemmingsen, *Libellus de conjugio, repudio, et divortio* (Leipzig: Steinman, 1578); Melchior Kling, *Matrimonialium causarum tractatus, methodico ordine scriptus* (Frankfurt am Main: Chr. Egenolphus, 1553); Basilius Monner, *Tractatus duo:1. De matrimonio; 2. De clandestinis conjugiis*, 2nd ed. (Jena: Steinmann, 1604); Johannes Schneidewin, *In institutionum imperialium titulum X: De nuptiis. . .* (Frankfurtam Main, 1571). See further detailed sources and discussion of the legal literature of Lutheran Germany in my *Law and Protestantism* and on the law in action in Ralf Frassek, *Eherecht und Ehegerichtsbarkeit in der Reformationszeit: Der Aufbau neuer Rechtsstrukturen im sächsischen Raum unter besonderer Berücksichtigung der Wirkungsgeschichte des Wittenberger Konsistoriums* (Tübingen: Mohr Siebeck, 2005).

76. See Harold J. Berman, *Law and Revolution, II: The Impact of the Protestant Reformations on the Western Legal Tradition* (Cambridge, MA: Harvard University Press, 2003), 100–130.

77. See Guido Kisch, *Consilia: Eine Bibliographie der juristischen Konsiliensammlungen* (Basel: Helbing & Lichtenhahn, 1970).

78. See examples of these in *Melanchthons Werke*, in Corpus reformatorum 1–28, ed. G. Bretschneider and H. E. Bindseil (Brunswick: C. A. Schwetschke & Filium, 1834–60), esp. 4:777–79; 5:306–8; 7:1002–4. Also see Johannes Brenz, "Ehegutachten," in idem, *Frühschriften*, ed. Martin Brecht, Gerhard Schäfer, and Frieda Wolf, 2 vols. (Tübingen: J. C. B. Mohr, 1970–74), 2:253–96; and discussion of Luther's marriage opinions in Walter Köhler, "Luther als Eherichter," *Beiträge zur sächsischen Kirchengeschichte* 47 (1947): 18.

79. Wiebke Schaich-Klose, *D. Hieronymus Schürpf: Leben und Werk des Wittenberger Reformationsjuristen, 1481–1554* (Trogen and Tübingen: F. Meili, 1967).

opinions. His posthumously published collection of some 800 *consilia* remained a standard reference book for more than two centuries thereafter.[80]

Third, from the early 1520s onward, numerous new marriage ordinances were promulgated—first as parts of the new church ordinances (*Kirchenordnungen*) and public policy ordinances (*Polizeiordnungen*) and increasingly in the later sixteenth century as freestanding marriage statutes (*Eheordnungen*).[81] The first Lutheran marriage laws appeared in 1523 in the towns of Zwickau and Leisnig and in 1524 in Magdeburg, Annaberg, and Meissen. By 1530, at least eight other cities had promulgated new marriage law, and by 1560 sixty other cities had joined them. Various principalities and duchies followed, first in Hesse and Saxony in the late 1520s and 1530s; by 1580 all major Lutheran territories had joined them.

The Lutheran Reformers did not leave the promulgation of these new marriage laws to the vagaries of the political process. Many of the leading theological lights of the Reformation—Luther, Melanchthon, Brenz, Bugenhagen, and several others—participated actively in both drafting and defending these laws. The most fertile legislative pen was that of the Wittenberg theologian and town pastor Johannes Bugenhagen, who drafted or shaped more than twenty major new marriage ordinances for Germany as well as the Kingdoms of Denmark and Norway, which moved decisively toward the Lutheran reformation of marriage.[82] The Reformers made ample use of scissors and paste in crafting this legislation. They regularly duplicated their own formulations and those of their closest coreligionists in drafting new laws. They corresponded with each other about marriage laws and frequently circulated draft laws among their inner circle for comment and critique. They referred to and paraphrased liberally the theological writings of the leading Reformers, particularly those of Luther, Melanchthon, Bucer, Bugenhagen, and Brenz. This close collaboration led to considerable uniformity among the marriage law provisions and considerable legal appropriation of the Reformers' cardinal theological ideas on marriage and the family.

Although the new Lutheran marriage laws were wide-ranging, three fundamental changes in the traditional canon law of marriage were common. The new civil law of marriage (1) modified the traditional consent doctrine and required

80. Hieronymus Schurpff [Schürpf], *Consilia seu reponsa iuris centuria I–III* (Frankfurt: Christian Egenolff [Egenolph], 1545–56, repr., 1564). On their influence, see Theodore Muther, *Aus dem Universitäts- und Gelehrtenleben im Zeitalter der Reformation* (Erlangen: A. Deichert, 1866), 186.

81. The best collections of this new legislation are in Arthur Kern, ed., *Deutsche Hofordnungen des 16. und 17. Jahrhunderts*, 2 vols. (Berlin: Weidmann, 1905); Aemilius L. Richter, *Die evangelischen Kirchenordnungen des sechszehnten Jahrhunderts*, repr., 2 vols. (Nieuwkoop: B. DeGraaf, 1967) (hereafter, Richter); Emil Sehling, ed., *Die evangelischen Kirchenordnungen des 16. Jahrhunderts*, vols. 1–5 (Leipzig: O. R. Reisland, 1902–13), and vols. 6–19 continued under the same title (Aalen: Scientia Verlag, 1955–2008) (hereafter, Sehling).

82. See Kurd Schulz, "Bugenhagen als Schöpfer der Kirchenordnungen," in *Johann Bugenhagen: Beiträge zu seinem 400. Todestag*, ed. Werner Rautenberg (Berlin: Evangelische Verlagsanstalt, 1958), 51; Anneliese Sprengler-Ruppenthal, "Bugenhagen und das kanonische Recht," *Zeitschrift der Savigny-Stiftung für Rechtsgeschichte: Kanonistische Abteilung* 75 (1989): 375.

the participation of others in the process of marriage formation; (2) sharply curtailed the number of impediments to engagement and to marriage; and (3) introduced absolute divorce on proof of cause, with a right of remarriage. Such changes, taken together, simplified the laws of marriage formation and dissolution, provided for broader public participation in this marriage process, and protected the public functions of the social estate of marriage.

The Law of Consent to Marriage

As in canon law, so in the new civil law, the marriage bond was to be formed by a free consensual union between two parties. Many of the Reformers, however, accepted the traditional consent doctrine only after (1) modifying the canonists' distinctions among the engagement or future promise to marry, the present promise to marry, and the consent to consummate the marriage through sexual intercourse; (2) requiring that parents and witnesses participate in the marriage process; and (3) enlarging the task of the church in the process of marital formation.

Luther was the most ardent advocate for these reforms. For Luther, the three forms of consent accepted at canon law were scripturally unwarranted, semantically confusing, and a source of public mischief. The Bible, said Luther, makes no distinction between the present and future promise of marriage. Any promise to marry, freely given in good faith, creates a valid and presumptively indissoluble marriage before God and the world; this marriage is consummated through sexual intercourse. Even before consummation, however, Scripture makes clear that breach of this promise through sexual relations with, or a subsequent marriage promise to, another is adultery.

Furthermore, the distinction between present and future promises of marriage depends upon "a scoundrelly game" (*ein lauter Narrenspiel*) in Latin words that have no equivalent in German and thus confuse the average person. The Catholic Church courts usually interpreted the declaration *Ich will Dich zum Weibe haben* or *Ich will Dich nehmen* or *Ich will Dich haben* or *Du sollst mein sein* as a future promise, though in common German parlance these were usually intended to be present promises.[83] A present promise, traditional church courts insisted, must use the Latin phrase *Accipio te in uxorem* or the German phrase *Ich nehme Dich zu meinem Weibe*, though neither phrase was popular in lay circles. Such a post hoc interpretation of promises, Luther charged, exploited the ignorance of the common people, disregarded the intent of the couple, and betrayed the presumption of the church courts against marriage. By interpreting many promises to be engagements and not marriages, church courts had availed themselves of the much more liberal rules for dissolving engagements and thus

---

83. *LW* 45:11, 274; and analysis in Rudolf Sohm, *Das Recht der Eheschliessung aus dem deutschen und kanonischen Recht geschichtlich entwickelt* (Weimar: Böhlau, 1875), 138–39, 197–98. The promises are ambiguous because the verbs *will* and *sollst*, though commonly understood to be in the present tense, can also be interpreted as future verbs.

had been able to dissolve numerous marriages. Through their combined doctrines of construing marriage promises as mere engagements and of permitting a religious vow to dissolve an engagement promise, the canon lawyers had thus covertly subsidized celibacy and monasticism.

To allay the confusion and reverse the presumption against marriage, Luther at first proposed that all promises to become married in the future (*sponsalia de futuro*) be viewed as binding marriage vows in the present (*sponsalia de praesenti*) unless either party had expressly stipulated some future condition or event. A promise in any language with a verb in the future tense was not enough to defeat the presumption. An expressly stated condition was required to preclude the merger of engagement and marriage promises. Luther later retreated a bit from this position. He eventually recognized the validity and importance of making distinctions between engagement and marriage promises, but he insisted that the interval between the two promises be very short (as had been the case in his own marriage with Katharina) and that a high burden of proof of cause be placed on either party who wished to break their engagement.[84]

Luther and his followers did not attach such solemnity and finality to the marriage promise without safeguards. First, they insisted that, before any such promise, the couple seek the consent of their parents on both sides or, if they were dead or missing, of their next of kin or guardian. Such consent, they argued, was mandated by Scripture (in the Commandment to honor one's parents) as well as by natural law, Roman law, and early canon law. But mandatory parental consent rules had been lost on the Catholic Church, leading to the current toleration for secret marriages. The parents of both the man and the woman played an essential role in the process of marriage formation, Luther argued. They judged the maturity of the couple and the harmony and legality of their prospective relationship. More important, their will was to reflect the will of God for the couple. Like the priest and like the prince, the parent had been given authority as God's agent to perform a specific calling in the institution of marriage. Parents are "apostles, bishops, and priests to their children."[85] By giving their consent to the couple, parents were, in effect, giving God's consent.

Marriages contracted without parental consent were, in the view of Luther and other Reformers, presumptively void.[86] But where parents withheld their consent unreasonably, ordered their child to lead a celibate life, or used their authority to coerce a child to enter marriage unwillingly, they no longer performed a godly task. In such cases Luther urged the child to petition a minister or a magistrate for approval and thereafter to be married despite a parent's objection.[87] If the magistrate or minister, too, was unreasonable or coercive, Luther urged the child to seek refuge in another place or simply to marry without such permission.

---

84. WA TR 2, No. 3179a. See also WA TR 3, No. 3921; *LW* 54:294–95.
85. *LW* 45:46.
86. *LW* 46:205; see Dieterich, *Das protestantische Eherecht*, 93–96.
87. WA TR 5, No. 5441; *LW* 54:424.

Luther stressed his teaching on parental consent and its limitations many times in his sermons, letters, *consilia*, and formal writings. An interesting example can be found in Luther's intervention in the case of a young Wittenberg law student, Johannes Schneidewin, who later would become a distinguished law professor at the University of Wittenberg and a strong supporter of Luther's reforms of marriage law. While studying at Wittenberg, Schneidewin was a tenant in Luther's home and with Luther's blessing had fallen in love with a local woman, Anna Dürer. Johannes had sought his widowed mother's permission to marry Anna in his hometown of Stollberg, but his mother had ignored his repeated queries. Luther then wrote thrice to Mrs. Schneidewin, asking her permission and assuring her that the parties were fit and ready to be married and very much in love:

> Some time ago, I wrote to you that your son John is attached by a great love to an honorable girl here. . . . I hoped to receive a favorable reply from you. I too have become impatient with your obstructing your son's marriage, and this has moved me to write to you once again. Because I too am fond of your son, I am unwilling to see his hope turned to ashes. The girl pleases him very much, her station in life is not unlike his, and she is, besides, a pious girl of an honorable family. Accordingly, I believe you have reason to be satisfied, especially because your son has submitted to you in filial obedience. . . . It therefore behooves you, as a loving mother, to give your consent. . . . I pray you not to delay your consent any longer. Let the good fellow have peace of mind. And I cannot wait much longer. I shall have to act as my office requires.[88]

Luther did not wait long to exercise his ministerial office. He married the couple less than two months later. An appreciative Professor Schneidewin later dedicated his first book on the law of marriage "to the memory of the honorable Dr. Martin Luther."[89]

Second, in addition to parental consent, Luther insisted that the promise to marry be made publicly, in the presence of at least two good and honorable witnesses. These witnesses could, if necessary, attest to the event of the marriage or to the intent of the parties and could also help instruct the couple in the solemnity and responsibility of their relationship—a function tied to Luther's doctrine of the priesthood of all believers.[90]

Third, Luther and his followers insisted that, before consummating their marriage, the couple repeat their vows publicly in the church, seek the blessing and instruction of the pastor, and register in the public marriage directory kept in the church. Luther saw the further publicizing of marriage as an invitation for others to aid and support the couple, a warning for them to avoid sexual relations with either party, and a safeguard against false or insincere marriage

---

88. WA BR 8:453–55, using the translation in Tappert, *Letters of Spiritual Counsel*, 287–88. See also WA BR 8:492–93, 499.

89. Schneidewin, *De nuptiis*, prooemium.

90. *LW* 46:268.

promises made for the purpose of seducing the other party. Just as the parental consent was to reflect God's will that the couple be married, so the pastor's blessing and instruction were to reflect God's will for the marriage—that it remain an indissoluble bond of love and mutual service.[91]

With these requirements of parental consent, witnesses, and church registration and solemnization, Luther deliberately discouraged the secret marriages that the medieval canon law had recognized (though not encouraged). He made marriage a public institution, advocating the involvement of specific third parties throughout the process of marriage formation. Luther did, however, insist that private vows followed by sexual intercourse should constitute a valid marriage if the woman was impregnated or if the intercourse became publicly known. This was to be a case-by-case exception to the usual rule that a private promise was not an adequate basis for a valid marriage. Luther made the exception to protect the legitimacy and life of the child and to prevent the woman from falling victim to "the strong prejudice [against] marrying a despoiled woman."[92]

Various Lutheran jurists worked out the legal implications of these reforms to the law of marital consent. Luther's conflation of future and present marriage promises found support only among later jurists who had joined the evangelical cause. Earlier jurists—such as Schürpf and two other Wittenberg colleagues Melchior Kling and Konrad Lagus—rejected this reform, despite Luther's heated arguments with them. They retained the traditional canon-law distinction between present and future promises to marry and insisted on a separate group of impediments for each promise. Although they urged courts to interpret promises in accordance with the common German language, they silently rejected Luther's other recommendations.[93] Only in the second half of the sixteenth century were Luther's teachings made, in Rudolph Sohm's words, "the general Protestant doctrine and praxis which lasted into the eighteenth century."[94] Schneidewin, Joachim von Beust, Basilius Monner, Konrad Mauser, and other later Lutheran jurists rejected or severely diminished the distinction between the present promise to marry and the public unconditional engagement promise, and they shortened the time between the formal engagement and the wedding. Like Luther, they inveighed against secret marriages, and many affirmed, for the same reason as Luther, the exception for private marriages whose consummation became publicly known or resulted in pregnancy.[95]

Luther's reforms of the law of marital consent also came to expression in the new civil law. Many statutes used the terms "betrothal" (*Verlöbnis*) and "marriage"

91. *LW* 53:110.

92. Ibid. See further Karl Michaelis, "Über Luthers eherechtliche Anschauungen und deren Verhältnis zum mittelalterlichen und neuzeitlichen Eherecht," in *Festschrift für Erich Ruppel zum 65. Geburtstag*, ed. Heinz Brunotte et al. (Hannover: Lutherhaus, 1968), 43, 51.

93. Dieterich, *Das protestantische Eherecht*, 121.

94. Sohm, *Das Recht der Eheschliessung*, 198.

95. See ibid., 233, and a good contemporary catalog of views in Joachim von Beust, *Tractatus connubiorum praestantiss*, vol. 1, folios 5a–5b.

(*Ehe*) interchangeably and deemed the public betrothal to be a completed (*geschlossen*) marriage.[96] Several other statutes, while retaining the traditional distinction between promises of betrothal and marriage, attached far greater importance and finality to public unconditioned betrothals, providing (1) that these promises take precedence over all secret betrothals (even those made subsequently); (2) that promiscuity by either betrothed party should be punished as adultery; and (3) that these promises can be dissolved only on grounds also permitted for divorce.[97] The functional distinction between future and present promises was thus considerably narrowed in the laws of a number of German polities.

The requirement of parental consent to marriages, particularly for children who had not yet reached the age of majority, won virtually unanimous acceptance in sixteenth-century Germany, among jurists and legislators alike. Parental consent was a particularly prominent topic of discussion among the jurists. They adduced evidence in support of mandatory parental consent from Roman law, early canon law, and Germanic law alike. For several of the early jurists, like Kling and Schürpf, who advocated closer allegiance to canon law, parental consent was highly commendable but not absolutely necessary. Couples who married without parental consent should be fined by the state and disciplined by the church, but neither the parents nor the new husband or wife should be able to annul the marriage because of this omission. Several later jurists, such as Monner, Mauser, and Schneidewin, argued that such secret marriages should be annulled, unless the parties had consummated their private vows; post hoc consent by the parties should have no effect. Virtually all the jurists urged that the couple seek the approval of both fathers and mothers. Where the parents were dead or missing, they assiduously listed, in the order of priority, the next of kin, tutors, curators, and others whose consent should be sought. Finally, the jurists discussed in detail the conditions that parents could attach to their consent. Reasonable conditions of time ("You may marry my daughter but only after a year"), of place ("only in the church of Wittenberg"), or of support ("only when you secure a job") were generally accepted by the jurists. But they carefully denied parents the opportunity to use the consent doctrine to place coercive demands or unreasonable restrictions on the couple. Monner and Mauser, in fact, argued that parents or guardians who abused their consensual authority be fined or even imprisoned in cases of serious abuse.[98]

Given the prominent attention to parental consent by theologians and jurists, it is not surprising that most of the new civil statutes required such consent.

96. See the Church Ordinances of Zurich (1529), Brandenburg-Nuremberg (1533), Württemberg (1536), Kassell (1539), Schwabisch-Hall (1543), Cologne (1543), and Tecklenberg (1588) as well as the Consistory Ordinance of Brandenberg (1573), in Richter, 1:135, 209, 270, 304; 2:16, 47, 476, and 381.

97. See the Goslar Consistory Ordinance (1555) and the Declaration of the Synod of Emden (1571) in Richter, 2:166, 340. See also the Opinions of the Wittenberg Court quoted in Sohm, *Das Recht der Eheschliessung*, 199–200.

98. See Dieterich, *Das protestantischen Eherecht*, 123–27.

Very few statutes, however, ordered that marriages contracted without parental consent be nullified.[99] The presence of witnesses or the public declaration of betrothal in a church was usually accepted as an adequate substitute, though several statutes ordered stern penalties for parties who failed to gain parental consent.[100] The ambit of the parents' authority in the marriage process was also carefully circumscribed in the new statutes. They prohibited parents from entering their unwilling children in cloisters or monasteries or from obstructing children who wished to leave their sacred orders. Children saddled with severe conditions or restrictions on their prospective marriages were granted rights of appeal to the local court; where the court found for the child, the parents (or guardians) were subject to fines and other penalties.[101] In most jurisdictions, parental consent was no longer required once the child reached the age of majority.[102]

The requirement of at least two good and honorable witnesses to the marriage promise was accepted by virtually all jurists and legislative draftsmen. A few early statutes denied outright the validity of an unwitnessed marriage promise, but in most jurisdictions, the validity of these promises was left to the discretion of the court.[103] At first, unwitnessed marriages were rarely dissolved. But as the scandal of premarital sex and pregnancy grew and courts were faced with time-consuming evidentiary inquiries into the relationship of litigating couples, these private promises were increasingly struck down. Parties who consummated their private promises were fined, imprisoned, and, in some jurisdictions, banished from the local community. In the later sixteenth century, a number of territories also began to require either that the couple invite a government official as one witness to their promises or that they announce their promises before the city hall or other specified civic building.[104]

99. See Marriage Ordinance of Württemberg (1537) in Richter, 1:280. The Wittenberg marriage court apparently also took this rigid stance, though absolute parental consent was not prescribed in the Wittenberg statute. See Dieterich, *Das protestantischen Eherecht*, 156–57.

100. See, e.g., the Church Ordinances of Basel (1529) and Brandenburg (1573) and the Declarations of the Synod of Emden (1571) in Richter, 1:125; 2:376, 340. See also the Reformation Ordinance of Hessen (1526), Marriage Ordinance of Württemberg (1553), and the Schauenburg Policy Ordinance (1615), quoted in Gustav Schmelzeisen, *Polizeiordnung und Privatrecht* (Münster and Cologne: Böhlau, 1955), 33–34.

101. See the Constitution of the Wittenberg Consistory Ordinance (1542), the Church Ordinance of Cellische (1545), the Marriage Ordinance of Dresden (1556), the Territorial Ordinance of Prussia (1577), the Marriage Ordinance of Kurpf (1582), and the Schauenburg Policy Ordinance (1615) in Sehling, 1:20, 292, 343, and in Schmelzeisen, *Polizeiordnung und Privatrecht*, 36. See also illustrative cases in Joachim von Beust, *Tractatus de iure connubiorum et dotium* (Frankfurt am Main: P. Schmidt, 1591), pt. 1, folios 82b–86a.

102. See, e.g., the Church Ordinance of Goslar (1555) in Richter, 2:165. The age of majority in that jurisdiction was 20 years for men, 18 for women; in some jurisdictions, the age of majority was as high as 27 for men and 25 for women; see Schmelzeisen, *Polizeiordnung und Privatrecht*, 35.

103. The Marriage Ordinance of Zurich (1525), copied in several south German cities, was the first to declare void ab initio all unwitnessed marriages. See Köhler, "Die Anfänge," 74. The more typical early statutes are the Church Ordinance of Ulm (1531) and the Marriage Ordinance of Württemberg (1537), in Richter, 1:158, 280.

104. Marriage Ordinance of Württemberg (1553) and Church Ordinance of Goslar (1555) in Richter, 2:129, 165. See discussion in Köhler, "Die Anfänge," 292.

In many jurisdictions, the church was assigned an indispensable role in the process of marriage formation. Couples were required, on pain of stiff penalty, to register their marriage with local church officials.[105] The public church celebration of the marriage and the pastor's instruction and blessing were made mandatory even for couples who had earlier announced their engagement in the community and received parental consent.[106] Several ordinances explicitly ordered punishment for engaged couples who consummated their marriages before participating in the church ceremony.[107] By the 1550s, this "anticipatory sex" was grounds for imprisonment or banishment from the community as well as excommunication from the church.[108]

These four interrelated reforms introduced into the German civil law of marriage—the growing conflation of unconditioned future and present promises to marry, along with the requirements of parental consent, of witnesses, and of church registration and celebration for marriage—remained standard provisions in the next three centuries, not only in Germany but also in many other Western nations. These reforms were partly based on the new theology of the Lutheran social model of marriage. But they were also based on earlier Roman law and canon-law provisions, which had fallen into desuetude by the eve of the Reformation. Indeed, as we saw in the last chapter, the Council of Trent in 1563 made comparable changes to the canon law of marital formation—appealing to many of the same early canon-law and Roman-law precedents adduced by the Reformers but grounding these reforms in the distinctive sacramental theology of the Catholic tradition.

The Law of Impediments to Marriage

Lutheran theologians and jurists strove with equal vigor to reform the canon law of impediments. For the Reformers, a number of these grounds for annulment of betrothals and marriage were biblically groundless. Several others, though grounded in the Bible, had in their view become a source of corruption and confusion.

According to the Bible, as the Reformers understood it, marriage is a duty prescribed by the law of creation and a right protected by the law of Christ. No human law could impinge on this divine duty or infringe on this "divine right" of marriage without the warrant of divine law.[109] No human authority could

105. See, e.g., Church Ordinance of Ulm (1531) in Richter, 1:159.

106. See the Zurich Chorgericht Ordinance (1525) and the Church Ordinances of Basel (1530), Kassel (1530), Ulm (1531), Strasbourg (1534), and the numerous later statutes quoted and discussed in Emil Friedberg, *Das Recht der Eheschliessung in seiner geschichtliche Entwicklung* (Leipzig: Bernhard Tauchnitz, 1875), 213–17.

107. See the Ordinances of Nürnberg (1537), Augsburg (1553), and Ulm (1557) described in Ozment, *When Fathers Ruled*, 36; Köhler, "Die Anfänge," 296.

108. See the Marriage Ordinance of Württemberg (1553) in Richter, 2:128 and the Church Ordinance of Palatine on the Rhine (1563) in Sehling, 6:133.

109. *LW* 36:100.

impede or annul a marriage without divine authorization.[110] As Melanchthon put it: "The union of male and female belong to [the order of] natural laws. Since natural law is immutable, the right to contract marriage (*ius contrahendi conjugi*) must always remain."[111] Hence impediments to marriage that were not clear commands of God and nature could not be countenanced. These included the canon-law impediments that protecting the sanctity of the marriage sacrament, for the Bible (as the Reformers understood it) does not teach that marriage is a sacrament. They also included impediments that privileged religious vows of celibacy or chastity over promise of marriage, for the Bible, in the Reformers' view, subordinates such vows to the calling of marriage.

Even the biblically based impediments of the traditional canon law had, in the Reformers' view, become sources of corruption and confusion. It had long been the official practice of the medieval church to relax certain impediments (such as consanguinity, affinity, and public honesty) where they worked injustice to the parties or to their children. Parties could receive a dispensation from these impediments and be excused from the legal strictures. This "equitable" practice met with little criticism and indeed was continued by the Reformers, as we just saw in the infamous bigamy case of Philip of Hesse. The Reformers' principal concern was with the abuse of this practice in certain bishoprics in Germany. Some corrupt bishops, in their judgment, had turned their proper "equitable" authority to their own financial gain by relaxing any number of impediments if the dispensation payment was high enough. This clerical bribery and trafficking in dispensations from impediments evoked caustic attacks from the Reformers. "There is no impediment to marriage nowadays," Luther charged, "which they cannot legitimize for money. These man-made regulations seem to have come into existence for no other reason than raking in money and netting in souls."[112] Such abuses not only desecrated the priestly office but also resulted in a liberal law of impediments for the rich and a restrictive law for the poor. Furthermore, the Reformers averred, the impediments had become so intricate that they were confusing to the common person. The confession manuals of the day were filled with ornate legalistic discussions of the impediments, incomprehensible to the uninitiated and frequently written in Latin, and not the language of the common people.[113]

Acting on these general criticisms, the Reformers developed a simplified and, in their view, more biblical law of impediments. They (1) adopted most of the physical impediments; (2) accepted, with some qualification, the impediments protecting the parties' consent; (3) adopted a severely truncated law of personal impediments; and (4) discarded the spiritual impediments protecting the sanctity of the sacrament.

110. See *LW* 36:96; 45:22.
111. *TC*, 366–67.
112. *LW* 36:96–106; 45:7–9.
113. Ibid. See also *LW* 45:22–30; Bucer, *RC*, chap. 17; and discussion of other views in Dieterich, *Das protestantische Eherecht*, 97–98.

Given the importance that the Reformers attached to the physical and sexual union of husband and wife, they readily accepted the canonists' physical impediments of permanent impotence and bigamy, on the strength of the same favorite passages in Moses, the Gospels, and Paul that the medieval canonists had used.[114]

The Reformers also accepted the traditional impediments that guaranteed the free consent of both parties to the engagement and marriage contracts. Thus a man and a woman who had been joined under duress, coercion, or fear were seen as "unmarried before God" and thus free to dissolve their union. Both Lutheran theologians and jurists, however, required that the pressure exerted on the couple be particularly pervasive and malicious—a requirement that they based on patristic authority. The Reformers, like the canonists, accepted errors of person as grounds for annulment. Luther, Bucer, and Brenz, however, urged Christian couples to follow the example of Jacob and Leah and accept such unions as a challenge placed before them by God—a recommendation that is repeated in some of the statutes. A number of Reformers also permitted annulment of marriage based on errors of quality, the mistaken assumption that one's spouse was a virgin. For, as the Mosaic law and Pauline teachings made clear, one's prior commitment to marriage, whether through a promise or through sexual intercourse, prevented one from entering any true marriage thereafter. Thus the second putative marriage was void from the start.[115]

In developing the civil law of personal impediments, the Lutheran theologians and jurists were far less faithful to the canon-law tradition. They rejected several of these impediments and liberalized others in an attempt to remove as many obstacles to marriage and as many obfuscations of Scripture as possible. First, the Reformers rejected impediments designed to protect the celibate and the chaste. The canon laws prohibiting marriage to clerics, monks, and nuns were unanimously rejected as unscriptural.[116] Several statutes explicitly condoned clerical marriage and enjoined subjects to accept the offspring of preachers as legitimate children and heirs.[117] Canon laws forbidding remarriage to those who had initially married a cleric, monk, or nun had no parallel in the new civil law. The traditional assumption that vows to chastity and celibacy automatically dissolved

---

114. Ibid.

115. See generally, ibid.; *LW* 45:22, 66, 102, 128; and discussion in Friedberg, *Das Recht der Eheschliessung*, 212; Kirstein, *Die Entwicklung*, 28, 57; Köhler, "Die Anfänge," 375. For statutory examples, see Consistory Ordinances of Brandenburg (1573) and Prussia (1584) in Richter, 2:383, 466, on impediments to protect free consent; Kurbrandenburg Church Ordinance (1540) in Richter, 1:323 on the impediment respecting errors of quality.

116. See, e.g., *LW* 35:138; 45:28; *Common Places of Martin Bucer*, trans. and ed. D. F. Wright (Appleford: Sutton Courtenay Press, 1972), 406; and discussion of other reformers' views in Dieterich, *Das protestantishen Eherecht*, 78, 110. Yet conservative jurists, such as Kling and Schürpf, rejected this impediment with great hesitation; by 1536, Schürpf considered the children of clerics to be illegitimate and recommended that legacies and inheritances not be bequeathed to them. See Stintzing, *Rechtswissenschaft*, 275.

117. Church Ordinances of Northeim (1539), Kurbrandenburg (1540), Braunschweig-Wolfenbüttel (1543) as well as the Consistory Ordinance of Wittenberg (1542) in Richter, 1:287, 323, 367; and 2:56.

engagements and unconsummated marriage promises found acceptance only among the early conservative jurists, such as Kling and Schürpf. They were uniformly rejected by Lutheran jurists and legislators after 1545.[118]

Second, the canon-law spiritual impediments, prohibiting marriages between godparents and their children found no place in the new Lutheran laws.[119] Third, the legal impediments, proscribing marriages between a variety of parties related by adoption, were liberalized and in some jurisdictions abandoned altogether.[120]

Fourth, the Reformers rejected or simplified the intricate restrictions on those related by blood, family, spiritual, and legal ties. Only early Lutheran jurists and legislators accepted the medieval canon-law formulation of the impediment of consanguinity that permitted annulment of marriages between parties related by blood to the fourth degree. Several Reformers permitted restrictions on parties related by blood only to the third or to the second degree, and both positions found statutory expression.[121] Luther's repeated arguments for adopting only the slender group of impediments of consanguinity set forth in Leviticus and Deuteronomy were routinely rejected—in no small part because this Mosaic law was considered to be incomplete, not even prohibiting relations between a father and daughter, between a grandson and a grandmother, or between first and second cousins.[122] Similarly, the canon-law impediments of affinity and public decorum—which annulled marriage between a person and the blood relative of a deceased spouse or fiancé(e) to the fourth degree—were accepted in qualified form only by early Lutheran jurists and legislators.[123] The arguments by theolo-

118. *LW* 36:97–99.

119. Ibid., 100, 136. Though most statutes silently ignored the spiritual impediments, a few later statutes explicitly denied their validity. See, e.g., the Church Ordinance of Lower Saxony (1585) and the Braunschweiger Policy Ordinance (1618), quoted in Schmelzeisen, *Polizeiordnung und Privatrecht*, 53.

120. This impediment was retained by a few early reformers such as Kling, Schürpf, and Brenz. Many later jurists who rejected the impediment still insisted that the adopted child be granted the full rights of protection and inheritance accorded the natural child. See Dieterich, *Das protestantische Eherecht*, 101, 137.

121. See a convenient table in Philipp Melanchthon, *De arbore consanguinitatis et affinitatis, sive de gradibus* (Wittenberg, 1540), folios aii–bii. For Andreas Osiander's position, which was influential in Lutheran Germany, see the summary in Judith W. Harvey, "The Influence of the Reformation on Nürnberg Marriage Laws, 1520–1535" (PhD diss., Ohio State University, 1972), 250. Impediments of consanguinity to the third degree were accepted by the Württemberg Marriage Ordinance (1537), the Cellisches Ehebedenken (1545), the Mecklenburg Church Ordinance (1557), the Hessen Reformation Ordinance (1572), the Mecklenburg Policy Ordinance (1572), the Lübeck Ordinance (1581), respectively, in Richter, 1:280; Sehling, 1:296; 5:212; Schmelzeisen, *Polizeiordnung und Privatrecht*, 50. Impediments of consanguinity to the second degree were accepted by the Saxon General Articles (1557) in Richter, 2:178.

122. See *LW* 45:3, 23; and corrections in WA BR 7:152–53. See esp. *LW* 45:3, 23; Bucer, *Common Places*, 410. The Levitical law of impediments of consanguinity was adopted by later statutes, e.g., the Brandenburg Ordinance (1694) and the Prussian Cabinet Order (1740), quoted and discussed in Schmelzeisen, *Polizeiordnung und Privatrecht*, 51–52.

123. See Dieterich, *Das protestantische Eherecht*, 135–36.

gians to reduce these restrictions to "in-laws" in the third, second, or even first degrees all came to legislative expression.[124]

Fifth, a number of jurisdictions that had accepted Luther's conflation of future and present marriage promises rejected the canon-law impediment of multiple relationships. The canonists had maintained that any engagement was dissolved if one of the parties made a subsequent marriage promise to another or had sexual relations with another. This rule was adopted by the Reformers only for conditional betrothal promises. They regarded unconditional public promises of engagement to be indissoluble and thus superior to any subsequent physical or verbal commitments of marriage.[125]

Finally, the Reformers rejected the spiritual impediments of unbelief and crime, which had been designed to protect the sanctity of the marriage sacrament. The canon law had prohibited marriage between Christians and non-Christians and permitted annulment where one party had permanently left the church. Only those couples who had been sanctified by baptism and who remained true to the faith could sacramentally symbolize the union of Christ and his church. To the Reformers, marriage had no such symbolic Christian function and thus no prerequisites of baptism or unanimity of faith.[126] The canonists had also prohibited marriage to the person who had done public penance (for mortal sin) or who was guilty of certain sexual crimes; that offender's marital union, the canonists argued, would be constantly perverted by this grave former sin, and thus neither the mortal sinner nor the spouse could receive the sanctifying grace of the sacrament. To the Reformers, marriage imparted no such sanctifying grace and thus required no such prerequisite purity. To be sure, Luther wrote, "sins and crimes should be punished, but with other penalties, not by forbidding marriage. David committed adultery with Bathsheba, Uriah's wife, and had her husband killed besides. He was guilty of both crimes, still he [could take] her to be his wife."[127] A number of jurists and legislators concurred.

The Law of Divorce and Remarriage

The Reformers' attack on the canon law of impediments was closely allied with their attack on the canon law of divorce. Just as they discarded many impediments as infringements on the right to enter marriage, they rejected the canon law of divorce as an abridgement of the right to end one marriage and to enter another.

Since the twelfth century, the Catholic Church had consistently taught that (1) divorce meant only separation of the couple from bed and board; (2) such

124. Ibid., 100, 161.
125. See the Cellisches Ehebedenken (1545), the Consistory Ordinance of Goslar (1555), and the Marriage Ordinance of Dresden (1556), in Sehling, 1:295; Richter, 2:166; Sehling, 1:343.
126. Dieterich, Das protestantische Eherecht, 68, 102.
127. LW 45:26.

separation had to be ordered by a church court on proof of adultery, desertion, or cruelty; divorce cannot be undertaken voluntarily; and (3) despite the divorce, the sacramental bond between the parties remained intact, and thus neither party was free to remarry until the death of the estranged spouse. Once properly established, the marriage bond could not be severed, even if the parties became bitter enemies.

The Lutheran Reformers rejected this traditional doctrine of divorce with arguments from Scripture, history, and utility. Scripture teaches, the Reformers insisted, that marriage is a natural institution of the earthly kingdom, not a sacramental institution of the heavenly kingdom. The essence of marriage is the community of husband and wife in this life, not their sacramental union in the life to come.[128] For a couple to establish "a true marriage" in this earthly life, declared Martin Bucer, "God requires them to live together and be united in body and mind. . . . The proper end of marriage is . . . the communicating of all duties, both divine and human, each to the other with the utmost benevolence and affection."[129] Irreconcilable separation of the parties was tantamount to dissolution of the marriage, for the requisite benevolent communion of marriage could no longer be carried out. The traditional teaching that permanently separated couples were still bound in marriage rested on the unbiblical assumption that marriage is a binding sacrament.

Furthermore, the Reformers charged, for the church to equate divorce with judicial separation and to prohibit the divorced from remarrying has no basis in Scripture. As used in Scripture, the term *divortium* means dissolution of marriage, not simply separation. No philological evidence from biblical or early patristic times suggests otherwise. Medieval writers had improperly introduced their interpretation of the term in order to support their sacramental concept of marriage.[130] Where Scripture permits divorce, the Reformers believed, it also permits remarriage. "In the case of adultery," for example, Luther wrote, "Christ permits divorce of husband and wife so that the innocent person may remarry."[131] Other Reformers considered the sentence of divorce and the right of remarriage to be "one and the same."[132] For the divorced individual, like any single person, needed to heed God's duty to form families and to accept God's remedy against incontinence and other sexual sins. To deprive those divorced of the spiritual and physical benefits of marriage, as the medieval church had done, could not be countenanced. It was unbiblical and led to all manner of sexual sin.

128. *LW* 46:276; CR 7:487; 21:1079; Johannes Bugenhagen, *Vom Ehebruch und Weglauffen* (Wittenberg, 1539–41), folio 171; Johannes Brenz, *Wie in Eesachen vnnd den fellen so sich derhalben zutragen nach Götlichem billichem rechten Christenlich zu handeln sey* (Nuremberg: Jobst Gutknecht, 1529; Wittenberg, 1531), folio 185; Schneidewin, *De nuptiis*, 484; Konrad Mauser, *Explicatio erudita et utilis X. tituli institutionem: De nuptiis* (Jena, 1569), 335; Monner, *Tractatus duo*, 1:203.

129. Bucer, *Common Places*, 465.

130. Ibid., 416–17; *LW* 46:275–81.

131. *LW* 45:30–31.

132. Quoted by Ozment, *When Fathers Ruled*, 84.

The Reformers bolstered these biblical arguments for divorce and remarriage with arguments from history. They adduced support for their biblical exegesis from the commentaries of the church fathers. They found a wealth of precedents for laws of divorce and remarriage in the Mosaic law based on Deuteronomy 24:1–4 (permitting divorce for "uncleanness") and the many decrees of the Christian Roman emperors. These historical laws of divorce, however, were hardly commensurate with the teachings of the gospel. Christ had permitted divorce only on grounds of adultery and only as a special exception to the general command "What . . . God has joined together, let not man put asunder."[133] In 1 Corinthians 7:15 Paul had hinted further that divorce might be permitted on grounds of desertion: "If the unbelieving partner desires to separate, let it be so; in such a case the brother or sister is not bound. For God has called us to peace."[134] The laws of Moses and of the Roman Empire, however, had put marriages asunder for many other reasons besides adultery and desertion. The Mosaic law had permitted divorce for "uncleanness," indecency, and incompatibility of all kinds. In Roman law, a person could divorce a spouse who was guilty of treason or iconoclasm, who had committed one of many felonies or fraudulent acts against third parties, or who had abused, deserted, threatened, or in others ways maltreated members of their family. Divorce was also permitted if a husband wrongly accused his wife of adultery or if a wife was guilty of shameful or immoral acts (such as abortion, bigamy, or exhibitionism); or became delinquent, insolent, or impotent; or persistently refused to have sexual relations. In the later Roman Empire, divorce was even permitted by mutual consent of the parties. The innocent party was, in most instances, permitted to remarry another.[135] Such liberal laws remained in constant tension with the New Testament command that all but the unfaithful must remain indissolubly bound.

The Lutheran Reformers resolved this tension by distinguishing between moral laws designed for Christians in the heavenly kingdom and civil laws designed for all persons in the earthly kingdom. Christ's command, the Reformers taught, is an absolute moral standard for Christians. It demands of them love, patience, forgiveness, and a conciliatory spirit. It sets out what is absolutely right, what the true law would be if the earthly kingdom were free from sin and populated only by perfect Christians. Yet the earthly kingdom is fallen, and many of its sinful citizens disregard the moral law. Thus it becomes necessary for civil authorities to promulgate laws that both facilitate and protect marriage and its social functions as well as maintain peace and order in sinful society. The positive laws of the German magistrates, like those of Moses and the Roman emperors, therefore must inevitably compromise moral ideals for marriage. They must allow for divorce and remarriage.[136] "It might be advisable

133. Mark 10:2–12 RSV; Luke 16:18; Matt. 5:31–32; 19:3–9.
134. See 1 Cor. 7:15 RSV.
135. See above, chap. 1, pp. 28–29.
136. *LW* 21:94; Bucer, *Common Places*, 411; and the views of Brenz and Bugenhagen discussed by Ozment, *When Fathers Ruled*, 89; Anneliese Sprengler-Ruppenthal, "Zur Rezeption des römischen

nowadays," Luther wrote, "that certain queer, stubborn, and obstinate people, who have no capacity for toleration and are not suited for married life at all, should be permitted to get a divorce, since people are as evil as they are, any other way of governing is impossible. Frequently something must be tolerated, even though it is not a good thing to do, to prevent something even worse from happening."[137] "The reality is that some households become broken beyond repair," Bugenhagen continued. This is "an eyesore both to the church and the state" and is better removed lest "it cause further evil."[138] The law of divorce and remarriage, like other positive laws, must thus be inspired by the moral norms of Scripture as well as by pragmatic concerns of utility and good governance.

By conjoining these arguments from Scripture, utility, and history, the Reformers concluded that (1) absolute divorce with a subsequent right to marry had been instituted by Moses and Christ; (2) the expansion of divorce was a result of sin and a remedy against greater sin; and (3) God had revealed the expanded grounds for divorce in history. On this basis, the Reformers advocated a new civil law of divorce and remarriage. They specified the proper grounds for divorce and the procedures that estranged couples had to follow.

The Lutheran Reformers and legislators of Germany unanimously accepted adultery as a ground for divorce, on the stated authority of Scripture and frequently also of Roman law and early canon law.[139] Theologians such as Luther and Bugenhagen, however, advocated that the couple first be given time to resolve the matter privately. They instructed adulterers to seek forgiveness and innocent spouses to be forgiving. They further urged pastors and friends to sponsor the mending of this torn marriage in any way they could. A number of marriage ordinances repeated the Reformers' prescriptions.[140] Criminal statutes provided that punishment of the adulterer could not commence until the innocent party sued for divorce. Absent such suits, a judge could begin criminal proceedings against an adulterer only if the violation was "open, undoubted,

Rechts in Eherecht der Reformation," *Zeitschrift der Savigny-Stiftung für Rechtsgeschichte: Kanonische Abteilung* 68 (1982): 395.

137. *LW* 21:94; see also Bucer, *Common Places*, 411–12, and discussion of other reformers in Aemilius Richter, *Beiträge zur Geschichte des Ehescheidungsrecht in der evangelischen Kirche* (Aalen: Scientia Verlag, 1958), 32.

138. Bugenhagen, *Vom Ehebruch und Weglauffen*, folios miii–oiii.

139. See the numerous church ordinances and other statutes quoted and discussed by Hans Dietrich, *Evangelisches Ehescheidungsrecht nach den Bestimmungen der deutschen Kirchenordnungen des 16. Jahrhunderts* (Erlangen: A. Vollrath, 1892), 12–14, 164; Hans Hesse, *Evangelisches Ehescheidungsrecht in Deutschland* (Bonn: H. Bouvier, 1960), 31–33; Friedrich Albrecht, *Verbrechen und Strafen als Ehescheidungsgrund nach evangelischem Kirchenrecht* (Stuttgart, F. Enke, 1903), 43–46. The Church Ordinance of Lübeck (1531) and Marriage Ordinance of Württemberg (1537), drafted by Brenz, as well as the Marriage Ordinance of Pfalz (1563) and Church Ordinance of Hüttenberg (1555) cite Roman law prominently alongside Scripture in support of this ground for divorce. See Sehling, 5:356; Richter, 1:280; 2:257, 163. Several times Melanchthon and Kling refer to earlier canonical and patristic writings in their discussions of adultery. See CR 21:103 and Kling, *Matrimonialium causarum tractatus*, folio 101v. On Kling's views, see also Richter, *Beiträge zur Geschichte des Ehescheidungsrecht*, 29–30.

140. *LW* 45:32. See discussion in Ozment, *When Fathers Ruled*, 85; Hesse, *Evangelisches Ehescheidungsrecht*, 32.

and scandalous."[141] Even in such cases, the civil authorities preferred less severe penalties (not banishment or imprisonment) that would still allow the couple to rejoin. Where efforts of private reconciliation failed and continued cohabitation of the parties yielded only misery and threats to the safety of the parties and their children, the innocent spouse could sue for divorce.

Husbands and wives had equal rights to sue for divorce. Thereafter the innocent party was permitted to remarry, after a time of healing—at least a few months or a year if there was any risk of pregnancy resulting from the first marriage. The adulterer faced stern criminal sanctions scaled to the egregiousness of the offense. These ranged from fines or short imprisonment to exile or execution in the case of repeat adulterers. The call by many Reformers to execute all divorced adulterers found little acceptance among the civil authorities, though many jurisdictions, in response, stiffened their penalties for adultery.[142] Only the egregious repeat offender was subject to execution.[143]

Though a few theologians and early legislators accepted adultery as the only ground for divorce, many others defended a more expansive divorce law.[144] Desertion or abandonment was a widely accepted ground for divorce among the Reformers. A party who deserted his or her spouse and family destroyed the bond of communal love, service, and support needed for the marriage to survive and for children to be properly nourished and reared. Not every absence of a spouse, however, could be considered a form of desertion. Theologians such as Bugenhagen and jurists such as Schneidewin insisted that the abandonment be notoriously willful and malicious, a requirement that was repeated in several

141. Bambergensis Halsgericht und rechtliche Ordnung, art. 145 (1507), repeated with revisions in Constitutio Criminalis Carolina, art. 120 (1532), in *Die peinliche Gerichtsordnung Kaiser Karls V: Constitutio criminalis Carolina*, ed. Josef Kohler and Willy Scheel (repr., Aalen: Scientia Verlag, 1968), 63.

142. See, e.g., Bugenhagen, *Vom Ehebruch und Weglauffen*, folios oiii–piii.

143. See, e.g., Bucer, *Common Places*, 410–11. On the reaction of the civil authorities thereto, see Dieterich, *Das protestantische Eherecht*, 105; Harvey, "The Influence,"113; Karl Kock, *Studium Pietatis: Martin Bucer als Ethiker* (Inaug. diss., Mainz, 1960), 141; Walter Köhler, *Zuercher Ehegericht und Genfer Konsistorium*, 2 vols. (Leipzig: Verlag von M. Hensius Nachfolger, 1942), 1:109. The Bambergensis and Carolina, however, ordered "death by the sword" as criminal punishment for adultery; these statutes further provided that innocent spouses who, on discovery of the philandering parties, immediately killed one or both of them, were not subject to penalty. Such provisions, which had been part of Germanic law for centuries, were only rarely enforced by the end of the sixteenth century. Even the adulterer who was spared, however, was denied the right to remarry and was subject to severe penalty when prosecuted for subsequent acts of prostitution, homosexuality, and other sexual crimes. See Schmelzeisen, *Polizeiordnung und Privatrecht*, 53–54.

144. This was the view of, e.g., Ambrosius Blaurer and Johannes Oecolampadus, among theologians, and Schürpf, Schneidewin, Kling, and the draftsmen of the Church Ordinances of Schwabisch-Hall (1531) and of Lower Saxony (1585), among jurists. Johannes Brenz initially permitted divorce only on this ground but later expanded the grounds for divorce. Even in this later period, however, Brenz permitted remarriage only to victims of adultery and exacted ecclesiastical penalties against church members who divorced for reasons other than adultery. See Köhler, "Die Anfänge," 302; Hesse, *Evangelisches Ehescheidungsrecht*, 32–33; Albrecht, *Verbrechen und Strafen*, 14–16; Schmelzeisen, *Polizeiordnung und Privatrecht*, 61.

statutes.[145] Thus no divorce was permitted if the absent partner was serving the prince's army, engaged in study or business abroad, or was visiting a foreign place. Divorce for desertion was permitted only where the partner's absence was completely inexcusable and inequitable, left the spouse and family in grave danger, or was so unreasonably prolonged that the party had presumably died or fallen into delinquency or adultery. In such cases the deserted spouse was free to remarry. The long-lost deserter who returned was presumed guilty of foul play until proven innocent and even then could not seek to break up the new marriage.[146] If the deserter never returned, the spouse could, after a designated period of time, petition for an ex-parte divorce and for the right to marry another. No legislature accepted Luther's recommendation that a deserted party of good reputation need wait only a year before bringing such an action, but few went so far as to require the full seven to ten years stipulated at Roman law.[147] Waiting periods of three years after desertion were the statutory norm.

Quasi-desertion, the unjustifiable abstention from sexual intercourse, found limited acceptance as a ground for divorce. Luther, Brenz, Bucer, and a few jurists argued that voluntary abandonment of such an essential aspect of marriage was tantamount to abandonment of the marriage itself. Furthermore, it violated Paul's injunction in 1 Corinthians 7 that spouses honor the conjugal debt and abstain from sex only by mutual consent. Luther counseled the deprived spouse to warn the other spouse of his or her discontent and to invite the pastor or friends to speak with the spouse. If the spouse remained abstinent, he permitted the deprived spouse to sue for divorce and remarry.[148] Only a few statutes adopted this teaching.[149]

At the urging of several more liberal Reformers, most notably Martin Bucer, numerous other grounds for divorce sporadically gained acceptance in Lutheran territories. Already in the 1520s, Zurich and Basel under Ulrich Zwingli's inspiration recognized, alongside adultery and desertion, impotence, grave incompatibility, sexually incapacitating illnesses, felonies, deception, and one spouse's serious threats against the life of the other spouse as grounds for divorce.[150] By the 1550s, confessional differences between the couple, defamation of a spouse's moral character, abuse and maltreatment, conspiracies or plots against a spouse, acts of incest and bigamy, delinquent frequenting of "public games" or places

145. Bugenhagen, *Vom Ehebruch und Weglauffen*, folios oiii–piii. See Church Ordinances of Pomerania (1535) and Lippische (1538), in Richter, 1:250; 2:499; and other statutes quoted and discussed in Hesse, *Evangelisches Ehescheidungsrecht*, 33–35; Dietrich, *Evangelisches Ehescheidungsrecht*, 17–25; Schmelzeisen, *Polizeiordnung und Privatrecht*, 60–61.

146. See, e.g., the Church Ordinances of Goslar (1531) and Cellische (1545) and the Consistory Ordinance of Mecklenberg (1571), in Richter, 1:156; Sehling, 1:295; 5:239.

147. See WA TR 3, No. 4499; WA TR 5, No. 5569.

148. *LW* 45:33–34. See also Dietrich, *Evangelisches Ehescheidungsrecht*, 25–31.

149. Church Ordinances of Lippische (1538), Göttingen (1542), Mecklenberg (1552), the Württemberg Marriage Ordinance (1553), and the Consistory Ordinance of Prussia (1584), in Richter, 1:365; 2:120, 130, 466, 499.

150. Ozment, *When Fathers Ruled*, 93.

of ill repute, and acts of treason or sacrilege all came to legislative expression as grounds for divorce.[151] Though no single marriage statute in this period explicitly adopted all these grounds for divorce, a few statutes did permit divorce "on any grounds recognized by Scripture and the Roman law of Justinian."[152]

The Reformers insisted that divorce, like marriage, be a public act. Just as a couple could not form the marriage bond in secret, so they could not sever it in secret. They had to inform the community and church of their intentions and petition a civil judge to order the divorce.[153] This requirement of publicity was a formidable obstacle to divorce. Couples who publicized their intent to divorce invited not only the counsel and comfort of friends and pastors but frequently also the derision of the community and the discipline of the church. Furthermore, judges had great discretion to deny or delay petitions for divorce and to grant interim remedies short of this irreversible remedy. Particularly in conservative courts, the petitioner had a heavy burden of proof to show that the divorce was mandated by statute, that all efforts at reconciliation had proved fruitless, and that no alternative remedy was available.

SUMMARY AND CONCLUSIONS

The Lutheran Reformation introduced a new social model of marriage into the Western tradition, alongside the Catholic sacramental model. Like the Catholics, Lutherans taught that marriage was a natural, created institution subject to godly law. But unlike the Catholics, Lutherans rejected the subordination of marriage to celibacy. The person was too tempted by sinful passion to forgo marriage. The family was too vital a social institution in God's redemptive plan to be hindered. The celibate life had no superior virtue and no inherent attractiveness vis-à-vis marriage and was no prerequisite for ecclesiastical service.

The Lutheran Reformers replaced the sacramental model of marriage with a new social model. Marriage, they taught, was part of the earthly kingdom, not the heavenly kingdom. Though a holy institution of God, marriage required no prerequisite faith or purity and conferred no sanctifying grace, as did true sacraments. Rather, it had distinctive uses in the life of the individual and of

151. See statutes in Dietrich, *Evangelisches Ehescheidungsrecht*, 31; Hesse, *Evangelisches Ehescheidungsrecht*, 35; Köhler, "Die Anfänge," 303. See a contemporary catalog in Monner, *Tractatus duo*, 1:54b–59.

152. See the Church Ordinances of Hanover (1536) and Hüttenberg (1555), and the Marriage Ordinance of Pfalz (1563), quoted in Dietrich, *Evangelisches Ehescheidungsrecht*, 31–32. A similar provision is recommended by Basilius [Erasmus] Sarcerius, *Corpus juris matrimonialis: Vom Ursprung, Anfang und Herkomen des Heyligen Ehestandts* (Frankfurt am Main: P. Schmidt, 1569), folio 216.

153. See, e.g., *LW* 36:102; 45:30; 46:311. See comparable practices in Switzerland described in Thomas Max Safley, "Canon Law and Swiss Reform: Legal Theory and Practice in the Marital Courts of Zurich, Bern, Basel, and St. Gall," in Helmholz, *Canon Law in Protestant Lands*, 187.

society. It deterred prostitution, promiscuity, and other public sexual sins. It revealed to humanity its sinfulness and its need for God's marital gift. It taught love, restraint, and other public virtues and morals. All fit men and women were free to enter such unions, provided they complied with the laws of marriage formation.

As an estate of the earthly kingdom, marriage was subject to the prince, not the pope. Civil law, not canon law, was to govern marriage. Marital disputes were to be brought before civil courts, not church courts. Marriage was still subject to God's law, but this law was now to be administered by the civil authorities, who had been called as God's vice-regents to govern the earthly kingdom. Church officials were required to counsel the magistrate about God's law and to cooperate with him in publicizing and disciplining marriage. All church members, as priests, were required to counsel those who contemplated marriage and to admonish those who sought annulment or divorce. But the church no longer had legal authority over marriage.

The reforms of German marriage law introduced during the Lutheran Reformation reflected this reconceptualization of marriage. Civil marriage courts replaced church courts in numerous Lutheran territories, frequently at the instigation of the Reformers. New civil marriage statutes were promulgated, many replete with Lutheran marriage doctrine and scriptural marriage laws. Lutheran jurists and moralists throughout Germany published treatises on marriage law, affirming and embellishing the basic marriage doctrine set forth by the theologians.

This new civil law of marriage had a number of important innovations that can be traced directly to the theology and advocacy of Luther and his fellow Reformers. Because the Reformers rejected the subordination of marriage to celibacy, they rejected laws that forbade clerical and monastic marriage, that denied remarriage to those who had married a cleric or monastic, and that permitted vows of chastity to annul vows of marriage. Because they rejected the sacramental nature of marriage, the Reformers rejected impediments of crime and heresy and prohibitions against divorce in the modern sense. For them, marriage was the community of the couple in the present, not their sacramental union in the life to come. Where that community was broken, for one of a number of specific reasons (such as adultery or desertion), the innocent husband or wife could sue for divorce. Because persons by their lustful natures are in need of God's remedy of marriage, the Reformers removed numerous legal, spiritual, and consanguineous impediments to marriage not countenanced by Scripture. Because of their emphasis on the godly responsibility of the prince, the pedagogical role of the church and the family, and the priestly calling of all believers, the Reformers insisted that both marriage and divorce be public occasions, involving a number of others. The validity of marriage promises depended upon parental consent, witnesses, church consecration and registration, and priestly instruction. Couples who wanted to divorce had to announce their intentions in the church and community and petition a civil judge to dissolve the bond. In the process of marriage formation and dissolution, therefore, the couple was subject to God's law, as appropriated in the civil law, and to God's will, as revealed in the admonitions of parents, peers, and pastors.

It must be stressed, however, that the Lutheran Reformers appropriated a great deal of the medieval canon law in their formation of the civil law of marriage. Canon-law doctrines that grounded marriage in the mutual consent of the parties continued with only minor changes. Canon-law prohibitions against unnatural relations and against infringement of natural marital functions remained in effect. Canon-law impediments that protected free consent, that implemented scriptural prohibitions against marriage of relatives, and that governed the couple's physical relations were largely retained. Such canon laws were as consistent with Roman Catholic as with Lutheran concepts of marriage, and they continued largely uninterrupted.

Moreover, Lutheran jurists and judges turned readily to canon-law texts and authorities in formulating their doctrines of marriage law. Professorial and court opinions of the late sixteenth century on cases of disputed betrothals, wife abuse, incest, child custody, desertion, adultery, divorce, annulment, and the like are chock-full of citations to Gratian's *Decretum*, the Decretals, and various canonists.[154] Legal dictionary and handbook entries on marriage, prepared by Lutheran jurists, cite Catholic theological and canon-law sources with great frequency and authority.[155] Learned tracts on marriage law, prepared by Lutheran jurists, often made greater use of canon law and Roman-law authorities than the new Protestant texts.

The 1543 *Tract on Matrimonial Cases* by Melchior Kling, Luther's friend and colleague at Wittenberg, illustrates and explains this appetite for traditional canon-law forms. Several times in this tract, Kling states that he accepts the "new [Lutheran] theology of marriage." But he said: "I have generally followed the canon law in this writing, which at the time of the [Roman] Empire was used to frame opinions in matrimonial cases. For even though other laws may have been extant, which might seem more worthy and outstanding—customs and examples both predating and following the time of Moses, the law of Moses itself, the New Testament, and Roman law—these are not completely sufficient or comprehensive for our time."[156] The canon law, Kling believed, had appropriated the most valuable parts of the Old and New Testaments, Roman law, and local custom and had refined its doctrine for centuries. "Surely, we could not go back to the simple Mosaic rules of marital impediments" or "return to the pre-Mosaic

154. See, e.g., cases collected in von Beust, *Tractatus de iure connubiorum*. In the cases and commentaries, von Beust draws eclectically from Protestant, Catholic, and Roman authorities. In instances of conflict of laws, authorities are generally listed side by side, with Protestant sources generally preferred to Catholic and legal opinions preferred to theological opinions. A catalog of authorities lists more than twenty canonists, including such leading lights as Gratian, Hostiensis, Innocent III, Innocent IV, Jason de Maino, Johannes Andreae, Joannes de Imola, Panormitanus, and Paulus de Castro.

155. See sources in my *Law and Protestantism*, chaps. 2, 4.

156. Kling, *Matrimonialium causarum tractatus*.

customs of concubinage and polygamy," he reasoned. "Nor could we easily follow both the Mosaic [and] . . . New Testament laws of divorce," let alone try to
"observe the multiple causes for divorce [recognized at Christian] imperial law."
The canonists had worked through all these conflicts of law and had systematized a "Christian and equitable" source of law, which evangelicals should not,
and could not, simply cast aside. To begin on a biblical tabula rasa is "foolish,"
Kling concluded. "We should begin with tradition" and amend and emend it
as the Bible and new theological doctrines compel.[157] Kling practiced what he
preached. Though he most frequently cited the Bible, the Digest, the "doctors,"
and the "theologians" (presumably of Wittenberg), his tract is peppered throughout with references to the *Decretum*, the Decretals, and sundry canonists.[158]

These caveats of Luther's own day warn us that the reformation of marriage
law in Lutheran Germany was not so radical as the early Reformers had envisioned and as some historians have assumed. The Lutheran Reformers worked
within the Western tradition of marriage. Their new theology of marriage,
though filled with bold revisions, preserved a good deal of the teaching of the
Roman Catholic tradition. Their new civil law of marriage was heavily indebted
to the canon law that it replaced. What the Lutheran Reformers offered was a
new social model for marriage, which stood alongside the traditional sacramental model and within the Western tradition.

---

157. Ibid., prooemium, A2–A3.

158. In this 44-folio page tract (ibid.), Kling cites Hostiensis 14 times, Panormitanus 31 times,
and Johannes Andreae 6 times. Though this work was taken as authoritative in Lutheran circles,
there is not one direct citation to any Lutheran theologian or jurist.

Chapter 6

Marriage as Covenant in the Calvinist Tradition

The theology and law of marriage developed in the Lutheran Reformation provided a paradigm for the Protestant tradition. The Lutheran Reformers defined the principal theological differences with the medieval Catholic tradition and drafted many of the enduring provisions of Protestant marriage law. Lutheran theological and legal tracts on marriage and family life enjoyed such wide circulation and authority in early modern Europe that one exuberant authority wrote: "All that the Reformation offered to the Western tradition of the family was born in Wittenberg."[1]

If Wittenberg was the Bethlehem of Protestant marriage law, Geneva was the Nazareth. This small independent city, newly converted to the Protestant cause in 1536, provided an ideal environment for the slow maturation of a distinctive law and theology of marriage that would come to dominate a good deal of the Protestant world in subsequent centuries. The leader of the Genevan reformation was John Calvin, an exiled French jurist and theologian, who joined the Protestant cause in the early 1530s. During his Genevan tenure from 1536 to

---

1. Rudolf Sohm, *Das Recht der Eheschliessung aus dem deutschen und kanonischen Recht geschichtlich entwickelt* (1875; repr. Aalen: Scientia Verlag, 1966), 266.

1538, and again from 1541 until his death in 1564, Calvin led a sweeping reformation of Genevan marriage and family life, alongside many other religious, political, and legal institutions. So profound and enduring was his influence on the Western legal tradition that, two centuries later, even a religious skeptic like Jean-Jacques Rousseau had only praise for his compatriot: "Those who consider Calvin only as a theologian fail to recognize the breadth of his genius. The editing of our wise laws, in which he had a large share, does him as much credit as his *Institutes [of the Christian Religion]*. . . . So long as the love of country and liberty is not extinct among us, the memory of this great man will be held in reverence."[2]

Calvin constructed a comprehensive new theology and jurisprudence that made marital formation and dissolution, children's nurture and welfare, family cohesion and support, and sexual sin and crime essential concerns for both church and state. Working with other jurists and theologians, Calvin drew the consistory and council of Geneva into a creative new alliance to govern sex, marriage, and family life. Together these authorities outlawed monasticism and mandatory clerical celibacy and encouraged marriage for all fit adults. They set clear guidelines for courtship and engagement. They mandated parental consent, peer witness, church consecration, and state registration for valid marriage. They radically reconfigured weddings and wedding feasts. They reformed marital property and inheritance, marital consent and impediments. They created new rights and duties for wives within the bedroom and for children within the household. They streamlined the grounds and procedures for annulment. They introduced fault-based divorce for both husbands and wives on grounds of adultery and desertion. They encouraged the remarriage of the divorced and widowed. They punished rape, fornication, prostitution, sodomy, and other sexual felonies with startling new severity. They put firm new restrictions on dancing, sumptuousness, ribaldry, and obscenity. They put new stock in catechesis and education and created new schools, curricula, and teaching aids. They provided new sanctuary for illegitimate, abandoned, and abused children. They created new protections for abused wives and impoverished widows. Many of these reforms of sixteenth-century Geneva were echoed and elaborated in numerous Calvinist communities, on both sides of the Atlantic, and a good number of these reforms found their way into modern civil law and common law alike.[3]

Calvin's reformation of marriage law and theology fell into two distinct phases. In the first half of his career, Calvin the *jurist* was primarily at work.

2. *Du contrat social* (1762), bk. 2, chap. 7n., reprinted in Jean-Jacques Rousseau, *The Social Contract and the Discourse on the Origin of Inequality*, ed. Lester G. Crocker (New York: Washington Square Press, 1967), 44n.

3. This is the main thesis of John Witte Jr. and Robert M. Kingdon, *Sex, Marriage, and Family in John Calvin's Geneva*, 2 vols. (Grand Rapids: Wm. B. Eerdmans Publishing Co., 2005–12) (hereafter, *SMF*). These two volumes provide detailed analysis and critical editions of hundreds of relevant materials on the reformation of marital formation, maintenance, and dissolution in Calvin's Geneva—including a large number of consistory court records. Though I sampled some of the court cases in the first edition of this volume, I have omitted them in this new edition because space is limited and other chapters herein omit court cases as well.

Content to repeat theological commonplaces on marriage drawn from Lutheran and other Protestant Reformers, he directed most of his energy to the establishment of a new marriage law and marriage liturgy for Geneva. A comprehensive Marriage Ordinance of 1546, together with several other statutes, brought old canon-law rules and new civil-law reforms into an impressive new synthesis. A Marriage Liturgy of 1545 elaborated the rules and rites of mandatory church weddings. The Ecclesiastical Ordinances of 1541 and 1547 brought the council and consistory into an imposing new alliance for the enforcement of these laws.

When these early legal and liturgical reforms met with widespread resistance in Geneva in the early 1550s, Calvin the *theologian* went to work. In a long series of letters, sermons, and biblical commentaries, Calvin laid out a covenant theology of marriage and family life that served to integrate and rationalize much of the new legal structure that he and his colleagues had built. This covenantal understanding of marriage eventually came to dominate Calvinist communities, not only in and around Geneva, but eventually in the widely dispersed Reformed communities of France, England, Scotland, the Netherlands, and their North American colonies.

THE CASE OF THE FRENCH NOBLEWOMAN

A 1552 case before the Geneva consistory provides a good opening view of this new law and theology of marriage and the tensions that lingered between these two normative systems in Calvin's mind. A "certain noblewoman from Paris," as she anonymously identified herself, sent a long letter to the consistory on June 24, 1552.[4] The noblewoman's choice of anonymity was deliberate, for she wrote to complain bitterly of her husband's "idolatry and persecution of Christians" and to inquire whether "the law of marriage compels her to live with her husband, or whether the Gospel permits her to leave him and to seek liberty [in Geneva]." The prevailing civil law of Geneva gave husband and wife alike an equal right to sue for divorce on proof of adequate cause—a procedural equality for which Geneva had already become quite famous. Thus, if she moved to Geneva, this noblewoman could easily press an ex-parte case against her husband for divorce. The prevailing popular stigma against divorce, however, rendered such suits very dangerous for a woman, particularly this one. By leaving her husband and homeland, she would at minimum put her liberty and property at risk. By filing a divorce suit against her husband, she would likely imperil her own life and limb as well.

Ten years earlier, this noblewoman had converted from Catholicism to the Protestant cause—contrary to her husband's confession and command. At first

4. "Letter d'une dame inconnue à la Compagnie des Pasteurs. De France, 24 juin 1555," in *Registres de la compagnie des pasteurs de Genève au temps de Calvin*, ed. Jean-Francois Bergier and Robert M. Kingdon (Geneva: Droz, 1964), 1:138–40 (hereafter, *RCP*). The editors speculate that the woman was Madame de Cany, with whom Calvin had corresponded several times before.

he had indulged her somewhat, she writes, "though he held her all the time to the papal idolatry, forcing her to go to Mass and to undertake journeys and pilgrimages and make vows to the saints." Six years later, however, he and his relatives began a ruthless campaign against her and her Protestant coreligionists. "Some he throws into prison; others he charge[s] before the judge and nobility." "He forbids [his wife] to speak to any of them." He censors her letters, shadows her movements, threatens her servants with "the fire" not to conspire in her heresy. He forbids her to perform charity or to "sing Psalms or hymns or anything else in the praise of the Lord." He forces her continued compliance with "papal idolatry." If she disobeys him, he "threatens to throw her into the water or some other secret death"—suggesting that he might "amuse himself by having her burned or killing her slowly in a permanent dungeon." Till now, she has suffered "in becoming Christian silence," she writes, indicating that she fears relating any more in her letter lest her husband find her out. She assures Calvin and his colleagues, however, that she has endured "grievous and severe assaults [and] . . . every kind of affliction of both spirit and body." She urges the Genevan consistory "to meet together to formulate a reply to her sad request so that she may have a resolution of her case, for she has no desire to live any longer in such idolatry."

Calvin's opinion, on behalf of the "unanimous" Geneva consistory, vacillated between pastoral gentleness and biblical legalism.[5] Calvin the pastor opened with a few lines of "pity and compassion" for the noblewoman's "most severe and cruel servitude" suffered on account of "her true and pure religion." "We bear in mind the perplexity and anguish in which she must be,. . . praying God that it would please Him to give her relief."

Calvin the jurist, however, had little relief to give her. "Since she has asked for our counsel, regarding what is permissible," he wrote, "our duty is to respond, purely and simply, on the basis of what God reveals to us in his Word, closing our eyes to all else." The new Genevan law followed the strict biblical view that divorce is permitted only on grounds of adultery (and in rare cases, malicious desertion). Cruelty and abuse were insufficient grounds for divorce, and "voluntary divorce" by either or both parties was out of the question. A marital couple's differences in religion were also an insufficient ground for divorce. To the contrary, said Calvin, citing 1 Corinthians 7:13 and 1 Peter 3:1, "a believing party cannot, of his or her own free will, divorce the unbeliever, . . . but should endure bravely and persevere with constancy . . . and make every effort to lead her partner into salvation." It would be an irony, said Calvin, "to abrogate the order of nature" in marriage for the sake of one form of Christianity over another. The parties must continue to live together, "and no matter how great his obstinacy

---

5. "Réponse de la Compagnie à la lettre précédente Genève, 22 juillet 1552," in ibid., 140–41, reprinted from *Ioannis Calvini opera quae supersunt omnia*, ed. G. Baum et al. (Brunswick: C. A. Schwetschke & Filium, 1892), 10:239–41 (hereafter *CO*). Though the opinion is unsigned, it bears Calvin's unmistakable tone and content.

might be, she must not let herself be diverted from the faith, but must affirm it with constancy and steadfastness, whatever the danger."

A little later in his opinion, Calvin the pastor softened this interpretation and seemed to be charting a road to relief. "If the party should be persecuted to the extent that she is in danger of denying her faith" or imperiling her life, he wrote, "then she is justified in fleeing." A spouse need not put soul and body in mortal jeopardy for the sake of the marriage, but may leave when faced with such a dire threat. "This does not constitute a voluntary divorce," said Calvin. The apostasy and cruelty together are tantamount to dissolution of the marriage itself, and an innocent party need not endure them. Given what the noblewoman had described in her letter—"grievous and severe assaults and every kind of affliction of both spirit and body"—this seemed to provide a rationale for finding in her favor.

Calvin the jurist had the final word in the case, and he found against her. His judgment rested on a rather technical legal point of notice, which he read into the same passages of 1 Corinthians 7:13 and 1 Peter 3:1, already cited. Contrary to what Scripture requires, Calvin concluded, the noblewoman had not given adequate notice to her husband of her religious dissatisfaction. "What she says in her letter is that she is only silent and dissimulates. When pressed to defile herself with idolatry, she yields and complies. This being so, she has no excuse for leaving her husband, without having made a more adequate declaration of her faith"—although, as Calvin recognized, she would doubtless have to endure "greater compulsion" as a consequence of such declaration. "If thereafter," Calvin concluded, "she finds herself in grave peril, with her husband persecuting her to death, she may avail herself of the liberty which our Saviour grants to His followers for escaping the fury of wolves."

This was a quite typical petition and a quite typical response.[6] With the deaths of Ulrich Zwingli, Martin Luther, and Martin Bucer by the early 1550s, Calvin had emerged alongside Philipp Melanchthon as the leading Protestant authority on the Continent. Private litigants and political magistrates from throughout Europe sought his counsel on sundry questions of marriage theology and law. A number of parties, particularly women, moved to Geneva to avail themselves of its more egalitarian marriage procedures and the possibilities of finding relief from oppressive homes and laws. Many of these parties, while not always so desperate in their plight as this French noblewoman, often raised

6. See comparable sentiments in Calvin's letters in *CO* 10/1:255–58, 264–66; 17:539. See discussion in Charmarie J. Blaisdell, "Calvin's Letters to Women: The Courting of Ladies in High Places," *Sixteenth Century Journal* 13, no. 3 (1982): 67–84; Nancy L. Roelker, "The Appeal of Calvinism to French Noblewomen in the Sixteenth Century," *Journal of Interdisciplinary Studies* 2 (1970–71): 405. For a list of these letters, see Charmarie J. Blaisdell, "Calvin's and Loyola's Letters to Women: Politics and Spiritual Counsel in the Sixteenth Century," in *Calviniana: Ideas and Influence of Jean Calvin*, ed. Robert V. Schnucker (Kirksville, MO: Sixteenth Century Journal Publishers, 1988), 235, 248–50.

the same kind of basic issue—how to balance biblical and civil laws on marriage and divorce, formal and equitable interpretations of the law, church and state responsibilities in the formation, maintenance, and dissolution of marriage.

Calvin's own vacillations in this case—between theological principles and civil precepts, pastoral equity and legal formality—capture in miniature the central tension of his broader reformation of marriage in Geneva. In 1552, Calvin was in the interim between the first phase of his reformation of marriage, which was focused on law, and the second phase of his reformation, which blended law more fully with theology. As he moved from his first to his second phase, Calvin often tempered his earlier legalism, even while confirming most of his laws. On questions of spousal oppression and apostasy, Calvin remained firm in his judgment not to grant a divorce unless the soul and body of the innocent spouse were truly imperiled.[7] This was consistent with (and perhaps even caused by) his judgment not to countenance revolt against oppressive and apostate magistrates unless the soul and body of the citizen were truly imperiled. On many other marital questions, Calvin's early legal views underwent considerable theological tailoring and tempering as he moved into the second phase of his career. It is to those two phases of his career in marital reformation that we now turn.

CALVIN'S EARLY THEOLOGY OF MARRIAGE

Calvin's first formulations on marriage drew heavily on the views of Luther, Melanchthon, Bucer, and Bullinger, whom we encountered in the last chapter. He also drew on Guillaume Farel, who had pioneered the reformation in Geneva. Calvin's first edition of his *Institutes of the Christian Religion* (1536) repeated, with only modest embellishment, the familiar Protestant attack on the prevailing Catholic theology of marriage. Like the Lutheran Reformers before him, Calvin grounded his views in the theory of the two kingdoms:

> There is a twofold government in man. One aspect is spiritual, whereby the conscience is instructed in piety and in reverencing God; the second is political, whereby man is educated for the duties of humanity and civil life that must be maintained among men. These are usually called the "spiritual" and the "temporal" kingdoms (not improper terms) by which is meant that the former sort of regime pertains to the life of the soul, while the latter has to do with the concerns of the present life—not only with food and clothing but [also] with laying down laws whereby a man

7. On Calvin's general views of civil disobedience, see sources in John Witte Jr., *The Reformation of Rights: Law, Religion, and Human Rights in Early Modern Calvinism* (Cambridge: Cambridge University Press, 2007), chaps. 1–2. On the analogy between marital and civic relations, see *CO* 29:549, 636–38, with discussion in Josef Bohatec, *Calvins Lehre von Staat und Kirche: Mit besonderer Berücksichtigung des Organismusgedankens* (Aalen: Scientia Verlag, 1968), 652–53.

may live his life among other men honorably and temperately. For the former resides in the mind within, while the latter regulates only outward behavior.[8]

Marriage, family, and sexuality are matters of the earthly kingdom alone, Calvin believed. Marriage is "a good and holy ordinance of God just like farming, building, cobbling, and barbering." Marriage serves to produce children, to remedy incontinence, and to promote "love between husband and wife."[9] Its morals and mores are subject to the laws of God, which are written on the "tablet" of conscience, rewritten in the pages of Scripture, and distilled in the Ten Commandments. Marriage, however, is not a sacrament of the heavenly kingdom. Though it symbolizes the bond between Christ and his church, Yahweh and his chosen people, marriage confirms no divine promise and confers no sanctifying grace, as do true sacraments. Though it is a righteous mode of Christian living in the earthly kingdom, it has no bearing on one's salvation or eternal standing.[10]

Moreover, celibacy is not an obligation of the earthly kingdom. The celibate life is a "special gift of God," commended only to those "rare persons" who are continent by nature. "It is the hypocrisy of demons to command celibacy" and "giddy levity" to exult the celibate state over the marital estate, Calvin charged. For the church to command celibacy is to "contend against God" and to spurn his gracious "remedy" for lust. For the church to subordinate marriage to celibacy is to commit the spiritual "arrogance" of supplanting God's ordinance with a human tradition.[11] Two decades earlier, such teachings were revolutionary. By the late 1530s, they were familiar Protestant refrains.

In his 1536 *Institutes*, Calvin also took up, with more originality, the Protestant attack on the Catholic canon law of marriage that he had learned as a law student in France. He issued a lengthy and bitter broadside against the arguments from Scripture, tradition, and the sacraments that the Catholic Church had adduced to support its ecclesiastical jurisdiction. "The power to frame laws was both unknown to the apostles, and many times denied the ministers of the church by God's Word," he insisted. "It is not a church which, passing the bounds of God's Word, wantons and disports itself to frame new laws and dream up new things" for spiritual life. The Bible alone is a sufficient guide for a person's Christian walk and a church's institutional life.[12] For the church to impose new laws upon its own members is to obstruct the simple

8. John Calvin, *Institution of the Christian Religion*, trans. Ford Lewis Battles (Atlanta: John Knox Press, 1975), 6.13 (hereafter *Inst.* 1536); see also ibid., 6.14; 6.35; and discussion in David Van Drunen, *Natural Law and the Two Kingdoms: A Study in the Development of Reformed Social Thought* (Grand Rapids: Wm. B. Eerdmans Publishing Co., 2010), 67–118.

9. *Inst.* 1536, 1.19; 1.22.

10. Ibid., 6.13.

11. Ibid., 5.68–71; 6.25.

12. Ibid., 6.17; 6.20.

law and liberty of the gospel. For the church to impose its own laws upon civil society is to obscure its essential pastoral, prophetic, and pedagogical callings. To be sure, Calvin wrote, quoting the apostle Paul, "all things [must] be done decently and in order" (1 Cor. 14:40). Certain rules and structures "are necessary for internal discipline [and] the maintenance of peace, honesty, and good order in the assembly of Christians." But the church has no authority to impose laws "upon consciences in those matters in which they have been freed by Christ"—in the so-called adiaphora, the external and discretionary things of life that do not conduce to salvation. Marriage and family life are among these adiaphora. Laws governing such matters lie within the province of the state, not the church.[13]

Particularly the Catholic Church's sacramental theology of marriage, Calvin argued, has led all Christendom down a "long legal trail of errors, lies, frauds, and misdeeds." Calvin singled out for special critique the familiar targets of earlier Protestant attacks: the Catholic Church's "usurpation" of marital jurisdiction from secular judges, its condonation of secret marriages of minors without parental consent, its restrictions on the seasons for engagement, its long roll of marital impediments beyond "the law of nations and of Moses," its easy dispensations from marital rules for the propertied and the powerful, its prohibitions against divorce and remarriage. "Papal tyranny" and "iniquitous laws," he wrote, have "so confused matrimonial cases . . . that it is necessary to review the controversies that often ensue therefrom in light of the Word of God" and "to make certain new ordinances by which [marriage] may be governed."[14]

GENEVA'S NEW LAWS ON MARRIAGE

The 1541 Ecclesiastical Ordinances and New Consistory

The Council of Geneva soon made "certain new ordinances" for the governance of marriage. The 1541 Ecclesiastical Ordinances of Geneva, drafted by Calvin and revised by the city councils, set out the church's new role in the governance of private and public life in Geneva. The church's four offices of pastors, teachers, elders, and deacons were to propound a purely biblical ethic of marriage and family life among its members—freed from the distortions of the canon law and free from the directions of a central episcopacy. Pastors were to expound relevant biblical passages from the pulpit. Teachers were to explain them more simply to students and catechumens. Elders were to discipline sexual license and marital discord among church members. Deacons were to aid orphans, widows, and the sexually abused. All church leaders were to set an example of sexual modesty, chastity, and integrity in their lives. Any pastor, the ordinance ordered, caught

13. Ibid., dedicatory epistle; and 6.4; 6.14–32.
14. Ibid., 5.71; 6.25; 6.31. See also CO 10/1:5, 13.

in fornication, "dissolute dancing," or sexual "scandal" was to be summarily dismissed from office and subject to separate criminal prosecution.[15]

The 1541 Ecclesiastical Ordinances established a consistory to work hand in hand with the Small Council of Geneva in the governance of sex, marriage, and family life.[16] The Small Council, which was the chief magisterial body of the city, operated with several standing specialty committees for finance, public works, charity, and the like.[17] The consistory was initially established as a new standing committee to aid the Small Council in its governance of the moral, religious, sexual, and familial life of the city. The presiding officer of the consistory was one of the four leading syndics of the Small Council. The members of the consistory included both laity and clergy, divided into two companies: (1) a Company of Elders (10–12 citizens elected from the three other representative city councils); and (2) a Company of Pastors (composed of up to 12 pastors drawn from local churches). The "Moderator" of the Company of Pastors was John Calvin, who by his ministerial office and by his legal learning exerted a formidable influence on the consistory's deliberations.

The consistory was designed to control the behavior of the entire population, to see to it that all Genevans not only accepted the new Reformed teachings set out in sermons and statutes but also lived them in their daily lives. It penetrated life in almost all of its variety in sixteenth-century Geneva. Some of the consistory's work was remarkably officious—intruding on the intimacies of bed and board with unusual alacrity. Some of its work was also remarkably solicitous—catering to the needs of the innocent, needy, and abused with unusual efficiency.

Well over half of the hundreds of cases heard by the consistory each year concerned issues of sex, marriage, and family.[18] Adultery and fornication, disputed engagements and weddings, and family quarrels were by far the most common of such cases. But intricate and tender issues concerning incest, polygamy, rape, sodomy, buggery, prostitution, voyeurism, public bathing, abortion, child neglect, child abuse, baptismal disputes, education disputes, wife abuse, mistreatment of maids, family poverty, embezzlement of family property, sickness, divorce, marital property disputes, inheritance, and others all crowded onto the

15. "Les Ordonnances ecclesiastiques de l'Église de Genève (1541)," in *RCP* 1:1. A slightly altered version appears in *Les sources du droit du canton de Genève*, ed. Émile Rivoire and Victor van Berchem, 4 vols. (Aarau: R. Sauerländer, 1927–35), vol. 2, item no. 794 (hereafter, *SD*). A truncated version was issued in 1547 for rural areas and is reprinted in *CO* 10/1:51–58.

16. Quote from Walter Köhler, *Zürcher Ehegericht und Genfer Konsistorium*, 2 vols. (Leipzig: M. Heinsius Nachfolger, 1942), 188. See studies in Cornelia Seeger, *Nullité de mariage, divorce et séparation de corps a Genève, au temps de Calvin: Fondements doctrinaux, loi et jurisprudence* (Lausanne: Méta-Editions, 1989), 199–304; Robert M. Kingdon, *Adultery and Divorce in Calvin's Geneva* (Cambridge, MA, and London: Harvard University Press, 1995), 7–30; E. William Monter, *Studies in Genevan Government (1536–1605)* (Geneva: Droz, 1964), 57–83.

17. *SMF*, 1:62–93.

18. Ibid. esp. 1:75–76, with tables showing how these issues were involved in 182 of the 309 cases heard by the Consistory in 1546; 253 of the 390 cases heard in 1552; and 323 of the 566 cases heard in 1557.

consistory's docket as well. Some of these cases were very intricate; a few required intense evidentiary investigation and legal disputation that went on for years.

Cases came before the consistory in a variety of ways. Sometimes they came on the initiative of an individual who sought relief. A jilted fiancée who wanted to have her engagement contract enforced or her dowry returned. A man who claimed his wife was cheating on him and wanted a divorce. A woman who limped into court with blackened eyes and broken teeth, asking for protection from her abusive husband. A child whose parents threatened to disinherit him unless he married a woman he did not want. In these cases, the consistory acted as a mediator, seeking to resolve the dispute amicably among the parties and referring suspected criminal activity like battery, adultery, and embezzlement to the city council for criminal investigation and possible prosecution.

Other cases began on the initiative of a government official, minister, or elder. Sometimes they alerted the Consistory to a serious need like poverty, sickness, unemployment, loneliness, neglect, or some comparable need that the consistory could address. More often, the complaint was about some moral irregularity, such as nonattendance or disruptiveness at worship services or failure to pay tithes; suspicion of polygamy, concubinage, or prostitution; public drunkenness, mixed public bathing, or nonmarital cohabitation; wild or blasphemous songs, obscene speech, plays, or publications; a raucous party or wedding featuring dancing and debauchery. Occasionally more serious offenses like rape, battery, sodomy, kidnapping, mayhem, torture, or homicide were also reported, though most of these cases went directly to the city council.

In all of these cases, the consistory served more as a grand jury and preliminary hearings court. The consistory had wide subpoena power to summon and investigate parties, witnesses, and documents. It would compile a detailed record and then reach a decision. Roughly half the cases each year were disposed of by use of spiritual sanctions alone: a private confession followed by a "remonstrance," a public confession or reparation before the congregation, a temporary ban from communion to induce remorse and confession. If the consistory found an individual to be guilty of a particularly serious offense or to be unduly recalcitrant or resistant to confession and reparation, they would send that person to the city council for criminal punishment or civil redress. In many of these cases, particularly the complicated ones, Calvin's legal skills shone through. His advice usually carried the consistory, and he was usually tapped to issue the remonstrances, to draft the complex orders, to write *consilia* for further guidance, or to report on serious legal cases to the city council.

The 1541 Ecclesiastical Ordinances and later ordinances, too, explicitly barred the consistory from exercising any formal jurisdiction over marriage—any power to make and enforce civil or criminal laws. The consistory could administer only spiritual sanctions of admonition, catechization, or public confession to conduct its affairs—a spiritual arsenal supplemented in the 1550s, after a long fight, with the power of excommunication. Cases or issues that required legal actions or orders concerning property, fines, corporal punishment, or imprisonment were referred to the city council for disposition. In such instances, the consistory's findings of fact and recommendations of legal action were probative but not binding on the council.

Critics of the day saw little distinction between this new Protestant consistory and the old Catholic Church courts that had enjoyed plenary jurisdiction over marital matters in Geneva until the Reformation. The Ecclesiastical Ordinances, however, sought to safeguard against such a "reversion" by appointing to the consistory both lay and ministerial officers, led by a powerful lay syndic, and by expressly curtailing the consistory's legal power: "Ministers have no civil jurisdiction and wield only the spiritual sword of the Word of God, as St. Paul commands them," the ordinance reads. "Disputes in marital cases are not spiritual matters but are mixed up with politics, and must remain a matter for the magistracy." "There must be no derogation by the consistory from the authority of the civil council or magistracy; the civil power must proceed unhindered."[19]

The civil power must not proceed unguided, however. Clear and comprehensive rules are "the sinews of the commonwealth [and] the souls of the civil power," Calvin believed. Such rules were especially critical for governing the tender subjects of sex, marriage, and family life.[20] Since the 1480s, the Genevan authorities had already supplemented a good deal of the medieval canon law of crimes with its own criminal prohibitions against sexual sins punishable by secular authorities: prostitution, adultery, fornication, rape, incest, bigamy, sodomy, bestiality, and the like.[21] These criminal laws were tightened and amended, in part at Calvin's urging, in the early 1540s.[22] But Geneva still lacked a civil law of marriage to replace the canon law of marriage that the city had formally rejected in 1536.

The 1546 Marriage Ordinance

A new ordinance on marriage was soon in place in Geneva. Calvin and four syndics of the city prepared a detailed Marriage Ordinance in 1545. This draft was slightly amended the next year, and that 1546 version circulated widely thereafter in Geneva and in surrounding towns.[23] Though not formally enacted until 1561, this 1546 draft Marriage Ordinance from the start guided the council and consistory. It provides a convenient overview of most of the reforms that

19. *RCP*, 1:9, 13.
20. *Inst.* 1536, 6.47, quoting in part from Cicero's *Laws*.
21. See the statutes of 1481–1536 collected in *SD*, vol. 2, item nos. 290, 294, 297, 300, 302, 345, 373, 398, 405, 420, 447, 485, 496, 510, 524, 562, 580.
22. See statutes of 1539–44 in *SD*, vol. 2, item nos. 756, 757, 775, 786, 795, 813. What survives of Calvin's efforts to pass a criminal code for Geneva (as well as ordinances on civil procedure, evidence, taxation, inheritance, contracts, and administrative law) is in *CO* 10/1:125–46. See discussion in Josef Bohatec, *Calvin und das Recht*, 2nd ed. (repr., Aalen: Scientia Verlag, 1991), 209–79.
23. *SMF*, 1:51–61, adapting translations of *RCP*, 1:30–38. For the drafting history of this ordinance, see *SMF*, 1:40–41.

Calvin and his Genevan colleagues introduced into the law of marital formation, maintenance, and dissolution.

Like the medieval canonists, Calvin built the Marriage Ordinance on the principle of freedom of marital contract. Marriage depended for its validity on the mutual consent of both the man and the woman; absent proof of free consent by both parties, there was no marriage. Calvin repeatedly defended this principle in his later commentaries and sermons. "While all contracts ought to be voluntary, freedom ought to prevail especially in marriage, so that no one may pledge his faith against his will."[24] "God considers that compulsory and forced marriages never come to a good end. . . . If the husband and the wife are not in mutual agreement and do not love each other, this is a profanation of marriage, and not a marriage at all, properly speaking. For the will is the principal bond."[25] When a woman wishes to marry, she must thus not "be thrust into it reluctantly or compelled to marry against her will, but left to her own free choice."[26] "When a man is going to marry and he takes a wife, let him take her of his own free will, knowing that where there is not a true and pure love, there is nothing but disorder, and one can expect no grace from God."[27] Dozens of such sentiments scattered throughout Calvin's writings attest to this principle of freedom of marital contract.[28]

Also like the medieval canonists, Calvin distinguished between contracts of engagement and contracts of marriage—or engagements and espousals, as he called them, following the tradition. Engagements were future promises to be married. Marriages were present promises to be married. But, unlike the medieval canonists, Calvin removed the need for the parties to use specific formulaic words: any clear indication of intent to marry would do. He softened the distinction and shortened the duration between engagements and marriages. He insisted that these contracts be both public and private in nature.[29] And although he recognized legitimate conditions to engagements, he made engagement contracts harder to break. This induced couples to spend more time courting and getting to know each other,[30] before taking the formal step of entering an engagement contract.

Because the consent of the couple was the essence of the engagement contract, Calvin took pains to secure it in the 1546 Ordinance. Engagement promises had to made "simply," "unconditionally," and "honorably in the fear of God." Such engagements were to be initiated by "a sober proposal" from the

24. Comm. Josh. 15:14; for English translations, which I have revised in part on review of the original French or Latin texts in CO, see *Calvin's Commentaries*, 47 vols. (Edinburgh: Oliver & Boyd, 1843–59).

25. Serm. Deut. 25:5–12; see Calvin's *Sermons sur la Genèse*, ed. Max Engammare, 2 vols. (Neukirchen-Vluyn: Neukirchener Verlag, 2000).

26. Comm. Gen. 24:57.

27. Serm. Deut. 25:5–12.

28. *SMF*, 1:120–30.

29. *SMF*, 1:119–63.

30. *SMF*, 1:94–118.

man, accepted by the woman, and witnessed by at least two persons of "good reputation." Engagements made in secret, qualified with onerous conditions, or procured by coercion were automatically annulled—and the couple themselves, and any accomplices in their wrongdoing, could face punishment. Engagements procured through trickery or "surprise," or made "frivolously, as when merely touching glasses when drinking together," could be annulled on petition by either party. Engagement promises extracted by or from minor children were presumptively invalid, though children could confirm them upon reaching majority. Engagements involving a newcomer to the city were not valid until the parties produced proof of the newcomer's integrity of character and eligibility for marriage. Absent such proof, the couple had to wait a year before they could marry.[31] In the next decades the consistory made firm and frequent application of all these rules.[32]

The consent of the couple's parents, or their guardians, was also vital to the validity of the engagement. The consent of fathers was the more critical; maternal consent was required only when fathers were absent and would be respected only if (male) relatives would concur in her views. In the absence of both parents, guardians would give their consent, again with priority for the male voice. Minor children—men under twenty, women under eighteen—who became engaged to be married without such parental consent could have their engagements unilaterally annulled by either set of parents or guardians. Adult or emancipated children could proceed without their parents' consent, though "it is more fitting that they should always let themselves be governed by the advice of their fathers." The ordinance made clear that parental consent was a supplement to, not a substitute for, the consent of the couple themselves. Parents were prohibited, on pain of imprisonment, from coercing their children into unwanted engagements or marriages or withholding their consent or payment of dowry until the child chose a favorite partner. They were further prevented from forcing youngsters into marriage before they were mature enough to consent to and participate safely in the institution. Minor children, "observing a modest and reverend spirit," could refuse to follow their parents' insistence on an unwanted partner or a premature engagement. Other children, confronting a "negligent or excessively strict" father, could "have him compelled to give a dowry" in support of their marriage.[33]

The consent of the broader state and church community also played a part in the engagements. Betrothed couples were to register with a local civil magistrate, who would post notices of their pending nuptials and furnish the couple with a signed marriage certificate. Couples were to file this registration thereafter with a local church, whose pastor was to announce their banns from the pulpit on three successive Sundays before the wedding. Such widespread notice was an open

31. *SD*, vol. 2, item 732.
32. *SMF*, 1:119–63, 202–19.
33. *SMF*, 1:164–201.

invitation for fellow parishioners and citizens alike to approve of the match or to voice their objections. Any objections to the engagement could be raised at this point. But all such objections, before the wedding service, had to be voiced privately to the consistory and only by citizens or by persons of good reputation. Such precautions helped to avoid the prospect of "defamation or injustice," particularly "to an honorable girl." Those who objected in an untimely or improper manner could be sued for defamation by the couple or their parents. A final call for objections to the marriage came during the wedding liturgy.[34]

While the consistory was given wide discretion to review these objections, the strong presumption was that engagement contracts, once properly made, could not be broken. Objections that raised formal impediments, however, required closer scrutiny and sometimes could result in orders of annulment or at least delay of the wedding. The impediments that came to prevail in Reformation Geneva fell into three clusters.

First, Calvin and his colleagues recognized three impediments of *capacity to contract marriage*: the impediment of infancy or impuberty, which precluded children under the age of puberty (roughly 14 for girls, 16 for boys) from contracting marriage even if their parents consented; the impediment of mental inability, which precluded marriage to those suffering from insanity or comparably chronic mental inability; and the impediment of polygamy or precontract, which precluded an already engaged or married person from engaging or marrying another. These three impediments of capacity were serious business. They could be pled by anyone at any time. They could be used to annul both engagements and fully consummated marriages. And the impediment of precontract could lead to charges of polygamy, a serious crime if done intentionally.[35]

Second, the Reformers recognized four impediments of *quality or fitness for marriage*: the lack of presumed virginity; the presence of a contagious disease; the incidence of sexual incapacity or dysfunction; and more controversially wide disparity of age between the man and the woman. These four impediments addressed the physical qualities of the parties to enter marriage, regardless of their legal capacities. They were serious business, too. At least the first three of these impediments of quality could be pled by the fit party to annul both an engagement and a newly contracted marriage. The fourth impediment, wide disparity of age, could annul at least an engagement contact, though Calvin failed in his repeated efforts to make this an absolute impediment to both an engagement and marriage contract.[36]

Third, the Reformers recognized a number of incest impediments, that is, blood or family ties between the two parties that rendered their engagement or marriage incestuous. Even if the parties were of proper age and mental ability to enter contracts and even if they had the requisite physical qualities to enter

34. *SMF*, 1:414–80.
35. *SMF*, 1:203–61.
36. *SMF*, 1:262–309.

marriage in general, their blood or familial ties prohibited them from marrying each other. Engagements or marriages contracted innocently yet in violation of these incest impediments were dissolved even if the parties objected. Those contracted knowingly could trigger severe criminal punishments. Though Calvin spent a great deal of time sifting through the biblical, classical, and natural law sources on incest, he ultimately settled on virtually all the same impediments of consanguinity and affinity as other Protestants of that period had come to recognize.[37]

The 1546 Marriage Ordinance did not recognize the canon-law impediments that prohibited interreligious marriage. Marriage outside the faith was imprudent, even foolish, Calvin and his colleagues argued, but it was not formally prohibited. Neither engagements nor marriages between parties of different faiths could be annulled on that ground alone. Nor did the ordinance recognize the spiritual impediments that broke the engagement or marital contract when one or both parties chose to enter a cloister or monastery or to seek ordination as a priest. Both these impediments rested on discarded assumptions that marriage was a sacrament and that celibacy was required of priests and monastics.[38]

The 1546 Marriage Ordinance also did not recognize the traditional impediment that an engagement contract could be dissolved by mutual consent. This was surprising. The medieval canonists had introduced this impediment not to encourage transient troth, but to give parties a final chance to walk away from the budding union if their relationship did not work out. Calvin and his colleagues provided no such escape: they forced into marriage many Genevan couples who had earlier been properly engaged but had now become alienated in their affections. This drove home a perennial lesson of the law of Calvin's Geneva: engagement contracts, like marital contracts, were "sacred contracts" that could not be entered or dissolved easily.[39] It also underscored Calvin's repeated counsel that prospective couples must meet, become well acquainted, and deliberate carefully with each other and their parents and peers before they became engaged to be married. To be sure, it was easier to get out of an engagement than a marriage in Reformation Geneva, for the roll of impediments to engagement was considerably longer than the roll of impediments to marriage. But it was even easier to get out of a courtship. Either courting party could simply leave, or the parties could mutually agree to sever their relationship. All this was a notable departure from the medieval tradition, which had allowed parties to dissolve engagement contracts by mutual consent. What was a two-stage process in the medieval tradition now became effectively a three-stage process in Reformation Geneva: courtship, betrothal, and marriage.

Theodore Beza—also a French theologian and jurist, who succeeded Calvin in Geneva and wrote two definitive tracts on marriage—summed up this

37. *SMF*, 1:310–53.
38. *SMF*, 1:354–82.
39. Serm. Deut. 22:25–30.

sentiment and explained the prevailing law of engagements and their annulment neatly in 1569:

> True and valid engagements cannot be dissolved any more than consummated marriages, since God's command also applies here: "What God has joined together, let man not put asunder." They cannot be broken by mutual consent of both parties, far less by the will of either party as once was tolerated by the Romans, and even by Moses because of the stubbornness of the Jews.
>
> Certain things that are called "engagements," however, are not binding, because they are invalid and void. These are of two sorts. Some bonds can never be valid—those that are incestuous because of a blood relationship or affinity [between the parties] that prohibits marriage, those initiated with the husband or wife of another, with a eunuch, or with someone laboring under some incurable disease that in fact removes all hope of consummating the marriage. Other bonds, though initially invalid, nevertheless may be confirmed afterward—those contracted between the sexually immature, those contracted without the authority of parents (or of those in place of parents), or those contracted by deception of the parties, or only for a future time, or with a condition added, or by force or fear. Finally, some [bonds] are initially valid but later are dissolved not so much by men as by God himself—when the [future] husband or wife commits adultery, when an unfaithful [future] spouse deserts a faithful one, when a woman betrothed as a virgin was not one, or when [one party betrays] madness or some other permanent and incurable disease that in fact removes all hope of carrying out the marriage, or when a contagious and incurable disease interferes with an engagement.[40]

The 1545 Marriage Liturgy

A Genevan couple, once properly engaged, had little time to waste and little room to celebrate. Neither their publicly announced engagement nor the civil registration of their marriage was sufficient to constitute a marriage. According to the 1546 Marriage Ordinance, a formal church wedding had to follow within six weeks of engagement. If the couple procrastinated in their wedding plans, they would be reprimanded by the consistory; if they persisted, they would be "sent before the council so that they may be compelled to celebrate it." If the prospective groom disappeared without cause, the woman was bound to her engagement for a year as a precaution against premarital pregnancy. If the prospective bride disappeared, the man could break off the engagement immediately—unless there was evidence that she had been kidnapped or involuntarily detained. Premarital sex and cohabitation in the brief engagement period were strictly forbidden to the parties, on pain of imprisonment. Pregnant brides-to-be, though spared prison, were required to do public confession for fornication before the wedding and to wear a veil signaling their sin of fornication on the

---

40. Theodore Beza, *De repudiis et divortiis,* in Beza, *Tractationum theologicarum,* 2nd ed. (Geneva: Eusthatii Vignon, 1582), 2:50, 204 (hereafter, Beza, *RD*).

day of the wedding.[41] Their lovers, too, were sometimes required to do public confession before the wedding liturgy.

Calvin elaborated on the rules and rites of weddings in his 1545 Marriage Liturgy.[42] Marriages without weddings were invalid in Reformation Geneva, the liturgy made clear. "The public and solemn" wedding ceremony was "essential" for a marriage to be "true and lawful."[43] "No marriages are lawful except those that are rightly consecrated."[44] For Calvin and his colleagues, weddings were essential confirmations not only that the couple privately consented but also that the church and the state publicly consented to the marriage. According to the 1545 Marriage Liturgy, all weddings had to be announced in advance by the publication of banns, and the banns were signed by a local magistrate and declared by a local minister for three successive Sundays before the wedding. Weddings took place either on Sunday or on a weekday when a public Bible lecture was scheduled and in the church where the banns had been pronounced. Weddings could not be held on the same Sunday for which the Eucharist was scheduled lest "the honor of the sacrament" be impugned. The local minister presided over the wedding, following a detailed liturgy that Calvin drafted. Marriages that had been secretly contracted or celebrated improperly elsewhere had to be announced and celebrated anew in a church wedding in Geneva.[45]

The banns were written announcements of the parties' pending wedding plans. The minister usually read them from the pulpit during the Sunday worship service. The publication of banns was an ancient practice of the church. What was new in Reformation Geneva, as compared to late medieval practice, was that the publication of banns was mandatory for every wedding. Marriages were not valid without weddings, and weddings could not proceed without banns. What was also new in Geneva, as compared to some other Protestant communities, was that banns were to be announced in the church, not in the public square or the city hall. A city official, called a syndic, had to sign the banns after the parties registered their betrothal in the local town hall. But the minister had to pronounce these signed banns in the church where the parties intended to be married. This underscored a central point of Calvin's marriage theology: that marriages were at once public and private, spiritual and temporal, ecclesiastical and political in nature.

The permission to celebrate weddings on any day, save on a Sunday when the Eucharist was celebrated, was a marked departure from the late-medieval Catholic tradition. Before the Reformation, the prince-bishop of Geneva prohibited weddings on any of the sixty odd holy days of the medieval religious calendar, as well as throughout the period of Lent. Several local synods also

41. *SMF*, 1:414–44.
42. *CO* 6:203–8. The 1545 edition largely repeats the 1542 edition but adds a lengthy preface and further instructions. Later editions of 1547, 1558, 1559, 1562, 1563, and 1566 are the same except for small variations of wording.
43. *CO* 6:203–4.
44. Comm. Gen. 24:59.
45. *SMF*, 1:445–80.

prohibited weddings on Sundays and discouraged them on Fridays.[46] But when church weddings were celebrated, the Eucharist had to be included in the wedding liturgy. Calvin and his colleagues eliminated most holy days and softened considerably the Lenten restrictions, freeing up days for weddings.[47] But more to the point, they allowed weddings on any days that the congregation gathered to hear biblical exposition, whether the Sunday sermon or the weekday lecture on biblical texts. This underscored an accent that Calvin's liturgy spelled out in more detail: weddings were congregational events that featured exposition of the Bible, not celebration of a sacrament.

Calvin's wedding liturgy began with biblical exhortation on marriage and its duties. The presiding minister offered the couple a rich mosaic of biblical teachings on marriage, citing and paraphrasing a dozen Old and New Testament passages. Man and woman were created for each other. The two shall become one flesh. Their voluntary union shall be permanent. The wife shall subject herself to her husband. Both husband and wife shall surrender their bodies to each other. Marriage protects both parties from lust. Their bodies are temples of the Lord, to be maintained in purity.

After this lengthy opening exhortation, the minister moved to a second phase, asking the man and the woman separately whether each consented to the marriage as so described. Part of the concern was to ensure that both the man and the woman fully and freely consented to the marriage and were not pursuing this marriage frivolously, fraudulently, or under any false illusions. Part of the concern was to ensure that each party had a detailed understanding of the nature and responsibility of the marriage institution that they were about to enter. The minister also asked the congregation whether they consented to the union or knew of any impediment. With all confirming their consent to go forward, the minister then administered the vows. Some of the phraseology of the vows will be familiar to Protestants today. But observe that these vows were taken before God and his congregation and that the parties were bound by God's Word. Notice, too, the disparities in the duties that the husband and wife owe each other:

> Do you, N., confess here before God and his holy congregation that you have taken and take for your wife and spouse N. here present, whom you promise to protect, loving and maintaining her faithfully, as is the duty of a true and faithful husband to his wife, living piously with her, keeping faith and loyalty to her in all things, according to the holy Word of God and his holy Gospel?
>
> Do you, N., confess here before God and his holy assembly that you have taken and take N. for your lawful husband, whom you promise to obey, serving and being subject to him, living piously, keeping faith and

46. See examples in Mark Searle and Kenneth W. Stevenson, *Documents of the Marriage Liturgy* (Collegeville, MN: Liturgical Press, 1992); J.-B. Molin and P. Mutembe, *Le rituel du mariage en France du XIIe au XVIe siècle* (Paris: Beauchesne, 1994).

47. Philip Benedict, *Christ's Churches Purely Reformed: A Social History of Calvinism* (New Haven, CT, and London: Yale University Press, 2002), 495.

loyalty to him in all things, as a faithful and loyal wife should to her husband, according to the Word of God and the holy Gospel?

The final phase of the liturgy combined blessing, prayer, and further biblical exhortation. The minister called on God to bless the new couple in the "holy estate" and "noble estate" to which "God the Father had called" them "for the love of Jesus Christ his Son." The minister quoted the familiar passage of Matthew 19:3–9, with its solemn warning "what God has joined together, let no man put asunder." He enjoined the couple to live together in "loving-kindness, peace, and union, preserving true charity, faith, and loyalty to each other according to the Word of God." The minister then led the couple and the congregation in a lengthy prayer. The prayer repeated much of the language of the opening biblical exhortation. It also called upon God to help the couple live together in holiness, purity, and uprightness, and to set good examples of Christian piety for each other and the broader community. The parties and congregation were then blessed with the final peace.

Compared to other Catholic and Protestant liturgies of the day, Calvin's wedding liturgy was long on instruction and short on ceremony. The liturgy was amply peppered throughout with choice biblical references, quotations, and paraphrases. The liturgy began and ended with lengthy biblical teachings on the respective duties of husband and wife. More biblical instruction was offered in the regular sermon for the day that followed immediately after the marriage liturgy. The lengthy vows again confirmed each party's godly duties in marriage, as did the concluding prayer. There was no Eucharist, no kneeling at the altar, no ritualistic clasping of hands, no lifting of the veil, no kissing of the bride, no exchange of rings, no delivery of coins, no music or singing—all of which were featured in other wedding liturgies of the day.[48] The Genevan wedding liturgy was to proceed, the preamble insisted, "respectably, religiously, and properly in good and decent order," so that the partners can "hear and listen to the holy Word of God that will be administered to them."

Calvin's wedding liturgy was a "beautiful collection of biblical texts," writes a leading historian of liturgy.[49] It was also a surprising collection, and not just because of its length and the number of biblical passages adduced. First, only two of the three traditional goods of marriage were referenced in the liturgy: mutual love and mutual protection from sexual sin. Nothing was said anywhere in the liturgy about the blessing and procreation of children. Though the liturgy referred to Genesis 1, it did not, like many other wedding liturgies, quote the familiar biblical instruction: "Be fruitful and multiply." Second, the natural qualities and duties of marriage were emphasized more than the spiritual. The opening exhortation did speak of "honorable holy matrimony instituted by God" and of the "sacred" obedience that a wife owed her husband. The final

48. See samples in Searle and Stevenson, *Documents;* Molin and Mutembe, *Le rituel du mariage.*
49. Kenneth Stevenson, *Nuptial Blessing: A Study of Christian Marriage Rites* (London: SPCK, 1982), 131.

blessing did speak of the "holy estate" and "noble estate" of marriage. But much
of the biblical exhortation, oaths, and final prayer were focused on the natural
qualities of marriage: its origins in creation, the mandate of fleshly union, the
need for mutual bodily sacrifice, the command of continence, the analogy of the
body as the temple of God, the need for bodily purity. Not even the familiar
analogies between marriage and the covenant between Yahweh and his elect
or Christ and his church were referenced. These emphases—together with the
express prohibition on any eucharistic celebration during the wedding, or even
on the day of the wedding—underscored Calvin's fervent belief that marriage
was both a natural and spiritual estate, but not a sacrament.

Calvin's wedding liturgy made it clear that the formation of marriage was a
fundamental concern of the church community.[50] For three Sundays before the
wedding, the church proclaimed the banns, which served as a general invitation
not only for anyone to raise impediments but also for everyone to attend the
wedding service. The wedding liturgy took place during a worship service. The
wedding took place *in* the church, not at the church door, as was customary in
some late medieval liturgies, and certainly not in a private home, as was also
customary in some Protestant and Catholic communities. The minister's duty,
reads the preamble to the marriage liturgy, was "to approve and confirm this
marriage before the whole assembly." The congregation was asked to consent to
the marriage. Both husband and wife were asked to confirm their consent and
to state their vows again "before God and his holy assembly." The congregation
was asked to join in congregational prayer for the blessing of the couple. While
the minister presided at the wedding, he stood with the couple on the same
level, not on the pulpit. His head was uncovered. He faced the couple and congregation throughout the ceremony. He made no turn to the altar, as had been
customary in medieval liturgies. And the entire liturgy was in the vernacular
language, so that all could understand in what they were participating. All this
underscored that in Calvin's Geneva a wedding liturgy was very much a church
affair, a public congregational event. Even the couple's parents and relatives had
no special place in the wedding liturgy.

Calvin did not create his wedding liturgy from whole cloth. A good bit of
this liturgy came from the "radical revision" introduced in Geneva by Guillaume
Farel in 1533.[51] And Farel's wedding liturgy was built, in part, on liturgical
reforms introduced in the 1520s in Bern, Strasbourg, Zurich, and other Protestant cities.[52] Calvin downplayed the novelty of his wedding liturgy. When the

50. Bryan D. Spinks, "The Liturgical Origins and Theology of Calvin's Genevan Marriage
Rite," *Ecclesia orans* 3 (1986): 195–210, here 195, 208–10.

51. Searle and Stevenson, *Documents*, 227; Henri Vuilleumier, *Histoire de L'Église Réformée du pays
de Vaud sous le régime Bernois*, 4 vols. (Lausanne: Éditions La Concorde, 1927–33), 1:310–14, 345–48.

52. See also the influence of Bucer's reforms of marriage law, lore, and liturgy discussed in Elf-
riede Jacobs, *Die Sakramentslehre Wilhelm Farels* (Zurich: Theologischer Verlag, 1978); Herman J.
Selderhuis, "Das Eherecht Martin Bucers," in *Martin Bucer und das Recht*, ed. Christoph Strohm
(Geneva: Droz, 2002), 185–99.

Council of Bern later charged him with liturgical iconoclasm, Calvin insisted: "The form of marriage has always remained in its original state, and I follow the order which I found established like one who takes no pleasure in making innovations."[53] Calvin was being forgetful or perhaps too modest, for he had revised Farel's 1533 liturgy. But Calvin also did not care too much about the exact form of the liturgy. Wedding liturgies, he wrote, concerned "things indifferent [adiaphora], wherein the churches have a certain latitude of diversity." "When one has weighed the matter carefully, it may be sometimes considered useful not to have too rigid a uniformity respecting them, in order to show that faith and Christianity do not consist in that."[54] The event of a church wedding liturgy was essential to the validity of marriage. The exact form of the liturgy, however, was open to local variation.

Divorce and Remarriage

Once it was properly contracted, consecrated, and celebrated, a marriage was presumed to be permanent. The married couple was expected to maintain a common home. According to the 1546 Marriage Ordinance, both parties could be called to account for privately separating from bed or board—particularly if there was suspicion of adultery, harlotry, concubinage, or sodomy. Couples who "wrangled and disputed with each other," the Marriage Ordinance went on, were to be admonished by the consistory to "live in peace and unity"; severe cases of discord were reported to the congregation for popular reproof or to the council for criminal punishment. Husbands were forbidden to "ill-treat," "beat," or "torment" their wives and were subject to severe criminal sanctions if they persisted. These sanctions became increasingly severe in later years as the consistory and council sought to clamp down on domestic abuse.[55] Yet the 1546 Marriage Ordinance made no provision, even in extreme cases, for the traditional halfway remedy of separation from bed and board (without divorce). An ethic of perpetual reconciliation of husband and wife coursed through the ordinance, with ministers, magistrates, and members of the broader community all called to foster this end.[56]

The presumption of permanent marriage was not irrebuttable, however. In instances of serious marital impediments or individual fault, a party could sue for annulment or divorce. A judgment of annulment of a consecrated and consummated marriage required proof that a putative marriage was void because of a serious impediment that was present at the time of the wedding but unknown to either of the marital parties. Either party could sue for annulment

53. *CO* 15:537–42; see also 10/1:82–84.
54. *CO* 15:537–42. On the meaning of adiaphora in Calvin's thought, see John L. Thompson, *John Calvin and the Daughters of Sarah: Women in Regular and Exceptional Roles in the Exegesis of Calvin, His Predecessors, and His Contemporaries* (Geneva: Droz, 1992), 227.
55. *SMF*, vol. 2, chaps. 5–6.
56. *SMF*, vol. 2, chaps. 10–11.

on discovery of an incestuous blood or familial relationship between them that violated biblical commands.[57] Upon annulment, both were left free to remarry. A husband could sue if he discovered that his wife lacked presumed virginity, was incurably diseased, or refused to correct a "defect of her body" that prevented intercourse—again, leaving both parties free to remarry. A wife could sue on grounds of the impotence or incurable disease of her husband—leaving her free to remarry but him "forbidden to misuse any woman again." In all such cases, the parties were expected to prepare a register of their individual and collective properties and, with appropriate judicial supervision, reach an "amicable" parting of property and person.[58]

Following Protestant conventions, Calvin and his colleagues also introduced absolute divorce on proof of adultery or desertion, and a subsequent right for the divorced parties to remarry, at least for the innocent party. In cases of adultery, husband and wife were accorded an equal right to sue—a deliberate innovation to "ancient practice," which the ordinance grounded in the apostle Paul's teaching that husband and wife have a "mutual and reciprocal obligation" in "matters of intercourse of the bed." Only an entirely innocent plaintiff could bring such a divorce suit; any evidence of mutual fault, fraud, or collusion in the adultery was fatal to the case. Failure to bring suit in a timely manner was taken as a sign of forgiveness and thus cut off the suit for divorce. After bringing suit, the plaintiff was urged to reconcile with the wayward spouse—and doubtless told that such reconciliation would likely exonerate the latter from criminal punishment. But the plaintiff could insist on the divorce, and in such instance, the case would be referred to the council for adjudication. The innocent party was free to remarry thereafter. The adulterer faced criminal punishment—imprisonment in the usual case, banishment or execution in an egregious case.

Parties could also sue for divorce on grounds of desertion. These divorce cases were procedurally more complicated and substantively less egalitarian in their treatment of husband and wife. In cases where the husband left home for a legitimate reason (such as for business or military service) but inexplicably did not return and could not be found, the wife had to wait ten years before he could be presumed dead and she permitted to remarry. In cases where the husband left "through debauchery or some other evil disposition," the wife was to find him and to request his return. If she could not find him, she would have to wait one year before proceeding further. If she did find him and he refused to return—or the year of waiting had expired—she was to request three biweekly announcements of his desertion, both by the minister in the church and by the lieutenant of the city council. If the husband still failed to respond, she was to summon two or three of his relatives or close friends to try to find him and urge his return. If that proved futile, she could appear before the consistory to state her case and, with their approval, petition the magistrate for an order of divorce. The return

57. See detailed sources in *SMF*, 1:310–53.
58. *CO* 10/1:139–43; and other sources in *SMF*, 1:383–413.

of the husband anytime before such an order was issued would end the proceedings. The husband would be admonished for his desertion. The wife would be compelled to welcome him back to bed and board. If the husband repeated his desertion, he faced prison. If he deserted his wife habitually, she could sue for divorce ex parte, with no further notification requirements.

A husband who brought suit for his wife's desertion followed the same procedures, but with three simplifications. First, cases of intentional abandonment of the home and a legitimate departure that went on longer than expected by the wife were treated alike. Second, husbands had no obligation to wait for one year (let alone ten) if he could not locate his wife; the public announcements of her departure and petition for divorce could commence immediately. Third, even if a wife returned, her husband could reject her if he had "suspicion that she has misconducted herself." The consistory would urge the couple to reconcile, but if he insisted, they would investigate her conduct while she had been away. If they found no evidence of misconduct, he would be compelled to accept her. If they reached "a very emphatic presumption that she committed adultery or kept bad and suspect company and did not conduct herself honorably as a good woman," the ordinance reads, "the husband's petition shall be heard, and he shall be granted what reason dictates."

The New Marriage Law in Comparative Perspective

The new marriage law of Geneva was a watershed in the evolution of Protestant marriage and family law. The ordinance collected and combined the most enduring provisions of medieval Catholic canon law and the most daring reforms of the new Protestant civil law. The ordinance retained the canonists' distinctions of betrothal, marriage, and consummation. Yet it imported various Protestant rules to simplify, abbreviate, and police the process. The ordinance repeated the canonists' requirement that the couple mutually consent to marriage. But it incorporated Protestant demands for the further consent of parents, parishioners, and citizens in the process. The ordinance accepted the canonists' biblically based impediments of consanguinity, affinity, and infirmity. But in typical Protestant fashion, it rejected the impediments rooted in Catholic sacramental theology. The ordinance repeated the canonists' injunction that marriage is an indissoluble estate. Yet it followed Protestant (and Roman law) views that adultery and desertion are themselves acts of marital dissolution, triggering rights for divorce and remarriage at least for the innocent party. The ordinance adopted the canon-law pattern of involving clergy in the governance of marriage. But it left to the Protestant magistrate both civil and criminal jurisdiction over sex, marriage, and family life.[59]

This marriage ordinance was more than a synthesis of earlier laws, however. Through this enactment, Calvin and his colleagues also introduced several

---

59. Seeger, *Nullité de mariage*, 135–82.

innovations, or novel emphases, in prevailing Protestant marriage law that came to have a formidable influence on the Western legal tradition.[60] A dozen such contributions deserve mention: (1) the strict prohibitions against frivolity, drunkenness, and conditionality in contracting betrothals; (2) the substantial protections of children from parental coercion into engagements; (3) the elevation of paternal over maternal consent in the process of betrothal; (4) the abbreviation and careful communal policing of the interim between engagement and marriage; (5) the absolute impediments of impotence and contagion to engagement and marriage; (6) the mandatory publication of banns by both magistrates and ministers; (7) the dual requirements of state registration and a church wedding to constitute marriage; (8) the deprecation of the right of separation from bed and board, and the strong emphasis on reconciliation between husband and wife; (9) the equal standing for women to sue for annulment on grounds of impotence and for divorce on grounds of adultery; (10) the disparate treatment of husbands and wives in suits for desertion; (11) the stern prohibition against wife abuse; and (12) the establishment of a mixed clerical and lay consistory, to serve as a hearings court of first resort and a mediator of last resort in marital cases.

Taken together, these innovations of Genevan marriage law helped to render both mental consent and sexual ability indispensable features of marriage. They helped to render engagement, marriage, and dissolution central concerns of church, state, and society alike. And they helped to promote what André Biéler once called a "differential equality"—such progressive gender equality on some issues that Geneva was named a "women's paradise," but such regressive patriarchy on other issues that Geneva was described at the same time as "a woman's abyss."[61]

CALVIN'S LATER COVENANT THEOLOGY OF MARRIAGE

Popular Contempt

"Rules without canons will either harden or wither over time," Lord Acton once said. "Whether hardened or withered, they come to little effect." Calvin learned this lesson the hard way in his reformation of Genevan marriage law. However refined his early legal and liturgical formulations on marriage may

---

60. See Köhler, *Genfer Konsistorium*, 2:642–45, who traces some of these Genevan "innovations" to the laws of Zurich (1525) and Basel (1529). See further Thomas Max Safley, "Canon Law and Swiss Reform: Legal Theory and Practice in the Marital Courts of Zurich, Bern, Basel, and St. Gall," in *Canon Law in Protestant Lands*, ed. Richard H. Helmholz (Berlin: Duncker & Humblot, 1992), 187.

61. Andre Biéler, *L'homme et la femme dans la morale Calviniste* (Geneva: Labor & Fides, 1963), 36, with sources and discussion in E. William Monter, "Women in Calvinist Geneva (1550–1800)," *Signs: Journal of Women in Culture and Society* 6 (1980): 189; Roger Stauffenegger, "Le Mariage à Genève vers 1600," *Mémoires de la société pour l'histoire de droit et des institutions de anciens pays bourguignons, comtois et romands* 27 (1966): 317.

have been, they did not admit of easy political adoption or popular acceptance. Genevan political officials dithered for nearly two decades before finally yielding to most of his legal reforms. Genevan parishioners and subjects resisted, with increasing contempt, the authority of Calvin and the consistory to deal with marital matters.

Cases of popular contempt appear already in the consistory register of 1546, when the marriage ordinance was first circulating. In one case, a man charged Calvin with posturing as "the new pope" of marriage.[62] In another case, a man flatly asserted that the consistory "lacked the authority" to dissolve his sister's engagement, punctuating his remarks with a few insulting jabs at Calvin.[63] In that same year, rioting broke out in Geneva when the city council, on Calvin's initiative, passed a new law governing what names a baptized child could be given: many popular local names were banned in favor of biblical names.[64] For many Genevans, such intrusions into private life were an outrage, and anticlericalism escalated in Geneva.[65] Why should ministers have such powers to probe the intimacies of bed and board? Why should the church consistory enjoy such authority over a civil estate like marriage? Why should the city magistrates be swayed by the pastors' teachings on sexuality and domesticity? Why should rights to participate in the sacrament of Eucharist turn on wrongs pertaining to the adiaphora of marriage? How was the magistrate or minister to parse and police the line between the pastoral functions of the consistory and the judicial functions of the council? Had not Calvin simply created a new church court under his authority, wielding much of the same power and prerogative as the former episcopal and inquisitorial courts of Catholicism but now lacking any final appeal to Rome? Dozens of litigants and pamphleteers voiced such criticisms in the later 1540s and 1550s. Calvin and his colleagues initially had no ready answers.

Not only the jurisdiction but also the substance of the new marriage law came under increasing challenge. Calvin may well have ingeniously cut and pasted what he considered to be the best of Catholic and Protestant laws and liturgies on marriage, suitably amended with his own favorite norms. But why should these rules and rites be binding on Geneva? Why could Geneva not adopt some of the more liberal rules of a Zurich or a Strasbourg, or the more conservative laws of a Rome or a Paris? What was to prevent piecemeal or wholesale reform or rejection of these new rules? What was to check the growing marital and sexual license in Geneva about which Calvin and other pastors complained bitterly: the

62. "Registres du Consistoire de Genève," ed. Robert M. Kingdon et al., 21 vols. (unpublished, in Meeter Center, Calvin College), 2:55.

63. Ibid., 2:98.

64. *RCP*, 1:29. See Barbara Pitkin, "'The Heritage of the Lord': Children in the Theology of John Calvin," in *The Child in Christian Thought*, ed. Marcia J. Bunge (Grand Rapids: Wm. B. Eerdmans Publishing Co., 2000), 160–93.

65. See generally Robert M. Kingdon, "Anticlericalism in the Registers of the Geneva Consistory, 1542–1564," in *Anticlericalism in Late Medieval and Early Modern Europe*, ed. Peter A. Dykema and Heiko A. Oberman (Leiden: E. J. Brill, 1993), 617.

sharp increases in adultery, desertion, and discord within the home; the escala-
tion of fornication, harlotry, and sumptuousness outside the home; the rapid
exploitation of the new rights to divorce and remarry by the Genevan elite; the
sharp increases in "ribaldry" of music and literature and "lewdness" of manner
and speech among the youth—pathos, which Calvin denounced with all the
passion and prescience of any modern-day Jeremiah.[66]

Such challenges sent Calvin scurrying to his library, pulpit, and letter desk
to develop and defend a more elaborate theology of marriage and family life
than he had earlier offered. In a long series of biblical commentaries, sermons,
consilia, and letters prepared in the last twelve years of his life, he provided a rich
theological apologia both for his marriage-law system as a whole and for many of
the individual rules that he had prescribed.[67] The centerpiece of his theological
synthesis was the biblical doctrine of covenant. Calvin's late-life ailments and
early death in 1564 at the age of 55 kept him from fully elaborating, let alone
systematizing, these new theological sentiments. But even in its somewhat scattered form, Calvin's new covenantal theology of marriage made an impressive
and enduring contribution to the Western tradition. Later Calvinist theologians
and jurists, in Europe and North America, elaborated many of the basic theological insights that he had adumbrated.

Covenant Theology of Marriage

Calvin's early theology of marriage had been grounded in the Lutheran doctrine
of the two kingdoms. Marriage, he had argued, was an institution of the earthly
kingdom alone—"a good and holy ordinance of God, just like farming, building, cobbling, and barbering."[68] Christians should participate in the institution—not to be justified or sanctified, but to keep themselves free from the sins
of lust and incontinence. Church leaders should cooperate in the governance
of marriage—not as spiritual lords of the Christian conscience, but as pastoral
aides to the Christian magistrate. This early theology may have allowed Calvin
to counter Catholic claims that marriage is a sacrament and thus subject to the
church's jurisdiction. But it did not allow him to counter either the political
laxness in marriage law or the popular license in marriage life that prevailed in
mid-sixteenth-century Geneva.

66. See, e.g., Comm. Lev. 20:10; 22:22–27; Serm. Deut. 5:18; 22:5–8, 13–25; Serm. Eph.
5:28—33; "Contra la Secte des Libertines," in *CO* 7:212.

67. For a chart of Calvin's preaching schedule, see T. H. L. Parker, *The Oracles of God: An
Introduction to the Preaching of John Calvin* (London and Redhill: Lutterworth Press, 1947), 160–62,
with sermons collected in *CO* and in *Supplementa Calviniani* (Neukirchen: Kreis Moers; Verlag der
Buchhandlungdes Erziehungsvereins, 1936–).

68. *Inst.* 1536, 5.68. But cf. John Calvin, *Institutes of the Christian Religion*, ed. John T. McNeill,
trans. Ford Lewis Battles (Philadelphia: Westminster Press, 1960), 4.19.34 (hereafter, *Inst.* 1559),
where Calvin repeats this language verbatim—and indeed the entire 1536 discussion of the section
on marriage as a "false sacrament." This language stood in considerable tension with that of his
sermons and commentaries discussed below.

Calvin's mature theology of marriage was grounded in the biblical doctrine of covenant. The idea of a divine covenant or agreement between God and humanity had long been taught in the Western church. Theologians, at least since the time of Irenaeus in the second century, had discussed the interlocking biblical covenants: (1) the covenant of works, whereby the chosen people of Israel, through obedience to God's law, are promised eternal salvation and blessing; and (2) the covenant of grace, whereby the elect, through faith in Christ's incarnation and atonement, are promised eternal salvation and beatitude. The covenant of works was created in Abraham, confirmed in Moses, and consummated with the promulgation and acceptance of the Torah. The covenant of grace was created in Christ, confirmed in the gospel, and consummated with the confession and conversion of the Christian.[69] These traditional teachings on the covenant were well known to the early Reformers, and Calvin had already used them to fortify his doctrines of sin and salvation, law and Gospel, man and God.[70]

In his later years, Calvin began to note with increasing regularity how often the Bible uses the term "covenant" to describe marriage. In the Old Testament, as we saw in chapter 2, Yahweh's covenantal relationship with Israel is analogized to the special relationship between husband and wife. Israel's disobedience to Yahweh, in turn, is frequently described as a form of "playing the harlot." Idolatry, like adultery, can lead to divorce, and Yahweh threatens this many times, even while calling his chosen to reconciliation. This set of images about marriage and divorce comes through repeatedly in the writings of the Old Testament prophets Hosea, Isaiah, Jeremiah, Ezekiel, and Malachi.[71] Between 1551 and 1564, Calvin preached, commented, or lectured on every one of these texts (except Ezek. 23), and he took increasing note of their lessons for modern-day understandings of marriage and divorce.[72]

The Bible, as we saw, also speaks about marriage as a covenant in its own right.[73] The prophet Malachi's formulation is the fullest:

> You cover the LORD's altar with tears, with weeping and groaning because he no longer regards the offering or accepts it with favor at your hand. You ask, "Why does he not?" Because the LORD was a witness to the covenant

---

69. See sources and discussion in Daniel J. Elazar, *Covenant and Commonwealth: From Christian Separation through the Protestant Reformation* (New Brunswick, NJ: Transaction Publishers, 1996).

70. *Inst.* 1559, 2.10–11; 4.15–16. For the covenant doctrines of other early reformers, see J. Wayne Baker, *Heinrich Bullinger and the Covenant: The Other Reformed Tradition* (Athens: Ohio University Press, 1980), 1–26, 181–216; Kenneth Hagen, "From Testament to Covenant in the Early Sixteenth Century," *Sixteenth Century Journal* 3 (1972): 1–24.

71. See sources in chap. 2 above, pages 38–45.

72. In the order of their appearance, see Comm. Isa. 1:21–22; 54:5–8; 57:3–10; 61:10–11; 62:4–5 (1551); Serm. Deut. 5:18; 22:22 (1555); Comm. Harm. Gosp. Luke 1:34–38 (1555); Comm. Ps. 16:4; 45:8–12; 82:1 (1557); Lect. Hos. 1:1–4; 2:19–20; 3:1–2; 4:13–14; 7:3, 9–10 (1557); Lect. Zech. 2:11; 8:1–2 (ca. 1560); Lect. Mal. 2:13–16 (ca. 1560); Lect. Jer. 2:2–3, 25; 3:1–5, 6–25; 13:27; 23:10; 31:32; 51:4 (1563); Comm. Harm. Law Deut. 11:26–32 (1563); and Lect. Ezek. 6:9; 16:1–63 (1564).

73. Calvin did not preach or comment on the book of Proverbs.

between you and the wife of your youth, to whom you have been faithless, though she is your companion and your wife by covenant. Has not the one God made and sustained for us the spirit of life? And what does he desire? Godly offspring. So take heed to yourselves, and let none be faithless to the wife of his youth. "For I hate divorce, says the LORD the God of Israel, and covering one's garments with violence, says the LORD, the God of hosts. So take heed to yourselves and do not be faithless."[74]

Using this passage, Calvin began to use the doctrine of covenant to describe not only the vertical relationships between God and humanity but also the horizontal relationships between husband and wife. Just as God draws the elect believer into a covenant relationship with him, Calvin argued, so God draws husband and wife into a covenant relationship with each other. Just as God expects constant faith and good works in our relationship with him, so God expects connubial faithfulness and sacrificial works in our relationship with our spouses. "God is the founder of marriage," Calvin wrote:

> When a marriage takes place between a man and a woman, God presides and requires a mutual pledge from both. Hence Solomon in Proverbs 2:17 calls marriage the covenant of God, for it is superior to all human contracts. So also Malachi [2:14] declares that God is, as it were, the stipulator [of marriage], who by his authority joins the man to the woman, and sanctions the alliance. . . . Marriage is not a thing ordained by men. We know that God is the author of it, and that it is solemnized in his name. The Scripture says that it is a holy covenant, and therefore calls it divine.[75]

God participates in the formation of the covenant of marriage through his chosen agents on earth, Calvin believed. The couple's parents, as God's "lieutenants" for children, instruct the young couple in the mores and morals of Christian marriage and give their consent to the union.[76] Two witnesses, as "God's priests to their peers," testify to the sincerity and solemnity of the couple's promises and attest to the marriage event.[77] The minister, holding "God's spiritual power of the Word," blesses the union and admonishes the couple and the community of their respective biblical duties and rights.[78] The magistrate, holding "God's temporal power of the sword," registers the parties, ensures the legality of their union, and protects them in their conjoined persons and properties. This involvement of parents, peers, ministers, and magistrates in the formation of the marriage covenant was not an idle or dispensable ceremony. These four parties represented different dimensions of God's involvement in the marriage

74. Mal. 2:13–16 RSV.
75. Serm. Eph. 5:22–26, 31–33; see also Serm. Deut. 5:18: "Marriage is called a covenant with God, . . . meaning that God presides over marriages."
76. Comm. Harm. Law Lev. 19:29; Serm. Deut. 5:16; Comm. 1 Cor. 7:36, 38; Serm. 1 Cor. 7:36–38; Serm. and Comm. Eph. 6:1–3.
77. Comm. 1 Thess. 4:3; Comm. 1 Pet. 2:9; *Inst.* 1559, 4.18.16–17.
78. Serm. Eph. 5:31–33.

covenant. They were essential to the legitimacy of the marriage itself. To omit any such party in the formation of the marriage was, in effect, to omit God from the marriage covenant.

The doctrine of covenant theology thus helped Calvin integrate what became universal requirements of valid marriage formation in the West after the mid-sixteenth century: mutual consent of the couple, parental consent, two witnesses, civil registration, and church consecration. It also provided a standing response to the centuries-long problem of secret marriage. Marriage was, by its covenantal nature, a public institution, involving a variety of parties in the community. To marry secretly or privately was to defy the very nature of marriage.

The Law of the Marriage Covenant

God participates in maintaining the covenant of marriage not only through the onetime actions of his human agents but also through the continuous revelation of his moral law. Calvin regarded the moral law as God's commandments, engraved on the conscience, elaborated in Scripture, and distilled in the Decalogue.[79] In his later years, he used sundry terms to describe this moral law: "the voice of nature," "the law of nature," "the natural order," "the inner mind," "the rule of equity," "the natural sense," "the sense of divine judgment," "the testimony of the heart," "the inner voice"—terms and concepts that he did not adequately sift or synthesize.[80] For our purposes, these are all largely synonyms to describe the basic norms created by God and confirmed in the covenant, for the right ordering of our marital and sexual lives.

The covenant of marriage is grounded "in the creation and commandments of God," and "in the order and law of nature," Calvin believed.[81] At creation, God ordained the structure of marriage to be a lifelong union between a fit man and a fit woman of the age of mature consent. God assigned to this marriage three interlocking purposes: (1) the mutual love and support of husband and wife, (2) the mutual procreation and nurture of children, and (3) the mutual protection of both parties from sexual sin.[82] In nature, man and woman enjoy a "common dignity before God" and a common function of "completing" the life and love of the other.[83] In marriage, husband and wife are "joined together

---

79. *Inst.* 1559, 2.7.1; 2.8.1; 4.20.15.

80. Among many other references, see ibid., 2.2.22; 2.7.3–4, 10; 2.8.1–2; 3.19.15–16; 4.20.3, 15, 16; Comm. Rom. 2:14–15; Serm. Deut. 4:44–6:4; 19:14–15. See discussion in Bohatec, *Calvin und das Recht*, 1–93; John Hesselink, *Calvin's Concept of the Law* (Allison Park, PA: Pickwick Publishers, 1992), 18–24, 51–85; and broader context and influence discussed in Christoph Strohm, *Calvinismus und Recht* (Tübingen: Mohr Siebeck, 2008).

81. Comm. Gen. 2:18; Comm. Deut. 24:1–4; Comm. Mal. 2:15; Comm. Harm. Gosp. Matt. 19:3–9; and Mark 10:2–12; Consilium in *CO* 10/1:239–41.

82. Comm. Gen. 1:27–28; 2:18, 21–22; Comm. 1 Cor. 9:11; Comm. Eph. 5:30–32; Serm. Eph. 5:28–30.

83. Comm. Gen. 1:27.

in one body and one soul," but then assigned "distinct duties" and "different authorities."[84] God has appointed the husband as the head of the wife. God has appointed the wife, "who is derived from and comes after the man," as his associate and companion—literally, his "helpmeet."[85] "The divine mandate [in paradise] was that the husband would look up in reverence to God, the woman would be a faithful assistant to him, and both with one consent would cultivate a holy, friendly, and peaceful intercourse."[86]

This created subordination of the wife to the husband was exacerbated by the fall into sin, Calvin believed. "The woman had previously been subject to her husband, but that was a liberal and gentle subjection. Now she is cast into servitude to man"—consigned perennially to a life of childbearing and domestic service, while the husband presides over her material and spiritual welfare and that of their children.[87] Calvin often reminded women of their God-given domestic roles—sometimes with a level of insult and misogyny that warrants criticism, even when judged by sixteenth-century standards.[88] But Calvin also made clear that husbands were not to abuse their superior offices within the marital estate, on pain of spiritual and civil sanctions.[89] He called marital couples repeatedly to the mutual love and nurture that God had prescribed for marriage.[90] More than once he insisted that the domestic vocation is equal in status to all other vocations. He further insisted that, despite the headship of the man within the home, the woman must enjoy both connubial and parental equality.[91] "While in other things, husband and wife differ both as to duty and as to authority," Calvin wrote, "with respect to their mutual obligations in bed, . . . they are bound to mutual benevolence."[92] And again, "Authority is distributed as much to one

84. Comm. Gen. 2:18, 22.

85. Comm. Gen. 2:18. See also Comm. 1 Cor. 9:8; 11:4–10.

86. Comm. Gen. 2:18.

87. Comm. Gen. 2:22, 25; 3:16; Serm. 1 Cor. 11:4–10; Comm. 1 Cor. 3:1–4, 6; 7:1–10; Comm. Eph. 5:22–26, 28–30; Serm. Eph. 5:31–33; Comm. 1 Tim. 2:13; 5:13–14; Serm. Titus 2:3–5. For analysis, see Claude-Marie Baldwin, "John Calvin and the Ethics of Gender Relations," *Calvin Theological Journal* 26 (1991): 133; Bohatec, *Calvins Lehre von Staat und Kirche,* 655–59; Biéler, *L'homme et la femme,* 35–42; Willis P. DeBoer, "Calvin on the Role of Women," in *Exploring the Heritage of John Calvin,* ed. David E. Holwerda (Grand Rapids: Baker Book House, 1976), 236–72.

88. See, e.g., Comm. 1 Tim. 2:9, deprecating women's vain apparel; Comm. Titus 2:3, castigating women outside the home as "prattlers and rumor-mongers"; Serm. Eph. 5:3–5, 22–26, bemoaning the "audacity" of women's dress, speech, and manner outside the home; Comm. 1 Pet. 3:3, saying the same.

89. Comm. Gen. 2:18; Serm. Deut. 24:1–4; Serm. Eph. 5:28–30.

90. Comm. Gen. 2:18; Comm. Gen. 29:18; Comm. Harm. Law Lev. 20:10; 22:22–27; Lect. Dan. 11:38–39; Comm. 1 Cor. 7:3; 9:11.

91. Comm. Gen. 2:18, arguing that this equality is implicit in the concept of Eve being "a helpmeet for Adam." But cf. Comm. 1 Cor. 11:4: "For in his home, the father of the family is like a king. Therefore he reflects the glory of God, because of the control which is in his hands"; Serm. Eph. 5:22–26, arguing that "husbands are advanced to the honor of superiority on condition that they should not be cruel toward their wives." See discussion in DeBoer, "Calvin on the Role of Women," 236–56.

92. Comm. 1 Cor. 7:3. See also Comm. Matt. 19:9; Serm. 1 Cor. 7:3–5; Serm. Deut. 24:5–6.

parent as to the other. . . . God does not wish the father alone to rule the child; the mother must also have a share in the honor and the preeminence."[93]

Calvin used this understanding of the created structure and purposes of marriage to integrate a variety of biblical morals and mores for life within the covenant of marriage. In Calvin's view, these biblical norms had different implications (1) for the believer versus the nonbeliever and (2) for the married couple versus the unmarried party. Calvin spelled out these distinctions in some detail, for to him they were critical to resolving some of the tensions that might appear between and within biblical and natural norms for marriage.

Calvin explained the first distinction—the differential impact of biblical marital norms on believers and nonbelievers—in the context of his broader theory of the "uses" of the moral or natural law.[94] Like other Protestant Reformers, Calvin believed that the moral law provides no pathway to salvation. Before the fall into sin, the law was a recipe for righteousness. But since the fall, no person has been capable of perfectly abiding by the law and thereby earning salvation by good works alone. Salvation now comes through faith and grace, not by works and the law, said Calvin. Nonetheless, from God's point of view, the moral law continues to be useful in this earthly life—to have "uses." God uses both its basic norms known to all persons and its more refined norms, known only to believers through the Bible to govern and guide humanity.[95]

On the one hand, said Calvin, the moral law has a "civil use" of defining for all persons what is absolutely necessary to maintain a modicum of civil and domestic order. In this sense, God uses "the moral law as a halter to check the raging and otherwise limitlessly ranging lusts of the flesh. . . . Hindered by fright or shame, sinners dare neither execute what they have conceived in their minds, nor openly breathe forth the rage of their lust."[96] The moral law thus imposes upon them a "constrained and coerced righteousness," a "civil morality."[97] Therefore "even the pagans" have always recognized the natural duties of sexual restraint, heterosexual monogamy, marital fidelity, procreation of children, bondage to kin, and the like, which are essential to the survival of marriage.[98]

93. Serm. Deut. 21:18–21; Comm. Gen. 2:18.

94. See sources and discussion in John Witte Jr., *God's Joust, God's Justice: Law and Religion in the Western Tradition* (Grand Rapids: Wm. B. Eerdmans Publishing Co., 2005), chap. 10.

95. Though Calvin had adumbrated this theory of the uses of the law already in the mid-1530s, his full elaboration came in his 1559 edition of the *Institutes*. There he distinguishes a "civil use of the moral law" (that yields civil morality through coercion), a "theological use" (condemning persons in their sin to repent), and an "educational use" (teaching spiritual morality to those who have repented). See *Inst.* 1559, 2.7.6–13. The fullest exposition of the doctrine before 1559 came in his *Sermons on Deuteronomy* of the mid-1550s, where Calvin is interpreting the Jewish laws of marriage, divorce, polygamy, adultery, and the like. See, e.g., Serm. Deut. 5:18, 21; 21:15–17; 22:25–30; 24:1–4. In this latter treatment, Calvin generally distinguished only the civil use and educational use (he calls it "spiritual" use), touching lightly on the "theological use" only in Serm. Deut. 5:21. My discussion, therefore, distinguishes only the first two uses.

96. *Inst.* 1559, 2.7.10; see also Serm. Deut. 24:1–4.

97. Ibid., see also 4.20.3.

98. Ibid., 2.8.6–10; Serm. Deut. 5:18, 21; 21:15–17.

On the other hand, the moral law has a "spiritual use" of defining for believers what is aspirationally needed to attain a measure of holiness or sanctification. Even the most devout saints, Calvin wrote, still need the moral law "to learn more thoroughly . . . the LORD's will [and] to be aroused to obedience."[99] In this sense, the moral law teaches them not only the "civil righteousness" that is common to nonbelievers but also the "spiritual righteousness" that is becoming of believers. The moral law not only coerces them against violence and violation but also cultivates in them charity and love. It not only punishes harmful acts of adultery and fornication but also prohibits evil thoughts of passion and lust.[100]

God's moral law for the covenant of marriage thus gives rise to two tracks of marital norms: civil norms, which are common to all persons; and spiritual norms, which are distinctly Christian. This moral law in turn gives rise to two tracks of marital morality: a simple "morality of duty," demanded of all persons regardless of their faith; and a higher "morality of aspiration," demanded of believers in order to reflect their faith.[101] In Calvin's mind, commandments and counsels, musts and shoulds, absolutes and adiaphora for marriage can thereby be distinguished.

This two-track system of marital morality, Calvin believed, corresponds roughly to the proper division of marital responsibility between church and state in this earthly life. It was the church's responsibility to teach aspirational spiritual norms for marriage and family life. It was the state's responsibility to enforce mandatory civil norms. This division of responsibility fit rather neatly into the procedural divisions between the consistory and the council in Calvin's Geneva. In marriage cases, the consistory would first call parties to their higher spiritual duties, backing their recommendations with (threats of) spiritual discipline. If such spiritual counsel failed, the parties were referred to the city council to compel them, using civil and criminal sanctions, to honor at least their basic civil duties for marriage.[102]

With this first distinction in mind, Calvin spelled out various biblical norms for married and unmarried parties, grounding and integrating many of these norms in the created structure and created purposes of marriage.

The Monogamous Structure of the Marriage Covenant

Calvin grounded various biblical rules against illicit sexual unions in the created structure of marriages as a lifelong monogamous union of a fit man and a fit woman. Citing Moses and Paul, he condemned as "monstrous vices" sodomy, buggery, bestiality, homosexuality, and other "unnatural" acts and

---

99. *Inst.* 1559, 2.7.12.

100. Ibid., 2.8.6.

101. The terms are from Lon L. Fuller, *The Morality of Law*, rev. ed. (New Haven, CT: Yale University Press, 1964). Calvin spoke of "civil morality" versus "spiritual morality." See *Inst.* 1559, 2.7.10; 4.20.3; Serm. Deut. 21:15–17.

102. See *Inst.*1559, 4.11.3–16; 4.20.1–2.

alliances—arguing cryptically that to "lust for our own kind" or "for brutes" was "repugnant to the modesty of nature itself."[103] He condemned as "incestuous" marriages contracted between the blood and family relatives identified in the Bible, which he amended a bit with arguments from natural law.[104] He argued that through his biblical and natural law, God had prohibited incestuous unions to avoid discord, abuse, rivalry, and exploitation among the relatives.[105] The Levitical law against incest, said Calvin, "was not simply a civil law of Israel . . . nor one of those laws which can be repealed in accordance with the circumstances of time and place. It flows from the very font of nature, and is grounded in the general source of all laws, which is permanent and inviolate."[106] Thus "unfit relatives" who were innocently married and later discovered their impediment must have their marriages immediately annulled.[107] Those who knowingly married in violation of these incest prohibitions must face not only annulment but also civil and spiritual sanctions.[108]

Calvin condemned, at greater length, the traditional Hebrew practice of polygyny, which had again become fashionable in a few experimental quarters of sixteenth-century Europe.[109] Calvin denounced polygyny because he believed that God had prescribed monogamy as part of the "order of creation." God created one man and one woman in paradise and brought them together in holy matrimony. This first marriage of Adam and Eve, he argued, set the norm and form for all future marriages, and it distinguished proper sexual relationships among humans from the random and multiple sexual associations of other animals. After recording the story of the creation and coupling of Adam and Eve, Moses wrote: "Therefore shall a man leave his father and his mother, and shall cleave unto his wife: and the two shall become one flesh." Christ repeated and confirmed this phrase of the two becoming one flesh in his interpretation of the Mosaic law, as did the apostle Paul in his instructions on Christian marriage.[110]

Calvin read the statement "The two *shall* become one flesh" as an imperative. In this phrase, God commanded monogamous marriage as the "most sacred" and "primal" institution. And God also condemned polygyny as "contrary to the order and law of nature," a teaching that Moses, Christ, and Paul all confirmed

---

103. Comm. Lev. 18:22; Serm. Deut. 22:13–24.

104. See detailed sources in *SMF*, 1:310–54.

105. Comm. Harm. Law Lev. 18 and 20, passim; Comm. Gen. 29:27; Serm. Deut. 22:25–30. See also Consilia in *CO* 10/1:231–38.

106. Consilium, *CO* 10/1:235–38. See also Serm. Deut. 22:25–30.

107. Comm. Lev. 18:6–18; Consilia, in *CO* 10/1:231–38.

108. Building on Calvin's doctrine, Beza elaborated these Levitical impediments at length in Beza, *RD*, 53–68.

109. See chap. 5 above, pp. 128–30. See further John L. Thompson, "Patriarchs, Polygamy, and Private Resistance: John Calvin and Others on Breaking God's Rules," *Sixteenth Century Journal* 35 (1994): 3, 7–15; Christopher Elwood, "Calvin, Beza, and the Defense of Marriage in the Sixteenth Century," in *Calvin, Beza, and Later Calvinism*, ed. David Foxgrover (Grand Rapids: Calvin Studies Society, 2006), 11–34.

110. *CO* 10/1:255, 258. See Gen. 2:24 KJV/NASB; Matt. 19:5–6; Eph. 5:31; and discussion above in chap. 2, pp. 32–35.

in their repeated references to this creation story. At creation, God could have made two or more wives for Adam, as he did for other animals. But he chose to create one. God could have made three or four types of humans to be the image of God. But he created two types: "male and female he created them." In the Mosaic law, God could have commanded his chosen people to worship two or more gods, as was common in that day, but he commanded them to worship one God and remain in exclusive covenant with him. In the gospel, Christ could have founded two or more churches to represent him on earth, but he founded one holy catholic and apostolic church, for which he made infinite loving sacrifices. Marriage, as an "order of creation" and a "symbol of God's relationship with his elect," involves two parties and two parties only. "Whoever surpasses this rule perverts everything, and it is as though he wished to nullify the very institution of God," Calvin concluded.[111]

Although monogamy had already been commanded at creation, polygyny had already become commonplace soon after the fall into sin. The first polygynist in the Bible was Lamech, a descendent of the first murderer, Cain. Calvin denounced Lamech, for he knowingly "perverted" the "sacred law of marriage" set by God that "two shall become one flesh." Whether driven by lust or by a lust for power, Lamech upset the "order of nature" itself in marrying a second wife. Lamech's sin of polygyny became the custom of subsequent generations of God's people. Indeed, said Calvin, the sin of polygyny has persisted to this day among Muslims, the descendents of Ishmael, the bastard son of Abraham's polygynous relationship with Hagar.[112] Many of Israel's great patriarchs and kings after Abraham—Jacob, Gideon, David, Solomon, Rehoboam, and others—succumbed to the temptation of polygyny just like Abraham. The Bible's account of the chronic discord of their polygynous households should be proof enough, Calvin argued, that their polygyny is against human nature and God's covenantal ideal of marriage. Each polygynist became distracted by multiple demands on his time and energy and multiple divisions of his affections. His wives competed for his attention and approval. His parents became torn in their devotion to their daughters-in-law. His children vied for his property and power. In King David's royal polygynous household, the sibling rivalry escalated to such an extent that the step- and half-children of his multiple wives raped and murdered each other. And that was after King David had already killed Uriah, the husband of Bathsheba, whom he lustfully coveted and wanted

---

111. *CO* 23:50–51; Calvin, *Sermons sur la Genèse*, 1:139–49; Comm. Gen. 1:27; *CO* 7:214; Serm. Deut. 21:10–14; Comm. Harm. Law Exod. 20:3–6; Comm. Eph. 5:31; Serm. Eph. 5:31; Lect. Ezek. 16; Serm. Deut. 21:15–17.

112. Comm. and Serm. Gen. 16:15–16; Comm. Gen. 25:12–18; Comm. Ps. 45:8; Comm. 1 Tim. 3:2. In Lect. Dan. 11:37, Calvin declares: "For Mohammed allowed to men the brutal liberty of chastising their wives and thus he corrupted that conjugal love and fidelity that binds the husband to the wife. Unless every man is content with a single wife, there can be no love, because there can be no conjugal happiness whenever rivalry exists between the inferior wives. As, therefore, Mohammed allowed full scope to various lusts, by permitting a man to have a number of wives, this seems like an explanation of his being inattentive to the love of women."

to add to his harem. Take one step on the slippery sinful slope of polygyny, Calvin concluded, and you slide all the way down into all manner of sinfulness.[113]

But it was not just kings with hundreds of wives who suffered from the compounding sins of polygyny, Calvin went on. Jacob's travails with his two wives, Rachel and Leah, was a simple but sobering illustration of these evils of polygyny under any circumstance. The biblical story is detailed, and Calvin returned to it often. Jacob's uncle Laban had tricked him into marrying his elder daughter, Leah, instead of Rachel, whom Jacob loved. Jacob, after working for seven years to earn this privilege, had reluctantly married Leah. Later, after another long stint of work, he finally gained permission to marry her sister, Rachel, as well. Both Laban and Jacob thereby "pervert[ed] all the laws of nature by casting two sisters into one marriage bed" and forced them to spend their "whole lives in mutual hostility." But it was not so much the incest as the polygyny that caused all the problems. After his second marriage, Jacob did not accord Leah "adequate respect and kindness"; indeed, he "hated" her. Yet the Lord "opened her womb" so that she produced many sons for him. Jacob loved and doted on Rachel to the point of fault, but she produced no children. Leah thus lorded her fertility over Rachel. Incensed, Rachel gave Jacob her servant Bilhah as a concubine in the hopes of having at least a surrogate child. Jacob obliged her and produced two sons by Bilhah. Leah countered by giving Jacob her servant Zilpah as a second concubine, with whom Jacob sired yet another son. All the while, Jacob continued to sleep with Rachel, who finally conceived and had a son, Joseph. This only escalated the feud between Rachel and Leah and their children and the children of their concubines.[114]

For Calvin, this entire scandalous affair proved that "there is no end of sinning, once the divine institution" and natural law of covenant marriage are breached. Jacob's fateful first step of committing polygyny led him to commit all manner of subsequent sins—rampant incest, concubinage, adultery, lust, and then even more polygyny. Jacob's initial sin was perhaps excusable; after all, he was tricked into marrying Leah and had worked and waited patiently seven years for a chance for Rachel to be his wife and to consummate his love for her. His subsequent sins, however, were an utter desecration of God's law. Calvin blamed Rachel as well, rebuking her for her "petulance," her blasphemy and lack of faith, her abuse of her servant Bilhah, and her complicity in Jacob's concubinage, adultery, and polygyny.

Jacob could well have mitigated his sin by divorcing Leah, before marrying Rachel, Calvin further argued. For divorce was "a lighter crime" than polygyny in ancient Israel. After all, God did allow Jewish men to divorce their wives in Deuteronomy 24, even if this was only a concession to their "hardness of heart" and perennial lust. God's provision for divorce created a hierarchy of proper marital conduct. Marriage for life was best. Divorce and remarriage were

---

113. Comm. Gen. 4:19; 16:1–6; 22:19; 26:34–35; 28:6–9; 29:27–30:34; 31:33–42; Lect. Mal. 2:15–16; Serm. 1 Sam. 1:6; Serm. 2 Sam. 13.

114. Comm. Gen. 29:27–30:3.

tolerable. Polygyny, however, was never allowed, for it was a desecration of the primal form and norm of marriage.[115]

Calvin drove home this argument by appealing to the biblical idea of marriage as a covenant. Malachi 2:14, he pointed out, defined marriage as an enduring covenant between a husband and wife, symbolizing the enduring covenant between God and his people. Malachi 2:14–15 then provided, rather opaquely, as the King James Version captures it: "Because the LORD hath been witness between thee and the wife of thy youth, against whom thou has dealt treacherously; yet she is thy companion, and the wife of thy covenant. *And did not he make one? Yet he had the residue of the spirit. And wherefore one? That he might seek a godly seed.*" Calvin read this passage as a confirmation of monogamy and as a condemnation of polygyny. The point of this passage, said Calvin, is that at creation God "breathed his spirit" of life into "one" woman, Eve. God had plenty of spirit left to breathe life into more women besides Eve. But God chose to give life to Eve only, who alone served to "complete" Adam, to be "his other half." And it was this union only that could produce "godly seed," that is, legitimate children.[116]

Both divorce and polygyny were deviations from this primal command of lifelong monogamy, Calvin recognized. But when compared, "polygamy is the worse and more detestable crime," and this shows in how the children of each were to be treated according to God's law. Divorce for cause was allowed by Moses, and even recognized by Christ and Paul. Polygyny enjoyed no such license. Children of divorce remained legitimate heirs. Indeed, the Mosaic law protected their inheritance against unscrupulous fathers who might be tempted to favor the children of their second wife. Children of polygyny, however, were illegitimate bastards, who deserved nothing. Indeed, Mosaic law barred such bastards "from the assembly of the LORD . . . until the tenth generation." Later passages ordered that bastards be "cast out" of their homes, just as Abraham had cast Ishmael out into the wilderness.[117]

Having made so much of this distinction between divorce and polygyny, Calvin dismissed out of hand traditional Catholic arguments that the remarriage of the divorced was a form of serial polygamy, or "digamy." "I do not consider polygamy to be what the foolish Papists have made it," Calvin declared derisively. Polygyny is about marriage to two or more wives at once, as is practiced today among Muslims. It has nothing to do with remarriage to a second wife after the first marriage is dissolved by divorce or death. For Calvin, that was the end of the matter, and he left it to Theodore Beza to elaborate this argument against the concept of serial polygamy.[118]

115. Lect. Mal. 2:14–16; Comm. Harm. Gospel Matt. 19:5–6.

116. Comm. Harm. Gosp. Matt. 19:5–6; Comm. 1 Tim. 3:2; Comm. Titus 1:6; Comm. Harm. Gosp. Matt. 19:3–9.

117. See Comm. Harm. Law Deut. 21:15–17; Comm. Harm. Law Deut. 23:2; Serm. Deut. 23:1–3; Comm. Gen. 21:8–18; Comm. Gal. 4:21–31.

118. See Theodore Beza, *De Polygamia,* in *Tractationum theologicarum,* 2nd ed. (Geneva: Eusthatii Vignon, 1582), 2:1–49, esp. 7, 11–26, 37–49.

Adultery and Divorce

Although Calvin went on at length to condemn polygyny, he saved his greatest thunder for the sin of adultery, outlawed in the Decalogue. He read the Seventh Commandment, "Thou shalt not commit adultery," expansively to outlaw various illicit alliances and actions, within and beyond the marital estate. Within marriage, the obvious case of adultery is sexual intercourse or "any other form of lewd sexual act" with a party not one's spouse.[119] Calvin regarded this form of adultery as "the worst abomination," for in one act the adulterer violates his covenant bonds with spouse, God, and the broader community.[120] "It is not without cause that marriage is called a covenant with God," Calvin thundered from his Geneva pulpit. "Whenever a husband breaks his promise which he has made to his wife, he has not only perjured himself with respect to her, but also with respect to God. The same is true of the wife. She not only wrongs her husband, but [also] the living God."[121] "She sets herself against his majesty."[122] Other parties are also vicariously injured. When a woman commits adultery, for example, "she injures her husband, exposes him to shame, despoils also the name of her family, despoils her unborn children, despoils those already born to her in lawful marriage."[123]

Given its disparate and devastating impact, Calvin argued, adultery had to be counted among the worst offenses—"even graver" than idolatry, heresy, or impiety. For "one can be idolatrous, heretical, or impious, and still hold to matrimonial obligation. But to be both adulterer and spouse, to be these two things at once, is impossible."[124] In Calvin's view, the moral law therefore pronounces "capital punishment for adultery," and he decried the modern-day habit of treating the offense more lightly. "The punishment of death was always awarded to adultery [in earlier times]. Thus it is all the more base and shameful that Christians do not emulate Gentiles at least in this. Adultery is punished no less severely by the Julian [i.e., Roman] law than by the law of God. Yet those who boastfully call themselves Christian are so tender and remiss that they punish this execrable offense only with a very light reproof."[125]

Though Calvin lamented this laxness of punishment, he directly addressed the consequences of adultery for the innocent spouse. Automatic execution of the adulterer would have left the innocent party with the stark but simple choice of remaining single or remarrying. Sparing the adulterer from execution complicated matters. The fate of the marriage should rest in the hands of the innocent

---

119. *Inst.* 1559, 2.8.41; Comm. Harm. Law Exod. 20:14.

120. Comm. Lev. 20:10; 22:22–27.

121. Serm. Deut. 5:18. See also Serm. Deut. 22:25–30; Serm. 2 Sam. 5:13–21; Comm. 1 Cor. 7:11.

122. Serm. Eph. 5:22–26.

123. Serm. Deut. 22:13–19.

124. Ibid. The quoted passage is from Beza, *RD*, 100.

125. Comm. Lev. 20:10, 22–27.

spouse, Calvin believed.[126] The innocent spouse should have the power either to forgive the fault and restore the marriage or to condemn the fault and confirm its dissolution.

The innocent spouse's confirmation of the dissolution of the marriage was expressed by filing for divorce on grounds of adultery. "Christ has allowed" the innocent spouse to seek divorce and even remarry thereafter if so inclined, said Calvin.[127] But a true believer should reconcile with the wayward spouse, following the example of Joseph's indulgence of the Virgin Mary when he first learned of her pregnancy.[128] God instituted divorce as "a concession" to our sinfulness, "permitting it only within the common civil order, which serves to bridle men here below," and not within the higher spiritual order "where the children of God ought to be reformed by the Holy Spirit. Though God does not punish those who divorce on reasonable and lawful grounds, he meant that marriage should always remain inviolable."[129]

Calvin refused to expand the grounds for divorce beyond adultery but was generous about entertaining divorce suits brought for adultery. Christ teaches that a proved case of adultery is the only "reasonable and lawful ground" for divorce, Calvin argued. To expand the grounds for divorce beyond adultery is both bad theology and bad policy. "Those who search for other grounds ought justly to be set at nought, for they choose to be wise above the heavenly teacher."[130] They also invite endless amendment to the moral law: "Some say that leprosy is a proper ground for divorce, because the contagion of the disease affects not only the husband but also the children. . . . Another man develops such a dislike of his wife that he cannot endure to keep company with her. Will [divorce or] polygamy cure this evil? Another man's wife falls into palsy or apoplexy, or becomes afflicted with an incurable disease. May the husband reject her under the pretense of incontinence?"[131] Obviously not, said Calvin, as he drew the line firmly at adultery alone as a legitimate ground for divorce.[132]

When properly pled on grounds of adultery, Calvin believed, divorce actions had to be made equally available to husband and wife. "The right to divorce belongs equally and mutually to both sides for both have a mutual and equal obligation to fidelity. Though in other matters the husband is superior [to the

---

126. Comm. Deut. 23:24–25; 24:1–4; Comm. Matt. 19:9 and discussion in Biéler, *L'homme et la femme*, 69–73. See also Beza, *RD*, 89: After adultery, "the bond of marriage, if it persists, is kept united by the will of the innocent spouse, and can be made strong again by the will of the innocent spouse."

127. Comm. Harm. Gosp. Matt. 19:3–9 and Mark 10:2–12.

128. Ibid. See also Beza, *RD*, 90.

129. Serm. Deut. 24:1–4. See also Serm. Deut. 21:15–17.

130. Comm. Harm. Gosp. Matt. 19:3–9 and Mark 10:2–12. See also Comm. Gen. 2:24: "Those who, for slight causes, rashly allow for divorces, violate, in one single particular, all the laws of nature and reduce them to nothing."

131. Ibid.

132. Calvin did, however, periodically recognize the legitimacy of divorce to avoid greater sins, such as incest and polygamy, discussed above, pp. 190–91.

wife], in matters of the marriage bed, the wife has an equal right. For he is not the Lord of his own body; and therefore, when, by committing adultery, he has dissolved the marriage, his wife is set at liberty."[133] The same is true in reverse for the husband. Once at liberty, the innocent spouse is free to remarry, said Calvin, following conventional Protestant teaching.

Calvin went beyond Protestant convention, however, in his surprising solicitude for the parties after divorce. Both parties, he wrote, would be severely tempted to sexual sin, and both should be granted relief to avoid still greater sin. For the innocent party, Calvin countenanced remarriage—even, if necessary, before issuance of the magistrate's final divorce decree: "If adultery is proved, *even if no sentence is passed*, a Christian church may proceed to marry those who can produce such hearings."[134] Likewise, the wayward party should eventually be allowed to remarry. "Adultery has not been punished as severely as it should have been, and the lives of those who violate the marriage bond have been spared," Calvin wrote glumly in a late-life letter. But then he turned quite pragmatic: "But it would be harsh to prohibit a man from marrying during his whole lifetime if his wife has divorced him for adultery, or to prohibit a woman who has been repudiated by her husband, especially if they have difficulty with being sexually continent; one indulgence necessarily brings the other along with it." Calvin would not allow the guilty party "to fly off immediately to another marriage. The freedom to remarry should be put off for a time, whether for a definite period of time or until the innocent party has remarried."[135]

Calvin considered various other acts within the marital estate—besides sexual intercourse with a third party—to be tantamount to adultery. On one extreme, he regarded sexual perversity with one's own spouse as a violation of the spirit of the Seventh Commandment. "We know to what end marriage was ordained— that persons should live honestly together, and that there should be no beastly looseness or coupling themselves together like dogs and bitches, or bulls and cows." Married couples "should show that they do not bear God's image in vain."[136] And again: "If married couples recognize that their association is blessed by the Lord, they are thereby admonished not to pollute it with uncontrolled and dissolute lust. . . . For it is fitting that a marriage, once covenanted in the Lord, be called to moderation and modesty."[137] Calvin saw this more as a spiritual law of sexual prudence than a civil law against marital prurience. But he did occasionally press the Genevan Council to reprimand couples who proved too sexually raucous, and issued several stern admonitions on sexual modesty to parishioners and correspondents alike.

On the other extreme, Calvin regarded one spouse's desertion of the other, or both spouses' voluntary separation from each other, as virtual forms of

---

133. Ibid.
134. *CO* 10/1:255–58, with added emphasis. See also Beza, *RD*, 88–89.
135. Consilium, in *CO* 10/1:231.
136. Serm. Deut. 22:13–19.
137. *Inst.* 1559, 2.7.44.

adultery. Husband and wife, he said flatly, "must live together and stay together till death."[138] Any undue separation from bed or board, beyond what is necessary for a spouse to carry out normal civic and vocational obligations, "is close to the appearance of adultery," particularly "if it is prompted by capriciousness or sexual desire."[139] Any abandonment of one's spouse is doubly suspect, especially if done angrily or maliciously.[140] Calvin pressed this logic not only for the simple reason that virile spouses, left on their own, might be tempted to adultery—in mind, if not in fact. He was also concerned that such separations violated God's literal command that husband and wife be joined together permanently in soul, mind, and body. "It is the law of marriage that when a man joins himself to a wife, he takes her to be a companion to live with her and die with her. If the nature of marriage is such,. . . a married man is only half a person, and he can no more separate himself from his wife than cut himself into two pieces."[141]

Calvin thus stood opposed to the traditional canon-law and civil-law remedy of separation from bed and board. He stood even more firmly opposed to the new social fashion of couples separating simply because "their manners were not congenial, or their appearance did not please, or some other [trivial] offense."[142] Calvin advocated perpetual union of bed and board between husband and wife—by force of law and arms, if necessary.[143] He ordered separated couples to reconcile with each other, deserting spouses to return to their homes, and abandoned spouses to forgive the desertion. Where reconciliation proved impossible, Calvin preferred to treat the marriage as dissolved by reason of the presumed adultery of one party, rather than perpetuated without the cohabitation of both parties.[144] This was consistent with his strict biblical reading that adultery is the sole ground for divorce granted by the moral law.

Calvin was not always consistent in his treatment of separation, however. As we saw in the opening story of the French noblewoman, where one party deviates from the faith and abuses the other, Calvin generally allowed only for separation by the innocent spouse, with no right of remarriage.[145] In cases of malicious desertion, he sometimes insisted that the innocent spouse bring proof of actual adultery before a divorce action could be filed.[146] Calvin was aware that he thereby left the innocent party subject to sexual temptation. He offered only a vague homily in reply: "Would it not be inhuman to refuse [the innocent party]

138. Comm. 1 Cor. 7:11. See also Serm. Deut. 24:1–4.
139. Consilium, CO 10/1:242–44.
140. Ibid; Comm. 1 Cor. 7:11.
141. Serm. Deut. 24:1–4. See also Comm. 1 Cor. 9:11: "If they be separated, they are like the mutilated members of the mangled body. Let them, therefore, be connected with each other by this tie of mutual aid and amicableness."
142. Comm. 1 Cor. 7:11; Consilium, in CO 10/1:242–44.
143. Ibid.
144. Ibid. See also Comm. Harm. Gosp. Matt. 19:9; Comm. 1 Cor. 7:11.
145. Comm. 1 Cor. 7:12.
146. See cases in Seeger, Nullité de mariage, 380–403; SMF, vol. 2, ch. 12.

the remedy of [re]marriage when constantly burning with desire? My answer is that when we are prompted by the infirmity of our flesh, we must have recourse to the remedy; after which it is the Lord's part to bridle and restrain our affections by his Spirit, [even] though matters should not succeed according to our desires."[147]

On this point, Theodore Beza was more insistent and consistent than Calvin in treating "desertion as adultery" and allowing divorce and remarriage to the innocent party. A party deserted "in soul," through a difference of religion, or "in body," through malicious abandonment, is like the innocent spouse in a case of adultery, said Beza. The innocent party has power either to forgive the fault and restore the marriage or to condemn the fault and confirm its dissolution. The innocent party should seek reconciliation with the wayward spouse "only so long as conscience allows." Thereafter, he or she can abandon the dissolved marriage by filing for divorce and then contract a new marriage, if so desired.[148]

For Calvin, the commandment against adultery was equally binding on the unmarried and equally applicable to both illicit sexual activities per se and various acts leading to the same. Calvin condemned with particular vehemence the sin of fornication—sexual intercourse or other illicit acts of sexual touching by a nonmarried party.[149] He decried at length the widespread practice of casual sex, prostitution, concubinage, premarital sex, nonmarital cohabitation, and other forms of bed-hopping that he encountered in modern-day Geneva, as well as in ancient Bible stories. "Today it is not only the common man who flatters himself into thinking that fornication is not such a great and mortal sin. We even see highborn persons making light of God by calling fornication a natural sin and a matter of little consequence. There are actually such shameless swine that talk that way."[150] All these actions, Calvin believed, openly defied God's commandment against adultery, and God's commendation of chaste and holy marriage.[151] Calvin had simple biblical counsel to offer against the "scourge of fornication": preach against it constantly, punish it severely by spiritual and criminal sanctions,[152] and portray everything from an individual case of syphilis to a community's encounter with pestilence as God's retribution for the offense.[153] He followed this counsel to the letter.

---

147. Comm. 1 Cor. 7:11.

148. Beza, *RD*, 95–99.

149. *Inst.* 1559, 2.8.41, 44; Comm. Harm. Law Lev. 20:10; 22:22–27.

150. Serm. Deut. 5:18.

151. *CO* 7:212.

152. In 1563, Geneva adopted the rule that when fornicating couples appear at the church for their wedding ceremony, "the minister make public declaration of their fault, which they ought also to recognize to undo the scandal" (*SD*, vol. 3, item no. 1042). Four months later, the penalty against fornication was raised from six days to nine, plus a fine; recidivists had also to appear before the sermon and make public confession of their sin and reparation to the shamed parties and families (ibid., vol. 3, item no. 1946).

153. Serm. Deut. 22:25–30; 28:25–29, 59–64; Comm. Harm. Law Lev. 20:10; 22:22–27; Lect. Ezek. 16:9, 20; Comm. 1 Cor. 6:18; Serm. Eph. 5:3–5.

Calvin stretched the reach of the Seventh Commandment far beyond the sin of actual fornication. For believers abiding by the spiritual law, such an extension was natural, for as Christ taught in the Beatitudes: "Continence involved not only keeping the body free from fornication, but also keeping a chaste mind."[154] But Calvin urged a comparable extension of the civil law of adultery. In his more exuberant moments, he tended to treat all manner of mildly sexual activities—lewdness, dancing, bawdy gaming, sexual innuendo, coarse humor, provocative primping, suggestive plays and literature, and much more—as forms of adultery, punishable by the state.[155] Calvin would not tie the sexy dresser and the insatiable playboy to the same stake for flogging or execution. He viewed milder forms of adventuresome sexual expression as forms of sumptuousness, punishable by admonition and fines.[156] But he insisted that even such attenuated sexual conduct was, in essence, a violation of the Seventh Commandment prohibition of adultery that deserved both spiritual reproof and criminal sanctions.

The Purpose of the Marriage Covenant

Starting with the created *structure* of the marriage covenant, Calvin was able to integrate various biblical and natural norms against bestiality, homosexuality, polygyny, adultery, desertion, and fornication and to smuggle in a tepid endorsement of divorce and firmer prohibition against separation. Turning to the created *purposes* of marriage—mutual love of husband and wife, mutual procreation of children, and mutual protection from lust—Calvin was able to integrate several other such norms, most of which he had already outlined in his 1546 Marriage Ordinance.

Sexual dysfunction, Calvin insisted, was an absolute barrier to marriage, for it vitiated all three purposes of marriage. Thus putative marriages of prepubescent children were null, even if the parties have reached sufficient maturity to consent to marry, for "the terms of the marriage cannot be carried out."[157] Marriages of "the frigid and eunuchs" were likewise null, for such unions "completely obviate the nature and purpose of marriage. For what is marriage except the joining of a male and female, and why was it instituted except to produce children and to remedy sexual incontinence?"[158] Calvin called for automatic annulment of any marriage of a permanently dysfunctional party and for penalties if the condition had been kept secret prior to the wedding.[159]

---

154. Quoted and discussed in Georgia Harkness, *John Calvin: The Man and His Ethics* (New York: Henry Holt, 1931), 130.

155. Serm. Deut. 22:5–8, 25–30; Serm. Eph. 5:3–5; Comm. 1 Pet. 3:3; Serm. Titus 2:3–5.

156. See Biéler, *L'homme et la femme*, 124–26, 138–45; W. Fred Graham, *The Constructive Revolutionary: John Calvin and His Socio-Economic Impact* (Atlanta: John Knox Press, 1978), 110–15.

157. Consilium in *CO* 10/1:231.

158. Ibid.

159. Ibid. See also Beza, *RD*, 72–73, 109–10; Seeger, *Nullité de mariage*, 116–18.

Calvin grounded a number of prudential norms for the *unmarried believer* in the created purposes of marriage. Citing both Moses and Paul, he counseled Christians against marrying unbelievers, for such unions would invariably jeopardize all three created functions of marriage. The unbeliever could not know the true meaning of love reflected in Christ, would not know how to raise children in the love of God, and might not resist the temptations to lust that marriage was supposed to remedy.[160] Calvin did not regard differences in religion as an absolute bar to the contracting of marriage, let alone a ground for annulment or divorce, as we have seen.[161] Instead, he simply wrote: "When a man is to marry, he should (so far as possible) choose a wife who will help him in the worship of God, . . . who knows God and his word, and who is ready to give up all idolatry." To do otherwise, said Calvin, was "spiritually unlawful," though civilly permissible.[162]

Citing Moses' account of the evil world on the eve of the flood—"The sons of God saw that the daughters of men were fair and took to wife such as them as they chose"—Calvin counseled further against entering engagements or marriages with undue levity or lust.[163] It was certainly good for men to have choices among women and freedom of choice, Calvin insisted. But the problem was that these men described in the Bible "did not choose those possessed of the necessary endowments" for marriage but chose indiscriminately. The modern message of this passage is that "temperance is to be used in contracting holy marriage."[164] Calvin continued in this vein in commenting on the Bible's account of Jacob's choice of Rachel over her elder sister, Leah. There was nothing wrong with Jacob's choosing Rachel because she was more beautiful, Calvin allowed. "Only excess is to be guarded against" for that leads to a "stifling of reason." A man who "chooses a wife because of the elegance of her form will not necessarily sin, provided reason always maintains the ascendancy." And reason teaches that a woman's "excellence of disposition" is the most important criterion in deciding whether to marry her.

Calvin thus recognized and even celebrated the importance of the sexual human body—though nothing on the order of the Renaissance artists and playwrights of his day.[165] He extolled "beauty," "comeliness," "handsomeness," "health," "elegance of form," and similar attributes many times—mostly in women, occasionally in men. He viewed attractive physiques as special creations and gifts from God. The body was "a temple of the Lord," the apostle Paul had written.[166] Some temples were more handsomely appointed than others. Some

---

160. See, e.g., letters in *CO* 13:307–11, 484–87.
161. See Comm. 1 Cor. 7:12, 14; *CO* 10/1:264–66.
162. Serm. Deut. 21:10–14. See also *CO* 13:487.
163. Comm. Gen. 6:2.
164. Ibid.
165. Biéler, *L'homme et la femme*, 81ff.
166. Comm. 1 Cor. 6:15–20. See also Comm. Gen. 39:6; Comm. Harm. Law Exod. 2:1–10. Calvin left no commentaries or sermons on Proverbs and the Song of Solomon (or Song of Songs), which are filled with (sometimes sultry) passages on the physical beauty of women.

were more beautiful on the inside than on the outside. Physical beauty was properly part of the natural calculus of courtship and marriage, Calvin believed. It was "not wrong for women to look at men."[167] Nor was it "wrong for men to regard beauty in their choice of wives."[168] For natural attraction helped to induce that "secret kind of affection [that] produces mutual love."[169] It was thus essential to Calvin that couples spend some time together before considering marriage so that their "natural disposition" toward each other "could be ascertained." If there was no natural and mutual attraction, there was no use for a couple to go forward toward marriage. Accordingly, Calvin opposed the late medieval tradition of arranged or child marriages between some couples, sight unseen.

As with all such natural gifts of God, however, physical beauty must be used moderately and modestly in courtship. Courting couples did not need to hide their physical beauty from each other. But they should not flaunt it either, lest others be tempted to sin. They did not need to avert their eyes from their partner's elegant form. But they should not dwell on it either, lest they be driven to lust.[170] They did not need to ignore physical attractiveness in deciding on a mate. But they should not make raw attraction their principal criterion of courtship or marriage. "Marriage is a thing too sacred to allow that men should be induced to it by the lust of their eyes." We "profane the covenant of marriage" when "our appetite becomes brutal, when we are so ravished with the charms of beauty, that those things which are chief are not taken into account."[171]

Calvin laid out "those things which are chief" in his account of what he sought in his own wife: "I am none of those insane lovers who embrace also the vices of those they are in love with, where they are smitten at first sight with a fine figure. This only is the beauty which allures me, if she is chaste, if not too nice and fastidious, if economical, if patient, if there is hope that she will be interested about my health," and if she could produce children.[172] Calvin could not have been surprised that this account did not bring an overwhelming response from eligible women. To everyone's great surprise, however, Calvin soon married Idelette de Bure, an Anabaptist widow with two children of her own. Idelette met Calvin's stated criteria of piety, modesty, frugality, and the like. But she was also savvy, sociable, respectable, and "actually pretty," Calvin's friend, Guillaume Farel noted with some surprise.[173] Calvin's first biographer, Theodore Beza, reports that Idelette and "Calvin lived in marriage about nine years in perfect chastity."[174] This has led some to speculate that they had a sexless spiritual marriage, as was

167. Comm. Gen. 39:6.

168. Comm. Gen. 6:2.

169. Comm. Gen. 29:18.

170. Comm. Gen. 12:11; 20:3; 34:1; 38:2; 39:3–6; Serm. 2 Sam. 11:1–5a.

171. See also Comm. Gen. 39:6; Comm. 1 Thess. 4:1–5.

172. Jules Bonnet, ed., *Letters of John Calvin*, 4 vols. (repr., New York: Burt Franklin, 1972), 1:139, 141.

173. *CO* 11:78–81. See also Bernard Cottret, *Calvin: A Biography*, trans. M. Wallace McDonald (Grand Rapids: Wm. B. Eerdmans Publishing Co., 2000), 141–42.

174. *CO* 21:37.

occasionally practiced by earnest Catholic couples of the day.[175] But the facts do not bear out such an austere picture, nor do they square with Calvin's repeated advice that married couples should enjoy each other sexually. Calvin reports that he and Idelette had a "very happy honeymoon" that was unhappily cut short by the plague.[176] Quarantined from Idelette, Calvin wrote in anguish that "my wife is in my thoughts day and night."[177] The couple had at least three children, maybe four. To their great grief, these children were all stillborn or died in their cribs.[178] Idelette's premature death in 1549 devastated Calvin. His pain was doubled by Idelette's premature death and his stepdaughter Judith's "lustful rush" into marriage and divorce a few years later on account of her adultery.[179]

Calvin chose thereafter to remain a widower and seemed to use this experience in advising other widows and widowers. Citing Paul, he urged the widowed to refrain from remarriage if they were beyond childbearing years and "altogether beyond the danger of incontinence."[180] For, in such instances, the marital purposes of procreation and perhaps even mutual love would be compromised, and "the inconveniences of mixed married life" might well not be worth it.[181] "Women are no less at liberty than men to marry a second time upon becoming widows," Calvin insisted, reiterating both his concern for gender equality in questions of sexuality and his condemnation of mandatory celibacy. But neither elderly widows nor elderly widowers should rush to marry too easily.[182] Building on this same moral, Calvin discouraged marriages between young men and elderly women, arguing that such unions "were contrary to the order of nature," for they would not yield children, and "contrary to the law of conscience," for they would tempt the young husband to adultery. He sometimes pressed this counsel in the obverse case as well, even to the point of condemning the late-life marriage of his dear friend and fellow reformer Guillaume Farel to a young woman less than half his age.[183]

Calvin also grounded several biblical norms for married parties in the created purposes of marriage. Most important, he urged that married couples retain

175. Agnès Walch, *La spiritualité conjugale dans le catholicisme français, XVIe-XXe siècle* (Paris: les Éditions du Cerf, 2002).

176. *CO* 11:83–86.

177. *CO* 11:174–79.

178. See letters in *CO* 11:419–20, 719; 12:322, 580; and William J. Bouwsma, *John Calvin: A Sixteenth-Century Portrait* (New York and Oxford: Oxford University Press, 1988), 23, 242n. In his *Respondio ad Balduini convicia* (*CO* 9:561–80), one of several attacks on the jurist Franciscus Baudouin, who had betrayed him, Calvin wrote: "Wishing to clear himself from the charge of a want of natural affection brought against him, Baudouin tweaks me for my lack of offspring. God had given me a son. But God had taken away my little boy." This suggests that Calvin had one son and two or three daughters.

179. See Richard Stauffer, *L'humanité de Calvin* (Neuchâtel: Delachaux & Niestlé, 1964), 19; Williston Walker, *John Calvin* (New York: Schocken Books, 1960), 357.

180. Comm. 1 Tim. 5:11.

181. Ibid.; Comm. 1 Cor. 7:1.

182. Comm. 1 Cor. 7:9. See also Comm. 1 Cor. 7:36; Comm. 1 Tim. 5:14.

183. See sources in *SMF*, 1:278–82.

a healthy sex life, even after their childbearing years. "Satan dazzles us . . . to imagine that we are polluted by intercourse," said Calvin.[184] But "when the marital bed is dedicated to the name of the Lord, that is, when parties are joined together in his name, and live honorably, it is something of a holy estate."[185] For "the mantle of marriage exists to sanctify what is defiled and profane; it serves to cleanse what used to be soiled and dirty in itself."[186] Husband and wife should not, therefore, "withhold sex from the other." Nor should they "neglect or reject" one another after intimacy or intercourse.[187] Couples may forgo their sexual obligations for a season, said Calvin, echoing the traditional position on the "Pauline privilege." But such abstinence should occur only by mutual consent and only for a finite period, lest one party be tempted to adultery by too long a wait.[188] The traditional option of maintaining a sexless "spiritual marriage" was anathema to Calvin.[189]

If a couple proved to be barren, Calvin urged them to accept this as God's providential design. "We are fruitful or barren as God imparts his power," he wrote. Those who are barren should sponsor or adopt orphans or find other ways of serving the next generation.[190] Calvin would hear nothing of concubinage or surrogate motherhood as a viable alternative to sterility, despite the example of Abraham and other Old Testament figures. In taking Hagar as his concubine, "Abraham took a liberty" that God had not countenanced, Calvin believed, and his reward was the perpetual strife between Sarah and Hagar, Isaac and Ishmael, and their many descendents. This, for Calvin, was proof enough that concubinage was no viable option for the modern day.[191] Calvin would also hear nothing of divorce on grounds of sterility. Procreation was only one created purpose of marriage, he counseled. Where it could not be achieved, a couple had to double their efforts to achieve the other purposes of mutual love and mutual protection from lust, "treating each other with chaste tenderness" even where God would not bless them with children.[192]

If, after a time, one marital party became incapable of sexual performance because of frailty, impotence, or sickness, Calvin urged understanding and patience on the part of the other spouse. Here, too, he would hear nothing of concubinage, separation, or divorce as a remedy or a result of this later sexual incapacitation.[193] There was a rather blurry line between automatic annulment

---

184. Serm. Deut. 5:18.

185. Serm. Deut. 22:13–19.

186. Serm. Deut., 5:18. See also Comm. 1 Cor. 7:6: "Marriage is a veil by which the fault of immoderate desire is covered over, so that it no longer appears in the sight of God."

187. Serm. Deut. 22:13–19; 24:5–6.

188. Comm. 1 Cor. 7:3, 5; Serm. Deut. 22:13–19; Comm. Harm. Gosp. Matt. 19:3–9 and Mark 10:2–12.

189. CO 7:212. See also Beza, RD, 82–83. For background, see Walch, La spiritualité conjugale.

190. Serm. and Comm. Gen. 1:28; Comm. Ps. 127:3; 128:3; Comm. 1 Tim. 5:14.

191. Comm. Gen. 16:1–6; Comm. Matt. 19:9. See also Beza, RD, 108.

192. Comm. Gen. 16:1–6. See also Beza, RD, 105–6.

193. Comm. 1 Cor. 7:11. See also Lect. Mal. 2:14.

of a new marriage where one party proved permanently impotent or frigid and automatic perpetuation of a long-standing marriage where a spouse once capable of intercourse later became incapacitated. Calvin did little to clarify the line. Theodore Beza and his colleagues on the Geneva consistory did, favoring perpetuation of any such marriage and opting for annulment only if the sexually active party sought it within a few months of the wedding and (obviously) only if the couple lacked children.[194]

If one party contracted leprosy or some other form of contagious disease, Calvin again urged "Christian patience" by the healthy party and sexual restraint by the afflicted party. He again flatly prohibited concubinage, separation, or divorce as options.[195] In one extreme case, Calvin did allow for separation from bed and board, where a husband had been afflicted with elephantiasis, a disease that dramatically increased his sexual appetite but was highly contagious and dangerous to his wife.[196] It would be "cruel," said Calvin, "to obligate the woman to share a home and marriage bed with a husband who is forgetful of all the laws of nature. We feel that she must be allowed to live as a widow, after a legal investigation by judges has intervened. Meanwhile, she should continue to attend her husband and perform any duties she can, provided that he does not require of her anything virtually unnatural."[197]

The Covenant Model of Marriage in Comparative Perspective

Calvin's covenant theology of marriage was neither very systematic nor entirely consistent. The foregoing account is no simple report from a chapter or two of Calvin's *Institutes* or other systematic works. It is a patchwork quilt, stitched together from many thin strands of argument strewn all over Calvin's late-life commentaries, sermons, letters, *consilia*, and legal fragments. And, even granting all of Calvin's close distinctions—between believers and nonbelievers, couples and singles, spiritual and civil laws, Old Testament customs and New Testament canons—this patchwork account is not free from anomaly.

For example, Calvin harvested a thick sheaf of modern-day prescriptions for marriage from the creation story of Adam and Eve, often reading the Genesis passages inventively and with anticipation of New Testament teachings and customs. But he would take no modern lessons from the Bible's descriptions of Abraham's concubinage, or Solomon's polygyny, condemning all such "unnatural" actions unequivocally. Calvin read into a few pastoral asides from Paul a very progressive understanding of equality of women in rights to marital sex, parentage, and divorce. But he squeezed out of the creation story a

---

194. See Beza, *RD*, 71–73; and cases summarized in Seeger, *Nullité de mariage*, 353–55.
195. Comm. Harm. Gosp. Matt. 19:9.
196. Consilium, in *CO* 10/1:241–42. But cf. Comm. Harm. Gosp. Matt. 19:9, where Calvin argues that a husband should not touch a leprous wife, but "I do not pronounce him at liberty to divorce."
197. *CO* 10/1:242.

general principle of subordination of women in all other matters, even to the point of denying women a right to propose marriage to a prospective husband.[198] Calvin insisted that any marital impediments of blood and family be grounded in a strict reading of the Bible or be discarded. But he imported, rather casually, various impediments of crime, religion, and quality that had only the shallowest grounding in the Bible. Calvin read the term *adultery* in the Seventh Commandment to include a fantastic range of illicit conduct—from a spouse's torrid affairs with a third-party relative to a bit of suggestive sexual innuendo between a happily married couple. But when discussing Christ's permission to divorce on grounds of the same term *adultery*, he read the term narrowly as proved illicit intercourse by one's spouse and a third party. Calvin was remarkably solicitous for the sexual needs and temptations of the divorced, even suggesting that they could remarry before the state had issued a divorce decree. But he offered only bland injunctions to "Christian patience" to allay the sexual burning of both single and married persons for whom no natural and licit sexual outlet was available. Even a sympathetic parsing of Calvin's opening distinctions and a generous appreciation for his sixteenth-century rhetorical style cannot explain away these and other anomalies in his presentation.

Such anomalies were inevitable and not fatal. Given the loose literary forums and forms in which Calvin worked, it was inevitable that loose ends and loose logic would remain, undetected. This was doubly inevitable given the conditions during which Calvin wrote in his later life: rapidly deteriorating health, escalating demands for his pastoral and political counsel, bitter controversies over the execution of Michael Servetus, and a proliferation of other demands associated with subjects of reform that had nothing to do with marriage and family life. In that context, it was remarkable that Calvin was able to rise to the level of refinement and comprehension that he did.

The profundity of Calvin's insights for marriage was not lost on his contemporaries or his followers. Even in prototypical form, Calvin's covenant theology of marriage proved to be a powerful Protestant model for marriage that exercised an enormous and enduring influence on the Western tradition.

Calvin's covenantal model mediated both the sacramental and the contractual models of marriage that pressed for recognition in his day. On the one hand, this covenantal model confirmed the sacred and sanctifying qualities of marriage, without ascribing to it sacramental functions. After his later-life reflections on the covenant of marriage, Calvin came to a far more elevated spiritual view of marriage than he had earlier offered. He described marriage in sweeping spiritual terms as "a sacred bond," "a holy fellowship," "a divine partnership," "a loving association," "a heavenly calling," "the fountainhead of life," "the holiest kind of company in all the world," "the principal and most sacred . . . of all the

---

198. See, e.g., Calvin, *Letters*, 2:110–11; and Calvin's sometimes officious matchmaking documented in *SMF*, 1:100–106.

offices pertaining to human society."[199] Conjugal love is "holy" when "husband and wife are joined in one body and one soul."[200] "God reigns in a little household, even one in dire poverty, when the husband and the wife dedicate themselves to their duties to each other. Here there is a holiness greater and nearer the kingdom of God than there is even in a cloister."[201] Calvin had come a long way from his earlier glum description of marriage as "a good ordinance, just like farming, building, cobbling, and barbering."

With this more spiritual view of marriage, Calvin also described more fully the biblical uses of marriage to symbolize the relationship of God and humanity. He analyzed at length the Old Testament image of Yahweh's covenant of marriage with Israel, and Israel's proclivity for "playing the harlot"—worshiping false gods and allying with Gentile neighbors, much as delinquent spouses abandon faith in God and faithfulness to each other.[202] He repeatedly returned to the New Testament image of Christ's marriage to the church, holding up Christ's faith and sacrificial love toward us as a model to which spouses and parents should aspire.[203] He went so far as to say that "marriage is the holiest bond that God has set among us," for it is "a figure of the Son of God and all the faithful," "a symbol of our divine covenant with our Father."[204] But then, almost in self-chiding, Calvin reiterated his earlier position that marriage, though symbolic of God's relationship with persons, is not a sacrament, for it does not confirm a divine promise. "Anyone who would classify such similitudes with the sacraments ought to be sent to a mental hospital."[205]

On the other hand, Calvin's covenantal model confirmed the contractual and consensual qualities of marriage, without subjecting it to the personal preferences of the parties. "It is the mutual consent of the man and the woman that . . . constitutes marriage," Calvin insisted, echoing traditional views.[206] Lack of true consent—by reason of immaturity, drunkenness, insincerity, conditionality, mistake, fraud, coercion, or similar impairment—perforce breaks the marriage contract, just as it breaks any other contract.[207]

But marriage is more than a contract and turns on more than the voluntary consent of the parties. God is a third party to every marriage, Calvin believed, and God has set its basic terms in the order and law of creation. "Other contracts

199. Serm. and Comm. Gen. 2:21, 24; 6:2; Serm. Deut. 21:10–14; Comm. Mal. 2:14, 16; Comm. Harm. Gosp. Matt. 19:11; Comm. 1 Cor. 7:14; 9:11; CO 7:212.

200. Comm. Gen. 2:18. But cf. *Inst.* 1559, 4.19, where Calvin sharply criticized Catholic sacramental views that regarded "carnal copulation" as an indispensable part of the sacrament of marriage.

201. Serm. 1 Tim. 5:3-16.

202. Lect. Ezek. 16; Comm. Mal. 2:14–15; Lect. Hos. 2:2; Serm. Deut. 21:10–14.

203. Serm. Eph. 5:28–33; Comm. Eph. 5:30–32.

204. Serm. Eph. 5:28–30; Lect. Ezek. 16:9, 17; Lect. Hos. 2:2; Serm. Deut. 21:10–14.

205. *Inst.* 1559, 4.19.34. This repeats verbatim what Calvin had written in *Inst.* 1536, 5.69.

206. Comm. Gen. 29:27; see also Comm. Gen. 2:18; Serm. Eph. 5:22–26; Consilium in CO 10/1:231–32.

207. CO 51:763. For Calvin's general views of contract, such as they are, see his "Fragments des travaux de Calvin relatifs à la législation civile et politique," in CO 10/1:126, 130–32, 139; with brief discussion of commercial contracts in Bohatec, *Calvins Lehre von Staat und Kirche*, 687–700.

depend on the mere inclination of men, and can be entered into and dissolved by that same inclination."[208] Not so the covenant of marriage. Our "freedom of contract" in marriage is effectively limited to choosing which party to marry from among the mature, unrelated, virile members of the opposite sex available to us. We have no freedom to forgo marriage—unless we have the rare gift of natural continence—for else we "spurn God's remedy for lust" and "tempt our nature" to sexual perversity.[209] We also have no freedom to abandon marriage, "for otherwise the whole order of nature would be overthrown."[210] "Consider what will be left of safety in the world—of order, of loyalty, of honesty, of assurance—if marriage, which is the most sacred union, and ought to be most faithfully guarded, can thus be violated," Calvin thundered.[211] "In truth, all contracts and all promises that we make ought to be faithfully upheld. But if we should make a comparison, it is not without cause that marriage is called a covenant with God," for it cannot be broken.[212]

Calvin's covenantal model of marriage not only mediated the sacramental and contractual models of marriage that he encountered in Geneva. It also modified the social model of marriage that he inherited from Wittenberg. Using the two-kingdom theory, Luther and his colleagues had treated marriage as a social estate of the earthly kingdom alone—an institution fundamentally earthly in nature, social in function, and civil in governance. Calvin echoed and endorsed these Lutheran teachings on marriage. But he also superimposed on this two-kingdoms framework a doctrine of marriage as covenant. The effect of this was to add a spiritual dimension to marriage life in the earthly kingdom, a marital obligation to spiritual life in the heavenly kingdom, and complementary marital roles for both church and state in the governance of both kingdoms.

Marriage was an earthly order and obligation for all persons, said Calvin, echoing Luther. But it also had vital spiritual sources and sanctions for Christians. Marriage required the coercive power of the state to preserve its integrity. But it also required the spiritual counsel of the church to demonstrate its necessity. Marriage was grounded in the will and consent of the parties. But it was also founded in the creation and commandments of God. Marriage deterred sinful persons from the lust and incontinence of this earthly life. But it also symbolized for them the love and sacrifice of the heavenly life. Marriage served the social purpose of procreation and protection from sin. But it also served the divine purpose of sanctification and edification by grace. None of these sentiments was altogether original with Calvin, nor were they entirely unknown to Luther.

208. Comm. 1 Cor. 7:11.
209. See *Inst.* 1559, 2.8.42; 4.19.34–37; Serm. and Comm. Gen. 2:18, 22; Comm. Harm. Gosp. Matt. 19:11:"The choice to marry is not put in our own hands, as if we were to deliberate on the matter"; Comm. 1 Cor. 7:7–8, 25–28; Comm. 1 Tim. 5:13. See also Calvin's correspondence in *CO* 5:330; 7:42, 670.
210. Serm. Deut. 22:25–30.
211. *CO* 7:212. See also Serm. and Comm. Gen. 2:24.
212. Serm. Deut. 5:18.

But, using the doctrine of covenant, Calvin was able to cast these traditional teachings into a new ensemble, with new theological emphases and new legal implications.

Calvin's covenantal model of marriage also helped to refine and rationalize many of the rules set out in the Marriage Liturgy of 1545, the Marriage Ordinance of 1546, and various other rules that Calvin and his colleagues had crafted in the early years of the Genevan Reformation. For example, the doctrine of covenant provided Calvin with a sturdy new rationale for the familiar Protestant requirement that the formation of marriages be intensely public affairs. Earlier Protestant Reformers (as well as later Catholic theologians at the Council of Trent) had described various parties' involvement in the formation of marriage as grounded in discrete biblical passages, with no general theory to integrate them. Parental consent was based on the Fifth Commandment of the Decalogue and Paul's admonitions to parents and children. Mandatory witnesses to betrothals and espousals was rooted in Peter's disquisitions on the priesthood of believers. Church consecration and celebration of the marriage was grounded in Christ's delegation of the power of the keys to Peter and the apostles. Civil registration and publication of marriage banns was based on Paul's general descriptions of state power in Romans 13. Calvin repeated, and also embellished, these familiar biblical rationales for the involvement of each party in the process of marriage formation.[213] But he also integrated these separate biblical rationales by treating all four of these parties as allied agents of God in forming the marital covenant. He thereby rebuffed the agitation in his day for the truncation of the public formalities and functionaries of marriage formation. He also helped to confirm the place of parents, peers, ministers, and magistrates in the marriage process for centuries to come. Subsequent generations of Reformed theologians and jurists—building on Calvin's work as well as that of his contemporary Heinrich Bullinger[214] and contemporaneous Anabaptist writers who espoused similar sentiments[215]—elaborated at length this covenantal conception of a public marriage process.

213. One such embellishment was that Calvin prioritized the father's consent over that of the mother, basing this on the headship of man over woman after the fall into sin. See, e.g., Consilium, CO 10/1:231–32, 238–39; Serm. Eph. 5:3–5; and detailed sources and analysis in SMF, 1:164–201.

214. See esp. Heinrich Bullinger, Der christlich E[h]estand (Zurich: Froschouer, 1540), discussed in chap. 7 below. Though Calvin and Bullinger corresponded regularly, I have found no evidence that Calvin used Bullinger's marriage tract in formulating his theology of marriage, let alone that Calvin had any influence on Bullinger's formulations. It is evident that Ulrich Zwingli, an important earlier reformer of marriage in Zurich, had at least adumbrated a comparable covenantal theology of marriage, which both Bullinger and Calvin knew. See his De vera et falsa religionis commentarius (1525), in Huldreich Zwinglis sämtliche Werke (Zurich: Theologischer Verlag, 1982–91), 3:590, and at 762–63 (brief section on marriage), with discussion and sources in Charles S. McCoy and J. Wayne Baker, Foundation of Federalism: Heinrich Bullinger and the Covenantal Tradition (Louisville: Westminster/John Knox Press, 1991).

215. See George Huntston Williams, The Radical Reformation, 3rd ed., Sixteenth Century Essays and Studies (Kirksville, MO: Sixteenth Century Journal Publishers, 1992), 755–98.

Similarly, the doctrine of covenant allowed Calvin to tighten the rules and standards for entering and exiting marriages. The 1546 Marriage Ordinance clearly distinguished between engagement and marriage, annulment and divorce. But at the same time, it conflated terms like rescission, dissolution, nullity, voidness, and the like, leaving unclear the precise legal effect of a given defect, impediment, or illicit action.[216] Calvin's and Beza's exposition on the moral law for the covenant of marriage made this somewhat clearer. Engagements and marriages were automatically annulled if the parties breached Levitical impediments or involved a sexually dysfunctional party. Engagements could be broken by either party, or at the instigation of a third party, for any number of reasons of Christian prudence—differences in religion or quality, concerns for compatibility, maturity, security, and the like. Marriages once entered were virtually permanent. The rules of Christian prudence that could annul betrothals could not annul marriages. Separation from bed or board was not an option, save in the most dire case of danger to an innocent spouse's body and soul. Divorce could be granted on strict biblical grounds of adultery or a fully proved case of malicious desertion that was tantamount to adultery.

This new covenantal understanding of marriage and family life did not remain confined to sermons, commentaries, and letters. In the course of the 1550s and thereafter, it also came to vivid legal application in the work of the Geneva consistory—led by Calvin, still serving as the moderator of the Company of Pastors and succeeded by Beza.[217] The pathbreaking work in the Genevan archives by Robert Kingdon, Cornelia Seeger, and Walter Köhler, among others,[218] shows how the consistory had seized upon its new marital jurisdiction with alacrity, especially in the aftermath of the 1555 riots in Geneva, which finally settled the city in favor of the Reformed faith.[219]

The consistory and council heard numerous cases of disputed betrothals. They automatically annulled betrothals on the discovery of a Levitical impediment of a blood or family relationship between the parties, potential bigamy by one party, or obvious impotence or other sexual dysfunction of one party. Parties who sought to conceal these conditions before marriage were subject to rather severe spiritual and criminal sanctions. The consistory and council generally annulled betrothals of minors who were immature, lacked parental consent, or were coerced or tricked into the betrothal—again, often sanctioning guilty parties in the process. They also generally annulled betrothals if one party contracted a contagious disease or was convicted for a crime or if the parties were separated by too great a difference of age, religion, quality, and in a few instances, even social status. They rarely

216. Seeger, *Nullité de mariage*, 97–101.

217. Eugène Choisy, *L'état chrétien calviniste à Genève au temps de Théodore de Bèze* (Geneva: C. Eggimann, 1902).

218. *SMF*, vols. 1 and 2. See further Köhler, *Genfer Konsistorium*, 2:626–45; Seeger, *Nullité de mariage*, 305–450.

219. See generally E. William Monter, "The Consistory of Geneva: 1559–1569," *Bibliothèque d'humanisme et renaissance* 38 (1976): 467–84.

annulled betrothals if parties failed to have their banns published, delayed their wedding unduly, cohabited or experimented sexually, were delinquent in dower payments, or disputed among themselves over jobs, property, or living arrangements. In most such instances, the consistory preferred to subject the parties to spiritual or civil sanctions, but compel them to get married. Malicious desertion of the betrothed generally broke the engagement and exposed the deserter to spiritual and civil sanctions. But a mere change of heart by either party was often not a sufficient ground for annulment of a betrothal, particularly if prenuptial contracts were executed and dower payments had been tendered.[220]

Although betrothals were relatively easy to annul, consummated marriages were not. The consistory and council did annul marriages on the stated statutory grounds of consanguinity, affinity, bigamy, or impotence. They generally dissolved marriages where, shortly after their wedding, the husband discovered that the woman taken to be a virgin was not so. They also lent a sympathetic ear to parties who, shortly after the wedding, complained that the spouse had become fiercely antagonistic and abusive, contracted a contagious disease, or was charged with a serious crime committed before the wedding. Most other pleas for annulment, even those brought by disheartened parents who learned of their minor children's marriage after the fact, were not successful, although the children could face serious spiritual and criminal sanctions for their disobedience and had little recourse if their parents chose to retaliate by disinheriting them.[221]

The consistory and council were even more reserved about granting divorces for consummated marriages. The only stated statutory grounds for divorce were proved adultery and malicious desertion, and the reported cases did nothing to create new grounds. The burden of proof on the innocent party was quite high—"absurdly high" for women petitioners, according to Cornelia Seeger.[222] Petitioners had to walk a tightrope between the consistory's spiritual counsel to be reconciled and the council's evidentiary demands to prove their spouse's wrongdoing and their own innocence at the same time. The vast majority of parties could not meet this burden of proof. Fewer than forty divorces were granted during Calvin's Geneva tenure from 1541–64, almost all with male petitioners, and most on grounds of adultery.[223] This was a very low rate of divorce, which persisted for the next two centuries. Divorce rates in Geneva at the *opening* of the twentieth century were a hundred times higher.[224]

One cause and consequence of such low divorce rates in sixteenth-century Geneva was that the Geneva Council and Consistory reinstituted the traditional

220. Seeger, *Nullité de mariage*, 305–31.
221. Ibid., 332–74.
222. Ibid., 464–65.
223. Ibid., 417; Kingdon, *Adultery and Divorce*, 176.
224. Ibid. See also Jeffrey R. Watt, "The Control of Marriage in Reformed Switzerland, 1550–1800," in *Later Calvinism: International Perspectives*, ed. W. Fred Graham, Sixteenth Century Essays and Studies (Kirksville, MO: Sixteenth Century Journal Publishers, 1994), 29; Antoinette Fauve-Chamoux, "Marriage, Widowhood, and Divorce," in *Family Life in Early Modern Times: 1500–1789*, ed. David I. Kertzer and Marzio Barbagli (New Haven, CT: Yale University Press, 2001), 221–56.

canon-law remedy of separation from bed and board, despite Calvin's strong protestations against it. In cases of severe wife or child abuse, perennial fighting between couples, habitual desertion, contagious disease, habitual frigidity, and the like, the consistory and council would simply separate the parties if all efforts at reconciliation failed.

THE PRESERVATION AND PLURALIZATION
OF CALVINIST MARRIAGE LAW

The reformation of marriage introduced in sixteenth-century Geneva did not die with John Calvin in 1564. Calvin and his followers had worked hard to preserve the new theology and law of marriage in a variety of media. The Geneva Bible included suggestive notes on marriage in the margins of the relevant texts of the Gospels and the Pauline Epistles. The Geneva Catechism and student hand-books of the Geneva Academy included ample discussions of marriage, divorce, and sexual conduct. A growing number of published letters, sermons, opinions, and biblical commentaries by Calvin and Beza placed before the reader a large cache of learned theological discussions of marriage. The Geneva Ecclesiastical Ordinance of 1561 incorporated Calvin's Marriage Ordinance of 1546, amply amended and emended with further norms suggested by the intervening years of litigation. "Change nothing!" was Calvin's famous deathbed instruction to his followers who had gathered to hear his final advice. On marriage matters, at least, his immediate followers obliged him.

This rich literary preservation of Calvin's reformation work not only ensured its survival in Geneva and surrounding rural communities in subsequent genera-tions, but it also helped in the colonization of Calvinist communities in various parts of Europe and eventually overseas to North America. A host of new com-munities, inspired by the writings of Calvin, Beza, and their Genevan colleagues, sprang up in the later sixteenth century and thereafter: French Huguenots, Dutch Pietists, Scottish Presbyterians, English and New England Puritans, and various smaller communities in the German Palatinate, Poland, Czechoslova-kia, Hungary, and eventually South Africa.[225] Many of the first leaders of these communities were educated in the Geneva Academy. Many later leaders were weaned on the rich corpus of Calvin's writings that became available to them, often in local translations. These far-flung Calvinist communities were not rep-licas of Geneva. Their leaders did not in every particular repeat the theological formulations of John Calvin and his colleagues. Indeed, while Lutheran com-munities in Germany and Scandinavia tended to settle into common routinized patterns in the seventeenth century, contemporaneous Calvinist communities tended to pluralize into a number of national and regional variations on Gene-van themes. The nature of these variations turned partly on the temperament of

225. See Menna Priest, ed., *International Calvinism* (Oxford: Clarendon Press, 1985); Benedict, *Christ's Churches Purely Reformed.*

their leaders, and partly on the historical and theological contexts in which the local reformations occurred.

Among the hallmarks of these later Calvinist communities was their preservation and their pluralization of Calvin's theology and law of marriage. Covenantal theologies of marriage sprang forth in ever-greater varieties in these early modern Calvinist communities. Genevan civil laws governing marriage formation, maintenance, and dissolution gave rise to a variety of local legal progeny. A great deal has been written on the new covenantal theology and civil laws of marriage among these later Calvinist groups in France, Germany, England, Scotland, and Germany. The Calvinist reformation of marriage in the Netherlands has not been part of the conventional literature. It deserves a few words both by way of introduction to English-speaking readers and by way of distillation of the main themes of the Calvinist reformation of marriage.

The Protestant Reformation came comparatively late to the Netherlands. The region had been under Spanish imperial rule until the mid-sixteenth century and was subject to the canon law of marriage administered by the bishop of Utrecht. After the violent upheaval against their Spanish rulers from 1566 to 1581, however, the seven northern provinces of the Netherlands abruptly turned to the Calvinist cause.[226] Civil authorities assumed jurisdiction over a variety of subjects previously governed by church courts, including marriage, promulgating a welter of new statutes and codes.[227] Civil jurists produced systematic syntheses of the new civil laws and offered learned opinions in explication and elaboration of these new laws.[228] The new legislation and learned law on marriage drew upon a variety of prototypes from Catholic canon law and Genevan civil law.[229]

226. See sources and discussion in Witte, *The Reformation of Rights*, chap. 3.

227. The most influential works on marriage included N. J. M. Dresch, "Plakkaat, betreffende huwelijk, echtbreuk enz. in Hollands Noorderkwartier, van 13 juni (1574)," in *Nederlands archief voor kerkgeschiedenis*, n.s., 39 (1952/3): 121; Politicke ordonnantie van Holland (1580), items 1–28, in A. S. de Blécourt and N. Japiske, *Klein plakkaatboek van Nederland* (Groningen: J. B. Wolters, 1919), 126; Politieke ordonnantie van Zeeland (1583), items 6–23, in *Klein plakkaatboek*, 129; *Echt-reglement, Over de Steden, ende ten platten lande, in de heerlijkheden en dorpen, staende onder de Generaliteit* (The Hague: Hillebrandt van Wouw, 1664).

228. For a good summary of the contemporary learned law, see Hugo Grotius, *The Jurisprudence of Holland*, trans. and ed. R. W. Lee (Oxford: Clarendon Press, 1926), bk. 1, chaps. v–xii. For a more exhaustive treatment, see Hendrik Brouwer, *De jure connubiorum, libri duo* (Delphis: Adrianum Beman, 1714). The best collection of cases is in C. van Bijnkershoek, *Observationes tumultuariae*, ed. E. M. Meijers et al., 4 vols. (Haarlem: Tjeenk Willink, 1926–62). See further sources in John Witte Jr., "The Plight of Canon Law in the Early Dutch Republic," in Helmholz, *Canon Law in Protestant Lands*, 135–64.

229. For good overviews, see L. van Apeldoorn, *Geschiedenis van het nederlandsche huwelijksrecht voor de invoering van de fransche wetsgeving* (Amsterdam: Uitgeversmaatschappij, 1925), 84–122, 126–70, 180–98; H. F. W. D. Fischer, "De gemengde huwelijken tussen Katholiken en Protestanten in de Nederlanden van de XVIe tot de XVIIe eeuw," *Tijdschrift voor rechtsgeschiedenis / Revue d'histoire du droit* 31 (1963): 463–85; Els Kloek, "Seksualiteit, huwelijk en gezinsleven tijdens de lange zestiende eeuw, 1450–1650," in *Familie, huwelijk en gezin in West-Europa: Van Middeleeuwen tot moderne tijd*, ed. Ton Zwaan (Amsterdam: Boom/ Open Universiteit, 1993), 107–38; Manon van der Heijden, *Huwelijk in Holland: Stedelijk Rechtspraak en kerkelijke Tucht, 1550–1700* (Amsterdam: B. Bakker, 1998).

The new Dutch civil law of marriage retained the traditional Catholic canon-law definition of the formal betrothal or engagement (*verloving, trouwbelofte*) as the first step to marriage. It also accepted the Catholic canon law and Protestant civil law's impediments to engagement that allowed either party to break the engagement without issue—if one party became a heretic or lunatic, became engaged to or was abducted by a third party, became physically or emotionally abusive of the other, or became impotent or deformed.

Following Genevan prototypes, however, the Dutch civil law rejected the canon-law rule that prior or subsequent religious vows to celibacy automatically annulled the betrothal. It also insisted on far more stringent formal requirements for the engagement, each enforced by stiff fines. Couples under the age of majority were required to receive consent from both sets of parents (or from guardians, tutors, or curators). They were required to announce their betrothals before at least two good and honorable witnesses. They were required to register their betrothal with the consistory of the local Reformed church, to receive spiritual instruction on marriage from the minister or an elder, and to request the minister to announce their betrothal banns from the pulpit for at least three successive Sundays before the wedding. They were required to petition the local magistrate in their domicile for a certificate showing that they were single, in good standing, and free from communicable disease and criminal delinquency. All these changes in the traditional law of betrothals reflected Calvin's axiom that marriage is an inherently public institution, in which parents, peers, and pastors all play a vital role.

The new Dutch civil law also accepted the basic canon-law definition of the marriage itself (*huwelijkssluiting*) as a free consensual union between a fit man and a fit woman. It likewise accepted the common Catholic and Protestant impediments that protected the free consent of both parties and annulled marriages based on fear, duress, fraud, and errors of person and quality. It accepted the physical impediments recognized at canon law that annulled marriages where one party was rendered impotent or physically impaired. It accepted the canon-law impediments of consanguinity and affinity, but only to the third degree, or in some provinces to the second degree.

Following Geneva prototypes, however, the Dutch civil law rejected the canon-law impediments that annulled marriages where one party had departed from the faith or committed a mortal sin. It also rejected canon-law impediments that prohibited remarriage to anyone who had previously married a cleric, monk, or nun.

The Dutch civil law departed from both pre-Tridentine canon law as well as Genevan civil law in requiring that parties solemnly repeat their vows before, and procure a marriage certificate from, either a Reformed minister or a magistrate. Calvin had insisted that marriage certificates be issued by the magistrates but that the wedding itself be celebrated in a church. Dutch Calvinists accorded equal authority to both church and state to certify and solemnize the marriage, leaving the choice of forum to the parties. This innovation became popular among seventeenth-century Calvinists in England and America.[230]

A similar blend of Catholic and Calvinist sources is evident in the Dutch civil law of divorce. Unlike Calvin, Dutch Calvinist authorities retained the traditional canon-law remedy of separation of bed and board. Indeed, seventeenth-century case law seems to show that they far preferred this remedy to that of outright divorce. Unlike the canonists, they ordered separation from bed and board for any number of causes: adultery, violence, contagion, wife and child abuse, confessional differences, defamation of a spouse's moral character, acts of incest or lewdness, habitual drunkenness and gaming, among other causes. Like Calvin, they allowed for outright divorce in the modern sense, with a right of remarriage to both parties. But while Calvin sought to restrict divorce to proved cases of adultery, the Dutch civil authorities recognized divorce on proof of desertion—not only physical desertion but also spiritual, sexual, emotional, and other forms of desertion as well. The expansive interpretation of the concept of desertion provided "the peg on which was later hung the doctrine of divorce by mutual consent in the Enlightenment era."[231]

230. A. J. M. van Overveldt, *De dualiteit van kerkelijk en burgerlijk huwelijk* (Tilburg: Bergmans, 1953). For a good example of comparable English Puritan reforms, see the marriage reforms in the 1552 Reformation of Ecclesiastical Law and 1653 Parliamentary Act, discussed in chap. 7 below, pp. 245–48 and 267–68. For comparable developments in New England, see Edmund S. Morgan, *The Puritan Family: Religion and Domestic Relations in Seventeenth-Century New England*, rev. ed. (New York: Harper & Row, 1966), 29ff.

231. Herman van den Brink, "The Married Life of Jan Klaasen en Katmn," in *The Charm of Legal History* (Amsterdam: Adolf M. Hakkert, 1974), 189, 198–99.

Chapter 7

Marriage as Commonwealth in the Anglican Tradition

The Lutheran and Calvinist reformations of marriage followed inverse patterns. The Lutheran Reformation began with a new theology of marriage that eventually assumed new legal forms. The Calvinist Reformation began with a new law of marriage that eventually attracted new theological norms. The Lutheran reformation of marriage was pluralistic at the start, led by scores of strong theologians and jurists, who inspired their own local brands of marital reformation. Over time, their reformation ordinances settled into a common legal pattern for Germany and Scandinavia. The Calvinist Reformation was more uniform at the start, centered in the work of Calvin and the Geneva Consistory. Over time, this Genevan reformation was colonized and pluralized in various Huguenot, Pietist, Presbyterian, Puritan, and Reformed communities of Europe and North America.

The Anglican reformation of marriage introduced a new, cyclical pattern of reform. Radical theological and legal reforms of marriage crashed onto the scene in one generation, only to be put down by the restoration of traditional forms in a subsequent generation. But in each of these cycles of reform and restoration, small changes were made in the prevailing theology and law of marriage, changes that gradually transformed the English marital tradition. This transformation of English marriage law was much slower than its Continental counterparts. What the Continental Reformers enacted over three decades, the English Reformers protracted over three centuries. But what the Continental Reformers provided for small integrated towns and territories, the English Reformers provided for a vast and diverse commonwealth, eventually on both sides of the Atlantic and into the Indian subcontinent too.

The first grand cycle of reform and restoration came in the sixteenth-century Tudor era. Catalyzed by the sensational divorce case of Henry VIII and Catherine of Aragon in 1527–33, reformers such as Thomas Cranmer and Thomas Becon set out to supplant the inherited canon-law tradition of marriage with new Protestant forms. They replaced the traditional sacramental model of marriage with various covenantal and social models drawn from the Continent, notably those of Heinrich Bullinger and Martin Bucer. They also imported familiar Protestant principles governing marriage, divorce, and remarriage. A good deal of ingenuity and energy was directed to legal reform. From 1533 onward, Parliament introduced a series of laws, culminating in the 1552 Reformation of Ecclesiastical Law. These legal reforms promised to bring sweeping liturgical, doctrinal, and canonical changes to the institution of marriage. This first effort at legal reform largely failed. Queen Mary's mid-sixteenth-century legal repeals broke the momentum of the reform. Queen Elizabeth's settlement after 1559 restored only a few piecemeal changes to the law of marriage. England in the later sixteenth century reverted to much of the marriage law of the medieval Catholic tradition. It largely spurned both the bold common-law reforms proffered by the Protestants and even the milder canon-law refinements promulgated by the Council of Trent.

A second grand cycle of reform came in the turbulent seventeenth-century reign of the Stuarts, a dynasty interrupted by the English Civil War of 1640–60 and terminated by the Glorious Revolution of 1689. The most dramatic changes affecting marriage in this second cycle of reform were theological. In an attempt to defend and extend the settled English law of marriage, English theologians developed a new commonwealth model of marriage. Leading Anglo-Puritans declared: "Marriage was made and appointed by God himself to be the foundation and seminary of all sorts and kinds of life in the commonwealth and the church."[1] The marital household is "a little commonwealth, by the good government, whereof Gods glory may be advanced, the commonwealth which standeth of several families, benefited, and all that live in [those] families may receive much comfort and commodity."[2] Such sentiments, typical in seventeenth-century English theology, embraced earlier sacramental, social, and covenantal models of marriage, yet went beyond them. Marriage was at once a gracious symbol

---

1. William Perkins, *Christian Oeconomie: Or, a Short Survey of the Right Manner of Erecting and Ordering a Family according to the Scriptures* (c. 1590), reprinted in *The Work of William Perkins*, ed. Ian Breward (Appleford: Sutton Courtenay Press, 1970), 3:418–19. For all the early English sources in this chapter, I have retained original titles but modernized the content's spelling and punctuation to make for easier reading.

2. Robert Cleaver, *A Godly Form of Householde Gouernment* (London: Thomas Creede, 1598), 1.

of the divine, a solemn covenant with one's spouse, and a social unit alongside church and state. But the essential cause, condition, and calling of marriage was that it simultaneously served and symbolized the commonwealth—that is, the common good—of the couple, the children, the church, and the state.

This commonwealth model of marriage initially provided a refined rationale for traditional English laws and structures of marriage. It helped to substantiate the traditional hierarchies of husband over wife, parent over child, church over household, state over church, and to integrate the sundry biblical duties that attached to each of these offices. The family was assigned a subordinate place in the natural hierarchy of social institutions, crowned by the king. Persons within the family were assigned their subordinate places in the natural hierarchy of family offices, headed by the paterfamilias.

But as the political concept of the English Commonwealth was revolutionized and democratized during the seventeenth century, so also was the theological concept of the family commonwealth. The traditional hierarchies of husband over wife, parent over child, and church over family were challenged with a revolutionary new principle of personal and institutional equality. The biblical duties of husband and wife and of parent and child were recast as the natural and contractual rights of each household member vis-à-vis the other. The traditional idea of a hierarchical natural order of marriage, society, and state was challenged with a new idea of marriages, societies, and states that were voluntarily contracted by free individuals in the state of nature. Just as the English Commonwealth could be rent asunder by force of arms when it abused the natural rights of the people, so the family commonwealth could be put asunder by suits at law when it abused the marital rights of either spouse. Just as the king could be relieved of his head for abuses in the English Commonwealth, so the paterfamilias could be removed from his headship for abuses in the domestic commonwealth.

This revolutionary construction of the commonwealth model, captured poignantly in the writings of English poet, John Milton, and English philosopher, John Locke, in the seventeenth century, provided a new rationale for the transformation of English marriage law. Inspired by this reconstructed commonwealth model, Parliament in 1653 introduced a series of reforms of marriage law and government that reflected the new principles of liberty and equality within the household, and that shifted marital jurisdiction from church courts to local magistrates. This experiment, too, largely failed. The 1653 law was repealed during the Restoration of 1660. Yet a few of its provisions on marital formation and divorce were retained, and more of them slowly soaked into English law and life in the next century. This reconstructed commonwealth model of marriage, together with the growing body of legal reforms, provided a key stepping-stone for the development of the Enlightenment contractarian model of marriage, discussed in the next chapter.

It is commonly argued that Anglican theology struck a via media, a middle way, between the teachings of Rome and Wittenberg, Paris and Geneva. This broad middle way allowed the Church of England to embrace a wide range of theological opinions that nudged against Catholic and Protestant poles on each side. As the great seventeenth-century Anglican poet John Donne put it:

> From extreme to extreme, from east to west, the angels themselves cannot come, but by passing the middle way between; from that extreme impurity in which Antichrist had dampened the church of God, to that intemperate purity in which Christ had constituted his church, the most angelical reformers cannot come but by touching, yea, and stepping upon some things in the way. . . . God reaches out his hand to the receiving of those who come towards him; and nearer to him, and to the institutions of his Christ, can no church, no not of the Reformation, be said to have come than ours does.[3]

While this via media image does not adequately capture many aspects of Anglican theology, it does help to describe the Anglican theology of marriage. From its start, the Anglican tradition contemplated a fantastic range of opinions on marriage, from the Anglo-Catholic to the Anglo-Puritan, from the sacramental to the contractarian. These differences in English theologies of marriage were sometimes quite profound. It is misleading simply to equate the teachings of the Church of England with those of the churches in England, particularly after the Toleration Act of 1689 gave license for English Protestant dissenters to maintain doctrines and practices that, by definition, lay beyond the boundaries of the established Anglican way.[4] But on questions of marriage, it has been the special genius of the Anglican tradition over the centuries to find a way to accommodate widely diverse and even discordant teachings and yet retain a distinct denominational identity and standard.

Today it is The Book of Common Prayer, with its timeless language, liturgy, and lectionary, that seems to hold worldwide Anglicanism together, albeit ever more tenuously. Historically, English law played a critical role as well. The law set the outer boundaries and defined the middle line of this theological via media. This was one virtue of establishing Anglicanism by law. Establishment laws defined the core theological doctrines of marriage, from which no dissent was tolerated. But these establishment laws also left the penumbral doctrines and practices of marriage, family, and sexuality open to wide speculation, experimentation, and variation. Invariably, what had been penumbral or even heretical doctrines in earlier generations eventually came to be established as core doctrines in later generations. It was this inherent fluidity and flexibility of

3. John Donne, *The Works*, ed. Henry Alford (Cambridge: Cambridge University Press, 1839), 4:485. See discussion on the concept of via media theology in Charles H. George and Katherine George, *The Protestant Mind of the English Reformation, 1570–1640* (Princeton, NJ: Princeton University Press, 1961), 375–418.

4. See John F. New, *Anglican and Puritan* (Stanford, CA: Stanford University Press, 1964), criticizing the Georges for an unduly ecumenical reading of early modern English theology. See further sources and discussion in Ian Breward, "Introduction," to Perkins, *Christian Oeconomie*, 1:1–33, 116–20.

the Anglican theology and law of marriage—grounded as it was in an emerging English epistemology of probability and reasonableness—that eventually gave the Anglican tradition a uniquely eclectic and dynamic quality.[5]

While the sacramental, social, and covenantal models of marriage eventually hardened with growing canonization, the commonwealth model inevitably softened with growing liberalization. In this we see the great irony of the Anglican contribution to the Western tradition of marriage: What began in the sixteenth century as the most conservative Christian tradition of marriage in all of Western Christendom ultimately gave birth to the most liberal Christian tradition of marriage three centuries later. To this ironic tale we now turn, analyzing a wider chronological swath of material than in the last two chapters in order to see the irony at last begin to unfold.

THE CASES OF HENRY VIII AND CATHERINE OF ARAGON

It is worth recounting King Henry VIII's mighty struggle to seek dissolution of his marriage with Catherine of Aragon. This dispute was the catalyst of the English Reformation in general and of the English reformation of marriage in particular. Given its sensational soap opera qualities, the case had a way of focusing the English mind on the arcane details of canon-law rules of marriage formation and dissolution—and the intense casuistry that could attend their application.[6]

The familiar facts of the case require a bit of historical background to appreciate. Henry VIII's father, Henry VII, had come to the English throne in 1485, a victor in the bloody War of the Roses over the question of royal succession. Henry VII's first son, Prince Arthur, was his heir apparent. Arthur's siring of a son was critical to ensuring a male successor to the English throne for at least two more generations. Prince Arthur was thus engageded as an infant to Catherine of Aragon, the daughter of Ferdinand and Isabella of Spain—an engagement that helped to seal favorable diplomatic relations between England and Spain. Arthur and Catherine were married in 1501. Prince Arthur died in 1502—childless.

Henry VII's second son, Henry (VIII), now became heir to the throne. In a continued effort to secure peace between England and Spain, the twelve-year-old

5. See Barbara J. Shapiro, *Probability and Certainty in Seventeenth-Century England: A Study of the Relationships Between Natural Science, Religion, History, Law, and Literature* (Princeton, NJ: Princeton University Press, 1983); idem, *"Beyond Reasonable Doubt" and "Probable Cause": Historical Perspectives on the Anglo-American Law of Evidence* (Berkeley and Los Angeles: University of California Press, 1991).

6. In the vast literature, see esp. Henry Ansgar Kelly, *The Matrimonial Trials of Henry VIII* (Stanford, CA: Stanford University Press, 1976); Diarmaid MacCulloch, *Thomas Cranmer: A Life* (New Haven, CT: Yale University Press, 1996), 41–78; V. Murphy, "The Literature and Propaganda on Henry's Divorce," in *The Reign of Henry VIII: Politics, Policy and Piety*, ed. Diarmaid MacCulloch (Basingstoke: MacMillan, 1995), chap. 6; Guy Bedouelle and Patrick LeGal, *Le "divorce" du Roi Henry VIII: Études et Documents*, Travaux d'Humanisme et Renaissance 221 (Geneva: Droz, 1987).

Prince Henry was engaged to his brother's widow, Catherine, in 1503. This engagement of a widow to her former brother-in-law raised a difficult legal question, however. The Mosaic law spoke thrice to the issue and not altogether clearly. Leviticus 18:16 stated: "You shall not uncover the nakedness of your brother's wife; she is your brother's nakedness" (RSV). Leviticus 20:21 underscored this prohibition with a threat of infertility: "If a man takes his brother's wife, it is impurity; he has uncovered his brother's nakedness; they shall be childless." But Deuteronomy 25:5 provided: "If brothers dwell together, and one of them dies and has no son, the wife of the dead shall not be married outside the family to a stranger; her husband's brother shall go in to her, and take her as his wife, and perform the duty of a husband's brother to her" (RSV). These Mosaic laws can be reconciled by reading the first two Leviticus passages to govern relations when both brothers are alive, and the Deuteronomy passage to govern only after one brother has died. But neither the rabbinical nor the canonical authorities over the centuries had accepted this reading unequivocally.

The prevailing Catholic canon law on the subject treated the relationship of a man and the widow of his brother as one of affinity. This relationship was an impediment to marriage and would lead to the involuntary annulment of a putative marriage contracted in violation of it. Already in the late thirteenth century, however, canonists had maintained that the pope, as final interpreter of the canon law, could grant a dispensation from this and other Levitical impediments in a specific case. Such dispensations were viewed as equitable exceptions to the usual rules. In this case of affinity, a dispensation could be especially compelling, given the injunction of care for a brother's widow in Deuteronomy 25:5. In the late fourteenth century, popes began to exercise this right of dispensation, waiving impediments of affinity in several cases of budding royal and aristocratic marriages. Indeed, Catherine's sister Isabella was granted precisely such a dispensation from an impediment of affinity in 1500, under pressure on the papacy by her father, Ferdinand.

On petition to Pope Julius II in 1504, therefore, Catherine was given a dispensation to marry her late husband's brother, Prince Henry. They were married in 1509, just after Henry VIII had succeeded to the English throne. Catherine gave birth to six children, including two princes, but they were all stillborn or died in infancy except Mary, born in 1516. Popular sentiment of the day described this ill fate as the scourge of childlessness promised by Leviticus 20:21. The lack of a male successor carried more than the usual disappointment to the hopeful couple and nation. Against the backdrop of the War of the Roses, it posed a real threat of renewed civil war. In desperation—or infatuation—Henry VIII had taken a mistress named Mary and sired an illegitimate son, Henry Fitzroy. But the claim of his bastard child to succeed to the throne was dubious at best.

Henry VIII grew disenchanted with Catherine. Already in 1524, word circulated of his desire to end his marriage with Catherine and to sire a legitimate son with another wife. By 1527, Henry and his advisers had come upon the legal formula to achieve this end. He announced that he had become convinced that his marriage to Catherine was against the law of God set forth in Leviticus 18. This law had been improperly waived by Pope Julius II's dispensation in 1504. It would violate his "scruple of conscience," Henry said, to continue his marriage in open violation of God's law.

Early in 1527, at Henry VIII's urging, the Archbishop of York, Cardinal Thomas Wolsey, convened a secret ex officio inquisitorial trial, which canon law empowered him to do. At trial, Henry was accused of violating the divine law of Leviticus 18, which prohibited his marriage to his brother's widow. Henry's defense was that the papal dispensation of Julius II granted him permission to marry. The promoter for the inquisitorial court then predictably attacked, at length, the procedural propriety and substantive legitimacy of the dispensation. Henry and his advisers evidently thought that this legal maneuvering would end the matter. Pope Julius's 1504 dispensation from the impediment of affinity would prove to be improper and be reversed. Henry's marriage to Catherine would thus be illegitimate and automatically annulled. He would perform a requisite penance for his sin of violating Leviticus 18. He would then be free to marry again. And a new woman to marry was at hand. Everyone thought that the intended new wife was to be Mary, Henry's former mistress. A marriage of Henry VIII and Mary would render their bastard son Henry Fitzroy's claim to the throne considerably stronger. Henry, however, secretly desired to marry not Mary, but Mary's sister, Anne Boleyn.

Confronted with these alarming new facts, Cardinal Wolsey suspended proceedings of the inquisitorial court and took the case under advisement. He soon learned that the case was not nearly so easy as Henry may have imagined. First, he discovered that the canon-law authorities were divided on whether an inquisitorial court could reverse a papal dispensation. The preponderance of authority was against him. Even if the inquisitorial court reversed the 1504 dispensation, therefore, it was unlikely that it would stand up on appeal to Rome.

Moreover, Catherine, who had since learned of the secret proceeding, stood up to fight for continuation of her marriage. She introduced a vital new fact that dramatically changed the legal question. Catherine claimed that her first marriage to Henry's brother, Arthur, had never been consummated through sexual intercourse. She was thus a virgin at the time of her marriage to Henry, she argued, and Henry in fact knew this. According to canonists who regarded consummation as critical to the formation of marriage, this meant she was technically not the wife or widow of Arthur, and no impediment of affinity precluded her marriage to Henry. According to other canonists who regarded the contract to be critical to the formation of marriage, this meant that the only impediment that stood in the way of her marriage to Henry was the impediment of public honesty. Dispensations from such a man-made impediment were routinely issued and could be covered by Julius's 1504 dispensation, or easily procured after the fact and applied retroactively. In either case, Catherine intimated, the validity of Pope Julius II's dispensation was not critical, and Henry's scruple of conscience was not pressing. Then to make the case even more difficult,

Catherine demanded, as canon law allowed, that she be made a party to the case and given legal counsel, not only from England but also from abroad. What was supposed to have been a bit of secret legal maneuvering had suddenly escalated well beyond what Henry and his advisers could have imagined.

The case was rendered even more complicated by Henry's secret desire to marry Anne Boleyn. The same impediment of affinity under dispute in Henry's relationship with Catherine also stood in the way of Henry's intended marriage to Anne Boleyn. By having already consensually consummated his relationship with Anne's sister Mary, Henry had, in effect, married her, albeit bigamously. His "marriage" to Mary created an impediment of affinity to marrying Mary's sister Anne Boleyn. For Leviticus 18 had likewise precluded a man from marrying his wife's sister while his first wife was still alive. Henry thus found himself in a most untenable position. In the case of his current wife, Catherine, he had just argued that the impediment of affinity could not be dispensed with, and an annulment must be granted. In the case of his intended new wife, Anne, he would have to argue that the impediment of affinity must be dispensed with, and permission to marry must be granted. The contradiction was too plain to ignore.

Henry sought to escape this dilemma by appealing to the new Pope, Clement VII, for a dispensation to marry Anne Boleyn. His counselors related Henry's intentions, together with several draft dispensations. Clement was trapped— both by precedent and by politics. According to prevailing canon-law authorities, the granting of a dispensation in this case was premature, given Henry's current marriage to Catherine. And dispensing with the impediment of affinity in this case would tacitly confirm the propriety of Julius II's dispensation from the impediment of affinity in 1504. Moreover, Clement had just surrendered to Catherine's nephew, Charles V, the Holy Roman Emperor, who had sacked Rome. Clement was in no position to alienate his captor by ill treatment of his captor's aunt, Catherine. Neither sovereign could be entirely disappointed, and Clement sought to assuage both. To assuage Henry, Clement granted him on April 13, 1528, a dispensation to marry Anne, pending resolution of his case with Catherine. To assuage Charles, Clement on the same day commissioned his own legatine inquisitorial court to rehear the case for annulment, taking the matter out of Cardinal Wolsey's discretion and placing it beyond Henry's immediate control.

The legatine court commenced a public inquisition in England on May 31, 1529. Both before and during trial, counsel for Henry and Catherine respectively debated at length the propriety of Julius II's 1504 dispensation that enabled the royal couple to be married. The former arguments continued—whether Catherine was a virgin at the time of her marriage to Henry and whether Pope Julius's dispensation was for the impediment of affinity or the impediment of public honesty. Counsel for Henry now added a third argument that brought a long rejoinder—that in 1504, the twelve-year-old Henry was too young to understand or consent to the dispensation and that the basis for the betrothal (continued peace with Spain) was fictional, since a peace treaty between the two countries was already contracted. Counsel for Henry also ventured a fourth argument—that the impediment of public honesty was not just a trivial man-made construction, but a serious natural-law impediment that Pope Julius had no power to dispense.

The legatine court ordered both Henry and Catherine to appear for testimony. Henry appeared; Catherine demurred. On June 16, 1528, Catherine appealed formally by mandate to Pope Clement VII to have the case moved from England to Rome—an appeal that Henry's functionaries in Rome delayed delivering to Clement for several weeks. On June 18 and 21, Catherine appeared before the legatine court and both formally protested the court's jurisdiction over her and the case and also pronounced in open court her virginity at the time of her marriage with Henry. She then withdrew and refused to appear again, despite charges of contumacy and the cajolery and threats issued by several royal and legatine visitors.

On July 16, 1529, Pope Clement VII responded to Catherine's appeal by suspending the legatine court sitting in England and ordering the entire case removed to Rome. This move was in accordance with the canon law procedure of advocation. On October 7, 1529, Clement responded to Catherine's claims of virginity by sending a private letter to Henry, inquiring into his view of the matter. Henry made no answer. On March 7, 1530, Clement amended his earlier dispensation and ordered Henry to suspend his planned marriage to Anne, pending the papal court's final resolution of his case against Catherine. When Clement learned that Henry was openly consorting with Anne, he issued a stern letter to Henry on January 25, 1532, threatening to excommunicate him if he did not leave Anne and return to Catherine.

These events set afoot the famous sequence of events that ultimately led to the break between England and Rome. Already in late 1529, both Henry and Clement began marshaling canon-law authorities from throughout England and the Continent to speak to the propriety of both Julius's 1504 dispensation and Clement's 1529 advocation. A number of English, French, and Italian faculties and professors of law and theology supported Henry's cause. The German faculties and individual professors from the rest of Europe sided primarily with the papacy. Despite intense negotiations—ultimately involving ambassadors from throughout the Continent—relations between Clement and Henry and between Catherine and Henry eroded. Henry refused to participate in the case in Rome. He refused to reconcile himself to Catherine.

On July 11, 1533, the papal court in Rome began hearings in the annulment case. After long argument, and adjournment, the papal court solemnly pronounced on March 23, 1534, that the marriage of Henry and Catherine "was and is valid and canonical."[7]

By this time, however, Henry had taken matters into his own hands. In the autumn of 1532, he had impregnated Anne—with the later Queen

---

7. Quoted by Kelly, *Matrimonial Trials*, 169.

Elizabeth—and on January 25, 1533, had secretly married her. In early March 1533, he pushed through Parliament the Act in Restraint of Appeals to Rome, which provided that all "causes of matrimony and divorces . . . shall from henceforth be heard and definitively adjudged and determined within the king's jurisdiction and authority."[8] The objections of Lord Chancellor Thomas More and Bishop Fisher led to their summary and savage execution.

On March 30, 1533, the King's favorite, Thomas Cranmer, was appointed archbishop of Canterbury. Within a month, Cranmer convened yet another ex officio inquisitorial trial on the propriety of Henry's marriage to Catherine. Cranmer summoned Henry and Catherine to appear to answer the charges against them of violating the Levitical law of impediments. Catherine refused to appear and was cited for contumacy. The same tired arguments on both sides, now swollen with supporting opinions collected from throughout Europe, were again presented. On May 28, 1533, Cranmer declared the marriage of Henry and Catherine annulled, accepting the arguments that Catherine had consummated her marriage with Arthur and that an impediment of affinity rendered void her marriage to Henry. Shortly thereafter, Cranmer ratified the secret marriage of Henry and Anne, saying nothing about the impediment of affinity between them.

On April 4, 1534, Parliament confirmed Archbishop Cranmer's sentences in the Act of Succession. The Act declared that Prince Arthur had "carnally known" Catherine, that the marriage between Henry and Catherine was thus "against the Laws of Almighty God" and "utterly void and annulled," and that the marriage of Henry and Anne "shall be established and taken for undoubtful, true, sincere, and perfect ever after."[9] This Act guaranteed the legitimacy of their daughter Elizabeth's claim to the throne. If any doubt of the pope's control lingered, Henry pushed through Parliament the Supremacy Act of 1534, declaring himself to be "the only supreme head in earth of the Church of England."[10]

Catherine died in 1536, under suspicious circumstances. When Anne Boleyn proved incapable of producing a male heir, she was condemned and executed for adultery in 1536. Henry then married Jane Seymour, who produced Edward VI in 1537, but died in childbirth. Edward VI would succeed Henry to the throne in 1547. Mary, daughter of Henry and Catherine, would succeed him in 1553. Elizabeth, daughter of Henry and Anne, would succeed her in 1559.

Few matrimonial cases, before or since, have reached this level of complexity, intrigue, and machination. Thomas Cranmer later called it "the case of the century," and for centuries thereafter historians and playwrights have sifted through its sordid and scintillating details to produce endless interpretations. For the average English soul in the 1520s and 1530s, the case was surely bewildering.

8. See 24 Henry VIII, c. 12. All these citations are Acts of Parliament, with the first number (24) indicating the year of the prevailing monarch's reign, and the last number (c. 12) indicating the chapter of the statute as it is compiled.

9. See 25 Henry VIII, c. 22.

10. See 26 Henry VIII, c. 1.

Arcane arguments about canon-law impediments; papal dispensations granted, modified, suspended, and reversed; sordid public discussions over whether Arthur and Catherine had sexual intercourse; ecclesiastical tribunals convened, suspended, and removed; learned canonists taking diametrically opposite positions on simple legal questions; great churchmen rewarded or beheaded for their views of the moment; the king's contumacy celebrated but the queen's contumacy castigated; the king's concubinage rewarded but his concubines executed—all this and much more could not have inspired much confidence in the prevailing system of theology or law.

After the dizzying events surrounding the birth of the English Reformation, theologians and jurists began to take stock of prevailing doctrines and to press for reforms that would both immunize England against such machinations in the future and routinize the salutary changes that had already taken place. The disputed doctrines of impediments, annulment, and divorce would loom large in these calculations.

THE TUDOR REFORMATION OF MARRIAGE THEOLOGY

Henry's celebrated marriage case triggered an explosion of new Protestant literature in England, both on marriage and its dissolution and on the canon law of marriage and its reformation.[11] Some of this literature was indigenous, building on a two-century tradition of English antipapalism and anticanonicalism inaugurated by John Wycliffe, William of Ockham, and others.[12] Some of this literature was Continental. The writings on marriage by Luther, Melanchthon, Bullinger, Bucer, Calvin, Beza, and many others enjoyed wide circulation in Tudor England—sometimes fully translated and reproduced with attribution, often excerpted in sermons and pamphlets or published under pseudonyms.[13]

Thomas Becon

The writings of Thomas Becon—student of Anglican divines Hugh Latimer and George Stafford and chaplain to Archbishop Cranmer—provide a good illustration of both types of literature on marriage. Becon peppered many of his seventy-odd surviving devotional and catechetical tracts with a variety of spicy Protestant sentiments on marriage, which he drew together in a circa-1560 title *The Booke*

11. See Chilton L. Powell, *English Domestic Relations, 1487–1653: A Study of Matrimony and Family Life in Theory and Practice as Revealed by the Literature, Law, and History of the Period* (New York: Columbia University Press, 1917), 207–24.

12. See Joan Lockwood O'Donovan, *The Theology of Law and Authority in the English Reformation* (Atlanta: Scholars Press, 1991), 11–80.

13. See a list of titles in George E. Howard, *A History of Matrimonial Institutions*, 3 vols. (Chicago: University of Chicago Press, 1904), 1:364–70; and discussion in Frederick J. Smithen, *Continental Protestantism and the English Reformation* (London: James Clarke, [1927]), 43–135; Eric Josef Carlson, *Marriage and the English Reformation* (Oxford: Blackwell, 1994), 3–9, 67–87.

of Matrimonie.[14] Several of Becon's tracts were bestsellers in Tudor and Stuart England and remain among the classics of Anglican theology. Becon also helped to produce English editions of the influential marriage tracts of Continental reformers Heinrich Bullinger and Martin Bucer; the Bullinger tract, in fact, was printed under Becon's pen name. In this range of writings, both the covenantal model and the social model of marriage developed on the Continent can be seen, together with the rudiments of a budding commonwealth model of marriage, which would come to full flower in England at the turn of the seventeenth century.

Becon's own prolific writings—like those of other Anglican divines in the early sixteenth century—propounded no fully systematic theology of marriage and family life. But they did provide a substantial cache of popular Protestant marriage principles. Like his Continental brethren, Becon inveighed bitterly against the decay of marriage in his day and laid much of the blame on the canon law. In Becon's view, the canon law had "most filthily corrupted, mangled, and defiled all the mysteries of God, of his holy word, and blessed Sacraments" and had "most vilely and most wickedly embased, cast down, and made almost of no reputation . . . the most holy state of godly matrimony."[15] "The glory of this Christian matrimony is now greatly obscured, yea almost utterly extinct and quenched through the abominable whoredom, stinking adultery, wicked fornication, and all kind of uncleanness which is used nowadays among us."[16]

On the one hand, Becon charged, the canon-law requirement of clerical celibacy had unleashed all manner of sexual pathos upon England. "The synagogue[s] of Satan are such and so great enemies to matrimony, that they had rather have their subdeacons, deacons, and priests, their monks and their friars, their canons and nuns . . . to be most filthy fornicators, abominable adulterers, stinking sodomites, and to be defiled with all kind of beastly and unnatural uncleanness, than once to suffer them to embrace holy wedlock." England's "plague" of prostitution, bastardy, homosexuality, syphilis, and much else was, in Becon's view, "aided and abetted" by the "evil command" of clerical celibacy.[17]

14. See *The Early Works of Thomas Becon, S.T.P.*, ed. J. Ayre for the Parker Society, 3 vols. (Cambridge: Cambridge University Press, 1843). This collection duplicates much from an earlier collection of Becon's writings, *The First Part of the Bokes, which Thomas Becon made* (London: J. Day, 1560–64), save one title, *The Booke of Matrimonie both Profitable and Comfortable for All Them that Entende Quietly and Godly to Lyue in the Holy State of Honorable Wedlocke* (ca. 1560), in ibid., 1, bk. 12, a tract of 236 folio pages (ESTC 1710). See discussion in D. S. Bailey, *Thomas Becon and the Reformation in England* (Edinburgh: Oliver & Boyd, 1952), 22, 57–58, 96, 111–15, 140, 147; Powell, *English Domestic Relations*, 75, 111–14, 125–29, 155–58, 244. Becon's *Booke of Matrimonie* must not be confused with Heinrich Bullinger's *The Golde Boke of Christen Matrimonye* (1542), which was frequently reprinted under Becon's pen name, Theodore Basille. Becon's tract includes many of the same themes as Bullinger's tract and a virtually identical preface, but the two works are quite distinct. Becon devotes more than half of the work to criticizing the canon law and scholastic theology; this critique finds virtually no place in Bullinger's tract. See esp. Becon, *Booke of Matrimonie*, Second Part, folios DCxvi–DCxlviii. (The capitalization and numbering of the folio pages in this volume are unusual, and because of that, I have retained them as cited.)

15. Ibid., folio CCCCClxxv.

16. Ibid., folios CCCCClx, CCCClxiii.

17. Becon, *Early Works*, 3:198. See also Becon, *Booke of Matrimonie*, folio DClxxvi.

On the other hand, Becon charged, the canon law had confused lay marital life through its imposition of unwieldy and unbiblical impediments to marriage, its recognition of secret marriages without church consecration, and its prohibitions against divorce for adultery and against the remarriage of widows and widowers.[18] With particular vitriol, Becon condemned the "evil canons" that allowed immature "child" marriages based on lust. When the inaptly married party comes to "see [an]other whom they could find in their heart to fancy and love better, . . . [then] many of them begin to hate one another." This in turn, Becon charged, ushered in an insidious pattern of easy annulments for the rich, who can pay for a dispensation, and of permanently unhappy households for the poor, who have no payment to dispense. Such households feature "frowning, overwharting, scolding, and chiding," and such prevalent abuse of wives and children "that the whole house is filled full of these tragedies even unto the top," and "shortly after the whole town is in a roar." "What a wicked and hell-like life."[19]

Becon offered familiar Protestant reforms to end this perceived wickedness. He summarized his suggestions in a series of pithy paragraphs contrasting "The Acts of Christ and of Antichrist [the Pope]" on questions of marital formation and dissolution:

> Christ saith: "Honor thy father and thy mother": in which commandment is required of children that they give not themselves to marriage without the consent of their godly parents. . . . Antichrist in the bestowing of children in marriage, requireth not the consent and good-will of the parents. . . .
>
> Christ, by being present at a marriage with his mother and with his disciples, teacheth evidently that matrimony ought to be solemnly and openly proclaimed and celebrated, and that it ought not to be done in corners. Antichrist, for money, granteth dispensations for all men for to marry where they will, when they will, and with whom they will. All things are decent and lawful, if money come. All things obey money.
>
> Christ in his doctrine did never forbid marriage to be contracted between any persons, except those degrees only which his heavenly Father had before forbidden by his servant Moses. Antichrist in his law prohibiteth many and divers degrees to marry together whom God hath set at liberty . . . except they purchase a license of him for money: for money maketh all things lawful in the court; neither are his laws any other thing than nets for money.
>
> [Christ] suffereth those that be god-fathers and god-mothers (as they term them) to be one child at baptism, to marry together, if they be loose and at liberty, and not forbidden by the law Levitical. [Antichrist] plainly forbiddeth this thing, and maketh the matter a spiritual consanguinity and a ghostly kindred, of much more force and strength than any carnal strength or fleshly consanguinity is.
>
> Christ freely permitteth marriage to all degrees, none excepted, if they have not the gift of continence: neither doth he appoint any time where it shall not be lawful to solemnize matrimony, but giveth liberty to all men at all times freely to marry. Antichrist . . . denieth marriage to all his clattering

18. Becon, *Booke of Matrimonie*, folios CCCCClxxv–Dxxii.
19. Ibid., folio CCCCClxiii.

clergy, rather suffering them to burn and run awhoring. . . . He forbids at certain times of the year to celebrate matrimony; insomuch that whosoever presumeth in those forbidden times to marry is not only accursed, but his marriage also is not lawful.

[Christ gives] liberty to the guiltless and innocent man, having an harlot to his wife, . . . not only to be divorced from that harlot, sometime his wife, but also to marry again. . . . Antichrist in his law saith, If a man have an whore to his wife, it shall be lawful for him to be divorced from her, both from bed and board; but he may by no means marry again, live as he may. . . .

[Christ gives] liberty to the faithful man or woman [to divorce an idolater and remarry]. Antichrist will by no means suffer any divorcement so to be made so that marriage shall follow, although the guiltless person burn so greatly.[20]

Each of these Protestant reforms of the canon law—parental consent to marriage,[21] church proclamation and consecration of marriage,[22] limitations of impediments to biblical forms,[23] permission for clergy to marry,[24] propriety of divorce for cause with rights of remarriage,[25] and propriety of remar-

---

20. Becon, *Early Works*, 2:532–33 (I have revised the order slightly); see also ibid., 3:198–99, 235–36. For a prototype of this Christ versus antichrist dialectic, see William Tyndale, *Doctrinal Treatises and Introduction to Different Portions of the Holy Scripture*, ed. H. Walter for the Parker Society (Cambridge: Cambridge University Press, 1848), 232–46.

21. See, e.g., Tyndale, *Doctrinal Treatises*, 23, 169–70, 199; *The Sermons of Edwin Sandys*, ed. J. Ayre for the Parker Society (Cambridge: Cambridge University Press, 1842), 2:50–51, 281, 325–26, 434, 455; *Early Writings of John Hooper*, ed. S. Carr for the Parker Society (Cambridge: Cambridge University Press, 1843), 126, 137–38, 149; *Sermons of Hugh Latimer*, ed. G. E. Corrie for the Parker Society (Cambridge: Cambridge University Press, 1844), 169–70. For later Anglican views on parental consent, see Richard L. Greaves, *Society and Religion in Elizabethan England* (Minneapolis: University of Minnesota Press, 1981), 155–77.

22. *The Remains of Edmund Grindal*, ed. W. Nicholson for the Parker Society (Cambridge: Cambridge University Press, 1843), 127, 143, 189; Hooper, *Early Writings*, 138. For later Anglican views, which were quite discordant on this point, see Greaves, *Society and Religion*, 177–90.

23. *Miscellaneous Writings and Letters of Thomas Cranmer*, ed. J. E. Cox for the Parker Society (Cambridge: Cambridge University Press, 1846), 94–95, 328–29, 359–60; Grindal, *Remains*, 127, 143, 175; John Jewell, *Works*, ed. J. Ayre for the Parker Society (Cambridge: Cambridge University Press, 1845–50), 3:1243–45.

24. Cranmer, *Miscellaneous Writings*, 168–69; T. Cooper, *An Answer in Defense of the Truth against the Apology of Private Mass* (1562), ed. W. Goode for the Parker Society (Cambridge: Cambridge University Press, 1850), 171; *Remains of Myles Coverdale*, ed. George Pearson for the Parker Society (Cambridge: Cambridge University Press, 1846), 483–85; William Fulke, *A Defence of the Sincere and True Translations of the Holy Scriptures into the English Tongue*, ed. C. H. Hartshorne for the Parker Society (Cambridge: Cambridge University Press, 1843), 71–72, 115–17, 471–91; idem, *Stapleton's Fortress Overthrown*, ed. R. Gibbings for the Parker Society (Cambridge: Cambridge University Press, 1848), 93–104; Jewell, *Works*, 2:727–28, 882–83, 989, 1128–29, 3:390–411, 805–10; *The Works of Nicholas Ridley*, ed. H. Christmas for the Parker Society (Cambridge: Cambridge University Press, 1843), 302–5; William Tyndale, *An Answer to Sir Thomas More's Dialogue*, ed. H. Walter for the Parker Society (Cambridge: Cambridge University Press, 1850), 29, 52–53, 151–60. See also John Ponet, *A Defence for Mariage of Priestes* (London: Reynold Wolff: 1549); and its rejoinder by Thomas Martin, *Traictise declarying and plainly provyng that the pretensed mariage of Priestes and professed persones is no marriage* (London: R. Caly, 1554).

25. Hooper, *Early Writings*, 378–87.

riage by the widowed[26]—while not unequivocally accepted, found substantial endorsement in the writings of the Anglican divines. William Tyndale, Thomas Cranmer, John Hooper, John Jewel, Hugh Latimer, and Edmund Grindal in particular adduced an ample arsenal of ancient Christian and classical sources in support of many of these reforms. Several others took the further familiar step, on which Becon dithered,[27] of denying the sacramental character of marriage altogether, thereby also questioning the propriety of the church's jurisdiction over marriage.[28]

Becon sketched out what he considered to be a more proper understanding of marriage. Marriage was not a condition to be despised or subordinated in dignity to the single, contemplative life. To the contrary, marriage is the "best estate," a "thing of great excellence and incomparable dignity," created by God to "maintain," "preserve," and "protect the commonwealth and also set forth the glory of God, of nature, and of man."[29] Marriage is a "great vocation and destiny," which clergy and laity alike should embrace and enjoy. Marriage is "an high, holy and blessed order of life, ordained not of man, but of God, . . . wherein one man and one woman are coupled and knit together in one flesh and body in the fear and love of God, by the free, loving, hearty, and good consent of them both, to the extent that they may dwell together, as one flesh and body of one will and mind in all honesty, virtue and godliness, and spend their lives in equal partaking of all such things as God shall send them with thanksgiving."[30] "Matrimony is instituted of God, celebrated in paradise, sanctified by the holy Ghost, and beautified with the first fruits of Christ's wonderful miracles."[31]

God ordained marriage for three causes, Becon wrote—love, procreation, and deterrence from sin, in that order of priority.[32] "The first cause" of marriage, Becon wrote, "is, that for as much as the solitary life is a sorrowful and uncomfortable life, and man in nature is desirous of company, and gladly liveth

26. Jewell, *Works*, 3:390–92. For later Anglican views, see Greaves, *Society and Religion*, 191–201.

27. Even in his *Booke of Matrimonie*, folio DCxlix.b, prepared after the Thirty-Nine Articles, Becon wrote of marriage as the man and woman "coupled in most high love, in permixtion of bodies, in the confederate bond of the sacrament, and finally in the fellowship of all chances."

28. See, e.g., Tyndale, *Doctrinal Treatises*, 1:254; Cranmer, *Miscellaneous Writings*, 115–16; Jewell, *Works*, 2:1125. Two decades later, this position was taken in the Thirty-Nine Articles, inspiring a torrent of homilies and commentaries on the subject. See, e.g., Thomas Rogers, *The Catholic Doctrine of the Church of England: An Exposition of the Thirty-Nine Articles*, ed. J. J. S. Perowne for the Parker Society (Cambridge: Cambridge University Press, 1844), 260. See summary in Carlson, *Marriage and the English Reformation*, 37–45.

29. Thomas Becon, Preface to [Heinrich Bullinger's] *The Golde[n] Boke of Christen Matrimonie* (London, 1542), folios A.ii.b., Aiii (ESTC 1723). For other Tudor Anglican views on the relative merits of marriage and celibacy, see Greaves, *Society and Religion*, 119–30; Carlson, *Marriage and the English Reformation*, 49–66.

30. Becon, *Booke of Matrimonie*, folio DCxvi.

31. Ibid., folio DCxvi.b.

32. But cf. ibid., folio DCxi, where he writes: "Who knoweth not, that the principal end, for which God instituted matrimony, is to be fruitful and to avoid fornication." This offhand comment was corrected by a later section of more than thirty folio pages devoted to exposition of all three causes of marriage.

not alone: God . . . appointed this most holy order of life, and commanded one man and one woman to live in the same, and that one of them might be a comfort, joy and help to another in all honest and godly things, . . . to have his family and name extended in great gladness and felicity, and the sweet consolation of travail."[33] Becon stressed these virtues of marital love several times, treating love as the sine qua non of marriage and the sacramental symbol and seal of Christ's love for his church.[34] The second cause of marriage, said Becon, is procreation, which serves not only to perpetuate one's family name but also to ensure that "the number of the elect and chosen people of God be fulfilled."[35] The third cause of marriage is to avoid "fornication, adultery, incest, sodomy, and all other kinds of uncleanness."[36]

Becon left it mostly to others to define the legal steps for forming and maintaining this ideal state of matrimony. His own advice—like that of many of his fellow divines—was mostly homiletic. To wit: "Art thou a father or mother, master or mistress? Bring then up thy family in the nurture of the Lord, and so art thou truly faithful. Art thou a married man? Look how thou cleave unto thy wife: love her as thy own flesh, and as Christ loved the congregation. So shall thy faith appear to be unfeigned. Art thou a married woman? Be obedient to thine own husband, and seek above all things to please him, and so shalt thou show thyself to be truly faithful."[37] In his catechism, he further urged husbands to love, support, and defend their wives and children in an exercise of true godliness, and wives, in turn, to obey their husbands, to educate their children, and "to be chaste, pure and honest in deed, in word, in gesture, in apparel and in all her behavior."[38]

Becon offered more substantial advice in his several glosses on the Commandment: "Thou shalt not commit adultery." Like his Catholic and Protestant contemporaries, he viewed this commandment as a source and summary of a biblical ethic on sexuality and marriage.[39] The commandment helped to systematize sundry biblical and natural commandments and counsels for married persons. Becon summarizes its lessons in sweeping terms:

33. Ibid., folios DCxlviii–xlix.

34. See long discussions of marital love in ibid., folios DCxxvi, DCxlvi.b–xlviii, DCi, DClxvi–lxvi.b.

35. Ibid., folios DCI.b–li.

36. Ibid., folio DCliv.b.

37. Becon, *Early Works*, 1:272. Cf. ibid., 371, on marital faithfulness. Becon did offer a more substantial digest of domestic duties grounded in the familiar passages of Paul and Peter. His 400-page *A New Catechism* (1560) devotes some 30 pages to the exposition of household duties: "Husbands toward Their Wives," "Wives toward Their Husbands," "Fathers and Mothers toward Their Children," "Children toward Their Parents," "Masters or Householders toward Their Servants." This is followed by sections on the offices and duties of widows, unmarried young men, maids, and young unmarried women. Becon, *Early Works*, 2:344–77, with summary in ibid., 3:130–35. He summarizes this section on duties in his *Booke of Matrimonie*, DClxiiii–lxxviii. But this contribution was largely derivative and duplicative of Tyndale's and Bullinger's work, discussed below.

38. Becon, *Booke of Matrimonie*, folios DClxiiii.b, DClxiiii–DClxxviii.

39. For later Anglican formulations, see Greaves, *Society and Religion*, 204–13, 228–36.

And forasmuch as matrimony is a holy state of life, God in the aforesaid precept requireth of all married persons, that they lead a pure, clean, and blameless life, that they be faithful and loving one to the other, that they break not the marriage vow, that they know not the company of any strange flesh, that they defile not themselves in mind with evil lusts and in the body with uncleanness; but that they be pure both in body and spirit, utterly estranged from all adultery, incest, whoredom, and whatsoever is unclean in the sight of God, living together in all godliness and honesty. And that the married folk may the better this do, God requireth also of them in this precept, that they suffer no fleshly thoughts to rise and rule in their hearts, but that they suppress them straightaway through earnest and hearty prayer, and through the diligent consideration of God's holy will, and through the fervent meditation of the sacred scripture; again, that they frequent the company of no lewd or ill-disposed persons, whereby they may be the rather provoked unto the breach of this commandment and unto dissolution of life: Item, that they avoid all wanton pasttimes, all filthy communications, all uncomely gestures, all nice and lascivious apparel, all reading of wanton books, all beholding of unpure images or pictures, all banqueting and excess of eating and drinking, and besides, whatsoever may entice or move unto the filthy pleasure of the flesh; and finally, that in all their words and deeds there appear nothing in them but gravity, modesty, and honest behaviour, unto the good example of such as be their youngers and inferiors, . . . that God may bless them and their marriage, and make them joyful parents of many children, which in this world may be good members of the Christian commonweal, and in the world to [be]come blessed citizens of that glorious and heavenly Jerusalem.[40]

The same commandment against adultery, Becon continued, similarly enjoins unmarried persons against the "mortal folly" of fornication, incest, "and such other corporal uncleanness" as well as "filthy talk, wanton countenances, singing of bawdy ballads, reading of amorous books, idle jesting, vain past times, and whatsoever maketh unto the provocation of fleshly appetite."[41] In other glosses on this same commandment, Becon thundered prophetically against "the loose and lascivious living" of his countrymen, particularly their habits of glibly contracting and dissolving marriages to "the great dishonor of God's institution." He even courted treason charges by intimating that the life of Henry VIII was both an illustration and instigation of undue sexual license. He called for a return to the "ancient biblical remedies" of severe punishment for sexual sinners, execution for convicted adulterers and fornicators.[42] In cases of proved adultery, he followed the Gospel literally, allowing the innocent spouse to divorce and remarry, after all attempts at reconciliation had failed.[43]

40. Becon, *Early Works*, 2:104, 97.

41. Ibid., 2:99.

42. Ibid., 3:5–6; Becon, "A Homily of Whoredome and Uncleannesse," in *Certayne Sermons, or Homilies Appointed by the Kynges Maiestie* (London: Richard Grafton, 1547), c.i–e.iii (ESTC 13639); Preface to Bullinger's *The Golde Boke*, folios A.iiii.b–B.vi.b. For Becon's related jeremiads against clerical abuses, sumptuousness, and economic exploitation, see Bailey, *Thomas Becon*, 58–67.

43. Becon, *Booke of Matrimonie*, folios DCxlii–DCLxxxii provides a long discussion of Catholic and Continental Protestant views, quoting at length from several church fathers and councils, and then Erasmus, Luther, Bucer, Melanchthon, Calvin, Bullinger, Brenz, and others.

Besides offering his own writings, Becon helped to introduce two systematic Protestant tracts from the Continent that came to work a considerable influence on later Anglican marriage theology: (1) *The Golde Boke of Christen Matrimonye*, by the Zurich reformer Heinrich Bullinger, an eighty-page exposition of a covenantal model of marriage;[44] and (2) *De regno Christi* (*On the Kingdom of Christ*), by the Strasbourg reformer Martin Bucer, nearly half of which was devoted to elaborating a social model of marriage.[45]

Heinrich Bullinger

Heinrich Bullinger's *Golde Boke* set out, in accessible pastoral terms, a covenantal model of marriage. Bullinger had built his covenant model of marriage on the foundation of Ulrich Zwingli's work and had effectively used this model to advocate several legal reforms in Zurich in the 1540s and 1550s. "Wedlock," he wrote, "is a covenant, a coupling or yoking together" of one man and one woman "by the good consent of the both."[46] "Holy wedlock was ordained of God himself in Paradise. . . . God was the first cause of wedlock, and [spliced] and knit them together, and blessed them."[47] It is thus an "honorable and holy" estate, enjoyed by the "holiest, and most virtuous, the wisest and most noble men" in the Bible, and commended to all persons today—clerical and lay, young and old, single and widowed, rich and poor.[48]

God created marriage so that a man and a woman "may live together honestly and friendly the one with the other, that they may avoid uncleanness, that they may bring up children in the fear of God, that the one may help and comfort the other."[49] Bullinger followed conventional arguments regarding the marital purposes of protection from lust and procreation of children, arguing that marriage is God's "remedy and medicine unto our feeble and weak flesh" and that children are "the greatest treasure" of a marriage.[50] But like Becon, he placed special emphasis on marital love and friendship, returning to the theme several

---

44. Heinrich Bullinger, *Der christlich E[h]stand* (Zurich: Froschouer, 1540); published as *The Christen State of Matrimonye* (London, 1541), trans. Myles Coverdale, one of the early translators of the Bible into English (ESTC 4045); and as *The Golde Boke of Christen Matrimonye* (London, 1542), under Thomas Becon's pseudonym, Theodore Basille (ESTC 1723).

45. Martin Bucer, *De regno Christi* (1555), in *Martini Buceri opera Latini*, ed. François Wendel (Paris: Presses Universitaires de France, 1955), vol. 25, with partial English translation in *Melanchthon and Bucer*, ed. Wilhelm Pauck (Philadelphia: Westminster Press, 1969), 155, 315–33 (bk. 2, chaps. 16–21, 47 on marriage); and in *The Judgement of Martin Bucer concerning Divorce* (1644), in *The Complete Prose Works of John Milton* (New Haven, CT: Yale University Press, 1959), 2:416–79 (bk. 2, chaps. 15–47, with some omissions) (hereafter, *CPW*).

46. Bullinger, *The Golde Boke*, folio v.

47. Ibid., folios i.b–ii, iii.

48. Ibid., folios xxi.b, xxiii, xxxvi.b, lxxvii.b–lxxviii. The chapter commending clerical marriage (and criticizing mandatory celibacy and chastity, with typical Protestant arguments) is included only in the 1541 edition, *The Christen State of Matrimonye*, 27.b–31.

49. Bullinger, *The Golde Boke* , folios bv–v.b.

50. Ibid., folios xix, xxi.b.

times in this and other writings.[51] At creation, he insisted, God planted in Adam and Eve "the love, the heart, the inclination and natural affection that it beseems the one to have toward the other." The "mouth of God thereby declares the duty knot and covenant of married folks, namely that the highest love, bond, and unity among them should be this, that no man separate them asunder, but only death. . . . The love therefore in marriage ought to be (next unto God) above all loves," with couples rendering to each other "the most excellent and unpainful service, diligence and earnest labor,. . . one doing for another, one longing, depending, helping and forbearing another, suffering, also like joy and like pain one with another."[52]

Such an ideal state of matrimony, Bullinger insisted, could be achieved only if the covenant of marriage were "framed right according to the word and will of God."[53] Bullinger recognized the conventional steps of betrothal, wedding, and consummation, and glossed each step with ample pastoral advice, often based on biblical sources. Parties should enter marriage only by a "mature and mutual consent" that is free from coercion, fraud, or the inducements of "carnal lust, money, good, [or] flattery."[54] They should marry only fellow believers who show true "fear of God" and godly virtues, for "marriage also concerns the soul and inward man."[55] They should avoid marriages with blood or family relatives listed in Leviticus, ending unions immediately if such a relationship is discovered.[56] They should procure their parents' consent, which ought to be given

51. See, e.g., *The Decades of Henry Bullinger: The First and Second Decades*, ed. Thomas Harding for the Parker Society (Cambridge: Cambridge University Press, 1849), Second Decade, Tenth Sermon, 397–98: "The first cause why matrimony was instituted is man's commodity, that thereby the life of man might be the pleasanter and more commodious."

52. Bullinger, *The Golde Boke*, folios iii.b–iiii. Bullinger returns to these themes of marital love in folios xxii–xxiiii, xxxvi.b–xxxviii. Contemporaneous Tudor divines sometimes offered similar sentiments on the purposes of marriage, with an emphasis on marital affection, love, and companionship. See, e.g., Sandys, *Sermons*, 315–16: "Marriage is honourable in respect of the causes for which it was ordained. . . . The first is mutual society, help, and comfort. And this were a cause sufficient to esteem of marriage if there were no other. . . . The second cause . . . is increase and propagation. . . . Another cause . . . is a remedy against uncleanness." Sandys then went on to expound "the duties of love" that couples owe to each other (ibid., 316–24, 329). See also Edmund Tilney, *A Brief and Pleasant Discourse of Duties in Marriage, Called the Flower of Friendshippe* (London: Henrie Denham, 1571), folios Biiibv–Biiic, Biiia, calling marriage a "true, and perfect love."

53. Bullinger, *The Golde Booke*, folios vi, vii.

54. Ibid., folios vi–vi.b, xv–xviii. Elsewhere he writes: "The holy Scripture diligently teacheth all men to have a special care, that they contract matrimony devoutly, holily, soberly, wisely, lawfully, and in the fear of God; and that no evil disposition or covetousness, desire of promotion, or fleshly lust, may lead and provoke them; and that wedlock be not entered into otherwise than either the laws of man or of God permit." See *The Decades of Henry Bullinger: The Fifth Decade*, ed. Thomas Harding for the Parker Society (Cambridge: Cambridge University Press, 1852), Tenth Sermon, 510.

55. Bullinger, *The Golde Boke*, folios vii–x. Among prerequisites, Bullinger includes "faith, God's glory, God's service, understanding or knowledge, prudence, truth, soberness, righteousness, liberality, chastity, humblenesse, honesty, and nurture, singleness, and diligence, and such like virtues" (ibid., folio xlii–xliii.b).

56. This chapter was dropped from the 1542 edition but included in the 1541 edition, *The Christen State of Matrimonye*, 12–20.

fairly, soberly, and with due admonition of the solemnity of the union.[57] They should be married in a public church wedding officiated by "God's minister" and "receive the blessing and commit themselves to the common prayers of the congregation, and intone the same."[58] By so doing, it is "openly declared in the sight of all the world, that it is God which knitteth the knot of marriage" and that "everyone is warned, faithfully to keep his promise, made and given to his spouse." After a suitable and "sober" celebration, they must enter their "first dwelling together."[59]

Bullinger did not leave the newly married couple untutored. The first few months of cohabitation are a "most dangerous" time, he believed, and he thus devoted a third of his tract to describing the interlocking "duties of domesticity" required by the marital covenant between husband, wife, and God.[60] Bullinger went on for several pages advising couples about sex, food, dress, and other details of domestic economy, warning against excess in any of these. He then set out the couple's respective duties of "ordinate obedience and conjugal love mutual," following New Testament leads and holding up the relationship of Christ and his church as a "mirror to the state of wedlock and conjugal covenantal love."[61]

The wife owes her husband the duties of obedience, service, respect, devotion, modesty, courtesy, support, faithfulness, and honesty.[62] The husband is the head of the wife, "her defender, teacher, and comforter," called to exhibit the selfless sacrificial love of Christ himself and the virtues of clemency, wisdom, integrity, and faithfulness.[63] The wife must give proper care to the home, exhibiting cleanliness, industry, thrift, and judiciousness in her treatment of servants and neighbors. The husband must "labor for the common weal" of his family, exhibiting industry, honesty, integrity, and charity.[64] Couples with children could turn to a dozen pages of Bullinger's instructions on the parental duties of breast-feeding, nurture, discipline, education, and dress of children, and later, their courtship and contracting of marriage with a suitable partner.

This genre of writing about the interlocking covenantal duties of husband and wife, and of parent and children within the households—blending catechism, confessional book, and instructional manual into a sort of spiritual "Dr. Spock" for new families—became a trademark of the Anglican tradition. The "duties of domesticity" that Heinrich Bullinger pressed into thirty pages of terse text in 1540 became the subject of some six hundred pages of prolix prose by William Gouge a century later.[65] Scores of such books appeared in the later

57. Ibid., folios x–xv.
58. Ibid., folio xlvi.b. See generally folios xlvi–l.b.
59. Ibid., folio l.b.
60. Ibid.
61. Quotes are from ibid., folios liii, lv.b.
62. Ibid., folios liii–lv, lxii–lxiii.b.
63. Ibid., folios lv–lvi.
64. Ibid., folios lxv.b–lxvii.
65. William Gouge, *Of Domesticall Duties: Eight Treatises* (London: John Haviland, 1622) (ESTC 12119).

sixteenth and seventeenth centuries, written by divines of both Anglo-Catholic and Anglo-Puritan inclination.[66]

Even properly contracted marriages and dutifully maintained households can be rent asunder, Bullinger continued. The "shameful, vicious and abominable" sins of adultery, harlotry, and lust can affect even the noblest couple and drive them to defy their "sacred covenantal duties" to God, spouse, and children.[67] In the event of one party's adultery or malicious desertion (which is tantamount to adultery), Bullinger wrote, "divorce is permitted of God." Christ allowed divorce "for the health and medicine of man, and for amendment in wedlock," even though this was a "perilous and pitiful" regimen.[68] This "medicine" of divorce could not be administered by the couple themselves, but by a disinterested judge, who had to hear their petitions and find adequate cause for the dissolution of their marriage. Adulterous parties must be severely punished—executed in egregious cases. Innocent parties must be free to remarry, for to prohibit remarriage is "violently to cast a snare about poor peoples' necks and to drive them unto vice and sin."[69]

The first English edition of Bullinger's tract was printed anonymously in 1541. It was immediately censored, doubtless because of its open advocacy of clerical marriage and of divorce and remarriage—teachings (let alone practices) that remained illegal in England until 1547.[70] The book was republished the following year under a new title, *The Golde Boke of Christen Matrimonye*, and (at the insistence of "the hungry printer") under Thomas Becon's famous pen name.[71] The suspect chapters on clerical marriage and divorce were quietly dropped from the new edition, together with two other controversial chapters on impediments to marriage. This Becon edition of Bullinger's tract was regularly reprinted, and various abridgments and summaries of it became standard texts for Anglican clerics for the next two centuries.[72]

Becon added a long preface to this 1542 edition of Bullinger's *Golde Boke*, which extolled marriage not only for the spiritual good of the couple and their children but also for the civil good of the commonwealth and church. By marriage, Becon wrote with ample bombast, "many noble treasures chance unto us, virtue is maintained, vice is eschewed, houses are replenished, cities are inhabited, the ground is tilled, sciences are practiced, kingdoms flourish, amity

66. See sources and discussion in John Witte Jr. and Heather M. Good, "The Duties of Love: The Vocation of the Child in the Household Manual Tradition," in *The Vocation of the Child*, ed. Patrick M. Brennan (Grand Rapids: Wm. B. Eerdmans Publishing Co., 2008), 266–94.

67. Bullinger, *The Golde Boke*, folios xxiiii–xxxvi.b.

68. Bullinger, *The Golde Boke*, 1541 ed., folio lxxvi.b.

69. Bullinger, *The Golde Boke*, folio lxxvii.b.

70. See editor's notes in Bullinger, *The Fifth Decade*, xviii–xix. 31 Henry VIII, c. 14 (1539), prescribed, inter alia, maintenance of clerical celibacy and vows of chastity. This was repealed by 1 Edward VI, c. 12 (1547), as well as subsequent legislation mandating the Thirty-Nine Articles.

71. Becon, *Early Works*, 1:29.

72. The work is summarized in Bullinger, *The Second Decade*, 393–435. In the 1586 Convocation, Archbishop Whitgift directed the lower clergy to study Bullinger's *Decades* as part of their theological training. Alec R. Vidler, *Christ's Strange Work: An Exposition of the Three Uses of God's Law*, rev. ed. (London: SCM Press, 1963), 34.

is preserved, the public weal is defended, natural succession remaineth, good arts are taught, honest order is kept, Christendom is enlarged, God's word promoted, and the glory of God highly advanced and set further."[73] On the stability of "this household's common weal" hangs the security of the whole Commonwealth of England.[74]

Martin Bucer

Becon's emphasis on the social utility of the "household's common weal" is central to Martin Bucer's 1550 manifesto *On the Kingdom of Christ* (*De regno Christi*). Bucer, as we saw in the prior two chapters, was one of the great Continental Protestants, an intimate associate of Luther and Melanchthon, an influential mentor of the young Calvin, and a leading reformer of the theology and law of Strasbourg. Through Becon's influence in part, Bucer had been appointed to a chair at Cambridge University in 1549. Bucer produced his *De regno Christi* shortly after his arrival, summarizing his lifelong reflections on the reformation of the earthly kingdom, including notably the reformation of marriage theology and law. The work was formally dedicated to the young English King Edward VI but was functionally more significant in helping to shape an emerging theology of marriage in England.[75]

Like Bullinger, Bucer taught that marriage is a "first and most sacred union of man and woman." Marriage is to be "established in a holy way" in accordance with the laws of God. Persons should enter into it "gravely, deliberately, religiously, as befits those who have professed piety."[76] Bucer set out many of the same rules for the proper contracting of marriage that Bullinger had out-

---

73. Becon, Preface to *The Golde Boke*, folio Aiiii.b.

74. See also Becon, *Booke of Matrimonie*, folio DCxlix: "For being that a city standeth of houses, and the common weal of private things, and of ruling of a household and family, the discipline to govern a common weal is ordained: how shall he rule a city that hath not learned to rule a house: how shall he govern a common weal that never knew his private and familiar business. . . . For truly matrimony giveth a great exercise to moral philosophy. For it has a certain household's commonwealth annexed, in ruling that which a man may soon learn and have experience of wisdom, temperance, love to God and his kin, and all other virtues." Ibid., folios CCCClxcvii–CCCClxcvix: "The order of wedlock . . . maketh kingdom's populace great. . . . It bringeth forth children, sons and daughters, to the commonwealth, . . . which at all times are not only ready to do good to the commonwealth but also to do for the conservation of the same. . . . They refuse no labor, no pain, to show their obedience toward their superiors, . . . to do good to all men, . . . to do God's good will & pleasure, in laboring, in calling upon God, in thanking God for his benefits, in mortifying the filthy lusts of the flesh, in wearing such apparel as becometh godliness, in relieving the poor and the needy, in visiting the sick, in dying unto sin and living unto righteousness.

75. See Charles Hugh Smyth, *Cranmer and the Reformation under Edward VI* (Cambridge: Cambridge University Press, 1926), 155–77. Bucer was especially influential on Archbishop Whitgift of Canterbury in his disquisitions over marriage questions with Cartwright. See, e.g., *The Works of John Whitgift*, ed. J. Ayre for the Parker Society (Cambridge: Cambridge University Press, 1852), 3:353–59. For Bucer's influence in England more generally, see Constantin Hopf, *Martin Bucer and the English Reformation* (Oxford: Basil Blackwell, 1946).

76. Bucer, *De regno Christi*, bk. 2, chaps. 15–16.

lined, periodically echoing Bullinger's description of marriage as a "compact" and "covenant" that symbolizes the loving union of Christ with his church.[77] He likewise endorsed Bullinger's rendition of the interlocking purposes of marriage—for mutual love and friendship, procreation of children, and protection from lust—with a similar emphasis on marital love, friendship, and sacrifice.[78]

Unlike Bullinger, however, Bucer placed special emphasis upon the social quality and utility of this divinely ordained institution. Following the conventions of the Lutheran two-kingdoms theory, he insisted that "marriage is a *res politica*," "a civil thing." It is an institution of the "earthly kingdom, not the heavenly kingdom." It is subject to godly norms, but directed to human ends. It is an institution created for the "common good"—both the "internal good" of members of the household and the "external good" of subjects of the commonwealth. "Holy wedlock [is] the fountain of and seminary of good subjects," designed for the "decency and well-being of the commonwealth," for the "springing up of good men, and a right constitution of the commonwealth." "Who knows not that chastity and pureness of life can never be restored or continued in the commonwealth, unless it first be established in private houses, from whence the whole breed of men is to come forth."[79]

This emphasis on the social utility of marriage was hardly startling. Many fellow divines, including Becon, said similar things, and one could trace these sentiments back to Greek philosophers, Roman jurists, and church fathers. But Bucer pressed this logic to conclusions radical for his own day and prescient of reforms urged a century later by John Milton. Marriage must be maintained if it caters to the common good, Bucer said. But it must be dissolved by divorce if it detracts from the common good of the couple, their children, or the broader community.[80] Bucer advocated the replacement of the medieval canon law of divorce with the more liberal divorce provisions of the earlier Christianized Roman law. He dismissed the canon-law remedy of separation from bed and board, with no right of remarriage, as just the kind of destructive custom that should be avoided. He likewise replaced the small list of causes for separation recognized at Catholic canon law with the more ample roll of causes recognized at Christianized Roman law. Bucer strongly intimated that divorce should be granted on grounds of "mutual consent alone," as earlier Roman law had (for a time) allowed.[81] Though he later seemed to retreat from this position, he confirmed a wide range of causes for divorce recognized at Roman law that were considered deleterious to the common good of family, state, or church:

> If the husband can prove the wife to be an adulteress, a witch, a murderess, to have bought or sold to slavery any one free born, to have violated

---

77. Ibid., bk. 2, chaps. 18, 19, 26, 38.
78. Ibid., bk. 2, chap. 38.
79. Ibid., bk. 1, chaps. 2, 5; bk. 2, chaps. 15, 21, 28, 47.
80. See above, pp. 132–33.
81. Bucer, *De regno Christi*, bk. 2, chap. 40.

sepulchers, committed sacrilege, favored thieves and robbers, desirous of feasting with strangers, the husband not willing, if she lodge forth without a just and probable cause, or frequent theaters and sights, he forbidding, if she be privy with those that plot against the State, or if she deals falsely, or offers blows [he may divorce her]. And if the wife can prove her husband guilty of any of those forenamed crimes, and frequent the company of lewd women in her sight, or he beat her, she had the like liberty to quit herself, with this difference, that the man after divorce might forthwith marry again, the woman not till a year after, lest she might chance to have conceived.[82]

All such pernicious conduct by a husband or a wife had to end the marriage, in Bucer's view, for to perpetuate the union thereafter served neither the internal good of the household nor the external good of the community.

Bucer's emphasis on the social dimensions of marriage, and its public utility in the earthly kingdom, also led him to advocate exclusive state jurisdiction over marriage. Bucer was in favor of local parishes and clerics maintaining internal codes of spiritual discipline to guide their members on questions of marriage and sexuality. But he stood firmly against any exercise of legal or political authority by the clergy over questions of marital formation, maintenance, and dissolution.[83] It was up to the Christian king, he wrote, "to take up the just care of marriages," following the tradition of the ancient Hebrew monarchs and Christian Roman emperors.[84] "Pious princes and commonwealths both may and ought [to] establish" a civil law of marriage.[85] To Bucer, this was self-evident, given that marriage was a "civil thing" of the earthly kingdom. "No wise man can doubt," he wrote confidently, "that it is necessary for princes and magistrates first with severity to punish whoredom and adultery; next to see that marriages be lawfully contracted, and in the Lord, then that they be faithfully kept; and lastly, when that unhappiness urges, that they be lawfully dissolved, and another marriage contracted, according as the law of God, and of nature, and the constitutions of pious princes have decreed."[86]

Becon, Bullinger, and Bucer set out many of the main themes of the emerging Anglican theology of marriage. From different perspectives, each of these influential writers insisted on chipping away various canon-law accretions from biblical and apostolic norms of marriage. Each criticized the sacramental construction of marriage, the subordination of marriage to celibacy, the inflation of impediments to betrothal and marriage, the restriction of divorce to separation from bed and board, among other canon-law institutions. Each insisted on the familiar Protestant requirements of mutual, parental, and communal consent

82. Ibid., bk. 2, chap. 37, with fuller exposition in chaps. 40–44.
83. Ibid., bk. 1, chaps. 8–9; bk. 2, chaps. 1–2.
84. Ibid., bk. 2, chaps. 1, 15.
85. Ibid., bk. 2, chap. 40.
86. Ibid., bk. 2, chap. 47.

to marriage, church consecration and registration of new unions, marriage for clergy and laity alike, divorce for cause, rights of remarriage for the innocent divorced person and for the widowed. Each treated marriage as a natural, contractual, social, and spiritual union that was held together by the mutual love and duties of husband and wife and by the mutual nurture of church and state. Each insisted that marriage was a covenant involving God, husband and wife, and the broader community, which was created to serve the ends of mutual love, mutual protection from sin, and mutual procreation and nurture of children.

Bullinger and Bucer added their own variations on these common themes. Bullinger stressed the internal covenantal duties of domestic love, devotion, and support between husband and wife, parent and child. Bucer stressed the external common goods of the household for the church, state, and broader commonwealth. Bullinger stressed the church's role in the communication and enforcement of biblical duties of the domestic covenant. Bucer vested the state with principal governance of the formation and dissolution of marriage. Bullinger adduced primarily biblical sources for his construction of marriage. Bucer added a variety of norms from natural law, the law of nations, and Christianized Roman law. Bullinger focused on marital formation and adumbrated various biblical norms governing engagements, weddings, and initial cohabitation. Bucer focused as well on marital dissolution and adduced various historical norms justifying separation, divorce, and remarriage.

In the mid-sixteenth century, the Church of England had not yet developed an integrated model of marriage to mediate among these variations on Protestant marriage doctrines. But the writings of Becon, Bullinger, Bucer, and other divines provided a fertile seedbed out of which would grow a rich theology of marriage in subsequent centuries. The companionate view of marriage, which is usually traced to seventeenth-century Puritan communitarianism and eighteenth-century "affective individualism," was already in place among Anglican theologians of the mid-sixteenth century.[87] The covenantal conception of the household, which is often treated as a unique contribution of seventeenth-century English Puritanism, was in fact already an integral part of Anglican thought by the mid-sixteenth century.[88] The commonwealth model of marriage as the prototype and progenitor of the English Commonwealth, which would become the paradigm of seventeenth-century marriage theology, had its roots in the writings of Becon and Bucer, and it can be traced to even earlier Protestant and Catholic prototypes.

87. See James T. Johnson, *A Society Ordained by God: English Puritan Marriage Doctrine in the First Half of the Seventeenth Century* (Nashville: Abingdon Press, 1970), 51–120, on Puritan views; Lawrence Stone, *The Family, Sex, and Marriage in England, 1500–1800* (New York: Harper & Row, 1979), 217–53, on affective individualism.

88. See Johnson, *A Society Ordained by God*; William and Malleville Haller, "The Puritan Art of Love," *Huntington Library Quarterly* 5 (1941–42): 235–72; Edmund Leites, *The Puritan Conscience and Modern Sexuality* (New Haven, CT: Yale University Press, 1986).

THE MODEST TUDOR REFORMATION
OF MARRIAGE LAW

It was left largely to Parliament to establish the preferred norms and habits for the church and the Commonwealth of England. The legislation passed in the heat of Henry's marital disputes with the papacy laid the constitutional groundwork for a robust legal reformation of marriage and many other topics. The 1533 Act in Restraint of Appeals barred the papacy's appellate jurisdiction over the English "empire" and declared that "all causes of matrimony and divorces" now lie exclusively "within the King's jurisdiction and authority."[89] The 1534 Supremacy Act declared the King to be "the only supreme head in earth of the Church of England," with "full power and authority . . . to reform" all doctrines, liturgies, and laws, including those affecting marriage.[90] Acts of 1533 and 1535 called for a Reform Commission of spiritual and temporal leaders of the commonwealth to recommend systematic reform of prevailing canon law, including the law of marriage.[91]

These rapid early legal reforms seemed to be a promising start to a comprehensive reform of English marriage law, on the scale and at the speed of the Continental Protestant reforms of marriage law. Despite this early headway, and promising draft legislation, the Tudor Parliaments ultimately made only a few modest legal reforms, which were sealed in 1604. Particularly the ambitious reforms to marriage law proposed by the Reform Commission in 1552 were rejected, and it would ultimately take more than three centuries thereafter for these reforms to find their way into English law.

Preliminary Legal Changes

Even before the Reform Commission began its work, Parliament made several piecemeal changes to the prevailing canon law of marriage, family, and sexuality that were consistent with the agitations of the Protestant Reformers. Impediments of consanguinity and affinity were restricted to those set out in Leviticus.[92] Judges and clerics were forbidden "to dispense with God's laws" on the subject, either by expanding these impediments beyond the Levitical degrees or by offering dispensations to parties to marry in violation of them.[93] The canon-law impediment of precontract, which had earlier allowed fully consummated marriages to be broken on discovery of a prior contract to marriage, could now

---

89. 24 Henry VIII, c. 12. See also 25 Henry VIII, c. 19.

90. See 26 Henry VIII, c. 1.

91. See 25 Henry VIII, c. 19; 27 Henry VIII, c. 15; 35 Henry VIII, c. 16.

92. See 32 Henry VIII, c. 38—repealing 25 Henry VIII c. 22 and 28 Henry VIII, c. 7; 1 Eliz. c. 1 s. 3. Archbishop Parker issued a table of forbidden degrees in 1563, which was adopted by the 99th Canon of 1604. See also the summary of accepted impediments in *The King's Book: or, A Necessary Doctrine and Erudition for Any Man* (1543; repr., London: S.P.C.K., 1932), 58–59.

93. 32 Henry VIII, c. 22.

be enforced only if the subsequently married couple had no children.[94] Parishes were ordered to keep a marriage registry, putting the public on notice of existing marriages.[95] Priests were granted freedom to marry, without prejudice to their person, property, or profession, and guaranteed the same punishment as the laity if convicted for adultery or fornication.[96] Children of properly solemnized and consecrated marriages were to be treated as presumptively legitimate; all others were to be treated as bastards and were subject to severe civil restrictions and deprivations.[97] Various sexual crimes, particularly buggery, bestiality, and sodomy, were newly and repeatedly condemned as capital offenses.[98] These piecemeal legislative changes were viewed by many as steps along the way to a more systematic reformation of the liturgy, doctrine, and discipline of marriage.

Liturgical Reform

Systematic liturgical reform came to the Church of England in The Book of Common Prayer. The Parliaments of 1549 and 1552 mandated versions of the Prayer Book, but these were repealed by Queen Mary.[99] Queen Elizabeth's First Parliament, however, promulgated a comprehensive new Prayer Book, which ultimately became a centerpiece of Anglican unity and identity.[100] This 1559 Book of Common Prayer provided a timeless distillation of prevailing sentiments on marriage, and a wedding ritual that is still widely practiced today:

> Holy matrimony . . . is an honorable estate, instituted of God in paradise in the time of man's innocence, signifying unto us the mystical union, that is betwixt Christ and his Church: which holy estate Christ adorned and beautified with his presence and first miracle that he wrought in Cana of Galilee, and is commended of St. Paul to be honorable among all men, and therefore is not to be enterprised nor taken in hand unadvisedly, lightly, or wantonly, to satisfy men's carnal lusts and appetites, like brute beasts that have no understanding, but reverently, discreetly, advisedly, soberly, and in the fear of God, duly considering the causes of which matrimony was ordained. One was, the procreation of children to be brought up in the fear of the Lord, and praise of God. Secondly, it was ordained for a remedy against sin, and to avoid fornication, that such persons as have not the gift

94. See 32 Henry VIII c. 38, repealed by 2 & 3 Edward VI, c. 3, and 1 & 2 Mary c. 8, both of which allowed for full enforcement of precontract impediments; partly revived by 1 Eliz. c. 1 s. 12, which was read to allow consideration of precontract impediments only if the present couple had no children.

95. Howard, *Matrimonial Institutions*, 1:360–63 (quoting a 1538 injunction of Thomas Cromwell, repeated in 1547 by Edward VI).

96. See 32 Henry VIII, c. 10, 19; 2 & 3 Edward VI, c. 21. See also 1 Edward VI, c. 12, repealing 35 Henry VIII, c. 5 (the statute calling for enforcement against clergy of the Six Articles of Religion, 31 Henry VIII, c. 14, which included a prohibition against the preaching or practice of clerical marriage).

97. See 25 Henry VIII, c. 21.

98. See 25 Henry VIII, c. 6; 2 & 3 Edward VI, c. 29; 5 Eliz. c. 17.

99. See 3 & 4 Edward VI, c. 10; 5 & 6 Edward VI, c. 1, repealed by 1 Mary 2, c. 2.

100. See 1 Eliz., c. 1.

of continency might marry, and keep themselves undefiled members of Christ's body. Thirdly, for the mutual society, help, and comfort, that the one ought to have of the other, both in prosperity and adversity.[101]

The Prayer Book repeated the traditional requirement of publication of banns of marriage on three successive Sundays or holy days prior to the wedding, during which occasion the couple, their parents, and other parties could voice objections to the budding union.[102] The wedding itself was to be celebrated as a public event, in a parish church, with a set liturgy. During the service, the officiating priest invited guests for the final time to state "any just cause why they may not be lawfully joined together." He admonished the couple that "if either of you do know any impediment why ye may not be lawfully joined together in matrimony, that ye confess it. For be ye well assured, that so many as be coupled together on [other grounds] than God's Word doth allow, are not joined together by God, neither is their matrimony lawful."[103] Thereafter the couple exchanged ritualized promises of marriage. The husband delivered the wedding ring to the woman. (The 1662 Prayer Book revision mandated exchange of rings.) The priest declared them married, adding the familiar warning of Matthew 19: "Those whom God hath joined together, let no man put asunder." There followed a series of ritualized blessings, prescribed Bible readings, set prayers, a homily, and public celebration of the Eucharist.

The 1559 Book of Common Prayer was passed by statute and mandated for use in all churches in England. All other prayer books and liturgies were declared to be "utterly void and of none effect."[104] Royal and local visitors were commissioned to ensure its uniform and universal adoption throughout England. Dissenters from the Prayer Book were subject to prosecution in church courts—sometimes vicious persecution, especially in the wake of anti-Catholic and antisectarian legislation in the 1570s and periodically thereafter.[105] The language and liturgy of the Prayer Book's section on the Solemnization of Matrimony remained virtually unchanged until the twentieth century, despite the comprehensive Prayer Book revisions of 1604 and 1661/62, and the 1789 adoption of a new Book of Common Prayer for the Protestant Episcopal Church in America.

101. "Form of Solemnization of Matrimony," in *The Book of Common Prayer 1559*, ed. John E. Booty (Charlottesville, VA: University of Virginia Press, 1976), 290–91.

102. Promulgated by the Synod of Westminster (1200) for England and the Fourth Lateran Council (1215) for the Church universal, with subsequent canons providing that if any clergyman celebrated a marriage without banns or license, he would be suspended for a year. One could also obtain a dispensation from the bishop, permitting the marriage to take place without publication of banns. This license, authorized already in the fourteenth century, was confirmed by 25 Henry VIII, c. 21.

103. See 32 Henry VIII, c. 38 (repealing 25 Henry VIII c. 22 and 28 Henry VHI, c. 7), and 1 Eliz., c. 1, s. 3.

104. See 1 Eliz. c. 2.

105. See Richard Burn, *Ecclesiastical Law*, 6th ed. (London: A. Stahan, 1797), 3:232–74; Ronald A. Marchant, *The Puritans and the Church Courts in the Diocese of York* (London: Longman's, 1960), 1–25. See acts against Catholic and sectarian dissenters in 13 Eliz. c. 2; 27 Eliz. c. 2; 35 Eliz. c. 1, 2.

Doctrinal Reform

Systematic doctrinal reform came to the Church of England in the Thirty-Nine Articles of Religion (1571). The Articles, however, said rather little about marriage and family life, save in two crucial passages. First, the Articles permitted clerical marriage as a matter of church dogma: "Bishops, Priests, and Deacons, are not commanded by God's law either to vow the estate of single life, or to abstain from marriage. Therefore it is lawful *also* for them, as for all Christian men, to marry at their own discretion, as they shall judge the same to serve better to godliness."[106] Second, the Articles explicitly denied the sacramental quality of marriage: Only baptism and Eucharist are the "two Sacraments ordained of Christ our Lord in the Gospel," the Articles read. The sacrament of marriage is a state of "life allowed in the Scriptures: but . . . not any visible sign, or ceremony, ordained of God."[107] The Thirty-Nine Articles said little else about marriage, save giving a nod to the homilies on marriage in the Prayer Book.[108]

Failed Reforms of Ecclesiastical Law

These relatively modest changes in the liturgy and doctrine of marriage left it to the Reform Commission to make the most radical changes in the inherited canon law-tradition. A body of thirty-two leading theologians, bishops, civilians, and common lawyers, led by Archbishop Thomas Cranmer, seemed equal to the task.[109] In 1552, they presented to Parliament a comprehensive Reformation of Ecclesiastical Law.[110]

---

106. The Thirty-Nine Articles of Religion of the Church of England, published A.D. 1571, Art. 23, in Philip Schaff, *The Creeds of Christendom*, 3 vols. (New York: Harper & Brothers, 1877), 3:486, 502–3; "Articles agreed on by the Bishoppes, and other learned menne in the Synod at London, . . . M.D. LII., Art. 31," in *Synodalia: A Collection of Articles of Religion, Canons, and Proceedings of Convocations in the Province of Canterbury*, ed. Edward Cardwell (Oxford: Oxford University Press, 1842), 1:18, 29–30.

107. In the 1571 Articles, Art. 25, following the language of the 1562 Articles in Cardwell, ed., *Synodalia*, 1:66. This doctrinal innovation was very recent. A statement of Convocation in 1557 (Cardwell, *Synodalia*, 2:448, 452) had unequivocally confirmed "the seven sacraments of the church." *The King's Book*, 57–65, in 1543 defended the sacrament of matrimony at some length. For earlier English texts from 1530 onward that deny or deprecate the sacramental quality of marriage, see Carlson, *Marriage and the English Reformation*.

108. In the 1571 Articles, Art. 25.

109. See Praefatio of John Foxe to the 1571 Reformation, in *The Reformation of the Ecclesiastical Laws*, ed. Edward Cardwell (Oxford: Oxford University Press, 1850), vii–viii, xxx; with a listing of Commission members in *The Reformation of the Ecclesiastical Laws of England, 1552*, ed. James C. Spalding, Sixteenth Century Essays and Studies (Kirksville, MO: Sixteenth Century Journal Publishers, 1992), 37–38. For the Commission's empowering legislation, see 25 Henry VIII, c. 19; 27 Henry VIII, c. 15; 35 Henry VIII, c. 16.

110. Reprinted and translated in Spalding, *1552 Reformation*, with relevant provisions "Concerning Marriage," "Concerning Degrees Prohibited in Marriage," "Concerning Adultery and Divorce," in ibid., 87–106. See also Cardwell, *1571 Reformation*, 39–58, with identical provisions on marriage, impediments, and divorce.

This *Reformatio* included a crisp primer on Protestant marriage theology and law. Softening the quasi-sacramental language of the Prayer Book, the *Reformatio* held up equality of partners, mutuality of obligations, and temporality of purposes as the main marks of marriage: "Marriage is a legal contract, inducing and effecting a mutual and perpetual union of a man with a woman, by the order of God, in which each surrenders to the other power over his body, for the purpose of begetting offspring or of avoiding harlotry, or of controlling life by means of reciprocal obligations."[111]

"Since marriage is a lawful and devout custom, and prevents the disgrace of many shameful things," the *Reformatio* continued, "we do not want to keep any persons of any condition, rank, or age whatsoever from marriage," including the clergy.[112] All parties are free to enter this union, provided they are fit for such unions and follow the conventional steps of betrothal and espousal. Parties may enter engagements once they have reached the age of consent—twelve for girls, fourteen for boys. Parents or guardians of both parties must give their consent to the pending union. Parish ministers must publicly announce the banns for marriage on three successive Sundays or holy days. Weddings must be public religious ceremonies in the parish church of either party, following the prescribed liturgy and ritualized exchange of oaths set out in the Prayer Book.[113] Engaged parties must postpone their cohabitation or consummation until after the ceremony. Violation of any of these rules automatically nullifies the marriage.

The *Reformatio* included a truncated list of impediments to betrothal and marriage. Discovery of a prior, undissolved marriage by either party or discovery of a blood or family relation between the parties proscribed in Leviticus leads to automatic annulment and potential punishment of the parties for bigamy or incest. Postmarital discovery of an error respecting the person or quality of one spouse or the impotence or another defect that precludes intercourse allows either party to bring an action for annulment. Proof of coercion or threats into marriage can also break betrothal or marriage. Insanity, contagion, and heresy are all sufficient grounds to break betrothals, but not consummated marriages. "Spiritual associations" by either party "ought not to impede at all the course of marriage"—a reversal of traditional canon-law rules respecting the superiority of vows of chastity and holy orders.[114]

The *Reformatio* granted both husband and wife an equal right to sue for complete divorce and the right to remarry, on proof of cause. Such causes include adultery, desertion, deadly hostility, and prolonged ill-treatment, with a hint

111. Spalding, *1552 Reformation*, "Concerning Matrimony," chap. 1. A later chapter, "Concerning Sacraments," recognizes only Eucharist and baptism. (This document is divided into unnumbered sections, and then each section has separate chapter divisions.)

112. Ibid., "Concerning Marriage," chap. 9. See also "Concerning Adultery and Divorce," chaps. 2, 4, regarding adultery by married clergy; "Concerning the Church, and the Ministers and Their Duties," chaps. 4–6, 13, referring to wives and families of clergy.

113. Ibid., chaps. 2, 4–5. See also "On Sacraments," chap. 7, on "solemn rites of marriage before the eyes of the whole church with the greatest gravity and fidelity."

114. Ibid., "Concerning Matrimony," chap. 7.

that even perennial "disagreements or grounds of offense" might ripen into a sufficient cause for divorce. In all such cases, couples are urged to reconcile and continue their marriage. Absent reconciliation, innocent parties may file a petition before an ecclesiastical judge. Innocent parties are warned against any conspiring in, or falsely charging, their spouses' marital fault, on pain of severe penalty. Husbands are required to continue to pay their wives "a seemly and fit allowance" while the divorce proceeding is pending, regardless of who was plaintiff.[115] A successful suit for divorce could bring criminal sanctions of banishment or imprisonment on the guilty party. Separation from bed and board is not a recognized remedy, nor is voluntary withdrawal from one's spouse a legitimate act. A couple is either to remain married and cohabiting or seek divorce following proper ecclesiastical procedures, thereby sundering the union permanently and leaving the former spouses free to remarry.

The *Reformatio* included traditional prohibitions against sexual offenses: adultery, fornication, bigamy, polygyny, incest, premarital sex, and conspiracy in the same. The church courts were to punish these with public penance, the ban, or excommunication. More serious sexual crimes of rape, sexual battery, kidnapping, and the like are left to the magistrate to punish, with corresponding spiritual sanctions where appropriate.[116] The proposed law urged "shotgun" weddings for betrothed parties whose premarital sex has led to pregnancy, on pain of a man's forfeiture of ample property and a woman's banishment or imprisonment. It demanded fathers to support illegitimate children that they have sired. It urges mothers, even of illegitimate children, to nurse their own children rather than send them to wet nurses.

Virtually every provision on marriage and divorce in the *Reformatio* had Lutheran and Calvinist precedents. Luther's and Calvin's emphases on formal engagements and the policing of the conduct of betrothed parties prior to the wedding are evident. Bullinger's emphasis on a highly ritualized consecration of marriage in church comes through clearly. Bucer's liberal doctrine of divorce, on grounds beyond adultery, and rights of remarriage are also clearly present. The Continental Reformers' common emphases on the civil qualities of marriage, clerical marriage, restricted impediments, and divorce rather than separation all find a place in the proposed law. These Protestant prototypes were well known to Cranmer and many of his colleagues, and they had skillfully appropriated them in the *Reformatio*. The only provisions not common in Continental Protestant marriage laws were the requirements of mothers to nurse their own children, husbands to support their wives during divorce suits, and fathers to support their illegitimate children—and these provisions were known at English canon law prior to the Reformation.

Though theologically commonplace, these provisions proved politically unpersuasive. The 1553 Parliament, which had already passed prototypes of the

---

115. Ibid., "Concerning Adultery and Divorce," chap. 14.
116. Ibid., "On Crimes."

Thirty-Nine Articles and The Book of Common Prayer, refused to promulgate this Reformation of Ecclesiastical Law. The 1571 Parliament likewise demurred. In each instance, it was a single strong layperson who led the opposition on largely political grounds—the Duke of Northumberland in the House of Lords in 1553, Queen Elizabeth herself in 1571. There is no evidence that the *Reformatio*'s articles on marriage and divorce themselves met with any serious criticism. But, as part of a more comprehensive reformation of the canon law and ecclesiastical structures of England, they did not pass muster.[117]

Traditional Legal Settlement

The rejection of the *Reformatio* was an affirmation of much of the medieval canon law of marriage. To be sure, earlier legislation allowing clerical marriage and restricting impediments of blood, affinity, and prior contracts remained in effect.[118] With the legal establishment of the Prayer Book and Thirty-Nine Articles, Parliament also indirectly sanctioned clerical marriage, publication of banns, and church consecration of marriages. But the early sixteenth-century Catholic canon law of marriage, as amended by Parliamentary statute, remained the law governing marriage in England, and this law looked very much like the medieval Catholic canon law of marriage before the reforms of Trent.[119]

Later sixteenth-century English law distinguished between engagement, marriage, and consummation. Parties could contract engagements after the age of seven, marriages after the age of twelve for girls, fourteen for boys—although in reality, the common practice of feudal wardships tended to extend the functional marriage age to sixteen and twenty-one respectively, and social custom discouraged marriages before parties had reached their midtwenties.[120] Legitimate engagements required a mutual promise to marriage in the future ("I shall take you for my husband/wife"). Public engagements, especially those backed by publicly stated mutual promises, were preferred, though private engagements were legitimate and enforceable. Consummation by the couple after their engagement led automatically to marriage. Absent consummation, the engaged parties could dissolve their engagement on the same grounds recognized by their medieval predecessors: by mutual consent; by reason of one party's desertion,

117. A. G. Dickens, *The English Reformation* (New York: Schocken Books, 1964), 244–54; Ralph Houlbrooke, *Church Courts and the People during the English Reformation, 1520–1570* (Oxford: Oxford University Press, 1979), 16–19.

118. This was confirmed by Acts and Proceedings of Convocation (1604), Canon 99, 102, in Cardwell, *Synodalia*, 1:245, 304–5.

119. As Zurich reformer Perceval Wibum reported glumly from England in circa 1571: "The greater part of the Canon law is still in force there, and all ecclesiastical censures are principally taken from it." See *The Zurich Letters*, ed. Hastings Robinson for the Parker Society (Cambridge: Cambridge University Press, 1842), 359.

120. See generally Joel Hurstfield, *The Queen's Wards: Wardship and Marriage under Elizabeth I* (Cambridge: Cambridge University Press, 1958).

fornication, abuse, cruelty, or crime; on discovery of coercion, fraud, infancy, contagion in either party; or by breach of a material condition (such as failure to deliver promised property). The couple's parents and third parties could also press the parties to forgo their union because of differences of status, person, or religion, and many other causes. Church courts could, on their own initiative, dissolve an engagement on discovery of a relationship of consanguinity, affinity, or precontract. All that was missing from the traditional canon law of engagement was the prohibitive impediment of a prior or subsequent vow of celibacy or chastity by either party. But, absent proof of an impediment of consanguinity, affinity, or precontract, the betrothed couple had the final word and act respecting their marriage. Legitimate marriages required only a mutual promise of marriage in the present ("I take you for my husband/wife"). No parental consent, testimony of witnesses, publication of banns, ceremony in church, or sexual consummation were necessary, although, again, it was customary to attend to each of these formalities.[121]

Marriages, once contracted, could be dissolved either by annulment (which allowed for remarriage) or divorce (which meant only separation from bed and board). An order of *annulment* required proof of one of the impediments to marriage that survived Tudor statutory reform—a blood or family relationship between the parties prohibited by Leviticus, a precontract to an earlier marriage by one of the parties, or the impuberty, frigidity, or impotence of either or both parties.[122] Annulments had hidden costs, however, beyond the costs of litigation. The annulment dissolved a woman's right to collect dower interests in her former husband's estate.[123] It reduced any children born of the union to the status of bastards.[124] And, if granted on grounds of precontract, the annulment could also expose the previously contracted party to prosecution for bigamy, which after 1604 was a capital offense.[125]

A decree of *divorce* required proof of adultery, desertion (for more than seven years), or protracted ill treatment—beyond the normal physical beatings that

121. For the law at the end of the Tudor Reformation, see Henry Swinburne, *A Treatise of Spousals or Matrimonial Contracts* (written circa 1591; London: S. Roycroft, 1686), 45–108; *The Lawes Resolutions of Womens Rights, or, The Lawes Provision for Women* (London: Assigns of John More, Esq., 1632), 51–115; *Baron and Feme: A Treatise of the Common Law concerning Husbands and Wives* (London: Assigns of Richard and Edward Atkyns, Esq., 1700), 28–50.

122. See 1597 Constitutions and Canons Ecclesiastical in Cardwell, *Synodalia*, 1:152–55, 161–63; and discussion in John Godolphin, *Repertorium canonicum*, 3rd ed. (London: Assigns of Richard & Edward Atkins, 1687). On the medieval enforcement of these impediments, see Richard H. Helmholz, *Marriage Litigation in Medieval England* (Cambridge: Cambridge University Press, 1974), 74–100.

123. Sir Edward Coke, *The First Part of the Institutes of the Lawes of England* (London, 1628), folios 32, 33v, 235; idem, *The Third Part of the Institutes of the Lawes of England* (London, 1644), 93. See also discussion in Martin Ingram, *Church Courts, Sex and Marriage in England, 1570–1640* (Cambridge: Cambridge University Press, 1987), 145.

124. Burn, *Ecclesiastical Law*, 1:118–35.

125. See 1 James c. 11.

English law allowed a husband to visit upon a recalcitrant or belligerent wife.[126] A judgment of divorce was an order for separation from bed and board alone, with no right of remarriage for either party while the other spouse was still alive.

The 1604 Canons

The 1604 Canons and Constitutions Ecclesiastical—the only major English legislation on marriage before passage of Lord Hardwicke's Act in 1753—both softened and hardened this inherited canon-law tradition for seventeenth-century England.[127] On matters of *marital formation*, the 1604 Canons softened the medieval canon law slightly. Seven years earlier, Convocation had thundered its support for the traditional canon-law rules of private consent, despite the problem of clandestine marriages: "consent in marriage is specially to be regarded, and credit of kindred, honor, wealth, contentment, and pleasure of friends be rather matters of convenience than necessity in marriage."[128] The 1604 Canons encouraged more publicity in marriage formation by confirming the Prayer Book's requirement of public banns and church consecration for marriage and by introducing the requirement that children under twenty-one years must procure the consent of their parents or guardians before contracting and consummating their marriage.[129]

The 1604 Canons, however, also confirmed the traditional licensing exception, which eventually undercut the effectiveness of these reforms as deterrents to secret marriages. Parties could be exempted from the publication and public consecration requirements by procuring a marriage license from an authorized ecclesiastical official.[130] "Licensed marriages" were initially conceived as narrow exceptions to the usual rules, reserved for instances where necessity, such as imminent travel or military service, demanded an abbreviated engagement. At first, only the Archbishop of Canterbury and a few of his delegates were formally authorized to issue marital licenses, and they were expected to demand the presence of two good and honorable witnesses, strict proof of no prior impediment or pending marital litigation affecting the couple, and formal proof of parental

---

126. See a contemporary critique in W[illiam] H[eale], *An Apologie for Women, or, Opposition to Mr. Dr. G. his Assertion . . . That it was Lawful for Husbands to Beate Their Wives* (Oxford: Joseph Barnes/Barres, 1609); and discussion in John M. Biggs, *The Concept of Matrimonial Cruelty* (London: University of London Press, 1962).

127. Some of these were anticipated in two canons: "De moderandis indulgentiis pro celebrations matrimonii absque trina bantiorum denunciations" and "De sententiis divortii non temere ferendis," in Cardwell, *Synodalia*, 1:147, 152–55.

128. Quoted by Ingram, *Church Courts*, 135.

129. Canons 100, 101, in Cardwell, *Synodalia*, 1:305. The age of consent for marriage was 12 years for girls, 14 for boys. Swinburne, *A Treatise of Spousals*, 45–54.

130. See Acts and Proceedings of Convocation (1604), item VI, in Cardwell, *Synodalia*, 2:580, 583 (only chancellors granted licenses for marriage). This was a different use of the marriage license than encountered in chap. 6 on Calvinism. In Geneva, and later Protestant polities, all betrothed parties had to procure a license from the magistrate and deliver it to the church to trigger publication of the banns. Procurement of the license was a prerequisite to any legitimate marriage, not an alternative to ecclesiastical marriage.

consent from both sets of parents.[131] In the course of the seventeenth century, however, this license exception came to be treated as an attractive alternative method of marrying without the involvement of church, family, or community. Licensing officials proliferated, licensing requirements eroded, and false licenses abounded. Couples who sought to marry secretly could easily steal away to a remote parish to be married or make their way to one of the many licensing booths that sprang up around the Fleet Prison and near the ports. This "underground marital industry," as Lord Hardwicke would later call it, thrived in the seventeenth and eighteenth centuries, despite the increasingly stern prohibitions of Parliament and Convocation against it.[132]

The problem of secret and premature marriages—which had earlier taxed the Catholic Church and led to the firm publicity requirements of the Council of Trent—thus continued to plague the Anglican commonwealth, too. It was now spurious and lax licensors and licenses, however, that provided parties with the convenient means for circumventing the laws requiring public marriage formation.[133] Parliament's opposition to such secret marriages had several motivations, not all entirely unselfish: the dangers of exploitation and abuse of youngsters; the social costs of inaptly formed marriages that would be impossible to dissolve; the parents' loss of control over their children and their properties; and the commonwealth's loss of revenue from license taxes and wedding fees, among other factors. The famous 1753 Parliamentary Act for the Better Preventing of Clandestine Marriage (Lord Hardwicke's Act) sought to put a forceful end to this practice by returning the licensing exception to its traditional limits and by requiring formal banns, church consecration, parental consent, and two witnesses as a condition for legitimate marriage—a late Parliamentary adoption of rules of public marital formation that had been commonplace in other Protestant and Catholic lands since the mid-sixteenth century.[134]

On matters of marital *dissolution*, the 1604 Canons held fast to the substance of medieval canon law and introduced reforms to ensure its faithful execution. Seven years earlier, Convocation had bitterly complained about an "epidemic" of "disorderly marriages" and annulments and divorces "slightly passed."[135] The 1604 Canons took steps to end the disorder and to obstruct easy marital dissolutions. All annulment and divorce proceedings were to be held in open church

131. Canons 101, 103. Per Canon 104, no parental consent was required for the marriage of an emancipated widow or widower.

132. See sample documents listing complaints in Cardwell, *Synodalia*, 1:380, 412; 2:707, 711–12, 724, 731, 770, 794.

133. For a picture of this practice by a later jurist, see Henry John Stephen, *New Commentaries on the Laws of England* (London: Henry Butterworth, 1842), 2:286–87.

134. See 26 Geo. II, c. 33. Also see Richard B. Outhwaite, *Clandestine Marriage in England, 1500–1850* (London: Hambledon Press, 1995); Lawrence Stone, *Road to Divorce: A History of the Making and Breaking of Marriage in England* (New York and Oxford: Oxford University Press, 1995), 96–137.

135. Cardwell, *Synodalia*, 2:579–80. See also 1597 Constitutions and Canons Ecclesiastical, in ibid., 1:152–55, 161–63.

court, staffed by a duly authorized ecclesiastical judge, with no secret dispensations or equitable tinkering with dissolution requirements allowed. Parties were required to offer testimonial, documentary, or physical evidence in support of their dissolution petitions. The uncorroborated testimony of the parties themselves, even if uncontested, was no longer deemed sufficient evidence to dissolve a marriage.[136]

In cases of divorce, the 1604 Canons were doubly insistent on the traditional remedy of separation alone, with no right of remarriage to the innocent party. Ecclesiastical judges were required to enjoin divorced parties to "live chastely and continently; neither shall they during each other's life, contract matrimony for any other person. And, for the better observation of this last clause, the said sentence of divorce shall not be pronounced, until the party or parties requiring the same have given good and sufficient caution and security into the court, and they will not any way break or transgress the said restraint or prohibition."[137] Judges were threatened with a one-year suspension of office for failure to extract this pledge.[138] Divorced parties who did remarry before the death of their ex-spouse (or presumed death in cases of desertion) faced prosecution for bigamy, a capital offense.[139] The firm measures were designed to put an end to the protracted disputes among jurists and theologians about the meaning of divorce and to cut off any further experimentation with granting divorced parties a right to remarriage.[140]

These restrictions on marital dissolution, confirmed by the 1604 Canons, worked a particular hardship on women caught in abusive marriages. Once emancipated from their childhood homes, most women were dependent on their husbands for security and support. Under the doctrine of coverture, their person and property effectively merged with that of their husbands. Absent special arrangements made through prenuptial contracts or the procurement of a special legal status of a feme sole (a legally independent single woman) or a feme covert (a married women with license to operate without her husband's consent), married women were restricted severely in their contractual, testamentary, commercial, and other legal capacities.[141] A major mitigating factor, however,

136. Canons 105–6.

137. Canon 107.

138. Canon 108.

139. See 1 James c. 11. In cases of unaccountable desertion for more than seven years, a party could remarry with immunity from the statute, on the presumption that the ex-spouse had died. Godolphin, *Repertorium canonicum*, 507–8.

140. Ibid., 494–98, 504–7. On the celebrated divorce cases of the Marquess of Northampton (1552) and Sir John Stawell (1572), which had granted the plaintiff rights of remarriage, see Sir Lewis Dibden and Sir Charles Chadwick Healey, *English Church Law and Divorce* (London: J. Murray, 1912), 62–69, 83–92. Just before promulgation of the 1604 Canons, Star Chamber had held that, at English law, divorce even for adultery entails only separation from bed and board. See *Rye v. Fuljambe* (1602), in Edmund Gibson, *Codex juris ecclesiastici Anglicani*, 2 vols., 2nd ed. (London: J. Baskett, 1713), 1:466.

141. See summary in William Blackstone, *Commentaries on the Law of England* (Oxford: Clarendon Press, 1765–69), 1:430; and discussion in Marylynn Salmon, *Women and the Law of Property in Early America* (Chapel Hill: University of North Carolina Press, 1986), 14–57.

was that the common law granted wives the rights of dower. This was a legal claim to at least a third of her husband's property held during his lifetime, a form of widow's insurance which even the most conniving and wastrel husband found hard to overcome. A wife's dower interests put a limit on his title to both land and other movable property, and she would have to be bought out if he insisted on selling an item of property.

The restrictions on marital dissolution put the right to dower in direct competition with the right to remarry. An annulment gave a woman the right to remarry but no right to collect her dower. A divorce preserved her right to dower but gave her no right to remarry.[142] Neither circumstance was attractive to a woman without independent wealth and "must have deterred many a woman from pursuing her legal rights against an abusive or adulterous husband."[143]

This intolerable circumstance led to one important reform of the prevailing ecclesiastical law at the turn of the seventeenth century—the introduction of the modern practice of awarding *alimony*. Historically, husbands could be required to make payments of daily maintenance to their wives while their divorce case was pending, a provision that found its way even into the proposed 1552 Reformation of Ecclesiastical Law. But now the obligation to pay alimony could be extended, temporarily or permanently, after issuance of the divorce decree. Innocent wives who had divorced adulterous or abusive husbands could petition a court to order the former spouse to make reasonable payments for their maintenance and support, for a set time or for life.[144] Courts insisted on proof of the wife's innocence and the husband's prior guilt before honoring any such petition and would hear nothing of a husband's suing for alimony from his wife. Any evidence of collusion or fraud by the wife would automatically cut off her rights to alimony. Once convinced of the wife's right to alimony, however, courts would calculate the award much in the same manner as they do today— weighing the length of the marriage, the size of the wife's premarital estate, the relative wealth and needs of the parties at the time of the divorce, the ages and needs of any children, the severity of the husband's fault during the marriage, among other factors.[145]

At first, only the Court of High Commission could hear petitions for alimony, and such awards were relatively rare. But in the course of the seventeenth century and thereafter, orders for alimony became a staple practice of lower ecclesiastical courts, despite the repeated attacks from common-law judges and jurists that church courts had no business in ordering transfers of property among the laity. The practice persisted in the church courts until the nineteenth

142. *Baron and Feme*, 89–90, 336–44. See modern discussion and sources in Susan Staves, *Married Women's Separate Property in England, 1660–1833* (Cambridge, MA: Harvard University Press, 1990).

143. Richard H. Helmholz, *Roman Canon Law in Reformation England* (Cambridge: Cambridge University Press, 1990), 77.

144. Ibid., 77–79; Godolphin, *Repertorium canonicum*, 508–13.

145. Helmholz, *Roman Canon Law*, 77–79.

century, when it was taken over by the common-law courts in the Matrimonial Causes Act of 1857.[146]

Given these modest changes in the prevailing law on the books, "marriage litigation in sixteenth- and seventeenth-century England continued to look much as it had during the Middle Ages."[147] Throughout this period, English church courts continued to enjoy plenary jurisdiction over questions of marriage, family, and sexuality—interrupted only briefly during the Commonwealth period of 1649–60. They adjudicated disputes over engagements and marriages, with the vast preponderance of cases involving contractual and property disputes between parties who had made clandestine or oral contracts of marriage and now sought specific performance or injunctive relief from the other. They heard petitions for annulment and divorce, although the new procedural and property restrictions rendered such actions considerably less common than they had been before the Reformation. They presided over cases of wife and child abuse, desertion, deprivation, and the like—often sharing such jurisdiction with various royal and common-law courts in serious cases involving crime. They meted out discipline for fornication, adultery, incest, premarital pregnancy, and the like, using the ecclesiastical censures of penance, admonition, ban, and excommunication—sometimes supplemented by heavy fines as well as corresponding criminal sanctions administered by the appropriate civil court.[148]

MARRIAGE AS COMMONWEALTH IN SEVENTEENTH-CENTURY ENGLAND

Traditional Theoretical Formulations

The legal settlement of marriage questions by the end of the sixteenth century also brought considerable theological settlement. Seventeenth-century English theologians—from the Anglo-Puritan to the Anglo-Catholic—generally agreed that marriage was not a sacrament, although it was a divinely ordained institution. Celibacy was not a prerequisite for clerical service, although it was a commendable state for the naturally continent.[149] Marriage was to serve the goals of

146. Ibid., 79.

147. Ibid., 69–70. For studies, see ibid., 70–79; Ingram, *Church Courts*; Ronald A. Marchant, *The Church under the Law: Justice, Administration, and Discipline in the Diocese of York, 1560–1640* (Cambridge: Cambridge University Press, 1969), passim; Carlson, *Marriage and the English Reformation*, 105–80. A compilation of some relevant statutes and cases is also provided in Burn, *Ecclesiastical Law*, 2:433–512; Godolphin, *Repertorium canonicum*, 492–513.

148. See sources in the preceding footnote and Richard B. Outhwaite, *The Rise and Fall of the English Ecclesiastical Courts* (Cambridge: Cambridge University Press, 2006). For the shifts toward secular courts in the eighteenth century, see Rebecca Probert, *Marriage Law and Practice in the Long Eighteenth Century: A Reassessment* (Cambridge: Cambridge University Press, 2009).

149. See, e.g., Richard Hooker, *Laws of Ecclesiastical Polity*, bk. 5, chap. 73.1, saying that the "single life be a thing more angelical and divine," but marriage is needed to increase citizens and

love, procreation, and continence, although these goals were variously described and prioritized. Mutual consent of a fit man and a fit woman was the essence of marriage, although arranged marriages, bordering on compulsion, were still commonly defended. The consent of parents or guardians was an essential step for the contracting of marriage, although marriages contracted without such consent were still tolerated. Contracts of engagement and marriage were still distinguished, although the length of time and the conduct of the parties in the interval were variously described.[150] Church consecration of marriage was an essential step to the formation of marriage, although the exchange of rings and the celebration of the Eucharist remained controversial ceremonies in some circles.[151] Impediments of consanguinity, precontract, impotence, or frigidity were the principal grounds for annulment of marriages, although impediments of crime and heresy were sometimes defended as well. The legal establishment of these core doctrines of marriage ended the heated theological debates about them. Those who could not accept these basic established doctrines had to keep silent or to leave—on pain of punishment.

Rancorous debate continued about the doctrine of divorce, however, despite the firmness of the law established by the 1604 Canons. Deuteronomy 24, Matthew 19, and 1 Corinthians 7 all taught that divorce was a proper remedy in certain cases—of "uncleanness," "fornication," or "departure of the disbeliever," respectively. The 1604 Canons had confirmed the traditional Catholic interpretation of these biblical passages; the term *divorce* meant only separation from bed and board, not absolute divorce with a right to remarriage. This traditional doctrine of divorce was forcefully defended by a variety of leading Anglican divines throughout the seventeenth century, and a few Puritans as well.[152]

The 1604 Canons, however, had not accepted the sacramental theology of marriage upon which this medieval interpretation had been founded. Therein

---

saints, in *The Work of Mr. Richard Hooker in Eight Books of the Laws of Ecclesiastical Polity with Several Other Treatises*, ed. Isaac Walton, 3 vols. (London: W. Clark, 1821); *The Works of George Herbert*, ed. F. E. Hutchinson (Oxford: Clarendon Press, 1941), 236–37; *The Works of the Right Reverend Father in God John Cosin*, vols. 1–4, ed. J. Sansom, vol. 5, ed. J. Barrow (Oxford: John Henry Parker, 1843–45), 1:48, 56.

150. See Swinburne, *Treatise of Spousals*; Matthew Griffith, *Bethel: or, A Forme for Families* (London: J. Days, 1633).

151. See, e.g., Hooker, *Laws*, bk. 5, chap. 73, describing the controversy and defending the Anglican position; William Bradshaw, *A Marriage Feast: A Sermon on the Former Part of the Second Chapter of the Evangelist Iohn* (London: Edward Griffin, 1620), defending church celebration and wedding feasts as the modern equivalent of the marriage feast of Cana, where Christ performed his first miracle.

152. See, e.g., Lancelot Andrewes, *Against Second Marriage after Sentence of Divorce with a Former Match, the Party Then Living* (c. 1610), edited by James Bliss and included in Lancelot Andrewes, James Bliss, Henry Isaacson, and Sir John Harington, *Two Answers to Cardinal Perron, and Other Miscellaneous Works*, Library of Anglo-Catholic Theology 11 (Oxford: John H. Parker, 1854), 106–10; and discussion of other writers in Derrick Sherwin Bailey, *The Man-Woman Relation in Christian Thought* (London: Longmans; New York: Harper & Bros., 1959), 215–31; Arthur Robert Winnett, *Divorce and Remarriage in Anglicanism* (New York: St. Martin's Press, 1958), 60–78.

lay the controversy. Historically the Catholic Church had prohibited complete divorce on the theory that marriage was an enduring sacrament between husband and wife. This sacramental bond of marriage symbolized the eternal bond of grace between Christ and his church. To allow absolute divorce and remarriage to an estranged couple was both to legitimate serial polygamy and to symbolize divine infidelity. Neither course could be countenanced. It was better for estranged couples to be separated from bed and board, yet remain married in this life. Even if the couple remained estranged for the rest of their temporal lives, their bond could still bring some measure of sanctifying grace to their children and the church, if not to themselves. God could use even a broken marriage to communicate his sacramental grace.[153]

By officially denying the sacramental character of marriage in the Thirty-Nine Articles, however, the Anglican Church and English Parliament had undercut this traditional rationale for prohibiting absolute divorce. No systematic substitute rationale was yet at hand. This inevitably led to strident theological attack against the established doctrine—not only from many Puritans but also from some Anglicans.[154] Some early seventeenth-century Anglican theologians, such as Vicar Edmund Bunny, simply returned to traditional sacramental rationales for this doctrine of limited divorce—in defiance of official Anglican dogma.[155] Others, such as Bishop Lancelot Andrewes, argued that the 1611 King James Version of the Bible had simply not captured the nuance of Christ's words in Matthew 19:9. The King James Version reads: "Whosoever shall put away his wife, except it be for fornication, and shall marry another, committeth adultery." But, properly understood, Andrewes argued, the verse should read: "He that putteth away his wife (which but for adultery is not lawful) and marrieth another, committeth adultery himself." This reading, together with the injunction, "What God hath joined together, let not man put asunder," said Andrewes, makes clear that the Bible grants only the right of separation, not remarriage.[156] But such counterdogmatic and countertextual logic could not be convincing in the long term. A new rationale was needed.

The *commonwealth model of marriage* provided the new rationale. This model served at once to rationalize and routinize the many marital doctrines that had been settled and to seek settlement over the disputed doctrine of divorce. The commonwealth model was not universally endorsed in seventeenth-century England. But it was a popular construction of the nature and purpose of marriage

---

153. See summary in *The King's Book*, 64–65.

154. For Anglican critique, see John Cosin, *Argument Proving that Adultery Works a Dissolution of the Marriage* (c. 1670); reprinted in *Works of Cosin*, 4:489. For Anglo-Puritan critique, see John Rainolds, *A Defence of the Judgement of the Reformed Churches, That a man may lawfullie not onlie put awaie his wife for her adulteries but also marrie another* (London, 1609) (ESTC 20607). See discussion in Bailey, *Man-Woman Relation*, 215; Winnett, *Divorce and Remarriage*, 79–117.

155. Edmund Bunny, *Of Divorce for Adulterie, and Marrying Againe: That There is no Sufficient Warrant so to do* (Oxford: Joseph Barnes, 1610).

156. Andrewes, *Against Second Marriage*, 108–9.

that appealed broadly to English theologians—from the Anglo-Catholic to the Anglo-Puritan.[157]

Early seventeenth-century theologians began where Thomas Becon and Martin Bucer had ended in the mid-sixteenth century—with the belief that "marriage is a little commonwealth," created "for the common good."[158] Already in 1590, William Perkins put it thus: "Marriage was made and appointed by God himself to be the foundation and seminary of all sorts and kinds of life in the commonwealth and the church. . . . Those families wherein the service of God is performed are, as it were, little churches; yea, even a kind of paradise on earth."[159] Robert Cleaver opened his famous 1598 tract *A Godly Form of Householde Gouernment* with an oft-repeated maxim: "A household is as it were a little commonwealth, by the good government whereof, God's glory may be advanced, the commonwealths which standeth of several families, benefited, and all that live in that families may receive much comfort and commodity."[160] William Gouge premised his massive 1622 tome *Of Domestical Duties: Eight Treatises* on the same belief that "the family is a seminary of the church and the commonwealth," and indeed in its own right, "a little church, and a little commonwealth, whereby a trial may be made of such as are fit for any place of authority, or subjection in church or commonwealth."[161] Daniel Rogers, a sharp critic of Gouge on many points, nonetheless embraced the commonwealth model of marriage: "Marriage is the preservative of chastity, the seminary of the commonwealth, seed-plot of the church, pillar (under God) of the world."[162] Such sentiments "represent the consensus" of those writing on marriage in the late sixteenth and early seventeenth centuries.[163]

Theologians predicated this commonwealth model on both natural and biblical arguments. Systematic theologians regarded the interlocking commonwealths of state, church, and family as something of an earthly form of heavenly government. Dudley Fenner, for example, suggested that "the divine polity of Father, Son, and Holy Spirit" was reflected in "the covenanted polities of state, church, and family." State authorities are the Father's vice-regents, called to rule in accordance with the natural laws of creation. Church authorities are the Son's

---

157. See Mary L. Shanley, "Marriage Contract and Social Contract in Seventeenth Century English Political Thought," *Western Political Quarterly* 32 (1979): 79–91; Susan Dwyer Amussen, *An Ordered Society: Gender and Class in Early Modern England* (Oxford: Basil Blackwell, 1988), 34–66, 134–79.

158. Becon, *Booke of Matrimonie*, folio DCxlix.

159. Perkins, *Works*, 3:418–19. See paraphrase in Robert Pricke, *The doctrine of superioritie, and of subjection, contained in the fift commandement of the holy law of almightie God* (London: Ephraim Dawson, 1609), A8–9.

160. Cleaver, *Householde Gouernment*, 1. Cleaver's book was reprinted at least eight times by 1630 and reprinted several times again in the eighteenth century. Haller and Haller, "The Puritan Art of Love," 241n.

161. William Gouge, *Of Domesticall Duties: Eight Treatises* (London: John Haviland, 1622), 17, 27, Epistle, sig. 2v.

162. Daniel Rogers, *Matrimoniall Honour* (London: Philip Nevil, 1642), 17.

163. Amussen, *An Ordered Society*, 38.

representatives, called to preach Christ's word and to administer his sacraments. Family authorities are the Spirit's agents, called to provide daily godly instruction, protection, and edification to its members. Just as the divine polity and persons of God are mutually dependent and edifying, so are these human polities.[164]

Biblical theologians grounded this commonwealth construction in the Fifth Commandment of the Decalogue: "Honor thy father and thy mother." This commandment, Robert Pricke maintained, was "the fundamental ground . . . of all Christian subjection and of like Christian government, as well in church and commonwealth, as in every school and private family."[165] This commandment, John Dod added, was also the "fundamental ground" of the Second Table of the Decalogue. It played much the same role that the First Commandment played for the First Table of the Decalogue. Only those who obey the First Commandment, "Thou shalt have no other gods before me," can fully obey the subsequent commandments on graven images, swearing, and the Sabbath. Likewise, only those who obey the Fifth Commandment, honoring parents, can fully obey the later commandments against killing, stealing, adultery, perjuring, and coveting.[166]

The domestic commonwealth was created as a hierarchical structure, traditionally minded English theologians believed. God had created Eve as "a helpmeet for" Adam (Gen. 2:18 KJV). God had called Adam and Eve to mutual society among themselves and mutual procreation of children. After the fall, God had commanded that Adam "shall rule over" Eve.[167] As heir of Adam, the modern husband was thus the head of his wife. As heir of Eve, the modern wife was his subject, his "helpmeet." Together husband and wife were the heads of their children and the rest of the household. Each of these offices in the family hierarchy was bound by a series of duties, rooted in the Bible and natural law.

The dozens of household manuals and catechisms published in the early seventeenth century copiously described this hierarchy of duties and offices within

164. Dudley Fenner, *Sacra theologica sive veritas quae est secundum pietatem* (London: T. Dawson, ca. 1585), bks. 4–8, on the divine, political, ecclesiastical, and familial covenant commonwealths. See also idem, *The Artes of Logike and Rhetorike . . . Together with Examples of the same for Methode, in the gouernment of the Familie* (Middleburg: R. Shiders, 1584), folio A, on the parallel internal duties and structures of "the families, church, or commonwealth"; and folios B–C, discussing "the common state of the familie" that serves "to further the peace and tranquillitie of the commonwealth but also of Religion and true holiness." See more generally E. M. W. Tillyard, *The Elizabethan World Picture* (New York: Vintage Books, 1944), on the theories of the hierarchical natural, social, political, and domestic order in early modern English literature.

165. Pricke, *The doctrine of superioritie*; the quote is the subtitle of the book. See also *Works of Cosin*, 1:48, 56: "Marriage is an honorable estate in all men, a state ordained by God himself in paradise, a state without which there can be no society in this world durable"; Thomas Gataker, *A Good Wife: God's Gift, and, A Wife Indeed: Two Marriage Sermons* (London: John Haviland, 1623), 27: "The Societie of Man and Wife [is] the main Root, Source, and Originall of all other Societies"(ESTC 11659).

166. John Dod and Robert Cleaver, *A Plaine and Familiar Exposition of the Ten Commandments, with a methodicall short Catechisme, Containing Briefly all the Principall Grounds of Christian Religion* (London: Thomas Man, 1604), 181 (ESTC 6968).

167. Gen. 3:16.

the domestic commonwealth. Robert Cleaver's four-hundred-page manual on *A Godly Form of Householde Gouernment* offered a typical description. "All government of a family," Cleaver wrote, must be directed to two ends: "First Christian holiness, and secondly the things of this life." "Religion must be stirring in Christian families, and that good government looketh to bring godly behavior into families, as well as thrift and good husbandry."[168]

The paterfamilias must play the leading role in achieving this domestic ideal, Cleaver believed. As a husband, he must "live with his wife discreetly." He must "cherish and nourish" her as Christ loves and supports his church. He must "use her in all due benevolence, honestly, soberly, and chastely." And he must "govern her in all duties, that properly concern the state of marriage, in knowledge, in wisdom, judgment, and justice." A husband must not be "bitter, fierce, and cruel" to his wife and must "never beat her" even if he, as her head, must reproach and admonish her. Instead, "as a man of knowledge," he must "edify her, both by a good example, and also, by good instructions."[169] As a father, the married man must lead his household in private devotions, daily prayer, catechization, and Bible reading. He must ensure that children and servants are faithful in public worship and Sabbath observance. He must be vigilant in offering his children instruction and admonition with wisdom, punishment, and rebuke with patience.[170]

The duty of the married woman is to be "faithful and loving" to her husband, "wise and prudent" to her family. She must "reverence her husband" and "submit herself unto him," as Scripture enjoins. She must not "wear gorgeous apparel beyond her degree and place." She must avoid sloth and the keeping of idle and untoward company. She must be thrifty, just, charitable, and prudent in her choice of friends. She must keep order and help maintain "the exercise of religion within the household." She must tend especially to the care of her daughters and maidens, teaching them and exemplifying for them the norms and habits of Christian womanhood.[171]

Husband and wife also have a variety of mutual duties to each other and to their children. Husband and wife "must love one another with a pure heart fervently." They must be "faithful" to each other, constantly "bending their wits, and all their endeavors, to the help of each other, and to the common good of the family." They must pray together, "admonish one another," and serve as "mutual helps to each other in matters concerning their own salvation, and the service of God." Together, they must "instruct and bring up their children even from their cradle, in the fear and nurture of the Lord, . . . in shame fastness, hatred of vice, and love of all virtue." When the children mature, they must "bring them up in some profitable and lawful calling, by which they may live honestly and Christianly, and not be fruitless burdens of the earth

168. Cleaver, *Householde Gouernment*, 6–7.
169. Ibid., 92, 114, 159, 202; Dod and Cleaver, *Plaine and Familiar Exposition*, 24, 226–28.
170. Cleaver, *Householde Gouernment*, 9–42.
171. Ibid., 52–91, 203–22; Dod and Cleaver, *Plaine and Familiar Exposition*, 221–22.

... or commonwealth." They must also "provide for the disposing of them in marriage," counseling them in their courtship and consenting to their marriage when they come of age and have chosen wisely among available spouses.[172] In response to this, "the duties of the natural child" are very simple: "reverence, obedience, and thankfulness"—exemplified notably in seeking their parents' consent to their own marriage, and in caring for their parents when they become elderly or disabled.[173]

Faithful maintenance of this hierarchy of offices and duties, Cleaver believed, was the best guarantee of order within the domestic commonwealth. "For as in a city, there is nothing more unequal, than that every man should be like equal: so it is not convenient, that in one house every man should be like and equal another. There is no equality in that city, where the private man is equal with the magistrate, the people with the senate, or the servants with the master, but rather a confusion of all offices and authority. The husbands and wives are lords of the house. . . . The husband without any exception is master over all the house, and hath as touching his family more authority than a king in his own kingdom. The wife is ruler of all other things, but yet under her husband."[174]

Faithful maintenance of these domestic duties and offices was also the best guarantee of order within the broader commonwealths of church and state, Cleaver insisted. Indeed, properly functioning marriages and households were indispensable to civic flourishing. "If masters of families do not practice at home catechizing, and [keeping] discipline in their houses and join[ing] their helping hands to magistrates and ministers," social order and stability will soon give way to chaos and anarchy.[175] "It is impossible for a man to understand to govern the commonwealth, that doth not know to rule his own house, or order his own person, so that he that knoweth not to govern, deserveth not to reign."[176]

This was common lore among Cleaver's fellow divines. "A conscionable performance of household duties . . . may be accounted a public work," William Gouge wrote. For "good members of a family are likely to make good members of church and commonwealth."[177] "Most of the mischiefs that now infest or seize upon mankind throughout the earth, consist in, or are caused by the disorders and ill government of families."[178] "There was never any disorder and outrage, in any family, church, or commonwealth" when domestic offices were respected and domestic duties discharged, Robert Pricke insisted. For domestic duty and discipline allow persons "to rise up to the knowledge of the sovereign Lord, and to give unto him the reverence and honor due to his divine majesty."

172. Cleaver, *Householde Gouernment*, 188–91, 243; Dod and Cleaver, *Plaine and Familiar Exposition*, 174–222.
173. Cleaver, *Householde Gouernment*, 186.
174. Ibid., 174–75.
175. Ibid., Preface, A4.
176. Ibid., 4–5.
177. Gouge, *Of Domesticall Duties*, 17, 27.
178. Richard Baxter, *A Christian Directory* (London: Robert White, 1673), as quoted by Shanley, "Marriage Contract," 79.

It also teaches them not only the personal virtues but also the civic habits that "upholdeth, and continueth all these estates, degrees, and orders" of the broader commonwealth.[179] Daniel Rogers wrote more generally that a stable marriage and household serve as "the right hand of providence, supporter of laws, states, orders, offices, gifts, and services, the glory of peace, . . . the foundation of countries, cities, universities, . . . crowns, and kingdoms."[180] In the mid-sixteenth century, Thomas Becon had described himself as "a veritable voice crying in the wilderness" of English divinity against the conventional deprecation and distortion of marriage. Half a century later, his prophetic voice was part of a loud ecumenical chorus extolling the domestic commonwealth for its indispensable personal, social, and moral goods.

Some writers pressed the commonwealth model to even further service and came to treat the domestic commonwealth not only as a valuable resource for political stability but also as the very source of political authority. Sir Robert Filmer (John Locke's famous antagonist, as we will see in a moment) posed this thesis forcefully in his defense of monarchical government. In his *Patriarcha,* published around 1638 as well as his later essays, Filmer sought to prove that the domestic and political commonwealths are essentially the same and that both are subject to the absolute authority of the male head.[181] Adam and Eve, Filmer believed, were the founders not only of the first marriage and family but also of the first state and society. Adam was the first husband and father but also the first patriarch and ruler. Eve was the first wife and mother, but also the first helper and subject. Together with their children, they composed at once a domestic and a political commonwealth.[182]

Over time, Filmer argued, this first domestic and political commonwealth of paradise was duplicated and differentiated. New marriages, new families, new societies, new states proliferated. But for all their diversity, these institutions retained the same basic patriarchal structure created by God for the first commonwealth. The highest authority within these institutions was vested in the eldest entitled male, the patriarch descended from Adam. Duties of obedience and subjection fell on all others, as they had fallen on Eve and in turn on her children. This pattern of authority and subjection was not a matter of a social contract or a voluntary

179. Pricke, *The doctrine of superioritie,* B2.

180. D. Rogers, *Matrimoniall Honour,* 17.

181. Robert Filmer, *Patriarcha and other Political Works,* ed. Peter Laslett (Oxford: Oxford University Press, 1949). See similar formulations in John Wing, *The Crown Conjugall; or, The Spouse Royall* (London: John Beale for R. Mylbourne, 1632) (ESTC 25845); Dudley Digges, *The Unlawfulnesse of Subjects taking up Armes Against their Soveraigne* ([London,] 1644); William Lawrence, *Marriage by the Morall Law of God Vindicated [and] The Right of Primogeniture in Succession to the Kingdoms of England and Scotland* (London, 1681). See James Daly, *Sir Robert Filmer and English Political Thought* (Toronto: University of Toronto Press, 1979); G. J. Schochet, *Patriarchalism in Political Thought: The Authoritarian Family and Political Speculation and Attitudes Especially in Seventeenth Century England* (New York: Basic Books, 1975).

182. Filmer, *Patriarcha,* chaps. 1, 7. See also idem, *Observations upon Aristotles Politiques Touching Forms of Government Together with Directions for Obedience to Governours in Dangerous and Doubtfull Times,* in *Patriarcha,* 185, 188: "Adam was father, king, and lord over his family."

choice by the ruler or the ruled, Filmer insisted. It was the nature of things, the design of God's creation. "Every man that is born is, . . . by his very birth, . . . a subject to him that begets him: under which subjection he is always to live, unless by immediate appointment from God, or by the grant or death of his Father, he becomes possessed of that power to which he was subject."[183]

On these premises, Filmer defended a monarchical form of government modeled on the domestic hierarchy. The hierarchy of the family under the paterfamilias is replicated in the political hierarchy of the state under the king, he believed. "Kings now are the fathers of their people."[184] "If we compare the natural duties of a father with those of a king, we find them to be all one, without any difference at all but only in the latitude or extent of them. As the father over one family, so the king, as father over many families, extends his care to preserve, feed, clothe, instruct, and defend the whole commonwealth."[185] The king enjoys "a natural right of a supreme Father over every multitude" and is deserving of the reverence, obedience, and subjection that natural children owe to their fathers. Thus the Fifth Commandment, "which enjoins obedience to kings is delivered in the terms of 'honor thy father' as if all power were originally in the father. If obedience to parents be immediately due by a natural law, and subjection to princes, but by the mediation of a human ordinance, what reason is there that the law of nature should give place to the laws of men, as we see the power of the father over his child gives place and is subordinate to the power of the magistrate[?]"[186]

Filmer recognized the inherent limitations of this extended interpretation of the commonwealth. Though analogous in hierarchy and duty, the modern commonwealths of state, church, and family were not identical. Each of these "commonwealths" had its own calling, constitution, and character that could not be conflated. The state had a unique power of the sword and the law. The church had a unique power of the Word and the sacrament. The marital household had a unique power of love and duty. Though he noted them, Filmer did not elaborate these differences among the political, ecclesiastical, and domestic commonwealths. Particularly in his later years, he tended increasingly toward a patriarchal monism.

Filmer's theological contemporaries did elaborate these differences and in so doing emphasized the unique "companionate" qualities of the domestic commonwealth. "There is no society more near, more entire, more needful, more kindly, more delightful, more comfortable, more constant, more continual, than the society of man and wife," wrote Thomas Gataker.[187] "Conjugal love,"

183. Robert Filmer, *Directions for Obedience to Government in Dangerous or Doubtful Times*, in *Patriarcha*, 231, 232.

184. Filmer, *Patriarcha*, chap. 5.

185. Ibid., chap. 7.

186. Ibid., chap. 6.

187. Gataker, *A Good Wife*, 27, listing the "purposes of marriage" as "societies" "assistance," "comfort and solace," "issue," and "remedy against incontinence" (cf. ibid., 31–38). See also ibid., 5: "Husband and wife are nearer than friends, . . . engrafted into the other, and so fastened together, they cannot again be sundered."

Daniel Rogers insisted, is the "main and joint duty of the married." Marital love is the highest love, for it is simultaneously spiritual and sensual, Christian and carnal—a sweet compound of both religion and nature."[188] "Marriage is the queen of friendships," Jeremy Taylor insisted, "in which there is a communication of all that can be communicated by friendships."[189] Even William Gouge, who rivaled Filmer in patriarchal sternness, could bring himself to say that "with true matrimonial love and affection," a man and a woman reach "the nearest of equality that may be," becoming "after a sort even fellows and partners."[190] Dozens of paeans to romance, sensuality, intimacy, tenderness, friendship, companionship, sharing, equality, and other soft affections between husband and wife flowed from the pens of seventeenth-century English writers. These writers were fully aware that marriage could also be what William Whately called "a little hell," featuring poverty, rape, violence, abuse, and other forms of pathos.[191] But marital love was an ideal to be held up. Even the rather reserved Book of Common Prayer of 1559 and 1662 commanded newly married couples to have "one accord of heart and mind" and to embrace "pleasant and sweet love." This passage, together with the more expansive biblical passages on love that the Prayer Book appointed for the marriage service, inspired many grand homiletic descriptions and prescriptions of marital love, affection, and companionship.[192]

Traditional Legal Formulations

The commonwealth model of marriage provided a sturdy new framework to rationalize the established law of marriage in England. English theologians repeated endlessly the biblical and traditional arguments for each of the rules of marital formation, maintenance, and dissolution, drawing on both medieval Catholic and various Protestant sources in so doing. But it was the commonwealth understanding of marriage—as the first society created by God, the foundation of the church and the commonwealth of England, the progenitor of civil society and morality—that gave these traditional interpretations a new sense of unity and gravity.

The steps for marital formation had to be carefully negotiated, for much was at stake in this union, both theological and political. The couple was not merely joining in covenant with each other and with God, as Continental Protestants

188. D. Rogers, *Matrimoniall Honour*, 146, 150, 157, 184.

189. Jeremy Taylor, *The Measures and Offices of Friendship*, 3rd ed. (London: R. Royston, 1662), 79.

190. Gouge, *Of Domesticall Duties*, 356.

191. William Whately, *A Bride-Bush, or, A Wedding Sermon: Compendiously Describing the Duties of Married Persons: By Performing Whereof, Marriage shall be to them a Great Help, Which Now Finde it a Little Hell* (London: William Jaagard for Nicholas Bourne, 1617) (ESTC 25296). See also Ingram, *Church Courts*, 144–45.

192. See illustrative sermons in *Sermons or Homilies Appointed to be Read in the Churches in the Time of Queen Elizabeth, of Famous Memory* (Liverpool: H. Forshaw, 1799), with discussion in Ingram, *Church Courts*, 142–45.

taught. They were not merely symbolically representing the mysterious union of Christ and his church, as Catholics taught. The couple was also, in effect, joining in covenant with the church and commonwealth of England—past, present, and future. They were promising, in William Heale's words, "to stake not only the temporal and eternal happiness of themselves and their children, but the very virtue, stability, order, and security of all England" on their marital promise.[193] A successful marriage would earn them and all others great reward; a failed marriage would bring great hardship.

Fraught as it was with personal, social, and eternal consequences, the step into matrimony thus required all the maturity, deliberation, and participation that the laws of marital formation demanded. Marriage required formal betrothals, with a delay before nuptials, so that all parties could calculate their companionability and compatibility.[194] It required the consent and counsel of parents and guardians, for they represented the wisdom of past generations of the commonwealth. It required the consecration of priests and approbation of magistrates, for they represented the current rulership of the commonwealth. It required the desire to procreate and the capacity to educate, for children would become the future generation of the commonwealth, to the benefit of family, church, and state alike.[195]

"They that enter into the state of marriage," Jeremy Taylor wrote, "cast a die of the greatest contingency, and yet of the greatest interest in the world, next to the last throw for eternity."[196] "Most gravely doth our Communion Book admonish such as come to be married that they ought enter into this estate, not rashly, lightly, unadvisedly . . . but discretely, advisedly, soberly, and in the fear of God," William Whately wrote. For persons who marry without full awareness of the gravity of their office do so "with much hazard to their souls, and much unquietness to themselves, families, and neighbors . . . [and] indeed the very commonwealth."[197] "Marriage of all humane actions is the one and only weightiest," William Heale continued.

> It is the present disposal of the whole life of man: it is a Gordian knot that may not bee loosed but by the sword of death: it is the ring of union whose poesie is pure and endless. In a word it is that state which either imparadizeth a man in the Eden of felicity, or else exposeth him unto a world of misery. Hence it is that so mature deliberation is required, before such an eternal bond be united. The mutual affection of each party, the

193. W[illiam] H[eale], *An Apologie for Women*, 2nd ed. (Oxford: Joseph Barnes/Barres, 1614), 105.

194. See esp. Cleaver, *Householde Gouernment*, 111–38; Swinburne, *Treatise on Spousals*, 11–14, 222–40.

195. See, e.g., Cleaver, *Householde Gouernment*, 154: "If they be well and virtuously brought up, God is greatly honored by them, the commonwealth is advanced: yea their parents and all other, fare the better for them."

196. Jeremy Taylor, *Eniautos*, 2nd ed. (London: Richard Royston, 1655), 2:224–25.

197. William Whately, *A Care-Cloth: or, a Treatise of the Cumbers and Troubles of Marriage* (London: Felix Kyngston for Thomas Man, 1624), A2 (ESTC 25299).

consent of parents, the approbation of friends, the trial of acquaintance: besides the especial observance of disposition, of kindred, of education, of behaviour. Now then if a man solemnize marriage upon these due respects, he can hardly make his choice amiss, because he is guided by virtue, which never faileth her followers.[198]

A similar argument was used to rationalize the restricted rules of marital dissolution and divorce. English theologians repeated and glossed biblical passages on the maintenance of a "godly household." They grounded the patriarchal structure of the household on the Fifth Commandment and the texts of Paul. They grounded the impediments of precontract, consanguinity, and frigidity on Old Testament commandments on bigamy, incest, and procreation. They grounded the limited doctrine of divorce on New Testament passages counseling faithfulness to one's spouse even in the face of poverty, oppression, heresy, sickness, and other adversity.

It was the commonwealth understanding of marriage, however, that gave these traditional biblical rules their urgency and integrity for many seventeenth-century writers. The domestic commonwealth was the foundation of the English commonwealth. Its hierarchy of offices and duties was the model, even the source, of political authority and civic obligation. Its patriarchal construction was the foundation on which the monarchy and episcopacy of England was built. Its definition and discharge of duties was essential for civic order, liberty, and rule of law. Such a progenitive union could not be broken unless it defied God's explicit laws for marital formation. To break marriage for any other cause was, in Bishop Lancelot Andrewes's words, to act "against nature," "against the church," "against the commonwealth," indeed, "against the whole state of mankind."[199]

This was a new rationale for the English law of limited divorce and dissolution. In Catholic sacramental theology, marriage was presumed to be permanent because God had chosen this instrument to dispense his grace on the church. In Anglican commonwealth theology, marriage was presumed permanent because God had chosen this institution to convey his law for the commonwealth. In Catholic theology, even a broken marriage had to be maintained lest a channel of God's grace be prematurely closed to the church. In Anglican theology, even a broken marriage had to be retained lest a source of God's law and order be permanently lost on the commonwealth. Catholic divorce doctrine tended to be more sacramental and otherworldly in inspiration. Anglican divorce doctrine tended to be more social and utilitarian.

---

198. Heale, *An Apologie for Women*, 10–11.

199. Andrewes, *Works*, 2:233–34. See also William Ames, *The Marrow of Theology*, translated from the 3rd Latin ed. (1629) and edited by John D. Eusden (Boston: Pilgrim Press, 1968), 319, items 34–35, arguing: "The perpetuity of marriage does not depend only upon the will and covenant of the persons contracting, for then by consent of both a covenant so begun might be broken, as is the case between master and servant. Rather, the rule and bond of this covenant is the institution of God, . . . which establishes the individual companionship of husband and wife [and] looks toward the good of mankind and its rightful conservation and their hereditary succession."

To be sure, Anglicans in the seventeenth century and thereafter continued to speak of the sacramental qualities of marriage. But this was more a revival of an Augustinian concept of *sacramentum* than the survival of a Catholic theology of sacramentalism. In Catholicism, marriage was presumed to be permanent because it was a sacrament. In Anglicanism, marriage was presumed to be sacramental because it was permanent.

Liberal Revisions and Experiments

Until the mid-seventeenth century, this commonwealth model had considerable intuitive appeal. The English commonwealths of family, church, and state, as conventionally understood and organized, had parallel hierarchical structures under a single head. The king, subject to God, stood at the head of the political commonwealth. The archbishop, subject to God and king, stood at the head of the episcopal commonwealth. The paterfamilias, subject to God, king, and bishop, stood at the head of the domestic commonwealth. With such a neat and orderly construction, it was easy for some to believe the speculation of Dudley Fenner that these three commonwealth hierarchies were somehow models of God's creation order, perhaps even of the triune Godhead itself.[200]

Such speculations were harder to follow when the English world—in Christopher Hill's apt phrase—"was turned upside down" by the English Revolutions of 1640 to 1689.[201] The 1640 Revolution was partly a rebellion against the excesses of the political commonwealth, headed by King Charles. The landed aristocracy and merchants chafed under oppressive royal taxation raised to support unpopular wars. Clergy and laity suffered under harsh new establishment laws that drove religious nonconformists first out of their families and churches, then out of England altogether. Much of the country resented the increasingly belligerent enforcement of royal measures by the prerogative courts—Star Chamber, Admiralty, High Commission, and Requests. When Parliament was finally called into session in 1640, after an eleven-year hiatus, its leaders seized power by force of arms. Civil war erupted between the supporters of Parliament and the supporters of the monarch. The Parliamentary party prevailed and passed an Act "declaring and constituting the People of England to be a commonwealth and free state." Parliament abolished the kingship, and the deposed King Charles was tried, convicted for treason, and executed. Parliament also abolished the aristocratic House of Lords and declared that "supreme authority" resided in the people and their representatives. Anglicanism was formally disestablished, and episcopal ecclesiastical structures were replaced with congregational and Presbyterian forms. "Equal and proportional

200. On hierarchical order in English society, see Louis B. Wright, *Middle Class Culture in Elizabethan England* (Chapel Hill: University of North Carolina Press, 1953).

201. Christopher Hill, *The World Turned Upside Down: Radical Ideas during the English Revolution* (New York: Viking Press, 1972).

representation" was guaranteed in the election of local representatives. England came under "the democratic rule" of Parliament and the Protectorate of Oliver Cromwell.[202]

After Cromwell died in 1658, the Commonwealth government eventually collapsed. King Charles II, son of Charles I, returned to England, reclaimed the throne in 1660, and restored traditional monarchical government and prerevolutionary law. This Restoration era was short-lived. When his successor, King James II, the other son of Charles I, began to abuse his royal prerogatives as his father had done, Parliament forced him to abdicate the throne in 1688 in favor of the new dynasty of William and Mary. This was the Glorious Revolution. It established government by the king *in Parliament* and introduced a host of new guarantees to English subjects, notably those set out in the Bill of Rights and the Toleration Act of 1689.[203]

The English Revolutions unleashed a torrent of both legal and literary experimentation respecting marriage and the family. Much of this experimentation was outlawed with the Restoration in 1660, but it was prescient of later legal developments and indicative of some of the customs of the English countryside and of the colonies.

In 1653, for example, the Commonwealth Parliament passed a statute that greatly simplified the contracting of marriage and largely removed it from the jurisdiction of the Church of England. Parties of the age of majority (sixteen for boys, fourteen for girls) who wanted to marry had to register with a local parish or justice of the peace. Their banns were to be thrice published at set intervals in the church or in the adjacent marketplace. Thereafter the couple had to procure a marriage certificate from the same office. If they were under twenty-one years, they also had to procure proof of their parents' or guardians' consent. Weddings were to be performed before a justice of the peace, with two or more witnesses present. The parties were to hold hands and exchange a simple prescribed oath, with no exchange of rings: "I, A.B., do here in the presence of God, the searcher of all hearts, take thee, C.D., for my wedded Wife [Husband], and do also in the presence of God, and before these witnesses, promise to be unto thee a loving and faithful Husband [loving, faithful, *and obedient* Wife]." The justice of the peace was to pronounce the couple "husband and wife." The signed marriage certificate was to be returned to the parish register. Defiance of any of these steps would render the marriage "void and of none effect."

Local justices of the peace not only conducted weddings in place of priests but were also given exclusive jurisdiction, in place of church courts, over the "hearing and determining of all matters and controversies touching contracts and marriages, and the lawfulness and unlawfulness thereof." They were specifically

202. See detailed sources and discussion in John Witte Jr., *The Reformation of Rights: Law, Religion, and Human Rights in Early Modern Calvinism* (Cambridge: Cambridge University Press, 2007), chap. 4.

203. See 1 William & Mary, st. 2, c. 2, c. 18.

authorized to seize "the whole estate, real and personal," of "any person" who "by violence or fraud shall steal or take away" another person under twenty-one years of age "with intent to marry."[204] Five years later, Parliament also claimed the power to grant private acts of divorce, with a right to remarry given to the divorced parties.

Much of this 1653 law was repealed during the Restoration of 1660. But marriages that had been contracted before 1660 in accordance with its procedures were validated by statute.[205] Moreover, the practice of granting divorce by private act of Parliament continued. The high costs and cumbersome procedures rendered such acts rare during the next century; there was on average only one divorce every five or six years. But after 1750, Parliament granted at least one such private act of divorce per year, a rate that slowly increased until the Divorce Reform Acts of 1857 and following years instituted causes of action for divorce in the common-law courts.[206]

This legal experimentation with traditional marriage law was matched by even bolder literary speculation. Freed temporarily from censorship laws during the Commonwealth era of 1640–60, English writers proposed all manner of alternatives to traditional habits and forms of marriage—from the salutary to the prurient. Gerrard Winstanley, the leader of the Diggers, suggested, against prevailing patterns of arranged and male-initiated marriages, that "every man and every woman shall have the free liberty to marry whom they love, if they can obtain the love and liking of that party whom they should marry, and neither birth nor portion shall hinder the match, for we are all of one family mankind." In a further effort to protect women, he urged that a man who impregnated a single woman be forced to marry her, and that convicted rapists and adulterers be executed.[207] A host of writers advocated absolute divorce on proof of cause, with a right to remarriage for both parties. Francis Osborne went further, proposing that marriages be made by annually renewable contracts, rescindable at will by either party. Henry Neville described a polygamous utopia, which featured "free love" and "open sex." John Hall, among others, advocated open "female nudism," arguing that "nakedness would be less provocative" than current women's fashions.[208] The English world had indeed been "turned upside down."

---

204. "How Marriages Shall be Solemnized and Registered . . ." (1653), in *A Collection of Acts and Ordinances of General Use Made in the Parliament*, ed. H. Scobell (London: Henry Hills & John Field, 1658), Pt. II, 236–38; confirmed in 1656, in ibid., 389.

205. See 12 C. II, c. 33.

206. See Stone, *Family, Sex, and Marriage*, 34–35, indicating only 17 such acts between 1670 and 1750; and 114 between 1750 and 1799. No woman received a private act of divorce until 1801. Salmon, *Women and the Law of Property*, 60. For the cumbersome procedures, see Allen Horstman, *Victorian Divorce* (New York: St. Martin's Press, 1985), 20.

207. Gerrard Winstanley, *The Law of Freedom in a Platform, or, True Magistracy Restored* (1652), ed. R. W. Kenny (New York: Schocken Books, 1941), 146.

208. Quoted in Hill, *The World Turned Upside Down*, 313–14.

JOHN MILTON AND JOHN LOCKE

It was in this revolutionary context that the great English poet John Milton and the great English philosopher John Locke turned the traditional commonwealth model of marriage "upside down." Traditional formulations treated the domestic commonwealth as a model, even a source, of the political commonwealth. Milton and Locke reversed the analogy. Milton focused on marital dissolution, arguing that failed English marriages, like the failed English Commonwealth, should be dissolved and the parties left free to reconstitute themselves. Locke focused on marital formation, arguing that marriages, like commonwealths, must be formed, maintained, and dissolved in accordance with the contract negotiated by a man and woman, who by nature are free and equal.

John Milton

Milton's efforts to reform the institution of marriage were part of his broader effort to reform the church and commonwealth of England altogether. Given that marriage and the family were the foundation of the church, state, and society, said Milton, it made little sense to call for the reformation of church and state without first attending to the reformation of the family.[209]

> The constitution and reformation of a commonwealth . . . is, like a building, to begin orderly from the foundation thereof, which is marriage and the family, to set right first whatever is amiss therein. How can there else grow up a race of warrantable men, while the house and home that breeds them, is troubled and disquieted under a bondage not of God's constraining . . . but laid upon us imperiously in the worst and weakest ages of knowledge, by a canonical tyranny of stupid and malicious monks: who having rashly vowed themselves to a single life, which they could not undergo, invented new fetters to throw on matrimony, that the world thereby waxing more dissolute, they also in a general looseness might sin with more favor.[210]

It was not revolutionary logic so much as personal crisis that drove Milton to pay close attention to domestic liberty and marital reform. His new bride had left him within a month of their wedding in 1642 and repeatedly resisted his attempts at reconciliation. Milton, his early biographer reports, "could ill bear the disappointment he met with by her obstinate absenting: And therefore thought upon a divorce, that he might be free to marry another."[211] But the English courts of his day still maintained the strict medieval canon law that forbad divorce and remarriage. Estranged spouses could separate from bed and board, but they could not marry another person during the lifetime of their

---

209. *CPW* 2:438–39.
210. Ibid., 2:438–39; see also 1:588; 2:431.
211. Ibid., 2:138.

spouse without courting charges of bigamy, after 1604 a capital offense. Their only hope for escape was to find an impediment—such as an incestuous blood tie between them—that would support a judgment of annulment. None of these options was available to Milton, and he felt unjustly enslaved in and to his marriage.

Thus, invoking "the right of nature and the liberty wherein I was born,"[212] Milton took his cause to the Parliament, addressing four books to them between 1643 and 1646 in an effort to convince them that he should be allowed to divorce and remarry in such circumstances. In his Address to Parliament, which opened his first tract, *The Doctrine and Discipline of Divorce*, Milton pressed a contractual argument for the right to divorce that followed the exact lines that Parliament had just used to justify their right to revolt against King Charles:

> He who marries, intends as little to conspire his own ruin, as he that swears allegiance [to the Crown]: and as a whole people is in proportion to an ill government, so is one man to an ill marriage. If [Parliament,] against any authority, covenant, or statute, may by the sovereign edict of charity, save not only their lives, but [also] honest liberties from unworthy bondage, as well may [the married man] against any private covenant, which he never entered to his mischief, redeem himself from unsupportable disturbances to honest peace, and just contentment: And much the rather, for that to resist the highest magistrate though tyrannizing, God never gave us express allowance, only he gave us reason, charity, nature, and good example to bear us out; but in this economical [that is, domestic] misfortune, thus to demean ourselves, besides the warrant of those four great directors, which doth as justly belong hither, we have an express law of God, and such a law, as whereof our Savior with a solemn threat forbid the abrogating. For no effect of tyranny can sit more heavily on the commonwealth, than this household unhappiness on the family. And farewell all hope of true Reformation in the state, while such an evil as this lies undiscerned and unregarded in the house.[213]

This was Milton's argument in a nutshell. The domestic commonwealth, like the political commonwealth, is formed by a contract or covenant between two parties, which may be dissolved if it fails in its fundamental purpose. This is the counsel of the "four great directors"—reason, charity, nature, and experience—in the case of political dissolutions. It is counseled by these same four great directors as well as by the Bible in the case of marital dissolutions. If such counsel is ignored, the whole commonwealth will suffer and each member within it.

The purpose of forming a political commonwealth is to protect liberty, establish order, and secure peace, Milton argued. When one or more of these purposes is irreconcilably frustrated, either by the tyranny of rulers or by the crime of subjects, the political commonwealth is broken, and either the rulers or the people may dissolve it—by force of arms, if necessary. Thereafter, the parties

212. Ibid., 2:580.
213. Ibid., 2:229–30.

can reorganize their political polity in a manner more consistent with the ideal purposes of liberty, order, and peace. It makes no difference that the political covenant between the people and their rulers is silent on the subject of dissolution, even when the main purpose of the covenant is frustrated. For both common sense and natural law are implied in the covenant and dictate that parties not be unconscionably held to bargains that were once right but have now gone irretrievably wrong:

> No understanding man can be ignorant that covenants are ever made according to the present state of persons and of things; and have ever the more general laws of nature and of reason included in them, though not expressed. If I make a voluntary covenant as with a man, to do him good, and he prove afterward a monster to me, I should conceive a disobligement. If I covenant, not to hurt an enemy, in favor of him and forbearance, and hope of his amendment, and he, after that, shall do me tenfold injury and mischief, to what he had done when I so covenanted, and still be plotting what may tend to my destruction, I question not but that his after actions release me; nor know I [a] covenant so sacred that withholds me from demanding justice on him. Howbeit, had not their distrust in a good cause, and the fast and loose of our prevaricating Divines overswayed, it had been doubtless better not to have inserted in a covenant unnecessary obligations, and words not works of a supererogatory allegiance to their enemy. . . . Protestants have done before, and many conscientious men now in these times have more than once besought the Parliament to do, that they might go on upon a sure foundation.[214]

Milton pressed the analogous argument in seeking "a sure foundation" from Parliament to reject those "prevaricating divines" against divorce and to grant him a "disobligement" of his marital contract because it had failed in its fundamental purpose.[215] The purpose of forming a marriage, Milton argued, is to foster love, create community, deter lust, and procreate children. Of these purposes, marital love is by far the most critical. "Marriage is a covenant," he wrote, "the very being whereof consists, not in forced cohabitation, and counterfeit performance, but unfeigned love and peace . . . and sweet and gladsome society."[216] "The apt and cheerful conversation of man with woman" is the "chief and noblest purpose of marriage."[217] "Where love cannot be, there can be left of wedlock nothing but the empty husk of an outside matrimony," dry, shriveled, and dispensable.[218]

Milton underscored this priority of marital love by describing marriage as a threefold society: at once religious, civil, and corporal in nature. As a religious society, marriage is a union of soul, spirit, and mind, between husband and

214. This quote is not from Milton's divorce tracts but from his *Tenure of Kings*, in *CPW* 3:231–32.
215. *CPW* 3:232.
216. Ibid., 2:254.
217. Ibid., 2:235; see also 2:246.
218. Ibid., 2:235, 256.

wife—a reflection of the perfect love of Adam and Eve in paradise, an expression of the perfect love between Christ and his church. As a civil society, marriage is a union of the couple's person and property, in which each spouse vows to support and protect the other in all things until death. As a corporal society, marriage is a union of bodies in intercourse, which serves to cool their passion and to conceive children if that is God's will.[219]

God appointed "the religious society" of marriage as "the highest and most excellent," Milton argued, for it dealt with the essential matters of the soul, the spirit, and the mind.[220] He appointed the corporal society of marriage as the "last and meanest," for this dealt with discretionary matters of the body and its passions.[221] "We know that flesh can neither join, nor keep together two bodies of itself; what is it then must make them one flesh, but likeness, but fitness of mind and disposition, which may breed the spirit of concord, and union between them?. . . For as the unity of mind is nearer and greater than the union of bodies, so doubtless is the dissimilitude greater, and more individual."[222] Without *agapē*, or soul love, a marriage is dead. Without eros or carnal love, a marriage can live. Think of the marriage of Mary and Joseph.[223]

Having posited this hierarchy of marital purposes, from the religious to the carnal, Milton thought it "preposterous ignorance and iniquity" that the law of his day should provide remedies "for the rights of the body in marriage but nothing for the wrongs and grievances of the mind."[224] Impotence and frigidity could lead to annulment. But frustration of "the superior and nobler ends both of marriage and the married persons . . . looses no persons" from marriage.[225] "What courts of concupiscence are these, wherein fleshly appetite is heard before right reason, lust before love or devotion."[226] If impotence, frigidity, and other frustrations of the base carnal society of marriage can lead to dissolution, then surely incompatibility, antagonism, and other frustrations of the higher religious society of marriage should lead to dissolution as well. To hold otherwise is to elevate the needs of the body above those of the soul, to privilege marital sex over marital love.[227]

Milton thus advocated divorce if either the religious or the carnal purposes of marriage were frustrated. Frustration of the religious purposes of marriage because of irreconcilable incompatibility provided the more compelling case for divorce, he believed. For the community and concordance of the couple's soul, spirit, and mind formed the first and foremost reason why God instituted marriage. Adam could not abide isolation, even in the perfection of paradise; no

219. Ibid., 2:235–56.
220. Ibid., 2:268–69; see also 2:606–7.
221. Ibid., 2:269.
222. Ibid., 2:605–6.
223. Ibid., 2:268–69, 605–9.
224. Ibid., 2:248.
225. Ibid., 2:599.
226. Ibid.
227. Ibid., 2:239–40, 248–50, 599.

person can abide it in this vale of tears. And a person trapped in a marriage with "a mute and spiritless mate" is even lonelier than the unmarried person.[228] The disaffected spouse becomes cold, dark, and sad, growing "not only in bitterness and wrath, the cancer of devotion, but in a desperate and vicious carelessness," falling victim to "dissimulation, suspicion, false colors, false pretenses."[229] In such circumstances, divorce is the better course. Who cannot see "how much more Christian it would be to break by divorce that which is more broken by undue and forcible keeping, . . . rather than that the whole worship of a Christian man's life should languish and fade away beneath the weight of an immeasurable grief and discouragement?"[230]

Frustration of the carnal purposes of marriage should likewise lead to divorce, Milton argued. In some instances, spouses willfully betray their bodies through adultery, cruelty, desertion, drunkenness, incest, sloth, violent crime, or other pathos that destroys any prospects of intimacy with their spouse. In other instances, one spouse suffers permanent impotence, frigidity, contagion, sterility, or disfigurement that precludes intercourse or conception. Where married parties cannot reconcile themselves to these conditions, they must be allowed to divorce, Milton argued. For the innocent or capable spouse who is not "heroically virtuous" will inevitably "despair in virtue and mutiny against divine providence"—testing the neighbor's bed, visiting the local brothel, or succumbing to various other "temptations, and occasions to secret adulteries, and unchaste roving."[231] Husbands, eager to perpetuate their family name, might be tempted to concubinage for the sake of having children—a temptation to which even the great patriarch Abraham succumbed, to his own misery as well as that of Sarai, Hagar, and Ishmael.[232] And if the couple already has children, the ills and evils of their marital discord will "undoubtedly redound upon the children . . . and the whole family. It degenerates and disorders the best spirits, leaves them to unsettled imaginations, and degraded hopes, careless of themselves, their household and their friends, inactive to all public service, dead to the commonwealth."[233]

"To enjoin the indissoluble keeping of a marriage found unfit against the good of man both soul and body," Milton concluded, "is to make an idol of marriage."[234] To be sure, "divorce is not rashly to be made, but reconcilement to be persuaded and endeavored."[235] But if such reconciliation cannot be achieved, it is better to take the painful step of divorce, to avoid even worse pain. This is for the good of the couple, their children, and the broader commonwealth. "Peace and love, the best subsistence of a Christian family, will return home

228. Ibid., 2:251.
229. Ibid., 2:260, 631.
230. Ibid., 2:259; see further 2:251–52, 259–60, 589–91, 630–31.
231. Ibid., 2:253–54, 632.
232. See Gen. 16:1–16; 21:8–21.
233. *CPW* 2:632.
234. Ibid., 2:276.
235. Ibid., 2:680.

from whence they are now banished; places of prostitution will be less haunted, the neighbor's bed less attempted, the yoke of prudent and manly discipline will be generally submitted to, sober and well ordered living will soon spring up in the commonwealth."[236]

Milton did not spell out the legal ramifications of these views on marriage and divorce. He instead reprinted, with his own long preface, the legal discussion of marriage and divorce in Martin Bucer's tract *De regno Christi*, which we saw earlier in this chapter. Milton endorsed Bucer's conflation of annulment and divorce, his insistence on the equal rights of husband and wife to petition for divorce on proof of cause, and his call for civil courts rather than church courts to handle all marriage and divorce litigation.[237] Milton also assembled a rather untidy heap of liberal divorce laws—from the ancient Judaic to the modern Protestant—to demonstrate the purported anachronism of prevailing English law against divorce.[238] Readers who wanted more, Milton said, should read the systematic legal discussion on the subject just published by the distinguished English jurist John Selden.[239]

Milton directed his main energies to the theological ramifications of these views of marriage and divorce. He spent a good deal of time deconstructing the conventional theological arguments for the indissolubility of marriage, dismissing them all derisively as the kinds of "silly superstition," "devilish doctrine," and "heinous barbarism" that a commonwealth dedicated to true liberty could not countenance.[240] Catholics first called marriage a sacrament because it is permanent, he argued, and then later insisted that marriage is permanent because it is sacrament, a sign of Christ's union with his church. But this sacramental symbolism of marriage only proves that it is the spiritual, rather than the corporal, union of marriage that is critical, Milton insisted. "For me I dispute not now whether matrimony be a mystery or no; if it be of Christ and his church, certainly it is not meant of every ungodly and miswedded marriage, but then only mysterious, when it is a holy, happy, and peaceful match. . . . Since therefore none but a fit and pious matrimony can signify the union of Christ and his church, there cannot be any hindrance of divorce to that wedlock wherein there can be no good mystery."[241]

Continental Protestants argue that marriage is indissoluble because it is a covenant in which God is a party. But this again proves only that the spiritual dimensions of marriage are the more pressing, Milton wrote. If marriage is a true covenant among husband, wife, and God, "so much the more it argues the chief

236. Ibid., 2:230; see further 2:276, 431, 680.

237. See Herman J. Selderhuis, *Marriage and Divorce in the Thought of Martin Bucer*, trans. J. Vriend and L. Bierma (Kirksville, MO: Thomas Jefferson University Press, 1999).

238. *CPW* 2:692–718.

239. Ibid., 2:350, referring to Selden, *De iure naturali et gentium*, bk. 5, ch. 7 in John Selden, *Opera omnia tam edita quam inedita*, 3 vols. (London: Guil. Bowyer, impensis J. Walthoe, 1726), 1:498–604.

240. *CPW* 2:235, 238, 248.

241. Ibid., 2:607; see further 2:236–37, 591, 601–2, 630–31, 732.

society thereof to be in the soul rather than in the body, and the greatest breach thereof to be unfitness of mind rather than defect of body, for the body can have less affinity in a covenant more than human."[242] Moreover, to call marriage a covenant is not to prove its indissolubility; quite the contrary, as is evident from the dissolved political covenants of our time, let alone every private covenant that can be dissolved for cause. "Equity is understood in every covenant, even between enemies, though the terms be not expressed. If equity therefore made it, extremity may dissolve it. But marriage, they used to say, is the covenant of God. Undoubted: and so is any covenant frequently called in Scripture, wherein God is called as witness. . . . This denomination adds nothing to the covenant of marriage, above any other civil and solemn contract: nor is it more indissoluble for this reason than any other against the end of its own ordination. . . . But faith they say must be kept in covenant, though to our damage. I answer, that only holds true when the other side performs."[243]

Anglicans are even less convincing, Milton charged, for they "dare not affirm that marriage is either a sacrament, or a mystery, though all those sacred things give place to man, and yet they invest it with such an awful sanctity, and give it such Adamantine chains, to bind with, as if it were to be worshipped like some Indian deity."[244] But this is an irrational and silly conformity to one particular of the Catholic tradition, which in many other particulars has been rejected.

Both Catholics and Protestants alike argue that marriage is indissoluble because Christ commands that "what God has joined together, let not man put asunder."[245] The point of this passage, however, said Milton, is not the prohibition against man's putting asunder. It is the requirement that God must join the couple together. "When is it that God may be said to join?" Milton asked rhetorically. "When the parties and their friends consent? No surely; for that may concur to lewdest ends, or is it when church rites are finished? Neither; for the efficacy of those depends upon the presupposed fitness of either party. Perhaps after carnal knowledge? least of all: for that may join persons whom neither law nor nature dares join; 'tis left, that only then, when the minds are fitly disposed, and enabled to maintain a cheerful conversation, to the solace and love of each other, according as God intended and promised in the very first foundation of matrimony, I will make a help meet for him."[246] "So when it shall be found by their apparent unfitness, that their continuing to be man and wife is against the glory of God, and their mutual happiness, it may assure them that God never joined them."[247]

Having deconstructed traditional Christian arguments about divorce, Milton set out to reconstruct a biblical argument for the right to divorce. The key passage, he insisted, is Deuteronomy 24:1–4. There God proclaimed through

242. Ibid., 2:275–76.
243. Ibid., 2:624; see also 2:245, 275–76.
244. Ibid., 2:277.
245. Matt. 19:6 KJV.
246. *CPW* 2:328.
247. Ibid., 2:276–77; see further 2:328, 650–51.

Moses: "When a man hath taken a wife, and married her, and it come to pass that she find no favour in his eyes, because he hath found some uncleanness in her: then let him write her a bill of divorcement, and give it in her hand, and send her out of his house"—leaving both parties free to remarry thereafter.[248] "Uncleanness" in this passage, said Milton, means "nakedness or unfitness" of body or of mind.[249] It implicates the whole range of corporal and religious grounds for divorce that he had already listed. Of these, religious grounds were the more important, for "what greater nakedness or unfitness of mind than that which hinders ever the solace and peaceful society of the marital couple[?]."[250] The ancient Hebrews had recognized this and built on this passage a comprehensive doctrine of divorce. Their interpretation was followed by the Greeks, the Romans, the early Christian emperors, and many others. This proves, said Milton, that Deuteronomy 24:1–4 is no special rule for the Jews. It is a universal moral law, "a grave and prudent law, full of moral equity, full of due consideration towards nature, that cannot be resisted; a law consenting with the laws of wisest men and civilest nations."[251]

Christ did not abrogate this moral law of divorce in his proclamation in Matthew 19:9: "Whosoever shall put away his wife, except it be for fornication, and shall marry another, committeth adultery; and whoso marrieth her which is put away doth commit adultery." This passage must be understood in context, Milton argued. Christ had already said in Matthew 5:18, "Till heaven and earth pass, one jot or one tittle shall in no wise pass from the law, till all be fulfilled." Moreover, his divorce proclamation was prompted, as Matthew 19:3 reports, by the Pharisees, tempting him and saying to him, "Is it lawful for a man to put away his wife for every cause?" Christ was giving a direct response to the scheming Pharisees. You, Pharisees, who might "in the hardness of your hearts" abuse the Mosaic law of divorce through inventive interpretation, you may divorce only on grounds of fornication.[252] But others, less hard of heart and less prone to casuistry, may do so on the fuller grounds allowed by Moses. Christ's "rigid sentence against divorce" was designed "not to cut off all remedy from a good man who finds himself consuming away in a disconsolate and unenjoyed matrimony, but to lay a bridle upon the bold abuses of those overweening rabbis."[253] Christ's words were not a timeless declaration for the church, but a terse denunciation of the Pharisees, who were testing him.[254]

If Christ's words are so understood, Milton continued, the apostle Paul's words can also be understood. In 1 Corinthians 7:15, Paul wrote: "If the

---

248. Ibid., 2:242, quoting Deut. 24:1–4 KJV. I am using the KJV in this and the next two paragraphs, since Milton's analysis turns on the exact wording of several of these passages.

249. *CPW* 2:244.

250. Ibid.

251. Ibid., 2:306; see further 2:239–44.

252. Ibid., 2:664; Scripture quotes in this paragraph and the next are from the KJV.

253. *CPW* 2:283; see further 2:661.

254. Ibid., 2:283, 621, 636, 661–62.

unbelieving [spouse] depart, let him depart. A brother or a sister is not under bondage in such cases: but God hath called us to peace." Paul was not contradicting Christ by adding desertion or disbelief as another ground for marital dissolution, Milton argued. He was simply confirming the traditional Hebrew practice that when the union of spirit between husband and wife is broken by a form of spiritual "uncleanness," the marriage is broken and the parties are freed from its bonds.[255] Indeed, Paul went beyond Moses by granting to both husband and wife alike this freedom to depart from a spiritually broken marriage—a suitable application of Paul's more general teaching that in Christ "there is neither male nor female."[256]

This was the heart of Milton's argument for domestic liberty. Over the next fifteen years, he embroidered these arguments a bit more. He called for the equal rights of men and women to enter marriages as to exit them through divorce. He called on husband and wives to love, support, and care for each other, and insisted that each had a right to claim these expanded conjugal debts from the other. He called for the rights of parents to nurture, discipline, and educate their children in their own faith but with due regard for each child's nature and gifts. He mentioned the need for greater privacy of the home, including freedom from illegal searches of the home and seizure of private papers. And he speculated, at some length and leisure, whether polygyny and concubinage were actually outlawed by God, though he said clearly that "homosexuality, fornication, violation, adultery, incest, rape, prostitution, and offences of a similar kind run counter" to God's law and cannot be countenanced at all.[257]

Milton's reconstruction of the commonwealth model of marriage was largely ignored in his day, and when it was recognized it was largely rejected. Even some of the radical writers of the Commonwealth era, who accepted the propriety of divorce and remarriage in cases of adultery and desertion, thought Milton's argument for divorce on the ground of irreconcilable differences proved too much. His books were dismissed for holding the "most dangerous and damnable tenets." If Milton had his way, his critics charged, "the bonds of marriage [will be] let loose to inordinate lust," and men will inevitably "quit of their wives for slight occasions" to the detriment of the couple, the children, the church, and the commonwealth alike. "What will all the Christian Churches through the world . . . think of our woeful degeneration in these deplored times, that so uncouth a design should be set on foot among us."[258]

---

255. Ibid., 2:681–83. "Uncleanness" or "indeceny" is the term in the Mosaic law of divorce, in Deut. 24:1–4.

256. *CPW* 2:338–39; see Gal. 3:28.

257. *CPW* 6:757; see further ibid., 2:393–413; 6:351–81, 755–57, 781–88.

258. Quotes from sources excerpted in William R. Parker, *Milton's Contemporary Reputation* (Columbus: Ohio State University Press, 1940), 74–79. See also ibid., 170–217, a facsimile reprint of an anonymous pamphlet, *An Answer to a Book [by John Milton], Intituled, The Doctrine and Discipline of Divorce* (London: William Lee, 1644), to which Milton responded in *Colasterion* (1645), in *CPW*, 2:719–58.

The 1644 Parliament not only rejected Milton's call for divorce reform, but also moved to censor and burn his *Doctrine and Discipline of Divorce*, among others. Such books, critics in Parliament and in pulpits pronounced, have converted religious and domestic liberties into "despicable licenses." They call for "a liberty of sensual lusts, and fleshly looseness" and "divorce at pleasure." "If any plead conscience for the lawfulness of polygamy (or for divorce for other cause than Christ and His apostles mention; of which a wicked book is abroad and uncensored, though deserving to be burnt, whose author hath been so impudent as to set his name to it, and dedicate it to ourselves) or for liberty to marry incestuously, will you grant toleration for this?"[259]

Some of the general ignorance of his work was perhaps a function of Milton's unfortunate choice of titles. By putting *Tetrachordon* and *Colasterion* on his book spines, Milton might have appealed to a stray Grecophile or two, but he could hardly have expected his books to jump into the hands of every passerby.[260] Some of the rejection by Parliament and the church was doubtless a function of Milton's rather pugnacious and prolix style: five hundred-plus pages of bare-fisted rhetoric in three years on a tender issue like divorce had to tax even the sympathetic reader. Some of this was doubtless also a function of Milton's iconoclasm. A reader could consider it clever to see one or two counterintuitive constructions of the commonwealth model of marriage. But Milton's gleeful overturning of a whole series of favorite Bible verses and traditional doctrines to support his argument about the nature of marriage and divorce had to have raised suspicions. Particularly since Milton left many of the theological niceties and legal nuances of his argument unexplored, it was easy to dismiss him. Later English reformers, both theological and legal, would look back to Milton as a brilliant prophet who anticipated many of the divorce reforms of 1857 to 1987.[261] But, in his own day, he was a prophet with little honor and little legal influence.

John Locke

John Locke's reconstruction of the commonwealth model of marriage in his *Two Treatises of Government* (1690) had a better immediate reception. In part, this was because Milton and other radical writers of the mid-seventeenth century had prepared the way for him, slowly liberalizing prevailing sentiment about marriage. In part, this was because Locke wrote after the Commonwealth

259. Quotes from 1643 and 1644 in William R. Haller, *Liberty and the Reformation in the Puritan Revolution* (New York: Columbia University Press, 1955), 78–134, esp. 125–26. For later reactions to Milton's views, see also Christopher Hill, *Milton and the English Revolution* (New York: Viking Press, 1978), 130–39, 222–30.

260. See W. Parker, *Milton's Contemporary Reputation*, 17–24.

261. See references to Milton in Lawrence Stone, *Road to Divorce: England, 1530–1987* (Oxford: Oxford University Press, 1990), 348–51, 407; and discussion on the Divorce Reform Acts in ibid., 368–422.

Parliament had experimented quite radically with English marriage law. In part, this was because Locke's reconstruction of marriage was only a by-product of his grand political argument in support of the Glorious Revolution, and what he wrote on marriage in his political writings was amply qualified by his discussion of marriage in his commentaries on the Bible.

In his *Two Treatises*, Locke set out to refute Robert Filmer's monarchical theory of government, which was among the strongest traditional formulations of the commonwealth model. Filmer had argued, as we saw, that God had created the patriarchal domestic commonwealth, headed by the paterfamilias, as the source of the hierarchical political commonwealth, headed by the King. God had created Adam and Eve as founders not only of the first marriage and family but also of the first state and society. Adam was the first husband but also the first ruler. Eve was the first wife but also the first subject. Together with their children, they composed at once a domestic and a political commonwealth. All persons thereafter were, by birth, subject to the highest male head, descended from Adam.

Locke responded to Filmer first by flatly denying any natural or necessary connection between the political and domestic commonwealths, between the authority of the paterfamilias and of the magistrate. "The power of a magistrate over a subject," he wrote, "may be distinguished from that of a father over his children, a master over his servant, a husband his wife, and a lord over his slave."[262] The "little commonwealth" of the family is "very far from" the great commonwealth in England "in its constitution, power and end." "The master of the family has a very distinct and differently limited power, both as to time and extent, over those several persons that are in it; . . . he has no legislative power of life and death over any of them, and none too but what a mistress of a family may have as well as he."[263]

Locke responded next by denying Filmer's patriarchal interpretation of the creation story. God did not create Adam and Eve as ruler and subject but as husband and wife, said Locke. Adam and Eve were created equal before God. Each had natural rights to use the bounties of paradise. Each had natural duties to each other and to God. After the fall into sin, God expelled Adam and Eve from the garden. He increased man's labor in his use of creation. He increased woman's labor in the bearing of children. He said to Eve in Genesis 3:16, "Thy desire shall be to thy husband, and he shall rule over thee" (KJV). According to Locke, these words, which Filmer had called "the original grant of government, were not spoken to Adam, neither indeed was there any grant in them made to Adam; they were a punishment laid upon Eve."[264] These words do not abrogate the natural equality, rights, and duties with which God created Adam and Eve,

262. John Locke, *Two Treatises of Government* (1690), ed. Peter Laslett (Cambridge: Cambridge University Press, 1960), II.2. For analysis, see sources and discussion in A. John Simmons, *The Lockean Theory of Rights* (Princeton, N J: Princeton University Press, 1992), 167–221.

263. Locke, *Two Treatises*, 11.86.

264. Ibid., 1.47.

and all persons after them. They do not render all wives eternally subject to their husbands.[265] And they certainly do not, as Filmer had insisted, give "a father or a prince an absolute, arbitrary, unlimited and unlimitable power, over the lives, liberties, and estates of his children and subjects."[266]

Men and women are born free and equal in the state of nature. But "God having made man such a creature, that, in his own judgment, it was not good for him to be alone, put him under strong obligation of necessity, convenience, and inclination to drive him into society," Locke argued. A person entered into society by entering into voluntary contracts with other persons of similar inclination. To that extent, the commonwealths of marriage, church, and state might be said to be related, said Locke. Each of these commonwealths was formed by the voluntary agreement of free and equal persons, moving from the state of nature to a social state.

"The first society" to be formed "was between man and wife, which gave beginning to that of parents and children."[267] This "conjugal society," like every other society, "is made by a voluntary compact between man and woman: and though it consists chiefly in such a communion and right in one another's bodies, as is necessary to its chief end, procreation; yet it draws with it mutual support and assistance and communion of interest too, as necessary not only to unite their care, and affection, but also necessary to their common offspring, who have a right to be nourished and maintained by them, till they are able to provide for themselves."[268] Marriage has no necessary form or function beyond this "chief end" of procreation, Locke argued against traditional understandings. Couples were free to contract about the rest of the relationship as they deemed fit. "Conjugal society might be varied and regulated by that contract, which unites man and wife in that society, as far as may consist with procreation and the bringing up of children till they could [provide] for themselves; nothing being necessary to any society, that is not necessary to the ends for which it is made."[269]

Locke thus combined a contractual and naturalist perspective on marriage—echoing some of the earlier arguments to the same effect by Thomas Aquinas that

265. In ibid., Locke did allow the thought that if Eve is understood "as the representative of all other women," God's words "will at most concern the female sex only, and import no more but that subjection they should ordinarily be in to their husbands." But, he immediately added, that such subjection is not necessary "if the circumstances either of her condition or contract with her husband should exempt her from it."

266. Ibid., 1.9. See also 1.98: "Paternal power, being a natural right rising only from the relation of father and son, is as impossible to be inherited as the relation itself, and a man may pretend as well to inherit the conjugal power the husband, whose heir he is, had over his wife, as he can to inherit the paternal power of a father over his children. For the power of the husband being founded on contract, and the power of the father founded on begetting, he may as well inherit the power obtained by the conjugal contract, which was only personal, as he may the power obtained by begetting, which could reach no farther then the person of him, that does not beget."

267. Ibid., 11.77.

268. Ibid., 11.78.

269. Ibid., 11.83.

we saw, but now casting them in "rights" terms.[270] It was a natural right for a man and a woman to enter into a marital contract. It was a natural duty for them to render procreation an essential condition of their marital contract. It was the natural right to survival of their child that imposed on parents a further natural duty to remain in their marriage once contracted till their children were self-sufficient.

> For the end of conjunction between male and female, being not barely procreation, but the continuation of the species, this conjunction betwixt male and female ought to last, even after procreation, so long as is necessary to the nourishment and support of the young ones, who are to be sustained by those that got them, till they are able to shift and provide for themselves. . . . Whereby the father, who is bound to take care for those he hath begot, is under an obligation to continue in conjugal society with the same woman longer than other creatures, whose young being able to subsist of themselves, before the time of procreation returns again, the conjugal bond dissolves of it self, and they are at liberty.[271]

The logical end of Locke's argument was that the childless couple, or the couple whose children were of age, should be free to divorce, unless they had found some other "communion of interest" to sustain their contract. Locke dithered on the question of divorce. It was not essential to his political argument to speak definitively on the subject, and he knew the dangers of loose literary speculation on it. In his private diary, he wrote quite brashly: "He that already is married may marry another woman with his left hand. . . . The ties, duration, and conditions of the left-hand marriage shall be no other than what is expressed in the contract of marriage between the parties."[272] In his *Two Treatises* and other publications, he only flirted with the doctrine of divorce and remarriage, suggesting delicately that the matter be left to private contractual calculation:

> The husband and wife, though they have but one common concern, yet having different understandings will unavoidably sometimes have different wills too; it therefore being necessary, that the last determination, i.e., the rule, should be placed somewhere, it naturally falls to the man's share, as the abler and the stronger. But the reaching out to the things of their common interest and property, leaves the wife in the full and free possession of what by contract is hers by peculiar right, and gives the husband no more power over her life, than she has over his. The power of the husband being so far from that of an absolute monarch, that the wife has, in many cases, a liberty to separate from him; where natural right, or their contract allows it, whether that contract be made by themselves in the state of nature, or by the customs or laws of the country they live in; and the children upon such separation fall to the father's or the mother's lot, as such contract does determine.[273]

270. See above chap. 4, pp. 83–87.
271. Locke, *Two Treatises*, 11.79–80.
272. Diary Entry, 1678, 1679, quoted in editor's note to ibid., 11.81, in Laslett, *Two Treatises*, pbk. ed., 364.
273. Locke, *Two Treatises*, 11.82.

The other logical end of this argument was that the state had little role to play within marriage and the family. For the state likewise was a voluntary assembly, formed by a governmental contract among like-minded parties. The state was formed after marriage and the family, and thus it was ultimately subordinate to it in priority and right. The marriage contract sets the terms of the agreement between husband and wife, parent and child. The state could intervene only to enforce these contractual rights and duties, and only to vindicate the natural rights and duties of each party within the household. "For all the ends of marriage being to be obtained under politick government, as well as in the state of nature, the civil magistrate doth not abridge this right or power of either naturally necessary to those ends, viz., procreation and mutual support and assistance whilst they are together; but only decides any controversy that may arise between man and wife about them."[274]

Locke did not press this contractarian reconstruction of the commonwealth model to the revolutionary ends that some Enlightenment philosophers would reach in the following centuries. Locke was a man of pious Puritan stock who remained firmly devoted to biblical teachings throughout his life. What he gave with his political hand, he took back with his theological hand. His famous *Letters on Toleration* and the *Reasonableness of Christianity,* together with his commentaries on several books of the Bible, were tracts of deep Christian conviction. In each of them, Locke called church and state to end their unhealthy alliance, to soften their belligerent dogmatism, to return to the simple moral truths of the New Testament. In each of these tracts, he also insisted on coating his doctrine of natural rights and duties with a number of classic Christian conceptions about the natural propriety of heterosexuality, monogamy, procreation, nurture and education of children, and the like. "He that shall collect all the moral rules of the philosophers and compare them with those contained in the New Testament," he wrote, "will find them to come short of the morality delivered by our Savior, and taught by his apostles. . . . Such a law of morality Jesus Christ hath given us in the New Testament [is] a full and sufficient rule for our direction, and conformable to that of reason."[275]

On the strength of these convictions, Locke endorsed a whole series of biblical teachings on marriage and sex that stood in considerable tension with his more radical statements on marriage in the *Two Treatises.* For example, Locke endorsed Christ's reading of the commandment against adultery as an injunction not only against "actual uncleanness, but all irregular desires [and] causeless divorces."[276] He endorsed Paul's injunctions against fornication, saying that such conduct "might be so unsuitable to the state of a Christian man, that a Christian society might have reason to animadvert upon a fornicator . . . as

274. Ibid., 11.83.

275. John Locke, *The Reasonableness of Christianity,* in *The Works of John Locke,* 12th ed. (London: C. & J. Rivington et al., 1824), 6:140–43. See also ibid., 11–15, and the fuller account in his *Essay on the Law of Nature,* trans. and ed. W. von Leyden (Oxford: Oxford University Press, 1954).

276. Locke, *Reasonableness of Christianity,* 115.

not comporting with the dignity and principles of that religion, which was the foundation of their society."[277] He glossed Paul's teachings in 1 Corinthians 7 on the relative merits of marriage and celibacy with a matter-of-fact tone that reflected comfortable acceptance of traditional Christian doctrine. Glossing Paul's statements on the rights and duties of husbands and wives, Locke wrote: "The woman (who in all other rights is inferior) has here the same power given her over the man's body, that the man has over hers. The reason whereof is plain; because if she had not her man, when she had need of him, as well as the man his woman, when he had need of her, marriage would be no remedy against fornication."[278] He paraphrased, without comment, Paul's requirement that husband and wife remain together till parted by death. He glossed Paul's later requirements that wives must submit to their husbands, and husbands to love their wives thus: "It is from the head that the body receives its vigorous constitution of health and life; this St. Paul pronounces here of Christ, as head of the church, that by that parallel which he makes use of, to represent the relation of husband and wife, he may both show the wife the reasonableness of her subjection to her husband, and the duty incumbent on the husband to cherish and preserve his wife."[279]

Locke stretched the commonwealth model of marriage—and indeed all prior Christian models of marriage—to the breaking point. On the one hand, he was a devout Christian, fully conversant with biblical teachings on marriage and sexuality, but not fully comfortable with their theological exposition or institutional expression in his day. On the other hand, he was a devoted liberal philosopher, fully supportive of the revolutionary reconstruction of the English commonwealth, but not fully satisfied with its philosophical foundation or its legal reification during the Glorious Revolution. From both perspectives, he pressed for a variety of reforms of marriage, family, and sexuality.

Locke the theologian and Locke the political philosopher agreed on many points of marital reform: greater freedom of marital contract, greater equality of husband and wife, greater emphasis on the procreation and education of children, greater restraint on the separation of couples with children, and greater protection of wives, children, and servants from abuse. On these twin theological and philosophical foundations, Locke helped to prepare the way for many of the legal reforms in English law, as well as American law, in the next centuries. His views on marriage, like Milton's, had no immediate legal impact, but they proved prescient and prophetic.

Locke the theologian and Locke the political philosopher, however, parted ways on many points as well. Locke the theologian emphasized the biblical norm of marriage as a hierarchical order headed by the husband, with subjection by

277. John Locke, *A Paraphrase and Notes on St. Paul's First Epistle to the Corinthians*, in *Works of Locke*, 7:118–19 (notes on 1 Cor. 6:12–13).

278. Ibid., 7:122–23 (notes on 1 Cor. 7:1–4).

279. Locke, *A Paraphrase and Notes on St. Paul's Epistle to the Ephesians*, in *Works of Locke*, 7:488 (notes on Eph. 5:23).

the wife. Locke the philosopher emphasized the voluntary organization of marriage as a negotiated contract between two equal parties. Locke the theologian vested both church and state with a prominent role in the guidance and government of marital and sexual conduct. Locke the philosopher countenanced no role for the church and a minimalist role for the state in policing the conduct of the household. Locke the theologian emphasized the duties of marital love, spiritual companionship, and sexual fidelity for life. Locke the philosopher emphasized the rights of marital equality, procreative capacity, and parental fidelity till children come of age.

Many skeptical readers of his day dismissed Locke as an intellectual schizophrenic, a man incapable of harmonizing his theological convictions and political speculations on marriage, and thus prone to intemperate remarks and indecisive principles on both scores. More sympathetic readers hailed Locke as a methodological genius, a man who liberated the theology and politics of marriage from each other.[280] By distinguishing a natural versus biblical discourse on marriage, and a political versus theological discourse, Locke broke the presumed organic connections between the domestic commonwealth and the political commonwealth, household and state, father and king, child and subject. The household could have its own order and organization based on the marital contract; the state could have its own offices and functions based on the social contract. The church could have its norms for marriage based on biblical revelation; the state could have its norms for marriage based on natural rights. The church could ground its norms of authority and obedience in the Fifth Commandment; the state could ground its norms for authority and obedience in the social contract. A pious Christian could accept the literal truths of the Bible for private life yet advocate the liberal reforms of the social contract for public law.

To accept Locke's method was to accept the proposition that it was no longer necessary to integrate the spiritual, natural, social, and contractual perspectives on marriage in an organic model—whether the Anglican commonwealth model or any of the other sacramental, social, or covenantal models. With Locke's method, natural and contractual perspectives on marriage could be fully expounded without reference to their religious and social implications. Religious and social perspectives on marriage could be fully defended without reference to their natural or contractual dimensions. Moreover, it was no longer necessary for state, church, or civil society to play an integrated role in the governance of marriage. Marriage was the first society a person entered from the state of nature, and the terms of the marital contract together with the person's natural rights and duties were superior to all other governing norms. If the married person chose to enter into a political, or an ecclesiastical, or a civil society, he or she could subscribe to the marital norms of that particular society. But these sets

---

280. See generally John W. Gough, *The Social Contract: A Critical Study of Its Development* (Oxford: Clarendon Press, 1936), 119–53.

of norms were independent of each other and subordinate to the natural and contractual norms of the marital contract.

Hugo Grotius, the seventeenth-century Dutch political philosopher on whom Locke partly relied for his philosophical constructions, once ventured the "impious hypothesis" that the law of nature could be valid even if "we should concede that which cannot be conceded without the utmost wickedness, that there is no God, or that the affairs of men are of no concern to him."[281] This idea was hardly original with Grotius and hardly acceptable to the establishment of his day. But Grotius's articulation of it in the midst of the bitter religious warfare and persecution of early seventeenth-century Europe proved propitious. It helped to set afoot the development of a law of nations and a law of the sea that did not depend upon a common theological foundation or necessary role for the church.

A similar claim might be made about Locke's "impious hypothesis" that a law of marriage could be valid even if God were not the founder of the marriage contract, or the church not an agent in its governance. This idea, too, was hardly original with Locke and hardly acceptable to the establishment of his day. But Locke's articulation of an independent naturalist and contractarian theory of marriage amid the revolutionary upheaval of English society also proved propitious. It helped to set afoot the development of an Anglo-American theory and law of marriage and the family that eventually no longer depended upon established theological doctrines or upon a necessary legal role for the church.[282]

Even cast in its most liberal formulation, the via media theology of the Anglican tradition could not ultimately contain Locke's dualistic understanding of marriage. The theological establishment thus steadfastly rejected such naturalist and contractual ideas of marriage, standing alone, for two more centuries. Even stretching traditional doctrines to their breaking point, the English law of marriage could not accommodate the legal reforms contemplated by Locke's more radical asides in his *Two Treatises*. The legal establishment thus resisted such reforms until well into the nineteenth century. It would take the Enlightenment articulation of a purely contractual model of marriage to effectuate these reforms fully. To that development we turn in the next chapter.

---

281. Hugo Grotius, *De jure belli ac pacis* (Paris: Buon, 1625), prolegommena, 11.
282. See Brian Tierney, *The Idea of Natural Rights: Studies on Natural Rights, Natural Law, and Church Law, 1150–1625* (Atlanta: Scholars Press, 1997), 317–24.

Chapter 8

Marriage as Contract in the Enlightenment Tradition

The laws born of the Catholic and Protestant models of marriage are not the artifacts of an ancient culture to be studied by antiquarians and archivalists alone. Until the twentieth century, this was our law in much of the West, notably in England and America, which will be the main focus of this final chapter. In the early twentieth century, leading legal authorities in England and America regularly spoke of marriage as a "state of existence ordained by the Creator," "a consummation of the Divine command to multiply and replenish the earth," "the highest state of existence," "the only stable substructure of social, civil, and religious institutions."[1] They described marriage as "a public institution of universal concern," in which "each individual marriage or its dissolution affects the rights not only of husband and wife, but of all other persons."[2] The United States Supreme Court still spoke regularly of marriage as "more than a mere contract," "a sacred obligation," "a holy estate," "the

1. W. C. Rodgers, *A Treatise on the Law of Domestic Relations* (Chicago: T. H. Flood, 1899); Joel Bishop, *New Commentaries on Marriage, Divorce, and Separation*, 2 vols. (Chicago: T. H. Flood, 1891), 1:3–7.
2. Ibid., 2:217.

foundation of the family and society, without which there would be neither civilization nor progress."[3]

Also in the early twentieth century, English and American legislatures treated marriage in much the same way that the Catholic leaders of Trent and the Protestant leaders of Wittenberg, Geneva, and Westminster had done in the sixteenth century. With ample variations across jurisdictions, English and American law generally defined marriage as a presumptively permanent monogamous union between a fit man and a fit woman of the age of consent, designed for their mutual love and support, for their mutual protection from sexual temptation, and for their mutual procreation and nurture of children. A typical state law in America required that engagements be formal and that marriages be contracted with parental consent, witnesses, and a suitable waiting period. It required marriage licenses and registration and solemnization before civil and/or religious authorities. It prohibited marriages between couples related by various blood or family ties identified in the Mosaic law. It discouraged, and in some states prohibited, marriage where one party was impotent or had a contagious disease that precluded procreation or endangered the other spouse. Couples who sought to divorce had to publicize their intentions, to petition a court, to show adequate cause or fault, and to make provision for the dependent spouse and children. Criminal laws outlawed fornication, adultery, sodomy, polygamy, incest, contraception, abortion, and other perceived sexual offenses. Tort laws held third parties liable for seduction, enticement, loss of consortium, or alienation of the affections of one's spouse. The church and broader community were given roles to play in the formation, maintenance, and dissolution of marriage and in the physical and moral nurture of children.[4]

By contrast, in the early twenty-first century, this traditional lore and law of the family has been largely spurned. Today a private contractual view of marriage has come to dominate Anglo-American law, lore, and life—largely unbuffered by complementary spiritual, social, or natural perspectives and largely unreceptive to much of a role for the church, state, or broader community. Marriage is viewed increasingly at law and at large today as a private bilateral contract to be formed, maintained, and dissolved as the couple sees fit. Requirements of parental consent and witnesses to the formation of engagement and marital contracts have largely disappeared. Mandatory waiting periods between engagement and marriage have also largely disappeared. Unilateral no-fault divorce statutes have reduced the divorce proceeding to an expensive formality. Payments of alimony and other forms of postmarital support to dependent spouses and children are giving way to lump-sum property exchanges, providing a clean break for parties to remarry.

3. U.S. Supreme Court Cases, *Maynard v. Hill*, 125 U.S. 190, 210–11 (1888); *Reynolds v. United States*, 98 U.S. 145, 165 (1879); *Murphy v. Ramsey*, 11 U.S. 15, 45 (1885).

4. For a detailed American overview, see Chester G. Vernier, *American Family Laws: A Comparative Study of the Family Law of the Forty-Eight States*, 5 vols. (Stanford, CA: Stanford University Press, 1931–38). For an English overview, see R. H. Graveson and F. R. Crane, eds., *A Century of Family Law, 1857–1957* (London: Sweet & Maxwell, 1957).

Court-supervised property settlements between divorcing spouses are giving way to privately negotiated or mediated settlements, often confirmed with little scrutiny by courts. The functional distinctions between the rights of the married and the unmarried couple, the straight and the gay partnership, the legitimate and the illegitimate child have all been considerably narrowed by an array of new statutes and constitutional cases. The roles of the church, state, and broader community in marriage formation, maintenance, and dissolution have been gradually truncated in deference to the constitutional principles of sexual autonomy, domestic privacy, and separation of church and state. Traditional criminal prohibitions against most sexual offenses have become dead letters in most states. Traditional prohibitions against contraception and abortion have been held to violate the constitutional right of privacy. Traditional tort suits for alienation of affections or interference with one's spouse or children have become largely otiose.[5]

These exponential changes in our marriage laws have been, in part, valiant attempts to bring greater equality and liberty within marriage and society, and to stamp out some of the patriarchy, paternalism, and plain prudishness of the past. These legal changes are also simple reflections of the exponential changes that have occurred in the culture and condition of American families—the stunning advances in reproductive and medical technology, the exposure to vastly different perceptions of sexuality and kinship born of globalization, the explosion of international and domestic norms of human rights, the implosion of the Ozzie and Harriet family born of new economic and professional demands on wives, husbands, and children. A fantastic range of literature—theological, ethical, political, economic, sociological, anthropological, and psychological—has emerged in the past five decades to vigorously describe, defend, or decry these legal changes.[6]

My explanation for these massive legal changes in Anglo-American marriage law is simple and, by the methodological design of this book, necessarily incomplete. What we have also been witnessing in the course of the past century is the gradual rise to legal prominence of an Enlightenment contractarian model of marriage. This model has slowly eclipsed Protestant and Catholic models of marriage, as well as the earlier classical and biblical ideas and institutions of marriage, on which the Western legal tradition of marriage was founded.

Enlightenment thinkers began where John Locke's "impious hypothesis" had ended. In his *Two Treatises on Government* (1690), as we saw in the last chapter, Locke had ventured the notion that marriage could be seen as a simple, bilateral

5. Numerous modern family-law texts are available. For American developments, see, e.g., Homer H. Clark Jr., *The Law of Domestic Relations*, 2nd ed. (St. Paul: West Publishing Co., 1988; pbk., 1998); Carl F. Schneider and Margaret F. Brinig, *Invitation to Family Law*, 3rd ed. (St. Paul: West Publishing Co., 2006). For English family law, see M. Masson, R. Bailey-Harris, and R. J. Probert, *Principles of Family Law*, 8th ed. (London: Sweet & Maxwell, 2008).

6. See the overview of recent literature in Don S. Browning, *Marriage and Modernization: How Globalization Threatens Marriage and What to Do about It* (Grand Rapids: Wm. B. Eerdmans Publishing Co., 2003); and in Don S. Browning and John Witte Jr., *From Private Contract to Public Covenant: What Can Christianity Offer to Modern Marriage Law?* (Cambridge: Cambridge University Press, forthcoming), chaps. 1–2.

contract between a man and a woman, who stood equal before each other in the state of nature. He had suggested that a natural and contractual perspective on marriage could be defended without necessary reference to spiritual perspectives on marriage. He had hypothesized that a law of marriage based on contract could be valid even if God were not viewed as the founder of the marriage contract, nor his church engaged as an agent in its governance. Locke had not pressed these ideas to their logical or legal conclusions, constrained as he was by his concerns for the natural rights of women and children. Indeed, in his theological writing, he had retreated to a literal biblical understanding of marriage, without the qualifications he had defended in his *Two Treatises*.[7] And for more than a century after him, Enlightenment philosophers and common-law jurists with them used arguments from natural law, common sense, and plain utility to maintain the traditional idea of marriage as a heterosexual and monogamous union, presumptively for life, and to reject adultery, fornication, prostitution, easy divorce, and other traditional sex crimes as deleterious to the needs of the family, particularly young dependent children.

In the later nineteenth and twentieth centuries, however, liberal thinkers pressed Locke's "impious hypothesis" to more radical logical and legal ends, a few of them today pressing for the abolition of marriage altogether. The essence of marriage, they argued, was not its sacramental symbolism, nor its covenantal associations, nor its social service to the community and commonwealth, as was traditionally taught. The essence of marriage was the voluntary private bargain struck between the two parties. The terms of their marital bargain were not preset by God or nature, church or state, tradition or community. These terms were set by the parties themselves, in accordance with general rules of contract formation and general norms of civil society. Such rules and norms demanded respect for the life, liberty, and property interests of other parties, and compliance with general standards of health, safety, and welfare in the community. But the form and function of their marriage relationship was to be left to the bargain of the parties themselves.[8]

EARLY ENLIGHTENMENT TEACHINGS ON SEX, MARRIAGE, AND FAMILY

The notion that marriage is a contract is certainly nothing new. From biblical and classical times forward, this idea has been part of the Western tradition. Roman law, canon law, civil law, and common law alike all confirmed that marriage is a contract that depends in its essence on the mutual consent of a man and a woman

7. See sources and discussion in chap. 7 above, pp. 278–85.

8. For later uses of Locke, see sources and discussion in Carole Pateman, *The Sexual Contract* (Stanford, CA: Stanford University Press, 1988); for other modern liberal thinkers and their influence, see sources and discussion in Brent Waters, *The Family in Christian Social and Political Thought* (Oxford: Oxford University Press, 2007), 60–82.

who have the fitness and capacity to marry each other. But the Western tradition has long regarded marriage not only as a private contract, but also as a natural, social, and spiritual association that served essential private and public goods in the community. This rendered traditional Western marriage something of an "adhesion contract." The structure and purposes of marriage were already predetermined by nature, society, and religion, and couples were given the freedom to accept or reject these terms but not to renegotiate any of them.

Many early Enlightenment philosophers, from 1650–1850, rejected the traditional religious dimension of marriage—the notion that marriage was a sacrament or covenant, subject to the governance or guidance of the church. This provided parties with more flexibility on where to make and how to maintain their marriage contracts. But the early Enlightenment philosophers continued to hold to the traditional view that marriage was at once a contractual, natural, and social institution. The demands of nature and society still set firm limits on what was permissible in their sex, marriage, and family lives. We could duplicate examples of these early Enlightenment arguments, but let us just focus on a couple of major Scottish and English Enlightenment philosophers who influenced the Anglo-American common law of marriage.

Henry Home and the Scottish Enlightenment

The writings of Henry Home, known as Lord Kames of Scotland (1696–1782), were particularly perceptive. A leading Scottish Enlightenment philosopher and a leading justice of the Scottish highest court, Home was best known for his brilliant defense of natural law, on empirical and rational grounds rather than on biblical or theological grounds. Home sought to prove the realities of virtue, duty, justice, liberty, freedom, and other natural moral principles, and the necessity for rational humans to create various offices, laws, and institutions to support and protect them. While his rationalist methodology rankled the orthodox Christian theologians of his day, Home wanted to win over even skeptics and atheists to his legal and moral arguments and to give enduring "authority to the promises and covenants" that helped create society and its institutions.[9]

Among many other institutions and "covenants," Home defended monogamous marriage as a "necessity of nature," and he denounced polygamy as "a vice against human nature." Home recognized that polygamy was commonplace among some animals.[10] He also recognized that polygamy had been practiced in

9. See esp. Henry Home, *Essays on the Principles of Morality and Natural Religion* (1779), ed. Mary Catherine Moran, 3rd ed. (Indianapolis: Liberty Fund, 2005), esp. pt.1, Essay 2, chaps. 6, 9; and the study of Ian Simpson Ross, *Lord Kames and the Scotland of His Day* (Oxford: Oxford University Press, 1972); William C. Lehmann, *Henry Home, Lord Kames, and the Scottish Enlightenment: A Study in National Character and in the History of Ideas* (The Hague: Martinus Nijhoff, 1971).

10. See Henry Home, *Sketches of the History of Man, Considerably Enlarged by the Latest Additions and Corrections of the Author*, ed. James A. Harris, 3 vols. (Indianapolis: Liberty Fund, 2007), bk.1, Sketch VI, Appendix: "Concerning Propagation of Animals and Care of Progeny."

early Western history and was still known in some Islamic and Asiatic cultures in his day. But, Home insisted, polygamy exists only "where women are treated as inferior beings" and where "men of wealth transgress every rule of temperance" by buying their wives like slaves and by adopting the "savage manners" of animals. Among horses, cattle, and other grazing animals, he argued, polygamy is natural. One superior male breeds with all females, and the mothers take care of their own young, who grow quickly independent. For these animals, monogamous "pairing would be of no use: the female feeds herself and her young at the same instant; and nothing is left for the male to do." But other animals, such as nesting birds, "whose young require the nursing care of both parents, are directed by nature to pair" and to remain paired till their young "are sufficiently vigorous to provide for themselves."[11]

Humans are the latter sort of creature, said Home, for whom pairing and parenting are indispensable. Thus humans are inclined by nature toward enduring monogamous pairing of parents—indeed, more so than any other creature, given the long fragility and helplessness of their offspring. Home expanded on the natural foundations of marriage, as they had been developed by Aquinas and Locke, and he added new insights as well from the science of cultural development (anthropology, as we now call it):

> Man is an animal of long life, and is proportionally slow in growing to maturity: he is a helpless being before the age of fifteen or sixteen; and there may be in a family ten or twelve children of different births, before the eldest can shift for itself. Now in the original state of hunting and fishing, which are laborious occupations, and not always successful, a woman, suckling her infant, is not able to provide food even for herself, far less for ten or twelve voracious children. . . . Pairing is so necessary to the human race, that it must be natural and instinctive. . . . Brute animals, which do not pair, have grass and other food in plenty, enabling the female to feed her young without needing any assistance from the male. But where the young require the nursing care of both parents, pairing is a law of nature.[12]

Not only is the pairing of male and female a law of nature, Home continued, but "matrimony is instituted by nature" to overcome humans' greatest natural handicap to effective procreation and preservation as a species—their perpetual desire for sex, especially among the young, at exactly the time when they are most fertile. Unlike most animals, whose sexual appetites are confined to short rutting seasons, Home wrote, humans have a constant sexual appetite which, by nature, "demands gratification, after short intervals." If men and women just had random sex with anyone, "like the hart in rutting time," the human race would devolve into a "savage state of nature" and soon die out. Men would make perennial and "promiscuous use of women" and not commit themselves

11. Ibid., Sketch V, 204; Sketch VI, 261, 263, 271, 278.
12. Ibid., Sketch VI, 263–64.

to the care of these women or their children. "Women would in effect be common prostitutes." Few women would have the ability on their own "to provide food for a family of children," and most would avoid having children or would abandon them if they did. Marriage is nature's safeguard against such proclivities, said Home, and "frequent enjoyment" of marital sex and intimacy "endears a pair to each other," making them want only each other all the more. "Sweet is the society of a pair fitted for each other, in whom are collected the affections of husband, wife, lover, friend, the tenderest affections of human nature."

> The God of nature has [thus] enforced conjugal society, not only by making it agreeable, but [also] by the principle of chastity inherent in our nature. To animals that have no instinct for pairing, chastity is utterly unknown; and to them it would be useless. The mare, the cow, the ewe, the she-goat, receive the male without ceremony, and admit the first that comes in the way without distinction. Neither have tame fowl any notion of chastity: they pair not; and the female gets no food from the male, even during incubation. But chastity and mutual fidelity [are] essential to the human race; enforced by the principle of chastity, a branch of the moral sense. Chastity is essential even to the continuation of the human race. As the carnal appetite is always alive, the sexes would wallow in pleasure, and be soon rendered unfit for procreation, were it not for the restraint of chastity.[13]

Polygamy violates this natural design and strategy for successful procreation through enduring marital cohabitation, Home argued. First, monogamy is better suited to the roughly equal numbers of men and women in the world. "All men are by nature equal in rank; no man is privileged above another to have a wife; and therefore polygamy is contradictory" to the natural order and to the natural right of each fit adult to marry. Monogamous pairing is most "clearly the voice of nature." It is echoed in "sacred Scripture" in its injunction that "two"—not three or four—shall become "one flesh" in marriage. If God and nature had intended to condone polygamy, there would be many more females than males.[14]

Second, monogamy "is much better calculated for continuing the race, than the union of one man with many women." One man cannot possibly provide food, care, and nurture to the many children born of his many wives. Their wives are not able to provide easily for their young when they are weakened from child labor and birth, needed for nursing, or distracted by the many needs of multiple children. Some of their children will be neglected; some will grow up impoverished, malnourished, or undereducated; some will inevitably die. "How

13. Ibid., Sketch VI, 264, 267, 269–70. Later, Home condemned mandatory celibacy and abstinence within marriage as "ridiculous self-denial," an "impudent disregard of moral principles," and the "grossest of all deviations, not only from sound morality, but [also] from pure religion" and natural law. See ibid., bk.3, Sketch III, 888–90.

14. Ibid., bk.1, Sketch VI, 265–66.

much better chance for life have infants who are distributed more equally in different families."[15]

Third, monogamy is better suited for women. Men and women are by nature equal, Homes argued at length, building on the egalitarian themes of Locke, among others. Monogamous marriage is naturally designed to respect this natural gender equality, even while recognizing the different roles that a husband and wife play in the procreation and nurture of their children. Thus marriage works best when a husband and wife have "reciprocal and equal affection" as true "companions" in life, who enjoy each other and their children with "endearment" and "constancy." Polygamy, by contrast, is simply a patriarchal fraud. Each wife is reduced to a servant, "a mere instrument of pleasure and propagation" for her husband. Each wife is reduced to competing for the attention and affection of her husband, particularly if she has small children and needs help in their care. One wife and her children will inevitably be singled out for special favor, denigrating the others further and exacerbating the tensions within the household, which causes the children to suffer, too. Packs of wolves might thrive this way, but rational humans cannot. Combining natural instinct with rational reflection, humans have discovered that monogamy is the "foundation for a true matrimonial covenant" between two equal adults.[16]

Fourth, monogamy is better designed to promote the fidelity and chastity that humans need to procreate effectively as a species. It induces husband and wives to remain faithful to each other and to their children, come what may. Polygamy, by contrast, is simply a forum and a catalyst for adultery and lust. If a husband is allowed to satisfy his lust for a second woman whom he can add as a wife, his "one act of incontinence will lead to others without end." Soon enough he will lust after yet another wife and still another—even the wife of another man, as the biblical story of King David's lust for Bathsheba tragically illustrates. The husband's bed-hopping, in turn, will "alienate the affections" of his first wife, who will embark on her own bed-hopping. Such "unlawful love" will only trigger more and more rivalries among husbands, wives, and lovers, in which all will suffer. Moreover, by sharing another man's bed, the wife might well get pregnant and require her husband "to maintain and educate children who are not his own." This most men will not do unless they are uncommonly smitten or charitable. Polygamy simply "does not work," Home wrote. "Matrimony between a single pair, for mutual comfort, and for procreating children implies the strictest mutual fidelity."[17]

Home's arguments were typical of the arguments from nature, reason, and experience that the Scottish Enlightenment mustered in favor of most traditional forms and norms of marriage. Frances Hutcheson, David Hume, Adam Smith, Gershon Carmichael, John Millar, David Fordyce, and several other

---

15. Ibid., Sketch VI, 266; Sketch VIII, 484.
16. Ibid., Sketch VI, 261, 267–68, 287–311.
17. Ibid., Sketch V, 204; Sketch VI, 270, 287–89.

Scottish philosophers in the eighteenth and early nineteenth centuries offered similar arguments about marriage.[18] For example, David Hume—in spite of all his skepticism about traditional morality and Christian theology—thought traditional legal and moral norms of sex, marriage, and family life to be both natural and useful. Hume summarized the natural-law argument for monogamous marriage crisply: "The long and helpless infancy requires the combination of parents for the subsistence of their young; and that combination requires the virtue of chastity and fidelity to the marriage bed."[19] Hume used many of the same arguments that Home had mustered against polygamy. This "odious institution" denied the natural equality of the sexes. It fostered "the bad education of children." It led to "jealousy and competition among wives," and more. Moreover, said Hume, polygamy forced a man, distracted by his other wives and children, to confine his other wives to the home—by physically threatening, binding, or even laming them; by isolating them from society; or by keeping them so poor and weak that they could not leave. All this is a form of "barbarism," with "frightful effects" that defy all nature and reason.[20]

Hume offered similar natural and utilitarian arguments against no-fault "voluntary divorce." Many in Hume's day argued for divorce as a natural expression of the freedom of contract and a natural compensation for having no recourse to polygamy despite a man's natural drive to multiple partners. "The heart of man delights in liberty," their argument went; "the very image of constraint is grievous to it." Hume would have none of this. To be sure, he recognized that divorce was sometimes the better of two evils, especially where one party was guilty of adultery, severe cruelty, or malicious desertion and especially when no children were involved. But outside of such narrow circumstances, he said, "nature has made divorce" without real cause the "doom of all mortals." First, with voluntary divorce, the children suffer and become "miserable." Shuffled from home to home, consigned to the care of strangers and stepparents "instead of the fond attention and concern of a parent," the inconveniences and encumbrances of their lives just multiply as the divorces of their parents and stepparents multiply. Second, when voluntary divorce is foreclosed, couples by nature

---

18. See, e.g., Gershom Carmichael, *Natural Rights on the Threshold of the Enlightenment: The Writings of Gershom Carmichael*, ed. James Moore and Michael Silverstone, trans. Michael Silverstone (Indianapolis: Liberty Fund, 2002), 128–37; David Fordyce, *The Elements of Moral Philosophy in Three Books* (1754), ed. Thomas Kennedy (Indianapolis: Liberty Fund, 2003), bk. 2, chaps. 2–3; John Millar, *The Origin of the Distinction of Ranks*, ed. Aaron Garrett (Indianapolis: Liberty Fund, 2006), 1.2–3; 2.1–2; Adam Smith, *Lectures on Jurisprudence* (1762), ed. R. L. Meek, D. D. Raphael, and P. G. Stein (Indianapolis: Liberty Fund, 1982), Lectures Feb. 7–8, 10–11, 1763; Frances Hutcheson, *Philosophiae moralis institutio compendiaria: With a Short Introduction to Moral Philosophy*, ed. Luigi Turco (Indianapolis: Liberty Fund, 2007), 218–22. See also Frances Hutcheson, *Logic, Metaphysics, and the Natural Sociability of Mankind*, ed. James Moore and Michael Silverthorne (Indianapolis: Liberty Fund, 2006), 206–7.

19. David Hume, *Enquiries concerning the Human Understanding and concerning the Principles of Morals* (1777), ed. L. A. Selby-Bigge, 2nd ed. (Oxford: Clarendon Press, 1902; repr., 1963), 206–7.

20. David Hume, *Essays Moral, Political, and Literary*, ed. Eugene F. Miller, rev. ed. (Indianapolis: Liberty Fund, 1987), Essay XIX, "On Polygamy and Divorces," 182–87.

become disinclined to wander and instead form "a calm and sedate affection, conducted by reason and cemented by habit; springing from long acquaintance and mutual obligations, without jealousies or fears." "We need not, therefore, be afraid of drawing the marriage-knot, which chiefly subsists by friendship, the closest possible." Third, "nothing is more dangerous than to unite two persons so closely in all their interests and concerns, as man and wife, without rendering the union entire and total. The least possibility of a separate interest must be the source of endless quarrels and suspicions." Nature, justice, and prudence alike require their "continued consortium."[21]

William Paley and the Utilitarians

The writings of Cambridge philosopher William Paley (1743–1805) provide a good illustration of how these same early Enlightenment arguments could be pressed in a more utilitarian direction. Paley sought to define those natural principles and practices of social life that most conduce to human happiness.[22] Marriage is among the "natural duties and rights of men and women," Paley wrote, for it provides a variety of "public and private goods." His list of marital goods is a nice distillation of traditional rationales:

1. The private comfort of individuals, especially of the female sex. . . .
2. The production of the greatest number of healthy children, their better education, and the making of due provision for their settlement in life.
3. The peace of human society, in cutting off a principal source of contention, by assigning one or more women [if the man became widowed or divorced] to one man, and protecting his exclusive right by sanctions of morality and law.
4. The better government of society, by distributing the community into separate families, and appointing over each the authority of a master of a family, which has more actual influence than all civil authority put together.
5. The same end, in the additional security which the state receives for the good behavior of its citizens, from the solicitude they feel for the welfare of their children, and from their being confined to permanent habitations.
6. The encouragement of industry . . . and morality.[23]

Paley worked systematically through the respective "natural rights and duties" of husband and wife, parent and child. In marriage, a husband promises

21. Ibid., 187–90.

22. William Paley, *Principles of Moral and Political Philosophy* (1785), ed. Dan L. LeMahieu (Indianapolis: Liberty Fund, 2002), 1–25. See further Dan L. LeMahieu, *William Paley: A Philosopher and His Age* (Lincoln: University of Nebraska Press, 1976).

23. Paley, *Principles*, 167–68.

"to love, comfort, honor, and keep his wife," and a wife promises "to obey, serve, love, honor, and keep her husband" "in every variety of health, fortune, and condition." Both parties further stipulate "to forsake all others, and to keep only unto one another, so long as they both shall live." In a word, said Paley, each spouse promises to do all that is necessary to "consult and promote the other's happiness." These are not only scriptural and traditional duties of marriage. They are also natural duties, as can be seen in the marital contracts of all manner of cultures, which Paley adduced in ample number. These natural duties, in turn, give the other spouse "a natural right" to enforce them in cases of adultery, "desertion, neglect, prodigality, drunkenness, peevishness, penuriousness, jealousy, or any levity of conduct which administers occasion of jealousy." What the apostle Paul called the "mutual conjugal rights" of husband and wife are simply one way of formulating the natural rights that husbands and wives enjoy in civilized societies the world over.[24]

If the couple is blessed with children, the parents have a "natural right and duty" to provide for the child's "maintenance, education, and a reasonable provision for the child's happiness in respect of outward condition." A parent's rights to care for their children "result from their duties" to their children, said Paley.

> If it be the duty of a parent to educate his children, to form them for a life of usefulness and virtue, to provide for them situations needful for their subsistence and suited to their circumstances, and to prepare them for those situations; he has a right to such authority, and in support of that authority to exercise such discipline as may be necessary for these purposes. The law of nature acknowledges no other foundation of a parent's right over his children, besides his duty towards them. (I speak now of such rights as may be enforced by coercion.) This relation confers no property in their persons, or natural dominion over them, as is commonly supposed.[25]

But a parent "has, in no case, a right to destroy his child's happiness," Paley went on, and those that do will suffer punishment, if not lose custody of their child. Moreover, while parents have a right to encourage and train their children to a given vocation and to give their consent to their children's marriages, "parents have no right to urge their children upon marriages to which they are averse." Children in turn have "a natural right to receive the support, education, and care" of their parents. They also have a "natural duty" to "love, honor, and obey" their parents, even when they become adults, and to care for their parents when they become old, frail, and dependent.[26]

Paley worked systematically through the various sexual sins that deviated from these private and public goods of marriage, and the natural rights and duties of the household—now marshaling natural, rational, and utilitarian

24. Ibid., 194–96.
25. Ibid., 209-10.
26. Ibid., 210.

arguments against them. His arguments against polygamy differed little from those of Home and Hume. More original were Paley's combinations of natural law and utilitarian arguments against fornication, prostitution, adultery, and easy divorce.

Paley opposed fornication, "sex or cohabitation without marriage," mostly because it "discourages marriage" and "diminishes the private and public goods" it offers "by abating the chief temptation to it. The male part of the species will not undertake the encumbrance, expense, and restraint of married life, if they can gratify their passions at a cheaper price; and they will undertake anything rather than not gratify them." Paley recognized that he was appealing to general utility, but he thought an absolute ban on fornication was the only way to avoid the slippery slope to utter sexual libertinism. "The libertine may not be conscious that these irregularities hinder his own marriage, . . . much less does he perceive how *his* indulgences can hinder other men from marrying; but what will he say would be the consequence, if the same licentiousness were universal? or what should hinder its becoming universal, if it be innocent or allowable in him?"[27]

Fornication furthermore leads to prostitution, Paley went on, with its accompanying degradation of women, erosion of morals, transmission of disease, production of unwanted and uncared-for children, and further irregularities and pathos. Fornication also leads naturally to a tradition of concubinage—"the kept mistress," who can be dismissed at the man's pleasure or retained "in a state of humiliation and dependence inconsistent with the rights which marriage would confer upon her" and her children. No small wonder that the Bible condemned fornication, prostitution, concubinage, and other such "cohabitation without marriage" in no uncertain terms, said Paley, with ample demonstration. But again, in these injunctions the Bible is simply reflecting the natural order and moral sense of mankind:

> Laying aside the injunctions of Scripture, the plain account of the question seems to be this: It is immoral, because it is pernicious, that men and women should cohabit, without undertaking certain irrevocable obligations, and mutually conferring certain civil rights; if, therefore, the law has annexed these rights and obligations to certain forms, so that they cannot be secured or undertaken by any other means, which is the case here (for, whatever the parties may promise to each other, nothing but the marriage-ceremony can make their promise irrevocable), it becomes in the same degree immoral, that men and women should cohabit without the interposition of these forms.[28]

Adultery is even worse than fornication, said Paley, because it not only insults the goods of marriage in the abstract but injures an actual good marriage, leaving the innocent spouse as well as their children as victims. For the betrayed spouse, adultery is "a wound in his [or her] sensibility and affections, the most painful and incurable that human nature knows." For the children it brings

27. Ibid., 168–69.
28. Ibid., 169–73.

shame and unhappiness since the vice is inevitably detected and discussed. For the adulterer or adulteress, it is a form of "perjury" that violates their marital vow and covenant. For all parties in the household, adultery will often provoke retaliation and imitation—another slippery slope to erosion of marriage and the unleashing of sexual libertinism and seduction. Both nature and Scripture thus rain down anathemas against it.[29]

Paley opposed "frivolous" or "voluntary" divorce as well. Like many others, he thought that divorce and remarriage of the innocent spouse was both natural and necessary in cases of adultery, malicious desertion, habitual intemperance, cruelty, and crime. But Paley was against voluntary divorces or separations for "lighter causes" or by "mutual consent," grounding his opposition in arguments from nature and utility. Such "lighter" divorces were "obviously" against natural law if the couple had dependent children, Paley thought. "It is manifestly inconsistent with the [natural] duty which the parents owe to their children; which duty can never be so well fulfilled as by their cohabitation and united care. It is also incompatible with the right which the mother possesses, as well as the father, to the gratitude of her children and the comfort of their society; of both which she is almost necessarily deprived, by her dismiss[al] from her husband's family."[30]

"Causeless," "voluntary," and "lighter" divorces, unilaterally sought, are not so obviously against natural law for childless couples, Paley argued, but they are still "inexpedient" enough to prohibit. The worry is, again, the mixed signaling of such a regime and the "gradual slide" down the slippery slope toward "libertinism." If such easy divorces are available, especially on a unilateral basis, each spouse will be tempted to begin pursuing their own separate interests rather than a common marital interest once the heat of their new love has begun to cool. Each will begin hoarding their own money, developing their own friendships, living more and more independently from the other. "This would beget peculation on one side, mistrust on the other, evils which at present very little disturb the confidence of married life" but eventually will destroy it from within. The availability of easy divorce will discourage spouses to reconcile their conflicts or "take pains to give up what offends, and practice what may gratify the other." They will have less incentive to work hard "to make the best of their bargain" or "promote the pleasure of the other."[31]

Limiting divorce to cases of serious fault will stop this inevitable downward spiral in a marriage, Paley believed. Forcing couples to stay together for better or worse, "though at first extorted by necessity, become in time easy and mutual; and, though less endearing than assiduities which take their rise from affection, generally procure to the married couple a repose and satisfaction sufficient for their happiness." In contrast, the availability of easy divorce will heighten the natural temptation of each spouse, especially the husband, to succumb to "new

29. Ibid., 176–80.
30. Ibid., 186, 190.
31. Ibid., 187–89.

objects of desire." However much in love they were with their wives on their wedding day and however hard they try, men are "naturally inclined" to wander after "the invitations of novelty" unless they are "permanently constrained" to remain faithful to their wives even as their wives lose their "youthful vigor and figure." Thus

> constituted as mankind are, and injured as the repudiated wife generally must be, it is necessary to add a stability to the condition of married women, more secure than the continuance of their husbands' affection; and to supply to both sides, by a sense of duty and of obligation, what satiety has impaired of passion and of personal attachment. Upon the whole, the power of divorce is evidently and greatly to the disadvantage of the woman: and the only question appears to be, whether the real and permanent happiness of one half of the species should be surrendered to the caprice and voluptuousness of the other.[32]

Paley's utilitarian arguments in favor of traditional understandings of sex, marriage, and family life would find enduring provenance among many utilitarians into the nineteenth century. The most famous of these utilitarians, Jeremy Bentham (1748–1832), endorsed most of these same propositions that Paley had set forth, even though Bentham famously eschewed the language of natural law and natural rights that had so inspired Paley's theory of marriage. Bentham thought most traditional sex, marriage, and family norms could be rationalized on utilitarian principles alone.[33]

Common-Law Formulations

Locke, Home, Hume, and Paley were only a few of the scores of Anglo-American writers from the seventeenth to the nineteenth centuries who defended traditional Western norms of sex, marriage, and family by using this surfeit of arguments from nature, reason, fairness, prudence, utility, pragmatism, and common sense. No doubt, some of these writers were inspired by their personal Christian faith, others by a conservative desire to maintain the status quo. But most of these writers pressed their principal arguments on nonbiblical grounds. And they were sometimes sharply critical of the Bible—denouncing Paul's preferences for celibacy, the Mosaic provisions on unilateral male divorce, and the many tales of polygamy, concubinage, and prostitution among the ancient biblical patriarchs and kings. Moreover, most of these writers jettisoned many other features of the Western tradition that, in their judgment, defied reason, fairness, and utility—notably including the establishment of Christianity by law and the political privileging of the church over other associations. Their natural-law

---

32. Ibid.

33. *The Works of Jeremy Bentham*, ed. John Bowring, 11 vols. (Edinburgh: William Tait, 1843), 1:119–21, 348–57; 2:499, 531–32; 3:73, 202–3; 6:63, 522; 7:579–81. See Mary Sokol, "Jeremy Bentham on Love and Marriage," *American Journal of Legal History* 30 (2009): 1.

theory of the family was not just a rationalist apologia for traditional Christian family values or a naturalist smoke screen for personal religious beliefs. They defended traditional family norms not out of confessional faith but out of rational proof, not just because they uncritically believed in these norms but because these norms worked.

It was precisely this rational, utilitarian, and even pragmatic defense of marriage that made it so appealing to English and American jurists as they sought to create a common law of marriage that no longer depended on ecclesiastical law or church courts. Particularly in America, the disestablishment of religion mandated by the state and federal constitutions of the later eighteenth and nineteenth centuries made direct appeals to the Bible and to Christian theology an insufficient ground by itself for cogent legal arguments. Even in England, which retained its Anglican establishment, many common lawyers were equally eager to cast their argument in the natural and utilitarian terms of the Enlightenment, rather than in the biblical and theological terms of the tradition. It was one thing to say that "Christianity was part of the common law," as Anglo-American lawyers had long said.[34] It was quite another thing to say that the common law was part of Christianity. That simply would not do. The Enlightenment arguments on sex, marriage, and family life, which deliberately eschewed biblical and theological proofs, were thus attractive to the common lawyers.

For example, William Blackstone, the leading English common lawyer of the eighteenth century, adverted regularly to these Enlightenment writings in his influential *Commentaries on the Law of England* (1765). Blackstone argued that exclusive and enduring monogamous marriages were the best way to ensure paternal certainty and joint parental investment in children, who are born vulnerable and utterly dependent on their parents' mutual care.

> The establishment of marriage in all civilized states is built on this natural obligation of the father to provide for his children: for that ascertains and makes known the person who is bound to fulfill this obligation: whereas, in promiscuous and illicit conjunctions, the father is unknown; and the mother finds a thousand obstacles in her way—shame, remorse, the constraint of her sex, and the rigor of laws—that stifle her inclinations to perform this duty: and besides, she generally wants [lacks] ability.

"The duty of parents to provide for the maintenance of their children is a principle of natural law," Blackstone continued. "The main end and design of marriage [is] to ascertain and fix upon some certain person, to whom the care, the protection, the maintenance, and the education of the children should belong."[35]

34. See Stuart Banner, "When Christianity Was Part of the Common Law," *Law and History Review* 16 (1998): 27–62.

35. William Blackstone, *Commentaries on the Laws of England*, 4 vols. (Oxford: Oxford University Press, 1765–69), 1.15.1; 1.16.1; 1.16.3. This quote is largely a paraphrase of Charles de Secondat, Baron de Montesquieu, *Spirit of the Laws* (French, 1748), 23.2; cf. trans. Thomas Nugent (1750, 1752), rev. J. V. Prichard (London: G. Bell & Sons, 1914), http://www.constitution.org/cm/sol.htm.

Much like his fellow Englishmen, William Paley and John Locke, Blackstone set out in detail the reciprocal rights and duties that the natural law imposes on parents and children. God and nature have "implant[ed] in the breast of every parent" an "insuperable degree of affection" for their child once they are certain the child is theirs, Blackstone wrote. The common law confirms and channels this natural affection by requiring parents to maintain, protect, and educate their children and by protecting their rights to discharge these parental duties against undue interference by others. These "natural duties" of parents are the correlatives of the "natural rights" of their children, Blackstone further argued. Once they become adults, children acquire reciprocal natural duties toward their parents:

> The duties of children to their parents arise from a principle of natural justice and retribution. For to those who gave us existence, we naturally owe subjection and obedience during our minority, and honour and reverence ever after; they, who protected the weakness of our infancy, are entitled to our protection in the infirmity of their age; they who by sustenance and education have enabled their offspring to prosper, ought in return to be supported by that offspring, in case they stand in need of assistance. Upon this principle proceed all the duties of children to their parents, which are enjoined by positive laws.[36]

While Blackstone's views had an enduring influence on the English common law of marriage, United States Supreme Court Justice Joseph Story's formulations were foundational for America law. Like Blackstone, Story was a student of Enlightenment theories of marriage, and he drew heavily on Scottish, English, and Continental writers in formulating his views. Story was also a deep student of comparative legal history and conflict of laws, and he studded his writings with all manner of ancient, medieval, and early modern sources on the origin, nature, and purpose of marriage.

> Marriage is treated by all civilized nations as a peculiar and favored contract. It is in its origin a contract of natural law. . . . It is the parent and not the child of society, the source of the city, a sort of seminary of the republic. In civil society it becomes a civil contract, regulated and prescribed by law, and endowed with civil consequences. In most civilized countries, acting under the sense of the force of sacred obligations, it has had the sanctions of religion superadded. It then becomes a religious, as well as a natural and civil contract; for it is a great mistake to suppose, that because it is the one, therefore it may [not] likewise [be] the other.[37]

Marriage is thus a civil contract dependent in its essence on the mutual consent of a man and a woman with the freedom and capacity to marry each

36. Ibid., 1.16.
37. Joseph Story, *Commentaries on the Conflict of the Laws, Foreign and Domestic, in Regards to Contracts, Rights, and Remedies, and Especially in Regard to Marriages* (Boston: Hilliard Gray, 1834), sec. 108.

other. But marriage is "more than a mere contract," Story insisted, for it also has natural, religious, and social dimensions, all of which the positive law of the state must take into account. The state's positive law of marriage must reflect the natural-law teaching that marriage is a monogamous union presumptively for life; that marriage channels the strong human sex drive toward marital sex, which serves to deepen the mutual love between husband and wife; that marriage provides a stable and lifelong system of support, protection, and edification for husbands and wives, parents and children. The positive law of the state must also reflect the teachings of nature—sometimes alone and sometimes "with religion superadded"—that civilized societies outlaw the practices of polygamy, incest, fornication, adultery, and "light divorce," all of which violate the other spouse's natural rights; as well as the acts of desertion, abuse, neglect, and disinheritance, which violate their children's natural rights.[38]

It is just because marriage has all of these natural goods and qualities embedded within it that it is "more than mere contract," Story went on. While all fit adults have the natural right and liberty to enter into a valid marriage contract, the form, function, and limits of this marriage contract are not subject to private bargain but preset by nature and society. In almost all civilizations and legal systems, marriage is "a unique contract, a contract sui generis." Story quoted at length from a Scottish case that distilled the views of Home, Hume, and others:

> The contract of marriage is the most important of all human transactions. It is the very basis of the whole fabric of civilized society. The status of marriage is *juris gentium* [part of the common law of nations] and the foundation of it, like all other contracts, rests on the consent of the parties. But it differs from other contracts in this, that the rights, obligations or duties arising from it are not left entirely to be regulated by the agreements of parties, but are, to a certain extent, matters of municipal regulation over which the parties have no control by any declaration of their will. It confers the *status* of legitimacy on children born in wedlock, with all the consequential rights, duties, and privileges, thence arising; it gives rise to the relations of consanguinity and affinity; in short, it pervades the whole system of civil society. Unlike other contracts, it cannot, in general, amongst civilized nations, be dissolved by mutual consent; and it subsists in full force, even although one of the parties should be forever rendered incapable, as in the case of incurable insanity, or the like, from performing his part of the mutual contract.[39]
> No wonder that the rights, duties, and obligations arising from so important a contract, should not be left to the discretion or caprice of the contracting parties, but should be regulated, in many important particulars, by the laws of every civilized country. . . . Many of the rights, duties, and obligations arising from it are so important to the best interests of morality and good government, that the parties have no control over them; but they are regulated and enforced by the public law.[40]

38. Ibid., secs. 108–99.
39. Ibid., secs. 109–10.
40. Ibid., secs. 110–12.

Story quoted another Scottish case that drew on Home and Hume for this proposition:

> Though the origin of marriage is contract, it is in a different situation from all others. It is a contract coeval with, and essential to, the existence of society; while the relations of husband and wife, parent and child, to which it gives rise, are the foundation of many rights acknowledged all the world over, and which, though differently modified in different countries, have everywhere a legal character altogether independent of the will of the parties. . . . The rights arising from the relation of husband and wife, though taking their origin in contract, have yet in all countries, a legal character, determined by their particular laws and usages altogether independent of the terms of the contract or the will of the parties at the time of entering into it.[41]

In the later nineteenth century, Anglo-American common lawyers frequently used the term *status* to signal this distinctive quality of the contract and relationship of marriage. As we saw in the introduction to this volume, *status* was a term that Sir Henry Sumner Maine had made famous in his provocative theory that modern law altogether was moving "from status to contract." Many American jurists accepted the concept of marriage as a status, yet without buying Maine's broader argument that marriage law was moving from "status to contract." Perhaps that movement could be seen in other areas of law where private contract was on the rise, American jurists argued, but the opposite was true in the law of marriage. Joel Bishop, a leading American family-law jurist, put it thus: "Marriage, as distinguished from the agreement to marry, and from the act of becoming married, is the civil status of one man and one woman legally united for life, with the rights and duties, which, for the establishment of families, and the multiplication and education of the species, are . . . assigned by the law of matrimony." The state law of matrimony, Bishop continued, fixes the terms of the marriage contract in accordance with the dictates of nature, morality, and society. Parties are free to accept or reject these basic terms, but they cannot rescind, condition, or modify them if they wish to enter a valid marriage. And once they marry, their status of being married is presumptively permanent and exclusive and carries with it built-in obligations of support and care for spouse, child, and other loved ones, which continue even after death. Marital parties cannot dissolve this union on their own *ipse dixit*, nor simply walk away from their obligations with impunity. The voluntarily assumed legal status of being a husband, wife, father, or mother is something that stays with them, even if they separate or divorce. The law still expects them to support and cooperate with each other in the care of their children, and sometimes to support each other through payment of alimony. And even after death the marital status of the decedent creates testamentary presumptions in favor of the surviving spouse, children, and natural kin.[42]

41. Ibid., secs. 111–12.
42. Joel P. Bishop, *Commentaries on the Law of Marriage and Divorce, and Evidence in Matrimonial Suits* (Boston: Little, Brown & Co., 1852), sec. 11, 13.

American jurist, James Schouler, put it succinctly in his authoritative treatise on domestic relations:

> This [marital] contract of the parties is simply to enter into a certain status or relation. The rights and obligations of that status are fixed by society in accordance with the principles of natural law, and are beyond and above the parties themselves. They may make settlements and regulate the property rights of each other; but they cannot modify the terms upon which they are to live together, nor superadd to the relation a single condition. Being once bound, they are bound forever; mutual consent cannot part them.[43]

By the later nineteenth century, this idea that marriage was a special civil status, defined by law, but entered into by voluntary contract, became the preferred common-law formula.[44] "The doctrine that marriage is a *status* is modern," wrote the distinguished American jurist William Nelson in 1895. By calling marriage a status, the American common law had settled on a halfway step between the traditional notion that "marriage was a sacrament to be solemnized by a religious ceremony of the church regardless of the faith of the parties" and the modern notion that marriage was merely a private "*civil* contract" in which the public has no interest. Marriage is a contract, but it is also more than a contract, Nelson insisted. Marriage is not a sacrament, but it does embrace some of the same qualities of faithfulness, exclusivity, and permanence that typified sacramental and covenantal marriages since the time of Augustine.[45]

LATER ENLIGHTENMENT CRITIQUE AND REFORMS

The key move made by the early Enlightenment philosophers before 1850 was to remove the religious dimension of marriage as necessary to provide a complete account of the institution. This liberalized the institution of marriage somewhat, and it liberated parties from the requirement of mandatory church weddings or pastoral care of their household. Parties were now given the choice of whether to involve the church or to obey the Bible in their sex, marriage, and family lives.[46]

---

43. James Schouler, *A Treatise on the Law of Marriage, Divorce, Separation, and Domestic Relations*, ed. Arthur W. Blakemore, 6th ed. (Albany, NY: Matthew Bender, 1921), sec. 1073.

44. See, e.g., Epaphroditus Peck, *The Law of Persons or Domestic Relations* (Chicago: Callaghan & Co., 1913), 3–4; Rodgers, *Domestic Relations*, 2–5; Walter C. Tiffany, *Handbook on the Law of Persons and Domestic Relations* (St. Paul: West Publishing Co., 1896), 4–7.

45. Tiffany, *Handbook*, sec. 5; Joseph Long, *A Treatise on the Law of Domestic Relations* (St. Paul: Keefe-Davidson Co., 1905), I.3–7.

46. See 5 & 6 Will. 4 c. 54. This law, passed in 1835–36, authorized both religious and civil forms of marriage. Parties who reached the age of consent could marry, as traditionally, in accordance with the ecclesiastical laws of England. But now Jewish, Quaker, and (later) Catholic parties could marry in accordance with the religious laws and customs of their own communities, being required only to register their marriages with the Superintendent Registrar's Office after the fact. Moreover, parties could forgo a religious marriage ceremony altogether by swearing a simple oath of marriage before an official in the Superintendent Registrar's Office.

But the early Enlightenment philosophers left in place the idea that marriage was at once a natural, social, and contractual association, with a number of its basic terms preset in order to protect the natural rights and duties of husbands and wives, parents and children.

The key move made by Enlightenment philosophers after 1850 was gradually to remove the necessary natural and social dimensions of marriage as well. This liberalized the institution of marriage even more, reducing it to a private contract between a man and a woman who had reached the age of consent. These parties were now free to enter, exercise, and exit their marriage contract without interference from church, state, or society. They were free to renegotiate the terms of their marital contract—through prenuptial agreements that set their own rules of behavior before, during, and after the marriage had ended. And they were free to live in various intimate relationships without any contracts at all.

John Stuart Mill

The most decisive statement of this later Enlightenment view of marriage was offered by John Stuart Mill, a leading English liberal and utilitarian philosopher, who also served for a time in the Parliament of England. Much of his writing about marriage was driven by the ferment in Parliament for the reform of the traditional English law of marriage, ferment that found equal force in state legislatures in America at the same time.[47] Several Parliamentary bills sought to liberalize marriage and divorce requirements, to liberate children from abusive households, and to provide wives with equal rights over marital property, minor children, and minimal maintenance. Mill was all for these changes, and many others, which he defended with arguments well known in English liberal and literary circles,[48] especially those influenced by Mary Wollstonecraft's feminist writings of the 1790s and thereafter.[49]

47. Among numerous sources, see, e.g., Mary Lyndon Shanley, *Feminism, Marriage, and the Law in Victorian England, 1850–1895* (Princeton, NJ: Princeton University Press, 1989); Lawrence Stone, *Road to Divorce: A History of the Making and Breaking of Marriage in England* (New York and Oxford: Oxford University Press, 1995); Graveson and Crane, eds., *A Century of Family Law*; Marylynn Salmon, *Women and the Law of Property in Early America* (Chapel Hill: University of North Carolina Press, 1986).

48. See especially several tracts in *Collected Works of John Stuart Mill*, ed. John M. Robson et al., 33 vols. (Toronto: University of Toronto Press, 1963–91), vol. 21; *On Liberty* (1859), chap. 5, in John Stuart Mill, *Utilitarianism, on Liberty, Essay on Bentham*, ed. Mary Warnock (1962; repr., New York: New American Library, 1974). See discussion in Gail Tulloch, *Mill and Sexual Equality* (Hertfordshire, UK: Harvester Wheatsheaf; Boulder, CO: Lynne Rienner Publishers, 1989); Susan Mendus, "The Marriage of True Minds: The Ideal Marriage in the Philosophy of John Stuart Mill," in *Sexuality and Subordination: Interdisciplinary Studies of Gender in the Nineteenth Century*, ed. Susan Mendus and Jane Rendall (London and New York: Routledge & Kegan Paul, 1989), 171–91.

49. Mary Wollstonecraft, *A Vindication of the Rights of Women* (1792), ed. Charles W. Hagelman Jr. (New York: W. W. Norton, 1967). See analysis in Jean Bethke Elshtain, *Public Man, Private Woman: Women in Social and Political Thought* (Princeton, NJ: Princeton University Press, 1981), 228ff.; Virginia Sapiro, *A Vindication of Political Virtue: The Political Theory of Mary Wollstonecraft* (Chicago: University of Chicago Press, 1992), 144ff. For Wollstonecraft's more general literary

Mill supported these new Parliamentary reforms in part because they promised to end the many abuses of the traditional system of marriage and family law. Though sometimes the traditional family is marked by "sympathy and tenderness," said Mill, "it is still oftener . . . a school of willfulness, overbearingness, unbounded self-indulgence, and a double-dyed and idealized selfishness" of the husband and father, with the "individual happiness" of the wife and children "being immolated in every shape to his smallest preferences."[50] Mill recited the many abuses that he saw. The traditional doctrine of parental consent to marriage, for example, gave parents a strong hand in the marital decisions of their children. Some enterprising parents used this as a means to coerce their children into arranged marriages born of their own commercial or diplomatic convenience or to sell their consent to the highest bidder for their children's affections. The traditional doctrine of common-law coverture, which folded the person and property of the wife into that of her husband, gave husbands the premier place in the governance of the household. Some enterprising husbands used this as a license to control closely the conduct and careers of their wives or, worse, to visit all manner of savage abuses on them and on their children, often with legal impunity. The traditional doctrine of adultery imposed upon innocent children the highest costs of their parents' extramarital experimentation. Children conceived of such dalliances were sometimes aborted in utero or smothered on birth. If they survived, they were declared illegitimate bastards with severely truncated civil, political, and property rights.

No system of marriage and family law that allows such abuses can be justified, Mill concluded. Mill himself formally renounced that law when he and Harriet Taylor were married in 1851:

> [I object to] the whole character of the marriage relation as constituted by law, . . . for this amongst other reasons, that it confers upon one of the parties to the contract, legal power & control over the person, property, and freedom of action of the other party, independent of her own wishes and will. . . . Having no means of legally divesting myself of these odious powers, . . . I feel it my duty to put on record a formal protest against the existing law of marriage, in so far as conferring such powers; and a solemn promise never in any case or under any circumstance to use them.[51]

But Mill's deeper attack on traditional English marriage law was theological—"laying bare the real root of much that is bowed down to as the intention of Nature and the ordinance of God," as Mill put it.[52] The prevailing theology and law of marriage and the family supports a threefold patriarchy, Mill charged. The

influence, see Shirley Foster, *Victorian Women's Fiction: Marriage, Freedom, and the Individual* (London: Croom Helm, 1985).

50. *Works of Mill,* 21:288–89.

51. Quoted and discussed in Shanley, *Feminism, Marriage, and the Law,* 3. See also F. A. Hayeck, *John Stuart Mill and Harriet Taylor: Their Friendship and Subsequent Marriage* (London: Routledge & Kegan Paul, 1951).

52. *Works of Mill,* 21:263.

church dictates to the state its peculiar understanding of nature. The state dictates to the couple the terms of their marital relation and abandons them once the terms are accepted. The man lords it over his wife and children, divesting them of all liberty and license in their person and property, thought and belief. "The aim of the law," Mill charged, "is to tie up the soul, the mind, the sense," and the body of the wife and children, together with their "material extensions."[53]

Nature does not teach bondage and subjection of women, said Mill, but the natural liberty and equality of all men and women. "The legal subordination of one sex to the other is wrong and ought to be replaced by a principle of perfect equality with no favour or privilege on the one side nor disability on the other."[54] "What is now called the [inferior] nature of women" and the superior nature of man "is an eminently artificial thing," born of social circumstances, not natural conditions.[55] "If marriage were an equal contract, . . . and if [a woman] would find all honourable employments as freely open to her as to men," marriages could be true institutions of liberty and affection, shaped by the preferences of wife and husband, not the prescriptions of church and state.[56]

Nature also does not teach parental tyranny and commodification of children but counsels parental nurture and education of children. Children are not items of property, to be sold on the market of marriage, nor simple conduits through which to pass the family name and fortune. Children are also not slaves or "animals," to be worked and whipped into submission and performance by their parents. "Children below a certain age *cannot* judge or act for themselves; up to a considerably greater age they are inevitably more or less disqualified for doing so—and they need constant nurture, girls as much as boys."[57] If the family were an open unit, where children could seek redress from neglect, abuse, and arbitrary rule, a real family could be realized, and true happiness for all parties involved could be attained. If the paterfamilias does not "fulfill his obligation to feed, nurture, and educate his child with love and patience," said Mill, the *paterpoliticus*, the state, as the child's protector under the social contract, "ought to see it fulfilled, at the charge, as far as possible, of the parent."[58]

Mill sought to infuse these contractarian principles of marriage and the family into the common law and public opinion of Victorian England and beyond. In his career as Parliamentarian, philosopher, and journalist, Mill advocated the reform of many familiar institutions of the Western legal tradition of marriage.[59]

53. Ibid., 21:37.

54. Ibid., 21:261.

55. Ibid., 21:263.

56. Ibid., 21:298.

57. Mill, *Principles of Political Economy*, in *Works of Mill*, 3:952–53. See also ibid., 16:1470; 17:1624, 1668–69; 19:401.

58. Mill, *On Liberty*, chap. 5, at 126, 238–39. See also the article of Harriet Taylor and J. S. Mill, in *Works of Mill*, 25:1172–76 (decrying child abuse and "domestic ruffianism").

59. See the collection of excerpts from his formal and informal writings in *Sexual Equality: Writings by John Stuart Mill, Harriet Taylor Mill, and Helen Taylor*, ed. Ann P. Robson and John M. Robson (Toronto: University of Toronto Press, 1994).

He urged the abolition of the requirements of parental consent, church consecration, and formal witnesses for marriage.[60] He questioned the exalted status of heterosexual monogamy and supported peaceable polygamy (though he
personally found the practice odious).[61] He called for the absolute equality of
husband and wife to receive, hold, and alienate property; to enter into contracts
and commerce; and to participate on equal terms in the workplace, education,
political life, and social circles.[62] He called for severe punishment of husbands
who assaulted, abused, or raped their wives, and for strict prohibitions against
prostitution and pornography.[63] He urged fathers to turn from their public
vocations and avocations to assist in the care and nurture of their children.[64] He
called for equal rights of husband and wives to sue for divorce and remarriage,
not only when one spouse committed adultery or desertion but any time (quoting Milton's words) the couple "become[s] conscious that affection never has
existed, or has ceased to exist between them."[65] He castigated the state for leaving annulment and other marital causes to the church and urged that the laws
of annulment and divorce be both merged and expanded under exclusive state
jurisdiction. He urged that paternal abuse of children be severely punished and
that the state intervene where necessary to ensure the proper physical and moral
nurture and education of children.[66]

This contractarian gospel for the salvation of Western marriage and family
law, preached by Mill and many others in the later nineteenth century, set out
much of the agenda for the transformation of Anglo-American family law along
Enlightenment lines. The transformation fell into two phases. The first transformation, from the 1850s forward, was designed to bring greater equality and
equity to the traditional family and civil society without denying the basic values
of the Western legal tradition of marriage. The second transformation, from
the 1950s forward, seems calculated to break the preeminence of the traditional
family and the basic values of the Western legal tradition that have sustained it.

Legal Reforms

The Enlightenment critique of traditional models of marriage brought many
reforms to Anglo-American marriage law, particularly on behalf of women and
children. Traditional marriage and family law, under both Catholic and Protestant models, had focused on the contracting and dissolving of marriages. The
governance of marriages and families once formed and once dissolved was left

---

60. *Works of Mill*, 21:46.

61. See, e.g., Mill, *On Liberty*, chap. 5, at 223–25.

62. *Works of Mill*, 21:287 See also collection of excerpts in Robson and Robson, *Sexual Equality*, 103.

63. *Works of Mill*, 17:1692–94.

64. Ibid., 21:299–322.

65. See collection of statements in Robson and Robson, *Sexual Equality*, 28–34, 53–102. Quote
is from Mill's article on Henri Saint-Simon, in ibid., 23; and in *Works of Mill*, 23:677–80.

66. *Works of Mill*, 25:1172–76; Mill, *On Liberty*, chap. 5, at 238–39.

largely to the discretion of the husband and father, operating with the counsel of the church and the broader Christian community. In the nineteenth and early twentieth centuries, this pattern shifted dramatically—partly inspired by the Enlightenment critique of prevailing norms and practices. Sweeping new laws were passed to reform marriage formalities, divorce, alimony, prenuptial contracts, marital property, wife abuse, child custody and support, and education of minors.

In England, Parliament passed the famous Matrimonial Causes Act of 1857, which set afoot a series of changes to traditional English marriage law.[67] The Act introduced three major reforms that had been unsuccessfully advocated in England since the sixteenth-century Reformation. First, the 1857 Act transferred all marriage and divorce jurisdiction from the church courts to the common-law courts. Only common-law courts could now hear cases and order legal relief in disputes over betrothal and marriage, marital cruelty and abuse, paternity and bastardy, petitions for child custody, alimony, and the like. Though the Church of England could maintain an internal body of canon law for voluntary use by its members, the church courts no longer held formal legal authority over English marriage life, and their rulings were not binding on the common-law courts.[68] In this, England was following the American example that had rejected ecclesiastical courts from the start.

Second, the 1857 Act authorized private suits for divorce on proof of cause, with a subsequent right to remarry for the innocent party. Parties could still press annulment suits on proof of an impediment of consanguinity, affinity, bigamy, or frigidity, and for separation from bed and board on proof of adultery, desertion, or cruelty. But innocent husbands and wives now also could sue for absolute divorce on proof of the adultery of the other party, with a right to remarry—and be spared the ardor and expense of trying to secure a private act of Parliament for the divorce. Initially such private suits were procedurally cumbersome and quite expensive. But this new cause of action for divorce did provide a passable road to relief and a fresh start to parties, of some means, who were trapped in marriages with faithless spouses. Through a series of amendments to the 1857 Act, culminating in the Divorce Acts of 1923 and 1937, procedures for divorce cases were simplified, costs for divorce suits were reduced, and the grounds for divorce were expanded to include desertion, cruelty, frigidity, habitual drunkenness, criminal conduct, and other forms of fault. As Lawrence Stone has demonstrated in a pathbreaking study, divorce rates accordingly slowly rose

---

67. 20 & 21 Vict. c. 85. See amendments in 21 & 22 Vict. c. 108; 22 & 23 Vict. c. 61; 23 & 24 Vict. c. 144; 27 & 28 Vict. c. 44; 28 & 29 Vict. c. 43; 29 Vict. c. 32; 30 Vict. c. 11; 41 & 42 Vict. c. 19; 7 Edw. 7 c. 12. For analysis of the formation of the Act and its inherent limitations, see Shanley, *Feminism, Marriage, and the Law*, 22–48. For subsequent reforms that expanded and equalized the rights of divorce, see Stone, *Road to Divorce*, 368–422.

68. For details, see A. K. R. Kiralfy, "Matrimonial Tribunals and Their Procedure," in Graveson and Crane, *A Century of Family Law*, 289–310.

in England. Divorce rates stood at 0.05 divorces per 1,000 marriages in 1870. They rose to 0.22 per 1,000 in 1920; 4.7 per 1,000 in 1970; 13.4 per 1,000 in 1985. At the same time, separation and annulment rates slowly dropped, with divorce increasingly viewed as the most effective and efficient remedy for broken marriages, particularly after the 1969 Divorce Act introduced divorce on the ground of "irretrievable breakdown," the cause for divorce that John Milton had advocated more than three centuries earlier.[69]

Third, the 1857 Matrimonial Causes Act ordered that, in cases of annulment or divorce, courts had discretion to place minor children in the custody of the parent who was best suited to provide their maintenance, nurture, and education. This reversed the traditional presumption that child custody belonged to the father—"however promiscuous, venereally diseased, brutal, or drunken" he might be.[70] The Act provided that the wife could claim custody, particularly where the children were of tender years or where the husband was found to be cruel, abusive, or unfit as a caretaker. Courts retained the traditional power to order guilty husbands to pay temporary or permanent alimony to innocent wives. Courts were also newly empowered to make "reasonable" allocations of marital property to the innocent wife and her custodial children. These 1857 provisions, together with subsequent Parliamentary legislation on infant custody, elementary education, and prevention of cruelty to children, slowly bent the law toward the presumption that custody of a child, particularly a minor, be granted to the mother and that the father be charged with support payments but entitled to visitation rights until the child reaches the age of majority.[71]

The reforms of marital property introduced by the 1857 Matrimonial Causes Act soon gave rise to more comprehensive legislation on women's rights to property. The Married Women's Property Acts of 1870, 1874, and 1882, plus subsequent revisions, slowly released married women from the traditional bonds of coverture that (at least formally) subsumed a woman's person and property into that of her husband's. Particularly after the 1882 Act, married women held title and control over the property they brought into the marriage or acquired after the wedding. They also gained increasing capacities to enter contracts of sale, lease, and mortgage of their properties, and the capacity to execute wills, trusts, and other forms of property disposition—in each case without necessary involvement of their husband and with ample protections against his intermeddling. Women also gained the capacity to sue or be sued regarding their property. Where such suits placed them in conflict with their husbands, traditional

69. Stone, *Road to Divorce*, 437–38. See also Max Rheinstein, *Marriage Stability, Divorce, and the Law* (Chicago: University of Chicago Press, 1971), 311–52.

70. Stone, *Road to Divorce*, 388.

71. See, e.g., 33 & 34 Vict. c. 75; 39 & 40 Vict. c. 79; 49 & 50 Vict. c. 27; 52 & 53 Vict. c. 44; 54 & 55 Vict. c. 3; 15 & 16 Geo. 5 c. 45. See discussion in Shanley, *Feminism, Marriage, and the Law*, 131–55; P. H. Pettit, "Parental Control and Guardianship," in Graveson and Crane, *A Century of Family Law*, 56–87.

rules of evidence that obstructed wives from testifying against their husbands were somewhat relaxed.[72]

These property law reforms brought ample rights to women who held ample wealth or who worked for more than subsistence wages outside the home. But the reforms were largely irrelevant to the large numbers of women who had no disposable property or who did not work outside the home.[73] Nonetheless, it was these early reforms of marital property law that strengthened the pursuit of the ideal of gender equality. In England at the turn of the twentieth century, property rights were still indispensable to social, economic, and political rights—for women as well as for men. As Millicent Garret Fawcett, a pioneer of women's rights, put it in 1886 with reference to the franchise: "Women's suffrage will not come, when it does come, as an isolated phenomenon; it will come as [a] necessary corollary of other changes which have been gradually and steadily modifying during this century the social history of our country. It will be a political change, not of a very great or extensive character in itself, based upon social, educational, and economic changes which have already taken place. It will have the effect of adjusting the political machinery of the country to the altered social conditions of its inhabitants."[74]

This proved to be a prophetic utterance. After their rights to property were enhanced, (married) women were able to gain broader rights and access to higher education, learned societies, trade and commercial guilds and unions, and a variety of professions, occupations, and societies historically closed to them. On the strength of these achievements, women ultimately gained the right to vote and to hold public office in 1918.[75] And in 1919, the Sex Disqualification (Removal) Act provided: "A person shall not be disqualified by sex or marriage from the exercise of any public function, or from being appointed to or assuming or carrying on any civil profession or vocation, or for admission to any incorporated society [or jury duty]."[76]

These sweeping legal changes in England implemented a number of the reforms advocated by Wollstonecraft, Mill, and a host of other exponents of the Enlightenment contractarian model. The Enlightenment gospel was by no means the only ideological catalyst for these reforms, nor was ideology the only impetus for reform. But it was the Enlightenment contractarian model of

72. See esp. 33 & 34 Vict. c. 93; 45 & 46 Vict. c. 75; 49 & 50 Vict. c. 52; 56 & 57 Vict. c. 71. See Shanley, *Feminism, Marriage, and the Law*, 103–30. For antecedent developments, see Susan Staves, *Married Women's Separate Property in England, 1660–1833* (Cambridge, MA: Harvard University Press, 1990).

73. Mary Ann Glendon, *The Transformation of Family Law: State, Law, and Family in the United States and Western Europe* (Chicago: University of Chicago Press, 1989), 111; see also generally idem, *The New Family and the New Property* (Toronto: Butterworths, 1981).

74. Quoted by Norman St. John-Stevas, "Women in Public Law," in Graveson and Crane, *A Century of Family Law*, 256–57.

75. See esp. Sandra Stanley Holton, *Feminism and Democracy: Women's Suffrage and Reform Politics in Britain, 1900–1918* (New York: Cambridge University Press, 1986).

76. 9 & 10 Geo. 6, c. 71.

marriage that helped to break traditional forms and introduce new reforms in English marriage and family law.

A similar legal transformation took place in America. In nineteenth-century America, family law authority Carl Schneider, writes,

> a family law answering a narrow range of questions about the legal (primarily property) relations of husbands and wives was gradually replaced by a family law that increasingly dealt with the termination of those relations, and that increasingly spoke to the relations between parent and child and between the state and the child. The breadth of this first transformation may be seen in the extraordinary range of family-law subjects that either originated or were wholly reformed in the nineteenth century: the law governing marriage formalities, divorce, alimony, marital property, the division of marital property, child custody, adoption, child support, child abuse and neglect, contraception and abortion.[77]

Other scholars have told various parts of this American story.[78] Mary Ann Glendon and Elaine Tyler May have demonstrated, in rich comparative perspective, the dramatic shifts in American law at the turn of the twentieth century toward greater freedom of contract in the formation and dissolution of marriage.[79] Marylynn Salmon and Michael Grossberg have documented, in exquisite detail, the gradual shifts toward equality of economic opportunity and proprietary capacity for married and unmarried women.[80] Frances Olsen and John Langbein have written at length on the "revolution in family wealth transmission" in early twentieth-century America.[81] Historians of children's rights have documented, from different archives, the emerging national concern for the protection and enhancement of children—a concern manifested in comprehensive new laws against child labor and child abuse, the rise of mandatory education for all children in public or private schools, the increased support, legitimation, and adoption opportunities for nonmarital children, and the expanding social welfare net for impoverished children and their families.[82] In

---

77. Carl E. Schneider, "Moral Discourse and the Transformation of American Family Law," *Michigan Law Review* 83 (1985): 1803, 1805.

78. For good overviews, see Michael Grossberg, *Governing the Hearth: Law and the Family in Nineteenth Century America* (Chapel Hill: University of North Carolina Press, 1985); Norman Basch, "Marriage and Domestic Relations," in *Cambridge History of Law in America*, ed. Michael Grossberg and Christopher Tomlins (Cambridge: Cambridge University Press, 2008), 245–79; Nancy F. Cott, *Private Vows: A History of Marriage and the Nation* (Cambridge, MA: Harvard University Press, 2000), 9–55.

79. See Glendon, *The Transformation of Family Law*; Elaine Tyler May, *Great Expectations: Marriage and Divorce in Post-Victorian America* (Chicago: University of Chicago Press, 1980).

80. Salmon, *Women and the Law of Property*; Grossberg, *Governing the Hearth*.

81. See, e.g., Frances Olsen, "The Family and the Market: A Study of Ideology and Legal Reform," *Harvard Law Review* 96 (1983): 1497; John H. Langbein, "The Twentieth Century Revolution in Family Wealth Transmission," *Michigan Law Review* 86 (1988): 722.

82. See Mary Ann Mason, *From Fathers' Property to Children's Rights* (New York: Columbia University Press, 1996); and sources and discussion in John Witte Jr., *The Sins of the Fathers: The Law and Theology of Illegitimacy Reconsidered* (Cambridge: Cambridge University Press, 2009), chap. 5.

some instances, such as divorce reform, American legislatures and courts were ahead of their English counterparts. On other topics, such as women's political and civil rights, the English Parliament blazed the trail.

This first wave of reforms brought many salutary changes to the Western legal tradition of marriage and the family, particularly for women and children. Marriages became easier to contract and easier to dissolve. Courts were more deferential to the wishes of the marital parties. Wives received greater protections in their persons and properties from their husbands, and greater access to and independence in their relationships outside the household. Ironically, the increased emphasis on the contractual nature of marriage also led to an increased solicitude for children—as protected third-party beneficiaries of both the marital contract of their parents and the social contract of their community. Children thus received greater protection from the abuses and neglect of their parents, and greater access to benefit rights of nurture, education, maintenance, and appropriate work. Young women, in particular, received greater freedom to forgo or postpone marriage, and greater access to social, political, and economic opportunities, regardless of their marital status.

Given the explosion of new legislation from the mid-nineteenth century forward, the state also came to replace the church as the principal external authority governing marriage and family life. The Catholic sacramental model of the family governed principally by the extended church, and the Protestant social model of the family governed by the congregation and broader Christian community gave way to a new model of marriage and the family ruled by the will of the parties subject to the limits of state law. To be sure, parties could still voluntarily subscribe to the internal marriage and family laws of their own religious communities and voluntarily accept the sexual discipline of the clergy. But the state's marriage and family laws were now supreme and in cases of conflict would preempt religious laws. This shift to state law became easy to rationalize in America with the rise to legal prominence of the maxim of "separation of church and state." But also in England, this preference for state governance of marriage came to dominate early twentieth-century discourse, even though the Church of England remained legally established.

It must be emphasized that this first wave of reforms, catalyzed by the Enlightenment contractarian model, sought to improve the Western legal tradition of marriage more than to abandon it. To be sure, the smug mockery of a Mill and the shattering iconoclasm of some Victorian radicals betrayed ample hostility to the tradition. But this radicalism was needed to fuel the reform movements of the nineteenth century—much as Luther's burning of the canon-law books in 1520 was needed to fuel the reforms of canon law in the sixteenth century. Just as Luther and his followers ultimately remained faithful to the Western legal tradition of marriage, so also did Mill and other nineteenth-century reformers.

Most legal reformers from 1850 to 1950 seemed to accept the ideal structure of marriage as a presumptively permanent union of a fit man and fit woman who had reached the age of consent. Most accepted the classic definition of the goods and goals of marriage: mutual love and affection, mutual procreation and nurture of children, mutual protection from spiritual and civil harms. The primary goal of these reformers was to purge the traditional household and community of its excessive paternalism, patriarchy, and prudishness, and thus to render the ideal structure and purpose of marriage into a greater reality for all. The changes inaugurated in this first wave of reform have been almost universally condoned in the West as salutary. Indeed, with the exception of the law of divorce and remarriage, almost all these legal changes in Anglo-American common law of marriage have now been incorporated into the modern theological platforms and social policies of Anglican, Protestant, and Catholic communities alike.[83]

MODERN LEGAL REFORMS IN AMERICA

The same judgment cannot be cast for the second transformation of Anglo-American marriage in the past half century. American reformers have been pressing the Enlightenment contractarian model of marriage to the more radical conclusions that Mill and others had suggested. The same Enlightenment ideals of individualism, freedom, equality, and privacy, which had earlier driven reforms of traditional marriage law, are now being increasingly used to reject traditional marriage laws altogether. The early Enlightenment ideals of marriage as a permanent contractual union designed for the sake of mutual love, procreation, and protection are slowly giving way to a new reality of marriage as a "terminal sexual contract" designed for the gratification of the individual parties.[84]

The Uniform Marriage and Divorce Act—both a "barometer of enlightened legal opinion" and a mirror of conventional custom on marriage[85]—reflects these legal changes. The Uniform Act defines marriage as "a personal relationship between a man and a woman arising out of a civil contract to which the consent of the parties is essential."[86] Historically, valid marriage contracts required the consent of parents or guardians, the attestation of two witnesses, church consecration, and civil licensing and registration. The Uniform Act requires only the minimal formalities of licensing and registration for all marriages, and parental consent for children under the age of majority. Marriages contracted in violation of these requirements are presumptively valid and immune from independent legal attack, unless the parties themselves petition for dissolution within ninety days of contracting marriage.[87] Historically, impediments of infancy, incapacity,

83. See sources and discussion in Don S. Browning and David A. Clairmont, eds., *American Religions and the Family: How Faith Traditions Cope with Modernization and Democracy* (New York: Columbia University Press, 2007); Don S. Browning and Bonnie Miller-McLemore, eds., *Children and Childhood in American Religions* (Rutgers, NJ: Rutgers University Press, 2009).

84. The phrase is from Pateman, *The Sexual Contract.*

85. Schneider, "Moral Discourse and Family Law," 1811.

86. See, e.g., Uniform Marriage and Divorce Act, s. 201 (hereafter, UMDA).

87. UMDA, ss. 202–6. Parents or guardians may seek dissolution of the marriage of their minor child or ward, provided the action is brought before the child reaches the age of majority. Ibid., s. 208.

inebriation, consanguinity, affinity, sterility, frigidity, bigamy, among several others, would nullify the marriage or render it voidable and subject to attack from various parties. Parties who married in knowing violation of these impediments would also be exposed to civil and criminal sanctions. The Uniform Act makes no provision for sanctions and leaves the choice of nullification to the parties alone. The Act does confirm the traditional impediments protecting consent—granting parties standing to dissolve marriages where they lacked the capacity to contract by reason of infirmity, mental incapacity, alcohol, drugs, or other incapacitating substances, or where there was force, duress, fraud, or coercion into entering a marriage contract.[88] But the Act limits the other impediments to prohibitions against bigamy and marriages between "half or whole blood relatives" or parties related by adoption.[89] And in many states that have adopted the Uniform Act, all impediments, save the prohibition against bigamy, are regularly waived in individual cases.

These provisions of the Uniform Marriage and Divorce Act reflect a basic principle of modern American constitutional law, first articulated clearly by the Supreme Court in *Loving vs. Virginia* (1967): "The freedom to marry has long been recognized as one of the vital personal rights essential to the orderly pursuit of happiness by free men. Marriage is one of the 'basic civil rights of man,' fundamental to our very existence and survival."[90] Using that principle, the Supreme Court has struck down, as undue burdens on the right to marry, a state prohibition against interracial marriage, a requirement that noncustodial parents obligated to pay child support must receive judicial permission to marry, and a requirement that a prisoner must receive a warden's permission to marry.[91] This same principle of freedom of marital contract, the draftsmen of the Uniform Act report, has led state courts and legislatures to peel away most of the traditional formalities for marriage formation.

The Supreme Court has expanded this principle of freedom of marital contract into a more general right of sexual privacy within the household. In *Griswold vs. Connecticut* (1965), for example, the Court struck down a state law banning the use of contraceptives by a married couple as a violation of their freedom to choose whether to have or to forgo children.[92] In a 1972 case, the Court stated its rationale clearly: "The marital couple is not an independent entity with a mind and heart of its own, but an association of two individuals,

88. Ibid., ss. 207–8.

89. Ibid., s. 207.

90. *Loving v. Virginia*, 388 U.S. 1, 12 (1967), quoting in part *Skinner v. Oklahoma*, 316 U.S. 535, 541 (1942). See also dicta in *Meyer v. Nebraska*, 262 U.S. 390, 399 (1923), and Universal Declaration of Human Rights (1948), art. 16–1: "Men and women of full age, without any limitation due to race, nationality, or religion, have the right to marry and found a family."

91. Respectively, *Loving v. Virginia*; *Zablocki v. Redhail*, 434 U.S. 374 (1978); *Turner v. Safely*, 482 U.S. 78 (1987).

92. See 381 U.S. 479 (1965). The same principle has been extended to protect access of unmarried couples, and even minors, to contraceptives. See *Eisenstadt v. Baird*, 405 U.S. 438 (1972); *Carey v. Population Services International*, 431 U.S. 678 (1977).

each with a separate emotional and intellectual makeup. If the right of privacy means anything, it is the right of the *individual*, married or single, to be free from unwanted governmental intrusion into matters so fundamentally affecting the person as the decision whether to bear or beget a child."[93] In *Roe vs. Wade* the following year, the Court extended this privacy principle to cover the right of abortion by a married or unmarried woman during the first trimester of pregnancy, without interference by the state, her husband, parents, or other third party. Still today, a married woman cannot be required to obtain permission from her husband to have an abortion.[94] In *Moore vs. East Cleveland* (1977), the Court struck down a municipal zoning ordinance that impaired members of an extended family from living together in the same household.[95] In *Kirschberg vs. Feenstra* (1981), the Court struck down a state statute that gave the husband as "head and master" of the family the right unilaterally to dispose of property held in common with his wife.[96] In all such cases, the private contractual calculus of the parties was considered superior to the general state interest in the health, safety, and welfare of its citizens.

State legislatures and courts have extended these principles of freedom of contact and sexual privacy to other aspects of marriage. Many states, for example, have abandoned their traditional reticence about enforcing prenuptial and marital contracts. The Uniform Premarital Agreement Act, adopted in roughly half the states today, allows parties to contract, in advance of their marriage, all rights pertaining to their individual and common property and "any other matter, including their personal rights and obligations, not in violation of public policy or a statute imposing a criminal penalty."[97] The Act does prohibit courts from enforcing premarital contracts that are involuntary, unconscionable, or based on less than full disclosure by both parties. But within these broad strictures, marital parties are left free to define in advance their own personal and property rights during marriage or in the event of separation, dissolution, or divorce.

Similarly, many states have left marital parties free to contract agreements on their own, or with a private mediator, in the event of temporary or permanent separation. The Uniform Marriage and Divorce Act provides that "parties may enter into a written separation agreement containing provisions for disposition of property owned by either of them, maintenance of either of them, and support, custody, and visitation of their children."[98] Such agreements are presumptively binding on a court, and absent a finding of unconscionability, courts will enforce

93. *Eisenstadt v. Baird*, 405 U.S. at 453.

94. See 410 U.S. 113 (1973). In *Planned Parenthood v. Casey*, 112 S. Ct. 2791 (1992), the Court upheld the right of abortion and struck down a state requirement of notification of one's spouse or the natural father as an "undue burden" upon this right.

95. See 431 U.S. 494 (1977).

96. See 450 U.S. 455 (1981).

97. Uniform Premarital Agreement Act, s. 3. The Act is duplicated in Walter O Weyrauch, Sanford N. Katz, and Frances Olsen, *Cases and Materials on Family Law* (St. Paul: West Publishing Co., 1994), 1111–1113.

98. UMDA, sec. 306(a).

these agreements on their own terms, reserving the right to alter those contract provisions that bear adversely on the couple's children. If the separation ripens into divorce, courts will also often incorporate these separation agreements into the divorce decree, again with little scrutiny of the contents of the agreement.

The same principles of freedom of contract and sexual privacy dominate contemporary American laws of divorce. Until the mid-1960s, a suit for divorce required proof of the fault of one's spouse (such as adultery, desertion, or cruelty) and no evidence of collusion, connivance, condonation, or provocation by the other spouse. Pleadings were public, and proceedings were recorded in public records. If plaintiffs met their burden of proof, the parties could be divorced. The innocent party, particularly the innocent wife, was generally granted custody of minor children. The guilty party, particularly the husband, was sometimes charged with ongoing obligations of alimony payments to the innocent spouse. The guilty party was also usually obligated to make child-support payments for dependent children. This law reflected the traditional view that marriage was ideally a perpetual bond of mutual love and support, that reconciliation of estranged spouses was the preferred remedy in cases of mutual fault, and that divorce was designed to relieve the innocent party of the company of a faithless spouse but to preserve at least some of the material benefits of the marriage.

Today this law of divorce has been abandoned. Every state has now promulgated a no-fault divorce statute, and virtually all states allow for divorce on the motion of only one party. The Uniform Marriage and Divorce Act has typical language, allowing for divorce if "both of the parties by petition or otherwise have stated under oath or affirmation that the marriage is irretrievably broken, or one of the parties has so stated and the other has not denied it."[99] Even if the innocent spouse forgives the fault and objects to the divorce, courts must grant the divorce if the plaintiff insists. The Uniform Marriage and Divorce Act and fifteen states have eliminated altogether consideration of the fault of either spouse, even if the fault rises to the level of criminal conduct. The remaining states consider fault only for limited questions of child custody, not for questions of the divorce itself. Husband and wife in effect have an unqualified "right to divorce."

Virtually all states have also ordered a onetime division of marital property between the divorced parties. Parties may determine their own property division through prenuptial or separation agreements, which the courts will enforce if the agreements are not unconscionable. But absent such agreements, courts will simply pool the entire assets of the marital household and make an equitable division of the collective property based on numerous factors. The Uniform Marriage and Divorce Act uses typical language:

> The court, without regard to marital misconduct, shall . . . equitably apportion between the parties the property and assets belonging to either or both however and whenever acquired, and whether the title thereto is in the name of the husband or wife or both. In making apportionment

99. UMDA, s. 305; see also ibid., ss. 302–3.

the court shall consider the duration of the marriage, any prior marriage of either party, antenuptial agreements of the parties, the age, health, station, occupation, amount and sources of income, vocational skills, employability, estate, liabilities, and needs of each of the parties, custodial provisions, . . . and the opportunity for each for future acquisition of capital assets and income.[100]

Such onetime divisions of property have largely replaced traditional forms of alimony and other forms of ongoing support, regardless of the fault, expectations, or needs of either party.[101]

These two reforms of the modern law of divorce serve to protect both the privacy and the contractual freedom of the marital parties. No-fault divorces free marital parties from exposing their marital discords or infidelities to judicial scrutiny and public record. Onetime marital property divisions give parties a clean break from each other and the freedom to marry another. Both changes, together, allow parties to terminate their marriages as easily and efficiently as they are able to contract them, without much interference from the state or from the other spouse.

These principles of contractual freedom are qualified in divorce cases involving minor children. The fault of the marital party does still figure modestly in current decisions about child custody. The rule introduced by the mid-nineteenth century reforms was that custody of children was presumptively granted to the mother, unless she was found guilty of serious marital fault or maternal incompetence. Proof of marital fault by the husband—particularly adultery, homosexuality, prostitution, or sexual immorality—virtually eliminated his chances of gaining custody, even if the wife was also at fault. Today the court's custodial decisions are guided by the proverbial principle of the "best interests of the child." According to the Uniform Marriage and Divorce Act, courts must consider at once the child's custodial preferences, the parents' custodial interests, "the interrelationship of the child with his [or her] parent or parents," "the child's adjustment to his [or her] home, school, or community," and "the mental and physical health of all parties involved."[102] "The court shall not consider the conduct of a proposed custodian that does not affect his relationship to the child," the Act concludes, setting a high burden of proof for the party who wants to make the spouse's marital fault an issue in a contested custody case. Under this new standard, the presumption of maternal custody is quickly softening, and joint and shared custody arrangements are becoming increasingly common.

Where one party is granted sole or principal custody, the noncustodial party is bound to make ongoing support payments—notwithstanding the current preference for a onetime marital property division. Indeed, several federal and state laws now mandate that noncustodial parents pay some 15–30 percent of

---

100. UMDA, s. 307 (Alternative A).
101. See ibid., s. 308, regarding temporary maintenance.
102. UMDA, s. 402.

their gross incomes in the form of child support and use unprecedented severity to punish delinquency in payment. Moreover, noncustodial parents are punished for their delinquency in caring for their children. Both federal and state laws punish deadbeat parents who shirk responsibilities of visitation and maintenance, neglect or abuse their children during temporary custody, and transport or detain their children against the wishes of the custodial parent.[103]

John Stuart Mill's ideal of marriage as "a private, bargained-for exchange between husband and wife about all their rights, goods, and interests" has become a legal reality in contemporary America. To be sure, courts do not enforce marital contracts as if they are simple commercial contracts. Some states, Milton Regan demonstrates, "will review the substantive fairness of certain antenuptial agreements at the time of enforcement to take account of changes in circumstances since execution. Some states will subject to particularly close scrutiny contract terms dealing with support, impose formalities beyond those required for ordinary contracts, or toll during marriage statutes of limitation relating to claims arising out of antenuptial agreements."[104] But the strong presumption in America today is that adult parties have free entrance into marital contracts, "free exercise" of marital relationships, and free exit from marriages once their contractual obligations are discharged.[105] Given the erosion of formalities for marriage formation and dissolution, these same freedoms of contract and sexual privacy are sometimes extended to other civil unions and domestic partnerships as well—a trend strongly encouraged by the American Law Institute's recent "Principles of the Law of Family Dissolution."[106] To be sure, parties are bound to continue to support their minor children, within and without marriage. But this, too, merely expresses another basic principle of contract law—that parties respect the reliance and expectation interests of their children, who are third-party beneficiaries of their marital or sexual contracts.

But John Locke's warning, echoing Thomas Aquinas, that the private contractualization of marriage will bring injustice and sometimes ruin to many women and children has also become a reality in America.[107] Premarital, marital, separation, and divorce agreements too often are not arm's-length

103. See, e.g., Uniform Child Custody Jurisdiction Act; Parental Kidnapping Prevention Act, 28 U.S.C.A. 1738A (1982), and further sources and discussion in Schneider, "Moral Discourse and Family Law," 1812–17; and Harry Krause, *Family Law in a Nutshell,* 3rd ed. (St. Paul: West Publishing, 1995), 225–332. The two acts are in Weyrauch et al., *Family Law,* 1114–25.

104. Milton C. Regan Jr., *Family Law and the Pursuit of Intimacy* (New York: New York University Press, 1993), 38; see also 148–52.

105. See, e.g., Martha Minow, "The Free Exercise of Families," *University of Illinois Law Review* (1991): 925.

106. American Law Institute, *Principles of the Law of Family Dissolution* (Newark, NJ: Lexis Nexis, 2002). See detailed analysis of this document in *Reconceiving the Family: Critique of the American Law Institute's Principles of Family Dissolution,* ed. Robin Fretwell Wilson (Cambridge: Cambridge University Press, 2006). I spend more time with the ALI Principles in Browning and Witte, *From Private Contract to Public Covenant.*

107. See Lenore J. Weitzmann, *The Marriage Contract: Spouses, Lovers, and the Law* (New York: Free Press, 1991).

transactions, and too often are not driven by rational calculus alone, however much courts and mediators insist that they are. In the heady romance of budding nuptials, parties are often blind to the full consequences of their bargain. In the emotional anguish of separation and divorce, parties can be driven more by the desire for short-term relief from the other spouse than by the concern for their own long-term welfare or that of their children. The economically stronger and more calculating spouse triumphs in these contexts. And in the majority of cases today, that party is still the man, despite the loud egalitarian rhetoric to the contrary.

"Underneath the mantle of equality [and freedom] that has been draped over the ongoing family, the state of nature flourishes," Mary Ann Glendon writes ominously.[108] In this state of nature, contractual freedom and sexual privacy reign supreme, with no real role for the state, church, or broader civil society to play. In this state of nature, married life has become increasingly "brutish, nasty, and short," with women and children bearing the primary costs.[109] The very contractarian gospel that first promised salvation from the abuses of earlier Christian models of marriage now threatens with even graver abuse.

Recall the statistics we recounted in the preface to this volume. Since 1975, roughly one-quarter of all pregnancies in America were aborted. One-third of all children were born to single mothers. One-half of all marriages ended in divorce. Two-thirds of all African American children were raised without fathers in their homes. Single mothers faced four times the rates of poverty, bankruptcy, and foreclosure. Children from broken homes were much more likely to have behavioral and learning problems, and suffered four times the rate of serious sexual or physical abuse. More than two-thirds of all juveniles and young adults convicted of major felonies since 1975 have come from single- or no-parent homes. While these numbers have improved somewhat in the past decade—owing in part to a strong new family-education movement and new family-policy initiatives—the burden of the modern family's breakdown falls disproportionately on women and children.

The modern welfare state has softened and spread out the costs of marital and family breakdown over the past two generations by supplying nonmarital children, single mothers, abandoned spouses, and aged parents with resources and

108. Glendon, *The Transformation of Family Law*, 146.
109. See, from different perspectives, Lenore J. Weitzman, *The Divorce Revolution: The Unexpected Social and Economic Consequences for Women and Children* (New York: Free Press, 1985); Barbara Dafoe Whitehead, *The Divorce Culture: How Divorce Became an Entitlement and How It Is Blighting the Lives of Our Children* (New York: Alfred A. Knopf, 1997); Paul R. Amato and Alan Booth, *A Generation at Risk: Growing Up in an Era of Family Upheaval* (Cambridge, MA: Harvard University Press, 1997); and Linda J. Waite and Maggie Gallagher, *The Case for Marriage: Why Married People Are Happier, Healthier, and Better Off Financially* (New York: Broadway Books, 2001); Elizabeth Marquardt, *Between Two Worlds: The Inner Lives of Children of Divorce* (New York: Three Rivers Press, 2005); David Blankenhorn, *The Future of Marriage* (New York: Encounter Books, 2007). For more recent literature, see detailed sources and discussion in Margaret Jane Brinig, *Family, Law, and Community: Supporting the Covenant* (Chicago: University of Chicago Press, 2010).

services traditionally supplied principally by their own natural kin. These are valuable advances that promote social justice and greater happiness for all. But the modern welfare state remains an expensive and risky modern experiment: it is not clear that it is a sustainable long-term solution even for the affluent West, let alone for underdeveloped or developing countries. In America today, those who depend on state social welfare often face bitter financial and emotional hardship and endless bureaucratic wrangling, and basic health insurance and decent public education are still beyond the reach of tens of millions. Better social welfare and health insurance systems are in place in Europe today. But these, too, depend on high median wealth in the population, all of which can disappear quickly, as the threats and realities of national bankruptcy in Iceland, Ireland, Greece, Spain, and Italy have recently reminded the world.

Perhaps we are simply witnessing today the birth pangs of a new marriage order that will feature the final removal of sexual stereotyping and exploitation; the real achievement of distributive justice to women, children, and the poor; the sensible pluralization of Western marriage laws to accommodate new global patterns of sexuality, kinship, and bonding. These are goals to which the Western legal tradition of marriage must surely aspire. And as Harold Berman reminds us, great legal revolutions always pass through radical phases before they reach an accommodation with the tradition that they had set out to destroy.[110]

It is hard to see the promise of these future benefits, however, in the current phase of the legal revolution of marriage in America. The rudimentary disquisitions on equality, privacy, and freedom offered by courts and commentators today seem altogether too lean to nourish the legal revolution of marriage and the family that is now taking place. The elementary deconstructions and dismissals of a millennium-long tradition of marriage and family law and life seem altogether too glib to be taken so seriously. The growing academic calls for the abolition of marriage seem so blind to the needs of children and to the dangers of depending on the benevolence of the state to carry on the work traditionally left to natural kinship networks.[111]

Yet the legal revolution marches on. And the massive social, psychological, and spiritual costs continue to mount up. The wild oats sown in the course of the modern sexual revolution have brought forth such a great forest of tangled structural, moral, and intellectual thorns that we seem almost powerless to cut it down. Chief Rabbi Jonathan Sacks of the United Kingdom puts it succinctly:

> Sex has become, for the first time since the conversion to Christianity of the Roman Emperor Constantine, an almost value-free zone. Whatever happens between two consenting adults in private is, most people now believe, entirely a matter for them. The law may not intervene; neither

---

110. Harold J. Berman, *Law and Revolution: The Formation of the Western Legal Tradition* (Cambridge, MA: Harvard University Press, 1983).

111. See arguments for and against the abolition of marriage illustrated in *Marriage Proposals: Questioning a Legal Status*, ed. Anita Bernstein (New York: New York University Press, 2006).

may social sanction. It is simply not other people's business. Together with a whole series of other changes, the result has been that what marriage brought together has now split apart. There has been a divorce between sex and love, love and marriage, marriage and reproduction, reproduction and education and nurture. Sex is for pleasure. Love is a feeling, not a commitment. Marriage is now deeply unfashionable. Nurture has been outsourced to specialized child carers. Education is now the responsibility of the state. And the consequences of failure are now delegated to social workers.[112]

112. Jonathan Sacks, *The Home We Build Together: Re[-]creating Society* (London: Continuum, 2007), 210.

Concluding Reflections

The foregoing chapters have recounted the rise of five theological models of marriage and their respective influences on the Western legal tradition: the Catholic sacramental model of the twelfth and thirteenth centuries, the Lutheran social model, the Calvinist covenantal model, the Anglican commonwealth model of early modern times, and the Enlightenment contractarian model of the past two centuries. These five theological models, each built in part on ancient classical, biblical, and patristic sources, have helped to drive the development of Western marriage and family law.

The foregoing chapters have emphasized the differences among these five models of marriage. *Theologically*, these differences can be traced to the genesis of these models in Catholic sacramental theology, Lutheran two-kingdom doctrines, Calvinist covenantal constructions, Anglican commonwealth theory, and Enlightenment contractarian theories, respectively. *Politically*, these differences can be seen in the shifts in marital jurisdiction. Catholics vested exclusive marital jurisdiction in the church. Anglicans left marital jurisdiction to church courts, subject to royal oversight and Parliamentary legislation. Calvinists assigned interlocking marital roles to local consistories and city councils. Lutherans consigned primary marital jurisdiction to the territorial prince or urban council.

Enlightenment thinkers reserved authority over marriage to the couple, subject to shrinking state oversight. *Legally*, these differences were most pronounced in the great debates over the form and function, and the length and limits, of rules governing marriage formation, maintenance, and dissolution; sexual alliances, preferences, and expression; spousal roles, rights, and responsibilities; and children's care, custody, and control.

To bring to light these historical Catholic, Protestant, and Enlightenment models, and their ancient prototypes, is neither to wax nostalgic about a prior golden age of the Western family, nor to write pedantic about arcane antiquities with no modern utility. These are the models that have shaped the Western family and the Western legal tradition, for better and for worse. These are the models that have to be dealt with—critically, constructively, and comprehensively—by jurists and theologians, preachers and politicians, activists and academics alike.

At minimum, it might be instructive to recognize that family transformations on a comparable scale to those we face today have been faced before—in the fifth, twelfth, sixteenth, and nineteenth centuries. Indeed, in some respects, the Western legal tradition of marriage in the past millennium has simply come full circle. Secret and private marriages were tolerated at the beginning of the last millennium, were condemned by Catholic and Protestant leaders in the middle of the millennium, but have now returned to prominence under Enlightenment theories of privacy. The single life was the celibate ideal of Catholics at the beginning of the millennium, was condemned by Protestants in the middle of the last millennium, and has now returned to social prominence under the inspiration of modern liberalism and privacy doctrine. Sexual pathos was prominent at the opening of this second millennium, with widespread concubinage, prostitution, voyeurism, polygamy, adultery, fornication, sodomy, wife and child abuse, teenage pregnancy, abortion, and much else. Sexual pathos has returned with equal pungency at the opening of the third millennium with the wildest frontiers of sexual prurience now only a mouse click way.

More fully conceived, these five traditional models, particularly those of Catholic and Protestant stock, have provided many enduring prescriptions for marriage that need to be pondered even in our day. First, these Western Christian traditions have seen that a marriage is at once a contractual, religious, social, and natural association, and that in order to survive and flourish, this institution must be governed both externally by legal authorities and internally by moral authorities. From different perspectives, Catholic and Protestant traditions have seen that marriage is an inherently communal enterprise, in which marital couples, magistrates, and ministers must all inevitably cooperate. After all, marital contracts are of little value without courts to enforce them. Marital properties are of little use without laws to validate them. Marital laws are of little consequence without canons to inspire them. Marital customs are of little cogency without natural norms and narratives to ground them.

The modern lesson in this is that we must resist the temptation to reduce marriage to a single perspective or to a single forum. A single perspective on marriage—whether religious, social, or contractual—does not capture the full nuance of this institution. A single forum—whether the church, state, or the household itself—is not fully competent to govern all marital questions. Marriage demands multiple forums and multiple laws to be governed adequately. American religious communities must think more seriously about restoring and reforming their own bodies of religious law on marriage, divorce, and sexuality instead of simply acquiescing in state laws. American states must think more seriously about granting greater deference to the marital laws and customs of legitimate religious and cultural groups that cannot accept a marriage law of the common denominator or denomination.[1]

Second, the Western tradition has learned to distinguish between betrothals and espousals, engagements and weddings. Betrothals were defined as a future promise to marry, to be announced publicly in the local community and to be fulfilled after a suitable waiting period. Espousals were defined as the present promise to marry, to be celebrated in a public ceremony before civil and/ or religious officials. The point of a public betrothal and waiting period was to allow couples to weigh the depth and durability of their mutual love. It was also to invite others to weigh in on the maturity and compatibility of the couple, to offer them counsel and commodities, and to prepare for the celebration of their union and their life together thereafter. Too long an engagement would encourage the couple to fornication. But too short an engagement would discourage them from introspection. Too secret and private a marriage would deprive couples of the essential counsel and gifts of their families and friends. But too public and routinized a marriage would deprive couples of the indispensable privacy and intimacy needed to tailor their nuptials to their own preferences. Hence the traditional balance of engagement and wedding, of publicity and privacy, of waiting and consummating.

The modern lesson in this is that we must resist collapsing the steps of engagement and marriage, and restore reasonable waiting periods between them, especially for younger couples. Today in most states, marriage requires only the acquisition of a license from the state registry, followed by solemnization before a licensed official—without banns, with little waiting, with no public celebration, without notification of others. So sublime and serious a step in life seems to demand a good deal more prudent regulation than this. It may well not be apt in every case to invite parents and peers, ministers and magistrates to evaluate the maturity and compatibility of the couple. Our modern doctrines of privacy and disestablishment of religion militate against this. But especially in the absence of such third parties, the state should require marital parties themselves to spend some time weighing their present maturity and prospective commitment. A presumptive waiting period of at least ninety days between formal engagement and

---

1. Joel A. Nichols, ed., *Marriage and Divorce in a Multi-Cultural Society: Multi-Tiered Marriage and the Boundaries of Civil Law and Religion* (Cambridge: Cambridge University Press, 2012); Rex Ahdar and Nicholas Aroney, eds., *Shari'a in the West* (Oxford: Oxford University Press, 2010).

wedding day seems to be reasonable, given the stakes involved—particularly if the parties are under twenty-five years of age. Comparable probationary waiting periods, particularly for younger parties, are routinely required to enter a contract for a home mortgage or to procure a license to operate a motor vehicle or handgun. Given the much higher stakes involved, marital contracts should be subject to at least comparable conditions.

Third, the Western tradition has learned to distinguish between annulment and divorce. Annulment is a decision that a putative marriage was void from the start, by reason of some impediment that lay undiscovered or undisclosed at the time of the wedding. Divorce is a decision that a marriage once properly contracted must now be dissolved by reason of the fault of the parties after their wedding. The spiritual and psychological calculus and costs are different in these decisions. In annulment cases, a party may discover features of their marriage or spouse that need not, and sometimes cannot, be forgiven—that they were manipulated or coerced into marriage; that the parties are improperly related by blood or family ties; that the spouse will not or cannot perform expected connubial duties; that the spouse misrepresented a fundamental part of his or her faith, character, or history. Annulment in such instances is prudent, sometimes mandatory, even if painful. In divorce cases, by contrast, the moral inclination (and for some, the moral imperative) is to forgive a spouse's infidelity, desertion, cruelty, or crime. In such instances, divorce might be licit, even prudent, but it often feels like, and is treated as, a personal failure even for the innocent spouse. The historical remedy was often calculated patience; early death by one spouse was the most common cure for broken marriages. In the modern age of fitness and longevity, this remedy is usually less apt.

The modern lesson in this is that not all marital dissolutions are equal. Today most states have simply collapsed annulment and divorce into a single action, with little procedural or substantive distinction between them. This is one (largely forgotten) source of our exponentially increased divorce rates; historically, annulment rates were counted separately. This is one reason why religious bodies have become largely excluded from the marital dissolution process; historically, annulment decisions were often made by religious bodies and then enforced by state courts. And this is one reason why no-fault divorce has become so attractive; parties often have neither the statutory mechanism nor the procedural incentive to plead a legitimate impediment. Parties seeking dissolution are thus herded together in one legal process of divorce—subject to the same generic rules respecting children and property, and prone to the same generic stigmatizing by self and others.

Fourth, the Western tradition has learned, through centuries of hard experience, to balance the norms of marital formation and dissolution. There was something cruel, for example, in a medieval Catholic canon law that countenanced easy contracting of marriage but provided for no escape from a marriage once properly contracted. The Council of Trent responded to this inequity in the *Tametsi* decree of 1563 by establishing several safeguards to the legitimate contracting of marriage—parental consent, peer witness, civil registration, and church consecration—so that an inapt or immature couple would be less likely to marry. There was something equally cruel in the rigid insistence of some early Protestants on reconciliation of all married couples at all costs, save those few who could successfully sue for divorce. Later Protestants responded to this inequity by reinstituting the traditional remedy of separation from bed and board for miserable couples incapable of either reconciliation or divorce.

The modern lesson in this is that rules governing marriage formation and dissolution must be balanced in their stringency, and separation must be maintained as a release valve. Stern rules of marital dissolution require stern rules of marital formation. Loose formation rules demand loose dissolution rules, as we see today. To fix the modern problem of broken marriages requires reforms of rules at both ends of the marital process. Today many states have tightened the rules of divorce, without corresponding attention to the rules of marital formation and separation. Such efforts, standing alone, are misguided. The cause of escalating divorce rates is not only no-fault divorce, as is so often said, but also no-faith marriage.

Fifth, the Western tradition has recognized that the household has multiple forms, that it can change over time and across cultures. The celebrated nuclear family of husband and wife, daughter and son is only one model that the Western tradition has cherished. It was common in the past to extend the theological and legal concept of the family to other kinds of units: the single household with one parent alongside children, stepchildren, adopted children, or grandchildren; the extended household, embracing servants, students, and sojourners or embracing three or four generations of relatives, with obligations of mutual care and nurture among them; the communal household of siblings or friends, single or widowed, with or without children; the spiritual household of brothers and sisters joined in the cloister, chantry, or charity, and dedicated to service of God, neighbor, and each other.

The modern lesson in this is that we must not cling too dogmatically to an ideal form of household. In the recent past, it was common for the establishment to look askance on the commune but approvingly on the community home, to look churlishly at the divorced but charitably on the widowed, to look suspiciously on the spinster but benevolently on the spurned. Today we accept, sometimes even admire, communes, the divorced, and spinsters—and make provision for them in our laws of taxation, property, and zoning as well as in our pastoral, diaconal, and pedagogical ministries. We now have other targets of suspicion, homosexuals and polygamists prominently among them.

Finally, the Western tradition has recognized that marriage and the family have multiple goods and goals. This institution might well be rooted in the natural order and in the will of the parties. Participation in it might well not be vital or even conducive to a person's salvation. But the Western tradition has seen that the marriage and family are indispensable to the integrity of the individual and the preservation of the social order.

In Catholic and Anglican parlance, marriage has three inherent goods, which Augustine identified as *fides, proles, et sacramentum*. Marriage is an institution of *fides*—faith, trust, and love between husband and wife, and parent and child, that goes beyond the faith demanded of any other temporal relationship. Marriage is a source of *proles*—children who carry on the family name and tradition, perpetuate the human species, and fill God's church with the next generation of saints. Marriage is a form of *sacramentum*—a symbolic expression of Christ's love for his church, even a channel of God's grace to sanctify the couple, their children, and the broader community.

In Lutheran and Calvinist parlance, marriage has both civil and spiritual uses in this life. On the one hand, the family has general civil uses for all persons, regardless of their faith. Marriage deters vice by furnishing a healthy sexual option to overcome the temptations of prostitution, promiscuity, pornography, and other forms of sexual pathos. Marriage cultivates virtue by offering love, care, and nurture to its members, and holding out a model of charity, education, and sacrifice to the broader community. Ideally, marriage enhances the life of a man and a woman by providing them with a community of caring and sharing, of stability and support, of nurture and welfare. Ideally, marriage also enhances the life of the child by providing the child with a chrysalis of nurture and love, with a highly individualized form of socialization and education. It might take a village to raise a child properly, but it takes a marriage to make one.

On the other hand, the family has specific "spiritual uses" for believers, ways of sustaining and strengthening them in their faith. The love of wife and husband can be among the strongest symbols we can experience of Yahweh's love for his elect, of Christ's love for his church. The sacrifices we make for spouses and children can be among the best reflections we can offer of the perfect sacrifice of Golgatha. The procreation of children can be among the most important words we have to utter.[2]

---

2. Cf. John E. Coons, "The Religious Rights of Children," in *Religious Human Rights in Global Perspective: Religious Perspectives*, ed. John Witte Jr. and Johan D. van der Vyver (The Hague: Martinus Nijhoff, 1996), 172: "In a faint echo of the divine, children are the most important Word most of us will utter."

Bibliography

Ahdar, Rex, and Nicholas Aroney, eds. *Shari'a in the West*. Oxford: Oxford University Press, 2010.

Albertus Magnus. *Quaestiones super animalibus*. Translated by Irven M. Resnick and Kenneth F. Kitchell Jr. as *Questions concerning Aristotle's "On Animals."* Washington, DC: Catholic University of America Press, 2008.

Albrecht, F. *Verbrechen und Strafen als Ehescheidungsgrund nach evangelischem Kirchenrecht*. PhD diss., Munich, 1903. Stuttgart: Enke, 1903. Reprint, Amsterdam: Schippers, 1962.

Amato, Paul R., and Alan Booth. *A Generation at Risk: Growing Up in an Era of Family Upheaval*. Cambridge, MA: Harvard University Press, 1997.

Ambrose of Milan. *Concerning Widows*. In *A Select Library of Nicene and Post-Nicene Fathers of the Christian Church: Second Series*, edited by Philip Schaff and Henry Wace, vol. 10. Reprint, Grand Rapids: Wm. B. Eerdmans Publishing Co., 1952.

American Law Institute. *Principles of the Law of Family Dissolution*. Newark, NJ: Lexis-Nexis, 2002.

Ames, William. *The Marrow of Theology*. Translated from the 3rd Latin ed., 1629, and edited by John D. Eusden. Boston: Pilgrim Press, 1968.

Amussen, Susan Dwyer. *An Ordered Society: Gender and Class in Early Modern England*. Oxford: Basil Blackwell, 1988.

Anciaux, Pierre. *The Sacrament of Penance*. New York: Sheed & Ward, 1962.

Andrewes, Lancelot. *Against Second Marriage after Sentence of Divorce with a Former Match, the Party Then Living*. Ca. 1610. Edited by James Bliss and included in Lancelot Andrewes, James Bliss, Henry Isaacson, and Sir John Harington, *Two Answers to Cardinal Perron, and Other Miscellaneous Works*. Library of Anglo-Catholic Theology 11. Oxford: J. H. Parker, 1854.

An Answer to a Book Intituled, The Doctrine and Discipline of Divorce. London: William Lee, 1644.

Apel, Johann. *Defensio Johannis Apelli ad Episcopum Herbipolensem pro suo coniugio*. Wittenberg: Johann Rau-Grunenberg, 1523.

———. *Isagoge per dialogum in quatuor libros Institutionum D. Justiniani Imperatoris*. Bratislaviae: A. Vincleri, 1540.

———. *Methodica dialectices ratio, ad jurisprudentiam accommodata*. Nuremburg: Fridericus Peypus, 1535.

Argula von Grumbach. *Ein christe[n]liche Schrifft einer erbaren Frawen, vom Adel*. Bamberg: [Erlinger], 1523.

———. *Grund und Ursach auss göttlichem Rechten, warumb Prior und Convent in Sant. Annen Closter zu Augspurg ihren Standt verändert haben*. Augsburg, 1526.

Aristotle. *The Ethics of Aristotle.* Translated and edited by J. A. K. Thomson. Reprint, New York: Penguin Books, 1965.

———. *The Politics of Aristotle.* Edited and translated by Ernest Barker. New York: Oxford University Press, 1962.

Arnórsdóttir, Agnes S. *Property and Virginity: The Christianization of Marriage in Medieval Iceland, 1200–1600.* Aarhus: Aarhus University Press, 2010.

Augustine of Hippo. *The City of God against the Pagans.* Translated by William M. Green. 7 vols. Cambridge, MA: Harvard University Press, 1963.

———. *On Marriage and Concupiscence.* In *A Select Library of Nicene and Post-Nicene Fathers of the Christian Church: Second Series,* edited by Philip Schaff and Henry Wace, vol. 5. Reprint, Grand Rapids: Wm. B. Eerdmans Publishing Co., 1952.

———. *On Original Sin.* In *A Select Library of Nicene and Post-Nicene Fathers of the Christian Church: Second Series,* edited by Philip Schaff and Henry Wace, vol. 5. Reprint, Grand Rapids: Wm. B. Eerdmans Publishing Co., 1952.

———. *Saint Augustine: Treatises on Marriage and Other Subjects.* Edited by R. J. Deferrari. Translated by Charles T. Wilcox. New York: Fathers of the Church, 1955.

———. *Sermons on New Testament Lessons.* In *A Select Library of Nicene and Post-Nicene Fathers of the Christian Church: Second Series,* edited by Philip Schaff and Henry Wace, vol. 6. Reprint, Grand Rapids: Wm. B. Eerdmans Publishing Co., 1952.

Baade, Hans W. "The Form of Marriage in Spanish North America." *Cornell Law Review* 61 (1975): 1–89.

Bailey, Derrick Sherwin. *The Man-Woman Relation in Christian Thought.* London: Longmans, New York: Harper & Bros., 1959.

———. *Thomas Becon and the Reformation in England.* Edinburgh: Oliver & Boyd, 1952.

Baker, J. Wayne. *Heinrich Bullinger and the Covenant: The Other Reformed Tradition.* Athens: Ohio University Press, 1980.

Balch, David, and Carolyn Osiek, eds. *Early Christian Families in Context: An Interdisciplinary Dialogue.* Grand Rapids: Wm. B. Eerdmans Publishing Co., 2005.

———. *Families in the New Testament World: Households and House Churches.* Louisville, KY: Westminster John Knox Press, 1997.

Baldwin, Claude-Marie. "John Calvin and the Ethics of Gender Relations." *Calvin Theological Journal* 26 (1991): 133–43.

Banner, Stuart. "When Christianity Was Part of the Common Law." *Law and History Review* 16 (1998): 27–62.

Baron and Feme: A Treatise of the Common Law concerning Husbands and Wives. London: Assigns of Richard and Edward Atkyns, Esq., 1700.

Basch, Norma. "Marriage and Domestic Relations." In *Cambridge History of Law in America,* edited by Michael Grossberg and Christopher Tomlins, 2:245–79. Cambridge: Cambridge University Press, 2008.

Bassett, W. J., ed. *The Bond of Marriage: An Ecumenical and Interdisciplinary Study.* Notre Dame, IN, and London: University of Notre Dame Press, 1968.

Baur, Jürgen. *Gott, Recht und weltliches Regiment im Werke Calvins.* Bonn: H. Bouvier, 1965.

Becon, Thomas. *The Booke of Matrimonie both Profitable and Comfortable for all Them that Entende Quietyly and Godly to lyue in the Holy State of honorable Wedlocke.* Ca. 1560. In Becon, *The First Part of the Bokes, which Thomas Becon made,* vol. 1. London: John Day, 1560–64. (2nd ed., in ESTC* 1710.)

———. *The Early Works of Thomas Becon, S.T.P.* Edited by J. Ayre for the Parker Society. 3 vols. Cambridge: Cambridge University Press, 1843.

---

* ESTC = English Short Title Catalogue, http://estc.bl.uk.

———. "A Homily of Whoredome and Unclennesse." In *Certayne Sermons, or Homilies, Appointed by the Kynges Maiestie.* London: Richard Grafton, 1547. (ESTC 13639.)

———. *A New Catechism.* 1560. In Becon, *The Early Works of Thomas Becon, S.T.P.,* edited by J. Ayre for the Parker Society, 2:1-410. Cambridge: Cambridge University Press, 1843.

———. Preface to [Heinrich Bullinger's] *The Golde Boke of Christen Matrimonye.* 1542. (ESTC 1723.)

Bels, P. "La formation du lien de mariage dans l'église protestante française (XVIe et XVIIe siécle)." In *Memoires de la société pour l'histoire de droit et des institutions de anciens pays bourguignons, comtois et romands* 27 (1966): 331–44.

Benedict, Philip. *Christ's Churches Purely Reformed: A Social History of Calvinism.* New Haven, CT, and London: Yale University Press, 2002.

Bentham, Jeremy. *The Works of Jeremy Bentham.* Edited by John Bowring. 11 vols. Edinburgh: William Tait, 1843.

Bergier, Jean-François, and Robert M. Kingdon, eds. *Registres de la compagnie des pasteurs de Genève au temps de Calvin.* 2 vols. Geneva: Droz, 1964.

Berman, Harold J. *Faith and Order: The Reconciliation of Law and Religion.* Grand Rapids: Wm. B. Eerdmans Publishing Co., 1993.

———. *Law and Revolution: The Formation of the Western Legal Tradition.* Cambridge, MA: Harvard University Press, 1983.

———. "The Religious Sources of General Contract Law." In *Faith and Order: The Reconciliation of Law and Religion,* 187–208. Atlanta: Scholars Press, 1993.

Bernstein, Anita, ed. *Marriage Proposals: Questioning a Legal Status.* New York: New York University Press, 2006.

Beust, Joachim von. *Tractatus connubiorum praestantiss: Iuris consultorum.* Vol. 1, Jena, 1606. Vols. 2–3, Frankfurt, 1617–18, 1742.

———. *Tractatus de iure connubiorum et dotium.* Frankfurt am Main: P. Schmidt, 1591.

Beza, Theodore. *De polygamia.* Ca. 1569. In *Tractationum theologicarum,* 2:1-49 2nd ed. Geneva: Eusthatii Vignon, 1582.

———. *De repudiis et divortiis.* 1568. In *Tractationum theologicarum,* 2:50-124 2nd ed. Geneva: Eusthatii Vignon, 1582.

Biéler, André. *L'homme et la femme dans la morale Calviniste.* Geneva: Labor & Fides, 1963.

Biggs, John M. *The Concept of Matrimonial Cruelty.* London: University of London Press, 1962.

Bishop, Joel P. *Commentaries on the Law of Marriage and Divorce, and Evidence in Matrimonial Suits.* Boston: Little, Brown & Co., 1852.

———. *New Commentaries on Marriage, Divorce, and Separation.* 2 vols. Chicago: T. H. Flood, 1891.

Blackstone, William. *Commentaries on the Law of England.* 4 vols. Oxford: Clarendon Press, 1765–69.

Blaisdell, Charmarie J. "Calvin's and Loyola's Letters to Women: Politics and Spiritual Counsel in the Sixteenth Century." In *Calviniana: Ideas and Influence of Jean Calvin,* edited by Robert V. Schnucker, 235–53. Kirksville, MO: Sixteenth Century Journal Publishers, 1988.

———. "Calvin's Letters to Women: The Courting of Ladies in High Places," *Sixteenth Century Journal* 13, no. 3 (1982): 67–84.

Blankenhorn, David. *The Future of Marriage.* New York: Encounter Books, 2007.

Blankenhorn, David, Don Browning, and Mary Stewart van Leeuwen, eds. *Does Christianity Teach Male Headship?* Grand Rapids: Wm. B. Eerdmans Publishing Co., 2004.

Blenkinsopp, Joseph. "The Family in First Temple Israel." In Leo G. Perdue et al., *Families in Ancient Israel,* 48–103. Louisville, KY: Westminster John Knox Press, 1997.

Bliss, James, ed. *Library of Anglo-Catholic Theology*. Oxford: J. H. Parker, 1854.

Blumenthal, David R. "The Images of Women in the Hebrew Bible." In *Marriage, Sex, and Family in Judaism*, edited by Michael J. Broyde and Michael Ausubel, 15–60. Lanham, MD: Rowman & Littlefield, 2005.

Bock, Kenneth. "The Moral Philosophy of Sir Henry Sumner Maine." *Journal of History of Ideas* 37 (1976): 147.

Boehmer, Iustus Henning. *Ivs ecclesiasticvm protestantivm vsvm modernvm ivxta seriem decretalium ostendens & ipsis rerum argumentiis illustrans*. 3 vols. Halle: Litteris et impendsis Orphanotrophei, 1714.

Bohatec, Josef. *Budé und Calvin: Studien zur Gedankenwelt des franzöischen Frühhumanismus*. Graz: H. Böhlaus Nachfolge, 1950.

———. *Calvins Lehre von Staat und Kirche: Mit besonderer Berücksichtigung des Organismusgedankens*. Aalen: Scientia Verlag, 1968.

———. *Calvin und das Recht*. 2nd ed. Reprint, Aalen: Scientia Verlag, 1991.

Boswell, John. *Same-Sex Union in Premodern Europe*. New York: Villard Books, 1994.

Bouwsma, William J. *John Calvin: A Sixteenth-Century Portrait*. New York: Oxford University Press, 1988.

Bradshaw, William. *A Marriage Feast: A Sermon on the Former Part of the Second Chapter of the Evangelist Iohn*. London: Edward Griffin, 1620.

Brecht, Martin. "Anfänge reformatorischen Kirchenordnungen bei Johannes Brenz." *Zeitschrift der Savigny-Stiftung für Rechtsgeschichte: Kanonistische Abteilung* 55 (1969): 322–47.

———. *Martin Luther*, trans. James L. Schaaf, 3 vols. Philadelphia and Minneapolis: Fortress Press, 1985-1993.

Breen, Quirinius. *John Calvin: A Study in French Humanism*. Grand Rapids: Wm. B. Eerdmans Publishing Co., 1931.

Brennan, Patrick M., ed. *The Vocation of the Child*. Grand Rapids: Wm. B. Eerdmans Publishing Co., 2008.

Brenz, Johannes. *Frühschriften*. Edited by Martin Brecht, Gerhard Schäfer, and Frieda Wolf. 2 vols. Tübingen: J. C. B. Mohr, 1970–74.

———. *Wie in Eesachen vnnd den fellen so sich derhalben zutragen nach Götlichem billichem rechten Christenlich zu handeln sey*. Nuremberg: Jobst Gutknecht, 1529; Wittenberg, 1531.

Brinig, Margaret Jane. *Family, Law, and Community: Supporting the Covenant*. Chicago: University of Chicago Press, 2010.

Brooke, Christopher N. L. *The Medieval Idea of Marriage*. Oxford and New York: Oxford University Press, 1991.

Brouwer, Hendrik. *De jure connubiorum, libri duo*. Delphis: Adrianum Beman, 1714.

Brown, Peter. *The Body and Society: Men, Women, and Sexual Renunciation in Early Christianity*. New York: Columbia University Press, 1988.

Browning, Don S. "Christian Ethics and the Family Debate: An Overview." *The Annual of the Society of Christian Ethics, 1995*, 251–62. Dallas: Society of Christian Ethics, 1995.

———. "Family Law and Christian Jurisprudence." In *Christianity and Law: An Introduction*, edited by John Witte Jr. and Frank S. Alexander, 163–84. Cambridge: Cambridge University Press, 2008.

———. *Marriage and Modernization: How Globalization Threatens Marriage and What to Do about It*. Grand Rapids: Wm. B. Eerdmans Publishing Co., 2003.

Browning, Don S., and Bonnie Miller-McLemore, eds. *Children and Childhood in American Religions*. Rutgers, NJ: Rutgers University Press, 2009.

Browning, Don S., and David A. Clairmont, eds. *American Religions and the Family: How Faith Traditions Cope with Modernization and Democracy.* New York: Columbia University Press, 2007.

Browning, Don S., and John Witte Jr. *From Private Contract to Public Covenant: What Can Christianity Offer to Modern Marriage Law.* Cambridge: Cambridge University Press, forthcoming.

Browning, Don S., et al. *From Culture Wars to Common Ground: Religion and the American Family Debate.* Louisville, KY: Westminster John Knox Press, 1997. 2nd ed., 2000.

Broyde, Michael J., and Michael Ausubel, eds. *Marriage, Sex, and Family in Judaism.* Lanham, MD: Rowman & Littlefield, 2005.

Bruce, Gustav M. *Luther as an Educator.* Westport, CT: Greenwood Press, 1979.

Brundage, James A. "Implied Consent to Intercourse." In *Consent and Coercion to Sex and Marriage in Ancient and Medieval Societies,* edited by Angeliki E. Laiou, 245–56. Washington, DC: Dumbarton Oaks Research Library and Collection, 1993.

———. *Law, Sex, and Christian Society in Medieval Europe.* Chicago: University of Chicago Press, 1987.

Bucer, Martin. *Common Places of Martin Bucer.* Edited by D. F. Wright. Appleford: Sutton Courtenay Press, 1972.

———. *De regno Christi.* 1555. Translated in *Melanchthon and Bucer.* Edited by Wilhelm Pauck. Philadelphia: Westminster Press, 1969.

Bugenhagen, Johannes. *Von dem ehelich en Stande der Bischoffe vnd Daiken.* Wittenberg: Josef Klug, 1525. Translated into Latin as *De coniugio episcoporum & diacorum.* Argentorati: I. Knoblouchus, 1526.

———. *Vom Ehebruch und Weglauffen.* Wittenberg, 1539–41.

———. *Was man vom Closter leben halten sol.* Wittenberg: Ge. Rhaw, 1529.

Bullinger, Heinrich. *The Decades of Henry Bullinger: The Fifth Decade.* Edited by Thomas Harding for the Parker Society. Cambridge: Cambridge University Press, 1852.

———. *Der christlich E[h]estand.* Zurich: Froschouer, 1540. Translated by Myles Coverdale as *The Christen State of Matrimonye.* London, 1541. (ESTC 4045.) Also translated by Miles Coverdale as *The Golde[n] Boke of Christen Matrimonye,* under Theodore Basille, pen name of Thomas Becon. London, 1542. (ESTC 1723.)

———. *The Decades of Henry Bullinger: The First and Second Decades.* Edited by Thomas Harding for the Parker Society. Cambridge: Cambridge University Press, 1849.

Bunge, Marcia, ed. *The Child in Christian Thought.* Grand Rapids: Wm. B. Eerdmans Publishing Co., 2001.

———, ed. *The Child in the Bible.* Grand Rapids: Wm. B. Eerdmans Publishing Co., 2009.

Bunny, Edmund. *Of Divorce for Adulterie, and Marrying Againe: That There is no Sufficient Warrant so to do.* Oxford: Joseph Barnes, 1610.

Burmeister, Karl Heinz. *Das Studium der Rechte im Zeitalter des Humanismus im deutschen Rechtsbereich.* Wiesbaden: G. Pressler, 1974.

Burn, Richard. *Ecclesiastical Law.* 6th ed. 4 vols. London: A. Stahan, 1797.

Cahill, Lisa Sowle. *Sex, Gender, and Christian Ethics.* Cambridge: Cambridge University Press, 1996.

Cairncross, John. *After Polygamy Was Made a Sin: The Social History of Christian Polygamy.* London: Routledge & Kegan Paul, 1974.

Calvin, John. *Calvin's Commentaries.* 47 vols. Edinburgh: Oliver & Boyd, 1843–59.

———. *Institutes of the Christian Religion.* 1559. Edited by John T. McNeill. Translated by Ford Lewis Battles. 2 vols. Philadelphia: Westminster Press, 1960.

———. *Institution of the Christian Religion.* 1536. Translated by Ford Lewis Battles. Atlanta: John Knox Press, 1975.

———. *Ioannis Calvini opera quae supersunt omnia*. Edited by G. Baum et al. 59 vols. Corpus reformatorum 29–87. Brunswick: C. A. Schwetschke & Filium, 1892.

———. *Letters of John Calvin*. Edited by Jules Bonnet. 4 vols. Reprint, New York: Burt Franklin, 1972.

———. *Sermons sur la Genèse*. Edited by Max Engammare. 2 vols. Neukirchen-Vluyn: Neukirchener Verlag, 2000.

———. *Supplementa Calviniana*. Neukirchen-Vluyn: Neukirchener Verlag des Erziehungsvereins, 1961–.

Capito, Wolfgang Fabricius. *Responsio de missa matrimonio & iure magistratus in religionem*. Argentorati: Per Vu. Rihelium, 1537.

Cardwell, Edward, ed. *The Reformation of the Ecclesiastical Laws*. Oxford: Oxford University Press, 1850.

———, ed. *Synodalia: A Collection of Articles of Religion, Canons, and Proceedings of Convocations in the Province of Canterbury*. Oxford: Oxford University Press, 1842.

Carlson, Eric Josef. *Marriage and the English Reformation*. Oxford: Basil Blackwell, 1994.

Carmichael, Gershom. *Natural Rights on the Threshold of the Enlightenment: The Writings of Gershom Carmichael*. Edited by James Moore and Michael Silverstone. Translated by Michael Silverstone. Indianapolis: Liberty Fund, 2002.

Catholic Church, Roman. *Catechism of the Catholic Church*. 2nd ed. Washington, DC: Libraria Editrice Vaticana, 2000.

———. *Catechism of the Council of Trent for Parish Priests*. Translated by John A. McHugh and Charles J. Callan. Rockford, IL: Tan Books & Publishers, 1982.

Chapais, Bernard. *Primeval Kinship: How Pair-Bonding Gave Birth to Human Society*. Cambridge, MA: Harvard University Press, 2008.

Chibi, A. A. "The Interpretation and Use of Divine and Natural Law in the First Marriage Crisis of Henry VIII." *Archiv für Reformationsgeschichte* 85 (1994): 265–86.

Choisy, Eugène. *L'état chrétien calviniste à Genève au temps de Théodore de Bèze*. Geneva: C. Eggimann, 1902.

———. *La theocratie à Genève au temps de Calvin*. Geneva: Droz, 1897.

Christoffersen, Lisbet, Kjell A. Modéer, and Svend Andersen, eds. *Law and Religion in the 21st Century: Nordic Perspectives*. Copenhagen: Djøf Publishing, 2009.

Chrysostom. *See* John Chrysostom.

Church of England. *The Book of Common Prayer*. 1559. Edited by John E. Booty. Charlottesville: University of Virginia Press, 1976.

———. *Sermons or Homilies Appointed to be Read in the Churches in the Time of Queen Elizabeth, of Famous Memory*. Liverpool: H. Forshaw, 1799.

Clark, Homer H., Jr. *The Law of Domestic Relations in the United States*. 2nd ed. St. Paul: West Publishing Co., 1988. Paperback, 1998.

Cleaver, Robert. *A Godly Form of Householde Gouernment*. London: Thomas Creede, 1598.

Clement. *The Instructor*. In *The Ante-Nicene Fathers*, edited by Alexander Roberts and James Donaldson, vol. 2. Reprint, Buffalo: Christian Literature Publishing Co., 1885.

———. *Stromata, or Miscellanies*. In *The Ante-Nicene Fathers*, edited by Alexander Roberts and James Donaldson, vol. 2. Reprint, Buffalo: Christian Literature Publishing Co., 1885.

Cocks, R. C. J. *Sir Henry Sumner Maine: A Study in Victorian Jurisprudence*. Cambridge: Cambridge University Press, 1988.

Code of Canon Law. Washington, DC: Canon Law Society of America, 1983.

Codex Theodosianus. Edited by Paul Krüger. 2 vols. Berlin: Weidmann, 1923–26.

Coing, Helmut, ed. *Handbuch der Quellen und Literatur der neueren europäischen Privatrechtsgeschichte*. 4 vols. Munich: Beck, 1973–88.

Coke, Sir Edward. *The First Part of the Institutes of the Lawes of England*. London, 1628.

————. *The Third Part of the Institutes of the Lawes of England*. London, 1644.

Coleman, Peter. *Christian Attitudes toward Marriage from Ancient Times to the Third Millennium*. London: SCM Press, 2004.

Colley, Linda. *Britons: Forging the Nation, 1707–1837*. New Haven, CT: Yale University Press, 1992.

Collins, John J. "Marriage, Divorce, and Family in Second Temple Judaism." In Leo G. Perdue et al., *Families in Ancient Israel*, 104–62. Louisville, KY: Westminster John Knox Press, 1997.

Coons, John E. "The Religious Rights of Children." In *Religious Human Rights in Global Perspective: Religious Perspectives*, edited by John Witte Jr. and Johan D. van der Vyver, 157–74. The Hague: Martinus Nijhoff, 1996.

Coons, John E., and Patrick M. Brennan. *By Nature Equal: The Anatomy of a Western Insight*. Princeton, NJ: Princeton University Press, 1999.

Cooper, Thomas. *An Answer in Defense of the Truth against the Apology of Private Mass*. 1562. Edited by W. Goode for the Parker Society. Cambridge: Cambridge University Press, 1850.

Corbett, Percy E. *The Roman Law of Marriage*. Oxford: Clarendon Press, 1930.

Corpus iuris civilis. Edited by Paul Krüger. 3 vols. Berlin: Weidmann, 1928–29.

Cosin, John. *The Works of the right reverend father in God John Cosin*. Vols. 1–4 edited by J. Sansom. Vol. 5 edited by J. Barrow. Library of Anglo-Catholic Theology 35–39. Oxford: John Henry Parker, 1843–55.

Cott, Nancy F. *Private Vows: A History of Marriage and the Nation*. Cambridge, MA: Harvard University Press, 2000.

Cottret, Bernard. *Calvin: A Biography*. Translated by M. Wallace McDonald. Grand Rapids: Wm. B. Eerdmans Publishing Co., 2000.

Coverdale, Myles. *Remains of Myles Coverdale*. Edited by George Pearson for the Parker Society. Cambridge: Cambridge University Press, 1846.

Crabites, Pierre. *Clement VII and Henry VIII*. London: George Routledge & Sons, 1936.

Cramer, Frédéric-August, ed. *Notes extraites des registres du Consistoire de l'Église de Genève, 1541–1814*. Geneva, 1853.

Cranmer, Thomas. *Miscellaneous Writings and Letters of Thomas Cranmer*. Edited by J. E. Cox for the Parker Society. Cambridge: Cambridge University Press, 1846.

Daly, James. *Sir Robert Filmer and English Political Thought*. Toronto: University of Toronto Press, 1979.

Davies, Kathleen M. "Continuity and Change in Literary Advice on Marriage." In *Marriage and Society: Studies in the Social History of Family*, edited by R. B. Outhwaite, 58–80. New York: St. Martin's Press, 1981.

D'Avray, David. "Marriage Ceremonies and the Church in Italy after 1215." In *Marriage in Italy, 1300–1650*, edited by T. Dean and K. J. P. Lowe, 107–15. Cambridge: Cambridge University Press, 1998.

————. *Medieval Marriage: Symbolism and Society*. Oxford: Oxford University Press, 2005.

Dawson, John P. *The Oracles of the Law*. Ann Arbor: University of Michigan Press, 1968.

Dean, T., and K. J. P. Lowe, eds. *Marriage in Italy, 1300–1650*. Cambridge: Cambridge University Press, 1998.

De Blécourt, A., and N. Japikse. *Klein plakkaatboek van Nederland*. Groningen: J. B. Wolters, 1919.

DeBoer, Willis P. "Calvin on the Role of Women." In *Exploring the Heritage of John Calvin*, edited by David E. Holwerda, 236–72. Grand Rapids: Baker Book House, 1976.

Deming, Will. *Paul on Marriage and Celibacy: The Hellenistic Background of 1 Corinthians 7*. 2nd ed. Grand Rapids: Wm. B. Eerdmans Publishing Co., 2004.

Demos, John. *A Little Commonwealth: Family Life in Plymouth Colony*. New York: Oxford University Press, 1970.

Dibden, Sir Lewis, and Sir Charles Chadwick Healey. *English Church Law and Divorce*. London: J. Murray, 1912.

Dickens, Arthur G. *The English Reformation*. New York: Schocken Books, 1964.

Didascalia Apostolorum. Translated by R. Hugh Connolly. Oxford: Clarendon Press, 1929.

Dieterich, Hartwig. *Das protestantische Eherecht in Deutschland bis zur Mitte des 17. Jahrhunderts*. Munich: Claudius, 1970.

Dietrich, Hans Gert. *Evangelisches Ehescheidungsrecht nach den Bestimmungen der deutschen Kirchenordnungen des 16. Jahrhunderts*. Erlangen: A. Vollrath, 1892.

Digges, Dudley. *The Unlawfulnesse of Subjects, taking up Armes Against their Soveraigne*. [London,] 1644.

Dixon, Suzanne. *The Roman Family*. Baltimore: Johns Hopkins University Press, 1992.

———. "The Sentimental Ideal of the Roman Family." In *Marriage, Divorce, and Children in Ancient Rome*, ed. Beryl Rawson, 99–113. Oxford: Oxford University Press, 1991.

Dod, John, and Robert Cleaver. *A Plaine and Familiar Exposition of the Ten Commandments, with a methodicall short Catechisme, Containing Briefly all the Principall Grounds of Christian Religion*. London: Thomas Man, 1604. (ESTC 6968.)

Donahue, Charles, Jr. *Law, Marriage and Society in the Later Middle Ages*. Cambridge: Cambridge University Press, 2007.

———. "The Policy of Alexander the Third's Consent Theory of Marriage." In *Proceedings of the Fourth International Congress of Medieval Canon Law*, edited by Stephan Kuttner, 251–81. Vatican City: Biblioteca Apostolica Vaticana, 1976.

Donne, John. *The Works*. 6 vols. Edited by Henry Alford. Cambridge: Cambridge University Press, 1839.

Duns Scotus, John. *Opera omnia*. Reprint, Farnborough: Gregg, 1969.

Dykema, Peter A., and Heiko A. Oberman, eds. *Anticlericalism in Late Medieval and Early Modern Europe*. Leiden: E. J. Brill, 1993.

Echt-reglement, over de steden, ende ten platten lande, in de heerlijkheden, ende dorpen staande onder de Generaliteyt. s'Gravenhage: Hillebrandt van Wouw, 1664.

Eells, Hasting. *The Attitude of Martin Bucer toward the Bigamy of Philip of Hesse*. New Haven: Yale University Press, 1924.

Elazar, Daniel J. *Covenant and Commonwealth: From Christian Separation through the Protestant Reformation*. New Brunswick, NJ: Transaction Publishers, 1996.

Elliott, Dyan. *Spiritual Marriage: Sexual Abstinence in Medieval Wedlock*. Princeton, NJ: Princeton University Press, 1993.

Elshtain, Jean Bethke. *Public Man, Private Woman: Women in Social and Political Thought*. Princeton, NJ: Princeton University Press, 1981.

Elwood, Christopher. "Calvin, Beza, and the Defense of Marriage in the Sixteenth Century." In *Calvin, Beza, and Later Calvinism*, edited by David Foxgrover, 11–37. Grand Rapids: Calvin Studies Society, 2006.

Enchiridion symbolorum, definitionum et declarationum de rebus fidei et morum. Edited by H. Denzinger and A. Schoenmetzer. 33rd ed. Fribourg: Herder, 1965.

Epstein, Louis M. *Marriage Laws in the Bible and the Talmud*. Cambridge, MA: Harvard University Press, 1942.

Erasmus. *See* Sarcerius, Basilius.

Erler, Adalbert, and Ekkehard Kaufmann, eds. *Handwörterbuch zur deutschen Rechtsgeschichte*. Berlin: E. Schmidt Verlag, 1984.

Esmein, Adhémar. *Le mariage en droit canonique*. 2nd ed. 2 vols. Paris: Sirrey, 1929–35.

Falk, Ze'ev W. *Jewish Matrimonial Law in the Middle Ages*. Oxford: Oxford University Press, 1966.

Fauve-Chamoux, Antoinette. "Marriage, Widowhood, and Divorce." In *Family Life in Early Modern Times: 1500–1789*. Edited by David I. Kertzer and Marzio Barbagli, 221–56. New Haven, CT: Yale University Press, 2001.

Fellhauer, David E. "The *consortium omnis vitae* as a Juridical Element of Marriage." *Studia canonica* 13 (1979): 7–171.

Fenner, Dudley. *The Artes of Logike and Rhetotike . . . : Together with Examples of the same for Methode, in the gouernment of the Familie*. Middleburg: R. Shiders, 1584.

———. *Sacra theologica sive veritas quae est secundum pietatem*. London: T. Dawson, ca. 1585.

Filmer, Robert. *Patriarcha and Other Political Works*. Edited by Peter Laslett. Oxford: Oxford University Press, 1949.

Finnis, John. *Aquinas: Moral, Political, and Legal Theory*. Oxford: Oxford University Press, 1998.

Firth, C. H., and R. S. Rait, eds. *Acts and Ordinances of the Interregnum, 1642–1660*. 3 vols. London: H. M. Stationery Printing Office, 1911.

Fischer, H. F. W. D. "De gemengde huwelijken tussen Katholiken en Protestanten in de Nederlanden van de XVIe tot de XVIIe eeuw." *Tijdschrift voor rechtsgeschiedenis / Revue d'histoire du droit* 31 (1963): 463–85.

Fordyce, David. *The Elements of Moral Philosophy in Three Books*. 1754. Edited by Thomas Kennedy. Indianapolis: Liberty Fund, 2003.

Foster, Shirley. *Victorian Women's Fiction: Marriage, Freedom, and the Individual*. London: Croom Helm, 1985.

Foxgrover, David, ed. *Calvin, Beza, and Later Calvinism*. Grand Rapids: Calvin Studies Society, 2006.

Francis, Mark. "Henry Sumner Maine: Victorian Evolution and Political Theory." *History of European Ideas* 19 (1994): 753–60.

Franzen, August. *Zölibat und Priesterehe in der Auseinandersetzung der Reformationszeit und der katholische Reform des 16. Jahrhunderts*. Münster: Aschendorff, 1969.

Frassek, Ralf. *Eherecht und Ehegerichtsbarkeit in der Reformationszeit: Der Aufbau neuer Rechtsstrukturen im sächsischen Raum unter besonderer Berücksichtigung der Wirkungsgeschichte des Wittenberger Konsistoriums*. Tübingen: Mohr Siebeck, 2005.

Friedberg, Emil, ed. *Corpus iuris canonici*. 2 vols. Leipzig: Bernhard Tauchnitz, 1879–81.

———. *Das Recht der Eheschliessung in seiner geschichtlichen Entwicklung*. Leipzig: Bernhard Tauchnitz, 1875. Reprint, Aalen: Scientia Verlag, 1968.

Friedman, Mordechai Akiva. *Jewish Marriage in Palestine: A Cairo Geniza Study*. 2 vols. Tel Aviv and New York: Jewish Theological Seminary of America, 1981.

Frier, Bruce W., and Thomas A. J. McGinn. *A Casebook on Roman Family Law*. Oxford: Oxford University Press, 2004.

Friesen, Joseph. *Geschichte des kanonischen Eherechts bis zum Verfall der Glossenliteratur*. 2nd ed. Reprint, Aalen: Scientia Verlag, 1963.

Fulke, William. *A Defence of the Sincere and True Translations of the Holy Scriptures into the English Tongue*. Edited by C. H. Hartshorne for the Parker Society. Cambridge: Cambridge University Press, 1843.

———. *Stapleton's Fortress Overthrown*. Edited by R. Gibbings for the Parker Society. Cambridge: Cambridge University Press, 1848.

Fuller, Lon L. *The Morality of Law*. Rev. ed. New Haven, CT: Yale University Press, 1964.

Gaius. *Gaius' institutiones*. Edited by Paul Krüger and William Studemund. Berlin: Weidmann, 1877.

Gamble, Richard C., ed. *Calvin's Work in Geneva*. New York and London: Garland Publishing Co., 1992.

Ganoczy, Alexandre. *Le jeune Calvin: Genèse et évolution de sa vocation réformatrice*. Wiesbaden: F. Steiner, 1966.

Gardner, Jane. *Women in Roman Law and Society*. London: Croom Helm, 1986.

Gataker, Thomas. *A Good Wife: God's Gift, and, A Wife Indeed: Two Marriage Sermons*. London: John Haviland, 1623. (ESTC 11659.)

Geffcken, Friedrich Heinrich. *Zur ältesten Geschichte und ehegerichtlichen Praxis des Leipziger Konsistoriums*. Freiburg: Mohr, 1894.

Gehrke, Heinrich. *Die Rechtsprechungs- und Konsilienliteratur Deutschland bis zum Ende des alten Reichs*. Frankfurt am Main, Universität, Diss. für das Fach Rechtswissenschaft, 1972.

George, Charles H., and Katherine George. *The Protestant Mind of the English Reformation, 1570–1640*. Princeton, NJ: Princeton University Press, 1961.

Gibson, Edmund. *Codex juris ecclesiastici Anglicani*. 2nd ed. 2 vols. London: J. Baskett, 1713.

Glendon, Mary Ann. *Abortion and Divorce in Western Law*. Chicago: University of Chicago Press, 1988.

———. *The New Family and the New Property*. Toronto: Butterworths, 1981.

———. *State, Law, and Family: Family Law in Transition in the United States and Western Europe*. Boston and Dordrecht: Martinus Nijhoff Publishers, 1977.

———. *The Transformation of Family Law: State, Law, and Family in the United States and Western Europe*. Chicago: University of Chicago Press, 1989.

Godolphin, John. *Repertorium canonicum*. 3rd ed. London: Assigns of Richard & Edward Atkins, 1687.

Gouge, William. *Of Domesticall Duties: Eight Treatises*. London: John Haviland, 1622. (ESTC 12119.) 2nd ed., London: John Beale, 1626.

Gough, John W. *The Social Contract: A Critical Study of Its Development*. Oxford: Clarendon Press, 1936.

Graebner, Otto. *Ueber Desertion und Quasidesertion als Scheidungsgrund nach dem evangelischen Kirchenrecht*. PhD diss., Leipzig, 1882. Colberg: C. Jancke and Dr. P. Jancke, 1882.

Graham, W. Fred. *The Constructive Revolutionary: John Calvin and His Socio-Economic Impact*. Atlanta: John Knox Press, 1978.

———, ed. *Later Calvinism: International Perspectives*. Kirksville, MO: Sixteenth Century Journal Publishers, 1994.

Gratian. *The Treatise on Laws with the Ordinary Gloss*. Translated by James Gordley and Augustine Thompson, OP. Washington, DC: Catholic University of America Press, 1993.

Graveson, R. H., and F. R. Crane, eds. *A Century of Family Law, 1857–1957*. London: Sweet & Maxwell, 1957.

Gray, Peter B., and Kermyt G. Anderson. *Fatherhood: Evolution and Human Paternal Behavior*. Cambridge, MA: Harvard University Press, 2010.

Greaves, Richard L. *Society and Religion in Elizabethan England*. Minneapolis: University of Minnesota Press, 1981.

Gregory of Nyssa. *On Virginity*. In *A Select Library of Nicene and Post-Nicene Fathers of the Christian Church: Second Series*, edited by Philip Schaff and Henry Wace, vol. 5. Reprint, Grand Rapids: Wm. B. Eerdmans Publishing Co., 1952.

Grey, Thomas C. *The Legal Enforcement of Morality*. New York: Knopf, 1983.

Griffith, Matthew. *Bethel: or, A Forme for Families*. London: J. Days, 1633.
Grindal, Edmund. *The Remains of Edmund Grindal*. Edited by W. Nicholson for the Parker Society. Cambridge: Cambridge University Press, 1843.
Grossberg, Michael. *Governing the Hearth: Law and the Family in Nineteenth Century America*. Chapel Hill: University of North Carolina Press, 1985.
Grossberg, Michael, and Christopher Tomlins, eds. *Cambridge History of Law in America*. 3 vols. Cambridge: Cambridge University Press, 2008.
Grotius, Hugo. *De jure belli ac pacis*. Paris: Buon, 1625.
———. *The Jurisprudence of Holland*. Translated and edited by R. W. Lee. Oxford: Clarendon Press, 1926.
Grubbs, Judith Evans. *Law and Family in Late Antiquity: The Emperor Constantine's Marriage Legislation*. Oxford: Clarendon Press, 1995.
———. "Marrying and Its Documentation in Later Roman Law." In *To Have and to Hold: Marrying and Its Documentation in Western Christendom, 400–1600*, edited by Philip L. Reynolds and John Witte Jr., 43–94. Cambridge: Cambridge University Press, 2007.
———. "Promoting Pietas in Roman Law." in *A Companion to Families in the Greek and Roman Worlds*, edited by Beryl Rawson, 377–92. Blackwell Companions to the Ancient World. Chichester: John Wiley & Sons, 2011.
Hagen, Kenneth. "From Testament to Covenant in the Early Sixteenth Century." *Sixteenth Century Journal* 3 (1972): 1–24.
Haller, William. *Liberty and Reformation in the Puritan Revolution*. New York: Columbia University Press, 1955.
Haller, William, and Malleville Haller. "The Puritan Art of Love." *Huntington Library Quarterly* 5 (1941–42): 235–72.
Harakas, Stanley. "Covenant Marriage: Reflections from an Eastern Orthodox Perspective." In *Covenant Marriage in Comparative Perspective*, edited by John Witte Jr. and Eliza Ellison, 92–123. Grand Rapids: Wm. B. Eerdmans Publishing Co., 2005.
Harkness, Georgia. *John Calvin: The Man and His Ethics*. New York: Henry Holt, 1931.
Harmless, William, SJ. "Christ the Pediatrician: Augustine on the Diagnosis and Treatment of the Injured Vocation of the Child." In *The Vocation of the Child*, edited by Patrick M. Brennan, 127–51. Grand Rapids: Wm. B. Eerdmans Publishing Co., 2008.
Harrington, William. *In this boke are conteyned the comendacions of matrimonye the manner & forme of contractyng solemonysynge and lyvyng in the same etc.* London: Roberte Redman, 1528.
Hartmann, Julius, and Karl Jager. *Johannes Brenz nach gedruckten und ungedruckten Quellen*. 2 vols. Hamburg: F. Petrus, 1840.
Harvey, Judith W. "The Influence of the Reformation on Nürnberg Marriage Laws, 1520–1535." PhD diss., Ohio State University, 1972.
Haskell, Paul G. "Premarital Estate Contract and Social Policy." *North Carolina Law Review* 57 (1979): 415–437.
Haverkamp, Alfred, ed. *Haus und Familie in der spätmittelalterlichen Stadt*. Tübingen: J. C. B. Mohr, 1984.
Hayeck, F. A. *John Stuart Mill and Harriet Taylor: Their Friendship and Subsequent Marriage*. London: Routledge & Kegan Paul, 1951.
H[eale], W[illiam]. *An Apologie for Women, or, Opposition to Mr. Dr. G. his Assertion . . . That it was Lawful for Husbands to Beate Their Wives*. Oxford: Joseph Barnes/Barres, 1609. 2nd ed., 1614.

Heaney, S. P. *The Development of the Sacramentality of Marriage from Anselm of Laon to Thomas Aquinas.* Washington, DC: Catholic University of America Press, 1963.

Heckel, Johannes. "Das Decretum Gratiani und das deutsche evangelische Kirchenrecht." *Studia Gratiana* 3 (1955): 483–538.

Helmholz, Richard H. "Canon Law in Post-Reformation England." In *Canon Law in Protestant Lands*, edited by Richard H. Helmholz, 203–21. Berlin: Duncker & Humblot, 1992.

———, ed. *Canon Law in Protestant Lands.* Berlin: Duncker & Humblot, 1992.

———. "Marriage Contracts in Medieval England." in *To Have and to Hold: Marrying and Its Documentation in Western Christendom, 400–1600*, edited by Philip L. Reynolds and John Witte Jr., 260–86. Cambridge: Cambridge University Press, 2007.

———. *Marriage Litigation in Medieval England.* Cambridge: Cambridge University Press, 1974.

———. *Roman Canon Law in Reformation England.* Cambridge: Cambridge University Press, 1990.

———. *The Spirit of the Classical Canon Law.* Athens: University of Georgia Press, 1996.

Hemmingsen, Niels. *Libellus de conjugio, repudio, et divortio.* Leipzig: Steinman, 1578.

Hendrix, Scott. "Masculinity and Patriarchy in Reformation Germany." *Journal of the History of Ideas* 56 (1995): 177–93.

Herbert, George. *The Works of George Herbert.* Edited F. E. Hutchinson. Oxford: Clarendon Press, 1941.

Hersch, Karen K. *The Roman Wedding: Ritual and Meaning in Antiquity.* Cambridge, MA: Harvard University Press, 2010.

Hesse, Hans. *Evangelisches Ehescheidungsrecht in Deutschland.* Bonn: H. Bouvier, 1960.

Hesselink, I. John. *Calvin's Concept of the Law.* Allison Park, PA: Pickwick Publishers, 1992.

Hill, Christopher. *The Century of Revolution, 1603–1714.* New York: W. W. Norton, 1961.

———. *The World Turned Upside Down: Radical Ideas during the English Revolution.* New York: Viking Press, 1972.

Hoffmann, H. *Das Kirchenverfassung der niederlandischen Reformierten bis zum Beginne der dordrechter Nationalsynode von 1618–1619.* 2nd ed. Tübingen: J. C. B. Mohr, 1907.

Holton, Sandra Stanley. *Feminism and Democracy: Women's Suffrage and Reform Politics in Britain, 1900–1918.* New York: Cambridge University Press, 1986.

Holwerda, David E., ed. *Exploring the Heritage of John Calvin.* Grand Rapids: Baker Book House, 1976.

Home, Henry. *Essays on the Principles of Morality and Natural Religion.* 1779. Edited by Mary Catherine Moran. 3rd ed. Indianapolis: Liberty Fund, 2005.

———. *Sketches of the History of Man, Considerably Enlarged by the Latest Additions and Corrections of the Author.* Edited by James A. Harris. 3 vols. Indianapolis: Liberty Fund, 2007.

Hooker, Richard. *The Work of Mr. Richard Hooker in Eight Books of the Laws of Ecclesiastical Polity with Several Other Treatises.* Edited by Isaac Walton. 3 vols. London: W. Clark, 1821.

Hooper, John. *Early Writings of John Hooper.* Edited by S. Carr for the Parker Society. Cambridge: Cambridge University Press, 1843.

Hopf, Constantin. *Martin Bucer and the English Reformation.* Oxford: Basil Blackwell, 1946.

Horstman, Allen. *Victorian Divorce.* New York: St. Martin's Press, 1985.

Houlbrooke, Ralph. *Church Courts and the People during the English Reformation, 1520–1570.* Oxford: Oxford University Press, 1979.

Howard, George Elliott. *A History of Matrimonial Institutions.* 3 vols. Chicago: University of Chicago Press, 1904.

Hugenberger, Gordon P. *Marriage as Covenant: A Study of Biblical Law and Ethics Governing Marriage Developed from the Perspective of Malachi.* Leiden: E. J. Brill, 1994.

Hugh of St. Victor. *De beatae Mariae Virginis virginitate.* In Patrologia latina, 176:857–76.

———. *On the Sacraments of the Christian Faith.* Translated by R. Deferrari. Cambridge, MA: Harvard University Press, 1951.

Hume, David. *Enquiries concerning the Human Understanding and concerning the Principles of Morals.* 1777. Edited by L. A. Selby-Bigge. 2nd ed. Oxford: Clarendon Press, 1902. Reprint, 1963.

———. *Essays Moral, Political, and Literary.* Edited by Eugene F. Miller. Rev. ed. Indianapolis: Liberty Fund, 1987.

Hunter, David G. *Marriage, Celibacy, and Heresy in Ancient Christianity: The Jovinianist Controversy.* Oxford: Oxford University Press, 2007.

———, ed. *Marriage in the Early Church.* Minneapolis: Fortress Press, 1992.

———. "Marrying and the *Tabulae Nuptiales* in Roman North Africa from Tertullian to Augustine." In *To Have and to Hold: Marrying and Its Documentation in Western Christendom, 400–1600,* edited by Philip L. Reynolds and John Witte Jr., 95–113. Cambridge: Cambridge University Press, 2007.

Hurstfield, Joel. *The Queen's Wards: Wardship and Marriage under Elizabeth I.* Cambridge: Cambridge University Press, 1958.

Hutcheson, Frances. *Logic, Metaphysics, and the Natural Sociability of Mankind.* Edited by James Moore and Michael Silverthorne. Indianapolis: Liberty Fund, 2006.

———. *Philosophiae moralis institutio compendiaria: With a Short Introduction to Moral Philosophy.* Edited by Luigi Turco. Indianapolis: Liberty Fund, 2007.

Ingram, Martin. *Church Courts, Sex and Marriage in England, 1570–1640.* Cambridge: Cambridge University Press, 1987.

Isidore of Seville. *The Etymologies of Isidore of Seville.* Translated by Stephen A. Barney. Cambridge: Cambridge University Press, 2006.

Jackson, Timothy P., ed. *The Best Love of the Child: Being Loved and Being Taught to Love as the First Human Right.* Grand Rapids: Wm. B. Eerdmans Publishing Co., 2011.

Jacobs, Elfriede. *Die Sakramentslehre Wilhelm Farels.* Zurich: Theologischer Verlag, 1978.

Jansen, Katherine L., Joanna Drell, and Frances Andrews, eds. *Medieval Italy: Texts in Translation.* Philadelphia: University of Pennsylvania Press, 2009.

Jerome. *Against Jovianus.* In *A Select Library of Nicene and Post-Nicene Fathers of the Christian Church: Second Series,* edited by Philip Schaff and Henry Wace, vol. 6. Reprint, Grand Rapids: Wm. B. Eerdmans Publishing Co., 1952.

———. *Letters.* In *A Select Library of Nicene and Post-Nicene Fathers of the Christian Church: Second Series,* edited by Philip Schaff and Henry Wace, vol. 6. Reprint, Grand Rapids: Wm. B. Eerdmans Publishing Co., 1952.

Jewell, John. *Works.* Edited by J. Ayre for the Parker Society. 4 vols. Cambridge: Cambridge University Press, 1845–50.

John Chrysostom. *St. John Chrysostom on Marriage and Family Life.* Translated by Catherine P. Roth and David Anderson. Crestwood, NY: St. Vladimir's Seminary Press, 1986

Johnson, James T. *A Society Ordained by God: English Puritan Marriage Doctrine in the First Half of the Seventeenth Century.* Nashville: Abingdon Press, 1970.

Justinian. *The Digest of Justinian.* Edited by Theodor Mommsen and Paul Krüger. Translated by Alan Watson. 4 vols. Philadelphia: University of Pennsylvania Press, 1985.

———. *Justinian's Institutes.* Edited by Paul Krüger. Translated by Peter Birks and Grant McLeod. Ithaca, NY: Cornell University Press, 1987.

Joyce, G. H., SJ. *Christian Marriage: An Historical and Doctrinal Study.* 2nd ed. London: Sheed & Ward, 1948.

Kelly, Henry Ansgar. *The Matrimonial Trials of Henry VIII.* Stanford, CA: Stanford University Press, 1976.

Kern, Arthur, ed. *Deutsche Hofordnungen des 16. und 17. Jahrhunderts.* 2 vols. Berlin: Weidmann, 1905.

Kingdon, Robert M. *Adultery and Divorce in Calvin's Geneva.* Cambridge, MA, and London: Harvard University Press, 1995.

———. "Anticlericalism in the Registers of the Geneva Consistory, 1542–1564." In *Anticlericalism in Late Medieval and Early Modern Europe,* edited by Peter A. Dykema and Heiko A. Oberman, 617–23. Leiden: E. J. Brill, 1993.

———. "Calvin and the Family: The Work of the Consistory of Geneva." In *Calvin's Work in Geneva,* edited by Richard C. Gamble, 93–106. New York and London. Garland Publishing Co., 1992.

Kingdon, Robert M., et al., eds. "Registres du Consistoire de Genève." 21 vols. of type-scripted records unpublished. In Meeter Center, Calvin College, being published in French as *Registres du Consistoire de Genève au temps de Calvin* / publiés par Thomas A. Lambert et Isabella M. Watt; sous la direction de Robert M. Kingdon, avec l'assistance de Jeffrey R. Watt. vols. 1- Genève: Libr. Droz, 1996- and translated as *Registers of the Consistory of Geneva in the Time of Calvin,* General Editor, Robert M. Kingdon; edited by Thomas A. Lambert and Isabella M. Watt; with the assistance of Jeffrey R. Watt; translated by M. Wallace McDonald. vols. 1–. Grand Rapids: Wm. B. Eerdmans Publishing Co., 2000– .

The Kings Book, or, A Necessary Doctrine and Erudition for Any Man. 1543. With an introduction by T. A. Lacey. Published for the Church Historical Society. London: SPCK, 1932.

Kirstein, Roland. *Die Entwicklung der Sponsalienlehre und der Lehre vom Eheschluss in der deutschen protestantischen Eherechtslehre bis zu H. Böhmer.* Bonn: Röhrscheid, 1966.

Kisch, Guido. *Consilia: Eine Bibliographie der juristischen Konsiliensammlungen.* Basel: Helbing & Lichtenhahn, 1970.

Kling, Melchior. *Matrimonialium causarum tractatus, methodico ordine scriptus.* Frankfurt am Main: Chr. Egenolphus, 1553.

Kloek, Els. "Seksualiteit, huwelijk en gezinsleven tijdens de lange zestiende eeuw, 1450–1650." In *Familie, huwelijk en gezin in West-Europa: Van middeleeuwen tot moderne tijd,* edited by Ton Zwaan, 107–38. Amsterdam: Boom; Heerlen: Open Universiteit, 1993.

Kock, Karl. *Studium Pietatis: Martin Bucer als Ethiker.* Inaug. diss., Mainz, 1960. Neukirchen-Vluyn: Neukirchener Verlag, 1962.

Koebner, Richard. "Die Eheauffassung des ausgehenden deutschen Mittelalters." *Archiv für Kulturgeschichte* 9 (1911): 136–98, 279–318.

Kohler, Josef, and Willy Scheel, eds. *Die peinliche Gerichtsordnung Kaiser Karls V.: Constitutio criminalis Carolina.* Pt. 1 of *Die Carolina und ihre Vorgängerinnen.* Aalen: Scientia Verlag, 1968.

Köhler, Karl. *Luther und die Juristen: Zur Frage nach dem gegenseitigen Verhältniss des Rechtes und Sittlichkeit.* Gotha: R. Besser, 1873.

Köhler, Walter. "Die Anfänge des protestantischen Eherechtes." *Zeitschrift der Savigny-Stiftung für Rechtsgeschichte: Kanonistische Abteilung* 30 (1941): 271–310.

———. "Luther als Eherichter." *Beiträge zur sächsischen Kirchengeschichte* 47 (1947): 18–27.

———. *Zürcher Ehegericht und Genfer Konsistorium.* 2 vols. Leipzig: M. Heinsius Nachfolger, 1942.

Kohls, Ernst-Wilhelm. "Martin Bucers Anteil und Anleigen bei der Auffassung der Ulmer Kirchenordnung in Jahre 1531." *Zeitschrift für evangelischen Kirchenrecht* 15 (1970): 333–60.

Konner, Melvin A. *The Evolution of Childhood: Relations, Emotions, Mind.* Cambridge, MA: Harvard University Press, 2010.

Korpiola, Mia. *Between Betrothal and Bedding: Marriage Formation in Sweden, 1200–1600.* Leiden: E. J. Brill, 2009.

———. "Lutheran Marriage Norms in Action: The Example of Post-Sweden, 1520–1600." In *The Lutheran Reformation and the Law,* edited by Virpi Mäkinen, 131–69. Leiden: E. J. Brill, 2006.

Kouri, E. I., and Tom Scott, eds. *Politics and Society in Reformation Europe.* New York: St. Martin's Press, 1987.

Krause, Harry D. *Family Law in a Nutshell,* 3rd ed. St. Paul, MN: West, 1995.

Laiou, Angeliki E., ed. *Consent and Coercion to Sex and Marriage in Ancient and Medieval Societies.* Washington, DC: Dumbarton Oaks Research Library and Collection, 1993.

Langbein, John H. *Torture and the Law of Proof.* Cambridge, MA: Harvard University Press, 1974.

Lape, Susan. "Solon and the Institution of the 'Democratic' Family Form." *Classical Journal* 98 (2002/3): 117–39.

Lasch, Christopher. *Haven in a Heathen World: The Family Besieged.* New York: Basic Books, 1977.

Latimer, Hugh. Sermons of Hugh Latimer. Edited by G. E. Corrie for the Parker Society. Cambridge: Cambridge University Press, 1844.

The Lawes Resolutions of Womens Rights: or, The Lawes Provision for Women. London: Assigns of John More, Esq., 1632.

Lawler, Michael G. *Marriage and the Catholic Church: Disputed Questions.* Collegeville, MN: Liturgical Press, 2002.

———. "Marriage as Covenant in the Catholic Tradition." In *Covenant Marriage in Comparative Perspective,* edited by John Witte Jr. and Eliza Ellison, 70–91. Grand Rapids: Wm. B. Eerdmans Publishing Co., 2005.

———. *Secular Marriage, Christian Sacrament.* New York: Twenty-Third Publications, 1985.

Lawrence, Ralph J. *The Sacramental Interpretation of Ephesians 5:32 from Peter Lombard to the Council of Trent.* Washington, DC: Catholic University of America Press, 1963.

Lawrence, William. *Marriage by the Morall Law of God Vindicated [and] The Right of Primogeniture in Succession to the Kingdoms of England and Scotland.* London, 1681.

Leclercq, Jean. *Monks on Marriage: A Twelfth-Century View.* New York: Seabury Press, 1982.

Leder, Hans-Gunter, ed. *Johannes Bugenhagen: Gestalt und Wirkung.* Bonn: Evangelische Verlagsanstalt, 1984.

Lehmann, William C. *Henry Home, Lord Kames, and the Scottish Enlightenment: A Study in National Character and in the History of Ideas.* The Hague: Martinus Nijhoff, 1971.

Leites, Edmund. *The Puritan Conscience and Modern Sexuality.* New Haven, CT: Yale University Press, 1986.

LeMahieu, Dan L. *William Paley: A Philosopher and His Age.* Lincoln: University of Nebraska Press, 1976.

Lemos, Tracy Maria. *Marriage Gifts and Social Change in Ancient Palestine, 1200 BCE to 200 CE.* Cambridge: Cambridge University Press, 2010.

Lettmann, Reinhard. *Die Diskussion über die klandestinen Ehen und die Einführung einer zur Gültigkeit verpflichtenden Eheschliessungsform auf dem Konzil von Trient.* Münster: Aschendorff, 1967.

Liermann, Hans. "Das kanonische Recht als Gegenstand des gelehrten Unterrichts an den protestantischen Universitäten Deutschlands in den ersten Jahrhunderten nach der Reformation." In Liermann, *Der Jurist und die Kirche: Ausgewählte kirchenrechtliche Aufsätze und Rechtsgutachten,* edited by Martin Heckel et al., 108–31. Munich: Beck, 1973.

———. "Evangelisches Kirchenrecht und staatliches Eherecht in Deutschland, Rechtsgeschichtliches-Gegenwartsprobleme." In *Existenz und Ordnung: Festschrift für Erik Wolf,* edited by Thomas Würtenberger, 109–21. Frankfurt am Main: Klostermann, 1962.

Lindberg, Carter. "The Future of a Tradition: Luther and the Family." In *All Theology Is Christology: Essays in Honor of David P. Scaer.* Edited by Dean O. Wenthe et al., 133–51. Fort Wayne, IN: Concordia Theological Seminary Press, 2000.

Linder, Klaus M. "Courtship and the Courts: Marriage and Law in Southern Germany, 1350–1550." ThD diss., Harvard University, 1988.

Locke, John. *Essay on the Law of Nature.* Translated and edited by W. von Leyden. Oxford: Oxford University Press, 1954.

———. *Two Treatises of Government.* 1689. Edited by Peter Laslett. Cambridge: Cambridge University Press, 1960.

———. *The Works of John Locke.* 12th ed. 9 vols. London: C. & J. Rivington et al., 1824.

Lohse, Berhard. "Die Kritik am Mönchtum bei Luther und Melanchthon." In *Luther und Melanchthon: Referate und Berichte des Zweiten Internationalen Kongresses für Lutherforschung Münster, 8–13. August 1960,* edited by Vilmos Vajtas, 129–45. Göttingen: Vandenhoeck & Ruprecht, 1960.

———. *Mönchtum und Reformation: Luthers Auseinandersetzung mit dem Mönchsideal des Mittelalters.* Göttingen: Vandenhoeck & Ruprecht, 1963.

Lombardus, Petrus. *Sententiae in IV libris distinctae.* 3rd ed. 2 vols. in 3. Spicilegium Bonaventurianum 4–5. Rome: Collegii S. Bonaventurae ad Claras Aquas, 1971–81.

Long, Joseph. *A Treatise on the Law of Domestic Relations.* St. Paul: Keefe-Davidson Co., 1905.

Luther, Martin. "Counsel in Questions of Marriage and Sex." In *Luther: Letters of Spiritual Counsel,* edited by Theodore G. Tappert, 258–94. Philadelphia: Westminster Press, 1955.

———. *D. Martin Luthers Werke: Briefwechsel,* 17 vols. Weimar: Bohlau, 1930–1983.

———. *D. Martini Luthers Werke: Kritische Gesamtausgabe.* 121 vols. 1883–2009.

———. *Luther's Works.* Translated and edited by Jaroslav Pelikan and Helmut T. Lehmann. American ed. 55 vols. Philadelphia: Muhlenberg Press / Fortress Press; St. Louis: Concordia Publishing House, 1955–86.

———. *Martin Luther: Selections from His Writings.* Edited by John Dillenberger. Garden City, NY: Doubleday, 1961.

Maccoby, Eleanor E., and Robert H. Mnookin. *Dividing the Child: Social and Legal Dilemmas of Custody.* Cambridge, MA: Harvard University Press, 1992.

MacCulloch, Diarmand, ed. *The Reign of Henry VIII: Politics, Policy and Piety.* Basingstoke: MacMillan, 1995.

———. *Thomas Cranmer: A Life.* New Haven, CT: Yale University Press, 1996.

Mackin, Theodore. *Marriage in the Catholic Church: Divorce and Remarriage.* New York: Paulist Press, 1984.

————. *Marriage in the Catholic Church: The Marital Sacrament.* New York: Paulist Press, 1989.

————. *Marriage in the Catholic Church: What Is Marriage?* New York: Paulist Press, 1982.

Mager, Inge. "'Es is nicht gut dass der Mensch allein sei' (Gen 2, 18): Zum Familienleben Philipp Melanchthons." *Arichiv für Reformationsgeschichte* 81 (1990): 120–37.

Mäkinen, Virpi, ed. *The Lutheran Reformation and the Law.* Leiden: E. J. Brill, 2006.

Marchant, Ronald A. *The Church under the Law: Justice, Administration, and Discipline in the Diocese of York, 1560–1640.* Cambridge: Cambridge University Press, 1969.

————. *The Puritans and the Church Courts in the Diocese of York.* London: Longmans, 1960.

Marquardt, Elizabeth. *Between Two Worlds: The Inner Lives of Children of Divorce.* New York: Three Rivers Press, 2005.

Marsilius of Padua. *Defensor pacis.* In Alan Gewirth, *Marsilius of Padua. The Defender of the Peace.* Vol. 2, *The Defensor Pacis.* Translated with an introduction. New York: Columbia University Press, 1956.

Martin, Thomas. *Traictise declarying and plainly provyng that the pretensed marriage of Priestes and professed persones is no mariage.* London: R. Caly, 1554.

Martos, Joseph. *Doors to the Sacred: A Historical Introduction to Sacraments in the Catholic Church.* Garden City, NY: Image Books, 1982.

Mason, Mary Ann. *From Fathers' Property to Children's Rights.* New York: Columbia University Press, 1996.

Masson, M., R. Bailey-Harris, and R. J. Probert. *Principles of Family Law.* 8th ed. London: Sweet & Maxwell, 2008.

Maurer, Wilhelm. "Reste des kanonischen Rechtes im Frühprotestantismus." *Zeitschrift der Savigny-Stiftung für Rechtsgeschichte: Kanonistische Abteilung* 51 (1965): 190–253.

Mauser, Konrad. *Explicatio erudita et utilis X. tituli institutionum: De nuptiis.* Jena, 1569; Wittenberg: Crato, 1569.

May, Elaine Tyler. *Great Expectations: Marriage and Divorce in Post-Victorian America.* Chicago: University of Chicago Press, 1980.

May, Henry F. *The Enlightenment in America.* New York: Oxford University Press, 1976.

McAreavey, John. *The Canon Law of Marriage and the Family.* Dublin: Four Courts Press, 1997.

McCoy, Charles S., and J. Wayne Baker. *Foundation of Federalism: Heinrich Bullinger and the Covenantal Tradition.* Louisville, KY: Westminster/John Knox Press, 1991.

McDevitt, Gilbert J. *Legitimacy and Legitimation: An Historical Synopsis and Commentary.* Washington, DC: Catholic University of America Press, 1941.

McSheffrey, Shannon. *Marriage, Sex, and Civic Culture in Late Medieval London.* Philadelphia: University of Pennsylvania Press, 2006.

Mejer, Otto. "Zur Geschichte des ältesten protestantischen Eherechts, inbesondere der Ehescheidungsfrage." *Zeitschrift für Kirchenrecht* 16 (1881): 35–106.

Melanchthon, Philipp. *De arbore consanguinitatis et affinitatis, sive de gradibus.* 1540. In Martin Luther et al., *Von Ehesachen.* Wittenberg: Josef Clug, 1540–41.

————. *De coniugio piae commonefactiones.* Wittenberg: Crato, 1551. Published in revised, expanded form as *Disputatio de conjugio.* Wittenberg, 1555. In *Loci praecipui theologici . . . cum appendice Disputationis de coniugio.* Leipzig: Bapst, 1554; Wittenberg: Krafft, 1555.

————. *Loci communes.* 1521. In *Melanchthon and Bucer,* edited by Wilhelm Pauck, 3–152. Philadelphia: Westminster Press, 1969.

————. *Loci communes, 1555.* In *Melanchthon on Christian Doctrine,* edited by Clyde L. Manschreck. New York: Oxford University Press, 1965.

————. *Werke*. In Corpus reformatorum 1–28, edited by G. Bretschneider and H. E. Bindseil. Brunswick: C. A. Schwetschke & Filium, 1834–60.

Menander of Laodicea. *Menander Rhetor*. Translated and edited by D. A. Russell and N. G. Wilson. Oxford: Oxford University Press, 1981.

Mendus, Susan. "The Marriage of True Minds: The Ideal Marriage in the Philosophy of John Stuart Mill." In *Sexuality and Subordination: Interdisciplinary Studies of Gender in the Nineteenth Century*, edited by Susan Mendus and Jane Rendall, 171–91. London and New York: Routledge & Kegan Paul, 1989.

Merzbacher, Friedrich. "Johann Oldendorp und das kanonischen Recht." In Merzbacher, *Recht-Staat-Kirche: Ausgewählte Aufsätze*, edited by Gerhard Koebler, 246–74. Vienna: Böhlau, 1989.

Meyer, Paul. *Der römische Konkubinat nach den Rechtsquellen und den Inschriften*. Leipzig: G. B. Teubner, 1895.

Meyendorff, John. "Christian Marriage in Byzantium: The Canonical and Liturgical Tradition." *Dumbarton Oaks Papers* 44 (1990): 99–107. Washington, DC: Dumbarton Oaks Research Library and Collection, 1990.

————. *Marriage: An Orthodox Perspective*. Crestwood, NY: St. Vladimir's Press, 1975.

Michaelis, Karl. *Das abendländische Eherecht im Übergang vom späten Mittelalter zur Neuzeit*. Göttingen: Vandenhoeck & Ruprecht, 1990.

————. "Über Luthers eherechtliche Anschauungen und deren Verhältnis zum mittelalterlichen und neuzeitlichen Eherecht." In *Festschrift für Erich Ruppel zum 65. Geburtstag*, edited by Heinz Brunotte et al., 43–62. Hannover: Lutherhaus, 1968. Reprint, Goldbach: Keip, 1995.

Mikat, Paul. *Die Polygamiefrage in der frühen Neuzeit*. Opladen: Westdeutscher Verlag, 1988.

Mill, John Stuart. *Collected Works of John Stuart Mill*. Edited by John M. Robson et al. 33 vols. Toronto: University of Toronto Press, 1963–91.

————. *Utilitarianism, On Liberty, Essay on Bentham*. Edited by Mary Warnock. 1962. Reprint, New York: New American Library, 1974.

Millar, John. *The Origin of the Distinction of Ranks*. Edited by Aaron Garrett. Indianapolis: Liberty Fund, 2006.

Milton, John. *The Complete Prose Works of John Milton*. 8 vols. New Haven, CT: Yale University Press, 1959.

Molin, J.-B., and P. Mutembe. *Le rituel du mariage en France du XIIe au XVIe siècle*. Paris: Beauchesne, 1994.

Monner, Basilius. *Tractatus duo: 1. De matrimonio; 2. De clandestinis conjugiis*. 2nd ed. Jena: Steinmann, 1603.

Monter, E. William. "The Consistory of Geneva, 1559–1569." *Bibliothèque d'humanisme et de la renaissance* 38 (1976): 467–84.

————. "Crime and Punishment in Calvin's Geneva, 1562." *Archiv für Reformationsgeschichte* 64 (1973): 281–87.

————. *Studies in Genevan Government (1536–1605)*. Geneva: Droz, 1964.

————. "Women in Calvinist Geneva (1550–1800)." *Signs: Journal of Women in Culture and Society* 6 (1980–81): 189–209.

Morgan, Edmund S. *The Puritan Family: Religion and Domestic Relations in Seventeenth-Century New England*. New York: Harper & Row, 1966.

Moughtin-Mumby, Sharon. *Sexual and Marital Metaphors in Hosea, Jeremiah, Isaiah, and Ezekiel*. Oxford: Oxford University Press, 2008.

Murphy, V. "The Literature and Propaganda on Henry's Divorce." In *The Reign of Henry VIII: Politics, Policy and Piety*, edited by Diarmond MacCulloch, chap. 6. Basingstoke: MacMillan, 1995.

Musonius Rufus. *Musonius Rufus: The Roman Socrates*. Translated and edited by Cora E. Lutz. New Haven, CT: Yale University Press, 1947.

Muther, Theodor. *Aus dem Universitäts- und Gelehrtenleben im Zeitalter der Reformation.* Erlangen: A. Deichert, 1866.

———. *Doctor Johann Apell: Ein Beitrag zur Geschichte der deutschen Jurisprudenz im sechzehnten Jahrhundert.* Köningsberg: Universitätsdruckerei, 1861.

Naphy, William G. *Calvin and the Consolidation of the Genevan Reformation.* Manchester and New York: Manchester University Press, 1994.

New, John F. *Anglican and Puritan.* Stanford, CA: Stanford University Press, 1964.

Nichols, Joel A., ed. *Marriage and Divorce in a Multi-Cultural Society: Multi-Tiered Marriage and the Boundaries of Civil Law and Religion.* Cambridge: Cambridge University Press, 2012.

Niebuhr, H. Richard. *Christ and Culture.* New York: Harper & Row, 1951.

Noonan, John T., Jr. *Canons and Canonists in Context.* Goldbach: Keip, 1997.

———. *Contraception: A History of Its Treatment by the Catholic Theologians and Canonists.* Cambridge, MA: Belknap Press, 1965.

———. "The Family and the Supreme Court." *Catholic University of America Law Review* 23 (1973): 255–74.

———. "Marital Affection in the Canonists." *Studia Gratiana* 12 (1967): 489–509.

———. "Novel 22." In *The Bond of Marriage: An Ecumenical and Interdisciplinary Study,* edited by W. J. Bassett, 41–96. Notre Dame, IN: University of Notre Dame Press, 1968.

———. "Power to Choose." *Viator* 4 (1973): 419–34.

———. *The Power to Dissolve: Lawyers and Marriages in the Courts of the Roman Curia.* Cambridge, MA: Belknap Press, 1972.

———. *A Private Choice: Abortion in America in the Seventies.* New York: Free Press, 1979.

Nörr, Knut Wolfgang. "Die Entwicklung des *Corpus iuris canonici.*" In *Handbuch der Quellen und Literatur der neueren europäischen Privatrechtsgeschichte,* edited by Helmut Coing, 1:835–56. Munich: Beck, 1977.

Novak, David. *Natural Law in Judaism.* Cambridge: Cambridge University Press, 1998.

O'Donnell, William J., and David A. Jones. *The Law of Marriage and Marriage Alternatives.* Lexington, MA: Lexington Books, 1982.

O'Donovan, Joan Lockwood. *The Theology of Law and Authority in the English Reformation.* Atlanta: Scholars Press, 1991.

Oldendorp, Johannes. *Collatio iuris civilis et canonici, maximam adferens boni & aequi cognitionem.* Cologne: Ioannes Gymnicus, 1541.

———. *Lexicon iuris.* Frankfurt: Chr. Egenolphus, 1546–53.

———. *Von Ratschlägen, wie man gute Policey und Ordnung in Stedten und Landen erhalten möge.* Rostock: Christoph Reusner, 1597. Facsimile reprint, Glashütten im Taunus, 1971.

Olsen, Frances. "The Family and the Market: A Study of Ideology and Legal Reform." *Harvard Law Review* 96 (1983): 1497–578.

Orenstein, Henry. "The Ethnological Theories of Henry Sumner Maine." *American Anthropologist* 70 (1968): 264–76.

Orme, Nicholas. *Medieval Children.* New Haven, CT: Yale University Press, 2001.

Otten, Willemien, and Karla Pollman, eds. *The Oxford Guide to the Historical Reception of Augustine.* Oxford: Oxford University Press, 2012.

Outhwaite, Richard B. *Clandestine Marriage in England, 1500–1850.* London: Hambledon Press, 1995.

———, ed. *Marriage and Society: Studies in the Social History of Family.* New York: St. Martin's Press, 1981.

———. *The Rise and Fall of the English Ecclesiastical Courts.* Cambridge: Cambridge University Press, 2006.

Owen, Eivion. "Milton and Selden on Divorce." *Studies in Philology* 43 (1946): 233–57.

Ozment, Steven E. *Ancestors: The Loving Family in Old Europe.* Cambridge, MA: Harvard University Press, 2001.

———. *Protestants: The Birth of a Revolution.* New York: Doubleday, 1992.

———. *When Fathers Ruled: Family Life in Reformation Europe.* Cambridge, MA: Harvard University Press, 1983.

Paley, William. *Principles of Moral and Political Philosophy.* 1785. Edited by D. L. LeMahieu. Indianapolis: Liberty Fund, 2002.

Palmer, Paul F. "Christian Marriage: Contract or Covenant." *Theological Studies* 33 (1972): 617–65.

Parish, Helen. *Clerical Celibacy in the West, c. 1100–1700.* Burlington, VT: Ashgate, 2010.

Parker, T. H. L. *The Oracles of God: An Introduction to the Preaching of John Calvin.* London and Redhill: Lutterworth Press, 1947.

Parker, William R. *Milton's Contemporary Reputation.* Columbus: Ohio State University Press, 1940.

Pateman, Carole. *The Sexual Contract.* Stanford, CA: Stanford University Press, 1988.

Patterson, Cynthia B. *The Family in Greek History.* Cambridge, MA: Harvard University Press, 1998.

Pauck, Wilhelm. *Das Reich Gottes auf Erden: Utopie und Wirklichkeit; Eine Untersuchung zu Butzers "De Regno Christi" und der englischen Staatskirche des 16. Jahrhunderts.* Berlin: W. de Gruyter, 1928.

———, ed. *Melanchthon and Bucer.* Philadelphia: Westminster Press, 1969.

Peck, Epaphroditus. *The Law of Persons or Domestic Relations.* Chicago: Callaghan & Co., 1913.

Pelikan, Jaroslav. *Reformation of Church and Dogma (1300–1700).* Chicago: University of Chicago Press, 1984.

———. *Spirit versus Structure: Luther and the Institutions of the Church.* New York: Harper & Row, 1968.

Perkins, William. *The Work of William Perkins.* Edited by Ian Breward. 3 vols. Appleford: Sutton Courtenay Press, 1970.

Pitkin, Barbara. "'The Heritage of the LORD': Children in the Theology of John Calvin." In *The Child in Christian Thought,* edited by Marcia J. Bunge, 160–93. Grand Rapids: Wm. B. Eerdmans Publishing Co., 2001.

Plato. *The Collected Dialogues of Plato, Including the Letters.* Edited and translated by Edith Hamilton and Huntingdon Cairns. New York: Pantheon Books, 1961.

Plutarch. *The Complete Works of Plutarch.* 6 vols. New York: Kelmscott Society, 1909.

———. *Plutarch's "Advice to the Bride and Groom," and "A Consolation to His Wife."* Edited by Sarah Pomeroy. New York: Oxford University Press, 1999.

———. *Plutarch's Lives.* Translated by Bernadotte Perrin. London: William Heinemann, 1928.

———. *Plutarch's Moralia.* Translated by L. Pearson. London: W. Heinemann, 1960.

Politische Reichs Händel, Das ist, Allerhand gemeine Acten, Regimentssachen, und weltliche Discursen. Compiled from the library of Melchior Goldast of Haiminsfeld. Frankfurt am Main: Johann Bringer, 1614.

Pomeroy, Sarah. *Families in Classical and Hellenistic Greece: Representations and Realities.* Oxford: Clarendon Press, 1997.

———, ed. *Plutarch's "Advice to the Bride and Groom," . . . See* Plutarch.

———. *Xenophon, "Oeconomicus": A Social and Political Commentary, with a New English Translation.* Oxford: Clarendon Press, 1994.

Ponet, John. *A defence for mariage of priestes: By Scripture and aunciente wryters.* London: Reynold Wolff, 1549.

Powell, Chilton L. *English Domestic Relations, 1487–1653: A Study of Matrimony and Family Life in Theory and Practice as Revealed by the Literature, Law, and History of the Period.* New York: Columbia University Press, 1917.

Pricke, Robert. *The doctrine of superioritie, and of subiection, contained in the fifth com-mandement of the holy law of almightie God.* London: Ephraim Dawson, 1609. (ESTC 20337.)

Priest, Menna, ed. *International Calvinism.* Oxford: Clarendon Press, 1985.

Probert, Rebecca. *Marriage Law and Practice in the Long Eighteenth Century: A Reassess-ment.* Cambridge: Cambridge University Press, 2009.

Pylkkänen, Anu. "Feminism and the Challenge to Religious Truths on Marriage: The Case of Nordic Protestantism." In *Law and Religion in the 21st Century: Nordic Perspectives,* edited by Lisbet Christoffersen, Kjell A. Modéer, and Svend Andersen, 525–45. Copenhagen: Djøf Publishing, 2009.

Rainolds, John. *A Defence of the Judgement of the Reformed Churches, That a man may law-fullie not onlie put awaie his wife for her adulterie but also marrie another.* London, 1609. (ESTC 20607.)

Rawson, Beryl, ed. *Marriage, Divorce, and Children in Ancient Rome.* Oxford: Oxford University Press, 1991.

Raymond of Penyafort [Raimundus de Pennaforte/Peñafort]. *Summa de iure canonico.* Edited by Xaverio Ochoa and Aloisio Díez. Rome: Commentarium pro religiosis, 1975.

———. *Summa on Marriage.* Translated by Pierre J. Payer. Toronto: Pontifical Institute of Medieval Studies, 2005.

Regan, Milton C., Jr. *Family Law and the Pursuit of Intimacy.* New York: New York University Press, 1993.

Reid, Charles J., Jr. *Power over the Body, Equality in the Family: Rights and Domestic Relations in Medieval Canon Law.* Grand Rapids: Wm. B. Eerdmans Publishing Co., 2004.

Reynolds, Philip L. *Marriage and the Schoolmen: The Emergence of the Sacramental Theol-ogy of Marriage during the Central Middle Ages.* (Forthcoming.)

———. *Marriage in the Western Church: The Christianization of Marriage during the Patristic and Early Medieval Periods.* Leiden: E. J. Brill, 1994.

Reynolds, Philip L., and John Witte Jr., eds. *To Have and to Hold: Marrying and Its Docu-mentation in Western Christendom, 400–1600.* Cambridge: Cambridge University Press, 2007.

Rheinstein, Max. *Marriage Stability, Divorce, and the Law.* Chicago: University of Chi-cago Press, 1971.

Richter, Aemilius. *Beiträge zur Geschichte des Ehescheidungsrecht in der evangelischen Kirche.* Aalen: Scientia Verlag, 1958.

———, ed. *Die evangelischen Kirchenordnungen des sechszehnten Jahrhunderts.* Reprint, 2 vols., Nieuwkoop: B. DeGraaf, 1967.

Ridley, Nicholas. *The Works of Nicholas Ridley.* Edited by H. Christmas for the Parker Society. Cambridge: Cambridge University Press, 1843.

Riisøy, Anne Irene. *Sexuality, Law and Legal Practice and the Reformation in Norway.* Leiden: E. J. Brill, 2009.

Rivoire, Émile, and Victor van Berchem, eds. *Les sources du droit du canton de Genève.* 4 vols. Aarau: Sauerlander, 1927–1935.

Robinson, Hastings, ed. and trans. *The Zurich Letters.* For the Parker Society. 2 vols. Cambridge: Cambridge University Press, 1842.

Robson, Ann P., and John M. Robson, eds. *Sexual Equality: Writings by John Stuart Mill, Harriet Taylor Mill, and Helen Taylor.* Toronto: University of Toronto Press, 1994.

Rodgers, William C. *A Treatise on the Law of Domestic Relations.* Chicago: T. H. Flood, 1899.

Roelker, Nancy L. "The Appeal of Calvinism to French Noblewomen in the Sixteenth Century." *Journal of Interdisciplinary Studies* 2 (1970–71): 391–418.

Rogers, Daniel. *Matrimoniall Honour*. London: Philip Nevil, 1642.

Rogers, Elizabeth Frances. *Peter Lombard and the Sacramental System*. PhD thesis, Columbia University, 1917. New York: n.p., 1917. Reprint, Merrick, NY : Richwood Publishing Co., 1976. http://www.archive.org/details/peterlombardsacr00rogerich.

Rogers, Thomas. *The Catholic Doctrine of the Church of England: An Exposition of the Thirty-Nine Articles*. Edited by J. J. S. Perowne for the Parker Society. Cambridge: Cambridge University Press, 1844.

Rosemann, Philipp W. *The Story of a Great Medieval Book: Peter Lombard's Sentences*. Peterborough, ON: Broadview Press, 2007.

Ross, Ian Simpson. *Lord Kames and the Scotland of His Day*. Oxford: Oxford University Press, 1972.

Rousseau, Jean-Jacques. *The Social Contract and the Discourse on the Origin of Inequality*. Edited by Lester G. Crocker. New York: Washington Square Press, 1967.

Sacks, Jonathan. *The Home We Build Together: Re[-]creating Society*. London: Continuum, 2007.

Safley, Thomas Max. "Canon Law and Swiss Reform: Legal Theory and Practice in the Marital Courts of Zurich, Bern, Basel, and St. Gall." In *Canon Law in Protestant Lands*, edited by Richard H. Helmholz, 187–201. Berlin: Duncker & Humblot, 1992.

———. *Let No Man Put Asunder: The Control of Marriage in the German Southwest; A Comparative Study, 1550–1600*. Kirksville, MO: Sixteenth Century Journal Publications, 1984.

Salmon, Marylynn. *Women and the Law of Property in Early America*. Chapel Hill: University of North Carolina Press, 1986.

Sandys, Edwin. *The Sermons of Edwin Sandys*. Edited by J. Ayre for the Parker Society. Cambridge: Cambridge University Press, 1842.

Sansom, J. *See* Cosin, John.

Sapiro, Virginia. *A Vindication of Political Virtue: The Political Theory of Mary Wollstonecraft*. Chicago: University of Chicago Press, 1992.

Sarcerius, Basilius [Erasmus]. *Corpus juris matrimonialis: Vom Ursprung, Anfang und Herkomen des Heyligen Ehestandts*. Frankfurt am Main: P. Schmidt, 1569.

Satlow, Michael L. *Jewish Marriage in Antiquity*. Princeton: Princeton University Press, 2001.

Schäfer, Hans Christoph. *Der Einfluss des kanonischen Eherechts auf die moderne staatliche Ehegesetzgebung*. Inaugural diss., Heidelberg University, 1963. Bamberg: R. Rodenbusch, 1963; reprint, 1969. Heidelberg: n.p., 1971.

Schäfer, Rudolf. "Die Geltung des kanonischen Rechts in der evangelischen Kirche Deutschland von Luther bis zur Gegenwart." *Zeitschrift der Savigny-Stiftung für Rechtsgeschichte: Kanonistische Abteilung* 5 (1915): 165–413.

Schaff, Philip. *The Creeds of Christendom*, 3 vols. New York: Harper & Bros., 1877.

Schaff, Philip, and Henry Wace, eds. *The Seven Ecumenical Councils*. Reprint, Grand Rapids: Wm. B. Eerdmans Publishing Co., 1952.

Schaich-Klose, Wiebke. *D. Hieronymus Schürpf: Leben und Werk des Wittenberger Reformationsjuristen, 1481–1554*. Trogen and Tübingen: F. Meili, 1967.

Scheidel, W. "A Peculiar Institution? Greco-Roman Monogamy in Global Context." *History of the Family* 14 (2009): 280–92.

Schillebeeckx, Edward. *Marriage: Human Reality and Saving Mystery*. New York: Sheed & Ward, 1965.

Schmelzeisen, Gustav. *Polizeiordnung und Privatrecht*. Münster and Cologne: Böhlau, 1955.

Schneider, Carl E. "Marriage, Morals, and the Law: No-Fault Divorce and Moral Discourse." *Utah Law Review* (1994): 503–85.

———. "Moral Discourse and the Transformation of American Family Law." *Michigan Law Review* 83 (1985): 1803–79.

———. "Rethinking Alimony: Marital Decisions and Moral Discourse." *Brigham Young Law Review* (1991): 197–257.

Schneider, Carl E., and Margaret F. Brinig. *Invitation to Family Law.* 3rd ed. St. Paul: West Publishing Co., 2006.

Schneidewin [Schneidewein], Johannes. *In institutionum imperialium titulum X: De nuptiis.* . . . Frankfurt am Main, 1571.

Schnucker, Robert V., ed. *Calviniana: Ideas and Influence of John Calvin.* Ann Arbor: University of Michigan Press, 1988.

Schochet, G. J. *Patriarchalism in Political Thought: The Authoritarian Family and Political Speculation and Attitudes Especially in Seventeenth-Century England.* New York: Basic Books, 1975.

Schouler, James. *A Treatise on the Law of Marriage, Divorce, Separation, and Domestic Relations.* Edited by Arthur W. Blakemore. 6th ed. Albany, NY: Matthew Bender, 1921.

Schremer, Adiel. "How Much Polygyny in Roman Palestine?" *Proceedings of the American Academy for Jewish Research* 63 (1997–2001): 181–223.

Schroeder, Henry Joseph, OP. *Canons and Decrees of the Council of Trent.* St. Louis: B. Herder Book Co., 1941.

Schulz, Kurd. "Bugenhagen als Schöpfer der Kirchenordnungen." In *Johann Bugenhagen: Beiträge zu seinem 400. Todestag,* edited by Werner Rautenberg, 51–63. Berlin: Evangelische Verlagsanstalt, 1958.

Schurpff [Schürpf], Hieronymus. *Consilia seu reponsa iuris: Centuria I–III.* Frankfurt: Christian Egenolff [Egenolph], 1545–56; reprint, 1564.

Schwab, Dieter. *Grundlagen und Gestalt der staatlichen Ehegesetzgebung in der Neuzeit bis zum Beginn des 19. Jahrhunderts.* Bielefeld: Verlag Ernst und Werner Gieseking, 1967.

Schwalb, Hans. *Beclagung eines Leyens genant Hanns schwalb uber vil missbrauchs christlichslebens.* Nuremberg: Johann Stuchs, 1521.

Schwarzenberg, Johann von. *Diss Büchleyn Kuttenschlang genant die Teüffels lerer macht bekant.* Nuremberg: Friedrich Peypus, 1526.

———. *Ein schöner Sendbrieff des wolgepornen und Edeln herrn Johannsen, herrn zu Schwartzenberg, an Bischoff zu Bamberg ausgangen.* Nuremberg: Hans Hergot, 1524.

Scobell, Henry, ed. *A Collection of Acts and Ordinances of General Use Made in the Parliament.* London: Henry Hills & John Field, 1658.

Scott, S. P., ed. *The Civil Law.* 17 vols. Cincinnati: The Central Trust Company, 1932.

Scribner, Robert W. "Police and the Territorial State in Sixteenth Century Württemberg." In *Politics and Society in Reformation Europe,* edited by E. I. Kouri and Tom Scott, 103–20. New York: St. Martin's Press, 1987.

Searle, Mark, and Kenneth W. Stevenson. *Documents of the Marriage Liturgy.* Collegeville, MN: Liturgical Press, 1992.

Seebass, Gottfried. *Das reformatorische Werk des Andreas Osiander.* Nuremberg: Verein für bayerische Kirchengeschichte, 1967.

Seeberg, Reinhard. "Luthers Anschauung von dem Geschlechtsleben der Ehe und ihre geschichtliche Stellung." *Luther-Jahrbuch* 7 (1925): 77–122.

Seeger, Cornelia. *Nullité de marriage, divorce et séparation de corps à Genève, au temps de Calvin: Fondements doctrinaux, loi et jurisprudence.* Mémoires et documents publiés par la société d'histoire de la Suisse romande. Lausanne: Méta-editions, 1989.

Sehling, Emil, ed. *Die evangelischen Kirchenordnungen des 16. Jahrhunderts.* Vols. 1–5. Leipzig: O. R. Reisland, 1902–13. Vols. 6–, under the same title. Aalen: Scientia Verlag; Tübingen: Mohr Siebeck, 1955–.

Selden, John. *De iure naturali et gentium, juxta disciplinam Ebraeorum libri septem.* London: Richardus Bishopius, 1640. (ESTC 22168.)

Selderhuis, Herman J. "Das Eherecht Martin Bucers." In *Martin Bucer und das Recht,* edited by Christoph Strohm, 185–99. Geneva: Droz, 2002.

———. *Marriage and Divorce in the Thought of Martin Bucer.* Translated by John Vriend and Lyle D. Biersma. Kirksville, MO: Thomas Jefferson University Press, 1999.

Shanley, Mary. *Feminism, Marriage, and the Law in Victorian England, 1850–1895.* Princeton, NJ: Princeton University Press, 1989.

———. "Marriage Contract and Social Contract in Seventeenth Century English Political Thought." *Western Political Quarterly* 32 (1979): 79–91.

Shapiro, Barbara J. *"Beyond Reasonable Doubt" and "Probable Cause": Historical Perspectives on the Anglo-American Law of Evidence.* Berkeley and Los Angeles: University of California Press, 1991.

———. *Probability and Certainty in Seventeenth-Century England: A Study of the Relationships Between Natural Science, Religion, History, Law, and Literature.* Princeton, NJ: Princeton University Press, 1983.

Sheehan, Michael M. *Marriage, Family, and Law in Medieval Europe: Collected Studies.* Edited by James K. Farge. Toronto: University of Toronto Press, 1996.

———. "Theory and Practice: Marriage of the Unfree and Poor in Medieval Society." *Mediaeval Studies* 50 (1988): 457–87.

Simmons, A. John. *The Lockean Theory of Rights.* Princeton, NJ: Princeton University Press, 1992.

Smith, Adam. *Lectures on Jurisprudence.* 1762. Edited by R. L. Meek, D. D. Raphael, and P. G. Stein. Indianapolis: Liberty Fund, 1982.

Smithen, Frederick J. *Continental Protestantism and the English Reformation.* London: James Clarke, [1927].

Smyth, Charles Hugh. *Cranmer and the Reformation under Edward VI.* Cambridge: Cambridge University Press, 1926.

Sohm, Rudolf. *Das Recht der Eheschliessung aus dem deutschen und kanonischen Recht geschichtlich entwickelt.* 1875. Reprint, Aalen: Scientia Verlag, 1966.

Sokol, Mary. "Jeremy Bentham on Love and Marriage." *American Journal of Legal History* 30 (2009): 1–21.

Söllner, Alfred. "Die Literatur zum gemeinen und partikularen Recht in Deutschland, Osterreich, den Niederlanden und der Schweiz." In *Handbuch der Quellen und Literatur der neueren europäischen Privatrechtsgeschichte,* edited by Helmut Coing, 2.1: 501–614. Munich: Beck, 1977.

Spalding, James C., ed. *The Reformation of the Ecclesiastical Laws of England, 1552.* Sixteenth Century Essays and Studies. Kirksville, MO: Sixteenth Century Journal Publishers, 1992.

Spangenberg, Cyriacus. *Ehespiegel: Das ist, Alles was vom heyligen Ehestande nützliches, nötiges, und tröstliches mag gesagt werden.* Strassburg: Samuel Emmel, 1563.

Spengler, Lazarus. *Eyn kurtzer ausszug aus dem Bebstlichen rechten der Decret und Decretalen, in den artickeln, die ungeverlich Gottes Wort un[d] Euangelio gemess sein.* Nuremberg: Jobst Gutknecht, 1530.

Spinks, Bryan D. "The Liturgical Origins and Theology of Calvin's Genevan Marriage Rite." *Ecclesia orans* 3 (1986): 195–210.

Sprengler-Ruppenthal, Anneliese. "Bugenhagen und das kanonische Recht." *Zeitschrift der Savigny-Stiftung für Rechtsgeschichte: Kanonistische Abteilung* 75 (1989): 375–400.

———. "Zur Rezeption des römischen Rechts in Eherecht der Reformation," *Zeitschrift der Savigny-Stiftung für Rechtsgeschichte: Kanonistische Abteilung* 68 (1982): 363–418.

Stackhouse, Max L. *Covenant and Commitments: Faith, Family, and Economic Life.* Louisville, KY: Westminster John Knox Press, 1997.

Staehelin, Adrian. *Die Einführung der Ehescheidung in Basel zur Zeit der Reformation.* Basel: Helbing & Lichtenhahn, 1957.

Stapleton, William. *Stapleton's Fortress Overthrown.* Edited by Richard Gibbings for the Parker Society. Cambridge: Cambridge University Press, 1848.

Stauffenegger, Roger. "Le Mariage à Genève vers 1600." In *Mémoires de la Société pour l'histoire de droit et des institutions des anciens pays bourguignons, comtois et romands* 27 (1966): 317–29.

Stauffer, Richard. *L'humanité de Calvin.* Neuchatel: Delachaux & Niestlé, 1964.

Staves, Susan. *Married Women's Separate Property in England, 1660–1833.* Cambridge, MA: Harvard University Press, 1990.

Stephen, Henry John. *New Commentaries on the Laws of England.* 4 vols. London: Henry Butterworth, 1842.

Stephen, James Fitzjames. *Liberty, Equality, Fraternity.* Edited by Stuart D. Warner. Indianapolis: Liberty Fund, 1993.

Stevenson, Kenneth W. *Nuptial Blessing: A Study of Christian Marriage Rites.* London: SPCK, 1982. Reprint, New York: Oxford University Press, 1983.

Stjerna, Kirsi Irmeli. *Women and the Reformation.* Malden, MA: Blackwell Publishers, 2009.

Stintzing, Roderich von. *Das Sprichwort "Juristen böse Christen" in seinen geschichtlichen Bedeutung.* Bonn: Marcus, 1875.

_____. *Geschichte der deutschen Rechtswissenschaft: Erste Abteilung.* Munich: Oldenbourg, 1880.

Stölzel, Adolf F. *Die Entwicklung des gelehrten Richtertums in den deutschen Tertitorien.* 2 vols. Aalen: Scientia Verlag, 1964.

Stone, Lawrence. *The Causes of the English Revolution, 1529–1642.* New York: Harper & Row, 1972.

———. *The Family, Sex, and Marriage in England, 1500–1800.* New York: Harper & Row, 1979.

———. *Road to Divorce: A History of the Making and Breaking of Marriage in England.* New York and Oxford: Oxford University Press, 1995.

———. *Road to Divorce: England, 1530–1987.* Oxford: Oxford University Press, 1990.

Story, Joseph. *Commentaries on the Conflict of the Laws, Foreign and Domestic, in Regards to Contracts, Rights, and Remedies, and Especially in Regard to Marriages.* Boston: Hilliard Gray, 1834.

Strauss, Gerald. *Law, Resistance, and the State: The Opposition to Roman Law in Reformation Germany.* Princeton, NJ: Princeton University Press, 1986.

———. *Luther's House of Learning: Indoctrination of the Young in the Lutheran Reformation.* Baltimore: Johns Hopkins University Press, 1978.

Strohm, Christoph. *Calvinismus und Recht.* Tübingen: Mohr Siebeck, 2008.

———, ed. *Martin Bucer und das Recht.* Geneva: Droz, 2002.

Sugarman, Stephen D., and Herma Hill Kay, eds. *Divorce Reform at the Crossroads.* New Haven, CT: Yale University Press, 1990.

Suppan, Klaus. *Die Ehelehre Martin Luthers: Theologische und rechtshistorische Aspekte des reformatorischen Eheverständnisses.* Salzburg: Universitätsverlag A. Pustet, 1971.

Swinburne, Henry (1551–1624). *A Treatise of Spousals or Matrimonial Contracts.* Composed ca. 1591; published posthumously from a draft found in Lincoln's Inn. London: S. Roycroft, 1686.

Taylor, Jeremy. *Eniautos.* 2nd ed. London: Richard Royston, 1655.

———. *The Measures and Offices of Friendship.* 3rd ed. London: Richard Royston, 1662.

The Teaching of the Twelve Apostles, Didache, or The Oldest Church Manual. Translated and edited by Philip Schaff. 3rd, rev. ed. New York: Funk & Wagnalls, 1889.

Telle, Émile V. *Érasme de Rotterdam et le septième sacrement*. Geneva: Droz, 1954.

Tentler, Thomas N. *Sin and Confession on the Eve of the Reformation*. Princeton, NJ: Princeton University Press, 1977.

Tertullian. *Against Marcion*. In *The Ante-Nicene Fathers*, edited by Alexander Roberts and James Donaldson, vol. 3. Reprint, Buffalo: Christian Literature Publishing Co., 1885.

———. *Apologeticus*. In *Tertullian*, translated and edited by Gerald H. Rendall. New York: G. P. Putnam's Sons, 1931.

———. *De Spectaculis*. In *Tertullian*, translated and edited by Gerald H. Rendall. New York: G. P. Putnam's Sons, 1931.

———. *Treatises on Penance*. Translated by William P. Le Saint. Westminster, MD: Newman Press, 1959.

Theophilus. *Institutionum graeca paraphrasis Theophilo antecessori vulgo tributa ad fidem librorum manu*. Edited by Cantadori Ferrini. Berlin: S. Calvary, 1884.

Thomas Aquinas. *On Love and Charity: Readings from the Commentary on the Sentences of Peter Lombard*, translated by Peter A. Kwasniewski, Thomas Bolin, and Joseph Bolin. Washington, DC: Catholic University Press of America, 2009.

———. *Sancti Thomae Aquinatis: Opera omnia*. Edited by Leonina. 13 vols. Rome: C. de Propagandae Fidei, 1882.

———. "Scriptum super libros Sententiarum Petri Lombardiensis." In Thomas, *Sancti Thomae Aquinatis: Opera omnia*, vol. 7.2.

———. *Summa contra Gentiles*. Translated by Vernon J. Bourke. 4 vols. Notre Dame: University of Notre Dame Press, 1975.

———. *Summa theologica*. Translated by Fathers of the English Dominican Province. First complete American ed. 3 vols. New York: Benziger Bros., 1947–48.

Thompson, John L. "Patriarchs, Polygamy, and Private Resistance: John Calvin and Others on Breaking God's Rules." *Sixteenth Century Journal* 35 (1994): 3–28.

Tierney, Brian. *The Idea of Natural Rights: Natural Rights, Natural Law, and Church Law, 1150–1625*. Atlanta: Scholars Press, 1997.

Tietz, Gerold. *Verlobung, Trauung und Hochzeit in den evangelischen Kirchenordnungen des 16. Jahrhunderts*. PhD diss., Tübingen, 1969. Tubingen: Fotodruck Prazis, 1969.

Tiffany, Walter C. *Handbook on the Law of Persons and Domestic Relations*. St. Paul: West Publishing Co., 1896. Reprint, Holmes Beach, FL: Baunt, 2011.

Tillyard, E. M. W. *The Elizabethan World Picture*. London: Chatto & Windus, 1943. Reprint, New York: Vintage Books, 1959.

Tilney, Edmund. *A Brief and Pleasant Discourse of Duties in Marriage, Called the Flower of Friendshippe*. London: Henrie Denham, 1571.

Timlin, Bartholomew T. *Conditional Matrimonial Consent: An Historical Synopsis and Commentary*. Washington, DC: Catholic University of America Press, 1934.

Tractatus universi iuris, duce, & auspice Gregorio XIII. 25 vols. Venice: Società dell'Aquila che si rinnova, 1584–86.

Treggiari, Susan. *Roman Marriage: Iusti Coniuges from the Time of Cicero to the Time of Ulpian*. Oxford: Clarendon Press, 1991.

Triglot Concordia: The Symbolic Books of the Evangelical Lutheran Church; German-Latin-English. St. Louis: Concordia Publishing House, 1921.

Trusen, Winfried. "Forum internum und gelehrten Rechts im Spätmittelalter: Summae confessorum und Traktate als Wegsbereiter der Rezeption." *Zeitschrift der Savigny-Stiftung für Rechtsgeschichte: Kanonistische Abteilung* 57 (1971): 83–126.

Tulloch, Gail. *Mill and Sexual Equality*. Hertfordshire, UK: Harvester Wheatsheaf; Boulder, CO: Lynne Rienner Publishers, 1989.

Tyndale, William. *An Answer to Sir Thomas More's Dialogue*. Edited by H. Walter for the Parker Society. Cambridge: Cambridge University Press, 1850.

———. *Doctrinal Treatises and Introductions to Different Portions of the Holy Scripture.* Edited by H. Walter for the Parker Society. Cambridge: Cambridge University Press, 1848.

van Apeldoorn, L. *Geschiedenis van het nederlandsche huwelijksrecht voor de invoering van de fransche wetgeving.* Amsterdam: Uitgeversmaatschappij, 1925.

van Bijnkershoek, C. *Observationes tumultuariae.* 4 vols. Edited by E. M. Meijers et al. Haarlem: Tjeenk Willink, 1926–62.

van de Kerckhove, P. Martinien, OM. "La notion de juridiction chez les Décrétistes et les premiers Décrétalistes (1140–1250)." *Études franciscaines* 49 (1937): 420–55.

van den Brink, Herman. *The Charm of Legal History.* Amsterdam: Adolf M. Hakkert, 1974.

van der Heijden, Manon. *Huwelijk in Holland: Stedelijk Rechtspraak en kerkelijk Tucht, 1550–1700.* Amsterdam: B. Bakker, 1998.

Van Drunen, David. *Natural Law and the Two Kingdoms: A Study in the Development of Reformed Social Thought.* Grand Rapids: Wm. B. Eerdmans Publishing Co., 2010.

van Overveldt, A. J. M. *De dualiteit van kerkelijk en burgerlijk huwelijk.* Tilburg: Bergmans, 1953.

Vernier, Chester G. *American Family Laws: A Comparative Study of the Family Law of the Forty-Eight States.* 5 vols. Stanford, CA: Stanford University Press, 1931–38.

Vidler, Alec R. *Christ's Strange Work: An Exposition of the Three Uses of God's Law.* Rev. ed. London: SCM Press, 1963.

Vinogradoff, Paul. *The Teaching of Sir Henry Maine.* Oxford: Oxford University Press, 1904.

Vuilleumier, Henri. *Histoire de L'Église Réformée du pays de Vaud sous le régime Bernois.* 4 vols. Lausanne: Éditions La Concorde, 1927–33.

Waite, Linda J., and Maggie Gallagher. *The Case for Marriage: Why Married People Are Happier, Healthier, and Better Off Financially.* New York: Broadway Books, 2001.

Walch, Agnès. *La spiritualité conjugale dans le catholicisme français, XVIe–XXe siècle.* Paris: les Éditions du Cerf, 2002.

Walker, Williston. *John Calvin.* New York: Schocken Books, 1960.

Ward, Roy B. "Musonius and Paul on Marriage." *New Testament Studies* 36 (1990): 281–89.

Waters, Brent. *The Family in Christian Social and Political Thought.* Oxford: Oxford University Press, 2007.

Watt, Jeffrey R. "The Control of Marriage in Reformed Switzerland, 1550–1800." In *Later Calvinism: International Perspectives,* edited by W. Fred Graham, 29–53. Sixteenth Century Essays and Studies. Kirksville, MO: Sixteenth Century Journal Publishers, 1994.

Weigand, Rudolf. *Die bedingte Eheschliessung im kanonischen Recht.* Munich: Max Hueber, 1963.

———. *Die Naturrechtslehre der Legisten und Dekretisten von Irnerius bis Accursius und von Gratian bis Johannes Teutonicus.* Munich: Max Hueber, 1967.

———. "Ehe- und Familienrecht in der mittelalterlichen Stadt." In *Haus und Familie in der spätmittelalterlichen Stadt,* edited by Alfred Haverkamp, 161–94. Tübingen: J. C. B. Mohr, 1984.

———. *Liebe und Ehe im Mittelalter.* Goldbach: Keip, 1993.

———. "Zur mittelalterlichen kirchlichen Ehegerichtsbarkeit: Rechtsvergleichende Untersuchung." *Zeitschrift der Savigny-Stiftung für Rechtsgeschichte: Kanonistische Abteilung* 67 (1981): 213–47.

Weitzman, Lenore J. *The Divorce Revolution: The Unexpected Social and Economic Consequences for Women and Children in America.* New York: Free Press, 1985.

———. *The Marriage Contract: Spouses, Lovers, and the Law.* New York: Free Press, 1991.

Wendel, François. *Le mariage à Strasbourg à l'epoque de la reforme, 1520–1692.* Strasbourg: Imprimerie Alsacienne, 1928.

Westermann, Claus. *Genesis 1–11: A Commentary.* Translated by J. J. Scullion, SJ. Minneapolis: Augsburg Publishing House, 1984.

Whately, William. *A Bride-Bush, or, A Wedding Sermon: Compendiously Describing the Duties of Married Persons: By Performing Whereof, Marriage shall be to them a Great Help, which now finde it a little Hell.* London: William Jaagard for Nicholas Bourne, 1617. (ESTC 25296.)

———. *A Care-Cloth: or, a Treatise of the Cumbers and Troubles of Marriage.* London: Felix Kyngston for Thomas Man, 1624. (ESTC 25299.)

Wheaton, Robert, and Tamara K. Hareven, eds. *Family and Sexuality in French History.* Philadelphia: University of Pennsylvania Press, 1980.

Whitehead, Barbara Dafoe. *The Divorce Culture: How Divorce Became an Entitlement and How It Is Blighting the Lives of Our Children.* New York: Alfred A. Knopf, 1997.

Whitgift, John. *The Works of John Witgift.* Edited by J. Ayre for the Parker Society. 3 vols. Cambridge: Cambridge University Press, 1852.

Williams, George Huntston. *The Radical Reformation.* 3rd ed. Sixteenth Century Essays and Studies. Kirksville, MO: Sixteenth Century Journal Publishers, 1992.

Wilson, Robin Fretwell, ed. *Reconceiving the Family: Critique of the American Law Institute's Principles of Family Dissolution.* Cambridge: Cambridge University Press, 2006.

Wing, John. *The Crown Conjugall; or, The Spouse Royall.* London: John Beale for R. Mylbourne, 1632. (ESTC 25845.)

Winnett, Arthur Robert. *Divorce and Remarriage in Anglicanism.* New York: St. Martin's Press, 1958.

Winroth, Anders. *The Making of Gratian's "Decretum."* Cambridge: Cambridge University Press, 2000.

Winstanley, Gerrard. *The Law of Freedom in a Platform, or, True Magistracy Restored.* 1652. Edited by R. W. Kenny. New York: Schocken Books, 1941.

Witte, John, Jr. *God's Joust, God's Justice: Law and Religion in the Western Tradition.* Grand Rapids: Wm. B. Eerdmans Publishing Co., 2005.

———. *Law and Protestantism: The Legal Teachings of the Lutheran Reformation.* Cambridge: Cambridge University Press, 2002.

———. "The Plight of Canon Law in the Early Dutch Republic." In *Canon Law in Protestant Lands,* edited by Richard H. Helmholz, 135–64. Berlin: Duncker & Humblot, 1992.

———. *The Reformation of Rights: Law, Religion, and Human Rights in Early Modern Calvinism.* Cambridge: Cambridge University Press, 2007.

———. *The Sins of the Fathers: The Law and Theology of Illegitimacy Reconsidered.* Cambridge: Cambridge University Press, 2009.

Witte, John, Jr., and Eliza Ellison, eds. *Covenant Marriage in Comparative Perspective.* Grand Rapids: Wm. B. Eerdmans Publishing Co., 2005.

Witte, John, Jr., and Frank S. Alexander, eds. *Christianity and Law: An Introduction.* Cambridge: Cambridge University Press, 2008.

Witte, John, Jr., and Heather M. Good. "The Duties of Love: The Vocation of the Child in the Household Manual Tradition." In *The Vocation of the Child,* edited by Patrick M. Brennan, 266–94. Grand Rapids: Wm. B. Eerdmans Publishing Co., 2008.

Witte, John, Jr., and Johan van der Vyver, eds. *Religious Human Rights in Global Perspective: Religious Perspectives.* The Hague and Boston: Martinus Nijhoff, 1996.

Witte, John, Jr., and Robert M. Kingdon. *Sex, Marriage, and Family in John Calvin's Geneva.* 2 vols. Grand Rapids: Wm. B. Eerdmans Publishing Co., 2005–12.

Wolgast, Eike. "Bugenhagen in den politischen Krisen seiner Zeit." In *Johannes Bugenhagen: Gestalt und Wirkung*, edited by Hans-Gunter Leder, 100–117. Bonn: Evangelische Verlagsanstalt, 1984.

Wollstonecraft, Mary. *A Vindication of the Rights of Women*. Edited by Charles W. Hagelman Jr. New York: W. W. Norton, 1967.

Wolter, Udo. "Amt und Officium in mittelalterlichen Quellen von 13. bis 15. Jahrhunderts." *Zeitschrift der Savigny-Stiftung für Rechtsgeschichte: Kanonistische Abteilung* 74 (1988): 246–80.

Wright, Louis B. *Middle Class Culture in Elizabethan England*. Chapel Hill: University of North Carolina Press, 1953.

Xenophon. *See* Pomeroy, Sarah.

Ziegler, Josef Georg. *Die Ehelehre der Pönitentialsummen von 1200–1350*. Regensburg: Friedrich Pustet, 1956.

Zwaan, Ton, ed. *Familie, huwelijk en gezin in West-Europa: Van Middeleeuwen tot moderne tijd*. Amsterdam: Boom; Heerlen: Open Universiteit, 1993.

Zwingli, Ulrich. *Huldreich Zwinglis sämtliche Werke*. 13 vols. Corpus reformatorum 88–101, 113–114. Zurich: Theologischer Verlag, 1982–91.

Index of Biblical Sources

Index of Subjects and Authors

abortion
 adultery and, 307
 canon law on, 5, 61, 63, 109
 Geneva consistory cases on, 167
 as grounds for divorce, 151
 natural law on, 83
 Roman law on, 55
 statistics on, x, 321
 in twentieth and twenty-first centuries, 288, 289
 U.S. Supreme Court on, 317
Abraham, 38, 44, 129, 185, 192, 194, 204, 205, 273
absolute (or diriment) impediments, 100–102
abuse and neglect. *See* child abuse and neglect; wife abuse
Act in Restraint of Appeals to Rome (1533; England), 226, 242
Acton, Lord, 182
Adam and Eve
 authority of Adam over Eve, 258, 261, 279
 Calvin on, 205
 as founders of first marriage and family, 4, 31, 32–35, 187, 191–92, 235, 258, 261, 272
 gender equality and, 33–34, 279–80
 Locke on, 279–80, 280n265
 monogamy of, 8, 37, 43, 187, 191–92, 194
 original sin of, 45, 68, 92
 procreation by, 4, 8, 31, 34–35, 43, 66, 80, 82, 121, 122, 258
 See also creation narratives in Genesis

adoption, 68, 68n46, 148, 204, 313, 316, 329
adultery
 Anglican view of, 233, 237, 246–47, 249, 254, 255
 Calvinist view of, 160, 169, 174, 180, 182, 195–200, 206, 210, 211
 canon law on, 58, 59–60, 62–63, 104, 112
 Council of Elvira on, 62–63
 double standard on, 21, 27, 59, 75
 in early-twentieth-century England and America, 288
 Enlightenment view of, 290, 298–99, 303, 310
 Geneva consistory cases on, 167, 168
 as grounds for divorce, 7, 29, 48, 57, 72, 80, 106, 112, 128, 132, 150–53, 153n144, 160, 162, 174, 180, 182, 195–200, 206, 210, 211, 215, 233, 237, 246–47, 249, 255, 310, 318
 impact of, on children, 298–99, 307
 Jesus Christ on, 47, 256, 282
 Lactantius on, 59
 Locke on, 282
 Lutheran view of, 7, 139, 143, 150–53, 157
 Mill on, 309
 Milton on, 273, 277
 Mosaic law on and Old Testament references to, 36, 37, 39–40, 45
 natural law on, 111
 at opening of second millennium generally, 326